THE

WILLARD J. GRAHAM SERIES

IN ACCOUNTING

BOOKS IN
THE WILLARD J. GRAHAM SERIES IN ACCOUNTING

CONSULTING EDITOR   ROBERT N. ANTHONY   *Harvard University*

Accounting for
Managerial Analysis

Accounting for Managerial Analysis

JAMES M. FREMGEN, D.B.A., C.P.A.
Professor of Accounting
Naval Postgraduate School

Revised Edition

1972

RICHARD D. IRWIN, INC. Homewood, Illinois 60430
IRWIN-DORSEY LIMITED Georgetown, Ontario

REVISED EDITION

First Printing, February, 1972

Previous edition published under the title
Managerial Cost Analysis

Library of Congress Catalog Card No. 79–168297

Printed in the United States of America

To Eleanor, Jim, and Steve

PREFACE

THIS text is a revision of an earlier volume entitled *Managerial Cost Analysis*. The new title more aptly describes the content and the objectives of the book—in the first edition as well as in this revision. It is intended primarily for a one-semester or one-quarter course in managerial accounting following a course in financial accounting or principles of accounting. It might also be used in a cost accounting course with a managerial emphasis. It is not a cost accounting text in the traditional sense, however, nor was the previous edition, although that may have been inferred from the old title. The main theme of the book is the usefulness of a variety of financial data and financial analyses to management in the functions of planning, control, and decision making. Obviously, cost data and cost analyses are important for these purposes; but they are not uniquely important. Management's needs for financial information extend far beyond costs alone. This text seeks to examine all of those needs.

Similarities to First Edition

In preparing this revision, I have attempted to make every change that I believed would make the book a better aid to the student's learning process. At the same time, I have tried to avoid making changes purely for the sake of change (except in the problem materials). The basic objectives and structure of the text are essentially unchanged. As noted above, the principal theme of the book is the same—management's uses of accounting information. The book still has three major parts dealing, respectively, with costs and cost accounting, financial data for planning and control, and financial analysis for decision making. There are still 19 chapters, although they are not all the same chapters that appeared in the first edition. The sequence of presentation of subject matter has been retained. Basis concepts of cost and the principles of cost accounting are discussed in the three chapters of Part I. The eight chapters in Part II deal primarily with budgets and standards and their uses in the managerial functions of planning and control. Finally, the seven chapters of Part III focus upon the uses of financial data in a variety of decision-making situations.

The distinction between planning and control on the one hand and decision making on the other is not a clear one. Obviously, planning involves making decisions; and so does control. Thus, the distinctions in the text are largely between logical blocks of subject matter rather than between separate management functions. The chapter on divisional performance measurement, for example, might be thought more appropriately classified under the heading of control than that of decision making. The placement of this particular chapter, thus, reflects its dependence upon prior material more than anything else.

Major Changes

Chapter 2 on cost concepts and classifications has been revised considerably to improve clarity and to reflect a greater degree of standardization of terminology than was recognized in the earlier edition. The comprehensive illustration of cost accounting in Chapter 3 is new and more complete. The discussion of the development of standards and standard costs in Chapter 5 has been substantially rewritten to make it less mechanical and more relevant to managerial concerns. The material dealing with the cost of capital in Chapter 8 has been expanded greatly. Some other materials in the chapters on budgeting have been condensed to avoid unnecessary repetition and to eliminate superfluous illustrations. The discussion of flexible budgets in Chapter 9 has been revised extensively, and the sections dealing with semivariable costs are entirely new.

Four chapters have been completely rewritten. Chapter 12, dealing with nonmanufacturing costs, is now organized around approaches to planning and controlling these costs rather than around functional classifications. A section describing the federal government's planning-programming-budgeting system has been added to illustrate how certain types of nonmanufacturing costs may be planned. A major feature in the revision is a substantial expansion of the material on capital budgeting. This is a matter of great concern to managers in all types of organizations. Chapters 15 and 16 are now devoted entirely to this topic. Techniques of capital investment analysis are presented in Chapter 15. The following chapter then develops some of the applications of these techniques and some of the problems that are encountered in capital budgeting. The material on the after-the-fact rate of return on investment in the first edition has been condensed and moved to Chapter 18. Chapter 18 also is new. It is now organized around different types of divisions and the methods of analyzing their performances. The section on transfer pricing has been expanded and tied more closely to the rest of the chapter.

The problems have been thoroughly revised. Every effort has been made to eliminate repetitive pencil-pushing exercises. There are more short problems illustrating key points in the text. There are also more that require the student to evaluate a situation or to criticize an analysis that has already been prepared. Hopefully, these problems will help students to see accounting information as a valuable aid to management and not merely the output of an accounting system. The short cases that appeared in a separate appendix in the first edition have been revised and placed at the end of appropriate chapters.

Suggested Course Outline

While every user of the text will undoubtedly wish to allocate time to topics and chapters according to the needs of his students and the objectives of his particular course, it may be useful to consider a suggested outline for a course with 42 class sessions in addition to examination periods. This outline would thus fit most three-semester-hour courses or four-quarter-hour courses.

Topic	Chapter(s)	Classes
Introduction	1	1
Cost concepts	2	2
Cost accounting	3 and 4	6
Standards	5	2
Comprehensive budgeting	6, 7, and 8	5
Flexible budgets	9	3
Standard costs and variances	10 and 11	4
Nonmanufacturing costs	12	2
Cost-volume-profit analysis	13	2
Incremental profit analysis	14	3
Capital budgeting	15 and 16	7
Pricing decisions	17	2
Divisional performance	18	2
Reporting to management	19	1
		42

Many variations on this schedule are possible, of course. Some of the early chapters (notably 4, 6, 7, and 8) can be covered more briefly than indicated above without impairing the student's preparation for the material in later chapters.

Acknowledgments

In addition to those persons recognized in the preface to the first edition, I am indebted to many people for their comments and suggestions in the preparation of this revision. First and foremost, I wish to thank my own students who were kind—and bold—enough to point out sections that they found unclear. Several other users of the first edition also sent me suggestions based upon their experiences with the text. For these, I am very grateful. Professor Robert N. Anthony of the Graduate School of Business Administration at Harvard University read the first edition and the draft of this revision very carefully and made numerous invaluable suggestions for improvement. I am much in his debt. Professors Clifford D. Brown of the Rochester Institute of Technology and Allan R. Drebin of Cornell University also commented extensively on the first edition. For assistance with the problem material, I appreciate the thorough and discerning work of Professors Robert Strawser of Virginia Polytechnical Institute and State University and Arthur Francia of The Pennsylvania State University. Finally, I must acknowledge the patience and understanding of my family, who learned the hard way that being a book widow and book orphans can be a recurring affliction.

January, 1972   JAMES M. FREMGEN

CONTENTS

Inventory Accounting Methods: *Perpetual, or Book, Inventory Method. Periodic, or Physical, Inventory Method. Comparison of Perpetual and Periodic Inventory Methods.* Inventory Cost Flow Assumptions: *First-in, First-out Assumption. Average Cost. Last-in, First-out Assumption. Comparison and Evaluation of Cost Flow Assumptions.* Cost Accounting Systems: *Job Order Cost System. Process Cost System.* Absorption and Variable Costing Compared: *The Development of Variable Costing. Arguments for and against Variable Costing. Internal and External Accounting Reports.*

Part II.   PLANNING AND CONTROL

Standards: *Price Standards. Quantity Standards. Degree of Precision in Standards. Review and Revision of Standards.* Standard Costs: *Materials and Labor. Overhead. Standard Cost Sheet. Nonmanufacturing Operations.* Variances: *Management by Exception.* Standards as Tools of Planning and Control.

Definition of a Budget. Purposes of Budgets. Framework for Budgeting: *The Budget Period. Environmental Factors. Company Policies.* Human Implications of Budgeting: *Personnel Involved in Budget Preparation. Budgets and Human Behavior.* Budgetary Review. Construction of the Budget: *Limiting Factor on Operations. Setting Budget Allowances.*

The Sales Forecast: *Factors Determining Sales. Developing the Sales Forecast in Detail. Budgeting Sales in Total Only. Long-Range Sales Planning.* Production Budgets: *Factors Determining Production. Summary of Production Budget. Labor Budget. Materials Budget. Departmental Overhead Budgets.* Budgets of Nonmanufacturing Costs. Budgeted Income Statements.

Planning Short-Term Capital: *Cash Budget. Working Capital Budget.* Long-Term Capital Planning: *Sources of Long-Term Capital. The Cost of Capital. Long-Term Capital Investments.* The Budgeted Balance Sheet. Budget Review Reports.

Construction of Flexible Budget: *Departmentalization of Costs. The Measure of Volume. Budget Cost Allowances. Normal Overhead Rates.* Establishing Budget Allowances: *Variable Costs. Fixed Costs. Semivariable Costs.* Departmental Expense Reports: *Report Form. Adjusting the Budget to Actual Volume. Variances from the Budget.*

Part III.   DECISION MAKING

Introduction

THE ROLE OF THE INDUSTRIAL ACCOUNTANT

I N ADDITION to his many sins against Christmas, Ebenezer Scrooge may be held accountable for a notable disservice to the profession of accountancy. By placing Bob Cratchit on a high stool, bent over a dusty ledger with a long quill pen in his hand and a green eyeshade over his brow, Scrooge perpetuated a caricature of the accountant which persisted long after that miser's reconciliation with his fellowmen. Happily, this image has been dispelled. Today, accountants guide the fortunes of some of the largest industrial corporations in America, and they have filled creditably some of the most responsible positions in the government. The basic reason for this advancement of the accountant's role in society is the fact that managers have come to appreciate the importance of accounting data and analyses in the effective administration of an enterprise. Accountants have become members in good standing of the management team. The central theme of this book is the usefulness of accounting information in the management of an organization. Most of the discussions and illustrations in this text are presented in the context of a business enterprise. However, very much the same type of data and analyses are equally useful in the management of a governmental or a nonprofit organization.

Managerial applications of accounting data are not the only important aspects of modern accounting development, of course. The responsibilities of the accountant, and particularly of the independent certified public accountant, extend far beyond the limits of a single firm. However, the uses of accounting information in management are sufficiently important and varied that it is appropriate to study them separately from other accounting practices. Thus, the accountant holding the center of the stage in this volume is the industrial accountant, whose primary concern is with the particular problems and needs of a specific firm. Various aspects of his job and his responsibilities will be considered in the pages that follow.

FUNCTIONS AND RESPONSIBILITIES OF THE INDUSTRIAL ACCOUNTANT

The Controller

The controller, or comptroller,[1] of a business enterprise is typically the top accounting executive in the firm. To be sure, the accountant may rise beyond the position of controller to those of executive vice president, president, and chairman of the board. In these latter positions, however, his areas of responsibility and authority would be so broad that it would not be accurate to continue to describe him as an accounting executive. While the role of the controller varies somewhat among firms, typically he occupies a staff position and reports directly to top management. Under his cognizance there is likely to be a large and diverse staff, responsible to him for the timely and efficient accomplishment of the various accounting functions of the firm. There is no single accepted listing of the functions of the controller's staff, but the following list is typical of most business enterprises:

1. Financial accounting.
2. Tax accounting.
3. Internal control.
4. Accounting systems design.
5. Management accounting.

Each of these will be considered briefly below.

Financial Accounting

Financial accounting encompasses a broad range of accounting practices and procedures related to the proper recording and reporting of the assets, liabilities, equities, revenues, and expenses of the firm. The end product of financial accounting is the financial report, the basic means of communicating financial information about the firm to those

---

[1] "Comptroller" is simply an older spelling of the word "controller." The pronunciation is the same regardless of the spelling, however. The word should be pronounced as "control" with "-er" added.

outside it. For this purpose, stockholders are regarded as "outsiders." In one sense, stockholders might be viewed as the most important "insiders," for they own the corporation. However, the corporate sector of our economy has developed to such an extent that the stockholders of most large companies are merely investors who provide a portion of the capital employed by corporate management in the conduct of the affairs of the firm. In this situation, it is reasonable to regard shareholders as outside parties, for their direct control over corporate activities is normally minimal.

Financial reporting is commonly accomplished in the form of published income statements, balance sheets, and funds statements, along with supporting data and explanations. Such reports are prepared in accordance with generally accepted accounting principles. These principles are derived chiefly from their wide acceptance in the accounting profession, although some of them stem from legal pronouncements. The Securities and Exchange Commission, for example, has rather broad powers to regulate accounting practices, although it has chosen to leave the selection of accounting principles, for the most part, to the accounting profession. Thus, the procedures of financial reporting are determined primarily by factors outside the firm. A certain degree of discretion is left to the reporting corporation, but the constraints upon individual firms' practices are fairly strict. It is entirely reasonable to demand that financal reports conform to specific accounting and reporting standards so that readers may interpret them in the light of accepted practices.

Financial accounting involves so many facets of a firm's operations that it is impossible to separate it from the other functions of the industrial accountant. Indeed, all of the functions discussed here are interrelated and overlapping. The separate discussions should not be interpreted as suggesting that these functions are clearly separable in practice.

Tax Accounting

For most businesses, tax accounting is concerned primarily with the federal income tax. This is not the only tax to which firms are subject, of course. Taxes imposed by states, municipalities, and foreign governments are important also. Business enterprises are subject to property taxes, excise taxes, and others. The federal income tax is different from these, however, in that the firm not only pays the tax but also assesses it. That is, the firm must determine how much tax is payable for a given tax period. The determination of the income tax liability is chiefly a function of the Internal Revenue Code and the supporting regulations, but there is some room for judgment and choice on the part of the taxpayer. It is, therefore, the responsibility of the tax accountant to determine the lowest possible income tax liability consistent with the law and regulations. Tax minimization (very different from tax evasion) is a perfectly legitimate objective of business management, and a great deal of time and effort is expended by accounting personnel to achieve that objective.

Except in those areas where the provisions of the income tax law conflict with generally accepted accounting principles for financial reporting, tax accounting is dependent largely upon the data developed within the financial accounting function.

Internal Control

The purposes of internal control are many and they involve matters which extend beyond the scope of accounting, as such. The basic objectives of internal control are

1. The safeguarding of assets,
2. The accuracy and reliability of accounting data,
3. The promotion of operating efficiency, and
4. The adherence to prescribed managerial policies.[2]

The safeguarding of assets, and particularly those assets, such as cash, which are especially susceptible to misappropriation, is a very important responsibility of the industrial accountant. Accuracy in the recording and reporting of accounting data is quite obviously essential to the effective fulfillment of any accounting function. The promotion of operating efficiency and compliance with established management policies should be regarded as responsibilities of every employee of a firm. The accountant's comprehensive overview of the firm's total operations, however, makes him peculiarly qualified to assume such responsibilities. In large firms, internal control may be so extensive and formalized that a separate subdivision of the controller's staff may be charged with the responsibility of maintaining its effectiveness. The specific responsibilities of this subdivison are commonly referred to as internal auditing. In some corporations, the internal auditing function is independent of the controller and the chief internal auditor reports directly to top management.

Accounting Systems Design

Integrally related to all of the other accounting functions listed here is that of accounting systems design. The primary purpose of this function

---

[2] Committee on Auditing Procedure, American Institute of Certified Public Accountants, *Auditing Standards and Procedures* (New York, 1963), p. 27.

is to develop systems which will efficiently and economically facilitate the other four functions. Systems design includes the structure of accounts within the firm and the processing of data through those accounts. The methods by which data are processed are also part of the job of systems design. As far as financial accounting is concerned, an accounts receivable ledger is the same regardless of how it is handled mechanically—handwritten in a bound ledger, machine punched on cards, or prepared by an electronic computer on magnetic tape. The mechanics are within the scope of the systems design function. The basic objective of systems design should be the most efficient possible recording, processing, and reporting of data at a reasonable cost.

While the substance and usefulness of the information generated by a system are of primary importance, the methods of processing data are also of considerable interest. Moreover, these matters are not unrelated. Certain methods of data processing make feasible some types of informational output that would not otherwise be practicable. The widespread use of computers in business firms has stimulated considerable interest in the concept of an integrated, or total, information system. Such a system would include accounting, but it would go far beyond the limits of present accounting systems. Whether it would properly fall within the purview of the accountant is a question that has been debated frequently—and sometimes hotly. The management of computer systems and data processing has often been delegated to controllers in large corporations. One reason for this practice is that most early applications of computers in business firms were in the area of accounting. As more and more nonaccounting uses of computers are found, it is possible that the management of computer systems will tend to pass from the hands of accountants. At present, however, many corporate controllers are charged with administrative responsibility for data processing operations.

Management Accounting

Discussion of the management accounting function has been deferred to the last here not because of the relative unimportance of the subject but to serve as a link to the main theme of the book. Management accounting is the function of the industrial accountant with which most of this volume will be concerned. Once again, this function cannot be separated completely from the other four. Many of the data relevant to financial accounting and to tax accounting are also pertinent to management accounting. The important feature which distinguishes management accounting from financial accounting is its point of view. Financial accounting is intended to serve as a means of communicating financial information to outsiders. Management accounting is a means of communicating financial data to managers. It need not be guided by generally accepted accounting principles but only by what the particular firm's management wants and needs. Any procedure or practice that proves helpful to management in the operation and control of the enterprise is good management accounting. It is in connection with this function that the industrial accountant is most importantly a member of the management team. His view here is focused on the interests and needs of his firm and not upon those of outside parties. This is as it should be. If accounting were of no direct use to management in the operation of the firm, then, from the point of view of management, it would be little more than a burden, a necessary evil. But accounting data are useful to management, and it is the responsibility of the management accountant to make them available in the form and at the time required by management.

COST ACCOUNTING

Cost accounting is an important part of the total accounting activities of a business firm, and particularly of a manufacturing company. It it not a sixth distinct function of accounting but, rather, a distinct activity related to the five functions discussed in the preceding section. Cost accounting is concerned with the proper recording, analysis, and reporting of the various costs incurred in the operation of an enterprise. Accounting systems design must conceive and structure procedures for the efficient accomplishment of these objectives. Internal control of costs and cost records is essential. It is in connection with the functions of financial and management accounting, however, that cost accounting is most often studied and employed. Through its financial accounting implications, cost accounting also relates to the tax accounting function.

It is impossible to draw a sharp and clear line between the financial and management accounting facets of cost accounting. Many of the cost data necessary for accurate financial reporting are of equal importance to management. However, there are some significant differences in points of view between financial and managerial reporting.

Financial Accounting Applications

As regards financial accounting, cost accounting activities are directed primarily toward the correct classification and measurement of the cost data which are reported on the income statement and on the balance sheet. These activities relate to the determination of periodic net income and to the valuation of inventories. They are guided by the dictates of generally accepted accounting principles. While financial reporting is not the central theme of the book, it is essential that the student have a basic knowledge of cost accounting as related to that function; for many of the managerial applications of cost information are derived from financial accounting practices. Chapters 3 and 4 present the fundamental concepts and procedures for the financial reporting aspects of cost accounting.

Management Accounting Applications

The managerial applications of cost accounting derive from and are determined by the needs of management in particular instances. Cost data are very useful to managers in planning, controlling, and evaluating business operations and in making specific decisions among alternative courses of action. In this context, costs should be reported in whatever manner best satisfies the requirements of management, regardless of compliance with or deviation from generally accepted accounting principles. Parts II and III of this book are concerned principally with the management accounting applications of costs. Particularly in Part II, however, the management and financial accounting aspects are so interwoven that their separate discussion can be based upon different points of view only, and not upon wholly different concepts.

COST CONTROL

A basic premise underlying most of the material discussed in this book is the presumption that the management of any organization wishes to control the costs that must be incurred in the conduct of its operations. As a practical matter, cost control may be thought of as equivalent to cost minimization. It is important to understand, however, that this does not mean simply cost avoidance. All costs can be avoided by terminating the existence of an organization. Cost control, then, is concerned with minimizing the costs that must be incurred in order to achieve the goals of the enterprise. The objective is to get the job done at the lowest possible cost. It is not acceptable, however, to reduce costs by doing a bad job. Cost control cannot be made meaningful unless and until standards of accomplishment have been specified for the organization.

In a business enterprise, cost control is commonly thought of as a corollary to the more basic objective of profit maximization. All other things being equal, profit will be increased as costs are reduced. However, cost control is in no way restricted to profit-seeking ventures. Governmental and nonprofit organizations have at least as much interest in cost control as do business firms. To the extent that these agencies seek to accomplish various objectives within the constraints imposed by a fixed or narrowly limited budget, cost control is critical to the effective achievement of their goals. A school district, for example, can provide a better education for its students if it minimizes the costs of providing each specific service, for it will then be in the position of having funds available to provide additional or improved services. If the Department of the Navy is able to minimize the cost of constructing a new aircraft carrier, it may find that it can more readily obtain the funds to construct escort vessels to protect the carrier. Socialist states have just as valid an interest in effective cost control as have private enterprises. Every society must cope with the problems of seemingly limitless needs and limited resources to fill them.

Many of the concepts and analytical procedures presented in this text are based upon the assumption that management wishes to minimize costs. The general validity of this assumption is apparent. Even when managers seem to be ignoring the most elementary notions of cost control, what they are really doing is estimating costs badly or, perhaps, exaggerating the benefits anticipated from a costly venture. Perhaps the world never really needed such costly failures as the Edsel, the Skybolt missile, and "Dr. Doolittle"; but the fault in these cases was certainly not that management wished to waste money. Rather, the estimated benefits anticipated proved to be overly optimistic. Of course, the fact that management carefully employs procedures designed to control costs does not guarantee that bad decisions will never be made. These are an unfortunate but inevitable consequence of managing in an uncertain world.

PROFESSIONAL ACTIVITY IN MANAGEMENT ACCOUNTING

Whether management is viewed as a profession, an art, or an occupation, it is unquestionably an important function in any business enterprise and in any economically developed society. Management affords a challenging and, potentially, very rewarding (in both the personal sense and the pecuniary sense) career. As already mentioned, accountants have become indispensable members of the top-management team in any large enterprise. And they are more and more assuming additional responsibilities which encompass far more than their own area of specialization. In keeping with this development, organizations of management accountants have developed to further the interests and personal effectiveness of their members. The three principal organizations in this area are the National Association of Accountants (formerly called the National Association of Cost Accountants), the Financial Executives Institute (formerly the Controllers Institute), and the Institute of Internal Auditors. Each of these associations has a widespread membership that participates in the activities of local chapters as well as in the national organization. Each publishes a monthly (quarterly in the case of the Institute of Internal Auditors) journal, containing articles and news items of particular interest to management accountants. In addition to these, such other organizations as the American Accounting Association and the American Management Association have turned their attentions to matters related specifically to management accounting.

In light of recent and prospective developments in American and international business, it is difficult to imagine that the role of the accountant and of accounting analysis in enterprise management will do anything but increase in importance. These developments do not mean that all managers will be accountants or that the business roles of other specialists will be eclipsed. The need for specialized knowledge and skill in such areas as production, distribution, engineering, research, and personnel administration will continue to grow also. Further, the role of the accountant as a specialist will not cease to exist as such; but his special functions will pervade more and more of the general operation of and decision making in business firms. Thus, while the manager need not be an accountant himself, he must be able to understand and interpret accounting information with considerable facility. The development and processing of accounting data are technical functions, but they are designed to support the more general managerial functions of planning, organization, and control. The accountant and the manager must be able to communicate freely and effectively. This requires that the manager be familiar with accounting practices and concepts, including their limitations, and that the accountant be conversant with all of the operations and problems of the firm. It is the author's hope that this volume will contribute to the manager's appreciation of how accounting can aid in his intelligent pursuit of the basic objective of the firm, to the accountant's understanding of the needs of management in various circumstances, and to the ability of both to adapt accounting procedures to meet the changing needs of business and nonbusiness enterprises.

QUESTIONS FOR DISCUSSION

1. "Management accounting is nothing but cost accounting with a fancy new name." Discuss this allegation.

2. What do you understand the functions of a controller to be? Is the controller an accountant or a manager?

3. What are the criteria for good financial reports to the public? What are the criteria for good reports to management? If they are not the same, explain why they are not.

4. "Accounting systems design is important, of course; but it really has nothing to do with management accounting. It is simply a technical matter of concern only to accountants." Discuss this statement.

5. "Cost control is not as important in government as it is in industry because governments don't have to make a profit." Discuss this argument.

6. "This can't be an accounting text. There wasn't a single number in that whole first chapter." Discuss this assessment.

PART I

Costs and
Cost Accounting

chapter 2

COST CONCEPTS AND CLASSIFICATIONS

I N FINANCIAL accounting, the term "cost," used without modifiers, has a fairly generally accepted meaning. In management accounting, however, there are a great many different concepts of cost, each intended to convey a very specific and distinct meaning. Unfortunately, cost terminology in this latter area has not been established with complete agreement. Different accountants use different terms to describe the same concept of cost, and a single term may be used to denote different concepts. The terminology employed in this volume follows that which appears to have attained a substantial degree of acceptance and which seems to be most useful.

HISTORICAL AND FUTURE COSTS

Historical Costs

Within the scope of the data-recording function of accounting, the term "cost" almost invariably means *historical cost* or *actual cost*. This is defined by the Committee on Terminology of the American Institute of Certified Public Accountants as follows:

Cost is the amount, measured in money, of cash expended or other property transferred, capital stock issued, services performed, or a liability incurred, in consideration of goods or services received or to be received.[1]

---

[1] Committee on Terminology, American Institute of Certified Public Accountants, *Accounting Terminology Bulletin No. 4: Cost, Expense, and Loss* (New York, 1957), p. 1.

In other words, historical cost is the measurable monetary value of goods or services given up in exchange for other goods or services. The measurability of the cost in monetary terms is essential to the concept. One of the traditional requisites of the recording function in accounting has been the existence of objective, verifiable evidence in support of each transaction to be recorded. As accounting deals with business information in terms of money, this objective evidence must not only demonstrate the reality of the transaction but also provide for its accurate measurement in monetary terms. The cost data reported in conventional financial statements are almost exclusively historical costs. The accurate measurement of the costs incurred is not the only problem concerning them, however. There is also the very important question of in which financial statment, the balance sheet or the income statement, they are to be reported.

Expired and Unexpired Costs. All historical costs may be classified as either unexpired or expired. An *unexpired cost* is one which has the capacity of contributing to the production of revenue in the future. It is the measured monetary value of the expenditure for goods or services which can be of use in the future revenue-producing activities of the firm. Thus, an unexpired cost is an asset and is reported on the balance sheet as of the end of an accounting period. The cost of salable merchandise on hand affords a good example of an unexpired cost. Such cost can contribute to the production of revenue in the future because the merchandise acquired at that cost can subsequently be sold. An *expired cost* is one which cannot contribute to the production of future revenues. Such revenue-producing capacity as this cost had has either already been consumed in the production of revenue or has been lost without benefit to the firm. The first type of expired cost, that which has been consumed in the production of revenue, is called an *expense*. An example is the cost of merchandise which has been sold. The second type, which has expired with no benefit to the enterprise, is generally described as a *loss*. An illustration of a loss is the cost of uninsured merchandise destroyed by fire. Both expenses and losses are reported in the income statement.

Many of the most complex and controversial accounting problems relate to the separation of expired and unexpired costs in preparing financial reports. Alternative accounting principles may resolve these problems differently. The measurement of cost expiration depends not only upon the occurrence of transactions but also upon the particular accounting theories and practices employed by a firm. In exactly the same circumstances, different procedures for handling a particular type of cost may result in materially different figures for expired and unexpired costs. The professional accountant must become very familiar with the various alternative procedures and, more importantly, must learn to evaluate them critically in light of specific facts and conditions.

While the manager need not have as complete a technical understanding of alternative accounting principles, he must have a basic knowledge of them in order for him to appreciate the significance and limitations of the accounting data with which he must work and upon which, in part, he must base his decisions. Some of these alternatives will be considered, as appropriate, in subsequent chapters.

Future Costs

If the preoccupation of financial accounting is with historical costs, that of management accounting is more likely to be with future costs. *Future costs* may be defined as those costs which are reasonably expected to be incurred in some future period or periods. Because these costs are expectations rather than accomplished facts, their actual incurrence is a forecast and their measurement, an estimate. Management is vitally concerned with future costs for the simple reason that they are the only costs over which managers can exercise any control. Historical costs can merely be observed and evaluated in retrospect. If they are regarded as excessive, management can ask only, "What went wrong?" Future costs, on the other hand, can be planned for—and planned to be reduced. If future costs are considered too high, management can ask the very important question, "What can be done about this?" If necessary, resources can be planned to meet the high costs; if feasible, plans can be made to reduce them. Despite the estimation inherent in the concept of future costs, the measurement of such costs is no less important than the measurement of historical costs. If anything, it is more important to management. The measurement of historical costs is basically a record-keeping activity, an essentially passive function insofar as management is concerned. The measurement of future costs, however, is critically associated with the active management functions of planning and control.

When a future cost is not merely expected but is incorporated formally into the overall operating plans for a specific period in the future, it is referred to as a *budgeted cost*. A detailed examination of budgeting will be deferred until later chapters. For the present it is sufficient to observe that budgets are formal, comprehensive, and coordinated plans relative to operations in specific future periods. Budgeted costs are important elements in these overall plans.

DIRECT AND INDIRECT COSTS

All costs incurred are, of course, identified with a particular enterprise. But this broad identification of costs with the firm is typically insufficient for purposes of determining periodic income and measuring asset values and for purposes of managerial analyses. For these purposes, it is necessary to associate costs with subcomponents or segments of the firm. These segments are referred to in this context as *costing units*. A costing unit is simply anything within a business enterprise to which it is both significant and practical to assign costs. Both criteria of significance and of practicality are important here. For example, it might prove practical to associate certain costs with rainy days; but such association may be of no significance whatever to anyone concerned with the enterprise. Conversely, it might appear significant to identify costs with moments of imaginative thinking by executives; but no practical means of doing so may be available. Some fairly common illustrations of costing units are the following:

1. An individual unit of product: for example, a 1,000-gallon batch of "Silverthorn Grey" latex interior wall paint.
2. A product line: for example, commercial paints.
3. A division of a corporation: for example, the Pontiac Division of General Motors Corporation.
4. A department within a plant: for example, the spray-paint shop of a major appliance manufacturer.
5. A sales territory: for example, the Northern California territory.
6. A particular channel, or method, of distribution: for example, sales to wholesalers.

There are three possibilities with respect to the relationship between a particular cost and a given costing unit. Certain costs can be traced logically and practically in their entirety to a costing unit; there is a directly determinable relationship. Such costs are called *direct costs*. An example of a direct cost would be the monthly salary of a divisional manager, where the division is the costing unit under consideration. Other costs can be identified partially with a costing unit, but not entirely. That is, they relate to the unit under study; but they also relate to other costing units. The amount of the cost which is properly identifiable with one unit is not readily determinable. Such costs are termed *indirect costs*. An example would be the monthly salary of a corporation's president, where one of several divisions is the relevant costing unit. The president's services benefit each division, but the proportion of his salary assignable to one particular division cannot be directly determined. Indirect costs are frequently called *common costs*, that is, costs which are common to, or shared by, two or more costing units. Finally, there are some costs which bear no identifiable relationship to a particular costing unit. Continuing the example of a corporate division, the salary of the manager of division B is neither a direct nor an indirect cost of division A. Thus, the direct and indirect costs of a particular costing unit do not necessarily include all of the costs incurred by the firm. Some costs may be totally unrelated to the costing unit in question.

From the foregoing discussion, it should be clear that whether a specific cost is direct or indirect depends upon the costing unit under consideration. Certain costs may be direct with respect to one costing unit and indirect with respect to another. Hence, the concepts of direct and indirect costs are meaningless without identification, at least implicitly, of the relevant costing unit. In financial accounting, the terms direct and indirect costs are sometimes used in such a way that the only costing unit suggested is the unit of product. To be sure, this is a very important costing unit in a business and one for which direct and indirect costs are typically ascertained. However, these concepts are also very useful with respect to many other costing units and will be used in their broader contexts throughout this volume. Thus, whenever direct and indirect costs are discussed, the relevant costing unit will be indicated.

COST ELEMENTS IN A MANUFACTURING ENTERPRISE

Manufacturing Costs

At one time, the study of cost accounting was concerned almost exclusively with the subject of manufacturing costs. While recent years have seen much greater attention devoted to nonmanufacturing costs, the costs of manufacturing remain the principal concern of both students and practicing cost accountants. There are two chief reasons for this emphasis on manufacturing costs. The first is the traditional practice of including only the costs incurred to manufacture goods in the valuation of the inventories thereof. The importance of accurate inventory valuation in financial accounting necessitates considerable detail in the development and classification of factory costs. The second reason is the fact that the processes of manufacture have become much more standardized and routinized than those of distribution, research, and administration. The greater uniformity of operations permits a higher degree of planning and control and, consequently, requires more detailed cost information. The manufacture of a large and diverse line of products, typical of so many modern corporations, involves the use of a wide variety of goods and services. For accounting purposes, however, each of these items is classified as one of three manufacturing cost elements: *materials, labor,* or *overhead.*

Materials.   Materials include a wide range of physical commodities that go into the making of a product. These are commonly described as raw materials. This term is by no means limited to basic natural resources. The raw material of one firm may be the finished product of another. For example, automobile tires are a finished product of a rubber company but a raw material of an automobile manufacturer.

For purposes of the accounting record-keeping function, the most important classification of materials cost is the distinction between direct and indirect materials, where the product is the relevant costing unit. *Direct materials* are those which can be identified, logically and practically, with the product. Only direct materials are classified as "materials." *Indirect materials,* those which cannot be traced directly to the product, are included in the classification of overhead.

The line between direct and indirect materials is not always an easy one to draw. To begin with, different cost accounting systems may result in different treatments of the same item. (Cost accounting systems will be discussed in Chapter 4.) Further, the direct identification of some materials with the product may be practical only at a prohibitively high cost. Hence, the distinction is commonly drawn on pragmatic as well as theoretic grounds. For example, in the manufacture of wooden chairs, the cost of the wood may be the only recognized direct material. Such materials as glue and screws, while logically traceable to the finished chair, may be treated as indirect simply because the expense of direct identification with the product would exceed the value to the firm of the added informational precision. This illustration points out a cardinal rule of accounting systems design. The benefit derived from an accounting technique must always at least equal the expense of that technique. A procedure that saves costs of $10,000 annually but itself costs $12,000 annually is clearly not justifiable on financial grounds.

Labor.   Like materials, the cost element "labor" includes only *direct labor,* that which can be identified directly with the product. *Indirect labor* is treated as a part of overhead. A simple illustration may assist in explaining the distinction here. A punch-press operator works directly on the product. He spends, on the average, a certain amount of time on each piece. His efforts can be logically traced to and reasonably measured in terms of units of product. Hence, his wages are accounted for as direct labor. Other workers in the same plant, such as foremen, janitors, and watchmen, do not work directly with the product. While their services are essential to production, there is no reasonable basis for measuring their efforts in terms of units of product. Hence, their wages and salaries are regarded as indirect labor cost, a part of overhead. In practice, there is considerable diversity with respect to the definition of direct labor. In some firms, labor-related costs, or fringe benefits, are treated as direct labor; in others, these costs are regarded as indirect. Supplementary unemployment benefit payments and guaranteed annual wage contracts present further complications in the classification of labor costs. All of these complications, however, are problems of practical application, not of basic concepts. Thus, the simplified presentation of labor cost accounting employed in this text will in no way limit the student's knowledge of the fundamental concepts involved.

Overhead.   For practical purposes, the cost classification of *overhead* may be defined simply as including all manufacturing costs other than direct materials and direct labor. Alternatively, overhead may be defined as indirect manufacturing costs. Among the items commonly included in this classification are the following: indirect materials, factory supplies, indirect labor, heat and power, depreciation on factory equipment, insurance on factory equipment, and machinery repairs and maintenance.

One unfortunate feature of overhead is the great diversity of terms which have been used to describe the concept. *Manufacturing expense, factory expense, burden, factory burden, loading, indirect expense, overhead, manufacturing overhead,* and other terms have all been used to denote exactly the same concept. The term overhead will be used consistently in this book. The student should, however, be aware of some of the different terms used and should recognize them when they are encountered. In view of the colloquial use of the term overhead to indicate operating costs in all types of enterprises, manufacturing and nonmanufacturing, profit and nonprofit, it might be considered preferable to prefix the word "overhead" with the qualifying adjective "manufacturing" to denote the indirect manufacturing costs discussed here. However, in cost accounting the term overhead, without a modifier, has a generally recognized technical meaning—indirect manufacturing costs—and will be used here in this way.

For certain purposes, it is useful to group materials and labor costs together and to identify this combination by a single term, *prime costs.* Similarly, labor and overhead costs together are commonly referred to as *conversion costs.* This latter term stems from the fact that labor and overhead costs are incurred in the process of converting raw materials into finished products.

Nonmanufacturing Costs

Despite their traditional preoccupation with manufacturing costs, cost accountants have come to devote more attention and effort to the nonmanufacturing costs incurred by business firms. One of the chief reasons for this change has been the recognition of the fact that nonmanufacturing costs account for the largest portion of every dollar spent by consumers. In other words, the sheer magnitude of the items involved makes it impossible to treat them casually. As more and more dollars are channeled into these nonmanufacturing activities, business managers are becoming increasingly aware of the need for efficient planning and control of such costs and, hence, for more complete and analytical data concerning them.

The subclassifications of nonmanufacturing costs are not as well defined as those of manufacturing costs. For purposes of discussion in this text, four such classifications are here proposed.

1. *Distribution costs* are those incurred in the performance of a wide range of activities generally categorized as marketing. These include selling, shipping, advertising, sales salaries, salesmen's travel expenses, etc.

2. *Administrative costs* include both executive and clerical costs which do not fit logically into some other classification (such as manufacturing or distribution). Examples are the salaries of top managers, directors' fees, general accounting costs, public relations costs, etc.

3. *Research and development costs* have frequently been included in administrative costs for want of a better classification. Recent years have witnessed a marked rise in overall business spending for these activities, however; and it is desirable to give them more individual attention. Especially in instances where efforts are directed toward basic research rather than simply toward product development, these costs seem to be sufficiently unique and significant to deserve separate classification.

4. *Financial costs* also have often been treated as part of administrative costs. These consist primarily of interest costs of one type or another. Also included in this classification are such costs as bank service charges, purchase discounts not taken, and stock and bond issue costs. Again, separate identification and treatment appear desirable.

The main focus of attention in Parts I and II of this volume will be on manufacturing costs. However, special consideration will be given to nonmanufacturing items throughout the text as appropriate and especially in Chapter 12. Many of the concepts and techniques widely applied to manufacturing costs are applicable also to nonmanufacturing costs with more or less modification.

THE BEHAVIOR OF COSTS WITH CHANGES IN VOLUME

One of the most commonly employed and useful of cost classifications is that on the basis of cost behavior with respect to changes in the volume of business activity. As volume changes, costs may either change with it or remain constant. Further, those costs which do change with volume may do so in different ways. Thus, classification of costs according to their behavior patterns with respect to changes in volume greatly facilitates the managerial functions of planning, controlling, and decision making. In this connection, costs are classified as *variable, fixed,* or *semivariable.*

Strict Definitions of Cost-Volume Relationships

In accounting literature, the three cost classifications relative to volume changes are typically defined as follows:

1. *Variable costs* are those costs which vary in total in direct proportion to changes in volume. Successive increases in units of volume result in parallel and proportionate increases in variable costs. Similarly, decreases in volume produce proportionate cost decreases. As an illustration, observe the following relationship between the cost of raw materials and the units of a particular product:

Units of Product	*Raw Materials Cost*
1.....................	$ 2.50
10.....................	25.00
100.....................	250.00
500.....................	1,250.00
842.....................	2,105.00
2,400.....................	6,000.00

Each change of one unit of product causes a change of $2.50 of materials cost. Materials cost in the illustration—and variable costs in general—change in direct proportion to volume. Expressed mathematically, there is a linear relationship between volume and cost.[2] As is apparent in the foregoing example, the directly proportional relationship between total materials cost and volume means that each additional unit of product has the same cost per unit as all other units. Thus, *variable costs vary in total in direct proportion to volume and, consequently, are constant per unit of volume.*

2. *Fixed costs* remain constant in total regardless of changes in volume. They are unaffected by volume changes. For example, the monthly rent on a computer installation may be $24,000 regardless of how many hours the equipment is used per month. Volume of operation may vary from no use at all to maximum monthly volume without altering the rental cost by one cent. Because it is fixed in total for the rental period, the rental cost of the equipment per hour of use decreases as the number of operating hours increases. This is apparent in the following comparison of several alternative monthly volumes of computer operation:

Total Monthly Rental	*Hours Operated per Month*	*Average Cost per Hour*
$24,000.....................	176	$136.36
24,000.....................	352	68.18
24,000.....................	480	50.00
24,000.....................	720	33.33

---

[2] It is entirely possible that some costs might actually be a nonlinear function of volume. At present, accounting treats such costs as semivariable. There is no reason why the definition of a variable cost could not be altered to include any cost that bears some known functional relationship to volume, whether that relationship is linear or not. As a practical matter, the linear relationship is an easy one to work with and appears to be valid in a very large number of cases.

There is an inverse relationship between volume and fixed cost per unit of volume. Hence, *fixed costs are constant in total as volume changes but vary per unit of volume inversely with volume.*

3. *Semivariable costs* are simply all costs which are neither perfectly variable nor absolutely fixed with respect to volume changes. Semivariable costs change in the same direction as volume but not in direct proportion thereto. They may remain constant over relatively small ranges of volume but increase as volume increases beyond these limited ranges. Hence, they might just as well be called semifixed costs. The term "semivariable" is more widely used, however, and will be employed consistently here.

FIGURE 2–1

Cost-Volume Relationships: Perfect

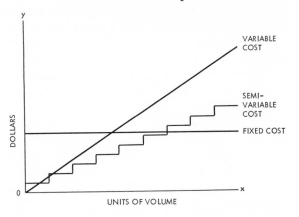

These three cost concepts are depicted graphically in Figure 2–1. Volume is measured on the horizontal axis of the chart; and dollars of cost on the vertical axis. Variable costs increase with volume in a steady, linear pattern. Fixed costs are totally unaffected by volume changes; they are the same at maximum volume as at none at all. (This, of course, assumes that the firm will continue to exist while not producing. All costs may be eliminated by going out of business.) Semivariable costs increase with volume but not in the same regular manner as the variable costs. The stair-step progression of these costs in Figure 2–1 is not necessarily typical. The various steps might be of less regular length and/or height, or the overall pattern of a particular semivariable cost might be better depicted by a nonlinear curve.

Relevant Concepts of Volume. In the foregoing discussion of cost-volume relationships, the term volume has been used in a general sense to denote business activity of some kind. It is readily apparent that the same concept of volume is not applicable to every cost item. Thus, raw materials cost was viewed as variable with respect to the volume of goods produced. Computer equipment rental was regarded as fixed with respect to the volume of use of the equipment. This rental charge would also be fixed with respect to the volume of goods produced, but such relationship might not be considered relevant. Materials cost could hardly be regarded as either fixed or variable with respect to computer hours. There simply is no significant relationship between the two quantities. Costs can be identified as variable, semivariable, or fixed only with reference to the volume of some activity to which those costs are pertinent. Manufacturing costs are typically evaluated in this connection in the light of the volume of goods produced. Selling costs are appraised with reference to the volume of goods sold. Administrative costs are usually viewed in relation to some relevant measure of work, such as the number of lines in letters typed or the number of payroll checks prepared. Throughout this text, when applied to manufacturing costs, the terms "variable" and "fixed" will have reference to cost behavior with respect to changes in the volume of units of product manufactured, unless otherwise indicated.

Cost-Volume Relationships in Practice

The definitions of variable and fixed costs in the previous section are very rigid. Any cost that is neither perfectly variable nor absolutely fixed would be classified as semivariable. As will be evident in subsequent discussions, these rigid definitions are necessary for the analytical employment of the concepts. However, in practice, it is likely that there are comparatively few costs which would be perfectly variable or absolutely fixed over *all* ranges of volume. Hence, the preponderance of costs in real business firms might well fall into the semivariable class. Because of the indefinite nature of this category, however, such classification of most business costs would greatly impair the analytical usefulness of cost-volume relations. Hence, in practice, many costs are classified as either variable or fixed despite the fact that they meet the strict definition of neither.

Raw materials cost is commonly treated as a variable cost. As a matter of fact, as the volume of production expands, it may be possible to obtain significant quantity discounts on the purchase of materials in large lots. Thus, materials cost per unit of product might decrease as volume reaches certain critical levels. Further volume increases may ultimately result in increased unit materials cost due to diseconomies of excessive size. Such a cost pattern is depicted by the variable cost curve in Figure 2–2. In a somewhat similar fashion, certain fixed costs may remain constant in total over significant ranges of volume. Again, however, there may be critical points beyond which additional costs may have to be incurred. This may be illustrated by the cost of supervision in a factory. There are critical points of operating volume at which it becomes necessary to employ additional supervisors to assure adequate control over expanding production. Such cost behavior is shown by the fixed cost curve in Figure 2–2.

Lest it appear that the variable and fixed cost classifications have no practical validity, it must be pointed out that, while a particular cost may not fit the strict definition of either classification, it may be both useful and operationally valid to treat it as variable or fixed, whichever is more nearly the case, for purposes of managerial analysis. First of all,

FIGURE 2–2

Cost-Volume Relationships: Imperfect

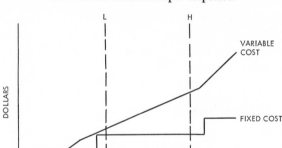

identification of costs as either variable or fixed is useful. It permits analyses which otherwise would not be feasible. Second, such identification may be valid for analytical purposes within limited ranges of volume. Notice that the cost curves in Figure 2–2, while not conforming to the strict definitions of variable and fixed over the entire range of volume, do so conform over significant ranges. It is quite possible that most cost items will prove to be very nearly perfectly variable or absolutely fixed over the relevant range of volume within which the firm is most likely to operate. Thus, in Figure 2–2, if the firm could reasonably expect that its volume of production would be no less than that indicated by the point L and no greater than that indicated by the point H, it is apparent that the costs whose behavior is charted would conform to the strict definitions of variable and fixed over the relevant range of activity. To be sure, Figure 2–2 is constructed deliberately to make this so; it could well be that the breaks in either or both cost curves would occur within the relevant range of volume. Nevertheless, this chart serves to illustrate an important point, namely, that cost behavior in the extreme ranges of activity may not be relevant for purposes of management analysis. Within the bounds of the minimum and maximum practical levels of output, many more cost items may prove to be either variable or fixed than would be so over the full range of technically possible (but practically improbable) operations.

The semivariable cost classification presents some peculiar problems. Certain costs fail to meet the criteria of either variable or fixed costs over any significant range of activity. Treating them as semivariable, however, does not admit of any definite analysis of their behavior in response to volume changes. But it is this very analysis that makes cost classifications with respect to volume changes so important to management. Thus, as a practical matter, many costs which actually appear to be genuinely semivariable are treated as though they were either variable or fixed, whichever they more nearly approximate, or as though they were made up of separable variable and fixed components. In other words, to meet the needs of management in analyzing cost behavior, the semivariable cost classification is not uncommonly completely eliminated. The procedures to accomplish this end will be discussed in Chapter 9, along with some consideration of the limitations which such practice places upon subsequent analyses.

COST CONCEPTS FOR CONTROL AND DECISION MAKING

Responsibility Costing

Historically, accounting was concerned largely with the reporting of economic facts relevant to an entire enterprise. Recent years have seen increased interest in the subdivision of the enterprise along responsibility lines for purposes of reporting to management. More and more management reports are emphasizing the association of economic data with the persons responsible therefor. This involves both the reporting of information to the executive responsible for the particular area of a business and also the reporting to higher management the results of operations in such a manner as to identify them with the responsible subordinates. This development has commonly been referred to as *responsibility accounting*. In cost accounting, it has resulted in the classification of costs along responsibility lines. Cost data are accumulated and reported according to areas of responsibility within a firm. These areas are commonly referred to as *responsibility centers*. Thus, reports indicate not only what costs have ben incurred but also who is responsible for them. This specific subdevelopment of responsibility accounting may be termed *responsibility costing* and is one of the most important cost classification schemes as far as business management is concerned. Responsibility costing facilitates greatly the practical implementation of management's cost control objective. It permits the translation of the basic objective into a program of action centered around people, and, after all, only people can make cost control a reality.

Controllable Costs. The concept of responsibility costing leads directly to the classification of costs as controllable or uncontrollable. Obviously, the controllability of a cost depends upon the level of responsibility under consideration. A *controllable cost* may be defined as one which is reasonably subject to regulation by the executive with whose responsibility that cost is being identified. Thus, a cost which is uncontrollable at one level of responsibility may be regarded as controllable at some other, usually higher, level. For example, the cost of factory maintenance may be uncontrollable at the level of the department supervisor, even though it may appear reasonable to trace some portion of that cost to the individual departments. At the level of the factory manager, on the other hand, maintenance costs may be viewed as controllable.

The controllability of certain costs may be shared by two or more executives. Thus, raw materials cost is generally considered to be a controllable cost. However, there are two distinct factors involved in materials cost. One is the price paid for the materials and the other is the usage of those materials. The responsibilities for these two factors may not be coincidental. The responsibility for prices may rest with the purchasing agent, while that for usage, with the production department supervisors.

It is important that cost controllability be understood in the proper sense. It does not involve eliminating costs, but rather keeping costs as close as possible to some desirable and reasonably attainable levels, or standards. Further, all deviations of actual costs from such standards must not be presumed to be controllable simply because the particular cost items in question are normally regarded as controllable. For example, raw materials cost in one period may be higher than normal because of unusually high prices. If these high prices were paid because materials were obtained from a distant supplier at higher than normal freight charges when local sources of supply were available, the deviation may be treated as positively controllable at the responsibility level of the purchasing agent. However, if the high prices can be traced to a market shortage due to the sudden discontinuance of certain foreign sources of supply, the deviation can hardly be considered controllable at any responsibility level within the firm. In summary then, it may be said that controllable costs are those which may be controlled by executives at a given responsibility level; but specific deviations from standards must be analyzed individually before they can be adjudged controllable or uncontrollable.

Costs Relevant to Alternative Choices

Business managers are frequently faced with decisions among two or more alternatives. These decisions may be fairly complex in terms of numbers of possible choices—for example, choosing among alternatives A, B, C, D, and E, all of which are mutually exclusive. Other decisions may involve simply the alternatives of accepting or rejecting a single proposal. Regardless of the degree of complexity of a particular decision, management must obtain all of the information relevant to the alternatives. This information will include, very importantly, cost data. It will also include many other facts which cannot be expressed quantitatively. For example, the impact of a decision upon employee relations or upon the corporate image is a crucial factor but is not normally subject to quantitative measurement. Thus, it must be kept in mind that, while cost data are important to a business decision, they are still only part of the basis for the final decision; they do not make the decision by themselves.

As is already apparent from the limited discussion in this chapter, there is a great variety of cost data available within a business firm. Not all of these data are likely to be relevant to the alternatives in a specific decision and, hence, not all should be reported to management for decision-making purposes. A surfeit of irrelevant information can be just as useless and misleading as a lack of significant facts. Accountants, therefore, must be able to develop those cost data which are relevant to the particular decision at hand and to report them to management in a manner which will facilitate analysis of the alternatives and formulation of a decision.

Relevant and Irrelevant Costs. A *relevant cost* is one which will be affected by a decision among alternatives. Hence, it is relevant to the analysis of that decision. The term *differential cost* is often used for the same concept because a relevant cost will be different in amount depending upon which alternative is chosen. An *irrelevant cost,* of course, is just the opposite of a relevant cost. It will be unaffected by a decision; it will be the same regardless of the choice that is made. Consequently, it has no relevance to the analysis for decision making. It can and should be ignored.

To illustrate these concepts, consider a decision to purchase or to rent a computer—given that the decision to acquire a computer has already been made. The rental contract would include installation, servicing, and maintenance by the manufacturer. The purchase price would include only the cost of the equipment delivered to the purchaser's plant. For the sake of simplicity, let us assume that all costs associated with the computer can be classified as one of the following:

1. Acquisition cost, including installation and debugging.
2. Service and maintenance cost.

3. Operating cost (labor, power, paper, and cards, etc.).
4. Space occupancy cost (depreciation, insurance, taxes, etc., on the portion of the plant in which the computer will be housed).

From the information given, it is apparent that acquisition costs will differ as between the two alternatives. Under the rental contract, the only acquisition costs would be the periodic rent payments. Under the purchase agreement, the acquisition costs would include the price of the equipment, installation charges, and debugging expenses. Service and maintenance cost would exist as a separate item only if the computer is purchased; the rent payments would include this item. The operating costs and the space occupancy costs would be the same regardless of the alternative chosen. The decision is, in essence, how to finance the acquisition of the computer. This decision will have no effect on the costs of housing and operating the equipment. Thus, the acquisition and the service and maintenance costs are relevant costs, while the operating and the space occupancy costs are irrelevant to the decision.

The reader should avoid the mistake of thinking of relevant costs as equivalent to variable costs and irrelevant costs as equivalent to fixed costs. In the computer illustration above, observe that the monthly rental charge, a typical fixed cost, is a relevant cost in the decision-making analysis. Conversely, the operating costs, which are likely to be largely variable with the volume of computer usage, are irrelevant costs in the analysis.

Incremental Cost.   The *incremental cost* of any one alternative in a decision-making situation is simply the additional cost that will be incurred if and only if that alternative is chosen. Since incremental cost is the added cost associated with a single alternative, it obviously derives from the concept of a relevant cost. In fact, it might be thought of as the net aggregation of all of the relevant costs peculiar to an alternative. The amount of the incremental cost in any case depends upon the reference point of the analysis. For example, suppose that the total output of a factory is now 100,000 units per year and the total annual cost in that factory is $500,000. A proposal has been made to increase annual output to 150,000 units and total annual cost to $650,000. The additional 50,000 units of output is the alternative that has been proposed—an alternative to no change in the present volume of production. The incremental cost of this alternative is the additional $150,000 of annual cost. The reference point for this analysis is the present production volume. Suppose, however, that management had already decided that output must be increased by 50,000 units annually and that the alternatives now being considered are different ways of accomplishing this objective. Alternative A would increase total annual costs by $150,000, while alternative B would increase them by $190,000. With respect to present operations, these two amounts represent the incremental costs of the alternatives. However, with respect to alternative A, the less costly of the two, the incremental cost of choosing alternative B is $40,000.

If incremental cost is associated with an alternative course of action which management may or may not adopt, it is a cost that may or may not be incurred. If the alternative is rejected, the incremental cost will be avoided. Similarly, if the proposed alternative is to eliminate some existing course of action rather than to add a new one, there would be certain existing costs that could be avoided. These are referred to as *avoidable costs*. For example, a proposal to reduce output would entail the avoidance of some costs. Actually, an avoidable cost is simply a variation of an incremental cost. Indeed, it might be defined as an incremental cost saving. The parallel concepts of incremental cost and avoidable cost are extremely important in decision making, for they are the cost effects of alternatives that might be chosen in the decision process.

Marginal Cost.   Literally, marginal cost and incremental cost are synonymous terms. Marginal cost has such a specific definition in economics, however, that it would be inaccurate and undesirable to use the terms interchangeably. In economics, marginal cost is the cost incurred in order to obtain one additional unit of output. This meaning is similar but not identical to that of incremental cost. In the preceding section, there was an example of an incremental cost of $150,000 associated with an increase of 50,000 units of output from a plant. This could not be called the marginal cost also. Marginal cost in this illustration would be the additional cost of producing each successive one of those 50,000 units. In this text, the additional costs associated with a particular alternative in a decision-making problem will consistently be referred to as incremental costs.

Out-of-Pocket Cost.   Any cost which will require the expenditure of cash as a consequence of a management decision may be referred to as an *out-of-pocket cost*. For example, the decision to exploit a mineral deposit presently owned by the company will result in certain costs such as wages and supplies which will require cash outlays. The same decision also results in the incurrence of the cost item depletion, the cost of the mineral resources exhausted as a result of mining operations. This cost, however, does not involve current cash expenditures. The cash payment (or at least the commitment to make a cash payment) for the mineral deposit was made earlier, at the time of acquisition of the property. Once the property has been obtained, such costs as depletion and depreciation are not out-of-pocket costs. Prior to purchase, however, the cost of the property does constitute an out-of-pocket cost of the decision to purchase. This particular cost concept is especially useful in analyses of future cash flows related to proposed investments.

Sunk Cost.   In the mineral deposit example in the preceding paragraph, the cost of depletion is a sunk cost. A *sunk cost* is one which is incurred simply as a consequence of a prior investment of capital; it requires no current outlay. Thus, it is essentially the opposite of an out-of-pocket cost. Depreciation, depletion, and amortization of intangibles are the principal examples of sunk costs. Despite the somewhat negative implications of the word "sunk," especially in maritime activities, a sunk cost should not be thought of as something bad or as a mistake of the past. Rather, it is the current evidence of a commitment made in the past. As such, it is an irrelevant cost for purposes of decision making.

MISCELLANEOUS COST CONCEPTS

Replacement Cost

The sustained and substantial price inflation in the United States since 1939 has given rise to considerable dissatisfaction with the traditional use of historical cost in financial reports. Many have argued that the actual cost of an asset, in terms of dollars expended at the time of its acquisition, is not significant at some later date when prices have changed materially. The merit of this argument is evidenced by the widespread and still growing concern among accountants and businessmen generally with the problem of appropriate recognition of price changes in accounting. One of the most frequently proposed solutions to this problem is the use of replacement cost instead of historical cost in financial reports. Unfortunately, such suggestions have largely failed to produce changes in business practice.

Replacement cost is the current market value of a specific asset, that is, what that asset would cost if it were to be acquired in its present condition in a free market transaction. It is the market value of the asset in its present condition, not the cost of the same asset when new or of some improved substitute asset. The fact that no market presently exists for a particular asset may make any measurement of replacement cost extremely difficult, but it does not alter the basic concept involved. The most familiar use of replacement cost in accounting practice today is in connection with the popular valuation of inventories at cost or market, whichever is lower. "Market" is here defined as the current replacement cost of that inventory, whether replacement would be effected by purchase or by production.

Opportunity Cost

In economic analysis, the word cost most commonly means opportunity cost. The *opportunity cost* of an economic good or service is the maximum amount which that good or service could yield if applied to some other purpose. Hence, opportunity cost is frequently defined as the revenue foregone in the most advantageous alternative use of capital as a consequence of employing it in its present use. So long as transactions take place in a basically free market, it is reasonable to assume that the actual cost (in the accounting sense of the term) of an asset is equal to its opportunity cost at the moment of acquisition. However, as economic conditions change, the cost of that asset as reported on the balance sheet at some future date (i.e., actual cost minus accumulated depreciation to date) is not necessarily equal to the opportunity cost of retaining it. Rather, the current fair market value, or replacement cost, of the asset may be taken as its opportunity cost then.

Obviously, the concept of opportunity cost is extremely important and useful to management in making decisions among alternatives. As a practical matter, however, it is normally impossible to identify with certainty the most advantageous alternative use of capital and, hence, impossible to determine opportunity cost, as such, quantitatively. Thus, practical business analyses must rely on such concepts as replacement cost and incremental cost to indicate the most advantageous uses of capital.

Imputed costs are particular types of opportunity cost. They are costs not actually incurred in an exchange transaction but still relevant to a particular business operation. For example, the use of cash already held in the company bank account to increase inventory levels results in certain actual costs, measured in exchange transactions. The price of the goods, the freight charges on them, and the rental of additional warehouse space for them are examples. Since cash was not borrowed to finance the inventory buildup, no actual interest payments will be made. However, if the cash on hand had been invested in some other way, it could have resulted in the receipt of interest revenue. This interest foregone on an alternative investment is referred to as imputed interest and is one of the most familiar illustrations of an imputed cost. An imputed cost is a real cost, even though current accounting practice would not record it in the accounts; and management must not ignore it in making decisions.

MULTIPLE COST CLASSIFICATIONS IN THE RECORDS

The discussions in this chapter should make it very clear that various schemes of cost classification are useful for various objectives. This is sometimes referred to as the concept of "different costs for different purposes." It is a very useful concept, and it should be incorporated in the design of the accounting system to the extent that it is feasible to do so. That is, the initial recording of a cost should seek to identify every class to which that cost might reasonably and usefully be assigned. The following is a purely illustrative listing of the classes to which a single cost item, the wages of a factory maintenance crew, might be assigned:

1. Cost item: wages and salaries, factory maintenance.
2. Functional classification: manufacturing, overhead, indirect labor.
3. Volume relationship: variable.
4. Responsibility: controllable by plant foreman.
5. Relationship to units produced: indirect.

When more than one category appears on a single line above, it reflects additional degrees of specificity in the classification of the cost. For example, the functional classification indicates that the wages of this crew are (a) manufacturing costs; (b) more specifically, overhead costs; and (c) most specifically, indirect labor costs.

Such a multiple classification system is obviously very useful for a great many purposes. It permits quick answers to questions such as this: "What variable overhead costs are controllable by the plant foreman?" Each cost item must bear an identification key for each classification to which it is assigned. Thus, the maintenance crew's wages in the illustration above must be accessible in the records according to any single classification or any combination thereof, as in the question suggested. Such detail in the accounting records cannot be attained at no cost. The more different classifications desired, the more costly will the accounting system be. Thus, management should require cost classifications that are called for with sufficient frequency to justify the cost of providing them. Information about costs that is needed only occasionally may be extracted from the records and underlying documents by special analysis. Of course, such an approach to information is not very efficient. However, it may be far less expensive than having readily available a great deal of information that is not likely to be used. A computer with random-access data storage greatly improves the practicality of multiple cost classifications. Such schemes will become increasingly practical as new storage devices with greater capacities and lower costs per record stored become available.

The reader will note that the illustrative listing above did not include any classification of the cost item as relevant or irrelevant. This omission was inevitable. It would be impossible to make such a classification without specifying the decision that was to be made. For example, the maintenance crew's wages might well be an irrelevant cost with respect to a decision to change the mix of products made in the factory; whereas it would be a relevant cost with respect to a decision to shut the factory down entirely.

QUESTIONS FOR DISCUSSION

1. "Management is vitally concerned with future costs for the simple reason that they are the only costs over which managers can exercise any control. Hence, historical costs are of no interest to management except to the extent that they may be useful in predicting future costs." Do you agree or disagree with this statement? Explain your position.

2. Define the concepts of direct and indirect costs. Can all of the costs incurred by a business enterprise be classified as either direct or indirect?

3. What is the difference between a cost and an expense? Is this a difference that is customarily recognized in common conversation as opposed to technical accounting discussions?

4. The Upsilon Corporation manufactures three products, Alpha, Beta, and Gamma, in its factory. Indicate whether you would expect each of the following cost items to be direct, indirect, or unrelated to product Beta, where Beta is the costing unit in question:
   a) Raw materials used to manufacture Beta
   b) Depreciation of factory and equipment
   c) Salary of factory manager
   d) Companywide advertising
   e) Wages of workers who package Beta
   f) Raw materials used to manufacture Gamma
   g) Federal income tax

5. For each cost item listed below, state whether you would expect it to be (1) variable in relation to production volume, (2) variable in relation to sales volume, (3) semivariable in relation to production volume, (4) semivariable in relation to sales volume, or (5) fixed. Briefly explain your reasoning in each case.
   a) Factory supervision
   b) Maintenance of office equipment
   c) Wages of production machine operators
   d) Bad debts
   e) Depreciation on factory equipment
   f) Manufacturer's federal excise tax on goods purchased
   g) Janitors' wages

6. "Both variable and fixed costs may be either controllable or uncontrollable costs." Do you agree or disagree with this statement? Explain your position and use examples if you feel they will help support your answer.

7. What are the basic requisites of effective responsibility costing?

8. The following production costs are expected to be incurred at the indicated monthly production volumes (measured in units of output):

Monthly Volume	Factory Wages	Maintenance	Supervision
10,000	$ 30,000	$10,000	$ 8,000
20,000	40,000	10,000	8,000
30,000	50,000	15,000	16,000
40,000	65,000	15,000	16,000
50,000	75,000	25,000	24,000
60,000	90,000	25,000	24,000
70,000	105,000	25,000	32,000
80,000	120,000	25,000	32,000
90,000	135,000	25,000	40,000
100,000	155,000	35,000	40,000

Barring some unusual occurrence, such as a strike, monthly production volume can be expected to fall somewhere between 60,000 and 90,000 units of product. As a practical matter, how would you recommend that each of these three cost items be classified—as variable, as fixed, or as semivariable? Why?

9. Jane Stewart is considering trading her sedan in for a new sports car. She bought the sedan two years ago for $3,000 and still owes $900 on it. The sports car would cost $4,200. Jane could sell or trade in her sedan for $1,600. If she does get the new car, however, she will have to abandon her plans to spend $1,200 on a Hawaiian vacation this year. With respect to Jane's decision, which costs are relevant and which are irrelevant? What would be the incremental cost (or the cost saving) of a decision to get the sports car rather than to keep the sedan?

10. Michael Renzik has invented an automatic pancake turner. He plans to go into the business of making and selling this device, which he has patented. He estimates that each turner will cost $1.25 for materials. He anticipates no direct labor cost, for he plans to do all of the work himself. To this end, he will quit his present job, at which he earns $600 per month. He will rent a vacant garage as his workshop at a monthly rental of $90. He has already purchased all of the tools he needs for $150. To buy the same tools now, Renzik would have to pay $180.

In the foregoing paragraph, identify one or more examples of each of the following types of costs. (A single cost item may, of course, be identified as more than one type of cost.)

a) Historical cost   f) Out-of-pocket cost
b) Future cost   g) Sunk cost
c) Variable cost   h) Opportunity cost
d) Fixed cost   i) Replacement cost
e) Relevant cost   j) Unexpired cost

11. "All out-of-pocket costs are avoidable costs." Discuss the validity of this statement.

12. "In the long run, all costs are variable." Is this true? If so, why? If not, why not?

13. Economists generally define "cost" as opportunity cost. Why don't accountants do the same?

14. If all of a firm's costs are either perfectly variable or absolutely fixed and if its selling price remains constant no matter how many units of product are sold, will the firm's profit before tax (a) decrease as volume increases, (b) increase at a slower rate than volume, (c) increase in direct proportion to volume, or (d) increase at a faster rate than volume? Explain your answer.

15. What does it cost a manufacturing firm to make one unit of product?

chapter 3

THE COST
ACCOUNTING CYCLE

THIS CHAPTER and the following one are concerned with the basic mechanics of recording and processing manufacturing cost data. These mechanics relate primarily to the financial accounting aspects of cost accounting—specifically, the valuation of inventories and the measurement of income in a manufacturing enterprise. At the same time, however, the manner of recording and classifying costs provides the key to effective cost control. Hence, cost accounting systems must be constructed with two important objectives in mind—accurate financial reports and effective cost control.

THE FLOW OF COSTS IN MANUFACTURING

At the moment of their incurrence, all costs may be regarded as essentially identical. They are all unexpired costs, incurred in the expectation that they will contribute to the production of revenue. What happens to costs after their incurrence depends upon their natures and also upon the particular accounting practices employed by the firm. With a very few exceptions (e.g., the cost of land), all costs ultimately expire or become expenses. The exact manner of their expiration, however, is determind by a number of factors, some of which are considered in the paragraphs that follow.

Cost Expiration in General

Long-Lived Assets. Some costs are incurred in order to acquire assets which can be expected to contribute to the production of revenues over fairly long periods of time. The cost of a factory building, for example, will remain a positive factor in the generation of revenue so long as the building is used in the manufacture of a salable product. The objective of income measurement requires that an appropriate portion of the cost of that building be charged to or matched with each dollar of revenue stemming from the sale of goods produced within its walls. Thus, only a portion of the building's cost will be matched with revenue in any one accounting period. The amount of such cost matched with revenue during any one period is the amount of the cost that expires during the period, that is, the amount which ceases to be an asset and becomes an expense. The process of periodically charging part of the cost of a long-lived asset to revenue is called *amortization*. The amortization of the cost of physical plant and equipment—buildings, machinery, vehicles, furniture, and fixtures, etc.—is called *depreciation*.

Current Operating Expenses.   Certain other costs follow a path almost diametrically opposed to that taken by long-lived assets. Such costs as salesmen's commissions and delivery costs are normally assumed to have contributed to the creation of revenue at the moment of their incurrence. Hence, they are charged immediately to expense accounts without their ever being classified as assets. Many costs are typically accorded this same treatment, even though their direct relationship to current revenues is not as obvious as in the case of salesmen's commissions. Thus, such cost items as advertising, executives' salaries, and product development are generally treated as expenses in the period in which they are incurred, even though a careful examination of their natures might suggest that they will enhance revenues in future periods as well as in the current one. Such treatment is a matter of practical convenience in most cases; in some instances, it is likely no more than a matter of habit. Whatever the reason, it is a fact that a great many costs are, as a matter of practice, expensed as soon as they are incurred.

Expiration of Manufacturing Costs

Cost Transformations.   In manufacturing accounting, it is a generally accepted principle that the costs of manufacturing a product are treated as an asset—inventory—until the product is sold, at which time those costs are matched with the revenue from the sale in the process of measuring income. This means that certain costs, such as materials and plant property, which are initially recorded as separate assets, are transformed into a new type of asset before they ultimately become expenses. The process by which an asset's cost is transferred to another asset category, the cost of manufactured goods, is referred to as *cost transformation*. This amounts to a temporary change of asset classification pending the sale of the product. For example, the amortization of the cost of long-lived manufacturing facilities involves an intermediate cost transformation prior to ultimate cost expiration when the manufactured product is sold.

The concept that the costs incurred in the manufacture of a product are combined in a new asset and expire only when that product is sold (or in some way damaged or otherwise rendered unsalable) is commonly stated as the principle that *costs attach.* Under this principle, elements of cost which could not be stored in an asset account in and of themselves—such as labor cost—may become parts of the asset representing the cost of the manufactured product. Thus, manufacturing inventory accounts contain elements of cost which are not inventoriable separately. Labor cannot be stored as a commodity awaiting employment, but the cost of labor already employed can be seen in the form of a manufactured product and treated as part of the total cost of that product.

Product and Period Costs. The foregoing paragraphs have explained how some costs in a manufacturing firm are included in the cost of the manufactured product, while others are treated as expenses of the accounting period in which they are incurred. The former type of cost is called a *product cost;* the latter is a *period cost.* It has already been observed that manufacturing costs are generally accepted as product costs. Nonmanufacturing costs, on the other hand, are treated as period costs. This distinction is generally accepted in current accounting practice, but it has not gone unchallenged. In recent years there has developed a significant movement away from this traditional approach to the product/ period cost distinction and toward an approach which treats as product costs only those manufacturing costs that vary in proportion to the volume of goods produced. In this newer approach, fixed manufacturing costs, along with nonmanufacturing costs, are treated as period costs.

Absorption Costing. The traditional method of accounting for manufacturing costs has included all of them as costs of the product, regardless of their behavior with respect to changes in volume. This method is called *absorption costing* or *full costing;* for the product "absorbs" the full amount of manufacturing costs. Fixed and variable factory costs are handled in exactly the same manner. The distinction between product and period costs is made only on the basis of the different functional areas of business activity; manufacturing costs being product costs and distribution, administrative, research, and financial costs being period costs. (Of course, certain nonmanufacturing costs, while not included as part of the cost of the product, may be deferred to future periods as assets rather than being treated as expenses of the current period. Costs of office furniture and of unexpired insurance on office buildings are examples.)

Variable Costing. In an increasing number of manufacturing enterprises, the traditional absorption costing technique is being replaced by the more recent innovation, *variable costing.* Under the variable costing method, only those manufacturing costs which vary with output are included in the cost of the product; fixed manufacturing costs are accounted for as period costs. Thus, this method distinguishes between product and period costs on the basis of cost-volume relationships as well as on the basis of the functional areas of business operations. Variable nonmanufacturing costs, it must be understood, are treated as period costs under variable costing, just as they are under absorption costing. In practice, direct materials and direct labor are almost always treated as variable costs. Hence, the actual distinction between absorption and variable costing lies in the accounting treatment of overhead and, specifically, fixed overhead. Variable overhead, like materials and labor, is treated as a product cost under both methods. Fixed overhead is treated as a product cost in absorption costing but as a period cost in variable costing.

In this chapter, the methodologies of both absorption and variable costing will be illustrated. A critical comparison of the two will be presented in the following chapter.

Manufacturing Inventory Accounts

In a merchandising enterprise, a single inventory account for all merchandise on hand is typical. This single account in the general ledger is supported by detailed records for stocks of individual items in inventory. But only one general ledger account is needed for merchandise inventory

FIGURE 3–1

Flow of Manufacturing Costs in Absorption Costing

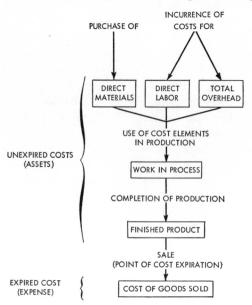

from the time it is purchased until it is sold. In a manufacturing firm, however, a single inventory account is not suitable. The function that distinguishes manufacturing from merchandising is the conversion of the materials purchased by the manufacturer into a new product. Thus, pig iron is converted to sheet steel; sheet steel, to automobile fenders; etc. At any one time, a manufacturing enterprise is likely to have on hand raw materials as yet unprocessed, goods in the process of manufacture but not yet completed, and finished products awaiting sale. Each of these stages of

FIGURE 3–2

Flow of Manufacturing Costs in Variable Costing

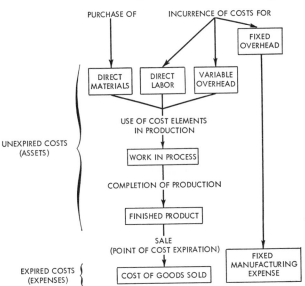

goods is normally accounted for in a separate inventory account. Raw materials are reported in a Materials Inventory account; uncompleted production, in a Work in Process account; and completed production, in a Finished Product account. Each of these is an inventory account and an asset. Each is a part of the sequential flow of manufacturing costs. Materials, as such, appear when they are purchased from suppliers. They become part of Work in Process at the time they are issued from the storeroom to the factory for use. Work in Process becomes Finished Product when the process of manufacture is completed. Finally, Finished Product is transferred to the Cost of Goods Sold account at the point of sale of the items in inventory. Sale is the point at which manufacturing costs expire (excepting fixed manufacturing costs under the variable costing method); hence, Cost of Goods Sold is an expense account.

This flow of manufacturing costs in the absorption costing method is presented diagrammatically in Figure 3–1. Notice that labor and overhead are included in this diagram in a position parallel to that of materials. While these two cost elements cannot be stored in inventory themselves, as can materials, they are costs of the product and are stored in the inventories of Work in Process and Finished Product. All three manufacturing cost elements finally become expenses as part of Cost of Goods Sold. Figure 3–2 repeats this cost flow diagram for variable costing. The only difference between the two is in the handling of fixed overhead.

ACCOUNTING FOR MANUFACTURING COSTS

Recording Costs by Responsibility

One of management's main objectives with respect to costs is their effective control. This objective can be implemented only by tracing costs to responsible executives, for cost control requires knowledge of who is responsible for costs as well as of the amounts of costs. Thus, costs are identified with the smallest significant units of managerial responsibility; such units are commonly called *responsibility centers*. A *cost center* is any component of a firm to which it is practical and useful to trace costs. Cost centers are not necessarily responsibility centers. A product line, for example, might be a cost center but not a responsibility center. For purposes of discussion, however, we shall assume that a cost center does coincide with a center of responsibility. A department in a factory is a typical example of a unit that is both a cost and a responsibility center. In cost accounting, all manufacturing costs are usually charged to production through one or more departments. Not every cost can be traced directly to a department, however. Depreciation on the plant building, for example, cannot be traced to any cost center smaller than the entire plant. Any identification of depreciation on the plant with one department therein must be based upon some arbitrary allocation scheme rather than upon direct traceability. Thus, there are commonly large cost centers which embrace two or more smaller ones. Normally, these larger cost centers correspond to higher levels of managerial responsibility.

The actual accounting processes for tracing costs to the pertinent cost centers may vary among firms. It is possible, for example, to have separate accounts for each cost element (i.e., materials, labor, and overhead) for each cost center. Alternatively, a single account may include all items of one cost element, subsidiary records and reports being employed to fix responsibility for costs by cost centers. In a large, decentralized firm, the former alternative would seem preferable. Whatever the methods used to accomplish it, the identification of costs with responsible executives and supervisors must be regarded as an imperative of good management accounting.

Accounting for Materials

Purchase. Accounting for materials begins when a need for a particular material is determined at some level of responsibility within the firm and a formal request is made that such material be purchased in the required amount. This formal request is commonly made on a standard form called a *purchase requisition.* This is an internal document, submitted by the department requesting the material to the purchasing department. A requisition may be initiated by one of the production departments which uses the item in question. More commonly, however, the requisition would be initiated by the materials storeroom when existing stocks of a material reach a preestablished minimum level which serves as a signal to reorder. No formal journal entry is prepared to record the issuance of a purchase requisition. However, the requisition sets into motion the activities which will ultimately result in the journalizing of a purchase.

If the purchase requisition is approved, the purchasing department will select the most advantageous supplier of the material needed and will issue a *purchase order* for the item. (It should be noted here that efficient purchasing normally involves issuance of purchase orders for several items at one time, where the orders for individual items are not large.) A purchase order is a document sent by the purchasing department to the supplier. It includes materials specifications, quantities ordered, and the date the items are needed. The supplier fills this order by shipping the materials requested and bills the purchaser for them by sending an invoice, which details the items purchased, the quantities shipped, and the prices. After the actual shipment has been compared with the invoice, called a *purchase invoice* in the hands of the purchaser, the invoice becomes the basis for the preparation of a journal entry to record the purchase, the invoice price (including freight charges, etc. where applicable) being the measured cost of the materials purchased. Such an entry follows:[1]

Materials Inventory xxx
    Vouchers Payable   xxx

In this entry and in similar ones throughout this text, it is assumed that a voucher system is used to control cash disbursements and, hence, that all

---

[1] In this entry and in those on the following pages, no dollar amounts are used. Only the accounts debited and credited are indicated. A later comprehensive illustration will repeat these entries with specific dollar amounts.

obligations incurred in the purchase of goods or services are credited to an account titled Vouchers Payable.

Usage. As materials are needed in the factory, the production departments issue *materials requisitions* (not to be confused with purchase requisitions) to the materials storeroom for the required quantities of the particular items. These materials requisitions, indicating the department requesting the items, are the bases for tracing materials costs to cost centers within the plant. The issuance of the materials to the factory by the storeroom signals a change in the inventory classification of those items. They now cease to be materials, as such, and become a part of the product in the process of manufacture. This results in a cost transformation from Materials Inventory to Work in Process. The following entry is made:

Work in Process... xxx
    Materials Inventory.................................... xxx

The foregoing entry assumes that the materials requisitioned are direct materials. This is not always the case. At the time of purchase, it is not always possible to distinguish between items that will be used as direct materials and those which will be used as indirect materials. And even if such distinction is possible, both direct and indirect materials may be included in the Materials Inventory account when purchased. When issued, however, indirect materials are not charged directly to the Work in Process account. To be sure, they will ultimately be charged to that account; but they are first accumulated along with other indirect manufacturing costs in an account for overhead costs in general. Thus, the requisition of indirect materials would be recorded as follows:

Overhead Control... xxx
    Materials Inventory.................................... xxx

At this point, the Overhead Control account may be taken simply as a temporary account for the accumulation of all indirect factory costs.

Accounting for Labor

For purposes of discussion, problems of accounting for labor may be classified in two categories: *Labor cost accounting* is concerned with the accounts and amounts to be charged (debited) for labor costs. *Payroll accounting* is concerned with the accounts and amounts to be credited in the recording and paying of obligations to employees for labor services. Because of the traditional emphasis in cost accounting upon manufacturing costs, labor cost accounting is concerned chiefly with manufacturing or factory labor. Payroll accounting, however, is just as concerned with administrative and sales employees as with factory workers.

In large firms, it is economically feasible to departmentalize many different activities and to accomplish considerable division of work. In such a firm, labor cost accounting may be handled by a factory accounting department and payroll accounting, by a payroll department. In such cases, some account common to both departments is needed so that the two separate accounting operations may be tied together and reconciled, to the extent that they both deal with the same basic data. This account may have different titles in different companies. In this text, it will be referred to as the Payroll Summary account. This is the account credited by the factory accounting department for the total of amounts debited to the various manufacturing cost accounts affected and the account debited by the payroll department for the total of credits representing obligations to employees and other parties entitled to some portion of the employees' earnings (e.g., the federal government). Obviously, except for lags or errors in bookkeeping procedures in the two departments, the debits and credits to the Payroll Summary account for any period of time will be equal.

Labor Cost Accounting. The proper charging of labor costs to manufacturing cost accounts requires that distinctions be made between direct and indirect labor costs and between labor costs incurred in different cost centers. The former distinction is largely a matter of definition; the latter, a matter of accurate record keeping. The maintenance of records which show the amounts of time worked by employees in various cost centers and the availability of hourly wage rate data permit the charging of factory labor costs by areas of responsibility. For the sake of simplicity, the discussions and illustrations in this chapter will assume that there is only one cost center—the entire factory—in the plant under study. This assumption does not alter the basic concepts involved or the mechanics of recording labor costs; it merely reduces the number of accounts to be handled.

As stated in Chapter 2, direct labor is that labor which can be traced logically and practically to the product. All other factory labor costs are regarded as indirect and are included in overhead. The wages of foremen, janitors, watchmen, factory clerks, and others whose work is not concerned directly with the product are usually treated as indirect costs. In addition, a number of payments made to direct laborers are commonly included in overhead rather than in direct labor. Wages paid to direct laborers while they are not actually performing productive work are usually accounted for as overhead. Examples of such wages are vacation pay, holiday pay, and idle-time pay. The reason for treating as overhead such payments to workers whose labor is normally regarded as direct is that these payments cannot be traced directly to units of product. Vacation pay and idle-time pay could hardly be charged directly to particular units of product, as no units are produced during the periods for which those costs are incurred. Premiums paid to direct laborers for overtime and double-time work and for night-shift work are normally included in overhead. If such premiums were charged directly to the units produced during overtime or night shifts, those units would have higher costs than those produced during the regular 40-hour week. Yet, the overtime and night-shift work is usually necessitated by a generally high level of production, not by specific units or jobs. Hence, it would not be meaningful to report units manufactured during overtime or night hours as more costly than their counterparts produced during the regular 8-hour day. Rather, overtime and night-shift premiums should be viewed as costs incurred because total production exceeds the capacity of the plant during a straight 40-hour week. As such, these costs are applicable to all units produced but directly traceable to none.[2]

The following journal entry illustrates the distribution of factory labor costs to the appropriate manufacturing cost accounts:

```
Work in Process............................................  xxx
Overhead Control..........................................  xxx
    Payroll Summary.......................................        xxx
```

The debit to Work in Process is to charge the direct labor cost to the product. Overhead Control is debited for indirect labor costs, overtime premiums, vacation pay, etc. The detail supporting this entry would be accumulated and classified on a labor cost distribution sheet.

Labor-Related Costs. In addition to wage and salary payments made to workers, employers incur a number of costs incidental to the employment of workers. These include such items as the employer's share of social security taxes, unemployment compensation taxes, insurance premiums, contributions to pension funds, and supplementary unemployment benefits. These are *labor-related costs* or *fringe benefits*. They are commonly treated as part of overhead, to the extent that they relate to manufacturing workers. Labor-related costs are incurred in connection with nonmanufacturing workers also. These, logically, are charged to nonmanufacturing expense accounts rather than to overhead. The entry to record labor-related costs applicable to factory employees is illustrated below:

```
Overhead Control..........................................  xxx
    Social Security Taxes Payable.........................         xxx
    Unemployment Compensation Taxes Payable..............         xxx
    Health Insurance Premiums Payable....................         xxx
    Etc..................................................         xxx
```

---

[2] An exception to this treatment of overtime premiums as overhead occurs when the overtime is necessitated solely in order to accelerate the completion of a specific job. For example, a ship owner may want to have his ship completed and put back into service faster than the shipyard's normal schedule would allow. Thus, he may require overtime simply to meet his own time schedule. In such a case, the overtime premium should be included in the direct labor costs charged to that specific job. Presumably, that customer would also have to pay a higher price to compensate the shipyard for the overtime pay.

There is no credit to the Payroll Summary account in this entry, for the labor-related costs do not involve direct payments to workers or withholdings from workers' earnings. Thus, labor-related costs are not involved in the payroll accounting process.

Some firms include labor-related costs in the classification of direct labor. This is accomplished by estimating the total average labor-related cost per direct labor hour and adding that average to the hourly wage rate to determine the total direct labor charge per hour. For example, assume that the direct labor wage rate in a plant is $2.50 per hour and that the average total labor-related cost is estimated to be $.65 per hour. Direct labor is then charged at a rate of $3.15 per hour. Since the $.65 portion of this charge is an estimate, it is likely that the total actual labor-related costs incurred would be somewhat more or less than the total charged to Work in Process. Such a difference would be disposed of by an adjustment at the end of the accounting period.[3] Including the labor-related costs applicable to direct labor wages in the classification of direct labor cost is unquestionably valid, and many accountants argue that it is distinctly preferable to including them in overhead. Nevertheless, most firms continue to treat labor-related costs as part of overhead. They will consistently be included in overhead in this text.

Regardless of how labor-related costs are classified for cost accounting purposes, their nature remains the same. The same procedures for controlling these costs would be employed no matter how they were classified in the accounts, and their significance in decision making is unaffected by their classification. Any decision that will have a direct impact upon direct labor cost will have a similar impact upon labor-related costs, and the latter are pertinent to that decision whether classified as direct labor or as overhead.

Evolving Problems of Labor Cost Accounting. Traditionally, labor has been regarded as a direct cost, incurred specifically because of the units of product manufactured. Likewise, it has generally been considered to be a variable cost, fluctuating in direct proportion to the volume of production. Where labor cost is incurred on a piece-rate basis—so much per unit of product manufactured—it clearly is both direct and variable with respect to production. Even where direct laborers are paid on an hourly basis, labor cost is essentially direct and variable if the workers are laid off when no production work is being done. However, if workers are regularly paid for a full 40-hour week, regardless of the amount of production, then labor cost would appear to be a fixed cost directly traceable to the firm's being in operation. It would not then vary with the vol-

---

[3] The manner of disposing of the difference between actual and estimated labor-related costs would be essentially the same as that illustrated later in this chapter for disposing of differences between actual overhead costs and normal overhead costs charged to production.

ume of production nor would it be directly traceable to units of product.

At the time of this writing, it would not be accurate to say that labor has truly become a fixed cost in American industry. There is a definite movement in that direction, however. Supplementary unemployment benefit payments and other wage continuation plans require employers to pay workers for time when they are not working. The demands for a guaranteed annual wage, or annual salary for production workers, recur in many labor contract negotiations. It is not unlikely that these demands will one day be met. Nor is this movement caused entirely by bargaining demands. Many employers have found numerous advantages in having a stable work force, even if it necessitates paying employees for nonproductive time.

Even if labor were, in effect, a fixed cost, it could be made to appear as a variable cost in the accounts. Direct labor could be charged to each unit of product at some normal rate; and labor cost of nonproductive time could be charged to overhead. In this case, however, labor cost is artificially made to appear direct and variable. The nature of the cost cannot be altered by the way in which it is accounted for. Charging idle-time labor costs to overhead is reasonable only when idle time is not a regular part of total labor cost. If labor were to become a true fixed cost, as in the case of annual salaries for production workers, it should be accounted for as such. It would then be an indirect cost insofar as the individual units of product are concerned and ought to be accounted for in the same way as fixed overhead costs. Such a method of accounting for labor cost would not change materially the final cost of manufactured products where absorption costing is used. Labor would still be charged to production, except that it would now be considered an indirect rather than a direct cost. If variable costing were used, however, labor, now being a fixed cost, would be treated as a period cost rather than as a cost of the product.

The problems associated with labor becoming a fixed cost are still beyond the frontier of accounting practice. Cost accountants have not devoted any great amount of attention to them. It may be that the present trend toward fixed labor costs will be halted and even reversed, but this does not now seem likely. Rather, it is likely that the trend will accelerate and that accountants will have to deal directly with the consequent problems.

Payroll Accounting.   The mechanics of payroll accounting are common to all enterprises which employ a significant number of workers. The payroll department handles the pay records of all employees, whether they receive hourly wages or weekly salaries, whether they are employed in production or in some nonmanufacturing activity. Basically, the payroll department's task is to determine who is to receive what amount of each employee's gross earnings and to prepare payroll checks. The federal government receives a portion of each worker's earnings in the form of income tax withheld from the worker's pay and also in the form of social security[4] tax withheld. In some states, income tax is also withheld for the account of the state government. Union dues are frequently "checked," or withheld by the employer for the union. There may be withholdings for insurance programs to which employees contribute, United Fund and similar donations pledged by the employees, and investment programs such as the bond-a-month plan for the purchase of U.S. savings bonds. Finally, after all withholdings, the balance is paid to the employee; this in his "take-home" pay. Following is a general journal entry to record the payment of a payroll in accordance with the foregoing discussion:

Payroll Summary...	xxx	
Federal Income Tax Withheld...........................		xxx
Social Security Taxes Payable..........................		xxx
Union Dues Withheld...................................		xxx
United Fund Contributions Withheld....................		xxx
Etc..		xxx
Vouchers Payable......................................		xxx

The credit to Vouchers Payable is for the amount of the employees' net "take-home" pay. This liability will be discharged when the payroll checks are drawn and disbursed. The liabilities for the amounts withheld will be discharged when remittances are made to the government, the union, the United Fund, etc.

Accounting for Overhead

Thus far, we have observed the actual recording of three items of overhead cost—indirect materials, indirect labor, and labor-related costs. There are a great many other items in the overhead classification, all of which must be accounted for as have these three. It is also necessary to charge overhead costs to the product, that is, to Work in Process. In this section, we shall examine first the accumulation and classification of overhead cost items and then the charging of overhead costs to the product.

Recording Variable and Fixed Overhead Costs. In the entries already illustrated, the three overhead items encountered were charged to a single account, Overhead Control. As already mentioned, it is desirable to accumulate these costs according to responsibility. Hence, each distinct cost center ought to have its own overhead account. Again, for simplicity, we shall pursue the discussion of overhead costs under an assumption that there is only one cost center in the plant under study. There is still a further classification of overhead costs which should be observed, how-

---

[4] The social security tax is also referred to as the OASI (Old Age and Survivors' Insurance) tax and as the FICA (Federal Insurance Contributions Act) tax.

ever. Traditionally, all overhead costs have been included in one account for each cost center. Recent years, however, have witnessed increasing interest on the part of management in having manufacturing cost data identified and recorded in the accounts as variable or fixed with respect to changes in output. Since materials and labor are almost universally regarded as variable costs, as a practical matter only overhead costs must be segregated into variable and fixed classifications. This can be accomplished by having two overhead control accounts for each cost center— Variable Overhead Control and Fixed Overhead Control. This separate recording of variable and fixed overhead can and should be effected under either an absorption costing or a variable costing system. From an accounting viewpoint, separate recording is essential only in variable costing. But, for purposes of management, it is equally desirable under both methods.

There is still the very important problem of identifying those costs which are variable and those which are fixed. In a practical situation, this distinction may present some very perplexing problems. Nevertheless, as mentioned in the previous chapter, the distinction is so useful to management that it must be made even if it involves a number of approximations. For purposes of illustration in this chapter, we shall consider only eight overhead cost items, including the three already encountered in connection with accounting for materials and labor. These eight items are listed below and classified as variable or fixed. The classifications of the individual cost items here are for illustrative purposes and do not purport to be applicable in manufacturing enterprises generally.

Variable Costs	*Fixed Costs*
Indirect materials	Indirect labor
Labor-related costs	Labor-related costs
Power and light	Depreciation
	Insurance
	Property taxes
	Repairs and maintenance

Labor-related costs are unique in this listing, as they are included both as variable and. as fixed. To the extent that they relate to direct labor, a variable cost here, they are variable. To the extent that they relate to indirect labor, a fixed cost here, they are fixed.

We must now retrace our steps and reconstruct some of the entries prepared earlier so that all overhead items will be identified and recorded as variable or fixed. The entry for the requisition of indirect materials now appears as follows:

```
Variable Overhead Control................................  xxx
    Materials Inventory....................................        xxx
```

The entry to record the distribution of labor costs, including indirect labor, is now prepared thus:

```
Work in Process..........................................  xxx
Fixed Overhead Control...................................  xxx
     Payroll Summary.......................................        xxx
```

The labor-related costs are now recorded as follows:

```
Variable Overhead Control................................  xxx
Fixed Overhead Control...................................  xxx
     Social Security Taxes Payable..........................        xxx
     Unemployment Compensation Taxes Payable...............        xxx
     Health Insurance Premiums Payable.....................        xxx
     Etc...................................................        xxx
```

Note that the only change in each of the three entries above is in the title(s) of the overhead account(s) debited. The remaining overhead items in our lists may be recorded by the following entries:

```
Variable Overhead Control................................  xxx
     Vouchers Payable (power and light bills)..............        xxx

Fixed Overhead Control...................................  xxx
     Accumulated Depreciation—Plant and Equipment..........        xxx
     Unexpired Insurance...................................        xxx
     Accrued Property Taxes Payable........................        xxx
     Vouchers Payable (repair and maintenance bills)........        xxx
```

These two entries assume that power and light and repair and maintenance bills are paid currently, that insurance is paid for in advance, and that property taxes are accrued and paid subsequently.

Charging Actual Overhead Costs to Production. Because overhead is indirect and in total is not perfectly variable with output, it is not possible to charge overhead costs to production in the same way as materials and labor. The materials and labor costs associated with a particular product or batch of production are determinable when the materials are used and the labor time recorded. The overhead costs associated with a particular product, however, can be determined only by some arbitrary allocation scheme, the total overhead costs being allocated among the units produced in some manner which appears reasonable. Total actual overhead cost, of course, cannot be determined until the end of the accounting period and, hence, cannot be allocated to the products until then. If there is no objection to such a delay in charging overhead costs, an entry can be prepared as of the end of each period to charge that period's production with its overhead costs. The entry depends upon the costing method employed in the firm—absorption costing or variable costing. Under absorption costing, both variable and fixed overhead are charged to production.

```
Work in Process..........................................  xxx
     Variable Overhead Control.............................        xxx
     Fixed Overhead Control................................        xxx
```

Under variable costing, only the variable overhead is treated as a product cost.

Work in Process... xxx	
Variable Overhead Control...............................	xxx

Fixed overhead is treated as an expense of the current period under variable costing and, hence, would not be transferred to Work in Process. Fixed Overhead Control, like other current expense accounts, would be closed at the end of the period to the Revenue and Expense Summary account.

Charging Normal Overhead Cost to Production. The practice of charging actual overhead to production after the end of the accounting period involves a number of difficulties. These stem from the facts that overhead is indirect and is composed, in part at least, of fixed costs. If all overhead were directly traceable to and perfectly variable with output, it could be charged to production in the same way as materials and labor. It is a fact, however, that overhead is partly fixed; and, as American manufacturers move more toward automation, it is reasonable to expect that the fixed-cost component of total overhead will become increasingly larger. Variable overhead is not readily traced to individual products either, even though it does vary in proportion to output. For example, the usage of indirect materials is commonly a function of the volume of production; but the usage of specific indirect materials cannot ordinarily be traced to specific products. Two of the most notable difficulties attendant upon the charging of actual overhead to production are discussed in the paragraphs which follow.

If a manufacturer contracts to produce special equipment or some other specialized product for a customer and to sell that special product at production cost plus some stipulated profit margin, no billing can be made until the total production cost of the order is determined. If actual overhead is charged to production, the total production cost of any order will be unknown until after the end of the period in which it is produced. This is clearly an intolerable situation if actual overhead were charged to production only at the end of each year. Even if it were charged monthly, the delay would only be reduced, not eliminated. Quite obviously, the customer would want to know as soon as the order was finished what he was going to have to pay for it. Similarly, the manufacturer would hardly care to wait until the end of the year before he could bill his customers. Hence, it is essential to have some regular method of determining the overhead applicable to an order or to any other batch of output as soon as the production process is finished. It is true, of course, that most production is sold at established list prices. However, there are enough sales at cost plus a profit margin to make this consideration a real one. For example, many defense contracts for new or custom-designed items provide for a price equal to cost plus some predetermined profit margin. While the number of such contracts is not very large, the dollar amounts involved are usually substantial.

Another disadvantage of charging actual overhead cost to production may be seen from an examination of a firm that experiences significant seasonal variations in the volume of its production. Such a situation is depicted in Table 3–1. For purposes of this illustration, all variable costs—materials, labor, and variable overhead—are included in a single figure *per unit of product;* it is the same each month. Fixed overhead, on

TABLE 3–1

Impact of Seasonal Output on Unit Cost

Month	Units of Product Produced	Fixed Cost in Total	Fixed Cost per Unit	Variable Cost per Unit	Total Cost per Unit of Product
January	1,000	$ 8,000	$8.00	$6.00	$14.00
February	2,000	8,000	4.00	6.00	10.00
March	2,500	8,000	3.20	6.00	9.20
April	4,000	8,000	2.00	6.00	8.00
May	6,000	8,000	1.33	6.00	7.33
June	8,000	8,000	1.00	6.00	7.00
July	8,000	8,000	1.00	6.00	7.00
August	6,000	8,000	1.33	6.00	7.33
September	4,000	8,000	2.00	6.00	8.00
October	3,500	8,000	2.29	6.00	8.29
November	2,000	8,000	4.00	6.00	10.00
December	1,000	8,000	8.00	6.00	14.00
	48,000	$96,000			

the other hand, is the same in total each month. Therefore, it varies, per unit of output, inversely with the volume of production. In months of low production, unit fixed cost and, consequently, total unit cost are relatively high. Conversely, in months of high production, unit cost is relatively low. Thus, marked differences in the unit cost of the product appear from month to month even though the product remains unchanged; only the quantities in which it is produced change. These variations in unit cost are likely to be misleading and to result in meaningless fluctuations in income from month to month, for selling price is not likely to change as unit cost changes. While the extent of the fluctuations in monthly output in Table 3–1 is admittedly extreme, it serves to illustrate the problem of charging actual overhead costs to production when output varies seasonally.

The reader should by now have recognized that the problem of unit cost fluctuating with seasonal variations in output exists only under absorption costing. Under variable costing, since no fixed costs are charged to the product, unit cost will be unaffected by volume fluctuations. The problem discussed with reference to the cost-plus-profit contract, however, is common to both absorption and variable costing.

If some overhead cost per unit that would be valid over the whole year could be determined in advance, it would solve the two problems described above. First, it would permit the charging of overhead cost to products as soon as they are completed. Hence, the cost-plus-profit contract could be billed as soon as the work is finished. Second, it would eliminate the seasonal fluctuations in unit cost due to the seasonal variations in output. For example, in Table 3-1, if the firm's accountant could have foreseen that a total of 48,000 units of product would have been produced during the year and that a total of $96,000 in fixed costs would have been incurred in that year, he could have predetermined that the fixed cost of producing each unit would be $2 as an average for the entire year. Therefore, the total unit cost would be $8 in each month. But can annual output and fixed costs be known in advance? While they cannot be predicted with certainty, they typically can be estimated in advance with reasonable confidence. As a matter of fact, if management is to plan business operations for a year, such estimates must be made. When these estimates are formalized, they are generally called budgets. For the present, we are concerned only with budgets for output and for fixed overhead. Given these two budgeted data, we can determine by simple division the budgeted unit fixed cost of the product for a period. When this budgeted unit cost is used in charging fixed overhead to production, it is referred to as a *normal fixed overhead rate.*

A *normal variable overhead rate* may be determined quite readily from observations of the variable overhead costs incurred per unit of output in the past, with adjustments for changing prices and circumstances. By virtue of the fact that it is variable, the variable overhead rate would be budgeted directly as an amount per unit of product. Budgeted output would be irrelevant here. The variable overhead rate would be the same at any level of output, whereas the fixed overhead rate will decline as higher levels of output are budgeted.

It must be understood that the use of normal overhead rates derived from budgeted data does not mean that the budget itself is recorded by means of a journal entry. The overhead charged to production in this case is the normal overhead rate(s) multiplied by the actual output for the period. Budgeted output is used only to determine the normal fixed overhead rate, not to charge overhead to production. The normal overhead rates are, in effect, estimates of what actual overhead per unit of output will be. The overhead cost actually charged to Work in Process, thus, is a function of the normal overhead rates and the actual output for the period.

Charging overhead costs to production at a normal rate means that the

Work in Process account will not consist entirely of literally *actual* costs. The normal cost element will carry through to the Finished Product and Cost of Goods Sold accounts. (Refer again to Figures 3–1 and 3–2 to see why this must be so.) This minor deviation from actual cost is widely accepted in business and, as a matter of fact, is typical of cost accounting systems. Because the use of normal overhead rates results in the charging to Work in Process of something other than actual overhead costs incurred, it is general practice to make the offsetting credits for that charge to accounts other than the overhead control accounts. These credits may be made to accounts titled Variable Overhead Applied and, under absorption costing only, Fixed Overhead Applied. Journal entries to record the charging of overhead at normal rates are illustrated below. Under absorption costing, both variable and fixed overhead are charged to the product.

```
Work in Process.............................................  xxx
     Variable Overhead Applied..............................         xxx
     Fixed Overhead Applied.................................         xxx
```

Under variable costing, only variable costs enter into the cost of the manufactured product.

```
Work in Process.............................................  xxx
     Variable Overhead Applied..............................         xxx
```

The Fixed Overhead Control account would again be closed directly to the Revenue and Expense Summary account, just as any other current expense.

As a result of the procedure described in the previous paragraph, there will be two accounts for variable overhead and, again only under absorption costing, two accounts for fixed overhead in the general ledger—the overhead control accounts with debit balances representing the actual costs incurred and the overhead applied accounts with credit balances representing the overhead cost charged to the product for the period. The balances in the two accounts for variable costs and, when appropriate, in the two accounts for fixed costs will be equal and offsetting only if the budgeted cost and output data prove to be exactly equal to the comparable actual data. Obviously, it is very unlikely that the budgeted and actual data will be identical. They may be very close to each other, but some discrepancy is virtually inevitable. Consequently, there will almost always be some differences between the debit balances in the overhead control accounts and the respective credit balances in the overhead applied accounts. These differences are termed *underapplied overhead* when actual costs exceed the costs applied and *overapplied overhead* when the costs applied are greater than the actual costs incurred. While there are alternative methods of disposing of under- or overapplied overhead, at this point we shall simply observe that it may be closed directly to the Revenue and Expense Summary account. This would be accomplished by closing both the overhead control accounts and the overhead applied accounts to Revenue and Expense Summary at the end of the fiscal year. The reporting of under- or overapplied overhead in financial statements is illustrated later in this chapter.

COMPREHENSIVE ILLUSTRATION

At this point, it may be helpful in understanding the basic cost accounting cycle (that is, the flow of manufacturing costs through the successive accounts) to study an illustration with specific production and cost data. These data pertain to the Wedgewood Products Company for the year 1972. Both absorption and variable costing are presented in this illustration.

TABLE 3–2

Variable Costs	Fixed Costs
Indirect materials	Indirect labor
Labor-related costs	Labor-related costs
Power and light	Depreciation
	Insurance
	Property taxes
	Repairs and maintenance

TABLE 3–3

	Absorption Costing	Variable Costing
Materials inventory.....	$ 80,000	$ 80,000
Work in process.......	200,000	150,000
Finished product......	300,000	225,000

The company has estimated that each unit of product will involve the incurrence of $1.50 of variable overhead costs. Hence, variable overhead will be applied to production at a normal rate of $1.50 per unit. Fixed overhead costs are budgeted at $750,000 for the year, and output is estimated at 300,000 units. Thus, under absorption costing only, fixed overhead will be applied to production at a normal rate of $2.50 per unit. The variable and fixed overhead cost items in this illustration will be those listed and classified on page 50 and repeated in Table 3–2.

The inventory balances at the beginning of the year are the starting point of the illustration. These balances, taken from the balance sheet as of December 31, 1971, are shown in Table 3–3. The inventory balances for Work in Process and Finished Product are greater under absorption costing than under variable costing, of course, for the former method includes fixed overhead in inventory while the latter method does not.

Journal Entries

Following are the transactions relevant to the Wedgewood Products Company's manufacturing operations during 1972 and the general journal entries to record them:

1. Raw materials costing $800,000 were purchased on account.

(1)

Materials Inventory.................................	800,000	
Vouchers Payable.............................		800,000

2. Materials costing $760,000 were issued to the factory for use. Of these, $680,000 were direct materials and $80,000 were indirect materials.

(2)

Work in Process......................................	680,000	
Variable Overhead Control...........................	80,000	
Materials Inventory............................		760,000

While detailed subsidiary records of cost items would also be maintained, all variable overhead items will be debited here to a single account, Variable Overhead Control, in the general ledger.

3. The factory payroll for 1972 totaled $1,400,000, of which $1,000,000 were the cost of direct labor and the balance was indirect labor.

(3)

Work in Process................................	1,000,000	
Fixed Overhead Control..........................	400,000	
Payroll Summary............................		1,400,000

4. Labor-related costs amount to 20% of the total payroll cost. To keep the illustration very simple, we shall not be concerned with the exact natures of these items. Rather, we shall credit the entire amount to a single liability account for fringe benefits. Labor-related costs associated with direct labor (20% of $1,000,000) are variable overhead, while those associated with indirect labor (20% of $400,000) are fixed overhead. The classification of labor-related costs as fixed or variable depends upon the classification of the labor costs to which they relate.

(4)

Variable Overhead Control...........................	200,000	
Fixed Overhead Control............................	80,000	
Liability for Fringe Benefits......................		280,000

Inasmuch as the payroll accounting procedures are not actually part of the cost accounting cycle, they are not included in this illustration. They would be handled in the manner illustrated on page 49.

5. The remaining overhead cost items are summarized as follows:

Variable costs:	
Power and light..................................	$130,000
Fixed costs:	
Depreciation on plant.............................	200,000
Insurance on plant...............................	20,000
Property taxes on plant...........................	10,000
Repairs and maintenance of plant..................	70,000

These items are recorded below, with both power and light bills and repairs and maintenance being credited to Vouchers Payable.

(5.1)

Variable Overhead Control.........................	130,000	
Vouchers Payable..............................		130,000

(5.2)

Fixed Overhead Control............................	300,000	
Accumulated Depreciation—Plant.................		200,000
Unexpired Insurance.............................		20,000
Accrued Property Taxes Payable.................		10,000
Vouchers Payable..............................		70,000

To this point in the illustration, all entries are identical under both absorption costing and variable costing. The remaining entries, however, deal with the application of overhead costs to production and with subsequent accounting for the full cost of the product. Hence, they will be different under the alternative costing methods. Entries for absorption costing will be keyed with the letter "A," and those for variable costing, with the letter "V."

6. Actual output for 1972 (i.e., the total production work actually performed during that year, whether the units were completed or not)[5] totaled 280,000 units of product. Overhead is applied to production at normal rates of $1.50 per unit for variable costs and, under absorption costing only, $2.50 per unit for fixed costs. Thus, the entry for absorption costing is as follows:

(6A)

Work in Process...................................	1,120,000	
Variable Overhead Applied....................		420,000
Fixed Overhead Applied.......................		700,000

Under variable costing, only the variable overhead is applied to production. Note that this results in a substantially lower cost in Work in Process.

(6V)

Work in Process.....................................	420,000	
Variable Overhead Applied......................		420,000

7. The total cost of production completed during a period is normally computed by determining the unit cost of goods produced in the period and multiplying that unit cost by the number of units completed. The methods of determining unit cost will be discussed and illustrated in Chapter 4. Thus, at this point, we shall simply assert that the unit cost in the Wedgewood Products Company for 1972 is $10 under absorption costing. Included in this figure, of course, is $2.50 of fixed overhead. Under variable costing, no fixed overhead is applied to production; hence, the unit cost would be $7.50. A total of 260,000 units of product were com-

---

[5] The distinction between production work done and units completed will be explained fully in the next chapter.

pleted in 1972. Under absorption costing, the following entry would be made to record the completion of 260,000 units at a cost of $10 each:

(7A)

Finished Product...............................	2,600,000	
Work in Process............................		2,600,000

Under variable costing, the same 260,000 units would be costed at only $7.50 per unit.

(7V)

Finished Product...............................	1,950,000	
Work in Process............................		1,950,000

8. During 1972, a total of 250,000 units of product were sold on account for $16 each. The unit costs of the goods sold were $10 under absorption costing and $7.50 under variable costing. Two entries must be made to record these sales. The first records the sales revenue and is the same regardless of the costing method used.

(8.1)

Accounts Receivable............................	4,000,000	
Sales.......................................		4,000,000

The second entry records the expiration of the cost of the goods sold. It records the transfer of production costs from the classification of assets to that of expense. This entry will be different under the alternative costing methods. Under absorption costing, the cost per unit of the 250,000 units sold is $10.

(8.2A)

Cost of Goods Sold............................	2,500,000	
Finished Product............................		2,500,000

Under variable costing, the unit cost is only $7.50.

(8.2V)

Cost of Goods Sold............................	1,875,000	
Finished Product............................		1,875,000

The transfer of the cost of goods sold from asset to expense effectively concludes the cost accounting cycle. All manufacturing costs now appear in accounts that are consistent with the manner in which they will be reported in the financial statements.

Ledger Accounts

Postings of the journal entries in the preceding section are shown in Figures 3–3 and 3–4. They are keyed by numbers and letters to the entries. Only those accounts that deal directly with the costs of manufacturing are included in these exhibits. Figure 3–3 depicts the flow of manufacturing costs through the accounts under the absorption costing method. Figure 3–4 repeats this illustration under variable costing. The only

FIGURE 3–4
Manufacturing Cost Accounts under Variable Costing

Materials Inventory

Bal.	80,000	760,000	(2)
(1)	800,000		
Bal.	120,000		

Work in Process

Bal.	150,000	1,950,000	(7V)
(2)	680,000		
(3)	1,000,000		
(6V)	420,000		
Bal.	300,000		

Finished Product

Bal.	225,000	1,875,000	(8.2V)
(7V)	1,950,000		
Bal.	300,000		

Cost of Goods Sold

(8.2V)	1,875,000	

FIGURE 3–3
Manufacturing Cost Accounts under Absorption Costing

Materials Inventory

Bal.	80,000	760,000	(2)
(1)	800,000		
Bal.	120,000		

Work in Process

Bal.	200,000	2,600,000	(7A)
(2)	680,000		
(3)	1,000,000		
(6A)	1,120,000		
Bal.	400,000		

Finished Product

Bal.	300,000	2,500,000	(8.2A)
(7A)	2,600,000		
Bal.	400,000		

Cost of Goods Sold

(8.2A)	2,500,000	

Payroll Summary

	1,400,000 (3)

Variable Overhead Control

(2)	80,000	
(4)	200,000	
(5.1)	130,000	
Bal.	410,000	

Fixed Overhead Control

(3)	400,000	
(4)	80,000	
(5.2)	300,000	
Bal.	780,000	

Variable Overhead Applied

| | | 420,000 (6V) |

Payroll Summary

	1,400,000 (3)

Variable Overhead Control

(2)	80,000	
(4)	200,000	
(5.1)	130,000	
Bal.	410,000	

Fixed Overhead Control

(3)	400,000	
(4)	80,000	
(5.2)	300,000	
Bal.	780,000	

Variable Overhead Applied

| | | 420,000 (6A) |

Fixed Overhead Applied

| | | 700,000 (6A) |

difference in the latter exhibit is the absence of a Fixed Overhead Applied account and, consequently, lower total costs in Work in Process, Finished Product, and Cost of Goods Sold. These two figures show exactly the same cost flows that are presented in Figures 3–1 and 3–2, except that ledger accounts are used instead of block diagrams. An inspection of the overhead accounts in Figure 3–3 shows that variable overhead was over-applied by $10,000 and that fixed overhead was underapplied by $80,000. The same $10,000 of overapplied variable overhead appears in Figure 3–4 under variable costing. However, under this method, there is no under-applied fixed overhead because fixed overhead is not applied to production at all.

OPERATING STATEMENTS FOR A MANUFACTURING ENTERPRISE

In a manufacturing concern, as in almost all business firms, the principal operating report is the income statement. However, in manufacturing, the development of the cost of goods sold figure is so involved that the income statement is usually supported by a detailed *statement of cost of goods manufactured and sold*. This latter statement summarizes the results of manufacturing operations for the period. It is a formal summary of the data processed through the cost accounting cycle. This supporting statement and the income statement of the Wedgewood Products Company for 1972 are illustrated below under both alternatives of absorption costing and variable costing. The data are taken from the comprehensive illustration in the preceding section.

Operating Statements under Absorption Costing

Table 3–4 is a statement of cost of goods manufactured and sold prepared in accordance with the absorption costing method. Table 3–5 is the income statement prepared under the same method. The formats of the statements presented here are not suggested as standard or as ideal. There is a considerable variety of forms used in practice. Those illustrated in this chapter are very widely used, however.

In Table 3–4, the cost of goods manufactured is equal to the cost of the goods that were completed and transferred from Work in Process to Finished Product (cf. entry 7A in the previous section). The final figure in Table 3–4, the cost of goods sold, is the amount transferred from Finished Product to Cost of Goods Sold (cf. entry 8.2A). In the calculation of the cost of direct materials used, it is necessary to deduct those items used as indirect materials, for they will be included in the total of variable overhead applied to production.

The income statement in Table 3–5 is prepared in the conventional format used under absorption costing. The only new data in this report

TABLE 3–4

WEDGEWOOD PRODUCTS COMPANY
Statement of Cost of Goods Manufactured and Sold
For the Year Ended December 31, 1972

Direct materials used:			
Inventory, January 1, 1972...........		$ 80,000	
Purchases.........................		800,000	
Available for use....................		$880,000	
Deduct:			
Inventory, December 31, 1972.......	$120,000		
Used as indirect materials...........	80,000	200,000	$ 680,000
Direct labor........................			1,000,000
Variable overhead applied..............			420,000
Fixed overhead applied................			700,000
Total current production costs..........			$2,800,000
Deduct increase in work in process:			
Inventory, December 31, 1972........		$400,000	
Inventory, January 1, 1972..........		200,000	200,000
Cost of goods manufactured............			$2,600,000
Deduct increase in finished product:			
Inventory, December 31, 1972........		$400,000	
Inventory, January 1, 1972..........		300,000	100,000
Cost of goods sold...................			$2,500,000

are the nonmanufacturing expenses and the income taxes. In this and other illustrations throughout the book, we shall assume that the applicable income tax rate is 40%. The net underapplied overhead ($80,000 underapplied fixed overhead minus $10,000 overapplied variable overhead) is shown in the income statement as an addition to the cost of goods sold. It might just as well have been added at the end of the statement of cost of goods manufactured and sold instead. Either way, the underapplied overhead (an element of manufacturing cost) is associated with the expired manufacturing costs of the period (i.e., with cost of goods sold). This is the conventional method of disposing of under- or overapplied overhead at the end of the fiscal year. If the amount of under- or

TABLE 3–5

WEDGEWOOD PRODUCTS COMPANY
Income Statement
For the Year Ended December 31, 1972

Sales...		$4,000,000
Cost of goods sold (cf. Table 3–4)................	$2,500,000	
Add net underapplied overhead..................	70,000	2,570,000
Gross margin...................................		$1,430,000
Nonmanufacturing expenses.....................		780,000
Income before tax.............................		$ 650,000
Income taxes (40%)............................		260,000
Net income....................................		$ 390,000

overapplied overhead is very material, treating it simply as an adjustment to cost of goods sold might distort reported income. In such a case, it would be allocated appropriately among Work in Process, Finished Product, and Cost of Goods Sold. The effect of this allocation would be to adjust the accounts so that actual overhead was effectively applied to production. The procedure for doing this will be discussed in Chapter 10.

Operating Statements under Variable Costing

The statement of cost of goods manufactured and sold under variable costing is nearly identical to that prepared under absorption costing. The only difference is that no fixed overhead is included in any of the data in the statement. Table 3–6 illustrates such a statement with the data under variable costing in the comprehensive illustration.

The income statement for variable costing is presented in Table 3–7. It differs significantly from the one used in absorption costing. Not only are different data involved in the determination of cost of goods sold and is fixed overhead reported differently, net income is different in amount. Moreover, the entire format of the statement is different. In absorption costing, the principal internal division of expenses is between manufacturing and nonmanufacturing expense items. The major intermediate measure of income is the gross margin, which is the excess of revenue over total manufacturing expense. In variable costing, expenses are separated in the income statement according to their behavior with respect to

TABLE 3–6

WEDGEWOOD PRODUCTS COMPANY
Statement of Cost of Goods Manufactured and Sold
For the Year Ended December 31, 1972

Direct materials used:			
Inventory, January 1, 1972...........		$ 80,000	
Purchases.........................		800,000	
Available for use....................		$880,000	
Deduct:			
Inventory, December 31, 1972.......	$120,000		
Used as indirect materials..........	80,000	200,000	$ 680,000
Direct labor.........................			1,000,000
Variable overhead applied.............			420,000
Total current variable production costs...			$2,100,000
Deduct increase in work in process:			
Inventory, December 31, 1972........	$300,000		
Inventory, January 1, 1972..........	150,000		150,000
Cost of goods manufactured............			$1,950,000
Deduct increase in finished product:			
Inventory, December 31, 1972........	$300,000		
Inventory, January 1, 1972..........	225,000		75,000
Cost of goods sold....................			$1,875,000

changes in volume. Variable and fixed expenses are separated, but no major distinction between manufacturing and nonmanufacturing expenses is recognized. The major intermediate income figure is called *variable profit,* the difference between sales revenue and variable expenses. (The terms "contribution margin" and "marginal contribution" are often used for the concept here called variable profit. This latter term is more accurately descriptive of the profit measure in question, however, and will be used throughout this book.) Since both sales revenue and variable expenses are direct functions of sales volume, so is the variable profit.[6] Thus, variable profit tends to be a very useful figure for managerial analysis. The only new data refinement in Table 3–7 is a separation of

TABLE 3–7

WEDGEWOOD PRODUCTS COMPANY
Income Statement
For the Year Ended December 31, 1972

Sales...		$4,000,000
Variable expenses:		
Cost of goods sold (cf. Table 3–6)...............	$1,875,000	
Less overapplied variable overhead..............	10,000	
	$1,865,000	
Variable nonmanufacturing expenses............	280,000	2,145,000
Variable profit..............................		$1,855,000
Fixed expenses:		
Fixed overhead..............................	$ 780,000	
Fixed nonmanufacturing expenses...............	500,000	1,280,000
Income before tax............................		$ 575,000
Income taxes (40%)...........................		230,000
Net income...................................		$ 345,000

the total nonmanufacturing expenses of $780,000 into a variable component of $280,000 and a fixed component of $500,000. Perhaps the most important quantitative difference in the variable costing income statement is the fact that net income is $45,000 less than it was under absorption costing. This is attributable to the fact that all of the fixed overhead costs actually incurred during the year are reported as expenses under variable costing. Under absorption costing, however, a portion of fixed overhead remains in the inventory accounts for Work in Process and Finished Product, both of which increased during the year.

The discussions of absorption costing and variable costing in this chapter have been limited to the basic accounting procedures employed and the accounting difference between the two methods. A critical comparison of the two methods will be made in the next chapter.

---

[6] A minor exception to this statement is caused by the fact that the overapplied variable overhead is not a direct function of sales volume. The quantitative effect of this item, however, is usually immaterial.

QUESTIONS FOR DISCUSSION

1. What is meant by the concept that *costs attach?* Which costs attach in absorption costing? Which costs attach in variable costing?

2. What is the difference between a product cost and a period cost? How does each type of cost become an expense?

3. Which accounts in the general ledger of a manufacturing firm may be expected to be different under variable costing as contrasted with absorption costing?

4. Several different schemes of classification of costs have been discussed in this chapter and in the preceding one. It is often desirable that these different classifications be incorporated in the recording of costs in the accounts. Identify these various cost classifications and state the purpose(s) of recording costs according to each.

5. Should labor-related costs be included as part of direct labor cost or should they be accounted for as part of overhead? Explain your answer.

6. If the direct labor costs of production were true fixed costs of the period, how would they be accounted for? How would these procedures differ, if at all, from current practice with respect to labor cost accounting?

7. What are the advantages of using normal overhead rates instead of actual rates? What are the disadvantages? On balance, do you believe the advantages outweigh the disadvantages or vice versa? Why?

8. "The use of a normal fixed overhead rate results in an artificial smoothing of unit production costs over the course of a year in which there occur significant seasonal fluctuations in output." To what does this allegation refer? How would you respond to it?

9. "Variable costing is preferable to absorption costing in that it results in lower inventory values and, therefore, lower inventory carrying costs (i.e., imputed interest on the investment in inventory)." Comment on this statement.

10. How would you explain the under- or overapplied overhead as a separate item appearing in the income statement?

11. What is the relationship between a statement of cost of goods manufactured and sold and the block diagrams of manufacturing cost flows in Figures 3–1 and 3–2?

12. "Absorption costing is clearly invalid. Since fixed overhead is charged to the inventory of manufactured products at a rate based on the number of units expected to be produced, the value of that inventory will be greater if the firm expects to produce fewer units. In other words, the fewer units a firm expects to produce and does produce, the more valuable each individual unit becomes. This is nonsense." Discuss this criticism of absorption costing.

13. "Variable costing is obviously invalid. Since only variable costs are charged to production, the more costs that are fixed, the lower will be the value of the inventory. Thus, if all costs were fixed, the inventory would be without value. That is ridiculous." Evaluate this criticism of variable costing.

PROBLEMS

1. The following data summarize the manufacturing operations of the Half Moon Company during its first year of operations:

Raw materials purchased........................	$150,000
Direct materials used...........................	142,000
Direct labor cost incurred.......................	220,000
Variable overhead costs incurred.................	90,000
Fixed overhead costs incurred...................	120,000
Variable overhead applied.......................	88,000
Fixed overhead applied..........................	110,000
Total cost of products completed.................	520,000
Total cost of products sold......................	450,000

The company has adopted the absorption costing method.

Required:

a) Show the manufacturing costs summarized above as postings to general ledger accounts.

b) What is the total manufacturing cost charged to expense during this first year of operations?

2. Complete the requirements of Problem 1 under the assumption that the company had adopted the variable costing method. Change the cost of products completed to $418,000 and the cost of products sold to $362,000. No fixed overhead is applied, of course.

3. The total factory labor cost of the Coos Bay Milling Company for the two-week period ended September 29, 1972, is $80,000. Of this amount, $65,000 is direct labor cost. The balance is indirect labor and is regarded as a fixed cost. The payroll department withholds a total of $12,000 from the employees for federal income taxes. The entire payroll is subject to the social security withholding rate of 6%. The only other item withheld is the employees' contribution to a pension plan; this amounts to 5% of the payroll. The company must match the employees' social security tax payments and their contribution to the pension plan. It must also pay unemployment compensation tax equal to 3% of the payroll.

Required:

Prepare general journal entries to record (a) the charging of labor costs to manufacturing cost accounts in the cost accounting department and (b) the distribution of the payroll in the payroll department.

4. The Winona Manufacturing Company charges overhead to production at normal rates and employs the absorption costing method. Past experience, adjusted for anticipated price changes, indicated that variable overhead would average $1.50 per unit of product in 1972. Fixed overhead for that year was budgeted at $5,000,000. Output for 1972 was budgeted at 2,000,000

units of product. Actual output for 1972 proved to be only 1,800,000 units. Actual overhead for the year included variable costs of $2,850,000 and fixed costs of $4,800,000.

Required:

Compute the under- or overapplied overhead for variable and fixed costs separately. State briefly what factors appear to have caused these under- or overapplied amounts.

5. The Naugatuck Products Corporation charges overhead to production at a normal rate and uses the variable costing method in accounting for production. Budgeted variable overhead for 1972 was $.80 per unit of product. Budgeted fixed overhead was $900,000. Budgeted output for the year was set at 600,000 units of product. Actual output for 1972 totaled 700,000 units. Actual variable overhead amounted to $600,000, and actual fixed overhead to $925,000.

Required:

Show all balances in overhead control and overhead applied accounts at the end of 1972. What is the amount of under- or overapplied overhead?

6. The operations of the Raritan Corporation for the year ended December 31, 1972, are summarized below. The corporation uses absorption costing.

Inventory balances, January 1, 1972:

Materials...	$ 20,000
Work in process.................................	25,000
Finished product...............................	40,000
Purchases of raw materials.........................	240,000
Direct materials used..............................	200,000
Direct labor cost incurred..........................	150,000
Overhead costs incurred (credit to "miscellaneous accounts"):	
Variable.......................................	55,000
Fixed...	120,000
Cost of completed production......................	480,000
Cost of products sold..............................	500,000
Revenue from sales on account.....................	750,000

Variable overhead is applied to production at a normal rate of $2 per unit of product. Fixed overhead is applied at a normal rate of $4 per unit. During 1972, a total of 25,000 units of product were manufactured.

Required:

a) Prepare general journal entries to record the corporation's operations for 1972.

b) Compute the ending balances in the three inventory accounts at December 31, 1972.

c) Compute the under- or overapplied overhead for the year.

7. The Bonham Manufacturing Company uses variable costing in accounting for its production costs. Following is a summary of the company's operations for the year ended December 31, 1972:

Inventories, January 1, 1972:	
Materials....................................	$ 10,000
Work in process.............................	0
Finished product............................	20,000
Purchases of materials.........................	250,000
Direct materials used..........................	180,000
Direct labor payroll...........................	150,000
Actual overhead (credit to "miscellaneous accounts"):	
Variable....................................	75,000
Fixed.......................................	200,000
Cost of goods completed.......................	400,000
Goods sold on account:	
At selling price.............................	600,000
At cost.....................................	360,000

During 1972, 400,000 units of product were manufactured. Variable overhead is applied to production at a normal rate of $.20 per unit produced.

Required:

a) Prepare general journal entries to record operations for 1972.
b) Compute ending balances in the inventory accounts at December 31, 1972.
c) Compute the under- or overapplied overhead for the year.

8. The Wachusett Corporation manufactures ceramic ash trays. The variable costing method is used in product cost accounting. The company began operations in January, 1972. Budgeted output for 1972 called for production of 10,000,000 ash trays. Budgeted overhead costs included $500,000 of fixed overhead and $.02 of variable overhead per ash tray. Actual production data for 1972 are summarized below:

(1) Raw materials in the amount of 12,500,000 pounds were purchased at an average cost of $.02 per pound. Issued to the factory for use in production were 12,000,000 pounds.

(2) The total factory payroll for the year amounted to $800,000. Of this total, $750,000 was direct labor and the balance was indirect. Indirect labor cost varies in proportion to the volume of goods produced. Federal income tax withheld totaled $120,000. The entire payroll is subject to a 5% social security tax; both the employees and the corporation must contribute this percentage. In addition, the corporation alone is liable for a 3% unemployment compensation tax.

(3) Other actual variable overhead costs incurred during 1972 were as follows:

Factory supplies purchased and used..............	$40,000
Electric power and water bills paid................	$18,000

(4)   Actual fixed overhead costs incurred during the year included the following items:

Depreciation on plant and equipment...............	$350,000
Property taxes on plant and equipment..............	50,000
(Half of these taxes have already been paid. The remainder is payable on or before March 20, 1973.)	
Insurance on plant and equipment.................	25,000
(This is the current year's portion of the premium on a three-year insurance policy purchased on January 2, 1972.)	
Repairs and maintenance........................	100,000
(All paid currently.)	

(5)   A total of 11,000,000 ash trays were produced in 1972. No uncompleted work was in process at the end of the year. Of the completed units, 10,000,000 were shipped to customers and billed at a selling price of $.25 per ash tray.

Required:

a)   Prepare general journal entries to record the operations of the Wachusett Corporation for 1972.

b)   Compute the under- or overapplied overhead for the year.

9.   The Klamath Cabinet Works manufactures wooden cabinets for television and stereo sets. Absorption costing is used. Budgeted production for 1972 was set at 50,000 cabinets. Fixed overhead was budgeted at $2,000,000 for that year, and variable overhead at $6 per cabinet. Actual operating data for 1972 are summarized below:

(1)   The cost of raw materials purchased during 1972 totaled $1,400,000. The cost of direct materials issued to the factory totaled $1,500,000.

(2)   The factory payroll for the year included $2,400,000 of direct labor and $600,000 of indirect labor, which is a fixed cost of production. Federal income taxes withheld totaled $360,000. The corporation also withholds payroll taxes equal to 5% of the employees' earnings. It must pay, in addition, 10% of the total payroll as its share of payroll taxes.

(3)   Indirect materials used cost $80,000 and were drawn from the inventory of raw materials. These are classified as variable costs.

(4)   Other actual fixed overhead costs included the following items:

Depreciation on factory facilities...................	$800,000
Heat, light, and power...........................	100,000
(All paid currently.)	
Property taxes on factory........................	50,000
(All payable in 1973.)	
Maintenance....................................	450,000
(All paid currently.)	

(5)   A total of 56,000 cabinets were produced during 1972. There was no inventory of work in process at either the beginning or the end of the year. All cabinets completed were shipped immediately to customers. The selling prices average $125 per cabinet.

Required:

a) Prepare general journal entries to record all of these transactions of 1972.

b) Compute the amount of under- or overapplied overhead for the year.

10. The following data are taken from the accounting records of the Campbell Corporation for the year ended December 31, 1972:

Inventories, January 1:	
Raw materials..................................	$ 30,000
Work in process...............................	15,000
Finished products.............................	65,000
Sales...	740,000
Purchases of raw materials........................	200,000
Materials issued to the factory:	
As direct materials............................	175,000
As indirect materials (variable cost)..............	15,000
Payroll:	
Direct labor....................................	180,000
Indirect labor (variable cost)....................	50,000
Salesmen's salaries (fixed cost)..................	90,000
Factory power and utilities (fixed cost).............	40,000
Advertising (fixed cost)...........................	30,000
Depreciation on factory (fixed cost)................	50,000
Inventories, December 31:	
Raw materials.................................	?
Work in process...............................	20,000
Finished products.............................	50,000

Overhead is applied to production at normal rates of $1.20 per unit of product for variable costs and $1.80 per unit of product for fixed costs. The actual output of 1972 totaled 50,000 units of product. The applicable federal income tax rate is 40%.

Required:

Prepare an income statement and a supporting statement of cost of goods manufactured and sold for the year ended December 31, 1972.

11. The data below are a summarization of the operations of the Alert Automotive Company for the year 1972:

Sales......................................	$830,000
Purchases of materials.......................	150,000
Payroll:	
Direct labor..............................	200,000
Indirect labor (fixed cost).................	50,000
Office and sales force (fixed cost)...........	100,000
Depreciation (fixed cost):	
On factory equipment.....................	60,000
On office furnishings and equipment.........	15,000
Maintenance (fixed cost):	
On factory equipment.....................	25,000
On office equipment......................	10,000
Supplies used (variable cost):	
In factory...............................	22,000
In office.................................	5,000
Labor-related costs........................	10% of payroll

Output for 1972 totaled 200,000 units of product. Variable overhead is applied to production at a normal rate of $.20 per unit. Fixed overhead is accounted for as a period expense.

Inventories at the beginning and the end of the year were as follows:

	January 1	December 31
Materials.........................	$20,000	$10,000
Work in process....................	5,000	10,000
Finished product...................	40,000	50,000

The applicable income tax rate is 40%.

Required:

Prepare an income statement and a supporting schedule of cost of goods manufactured and sold for the year 1972.

12. Below is the statement of cost of goods manufactured and sold of the Travis Company for the year 1972:

TRAVIS COMPANY
Statement of Cost of Goods Manufactured and Sold
For the Year Ended December 31, 1972

Direct materials:		
Inventory, January 1......................	$ 8,000	
Purchases...............................	60,000	
Available for use.........................	$68,000	
Deduct: Inventory, December 31.............	$10,000	
Used as indirect materials...........	2,000	
	$12,000	$ 56,000
Direct labor...................................		70,000
Variable overhead applied.....................		28,000
Fixed overhead applied.......................		42,000
Total current production costs.................		$196,000
Add decrease in work in process:		
Inventory, January 1......................	$ 9,000	
Inventory, December 31...................	6,000	3,000
Cost of goods manufactured..................		$199,000
Deduct increase in finished product:		
Inventory, December 31...................	$18,000	
Inventory, January 1......................	11,000	7,000
Cost of goods sold...........................		$192,000
Add underapplied fixed overhead..............	$ 6,000	
Less overapplied variable overhead...........	3,000	3,000
Net cost of goods sold.......................		$195,000

Required:

Reconstruct the ledger accounts for manufacturing costs in the Travis Company for the year 1972.

13. Following is the adjusted trial balance of the Yeaton Manufacturing Corporation as of December 31, 1972:

	Debit	Credit
Cash...................................	$ 18,000	
Accounts receivable.....................	26,000	
Raw materials..........................	30,000	
Work in process........................	12,000	
Finished product.......................	44,000	
Land...................................	120,000	
Plant property and equipment............	380,000	
Accumulated depreciation—plant property and equipment.......................		$ 60,000
Patents................................	21,000	
Vouchers payable.......................		30,000
Accrued expenses.......................		25,000
Mortgage bonds payable.................		150,000
Common stock..........................		200,000
Retained earnings......................		170,000
Sales..................................		460,000
Cost of goods sold......................	288,000	
Variable overhead control................	36,000	
Fixed overhead control..................	43,000	
Selling expenses........................	50,000	
General administrative expenses..........	80,000	
Variable overhead applied................		39,000
Fixed overhead applied..................		42,000
Interest expense.......................	10,000	
Federal income tax.....................	18,000	
	$1,176,000	$1,176,000

In addition, the cost records show that materials costing $120,000 were purchased during 1972 and that the inventories at January 1 were as follows:

Materials...............................	$20,000
Work in process.........................	5,000
Finished product........................	32,000

Required:

Prepare an income statement and a statement of cost of goods manufactured and sold for the year ended December 31, 1972.

14. The adjusted trial balance of the Taney Milling Company as of December 31, 1972, appears as follows:

	Debit	*Credit*
Cash...................................	$ 3,500	
Accounts receivable.......................	12,400	
Raw materials inventory....................	22,200	
Work in process..........................	4,800	
Finished product..........................	11,700	
Land..................................	29,000	
Buildings...............................	68,500	
Accumulated depreciation—buildings.........		$ 34,900
Machinery and equipment..................	114,000	
Accumulated depreciation—machinery and equipment.............................		52,600
Accounts payable.........................		9,900
Accrued expenses.........................		1,800
Bank note payable........................		15,000
C. G. Taney, capital......................		172,200
Sales..................................		401,600
Cost of goods sold........................	253,800	
Variable overhead control..................	36,000	
Fixed overhead control....................	84,400	
Variable marketing expenses................	16,200	
Fixed marketing expenses..................	28,000	
Fixed administrative expenses..............	42,000	
Variable overhead applied..................		39,400
Interest expense.........................	900	
	$727,400	$727,400

Materials were purchased at a total cost of $145,000 during 1972. The direct labor charges for the year were $54,100. Inventories at January 1, 1972, were as follows:

Materials................................	$24,000
Work in process..........................	14,000
Finished product.........................	16,000

Required:

Prepare an income statement and a statement of cost of goods manufactured and sold for the year ended December 31, 1972.

15. At December 31, 1972, the Inventory of Manufactured Products account of the Mackinaw Corporation contained the following summarized data:

Inventory of Manufactured Products

Balance, January 1, 1972	130,000	1,989,475	Cost of goods sold
Raw materials purchased	480,000		
Factory payroll	740,000		
Budgeted overhead	750,000		
Balance, December 31, 1972	110,525		

Unfortunately, the corporation's bookkeeper withdrew from his one and only accounting course in college after getting a grade of 13 (out of 100) on his first examination. The intent of this account is to use the absorption costing method and to apply overhead to production at normal rates. The cost of goods sold is calculated by summing all debits to the account, dividing that sum by the total number of units available during the year, and multiplying the resultant unit cost by the number of units sold.

You have made an independent examination and have determined that all debits in the account above are correct in amount, although incorrectly handled. You have discovered the following additional information:

Production for 1972 was budgeted at 50,000 units of product. Variable overhead was budgeted at $5 per unit, and fixed overhead at $500,000 for the year.

Actual production during 1972 totaled 55,000 units. Actual production costs other than materials were as follows:

Direct labor	$660,000
Indirect labor (fixed cost)	80,000
Other fixed overhead	440,000
Variable overhead	295,000

The correct inventory balances at the beginning of the year were as follows:

Raw materials	$ 30,000
Finished product	100,000

The inventory of raw materials at December 31 had a cost of $70,000. Because of the short production process, there is never any inventory of work in process at the end of a period.

The goods sold during the year included the 3,000 finished units in inventory at the start of the year plus 52,000 of the 55,000 units produced during the year.

Required:

Determine the correct balances in the Materials Inventory, Work in Process, Finished Product, and Cost of Goods Sold accounts as of December 31, 1972.

16. The Hawthorn Metal Products Corporation manufactures a variety of small machined parts. Output is measured in pounds of finished product. The absorption costing method is used.

   The budgeted output for 1972 was set at 600,000 pounds. The budget for overhead cost for the year was prepared as follows:

Variable cost items (per pound):	
Indirect materials and supplies	$.11
Indirect labor	.40
Labor-related costs	.18
Power and light	.06
	$.75
Fixed cost items:	
Depreciation	$500,000
Plant supervisors' salaries	80,000
Labor-related costs	8,000
Maintenance	150,000
Property taxes	30,000
Property insurance	12,000
	$780,000

The following inventory balances appeared in the firm's balance sheet at December 31, 1971:

Materials................................	$120,000
Work in process..........................	50,000
Finished product.........................	400,000

Raw materials purchases for the year 1972 totaled $900,000. A summary of storeroom issue slips for the year shows that $800,000 of direct materials and $60,000 of indirect materials and supplies were issued from the materials inventory to the factory.

The payroll for 1972 is summarized below:

Direct labor.............................	$ 750,000
Indirect labor...........................	250,000
Plant supervisors' salaries...............	80,000
Salesmen's commissions..................	200,000
Administrative salaries..................	300,000
	$1,580,000

Federal income tax in the amount of $250,000 was withheld from employees' earnings. Social security taxes were withheld in an amount equal to 6% of the total payroll. The company matches the employees' social security contributions and pays an unemployment compensation tax equal to 4% of the total payroll.

The following additional expenses were paid in cash during 1972:

Power and light..........................	$ 35,000
Maintenance bills........................	160,000
Property taxes for 1972...................	20,000
Property insurance premium on three-year policy covering 1972, 1973, and 1974......	30,000
Advertising bills.........................	90,000
Miscellaneous administrative expenses.......	70,000
Interest on long-term notes payable.........	8,000

Depreciation on the factory and on the office furnishings were recorded in the amounts of $525,000 and $50,000, respectively.

Production records showed that 520,000 pounds of products were actually produced during 1972. The total cost of completed production was $2,600,000. The cost of goods shipped and billed to customers was $2,500,000. These goods shipped were billed at selling prices totaling $4,150,000.

Required:

a) Prepare general journal entries to record the operations of Hawthorn Metal Products Corporation for 1972.

b) Prepare an income statement and a supporting statement of cost of goods manufactured and sold for the year.

c) Calculate the under- or overapplied overhead for 1972 and explain as best you can how it came to be.

17. The Gresham Company produces concrete funeral vaults. Only variable production costs are charged to the inventories of goods produced.

Budgeted sales and production volumes for 1972 were both set at 300,000 units of product. Expenses for the year were budgeted as follows:

Raw materials...................... $15 per unit produced
Direct labor........................ $4 per unit produced
Indirect labor...................... $1 per unit produced
Indirect materials.................. $.80 per unit produced
Shipping and billing expenses.......... $.40 per unit sold
Salesmen's commissions.............. 10% of sales revenue
Administrative salaries............... $300,000
General office expenses.............. $150,000
Depreciation on factory.............. $200,000
Depreciation on office................ $100,000
Labor-related costs................. 10% of payroll

During 1972, a total of 340,000 units were produced and 350,000 units were shipped to customers. The selling price was $30 per unit.

Inventory balances at the beginning and the end of the year were as follows:

	Dec. 31, 1971	Dec. 31, 1972
Materials....................	$300,000	$150,000
Work in process.............	50,000	100,000
Finished product............	250,000	150,000

Materials were purchased for $5,000,000 during 1972. Direct materials used cost $4,900,000, and indirect materials used cost $250,000. Both were drawn from the same materials inventory account.

The following items were paid in cash during the year:

Payroll:
  Direct labor............................... $1,500,000
  Indirect labor............................. 400,000
  Administrative salaries..................... 315,000
  Salesmen's commissions.................... 10% of sales
Shipping and billing expenses.................. $ 125,000
General office expenses....................... 160,000

The entire payroll is subject to social security tax payments of 6% by both the employees and the company. In addition, the company withheld $538,500 in income taxes from employees' earnings. The company itself is also required to pay unemployment compensation tax equal to 4% of the payroll.

Depreciation charges for 1972 were recorded as follows:

On the factory................................. $200,000
On the office.................................. 120,000

The applicable income tax rate is 40%.

Required:

a) Prepare general journal entries to record the operations of the Gresham Company for 1972.

b) Prepare an income statement and a supporting statement of cost of goods manufactured and sold for the year.

c) Calculate the under- or overapplied overhead for 1972.

—————————————————— chapter 4

INVENTORY COSTING

F ROM THE discussion of the cost accounting cycle in the previous chapter, the reader can see that one of the most important implications of that cycle for financial accounting is the assignment of manufacturing costs to inventory accounts. This chapter will treat several aspects of accounting for costs in inventory. Specifically, the following matters will be considered:

1. Inventory accounting methods.
2. Inventory cost flow assumptions.
3. Cost accounting systems.
4. Absorption and variable costing—a critical comparison.

The latter two points involve considerably more than just inventory accounting and will be considered in broader contexts.[1]

INVENTORY ACCOUNTING METHODS

Perpetual, or Book, Inventory Method

The illustrations of the cost accounting cycle in Chapter 3 were prepared, without specific mention of the fact, in accordance with the *perpetual inventory method*. Under a perpetual, or book, inventory method, the costs of all items placed into inventory are debited immediately to the inventory account and the costs of items removed from inventory are credited promptly to that account. Thus, so long as all postings are com-

---

[1] Students who have recently completed a course in financial accounting or principles of accounting should find the material discussed under the first two points already familiar to them. However, it is probably well for them to read it as a quick review.

plete, the inventory account will, at all times, show the cost of the inventory on hand. There is a perpetual record in the books of the balance in inventory. This method measures directly the flows of costs into and out of inventory. A perpetual inventory record can be incorporated effectively in a system of inventory control. Accurate and up-to-date records of inventory receipts and issues, coupled with adequate physical safeguarding of stocks on hand, provide simultaneously the bases for good inventory control and correct inventory cost data.

Periodic, or Physical, Inventory Method

In a *periodic inventory method,* actual stocks on hand are counted at the close of each accounting period (typically one year). The sum of the stock at the close of the previous year and the purchases during the current year is the amount of inventory available for use or sale (depending upon the nature of the inventory) during the current period. Subtracting from this sum the stock counted as of the end of the current year, one determines the amount of the inventory issued—whether for use or for sale—during the current year. This method does not provide information as to inventory balances except when physical counts of inventories are taken. Between physical counts, existing inventory balances can only be estimated. This does not imply that no physical control over inventory is exercised during the period. On the contrary, physical control may be just as sound under a periodic inventory method as under a perpetual method.

Comparison of Perpetual and Periodic Inventory Methods

In general, the perpetual and periodic inventory methods may be viewed as alternative approaches to the same end, not as alternative ends. The periodic inventory method involves an absolutely essential physical count of stocks on hand as of the end of the accounting period. The perpetual inventory method does not. Thus, the end-of-year closing procedures may be substantially simplified by the use of the perpetual method. This does not mean, however, that no physical counts need be taken under the perpetual inventory method. Such counts must be made annually in either method, but in the perpetual method, they may be made at any time and not necessarily as of the end of the period. The inventory count in the perpetual method may be made continually throughout the year— different classes of inventory being counted each month. This practice tends to avoid delays or shutdowns due to a full-scale annual physical count. The book inventory accounts should be adjusted for any discrepancies revealed by the physical count. Such discrepancies are almost inevitable in any business firm; hopefully, they will not be material in amount.

INVENTORY COST FLOW ASSUMPTIONS

To this point, the flow of costs through inventory accounts has been considered in a very general way, and primarily in terms of aggregate dollar amounts. As a matter of fact, however, those aggregate quantities typically comprise individual items in inventory and their individual costs. If each item that passed through a particular inventory account bore exactly the same cost per unit, the determination of the aggregate costs charged and credited to the account would be a simple matter of multiplying physical quantities by the uniform unit cost. Business experience, however, has shown that unit costs are not likely to remain unchanged indefinitely. Changes in the general price level, in prices in specific commodity markets, and in the physical quality and composition of commodities all tend to produce variations in unit costs over time. Thus, at any one time, an inventory may comprise physically homogeneous items having different unit costs. For example, suppose that the inventory of raw materials of a manufacturing company includes 500 pounds of material X, purchased at different times and different prices, as follows:

Purchased in December, 1971.........	100 lbs. @ $5 =	$ 500
Purchased in January, 1972..........	200 lbs. @ $6 =	1,200
Purchased in February, 1972.........	200 lbs. @ $7 =	1,400
	500 lbs.	$3,100

During March, 1972, 300 pounds of material X are issued to the factory. From Chapter 3, we know that the cost of these 300 pounds will be charged to Work in Process and credited to Materials Inventory. The question now is which pounds at which unit cost were issued.

One way of determining which units are issued from inventory is *specific identification.* This would require that each physical unit of material be separately identified with its unique unit cost. Then, as that physical unit is removed from inventory, its cost would be charged to Work in Process. Specific identification is feasible where the inventory consists of small quantities of physically separable items. It becomes impractical where the quantity of items is large, as in the case of a bin of bolts. It is impossible in inventories of fungible goods, such as liquids and grains stored in a single tank, elevator, or other container. Even where specific identification is possible, it is questionable whether it is desirable. If there are marked differences among the unit costs of goods in inventory, management might be able to manipulate income from period to period by judicious selection of the specific items to be drawn from stock.

What then is the alternative to specific identification? As a practical matter, some assumption must be made as to the sequence in which costs flow out of inventory. Current accounting practice recognizes three basic cost flow assumptions as generally acceptable. These will be discussed in turn below. It must be emphasized that these are *cost flow* assumptions. Their whole purpose is to determine the costs to be credited to inventory accounts for items removed from stock and, consequently, cost balances remaining in inventory. They are not intended to depict nor should they be interpreted as depicting the physical flow of goods in inventory. Physical and cost flows may parallel each other, but generally accepted accounting principles allow the use of a cost flow assumption which is clearly at variance with the observable physical flow.

First-in, First-out Assumption

The first inventory cost flow assumption to be considered here is the *first-in, first-out* assumption, or Fifo. As the name implies, Fifo assumes that the earliest units received in inventory are the first ones to be issued. Thus, under Fifo, the 300 pounds of material X issued in the illustration above would be assumed to consist of the 100 pounds purchased in December plus the 200 pounds purchased in January. The cost of materials issued and of materials left in inventory after the issue in March would then be determined as follows:

```
Materials issued:
  100 lbs. @ $5.....................................  $  500
  200 lbs. @ $6.....................................   1,200    $1,700
Materials remaining in inventory:
  200 lbs. @ $7.....................................             1,400
                                                               $3,100
```

Each purchase is kept separate in the inventory records, and the order in which it was received determines the order of its issuance. Perhaps the principal appeal of the Fifo assumption is that it is likely to conform to the physical flow of goods in the majority of instances. However, it must be remembered that the selection of a cost flow assumption is not necessarily tied to the physical flow of the goods in the inventory under current accounting principles. Some accountants have argued that the cost flow *should* follow the physical flow, but this position has not become generally accepted.

Average Cost

A second cost flow assumption states, in effect, that all units in inventory are so commingled as to render identification of specific purchases irrelevant. Consequently, all additional purchases are added in with the inventory already on hand to determine an average unit cost for all of the units in stock. This is the *average cost* assumption. Since each new purchase is averaged with the goods already on hand to determine unit cost, there is only one unit cost in an inventory account at any one time; and all units issued from that inventory are credited to the account at the then current average unit cost. Continuing with the illustration of material X developed in the previous sections, the unit cost in inventory at the end of December, 1971, is $5; for that is the only unit cost encountered at that point. The purchase in January, 1972, causes the computation of a new unit cost, however. This will be the quotient of the total cost in inventory ($500 + $1,200 = $1,700) divided by the total physical quantity in stock (100 lbs. + 200 lbs. = 300 lbs.). The new average unit cost is then $5.67 ($1,700 ÷ 300). As it happens, this unit cost is never used in connection with an issue of material, for no materials were issued prior to the next purchase in February. With the February purchase, the unit cost is once more recomputed and found to be $6.20 ($3,100 total cost ÷ 500 total units). This unit cost is then employed when 300 pounds are issued to the factory in March. Under the average cost assumption, the costs of material X issued and still on hand would then appear as follows:

Materials issued:
300 lbs. @ $6.20. . . . . $1,860
Materials remaining in inventory:
.200 lbs. @ $6.20. 1,240
$3,100

This illustration reveals the basic methodology of the average cost method. Only one unit cost figure appears in each inventory account at one time. This average unit cost is recomputed each time additional units are received in inventory. It is not changed by issues from inventory. Issues are credited to the inventory account at the current average unit cost. The average unit cost is always a *weighted average,* that is, the total dollar cost of the inventory is divided by the total number of units on hand. Hence, the unit prices in purchases of large quantities have relatively greater impacts upon average unit costs than the prices in purchases of small quantities. (Observe the unit cost computation on the occasion of the January purchase as a demonstration of this weighting effect.)

Last-in, First-out Assumption

The third cost flow assumption to be considered is the *last-in, first-out,* or Lifo assumption. It is exactly the converse of the Fifo assumption. The most recent acquisitions in inventory are assumed to be issued first. Thus, any ending inventory balance will be assumed to consist of the oldest items purchased, as long as the entire stock has not been liquidated at one time. Obviously, the last-in, first-out assumption is not likely to correspond with the physical flow of goods except in unusual instances. For perishable items, a last-in, first-out physical flow would be impossible. Nevertheless, current accounting practice would accept the use of Lifo in such a situation. Lifo, like Fifo and average cost, is a *cost flow* assumption; and there is no requirement that the assumed cost flow correspond to the observable physical flow.

The mechanics of Lifo are illustrated in connection with the example used before. The 300 pounds of material X issued in March would be assumed to include the last 200 pounds purchased during February plus 100 of the 200 pounds purchased in January. The balance of 200 pounds remaining in stock would consist of the oldest 100 pounds, purchased in December, plus the remaining 100 pounds from the January purchase. The costs of materials issued and on hand after the March issue would be as follows:

Materials issued:		
200 lbs. @ $7	$1,400	
100 lbs. @ $6	600	$2,000
Materials remaining in inventory:		
100 lbs. @ $5	$ 500	
100 lbs. @ $6	600	1,100
		$3,100

The mechanics of the three cost flow assumptions illustrated here, and particularly those of Lifo, can become considerably more complex. The basic concepts, however, are always as shown here. From the viewpoint of management, the consequences of these various cost flow assumptions are of much more interest than the mechanics, although a fundamental understanding of the procedures is obviously essential to any appreciation of the implications thereof.

Comparison and Evaluation of Cost Flow Assumptions

The illustrations of Fifo, average cost, and Lifo above show that the different assumptions produce different figures for the cost of goods issued and for the inventory balance as of the end of a period. In the example of material X, Fifo results in a cost of goods issued of $1,700; average cost, $1,860; and Lifo, $2,000. If the inventory involved were one of finished goods instead of raw materials, the respective costs of goods issued would represent the cost of goods sold. But the greater the cost of materials used, the greater ultimately will be the cost of goods sold. Hence, regardless of the inventory involved, the same general impact upon cost of goods sold will obtain for each cost flow assumption. Consequently—and most importantly—income will be affected by the selection of an inventory cost flow assumption except in the rare instance where all items acquired for inventory have the same unit price. Since price change rather than price stability has characterized the economic experience of most modern countries, it is a safe generalization that the cost flow assumption used will be a partial determinant of net income and, hence, of income taxes. For purposes of this discussion, we may regard income taxes as a direct function of net income. The direction of the impact upon income and income taxes of the cost flow assumption chosen depends upon the direction of movement of the prices for the inventoried commodities.

In an inflationary period, the Lifo inventory assumption tends generally to produce lower income and income taxes than either Fifo or average cost. The reason for this is that, under Lifo, the most recent costs, which in inflation are the higher costs, are charged against revenue in the income determination process. The early, lower costs remain in inventory. Under Fifo these lower costs would be charged to revenue. The average cost assumption lies somewhere between Fifo and Lifo in this connection, but its impact is generally closer to that of Fifo than to that of Lifo. In deflation, of course, the results are just the opposite; Lifo will tend to produce higher income figures than Fifo or average cost. From the standpoint of economic logic, deflation may be regarded as just as much a possibility as inflation. The experience of the American economy since 1939, however, has tended to create an inflationary bias in the thinking of most businessmen and consumers. Coincidentally, Lifo has existed as a practical alternative in inventory costing since 1939. The combination of persistent inflation and high income tax rates in the three decades after 1939 has led to widespread adoption of Lifo. It would be fair to state that the current usage of Lifo is attributable almost entirely to its tax advantages during a period of rising prices. Certainly, it makes sense for management to adopt whatever legitimate means are available to minimize income tax payments. The tax savings associated with the use of Lifo may be substantial, particularly when viewed in the aggregate over a period of many years.

The tax-saving aspects of Lifo are not completely free of danger for the taxpayer, however. Should inflation halt and deflation set in, the taxpayer may well find that he would then be better off using the Fifo assumption; but he might not be able to secure permission from the Commissioner of Internal Revenue to change his method of inventory accounting. Further, even if inflation continues, a substantial liquidation of inventory in any one year might result in the charging to revenue of the old, low costs in inventory and a consequent increase in net income and income tax. These considerations must be weighed by management, along with the favorable factors, in making the decision to adopt Lifo. And the decision as to the adoption of the Lifo cost flow assumption must be regarded as a management decision, not merely a technical accounting decision. Despite any doubts as to the theoretical validity of Lifo—and many accountants have such doubts—its tax-saving potential (including due consideration of the possible adverse tax implications) should be viewed as the dominant factor in the decision to adopt or reject it.

COST ACCOUNTING SYSTEMS

Any cost accounting system involves the basic cost accounting cycle explained in Chapter 3. However, the mechanics of processing cost data through this cycle and the manner in which these data are accumulated differ between the alternative systems. While many variations exist, the vast majority of cost accounting systems may be classified as one of two types—*job order* or *process*. In both types, manufacturing cost data are accumulated and charged to inventory accounts for the cost of goods produced. The problems of inventory costing differ somewhat between these two types of systems, as do other accounting procedures. More important than these differences, however, are the fundamental objectives common to both systems. They are alternative procedures for accomplishing essentially the same ends—the accurate and meaningful accumulation of cost data, the valuation of inventories, and the determination of income. Both absorption and variable costing, incidentally, can be employed effectively under either type of cost accounting system.

Job Order Cost System

A *job order cost system* is a system in which production is viewed and accounted for as a series of separate and distinct lots, batches, or jobs. Costs are accumulated for each individual job, and a unit cost is computed for each job. Job order costing is normally used where production is undertaken to fill specific customers' orders—such as in construction, printing, and shipbuilding. Such a system permits the manufacturer to match the revenue from an order with the costs incurred to produce it. Job order cost systems are by no means limited to instances of production to customers' orders, however. They are implemented in many industries where production is for inventory (to be sold subsequently to as yet undetermined buyers) but is accomplished in a discontinuous series of jobs. For example, in a furniture factory, the productive facilities of the plant may be employed serially for the manufacture of a lot of 100 maple bedsteads, then a lot of 100 maple dressers, then 500 walnut chairs, then 200 oak tables, and finally 100 upholstered couches. Obviously, it is not reasonable to say that 1,000 units of a homogeneous product have been produced. There are significant differences among these various products and the costs of producing them. Simply to identify a certain amount as the total cost of manufacturing these five jobs would not be particularly meaningful. And to divide such a total cost by 1,000 units of product would result in a wholly spurious figure for unit cost. Hence, cost data are developed for and charged to each job order individually. Even where several jobs for the same item are completed during one accounting period, the element of discontinuity of production (time lapses between the several jobs) makes it necessary to accumulate costs by jobs separately. Each job has its own unit cost, the total cost of the job divided by the number of units produced for it. Different job orders for the same product will very likely have slightly different unit costs, for the human element in production and price changes over time will have some effect upon costs.

Job Order Cost Sheets.   The costing unit in a job order system is the individual job. Direct manufacturing costs, therefore, are those which can be traced logically and practically to the units manufactured on a particular job order. Direct materials costs are traced to individual jobs by indicating job order numbers on materials requisitions issued by the plant to the materials storeroom. Direct labor charges to the several jobs are determined by the preparation of labor time tickets which indicate the amount of time spent by a worker on a particular job and his hourly wage rate. Overhead is typically applied at a normal rate when the job is completed. It must also be applied to incomplete jobs at the end of a fiscal year in order to avoid an erroneous underapplication of overhead for that period.

All manufacturing costs, direct and indirect, are accumulated for each job order on a *job order cost sheet.* This sheet indicates an identifying number for the job so that it may readily be traced, the product being produced, the number of units of product required for the job, the purpose for which the job is undertaken (i.e., for customer's order or for inventory), the date by which completion is necessary, and all of the costs incurred in the production of the job. All costs charged to production during any given period must appear on some job cost sheet. Hence, the total charges to Work in Process during the period will be equal to the total of all charges to job order cost sheets in that period. Similarly, the credits to Work in Process and corresponding debits to Finished Product will represent the sum of all costs charged to job cost sheets for completed jobs. Then, the ending balance in Work in Process will be equal to the sum of all costs accumulated to date on open cost sheets (i.e., sheets for uncompleted jobs) as of the end of the period. The file of job order cost sheets is, in effect, a subsidiary ledger supporting the general ledger account, Work in Process. Unit costs are determined only for completed jobs, and a job may be started in one period and completed in a subsequent one. Consequently, the calculation of unit cost on any one job may involve cost data spanning two or more accounting periods. The only constraint on this calculation is the job.

The necessity for maintaining numerous job order cost sheets and the necessary supporting documents, such as labor time tickets, means that the clerical work involved in a job order cost system is likely to be substantially greater than that required for a process cost system. This does not mean, of course, that a process system is always preferable. In many industries, only the job order system is feasible, regardless of the greater cost of implementing it.

Overhead Costs in Job Order Systems. The use of normal overhead rates, predetermined on the bases of budgeted costs and budgeted volume, is typically regarded as essential to the smooth functioning of a job order cost system. Normal overhead rates permit the determination of the total cost and, hence, unit cost of a job as soon as it is completed. Actual overhead rates could not be applied until the end of the accounting period. As explained in Chapter 3, such a delay is simply not practical.

Where several materially different products are manufactured in the same plant, it is not valid to charge overhead to all of these products by means of one overhead rate or a single set of rates *per unit of product.* One product may involve considerably more processing for each unit than another product; obviously, the former should be charged for proportionately more overhead. In other words, the unit of product may not be a suitable "common denominator" for the application of overhead costs to production in a multiproduct firm. Where such is the case, the volume of production may be stated in terms of some unit which is common to all products. In business practice today, direct labor hours are widely used as the basis for charging overhead costs to production. Volume is budgeted in terms of expected labor hours and normal rates per hour are set. The overhead charged to any one job is then the product of the number of labor hours actually worked on that job times the normal overhead rates per hour.

Job Order Costing and Responsibility Costing. The fact that cost data are accumulated for job orders does not mean that they are not also accumulated for each cost center in the plant. The choice of a cost accounting system does not change the need for the development of cost data along responsibility lines. Thus, there may be as many charges for labor and overhead on a job order cost sheet as there are cost centers involved in the production of the job. Each cost center would distribute its own costs to the jobs worked on in that center during the period. Since materials are not necessarily added to production in each cost center, there may be fewer charges for materials than there are cost centers.

Job Order Cost Sheet Illustrated. Table 4–1 is an illustration of a job order cost sheet for a manufacturer of paper novelty products. Among the company's products are jigsaw puzzles. The heading of the job cost sheet identifies the job, the product, and other pertinent informa-

TABLE 4–1

SHERMAN MANUFACTURING COMPANY
Job Order Cost Sheet

Job No. P750–69	*Product* Series 808 jigsaw puzzle
Date started 8/15/72	*Units required* 1,200
Date required 8/25/72	*Purpose* for inventory
Date completed 8/24/72	*Job authorized* J.F.C.

Job Costs

Raw materials:

		Cost	
	Requisition number		
Picture prints	3607	$180.00	
Cardboard backing	3608	66.00	
Boxes	3612	35.00	
Box labels	3612	48.00	$329.00

Direct labor:
Cutting department–25 hrs @ $2.00	$ 50.00	
Boxing department–40 hrs @ $1.75	70.00	120.00

Variable overhead:
Cutting department–25 hrs @ $ .32	$ 8.00	
Boxing department–40 hrs @ $ .40	16.00	24.00

Fixed overhead:
Cutting department–25 hrs @ $ .84	$ 21.00	
Boxing department–40 hrs @ $ .60	24.00	45.00
Total job costs		$518.00
Unit cost		$ .431667

Inspected and approved R. W. E.

tion. Each job has a distinctive number. In this illustration, the number partially identifies the product. The "P" shows that the job is for puzzles, and the "750" indicates the number of pieces in the puzzles. The final two digits of the job number simply show that this is the 69th job for 750-piece puzzles. The heading also describes the product and indicates how many units are required for the job. This particular job is being produced for inventory. Others may be produced to a specific customer's order. The production manager initials the cost sheet to authorize production of 1,200 units of this particular product. The date on which the finished units are required is entered along with the date on which the job is started.

All costs incurred in connection with this job are reported on the job order cost sheet. Raw materials costs are traced to the job by means of materials requisitions. Each requisition identifies not only the items being issued and their costs but also the job number for which they were issued. A summary of requisitions for Job No. P750–69 is entered on the cost sheet. Direct labor time is accumulated in each production department on labor time tickets. These tickets indicate the amount of time spent on a particular job. All tickets for a job are then summarized in each department and the departmental time totals entered on the job cost sheet, along with the departmental wage rates. Variable and fixed overhead are applied on the basis of normal rates per direct labor hour in each department. These normal rates are predetermined at the start of the fiscal year. The actual labor hours to which they are applied are taken from the summary of labor time tickets. The illustration assumes that the Sherman Manufacturing Company uses absorption costing. If variable costing were used, the section for fixed overhead would simply be deleted from the cost sheet, and total job costs would be less. When production is completed, the date is entered in the heading and the factory inspector initials the cost sheet to indicate that the job has been approved and the units transferred to the finished product storeroom.

Process Cost System

Process cost accounting systems regard production as a continuous flow rather than as a series of identifiable lots. Hence, this type of system is employed in industries where production processes are of a continuous and repetitive nature. Examples of such industries are basic steel, cement, flour milling, and petroleum refining. The simplest illustration of a process cost system is in a firm producing a single product or a single line of homogeneous products. However, process costing may be used effectively in a firm which produces a variety of products so long as the overall production process can be broken down into suboperations of a continuous, repetitive nature. For example, the spray-paint shop in a major appliance manufacturer's plant may perform essentially the same operations regardless of whether ranges, refrigerators, or washers are being painted. These suboperations are commonly referred to as *processes,* or *departments* in process costing. For purposes of the present discussion, processes may be identified with cost centers. Hence, the accumulation of cost data by responsibility will also provide the necessary cost information for the process cost accounting system.

Determination of Unit Cost. In a process cost system, the costing unit is the production in a particular department, or cost center, during a specified period of time, commonly one month. Thus, direct manufacturing costs are those which can be traced to the cost center. Consequently, certain costs which would be indirect in a job order system may be direct under process costing. For example, the wages of a janitor whose work is confined to one cost center would be treated as part of direct labor in a process cost system, even though the janitor does not actually work on the product. The important point is that he works directly in the department.

The unit cost under process costing is the quotient of the manufacturing costs incurred in a given center during a given period of time divided by the units of product manufactured in that center during that time period. This calculation is subject to two constraints, the cost center and the time period. The basic formula for unit cost determination is very simple.

$$\text{Unit cost} = \frac{\text{Total costs in department during period}}{\text{Units produced in department during period}}$$

While this basic formula is always valid, the determination of the units produced may be somewhat complex.

Equivalent Units of Production. Since one of the constraints upon the unit cost computation is the time period, the units produced during a particular period must be identified. If there is an inventory of unfinished production (i.e., Work in Process) at the beginning and/or at the end of the period, the determination of units produced involves some additional computations. Obviously, the total number of units of potential finished product in the inventory at the end of the month may not be included among the units produced during that month, for such inclusion would imply that they were completed when this is patently not so. Similarly, the total number of units in beginning inventory cannot be treated as part of current production; to do so would be to ignore the fact that those units were partially completed during the previous month. Thus, some unit is needed to measure the amount of productive work actually done during one period. The unit of measure for this purpose is the *equivalent unit of production.*

Equivalent units of production measure the amount of work accomplished during a given period. They are units of product, but not necessarily whole units. For example, assume that the drill press department of the Coppelius Manufacturing Company finished 42,000 units of product during the month of March, 1972. The inventory of Work in Process in the department at the end of February consisted of 14,000 units that were then half completed. The inventory of Work in Process at the end of March comprised 15,000 units that were one-third complete. The 42,000 units completed during the month do not include any part of the ending inventory, but that inventory was partially manufactured during the month. On the other hand, the 42,000 units do include the

14,000 units in beginning inventory; but half of the work on those units was completed in the previous month. Hence, the work done (equivalent units) during March consists of the units finished during that month plus the work done on the ending inventory minus the work done in February on the beginning inventory. Equivalent units produced, then, are equal to the total units completed during a period plus the total units in the ending inventory of Work in Process times the fraction that the inventory is completed and minus the total units in the beginning inventory of Work in Process times the fraction that they are already complete at the start of the period. Using the data from the example above, the equivalent units produced in the drill press department during March would be computed as follows:

Units completed during March	42,000
+ Units in ending inventory times fraction completed (15,000 units × ⅓)	5,000
	47,000
− Units in beginning inventory times fraction completed (14,000 × ½)	7,000
= Equivalent units produced	40,000

Unit cost would then be equal to the total costs incurred in the department during March divided by the 40,000 equivalent units.

The problem of equivalent units may be complicated further by the fact that not all of the cost factors of production are the same fraction complete in a given inventory of Work in Process. For example, all of the materials may be put into the production process at its inception; whereas the labor and overhead are added throughout the process. Hence, any inventory of Work in Process would be fully complete with respect to materials but might be any fraction complete with respect to labor and overhead. In such a case, no single figure for equivalent production would be valid. Rather, there would have to be one such figure for materials and a different one for labor and overhead. It should be noted here that labor and overhead will not necessarily be at the same degree of completion in an inventory. If they were not, there would have to be three separate figures for equivalent units. For purposes of the present discussion, we will assume that labor and overhead are at the same stage of completion. Obviously, this would be the case where overhead is applied to production on the basis of direct labor hours. Thus, a single figure for equivalent units and a single unit cost figure could be used for the combination of labor and overhead, commonly referred to as conversion costs. In the example in the previous paragraph, assume that all materials are placed into production at the start of the process (and, hence, are fully complete in any inventory) and that the fractions of completion indicated apply only to the conversion costs. The calculation of equivalent units would then appear as follows:

	Materials	Labor and Overhead
Units completed during March....................	42,000	42,000
+ Units in ending inventory times fraction completed:		
Materials (15,000 × 1).......................	15,000	
Labor and overhead (15,000 × ⅓).............		5,000
	57,000	47,000
− Units in beginning inventory times fraction completed:		
Materials (14,000 × 1).......................	14,000	
Labor and overhead (14,000 × ½).............		7,000
= Equivalent units produced....................	43,000	40,000

As a general rule, the concept of equivalent units must be related to a particular cost factor in order for it to be operationally meaningful. Consequently, unit costs typically can be computed only for each cost factor separately. Total unit cost is then the sum of the unit costs for the individual cost factors.

Process Costing Illustration. The determination of unit costs in a process system and the applications of these data are illustrated below for the drill press department of the Coppelius Manufacturing Company. The equivalent units of production for materials and for labor and overhead in this illustration are those computed in the preceding paragraph (i.e., 43,000 units with respect to materials and 40,000 units with respect to conversion costs). Cost data for the drill press department for the month of March are as follows:

Cost in the beginning inventory................		$ 88,000
Costs charged to production during March:		
Materials.....................................		172,000
Conversion costs:		
Direct labor..............................	$100,000	
Variable overhead applied.................	40,000	
Fixed overhead applied....................	60,000	200,000
		$460,000

It would be possible to treat each item of cost separately. However, since the same number of equivalent units are applicable to all conversion cost items, it is also possible to treat them together for purposes of unit cost computations. The latter approach will be used here, largely to keep the illustration small and simple. Thus, unit costs of production will be determined in two categories only—materials and conversion costs.

The equivalent units of production for March include only the work actually accomplished during the current month. The work done on the beginning inventory during February is excluded from the computation of equivalent units. Since total costs will be divided by equivalent units in the calculation of unit costs, logically the total costs used in the computation must parallel the units used. Thus, only the costs incurred during March are included in the determination of unit costs. Costs incurred during February on the beginning inventory of March are excluded. However, these costs incurred during February must be accounted for during March. While they are not employed in the current unit cost computation, they must not be ignored altogether.

The determination of unit cost is not a final end in itself, of course. It serves two fundamental purposes: First, it affords some basis for cost control. Unit costs of several months may be compared, trends noted, and differences evaluated with a view toward cost control. Actual unit costs may also be compared with some standards for unit costs in order to appraise the efficiency of manufacturing operations during the period. Second, the unit cost is necessary to determine the cost of goods completed in the department and transferred to the next step in the production process and also the cost of goods remaining in the departmental inventory of Work in Process at the end of the period. The calculation of unit costs and the application of such unit costs to production are illustrated in Table 4–2, a production cost report for the drill press department for the month of March. This report includes the costs in the beginning inventory, but it does not incorporate them in the computation of unit costs for March. Notice in Table 4–2 that there is no single figure for equivalent units which can be divided into total costs to produce the total unit cost of $9. Individual unit costs are determined for materials and for labor and overhead, and the sum of these is the total unit cost for March.

Obviously, the total costs incurred must be accounted for. There are only two possible dispositions of costs charged to a cost center. They may either be transferred to the next stage of the production process as the cost of completed production or remain in the center as the cost of the ending inventory of Work in Process. Table 4–2 shows the cost of completed production as comprising the cost of the beginning inventory, both the costs incurred in the previous month and the costs incurred currently to complete those units, and the cost of the units which were both started and completed during the current month. The inventory at the end of the month, therefore, consists of units started during the current month, and, consequently, of current costs. The reader should recognize that this illustration employs the first-in, first-out, or Fifo cost flow assumption. The average cost and the last-in, first-out assumptions may also be used in connection with inventories of work in process under a process cost system. While the basic approach is the same regardless of the cost flow assumption employed, there are enough technical distinctions among the three that the elementary picture intended here would be unduly clouded if all three assumptions were illustrated.

The cost report in Table 4–2 is divided into two sections, one showing the total costs incurred and the determination of unit costs and the other showing the disposition of these total costs. Unit costs are computed by dividing the total costs incurred during the current period for each cost factor by the equivalent production of the period for each factor. The costs accounted for include those charged to completed production and

TABLE 4–2

COPPELIUS MANUFACTURING COMPANY
Drill Press Department
Production Cost Report for the Month of March, 1972

	Total Costs	Equivalent Units	Unit Cost
Total costs incurred			
Beginning inventory..................	$ 88,000		
Current charges:			
Materials.........................	172,000	43,000	$4
Conversion costs...................	200,000	40,000	5
Total........................	$460,000		$9
Total costs accounted for			
Completed production:			
Units from beginning inventory			
Costs incurred in previous month...	$ 88,000		
Current cost to complete..........	35,000	7,000	$5
	$123,000	14,000	
Units started currently..............	252,000	28,000	9
Total units completed..............	$375,000	42,000	
Ending inventory			
Materials.........................	$ 60,000	15,000	4
Conversion costs...................	25,000	5,000	5
	$ 85,000		
Total........................	$460,000		

those in inventory at the end of the month. The cost of completed production is composed of the costs applied to the beginning inventory during the previous month, the current cost to complete the beginning inventory, and the current costs of units started and finished during the current month. The costs applied to the beginning inventory in February totaled $88,000. Since the beginning inventory was completed with respect to materials in the previous month, no current materials cost is charged to it. As it was only half completed with respect to labor and overhead, however, an additional 7,000 equivalent units of labor and overhead must be added during March at the current cost of $5 per unit. Adding these costs to complete ($35,000) to the costs of the previous month ($88,000) yields a total cost of $123,000 for the 14,000 units in beginning inventory, now completed. The remaining 28,000 units completed during March were started currently and, hence, can be charged entirely at the current total unit cost of $9. The total cost of these units is then $252,000. The total unit cost of $9 can be applied to the 28,000 units started and completed currently because they are all at the same stage of completion. The 15,000 units in ending inventory, on the other hand, are fully complete as to materials but only one-third complete as to conversion costs. Consequently, the cost of the ending inventory is the sum of 15,000 equivalent units of materials at the current unit cost of $4 plus 5,000 equivalent units of labor and overhead at the current unit cost of $5.

Journal Entries. Unlike the job order system, it is customary in process costs systems that there be as many Work in Process accounts as there are cost centers. Raw materials drawn from the storeroom, direct labor, and overhead are charged to the appropriate Work in Process accounts, as already illustrated in Chapter 3. In addition, the costs of units completed in one department and transferred to another department for further processing are charged to the Work in Process account of the latter department and credited to the account of the former. Referring again to the illustration in the foregoing sections, assume that the drill press department is only the first stage in the production process of the Coppelius Manufacturing Company. The product is transferred from that department to the assembly department, where the production process is finished. Goods are then transferred to the warehouse for finished products. On March 1, there was a debit balance of $88,000 in the account titled Work in Process—Drill Press Department. Journal entries to charge the current costs to that account would be as follows:

Work in Process—Drill Press Department.............. 372,000		
Materials Inventory.............................		172,000
Payroll Summary................................		100,000
Variable Overhead Applied.......................		40,000
Fixed Overhead Applied.........................		60,000

This entry, as well as the cost report in Table 4–2, assumes that the Coppelius Manufacturing Company uses absorption costing. If variable costing were used, fixed overhead would be excluded from the Work in Process account and, hence, from the computation of unit cost. Consequently, both unit cost and total inventory cost would be lower. In all other respects, however, the illustration would be the same.

The transfer of the semifinished product from the drill press department to the assembly department would be recorded thus:

Work in Process—Assembly Department............... 375,000		
Work in Process—Drill Press Department..........		375,000

Other costs incurred in the assembly department—perhaps additional materials and certainly labor and overhead—would be charged to the Work in Process account for that department in the usual way. Finally, the cost of goods completed in the assembly department would be credited to Work in Process for that department and debited to Finished Product. This last entry, of course, would require prior determination of the unit cost in the assembly department. The procedure for computing unit cost here would be exactly the same as that illustrated in Table 4–2.

ABSORPTION AND VARIABLE COSTING COMPARED

The Development of Variable Costing

Absorption costing is generally accepted in current accounting practice as *the* way of accounting for manufacturing costs and, specifically, fixed overhead costs. For many years, in fact, there was not even any significant suggestion of an alternative. During the 1930s, however, the method we know here as variable costing was proposed and given some small notice. But the growth of variable costing was slow in coming. The urgency of World War II caused a great many less critical considerations to be pushed out of men's minds, and the virtual pandemonium of the immediate postwar years was hardly conducive to careful consideration of something so technical as a method of accounting for fixed costs. Thus, the real development of the variable costing technique did not occur until the decade of the 1950s.

To begin with, the author must confess that variable costing is not widely known by that name at all. Rather, the concept has developed and is most popularly known today as *direct costing*. This has been an unfortunate choice of terminology, however; for the distinction which is at the heart of the method is not that between direct and indirect costs, but that between variable and fixed costs. "Variable costing," although not so widely employed, is a much more descriptive term and will be used throughout this volume. The same concept is known as *marginal costing* in Great Britain. Again, the selection of the term seems to be unsatisfactory. Variable costs cannot necessarily be identified with marginal costs, and, as already pointed out, marginal cost has so explicit a meaning in economic theory that the author prefers to avoid its use altogether in accounting.

Arguments for and against Variable Costing

The development of variable costing has progressed very rapidly in recent years. Advocates of the method have raised a number of arguments in its favor. Some of these will be considered, along with counterarguments where appropriate, in the paragraphs that follow.

Separate Accounting for Variable and Fixed Costs. One argument offered in support of variable costing is that it causes separate identification and recording of variable and fixed costs in the accounts and, hence, greater realization on the part of accountants and managers of the importance of volume in the determination of costs. There can be little question that the separate recording of variable and fixed costs is useful to management. As has been demonstrated in the preceding chapter, this separate recording can be effected just as well under absorption costing as under variable costing. The fact is, however, that a clear distinction between variable and fixed costs has only infrequently been made in the accounts of firms employing absorption costing. In other words, although the separation can be made in either costing method, it typically has accompanied only the variable costing method.

Emphasis on Cost-Volume Relationships. Perhaps the most important and unassailable argument in favor of variable costing is that it emphasizes the distinction between variable and fixed costs in reports to management and to others. A comparison of Tables 3–5 and 3–7 in Chapter 3 will testify to the validity of this point. Under absorption costing, the principal intermediate profit figure on the income statement is the gross margin, a residual after the deduction from revenue of both variable and fixed costs of manufacturing. The principal intermediate figure on the variable costing income statement is the variable profit, the difference between the revenue (which, of course, varies with sales volume) and those costs which vary with the volume of sales (variable cost of goods sold, variable selling expenses, etc.). Thus, variable profit, in itself, bears a direct relationship to volume. No such relationship exists between gross margin and volume. This undeniable emphasis upon cost-volume relationships is particularly useful to management, which has the power (not without limit, of course) to effect changes in costs and/or in volume. Whether the same emphasis is equally useful to others, such as stockholders and creditors, is problematic.

Some opponents of the variable costing method have pointed out that by excluding fixed costs from the cost of the product, the method emphasizes variable costs to the prejudice of fixed costs and that fixed costs are likely to be ignored or, at least, minimized in importance by management. This argument is particularly unsatisfactory, however; for it seems to rest upon the unattractive premise that managers are not very bright. But just the opposite would appear to be true. The general prosperity and profitability of American business enterprises hardly suggest the presence of managers who would be likely to overlook fixed costs—or any other costs, for that matter.

Effect of Inventory Changes on Reported Net Income. Under absorption costing, an increase in finished product inventory levels (i.e., ending inventory greater than the beginning balance) in a year of declining sales can have the effect of mitigating a decline in income, because fixed manufacturing costs incurred during the period are partially deferred in inventory until some subsequent period when the goods are sold. Conversely, a reduction in inventory levels (i.e., ending inventory less than the beginning) has the effect of charging to the revenues of that period fixed manufacturing costs incurred in some previous period. In other words, changes in inventory balances from the beginning to the end of a period have an identifiable impact upon income under absorption costing. Advocates of variable costing have argued that such an effect is artificial and may be misleading. They point out that variable costing avoids any income effect resulting from inventory increases or decreases.[2]

TABLE 4–3

Comparative Income Measurements
(all amounts in thousands)

	First year		Second year		Third year	
	Absorption Costing	Variable Costing	Absorption Costing	Variable Costing	Absorption Costing	Variable Costing
Unit sales volume.............	60	60	60	60	60	60
Unit production volume........	75	75	60	60	48	48
Sales revenue.................	$240	$240	$240	$240	$240	$240
Costs charged to revenue:						
Variable...................	$150	$150	$150	$150	$150	$150
Fixed.....................	48	60	60	60	69	60
Total costs............	$198	$210	$210	$210	$219	$210
Net income...................	$ 42	$ 30	$ 30	$ 30	$ 20	$ 30

The substance of this particular argument can best be seen from a simple illustration. Table 4–3 compares reported incomes under absorption costing and variable costing for the same company for three years. In the first year, more units are manufactured than sold; inventory is increased. In the second year, manufacturing volume and sales volume are identical; inventory balances remain unchanged. Finally, in the third year, sales volume exceeds the volume of production; inventory is decreased. The sales volume is the same (60,000 units) in each year, and the selling price remains stable at $4 per unit. The variable manufacturing costs total $2.50 per unit in each year, and the fixed manufacturing costs total $60,000 each year. No nonmanufacturing costs are included in the illustration because, since they are treated in the same way under

---

[2] This feature of variable costing, in contrast with absorption costing, was the central point in the earliest published article that advocated use of variable costing in reports to management. See Jonathan N. Harris, "What Did We Earn Last Month?" *N.A.C.A. Bulletin,* Vol. XVII (January 15, 1936), pp. 501–22.

both absorption and variable costing, they would have no effect upon the comparison.

Certain technical aspects of Table 4–3 must be seen clearly in order to understand fully the comparison being made. Under both costing methods, the variable costs charged to the revenue of the period are $150,000 (the 60,000 units sold each year at the unit variable cost rate of $2.50). Under variable costing, the fixed cost charged to revenue in each year is simply the total of fixed costs incurred in that year— $60,000. Under absorption costing, however, the fixed costs charged to revenue are the fixed costs of the goods sold and may be more or less than the $60,000 of fixed costs incurred in each year. In the first year, the fixed costs averaged $.80 per unit ($60,000 ÷ 75,000 units produced). Thus, the fixed cost of goods sold is $48,000 (60,000 units sold at a fixed cost rate of $.80 each). In the second year under absorption costing, fixed costs average $1 per unit ($60,000 ÷ 60,000 units produced); and the fixed cost of goods sold is $60,000 (60,000 units sold @ $1). Finally, the fixed costs per unit in the third year amount to $1.25 ($60,000 ÷ 48,000 units produced). The fixed costs of goods sold in the third year includes the fixed cost incurred in the third year (48,000 units sold × $1.25 = $60,000) plus some of the fixed costs incurred in the first year and deferred in inventory (12,000 units sold × $.80 = $9,600). This is a total of $69,600. In each year, the first fixed costs charged to revenue are those applicable to the current production. This means that the inventory is accounted for in accordance with the Lifo cost flow asumption. Year-to-year fluctuations in income under absorption costing would appear with either the Fifo or the average cost flow assumption also; only the amounts of the fluctuations would be different.

Table 4–3 implicitly assumes that budgeted and actual fixed overheads are equal each year and also that budgeted and actual production volumes are the same each year. The effect of these assumptions is that there is no under- or overapplied overhead in any year. These assumptions are not necessary for the illustration; they merely keep it simple.

The basic point of the illustration can now be seen quite simply. During the three-year period shown, there were no changes in sales volume, selling prices, variable costs per unit, or total fixed costs. The only change was in the volume of production and, consequently, in the levels of inventory. Under variable costing, changes in inventory levels have no effect upon income. Under absorption costing, on the other hand, income is different in each of the three years as a result of the changes in inventory levels. The proponents of variable costing argue that these fluctuations in income are meaningless and potentially misleading and, hence, that variable costing is superior to absorption costing insofar as each is concerned with the measurement of periodic net income.

The validity of this particular argument in favor of variable costing rests upon the validity of the basic premise of the method, namely, that fixed manufacturing costs are period costs and not product costs. Supporters of variable costing contend that such is indeed the case, that fixed overhead is the cost of providing productive capacity, of making production possible during a particular period, but not a part of the cost of the units actually produced in that period. Advocates of absorption costing, on the other hand, argue that the fixed costs of manufacturing are just as much costs of the product as are variable costs. They argue that the utilization of factory facilities, as represented by the cost item depreciation, is just as essential to the product as are direct materials and labor. Which of these positions is the correct one has been argued frequently and vehemently. As mentioned earlier, absorption costing is generally accepted in current accounting practice, while variable costing is not. This fact does not necessarily demonstrate the theoretic superiority of absorption costing, however. It could be interpreted simply as a reflection of the facts that absorption costing has long been entrenched in accounting practice and that accounting practices are not changed overnight.

It is important that the reader understand that the fluctuations in income shown in Table 4–3 under absorption costing are correct and proper if fixed overhead is truly a product cost as absorption costing suggests. As a matter of fact, if fixed overhead is properly treated as a product cost, then the use of variable costing would result in an *artificial* equalization of income over time; and such practice is generally agreed to be improper. Whether income fluctuations caused by changes in inventory levels are valid or not depends upon whether fixed overhead is a product cost or a period cost. At this writing, it is fair to say that the latter question remains a disputed point.

Internal and External Accounting Reports

The development of variable costing has centered around its usefulness in reports to management. Only recently has considerable interest arisen in its use also in reports to stockholders, creditors, and other outside parties. With respect to internal reports submitted to management, the decision as to the use of variable costing is a simple one. The criteria which should guide the selection of accounting techniques in reports to management are utility and effectiveness. If variable costing proves to be useful and effective in management reports, then, by all means, it should be used. Variable costing is good management accounting if it facilitates management's achievement of its basic objectives. The increasing popularity of the method in practice is considerable evidence of its usefulness.

Where external reports to stockholders and others are concerned, the criteria determining the selection of accounting practices are *generally accepted accounting principles*. These consist of various concepts, rules, and practices which have attained acceptance in business. At the time of this writing, variable costing has not attained the status of a generally accepted accounting principle. This does not mean that it never will; accounting principles are not immutable.[3] For the present, however, the reader should be aware that variable costing is not considered acceptable in external financial reports.

A firm which wishes to employ variable costing in its internal reporting system but must adhere to absorption costing for its external reports is not condemned to maintaining two separate sets of books. Costs may be accumulated in the accounts and internal reports prepared in accordance with the variable costing technique. When external reports are prepared, a simple adjustment may be made to add to inventory a proportionate share of the fixed overhead of the period and to remove such amount from the current fixed overhead expense account. For example, if the Fixed Overhead Control account had a balance of $750,000 at the end of a year and it was determined that, under absorption costing, 10% of that total should be deferred in inventory, a simple adjustment would transfer $75,000 of the fixed overhead to the appropriate inventory accounts—Work in Process and/or Finished Product. The remaining $675,000 would be reported as part of the cost of goods sold on the absorption costing income statement. This adjustment would be made only in the external financial statements, of course, not in the ledger accounts, which would be maintained consistently in accordance with variable costing.

QUESTIONS FOR DISCUSSION

1. Should management have any interest in the decision whether a perpetual or a periodic inventory method is to be used, or is this simply a technical accounting decision? Explain your answer.

2. You have been appointed controller of a newly organized electronics firm. The company will manufacture and distribute a variety of electronics components. It will be necessary to maintain fairly large inventories of raw materials and of finished products. Which inventory cost flow assumption would you recommend that this firm use—Fifo, average cost, or Lifo? Why? What assumptions, if any, underlie your recommendation? Might you recommend a different method of inventory costing if these assumptions were different?

---

[3] In view of the increasing popularity of variable costing among manufacturing firms, it is not unlikely that it will become generally accepted in external financial reports in the fairly near future. Its acceptance in financial reporting would depend to a considerable extent upon its acceptability in income tax reports also.

3. "In light of income tax considerations, Lifo is, as a practical matter, invariably preferable to Fifo." Comment on the validity of this statement.

4. "A manufacturer using a job order cost accounting system is compelled to use Fifo, for the first jobs started would normally be the first ones completed. And no job would ever be left incomplete for an indefinite period, as the Lifo assumption would suggest." Evaluate this position.

5. What are the comparative merits of using normal overhead rates rather than actual rates in job order cost systems and in process cost systems?

6. Why are equivalent units of production essential to an accurate determination of unit cost in a process cost system but not in a job order system?

7. Is process costing more compatible with the objective of responsibility costing than job order costing? Explain.

8. Of what value is an accounting system that records and reports fixed and variable costs separately.

9. Why might the net income of a firm in a single period be reported differently under absorption costing as compared with variable costing?

10. Assume that you have been engaged as a consultant to a medium-sized manufacturer. The president has asked you to study his operations and to recommend a basic cost accounting method—either absorption costing or variable costing. Production costs during the most recent year totaled $50 million, about 60% of which were variable costs and the remainder, fixed. Which method would you recommend? Why? If you would want any additional information before making your recommendation, specify what that information would be.

11. The sales of the Pickwick Company in 1971 were somewhat disappointing in light of recent years' experience. However, a substantial inventory of finished products was accumulated during that year in anticipation of much improved sales in 1972. Actual sales in 1972 proved to be even greater than expected. All of the current output and most of the inventory accumulated in 1971 were sold. Still, when the financial statements for the year were prepared, the net income was less than it had been in 1971. The chairman of the board was very unhappy with this report and demanded an explanation from the controller. The controller explained that under the absorption costing method long used in the firm, a major liquidation of inventory of finished products, such as occurred in 1972, tended to depress income. When the chairman discussed the situation with the firm's independent auditor, the auditor suggested that they prepare and examine revised income statements for 1971 and 1972 under the variable costing method. These revised statements showed a lower income for 1971 and a substantially higher income for 1972. The chairman of the board was so pleased with these revised statements that he fired the controller and replaced him with the auditor.

In 1973, sales declined sharply. This decline was believed to be only temporary, however. Upon the recommendations of the sales manager, production was maintained at the same level as in the preceding two years. It was agreed that any inventory accumulated in 1973 would be sold the following year. When the financial statements under variable costing were prepared at the end of 1973, the income statement showed a net loss. The chairman of the board asked for an explanation of this loss. The new controller said that it was simply a normal consequence of the variable costing method in such a year. A new independent auditor had been engaged, and he pointed out to the chairman that a profit would have been reported for 1973 under the old absorption costing method. Upon hearing this, the chairman bolted from the room, went directly to the corner tavern, downed six martinis, and then stretched himself across the Southern Pacific tracks.

Quickly, before the next train comes along, explain to the chairman why the alternative costing methods resulted in such different income figures over the three-year period. Tell him how he can go on living in reasonable sobriety with one or the other of these two methods.

PROBLEMS

1. The Jaggers Manufacturing Company's inventory records reveal the following transactions involving one of its principal raw materials during the month of January:

Balance, January 1	1,000 units @ $5.00
Purchase, January 8	4,000 units @ $5.25
Issue, January 10	2,200 units
Issue, January 20	2,000 units
Purchase, January 25	3,200 units @ $5.50
Issue, January 30	1,500 units

    The company uses a perpetual inventory system.

    Required:

    Compute the cost of the inventory of this raw material on January 31 under each of the following cost flow assumptions:
    a) Fifo
    b) Average cost
    c) Lifo

2. Complete the requirements of Problem 1 above on the assumption that the company uses a periodic inventory system.

3. The Gargery Forge Company's record of finished products shows the following activity during the year 1972:

	Completed Production		
Quarter	Units	Unit Cost	Units Sold
First	2,000	$12.00	1,000
Second	3,500	16.00	3,000
Third	4,500	20.00	5,000
Fourth	4,000	24.00	4,400

The inventory of finished products at January 1, 1972, consisted of 1,000 units with a unit cost of $10.80.

Required:

a) Assuming that the company uses a perpetual inventory system, compute the cost of the ending inventory of finished products and the cost of goods sold for 1972 under each of the following cost flow assumptions:

    (1) Fifo
    (2) Average cost
    (3) Lifo

b) Assuming now that the company uses a periodic inventory system, compute the cost of the ending inventory of finished product and the cost of goods sold for 1972 under each of the same three cost flow assumptions.

4. The Mycroft Company uses a job order cost accounting system and absorption costing. The schedule below shows the number of units produced on each job order during the first month of the firm's operations, the number of labor hours worked on each job, and the direct costs charged to each job.

	Job Number			
	1	*2*	*3*	*4*
Units of product.......	800	1,200	1,100	1,000
Direct labor hours......	800	1,500	1,200	400
Direct materials cost...	$6,400	$9,900	$9,200	$3,000
Direct labor cost.......	4,000	7,500	6,000	2,000

Overhead is applied to production at predetermined rates per labor hour worked. These rates are as follows:

    Variable.................................... $ .50
    Fixed...................................... 1.50

Jobs 1, 2, and 3 were completed during the month. Job 4 is less than half finished.

Required:

a) Compute the amount of overhead charged to each job.
b) Compute the unit cost of each completed job.
c) Prepare the journal entry to record the transfer of the completed jobs to Finished Product.
d) Determine the balance in Work in Process at the end of the month.

5. The Watson Tool Corporation, which commenced operations on August 1, 1972, employs a job order cost system. Overhead is charged to production at normal rates per direct labor hour, as follows:

Per Hour

Variable overhead.......................... $1.50
Fixed overhead............................ 2.00

Actual operations for the month of August, 1972, are summarized below:

(1) Purchases of raw materials: 50,000 pieces at $1.
(2) Prime costs charged to jobs and units produced:

			Direct Labor	
Job No.	Units	Materials	Cost	Hours
201...........	500	$5,000	$ 8,000	2,000
202...........	800	6,000	9,600	2,400
203...........	1,500	9,000	14,400	3,600
204...........	500	4,750	6,000	1,500
205...........	1,000	6,400	3,200	800

(3) Actual overhead costs incurred (credit to "miscellaneous accounts"):

Variable.................... $16,000
Fixed..................... 22,000

(4) Completed jobs: Nos. 201, 202, 203, and 204.
(5) Sales revenue: $120,000. All units produced on jobs 201, 202, and 203 were sold; 200 units produced on job 204 were sold.

Required:

a) Prepare general journal entries to record the operations for August, 1972.
b) Compute the unit cost of each completed job.
c) Compute the balance in Work in Process at August 31. Prove the accuracy of this balance by showing its composition (i.e., materials, labor, and overhead by jobs).

6. The Holmes Products Company uses a job order cost system and variable costing. Variable overhead is charged to production at a normal rate of $1 per direct labor hour. The inventories on May 1, 1972, were as follows:

Materials.. $25,000
Work in process:

Job No.	Materials	Labor	Overhead	
327	$4,300	$ 5,000	$2,000	
329	2,360	4,000	1,600	
330	1,200	1,000	400	
	$7,860	$10,000	$4,000	21,860

Finished product.................................. 50,000

Operations for the month of May, 1972, are summarized below:

(1) Materials costing $9,000 were purchased on account.
(2) A summary of materials requisitions shows the following charges to jobs:

Job No.	Materials Cost
330.....	$2,100
331.....	6,720
332.....	8,800
333.....	5,500
334.....	1,200

(3) The payroll for the month of May was distributed as follows:

Direct Labor

Job No.	Labor Hours	Labor Cost
327.....	200	$ 500
329.....	400	1,000
330.....	1,000	2,500
331.....	2,400	6,000
332.....	4,000	10,000
333.....	1,600	4,000
334.....	400	1,000

Variable indirect labor hours were 2,500 and cost $7,500.
(4) Labor-related costs amount to 10% of the payroll.
(5) Actual fixed overhead totaled $25,000 (credit to "miscellaneous accounts").
(6) The following jobs and units were completed during May:

Job No.	Units
327.....	6,000
329.....	4,800
330.....	4,000
331.....	7,200
332.....	12,000

(7) The cost of goods sold during May totaled $75,000.

Required:

a) Prepare journal entries to record the operations of the month of May.
b) Compute the unit cost of each completed job.
c) Compute the balance in Work in Process at May 31 and show its composition (i.e., materials, labor, and overhead by jobs).

7. The Moriarty Manufacturing Corporation produces a variety of power garden tools. A job order cost system is used. On June 1, 1972, the factory ledger showed the following inventory balances:

Materials.....	$ 60,000
Work in process.....	125,000
Finished product.....	180,000

Open job order cost sheets on June 1 contained the following charges:

Job M-1015.............................	$70,000
Job C-908..............................	30,000
Job T-750..............................	25,000

Transactions for the month of June are summarized below.

(1) Materials were purchased at a cost of $140,000.
(2) A summary of materials issues is as follows:

Job C-908........................	$ 20,000
Job T-750........................	12,000
Job M-1016......................	44,000
Job T-751........................	25,000
Job M-1017......................	30,000
Indirect materials	
(a variable cost)................	19,000
	$150,000

(3) Factory labor costs were distributed as follows:

Job M-1015......................	$ 21,000
Job C-908........................	15,000
Job T-750........................	6,000
Job M-1016......................	36,000
Job T-751........................	3,000
Job M-1017.....................	9,000
Indirect labor	
(a variable cost)...............	30,000
	$120,000

All factory workers are paid a uniform wage rate of $3 per hour.
(4) Labor-related costs included the following items:

Social security tax...........................	$6,000
Unemployment compensation tax.............	3,000

(5) The payroll department reported the following summary distribution of payroll credits:

Payroll checks disbursed....................	$92,000
Federal income tax withheld.................	18,000
Social security tax withheld.................	6,000
Health insurance premiums withheld.........	4,000

(6) The actual fixed overhead costs incurred during June included the following charges:

Depreciation on plant and equipment.........	$50,000
Property taxes and insurance................	10,000
Maintenance..............................	20,000

(7) Variable overhead is applied to production at a normal rate of $2 per direct labor hour. Fixed overhead is applied at a normal rate of $2.50 per hour.
(8) Jobs M-1015, C-908, T-750, and M-1016 were completed during June.

(9) Goods were sold for $550,000.

(10) The balance in Finished Product on June 30 was $150,000.

Required:

a) Prepare general journal entries to record the operations for the month of June.

b) Prepare a statement of cost of goods manufactured and sold for the month ended June 30, 1972.

8. The Lestrade Company manufactures two products, A and B. A job order cost system is employed. The letter prefix to the job number identifies the product being produced on that job. Work in process is accounted for by individual job orders. Raw materials and finished product are costed under the last-in, first-out assumption. A perpetual inventory system is used.

On January 31, 1972, the company's inventory accounts showed the following balances:

Raw materials (50,000 lbs. @ $.40)......... $20,000

Work in process:
Job A-29 (3,000 units)................. $15,000
Job B-63 (5,000 units).................   5,000   20,000

Finished product:
Product A (2,000 units @ $7.50)......... $15,000
Product B (3,000 units @ $2.00).........   6,000   21,000

The following raw materials purchases were made during the month of February:

February 10: 40,000 lbs. @ $.42
February 20: 50,000 lbs. @ $.44

Materials were issued during the month as follows:

February 15: 35,000 units for Job A-30
February 25: 45,000 units for Job B-64

Direct labor costs during February were charged to jobs as follows:

Job	Hours	Cost
A-29.........................	1,200	$ 5,400
A-30.........................	3,000	13,500
B-63.........................	800	3,600
B-64.........................	2,000	9,000

Actual overhead for the month included $24,000 of variable costs and $40,000 of fixed costs. Variable overhead is applied to production at a normal rate of $3 per direct labor hour. Fixed overhead is accounted for as a period expense.

Jobs A-29 and B-63 were completed about the middle of the month. On the last day of the month, 2,500 units of Product A and 6,000 units of Product B were sold to customers.

Required:

Prepare analyses of the ledger accounts for Raw Materials, Work in Process, Finished Product, and Cost of Goods Sold for the month of February, 1972. Show all debits and credits to each account and the ending account balances. Include any supporting schedules or computations that may be necessary.

9. The Spalanzani Steel Company uses a process cost accounting system. During the second quarter of 1972, 600,000 tons of steel were completed. On April 1, 90,000 tons had been in process; they were complete with respect to raw materials but only half complete with respect to labor and overhead. The inventory in process on June 30 consisted of 120,000 tons, 75% complete with respect to materials and 25% complete with respect to labor and overhead.

Required:

Compute the equivalent units of production during the second quarter.

10. Olympia Products, Inc., employs a process cost accounting system. During the month of August, 1972, the firm completed 10,000,000 pounds of product. On August 1, the inventory of work in process included 3,000,000 pounds of product; they were one-half complete with respect to materials and one-third complete with respect to conversion costs. On August 31, there were 2,000,000 pounds in process; they were one-fourth complete with respect to materials and one-fifth complete with respect to conversion costs.

Required:

Compute the equivalent units of production for the month of August.

11. The Nicklausse Corporation produces liquid soap in a single, continuous process. A process cost accounting system and absorption costing are employed. All inventories are costed under the Fifo assumption. At February 29, 1972, the corporation had an inventory of 3,000 gallons of soap in process. All materials required for these 3,000 gallons were already in process, and the inventory was estimated to be two-thirds complete with respect to labor and overhead. The costs in this inventory were as follows:

Materials...................... $2,700
Labor......................... 1,300
Overhead...................... 900

During March, 1972, 42,000 gallons of soap were completed and transferred to the finished stock warehouse. On March 31, 4,000 gallons remained in process. They were complete with respect to materials but only one-fourth complete with respect to labor and overhead. Charges to Work in Process during the month of March were as follows:

Materials........................	$30,100
Labor...........................	14,600
Overhead.......................	5,900

Required:

a) Compute the equivalent units produced during the month of March, 1972.
b) Compute the unit costs of production for the month.
c) Compute the costs of the soap completed during March and of the inventory in process at March 31.

12. The Hoffman Manufacturing Company produces a single product in one continuous production operation. A process cost accounting system and the Fifo cost flow assumption are used. Both variable and fixed overhead are charged to production at normal rates per direct labor hour of $1.20 and $1.80, respectively.

Physical production records for April, 1972, are summarized below:

Work in process, April 1: 500 units, complete with respect to materials and 40% completed with respect to labor and overhead.

Started into process during April: 6,500 units.

Work in process, April 30: 1,500 units, complete with respect to materials and one-third complete with respect to labor and overhead.

No units are lost or spoiled in the production process.

Production costs in the inventory of work in process on April 1 totaled $37,400. Current manufacturing costs included the following:

Materials issued to the factory............	$312,000
Direct labor............................	60,000 hrs.
	@ $3.96
Actual variable overhead.................	$ 75,000
Actual fixed overhead...................	$120,000

Required:

a) Compute the equivalent units of production for the month of April.
b) Compute the unit production costs for April.
c) Compute the total costs of goods completed during the month and of work in process at the end of the month.

13. The Miracle Shortening Corporation produces a liquid cooking oil in two successive production processes: blending and bottling. Only variable manufacturing costs are charged to products in the company's process cost accounting system. Inventories are costed under the Fifo assumption. The following cost data are taken from the records of the two production processes for the month of August, 1972:

	Blending	Bottling
Direct materials used	$88,800	$64,000*
Direct labor	96,400	35,000
Actual variable overhead	40,000	25,200
Variable overhead applied	42,200	21,000
Actual fixed overhead	50,000	70,000

*The cost of goods completed in the blending process and transferred to bottling is also accounted for as a direct materials cost. It is not included in this $64,000, which represents only the costs of bottles, caps, and labels.

Production statistics (in gallons) for the two processes are as follows:

	Blending	Bottling
Inventory, August 1	10,000	0
Completed during August	80,000	80,000
Inventory, August 31	4,000	0

Both the beginning and the ending inventories in the blending process were complete with respect to materials and one-half complete with respect to labor and overhead. The balance in Work in Process—Blending on August 1 was $21,000.

The inventory of finished product on August 1 included 50,000 gallons at a cost of $4.40 per gallon. During August, 70,000 gallons were sold at a net selling price of $9 each. Variable selling expenses average $.40 per gallon sold. Fixed selling and administrative expenses totaled $80,000 for the month. The applicable income tax rate is 40%.

Required:

a) Prepare a production report for the blending process for August, 1972. This report should include computations of equivalent units produced, unit production costs, and total costs of completed production and ending inventory.

b) Prepare an income statement and a supporting statement of cost of goods manufactured and sold for the month of August.

14. The Crespel Company manufactures an antiseptic powder in two successive production processes: compounding and packaging. A process cost accounting system is employed. Inventories are costed in accordance with the absorption costing method and the Fifo cost flow assumption.

At December 31, 1971, the company's inventory balances were as follows:

Raw materials	$180,000
Work in process—compounding	115,000
Work in process—packaging	92,000
Finished product (50,000 lbs.)	250,000

In the compounding department, the first production process, the inventory consisted of 60,000 pounds of product, two-thirds complete with respect to materials and half complete with respect to labor and overhead. In the packaging department, the beginning inventory consisted of 20,000 pounds, complete with respect to materials and half complete with respect to labor and overhead.

During 1972, raw materials purchases totaled $1,400,000. Raw materials were issued to the two production departments in the following amounts:

Compounding....................... $1,200,000
Packaging........................... 290,000

In addition, the finished output of the compounding department is accounted for as a raw material in the packaging department.

Direct labor costs in the two departments were as follows:

Compounding...................... 150,000 hrs. @ $3.00
Packaging......................... 120,000 hrs. @ $2.50

Actual overhead costs incurred in each department during 1972 were as follows:

	Compounding	Packaging
Fixed:		
Supervision.........................	$ 60,000	$ 40,000
Repair and maintenance..............	40,000	50,000
Depreciation.......................	175,000	150,000
Variable:		
Factory supplies....................	50,000	20,000
Indirect labor......................	90,000	50,000
Power and light....................	30,000	40,000

Overhead is applied to production at the following rates per direct labor hour:

	Compounding	Packaging
Variable...............	$1.10	$1.00
Fixed..................	1.70	2.00

During 1972, a total of 560,000 pounds of product were completed in the compounding department and transferred to packaging. At the end of the year, 100,000 pounds remained in process in compounding. This inventory was 80% complete with respect to materials and 50% complete with respect to labor and overhead. In the packaging department, a total of 540,000 pounds of product were completed and transferred to the warehouse for finished product. The inventory in process at the end of the year comprised 40,000 pounds, complete as to materials and half complete as to labor and overhead.

During the year, 500,000 pounds of product were sold.

Required:

a) Prepare journal entries to record all of the operations for 1972. Present all necessary supporting schedules and computations.

b) Prepare a statement of cost of goods manufactured and sold for the year ended December 31, 1972. Any net under- or overapplied overhead should be added or deducted at the end of this statement.

15. The Darnay Company uses the absorption costing method. During 1972, 80,000 units were produced and 72,000 units were sold. The following data were extracted from the company's adjusted trial balance at December 31, 1972:

	Debit	*Credit*
Sales.............................		$720,000
Cost of goods sold..................	$480,000	
Variable overhead control...........	55,000	
Fixed overhead control.............	150,000	
Variable selling expenses............	40,000	
Fixed selling expenses..............	60,000	
Fixed administrative expenses.......	40,000	
Variable overhead applied ($.75 per unit of product)..............		60,000
Fixed overhead applied ($2 per unit of product)..................		160,000
Income tax expense................	46,000	

The same normal overhead rates used in 1972 were used in all prior years.

Required:

a) Compute the net income of the company for 1972 under absorption costing. A formal income statement is not necessary.

b) Compute the net income of the company for 1972 under variable costing. A formal income statement is not necessary. (The income tax will be the same as under absorption costing.)

c) Reconcile the incomes under these two costing methods if they are not the same.

16. A. Manette & Co, Inc. commenced operations on January 1, 1970. Following is a summary of its operations during the first three years of the company's existence:

	1970	*1971*	*1972*
Volume in units:			
Sales......................	25,000	30,000	20,000
Production................	30,000	35,000	12,000
Selling price per unit.......... $	16	$ 16	$ 16
Variable costs per unit:			
Selling....................	2	2	2
Production................	6	6	6
Annual fixed costs:			
Selling....................	60,000	60,000	60,000
Production................	120,000	120,000	120,000

Under the absorption costing method, fixed overhead would be applied to production at a normal rate of $4 per unit of product in each of the three years.

Required:

a) Compute the income in each of the three years under both absorption costing and variable costing.

b) Explain any differences in incomes under these alternative costing methods for each year individually and for the three-year period in total.

c) Which alternative do you believe presents the more useful statement of the company's income? Why?

17. Following is the income statement of the Carton Products Company for 1972:

CARTON PRODUCTS COMPANY
Income Statement
For Year Ended December 31, 1972

Sales.....................................		$820,000
Cost of goods sold:		
Finished product, January 1 (12,000 units)...............................	$ 72,000	
Cost of goods manufactured during January (90,000 units).................	540,000	
	$612,000	
Finished product, December 31 (2,000 units).............................	12,000	
	$600,000	
Less overapplied fixed overhead............	10,000	590,000
Gross margin.............................		$230,000
Selling and administrative expenses...........		150,000
Net operating income......................		$ 80,000
Federal income tax........................		32,000
Net income..............................		$ 48,000

Sidney Carton, the company's president, is disappointed at this report, for it reflects a decline in income from the previous year despite an increase in sales volume.

An examination of the cost records shows that variable overhead has been applied at a rate of $1 per unit of product and that fixed overhead has been applied at a rate of $2 per unit. Variable selling and administrative expenses average $.60 per unit sold. All of these rates have been in effect since the company was founded.

Required:

a) Prepare an income statement for Carton Products Company for 1972 in accordance with the variable costing method. This method will not be accepted for income tax purposes, however.

    b) Explain with appropriate computations and comments any difference between the reported incomes under the two methods of costing.

18. Jerry Cruncher started manufacturing operations in a small plant early in 1972. At the end of this year, his accountant prepared the following income statement:

CRUNCHER CRACKER COMPANY
Income Statement
For Year Ended December 31, 1972

Sales (90,000 units)............................		$81,000
Variable expenses:		
Cost of goods sold.........................	$36,000	
Marketing expenses........................	18,000	54,000
Variable profit..............................		$27,000
Fixed expenses:		
Manufacturing expenses....................	$30,000	
Administrative expenses...................	5,000	35,000
Net loss.....................................		$(8,000)

As the company is unincorporated, income taxes need not be considered in its financial statements.

Cruncher was discouraged with the results of his first year of operations. A well-meaning friend suggested that his mistake was in adopting variable costing. He contended that a switch to absorption costing would be a profitable move for Cruncher.

Production for 1972 totaled 150,000 units of product.

Required:

    a) Recompute the company's 1972 income under absorption costing. Was Cruncher's friend right? Explain.

    b) Assume that Cruncher again produces 150,000 units in 1973 but sells 200,000 units. Assume also that all costs and expenses adhere to the same patterns as in 1972. Which costing method will result in the higher net income in 1973? Support your answer with appropriate computations.

19. This problem has been adapted from an article entitled "Try This on Your Class, Professor," by Raymond P. Marple, in *The Accounting Review* for July, 1956.

The Defarge Company purifies and bottles rain water for sale directly from its plant. Hence, its raw material is free and it incurs only production costs. As the plant is fully automated, all production costs are fixed in the amount of $240,000 per year. The water is sold at a price of $30 per barrel.

Consider two alternative cases for the firm's operations during its first two years in business:

Case 1. Business is slow.

	1971	1972
Barrels produced..............	20,000	0
Barrels sold.................	10,000	10,000

Case 2. Business is booming.

	1971	1972
Barrels produced..............	20,000	20,000
Barrels sold.................	10,000	30,000

Required:

a) Compute income before tax in dollars and as a percentage of sales revenue under both absorption costing and variable cost first for Case 1 and then for Case 2. Which costing method should the company use? Why?

b) Are you sufficiently curious about the point in Marple's article to go over to the library and read it?

20. The Two Cities Steel Company maintains its ledger and prepares all internal reports in conformity to the variable costing method. For its annual report to stockholders, however, the company's independent auditor insists that it use absorption costing. The conversion from variable to absorption costing is made by debiting or crediting (as appropriate) an account entitled "Fixed Overhead in Inventory" in an adjusting entry made at the end of each year. No other entry is ever made to this account. This account is then included along with Work in Process and Finished Product, which contain only variable costs, in the published balance sheet. Any under- or overapplied fixed overhead which appears as a result of the conversion to absorption costing is debited or credited to "Under/Overapplied Overhead," an account that is closed at the end of each year.

The following pertinent data were taken from the internal reports for the first three years of the company's operations:

	1970	1971	1972
Tons of steel:			
Sold.....................	80,000	140,000	200,000
Actual output..............	100,000	150,000	180,000
Budgeted output...........	100,000	150,000	200,000
Fixed overhead cost:			
Actual....................	$500,000	$560,000	$650,000
Budgeted.................	500,000	600,000	700,000

For purposes of the conversion to absorption costing, a normal fixed over-head rate is computed in the usual way.

The company's inventories are costed under the first-in, first-out as-sumption.

Required:

Prepare the necessary adjusting entry at the end of each of the three years to convert the company's accounts from variable costing to absorp-tion costing. Present computations to support these adjustments.

21. Put your pencil away! The following short case requires no computations at all—just careful thought and sound reasoning.

Late in 1971, the Contour Oil Company completed construction of a major oil refinery at Smog Harbor, California. The total cost of the re-finery was $60 million, and the facilities are expected to have an economic life of 15 years. The maximum productive capacity of the refinery is 6 million barrels of crude oil per year. However, during 1972, the first year of operations, it is estimated that actual production will be only two thirds of capacity.

Refinery operations will be largely automated. Hourly employees for the first year of operations have been planned as follows:

Position	Number	Hourly Wage
Refinery operator	250	$3.60
Maintenance man	80	2.75
Watchman	40	2.00
Shipping-dock worker	75	2.80
Boat crewman	12	3.00

There will be 255 16-hour working days in each year. Refinery operators run the refining machinery. Maintenance men perform routine repair and maintenance work on buildings and equipment. Shipping-dock workers load tank trucks which carry finished products to Contour Oil Company's bulk stations for further distribution. Boat crews assist tankers delivering crude oil to the refinery and tend the subsurface pipeline from the offshore tanker anchorage to the crude oil storage tanks. In addition to hourly wages, the following monthly salaries are anticipated:

Administration	$120,000
Refinery foremen	15,000
Shipping-dock foreman	750
Boat captains	1,750

The only significant raw material used by the refinery will be crude oil. It is expected to have an average cost of $.48 per barrel, delivered.

On the basis of its experience with other refineries, the company has estimated that other refinery overhead and operating expenses will be as follows:

Variable overhead........................ $.15 per bbl. of crude oil
Fixed overhead (excluding depreciation)...... $175,000 per mo.
Miscellaneous administrative expenses........ $80,000 per mo.

Although the refinery is a "modern" one with pollution control devices, emission of air pollutants from time to time is inevitable. A county ordinance requires that the refinery be shut down after any four hours of pollutant emission until the situation is corrected. The company's labor agreement requires that all hourly employees be paid in full if they are on the premises during such shut-down periods.

Required:

a)   Should Contour Oil Company use a job order or a process cost system for this refinery? Explain.

b)   Should the output of the refinery be costed by the absorption costing method or by the variable costing method? Explain.

c)   Should the wages of the shipping-dock workers be accounted for as direct labor? Explain. If not as direct labor, how should they be classified?

d)   How should the wages and salaries of the boat crewmen and captains be accounted for?

e)   During 1972, the refinery was shut down because of air pollutant emission for a total of 20 working days. How should employees wages paid for these 20 days be reported in the company's annual report?

PART II
Planning and Control

chapter 5

STANDARDS AND
STANDARD COSTS

DISCUSSIONS IN the preceding two chapters have dealt with various aspects of accounting for costs that have actually been incurred. The principal questions raised have concerned the classifying, recording, and reporting of actual cost data. Cost accounting involves the measurement of costs but not the critical appraisal of the amounts so measured. Cost planning and control involve the analysis and evaluation of costs. Planning and control are managerial functions dependent largely upon accounting information and procedures. These functions are concerned with what costs have actually been in the past, but with an eye to the future. With respect to the future, management is interested not merely in what costs may reasonably be expected to be but also in what costs ought to be. Knowledge of what costs should be provides a basis for intelligent planning and effective control. This chapter and the others in Part II are concerned with cost planning and control. The principal tools of planning and controlling costs are standards and budgets. Standards are discussed in the present chapter. Budgets will be considered in detail in Chapters 6 through 9.

STANDARDS

In general, *standards* may be defined as measured quantities which *should be* attained in connection with some particular operation or activity. The amount which should be attained is determined by management in accordance with its best judgment. Standards are not determined according to unquestioned and immutable natural laws. They are set by human judgment and, consequently, are subject to the same fallibility which attends all human activity. In the paragraphs that follow, we shall consider some of the quantities for which standards are frequently established in manufacturing enterprises and also the degrees of accuracy and precision implicit in standards.

Price Standards

Materials Price Standards. In most manufacturing operations, one of the most important cost elements is the cost of purchased raw materials. Management is interested in keeping this cost as low as possible, consistent with the need to maintain product quality. Part of the control of materials cost depends upon efficient purchasing and obtaining the most favorable possible price for the materials needed. A *materials price standard* is the price which should be paid for a particular raw material under the most favorable possible conditions. "The most favorable possible conditions" must be interpreted in light of the individual firm. The best price for one firm for a particular material may be either lower or higher than the best price for another firm for the identical item. In most cases, materials price standards can be set only for the firm, not for the industry as a whole.

Included in the standard materials price are all components of the amount which must be expended in order to acquire a particular material. Different suppliers may sell the same materials at different list prices. Assuming no differences in the qualities of the goods or in the services rendered by the various suppliers, the supplier offering the lowest price would be selected; and the materials price standard would be established on that basis. Differences in quality or in service may justify the selection of a higher price supplier, however. Thus, a supplier who cannot be relied upon to deliver materials when needed ought not be chosen simply because he sells materials at lower prices than his more dependable competitors. To the extent that his lower prices are reflected in unsatisfactory service, they are false savings to the buyer.

Freight charges are part of the purchase cost of materials, and they normally vary with the distance between the supplier and the purchaser. Thus, in setting materials price standards, a firm should look to the closest reliable sources of supply (presuming that all other factors are equal). Where materials are purchased from foreign suppliers, there may be import duties involved. These should be included as part of acquisition costs and incorporated in price standards.

Where discounts are available to the purchaser of materials, they should be included in the determination of price standards. *Quantity discounts* are granted for purchases of materials in relatively large lots. For example, the price per unit of an item may be lower when it is purchased in carloads than when it is purchased in smaller quantities. To the extent that quantity discounts are reasonable in the circumstances of the individual purchaser, they should be included in the calculation of the standard materials price. Obviously, it would be unreasonable for a firm to set materials price standards on the basis of carload discounts when carload quantities would represent supplies for excessively long periods of time and would involve undue storage and handling costs.

Cash discounts are granted for prompt payment of invoices, typically within 10 to 15 days. For example, the terms "2/10, n/30" on an invoice mean that the purchaser may deduct a 2% discount from the billed price if he pays within 10 days and that in any event the amount billed is due within 30 days. In the past, the materials cost in such a case was generally considered to be the gross amount billed, and the 2% discount, if taken by the purchaser, was treated as an adjustment to the cost of goods sold for the period. More recently, accountants have come to view the actual price of such materials as the net invoice price after deduction of the discount. This would be 98% of the gross amount billed in the example above. This view assumes that all cash discounts will be taken by a profit motivated firm. Any discounts not taken (accounts not paid within the allowed discount period) are then regarded as financial costs attributable to a lack of proper planning of cash resources and not to improper purchasing practices. In our discussion, we shall accept this latter view of cash discounts and shall incorporate them in price standards.

Let us now consider a simple illustration of the setting of a materials price standard. The Rackstraw Marine Corporation uses only one raw material, steel, in the manufacture of its product. It has investigated alternative sources of supply and has determined that the Bobstay Company is the most advantageous supplier. Bobstay's regular list price for steel is $182 per ton, f.o.b. shipping point (i.e., the purchaser pays the freight charges). However, there is a $7 quantity discount per ton for carload orders of 20 tons. The volume of Rackstraw's business is sufficient to make it economical for the corporation to purchase steel in carload lots. Hence, Rackstraw would base its price standard on the carload price. The Bobstay Company also allows a 2% cash discount for payment within 15 days. Finally, there is a freight charge of $170 per carload; this is paid directly to the carrier and is not eligible for any cash discount. Rackstraw's computation of its standard materials price is as follows:

Carload price ($182 − $7)	$175.00
Less cash discount (2% × $175)	3.50
	$171.50
Add freight charges ($170 ÷ 20 tons)	8.50
Standard price per ton	$180.00

This standard price provides a basis for planning future materials costs and for controlling current costs by providing a criterion against which actual prices paid for materials may be evaluated.

Labor Rate Standards. The price paid for labor is usually stated as a wage rate per hour or per piece of production or as a weekly or monthly salary. While it is possible to conceive of a standard weekly or monthly salary, such labor costs are normally not stated in terms of standards. Salaries are typically controlled by means of budgets rather than standards. Thus, labor price standards may be thought of as *wage rate standards* only. The rate may be either an hourly rate or a piece rate.

Wage rate standards are normally either a matter of company policy or the result of negotiations between management and a union. In either case, the accountant simply incorporates the rate established, however it may have been determined, in his work as appropriate. Deviations from established wage rates are unlikely to occur without foreknowledge on the part of management. A contractual wage increase due to a rise in the consumer price level, for example, may be predicted and planned for by observation of the trend of the Consumer Price Index.

In most manufacturing firms there will be several different wage rates. Rates will vary depending upon the degree of skill necessary for a particular job, the element of danger (if any) involved in a specific task, and other characteristics of the various workers. Both hourly rates and piece rates may be paid in the same plant. Thus, there is typically a series of standard wage rates rather than a single rate. In most of the illustrations in this text, however, only one or two rates will be used. This is done for the sake of simplicity and brevity of the illustrations, and it in no way detracts from the validity of the discussions. For the understanding of the development and handling of one standard wage rate can be extended very readily to any number of rates.

In the Rackstraw Marine Corporation (the illustration begun in the preceding section) there are two production departments. In the first, the molding department, the current standard wage rate is $3.20 per hour. In the second, the grinding department, the standard wage rate is $3.60 per hour. The difference between these two rates reflects a higher level of skill required of workers in the grinding department.

Quantity Standards

Materials Usage Standards. The cost of materials used by a manufacturer is a function of two factors, the price paid for the materials and the quantity of the materials used. Materials price standards have already been discussed. The quantity of materials used for the production of a particular product can also be subjected to standardization. Of course, there will be different quantity standards for different materials; and different standards may apply to the usage of a single material in different products or in different departments. *Materials quantity standards,* or *materials usage standards,* are established on the basis of necessary input-output relationships between materials and products and also upon observations of actual experience. For example, it may be a simple fact that a two-pound hammerhead requires two pounds of steel. It may also be a fact that the firm's experience shows that a two-pound hammerhead can be manufactured only by using slightly more than two pounds of steel in order to allow for weight losses due to scraping and smoothing. Both of these facts should be incorporated in the materials usage standard for hammerheads. These standards do not represent the minimum possible use of materials in production but the minimum efficient use after due allowances for materials shrinkage and loss. Any time that a liquid is boiled, for example, there will be some quantity loss due to evaporation. It would be clearly unrealistic and useless in such a case to set a materials quantity standard that did not allow for the evaporation loss.

The Rackstraw Marine Corporation produces a single product, capstan heads. As indicated before, the only raw material used in the manufacture of this product is steel. Each finished head weighs 40 pounds. However, in the grinding department, part of the steel that comes out of the molds is removed as the heads are ground and smoothed. Thus, it is necessary to use more than 40 pounds of steel in order to get a 40-pound finished product. Past experience coupled with careful engineering studies has shown that a steel input equal to 105% of the desired output is proper if the grinding process is performed efficiently. Thus, the standard materials usage per unit of product is as follows:

Weight of finished product.	40 lbs.
Allowance for normal loss in grinding (5% × 40).	2
Standard materials usage.	42 lbs.

This standard quantity does not provide for loss of materials due to careless handling, damage to units in process, or other undesirable circumstances. Indeed, these are the types of materials losses that use of the standard is intended to help eliminate.

Labor Time Standards. Labor quantities are measured in units of time, generally the time required to complete a particular operation. Thus, *labor time standards,* or *labor efficiency standards,* are the amounts of time which particular productive operations should take. The labor time standard for a product is the sum of the time standards for all operations necessary to the completion of the product. Labor time standards are normally established on the basis of observations of actual operations and a critical evaluation of whether or not those operations are being performed as efficiently as is feasible. Labor time standards typically include provisions for a reasonable amount of time lost simply because human beings are not mechanical devices and cannot utilize every second on the job for actual production. However, labor efficiency standards ought not provide for prolonged periods of idleness or for incompetence. If such time losses were incorporated in them, the standards would be of little value to management for purposes of cost control.

Labor time standards are commonly set on the basis of engineering studies of how long it should take an efficient worker to perform a particular task. A fairly familiar example of this process is a time and motion study. In this study, an engineer observes many workers performing a particular task many times. Through these observations, he determines what is the most efficient way to perform each step in the total operation. For example, if the worker must turn from a machine to pick up a piece of material, the time and motion study might determine when the worker should turn, in which direction he should turn, and where the stack of materials should be located so as to minimize his total time and effort. The final time standard is then the sum of the times required for each step in the operation. To some extent, time standards usually reflect an average of numerous actual observations. That is, if one worker was once able to complete an operation in a very short time, this single observation might not be a realistic and useful basis for setting the standard. Although labor time standards deal directly with workers' time, they may be affected by factors other than the workers themselves. If a worker performs an operation with a machine or a hand tool, the labor time standard for that operation will be controlled partly by the performance characteristics of the machine or the tool. For example, a laser can cut steel faster than an acetylene torch can. Thus, technical features of equipment are also relevant to setting the standard.

Engineering studies in the Rackstraw Marine Corporation have shown that each capstan head should be produced in one fourth of an hour in the molding department and one half of an hour in the grinding department. Each of these standards is the summation of times required for individual operations. For example, in the molding department, steel is first melted in caldrons. The molten metal is then poured into molds. When a mold has cooled, it is opened and the molded head is removed. The head is then washed with a mild acid solution and placed on a conveyor belt that takes it to the grinding department. Each operation in this process was studied and a standard time determined. The sum of those standard times is the quarter-hour time standard. A similar procedure was required to set the time standard in the grinding department.

Rework Costs. In many production operations, a portion of the goods manufactured are spoiled or damaged during the process. Such goods may have to be discarded or sold as scrap. Alternatively, they may be salvageable if they are reworked. Whatever the case, there will be costs incurred in the production of units which never become finished products or are finished only after extra work is done on them. To the extent that spoilage is unavoidable, such costs should be incorporated in the standard cost of the good units produced. If some of the units produced have to be scrapped, the costs incurred to produce them may simply be allocated equally among the good units that are completed. If rework is necessary on some units, the normal amount of rework should be charged equally to all units produced. In other words, there should be a standard rework charge. If rework also involves the use of additional materials, this materials cost should be allocated among the good units produced.

In the Rackstraw Marine Corporation, an average of 1 out of every 20 capstan heads removed from molds is spoiled. This may be caused by cracking when the mold is opened or by air pockets formed during the cooling process. These spoiled heads are simply thrown back into the caldron to be remelted and poured again. Hence, there is no loss of materials associated with the spoilage; but there is rework time. The time required to put a defective head back into the caldron is the same as the time required to rinse a good head and load it onto the conveyor belt. Thus, it is necessary to work one fourth of an hour in the molding department 21 times in order to produce 20 good heads. So long as this rate of spoilage is considered unavoidable, the additional time should be included in the determination of the standard cost. One way to do this is to compute the standard labor cost in the molding department in two steps. The first step computes the cost of one fourth of an hour at the standard wage rate of $3.20 per hour. The second step adds a standard rework charge equal to one twentieth of this cost. Thus, the final standard labor cost per head would be as follows:

$$
\begin{array}{lr}
\text{Basic labor cost } (\tfrac{1}{4}\text{ hr.} \times \$3.20)\ldots\ldots\ldots & \$.80 \\
\text{Plus rework charge } (1/20 \times \$.80)\ldots\ldots\ldots & \underline{.04} \\
& \overline{\underline{\$.84}}
\end{array}
$$

Alternatively, the rework time could be included directly in the labor time standard. Thus, the initial standard time would be one fourth of an hour. This would then be increased by one twentieth of one fourth. The resultant standard labor cost would be exactly the same as that computed under the first method.

$$\tfrac{1}{4}\text{ hour} + (\tfrac{1}{4}\text{ hr.} \times 1/20) = 21/80 \text{ hour}$$
$$21/80 \text{ hour} \times \$3.20 = \$.84$$

This latter method will be used in subsequent considerations of this same illustration throughout the chapter.

Degree of Precision in Standards

The discussion of quantity standards in the preceding paragraphs has suggested that these standards be set in light of reasonable circumstances and not in accordance with some determination of perfect performance. Most standards, in practice, do provide for reasonable amounts of excess quantities. Such standards are described as *current attainable standards.* They reflect quantities which can reasonably be attained under current conditions. They provide for lost time and materials due to circumstances which cannot reasonably be corrected. This does not mean that they are based simply upon what is actually done presently, but rather, upon what can be done by efficient performance of tasks. For example, a labor time standard may be set according to the conclusions drawn from a time and motion study as to the length of time required for a competent and experienced worker to perform an operation, with due allowances for normal lost time. If the firm has several inexperienced workers performing this operation at a particular time, it is highly improbable that the time standard will be met. This does not invalidate the standard, nor does it necessarily mean that these workers' performance is bad. The workers' inexperience serves to explain a temporary deviation from the standard. It may be expected that these deviations will diminish and ultimately disappear as the workers reach the standard level of experience.

The principal alternatives to current attainable standards are *perfection standards,* which allow only those quantities of materials or time which are absolutely essential to the accomplishment of a job. For example, it may be mathematically possible to obtain 324 brass disks of a 2-inch diameter from 1 square yard of sheet brass. The shortcomings of both humans and machines are such, however, that it is extremely unlikely that so many could actually be obtained. Nevertheless, a perfection standard would ignore this fact and would be based upon the maximum possible yield of disks. A current attainable standard, on the other hand, would allow for additional lost materials in light of what can be ascertained to be reasonable. The perfection standard, it should be observed, does allow for materials loss in this illustration, but only that loss which is technologically unavoidable. Obviously, not all of the brass in a sheet can actually be used in the cutting out of round pieces.

Some businessmen have contended that perfection standards are preferable to attainable standards because they provide a stimulus, or incentive, to workers to achieve the best possible performance. While this may prove true in some instances, it is more likely that a perfection standard, never attained, will result only in discouragement and resentment on the part of workers and, thus, defeat its own avowed purpose. A better incentive may be provided by an attainable standard which is set as "tight" as appears to be reasonable. Thus, while it may not be met often, it at least offers the workers a goal which they feel can be reached. Urging a runner to a four-minute mile may stimulate his competitive spirit; urging him to a three-minute mile may only frustrate him.

Review and Revision of Standards

A standard set at one moment of time may be reasonably attainable and may be a suitable criterion for the evaluation of actual performance at that moment. At some later time, however, the standard may no longer be attainable; or it may be so easily bettered that it is useless for purposes of planning and control. As market conditions change, prices change. A materials usage standard and/or a labor time standard may be rendered obsolete by technological innovations. Hence, standards must not be regarded as static quantities. As conditions change, relevant standards must change with them in order to remain useful. This means that all standards must be reexamined frequently and, when necessary, altered to conform to new circumstances. It is not necessary that standards be altered every time there is some slight change in the factors which bear upon them. If this were attempted, a company might find that its principal products were standards and that a technique originally adopted to control costs had become excessively costly itself. While minor changes in conditions do invalidate standards slightly, such minor changes can be compensated for in management's evaluation of actual performance against standards. Temporary changes in conditions, even if material in their effects, should not cause changes in standards. For example, a temporary shortage of a particular commodity may increase its price substantially, but not permanently. Many firms which employ standards adhere to a practice of frequent (perhaps quarterly) review of standards but revision of standards only as of the beginning of a new fiscal year, except where a substantial and permanent change in circumstances makes earlier revision appear desirable.

STANDARD COSTS

Materials and Labor

In line with the foregoing discussion of standards, *standard costs* may be defined as costs that reasonably should be incurred in the manufacture of a product. Thus, standard costs are quantities associated with units of output (i.e., products), whereas standards are measures associated with units of output (i.e., materials and labor). The standard direct materials cost and the standard direct labor cost of a product are based upon price and quantity standards. They are computed by multiplying price standards by quantity standards. Standard materials and labor costs are illustrated below for the continuing illustration of the Rackstraw Marine Corporation.

We have seen previously that the standard price paid for steel by Rackstraw is $180 per ton. The standard usage of steel is 42 pounds per finished unit of product. Obviously, these two standards are not directly compatible. The price standard must first be reduced to an amount per pound of steel before it can be used to determine the standard materials cost. The standard price per pound is $.09 ($180 ÷ 2,000 lbs.). Thus, the standard materials cost for one unit of product is $3.78 (42 lbs. of steel @ $.09).

Standard labor costs are computed in the same way. Standard wage rates are multiplied by standard labor times. In the Rackstraw Marine Corporation, there are two separate production departments, each with its own standard wage rate and standard labor time. Thus, the standard labor cost per unit of product must be calculated in two steps. First, in the molding department, the standard wage rate is $3.20 per hour. The standard labor time is one fourth of an hour plus an additional one twentieth of that time for unavoidable rework. This makes a total of 21/80 of an hour in the department. The standard labor cost in the molding department, then, is $.84 per unit (21/80 hr. @ $3.20). In the grinding department, the standard wage rate is $3.60 per hour and the standard labor time is one-half hour per unit. Thus, the standard labor cost is $1.80 per unit of product (½ hr. @ $3.60). The total standard labor cost, then, is the sum of these two departmental costs.

Overhead

The standard materials and labor costs of a product are based upon price and quantity standards. This is possible because there is a functional relationship between the number of units of the product produced and the quantities of materials and labor required, and because each material has its standard price and each worker his standard wage rate. No such functional relationship exists between the units produced and total overhead cost, however. Even that portion of overhead which varies with the volume of production cannot be closely related thereto as can direct materials and labor. As a consequence, standard costs for overhead are based upon budgets, not upon standards. Again, a proper understanding of the distinction between standards and standard costs is important. The latter can exist without the former, and they do in the case of overhead.

Variable overhead costs are budgeted per unit of volume on the basis of the firm's past experience, adjusted for observed and projected changes in conditions. This budgeted variable overhead cost per unit then becomes the standard variable overhead rate. Fixed overhead costs are budgeted in total for a fiscal period, typically one year. The standard fixed overhead rate is then computed by dividing the total budgeted fixed costs by budgeted production volume for the period. In other words, the determination of standard overhead rates is essentially the same as the determination of normal overhead rates in Chapter 3.[1] There would be a standard fixed overhead rate only under absorption costing, of course. Under variable costing, total fixed overhead would be treated as a period expense; it would not be related to the units of production at all.

Where many different products are produced in the same plant, it is likely that units of product would not be a suitable base (or common denominator) for the application of overhead to production. In such a case, some measure of units of input is likely to be used. Direct labor hours, direct labor cost, and machine-hours are widely employed for this purpose. Which one is actually used will depend upon the particular circumstances of the company. If overhead is applied on the basis of direct labor hours, standard overhead rates will be determined initially in terms of overhead cost per labor hour. Standard overhead cost per unit of product will then be computed by multiplying the standard labor hours per unit produced by the standard overhead rates. This is illustrated below in a continuation of the example used in previous sections.

Variable overhead is budgeted at $1.60 per direct labor hour in the molding department of the Rackstraw Marine Corporation. Fixed overhead is budgeted at a total of $160,000 per year, and production volume is budgeted at 40,000 direct labor hours per year. Thus, the standard fixed overhead rate is $4 per hour. Standard labor time in the molding department is 21/80 hour per unit produced. Multiplication of this time standard by the standard overhead rates produces standard overhead costs per unit of output of $.42 for variable overhead (21/80 hr. @ $1.60) and $1.05 for fixed overhead (21/80 hr. @ $4). In the grinding department, variable overhead is budgeted at $1 per direct labor hour and fixed overhead at $120,000 per year. Production volume is expected to total 80,000 labor hours per year. The standard fixed overhead rate, then, is $1.50 per labor hour. Standard labor time is one-half hour per unit of output. Thus, the standard variable overhead cost per unit is $.50 (½ hr. @ $1) and the standard fixed overhead per unit is $.75 (½ hr. @ $1.50). Obviously, Rackstraw uses absorption costing. If variable costing were used, there would be no standard fixed overhead costs.

---

[1] In Chapter 10, we shall see a slightly different way of determining the standard fixed overhead rate. Essentially, the difference will involve using a measure of production volume that is representative of normal production operations over a longer period of time than one year. The mechanics of the computation, however, are exactly the same.

Standard Cost Sheet

The total standard cost of a product is usually summarized on a *standard cost sheet* or *standard cost card*. This is simply a listing of the various raw materials, classes of labor, and departmental overhead charges that make up the total standard cost of the product. It is illustrated for the Rackstraw Marine Corporation in Table 5–1.

In this particular illustration, standard cost is determined for an individual unit of product. This need not always be the case. Especially where each unit is small and inexpensive, standard production cost may be expressed in terms of some group of units (e.g., one gross, one case, one

TABLE 5–1
RACKSTRAW MARINE CORPORATION
Standard Cost Sheet for One Capstan Head

Direct materials:		
Steel (42 lbs. @ $.09)		$3.78
Direct labor:		
Molding department (21/80 hr. @ $3.20)	$ .84	
Grinding department (½ hr. @ $3.60)	1.80	2.64
Variable overhead:		
Molding department (21/80 hr. @ $1.60)	$ .42	
Grinding department (½ hr. @ $1.00)	.50	.92
Fixed overhead:		
Molding department (21/80 hr. @ $4.00)	$1.05	
Grinding department (½ hr. @ $1.50)	.75	1.80
		$9.14

thousand, etc.). Also, the budgeting of overhead costs in this illustration is oversimplified. A more refined and more useful method of budgeting overhead will be discussed in Chapter 9.

Nonmanufacturing Operations

Historically, standards and standard costs have been related almost exclusively to manufacturing. In recent years, considerable interest has been demonstrated in methods of setting and using standards for nonmanufacturing operations. Obviously, standards can be established only for routine, repetitive operations. Certain nonmanufacturing activities do not lend themselves to standardization. It would be impossible to establish a useful standard cost for the retail sale of one automobile, for example. No two customers and, hence, no two sales are exactly the same. It may not be impossible to set standards for certain automobile servicing functions, however, or for the routine processing of customers' accounts. Conceivably, the cost of certain nonmanufacturing supplies may be controllable by the use of price and quantity standards, much in the same way as are materials. Some administrative work may lend itself to the establishment of wage rate and labor time standards. More often, however, administrative employees receive weekly or monthly salaries that do not vary with the amount of work done. Thus, while some standard costs for nonmanufacturing operations may be feasible on the basis of price and quantity standards, most commonly such standard costs would have to be based upon budgets in a manner similar to the setting of standard overhead costs. A more expansive treatment of this subject will be deferred until Chapter 12. The reader should be aware, however, that standards and standard costs are not necessarily restricted to manufacturing costs, even though the vast majority of their applications has been in that area.

VARIANCES

Insofar as cost control is concerned, the most important concepts in the use of standard costs are *variances,* the differences between actual costs and standard costs. Variances are dollar amounts. They are favorable when actual costs are less than standard costs, and they are unfavorable when actual costs exceed standard costs. The terms favorable and unfavorable are used here in a specialized and purely directional sense and should not be interpreted in the ordinary sense. Thus, all excesses of actual cost over standard cost are not necessarily unfavorable to the enterprise's economic welfare. For example, a wage rate increase may be more than justified by improvements in productivity and completely agreeable to management; but until it is reflected in a revised labor rate standard, it will cause an unfavorable variance. Likewise, not all favorable variances represent actual benefits to the firm. For example, if actual materials cost is lower than the standard cost because a low-grade substitute material is temporarily being used in the manufacture of the product, the adverse implications of lower product quality may greatly outweigh the apparent cost saving. When applied to variances, the terms favorable and unfavorable should be interpreted only as indicating the directions of variances from standard costs and not as suggesting good and bad results.

Management by Exception

Variances are particularly useful tools in the implementation of the concept of *management by exception.* This concept is founded on the very simple and logical premises that the limited time of business executives should be employed as profitably as possible and that their time may most profitably be spent in seeking ways to correct conditions which are not as they should be. In other words, the basic rule of management by exception is to concentrate on those operations and segments of an enterprise which appear to be unsatisfactory rather than to spend a lot of time reviewing satisfactory performance. Variances indicate instances where actual costs have failed to meet established standards. As suggested in the previous paragraph, favorable variances may call for correction just as well as unfavorable ones; and not all unfavorable variances require corrective action.

Variances are just as useful to management in the implementation of its cost control objective as the standards from which they stem are valid. If standards are current and attainable quantities, then variances may be regarded as useful bases for the evaluation of actual performance. If standards are out-of-date, the usefulness of the resultant variances will be impaired. Where perfection standards are employed, there is little point in management's attempting to eliminate all variances, for the standards cannot reasonably be expected to be met. In this case, management must be able to distinguish between that portion of a variance which is potentially controllable and that portion which is to be expected. Thus, perfection standards must be accompanied by standard variances, that is deviations from standard amounts that are regarded as unavoidable. These standard variances would, in effect, convert the perfection standards to attainable standards. And only reasonably attainable standards are useful to management as bases for cost control.

STANDARDS AS TOOLS OF PLANNING AND CONTROL

Throughout this chapter, frequent references have been made to the use of standards and standard costs for purposes of cost control. Standards provide bases for the evaluation of actual data. The differences between actual and standard costs may be analyzed by management in an effort to eliminate such differences in the future. Standards are also very useful in planning future operations. If standard costs for materials and for labor and a standard variable overhead rate are available, an estimate of volume in the future can be converted to an estimate of future variable manufacturing costs by simple multiplication. Materials usage standards, along with volume estimates, can provide the bases for purchase planning. Hiring policies can be better formulated if volume estimates can be coupled with labor time standards.

As a final note, it is often argued that standards and standard costs are pertinent only to large firms, that a small firm cannot afford the added costs of implementing a standard cost system. There is some truth in this point, but it should not be taken as conclusive proof that small companies cannot use standards. A small organization may be able to make effective use of very limited standards at a proportionately limited cost. Thus, only materials price standards might be used in a particular case; or, perhaps, materials price and usage standards might be feasible for a given firm. An extensive and integrated standard system is not necessary in all cases. Standards and standard costs are, primarily, tools of management. As such, they should be used to the extent they are economical and useful—no more and no less. In the areas of cost planning and control, as in so many other contexts, something is infinitely better than nothing.

QUESTIONS FOR DISCUSSION

1. What is the difference between a standard and a standard cost?
2. Why might a standard cost differ from the corresponding actual cost?
3. What is the nature of the fundamental difference between standard costs for direct materials and labor and standard overhead costs? What causes it?
4. How do standards and standard costs facilitate the managerial functions of planning and control?
5. "If standard costs are to be useful techniques for improving cost performance and for tightening cost control, they must be based upon perfection standards. Anything less will only encourage inefficiency." Do you agree with this statement? Explain your position.
6. The basic notion underlying the concept of management by exception is applicable to much of human activity, both in business and in nonbusiness affairs. How does the concept of management by exception apply to each of the following situations: (*a*) a purchasing agent reviewing purchase orders before approving them; (*b*) a football coach viewing films of last Saturday's victory; (*c*) a housewife caring for her baby; and (*d*) a foreman studying labor time reports for his department? How do standards and standard costs relate to the notion of management by exception?
7. "Sometimes, from the point of view of management, unfavorable variances from standard costs may be preferable to favorable variances." Comment on this assertion.
8. If reasonable standards are carefully established, why should it ever be necessary to change them? How often, if ever, should standards be changed?
9. What factors should be considered in setting a materials price standard? A materials usage standard?
10. In a large manufacturing firm, whom would you expect to be responsible for setting price and quantity standards for direct materials and labor?
11. Are standards and standard costs applicable to nonmanufacturing activities? Discuss.

PROBLEMS

1. The Domingo Corporation manufactures ornamental brass lamp bases in a single production process. The only raw material is brass, which is purchased in cases of 24 sheets at a price of $12 per case. Six sheets are used

in the manufacture of each lamp base. The production process requires 2½ hours for each lamp base by workers who are paid an hourly wage rate of $3.60. Variable overhead is applied to production at a rate of $.80 per labor hour, and fixed overhead at a rate of $2 per labor hour.

Required:

Prepare a standard cost sheet for one lamp base.

2. Stewart Enterprises produces a high-strength adhesive for use in the installation of linoleum and floor tiles. It is a mixture of powder and oil that is heated and stirred until it forms a thick but pliant paste. Each can of this adhesive requires 2 pounds of powder and 8 ounces of oil. The production process takes a half hour of work by a team of six men and results in the production of 24 cans of adhesive. Overhead is applied to production at standard rates per labor hour.

The standard cost sheet for one can of adhesive is summarized below:

Materials:		
Powder	$4.50	
Oil	3.20	
Can and label	.25	$7.95
Direct labor		.60
Overhead:		
Variable	$ .20	
Fixed	.50	.70
		$9.25

Required:

What is the standard price per pound of powder, the standard price per ounce of oil, the standard wage rate per hour, the standard variable overhead rate per hour, and the standard fixed overhead rate per hour?

3. The Tucker Company manufactures a paint thinner from a single raw material. This material is regularly purchased in half-carload lots of 500 drums. Each drum contains 80 gallons. The most advantageous supplier's list price for this material is $1.50 per gallon. He allows a discount of 2% for payment of invoices within 15 days. In addition, the purchaser is billed $16 for each drum shipped; this is a deposit on the drum itself. The purchaser receives full credit of $16 for each drum returned to the supplier. On the basis of experience, it is reasonable to anticipate that 10% of the drums received will unavoidably not be returned for credit. No discount is allowed on drum deposits forfeited. The freight for a half-carload is $2,400.

The paint thinner is produced in standard lots of 180 gallons of finished product. Experience has shown that 10% of the materials put into the production process are unavoidably lost due to evaporation.

Required:

Compute the standard price per gallon of raw material, the standard usage of raw materials per 180-gallon lot of production, and the standard materials cost per gallon of finished product.

4. The Sills Manufacturing Company produces Product A from an input of two raw materials, X and Y. Material X is purchased in 25-pound bags at a list price of $80 per bag and on credit terms of 1/15, n/30. Freight charges average $1,350 per truckload of 750 bags.

   Material Y is imported from South America. Its list price is $6 per gallon. Import duties of $.45 per gallon must be paid by the purchaser. The average freight cost for a shipment of 800 gallons is $120.

   Product A is manufactured in standard batches of one gross of pint jars each. (One gross equals 144.) Jars are purchased in cases of 240 at a standard price of $10.80 per case. Ten percent of the jars received are broken before they can be filled; this breakage is regarded as normal. For each batch of Product A, 20 pounds of Material X and 15 gallons of Material Y are required.

   Required:

   Compute the standard materials cost per pint of finished product.

5. The Shirley Office Furniture Company manufactures five-shelf steel bookcases in four successive production processes. These processes and their respective labor time and wage rate standards are as follows:

Frame forming:	$\frac{1}{8}$ hr. per frame @ $2.70 per hr.
Shelf cutting:	$\frac{1}{10}$ hr. per shelf @ $2.50 per hr.
Assembling:	$\frac{1}{4}$ hr. per bookcase @ $3.00 per hr.
Painting:	$1\frac{1}{2}$ hrs. per rack @ $2.40 per hr.

   In the assembling process, five shelves are welded to a frame. The completed bookcase is then hung on a large rack. When 20 bookcases have been placed on a rack, that rack is wheeled into the paint shop where all of the bookcases on it are spray-painted and then baked dry. The finished units are then transferred to the warehouse pending shipment to customers.

   Required:

   Compute the standard labor cost per finished bookcase.

6. The Milnes Company produces a liquid sweetener in three successive production departments: blending, cooking, and bottling. The operations of each department have been studied, and time study reports reveal the following data for the completion of a standard 100-gallon batch of the sweetener:

	Blending	Cooking	Bottling
Minimum possible time....................	2.00 hrs.	3.75 hrs.	.50 hrs.
Normal time by trained and experienced personnel............................	2.10	4.00	.56
Average time recently.....................	2.05	4.25	.60
Standard hourly wage rate.................	$3.60	$2.80	$3.00

   On the basis of past experience and an evaluation of future production requirements, it has been estimated that overtime work will be required in each department. Expected overtime will average 10% of the total time worked in each department. Each hour of overtime is paid at one and one-half times the regular standard hourly wage rate.

Required:

Compute the total standard labor cost of one batch of the liquid sweetener.

7. The Dooley Tool Corporation manufactures hammers in three production processes. Each finished hammer consists of a steel head weighing exactly one pound and a wooden handle. The standard purchase prices of the raw materials used are as follows:

Steel............................ $220 per ton
Lumber......................... $ .54 per bd. ft.

In the process of cleaning the molded hammerheads, approximately .05 pounds of steel are necessarily scraped away. Twenty handles are cut from one board foot of lumber, and 10% of the handles cut are broken or otherwise spoiled before they are finished. This loss is considered unavoidable.

The direct labor times and rates in the three production processes are as follows:

Process	Time	Hourly Rate
Head molding:		
Mold pouring...............	.08 hrs. per head	$2.50
Mold cleaning..............	.25 hrs. per head	3.20
Handle shaping:		
Cutting....................	.10 hrs. per handle	2.80
Finishing..................	.15 hrs. per handle	3.00
Assembly....................	.05 hrs. per hammer	2.50

Both variable and fixed overhead costs are charged to production at standard rates per direct labor hour. The budgeted overhead costs and labor hours, by processes, are as follows:

	Head Molding	Handle Shaping	Assembly
Variable overhead per hour....	$1.20	$.90	$1.60
Fixed overhead per year.......	$82,500	$60,000	$48,000
Labor hours per year.........	66,000	50,000	10,000

Required:

Prepare a standard cost sheet for one hammer.

8. The Price Beauty Products Company makes a mild astringent for cosmetic use. It is sold to distributors in cases of two dozen 5-ounce bottles. The company uses variable costing in its production accounting system.

The principal raw material is a special chemical purchased in 50-gallon drums at a list price of $7 per gallon. The supplier allows a 2% discount on the list price for payment of invoices within 10 days. Freight charges average $8 per drum.

Bottles cost $3.42 per gross. Five percent of the bottles purchased are broken in handling. This breakage is considered normal.

The astringent is manufactured in 60-gallon batches. One sixteenth of the material put into process is lost due to normal spillage and evaporation.

Direct labor costs are incurred as follows:

> Distilling: 6 man-hrs. @ $4.56 per 60-gal. batch
> Bottling: ½ man-hr. @ $4 per case

Budgeted overhead costs are as follows:

> Distilling: $1.20 per labor hr. plus $12,000 per mo.
> Bottling: $.80 per labor hr. plus $36,000 per mo.

Direct labor hours were budgeted at 3,000 per month in distilling and at 16,000 per month in bottling.

Required:
Compute the standard cost per case of finished product.

9. A new product of the Elias Toiletries Corporation is Lux-a-Soft Skin Lotion, to be marketed in 4-ounce bottles at a suggested retail price of $.59 per bottle. Cost and production studies show the following estimated costs:

Raw Materials

Item	Cost	Comments
Container:		
4-oz. bottle..........	$7.50 per gross	Allow additional 2% for breakage
Label...............	$4.50 per 1,000	Allow additional 3% for waste
Ingredients:		
Compound HX107....	$50 per 100 lbs.	70 lbs. used per 125-gal. batch
Alcohol and glycerine..	$25 per 100 gals.	80 gals. used per 125-gal. batch
Perfume oil.........	(see below)	5 lbs. used per 125-gal. batch

Perfume oil is produced in 90-pound batches by another division of the corporation. The standard cost of one such batch is $1,026.

An allowance for lost ingredients due to overfilling, waste, and bottle breakage is made in the amount of 5% of total ingredients cost before consideration of this loss.

Direct Labor per Gross

> Compounding department.................... 1½ hrs. @ $4
> Filling and packing department.............. 1 hr. @ $3.60

Overhead

(Per Standard
Labor Hour)

Variable:
Compounding department..................... $2.40
Filling and packing department................ $1.60
Fixed:
Compounding department..................... $1.80
Filling and packing department................ $2.50

Required:

Prepare a standard cost sheet for one gross of 4-ounce bottles of Lux-a-Soft Skin Lotion.

(Adapted from CPA Examination)

10. Vickers, Ltd., manufactures steel automobile jacks in three successive production departments. In the stamping department, parts are stamped out on large presses. In the parts finishing department, these parts are ground and smoothed. In the assembly department, the parts are assembled into complete jacks, which are tested and, if accepted, packed for shipping.

Following are the standard prices of materials and the standard labor and overhead rates per hour by departments:

	Stamping	Parts Finishing	Assembly
Steel...............	$240 per ton		
Packing materials.....			$ .15 per jack
Direct labor..........	$3.60 per hr.	$3.80 per hr.	$3.20 per hr.
Variable overhead....	.60 per hr.	.80 per hr.	1.20 per hr.
Fixed overhead.......	1.80 per hr.	1.20 per hr.	.40 per hr.

Each finished jack contains 8 pounds of steel. In the stamping department, another pound per jack is unavoidably lost in the presses.

After assembly, each jack is tested. If it does not function properly, it is rejected. The defective part(s) is identified and thrown into a scrap bin. The good parts are returned to the beginning of the assembly process and reused. Experience has shown that about 5% of the total quantity of jack parts, by weight, is defective and must be scrapped. Jacks that are tested and accepted are then packed and transferred to the warehouse.

Both the steel lost in the stamping department and the defective parts in the assembly department are accumulated and sold to scrap dealers for $100 per ton.

Standard production times by departments for one good jack are as follows:

Stamping.......................... 1/30 hr. per lb. of steel
Parts finishing..................... 1/10 hr. per lb. of steel
Assembly:
   To assemble and test.............. 1/4 hr. per jack
   To pack....................... 1/20 hr. per jack

Required:

Prepare a standard cost sheet for one finished jack. Show all necessary supporting computations.

chapter 6

BUDGETS: TOOLS OF PLANNING AND CONTROL

Discussions in Chapters 3 and 5 explained how normal and standard fixed overhead rates are based upon budgeted cost data. This is only one special application of budget data, however. In their broadest contexts, budgets relate to every activity and every segment of a business enterprise. Properly understood and implemented, they can be extremely useful tools of management in the planning and control of business operations and in the efficient allocation of capital resources.

Definition of a Budget

In a business enterprise, a budget is a comprehensive and coordinated plan, expressed in financial terms, for the operations and resources of an enterprise for some specified period in the future.[1] It is not suggested that the student memorize this definition verbatim but that he understand the essential elements of it. These elements are discussed in some detail below.

---

[1] This definition is also applicable to governmental units and to certain nonprofit institutions, although in these cases it is not really complete. In such organizations, budgets represent authorizations of and limitations upon the conduct of operations during the budget period. Thus, they are more than plans; they are legislative mandates. For example, it is an unlawful act, punishable by fine and/or imprisonment, for any officer of the federal government to spend more than the Congress has appropriated for his department in the annual budget.

Comprehensive. A budget is comprehensive in that it takes into account all of the many facets and activities of the enterprise. It is a plan for the firm as a whole rather than for only one segment of the firm. It is true that we very commonly encounter such things as departmental budgets and advertising budgets. This terminology is perfectly correct, but implicit in it is the assumption that a departmental or advertising budget is but one component of a total budget for the firm. Clearly, one segment of a company cannot have any very significant plan of its own unless that plan is a part of a master plan for the entire enterprise. The total plan will be referred to here as the *master budget;* the component budgets, as *budget schedules.*

Coordinated. If a comprehensive plan for an even moderately complex organization is to be useful, it must consider all segments of that organization and recognize the situation and problems of each segment. The plans for the various segments of the firm must be prepared jointly and in harmony with one another. If these component plans are not coordinated logically and practically, the whole will not be equal to the sum of the parts and the master plan will evoke only confusion.

Plan. In the foregoing paragraphs, the word "plan" has been used without amplification. While it is a word the meaning of which is commonly understood, it has some very specific connotations when used in connection with budgeting. A housewife plans a menu, something which is totally within her discretion. She also plans for winter, the occurrence of which is completely beyond her control. Planning the menu is a matter of active intent; planning for winter is one of passive expectation. A business budget normally is somewhere between these two notions of planning. Some of the factors which will determine a firm's future operations are entirely within its own discretion and control—such as promotional programs, manufacturing processes, and executives' bonuses. Other determinants of future activities are wholly beyond the control of the firm—general business conditions, governmental regulatory policies, and shifts in population age groups, for examples. Thus, a business budget is an expression partly of what the firm's management expects will happen and partly of what management intends to make happen. This does not suggest that mere wishing can make something come true, but careful planning and preparation can bring about a result that would not otherwise be obtained. In other words, good budgeting can not only suggest what will happen but can also make things happen.

Financial Terms. Business budgets are stated in terms of the monetary unit (the dollar in the United States). This is essential if a budget is to be comprehensive, for the monetary unit serves as the common denominator of business activities. A materials budget, for example, may deal with tons of steel; and a labor budget will involve men and man-hours. But tons and man-hours cannot be summed to any significant quantity. Similarly, the advertising budget may deal with such quantities as hours of network television time, pages of national magazine space, and thousands of direct mail brochures; but some common denominator is needed to express a total amount of planned advertising effort. A wide variety of quantities are likely to be involved in the basic development of a budget, but the final budget must express business plans in terms of money.

Operations. One of the fundamental objectives of a budget is the quantification of the revenues that will be realized and the expenses that will be incurred in the future. This information must be provided in detail. Revenues should be related to particular products sold or services rendered. Expenses should be identified with specific goods and services employed in the production of those revenues. The development of budgets for operations is discussed in detail in Chapter 7.

Resources. It is not sufficient simply to plan revenues and expenses for the future. The enterprise must also plan the resources necessary for the operating plans to be realized. Basically, the planning of financial resources involves planning for the various types of assets (cash, inventory, plant property, etc.) in the proper amounts for the efficient operation of the firm and planning the sources of the capital to be invested in these assets. Various aspects of planning for capital resources will be discussed in Chapter 8 and also in Chapters 15 and 16.

Specified Future Period. A budget is meaningless unless it is related to a particular period of time. It is not helpful for management to know that $10,000,000 of sales will be made unless it also knows *when* these sales will be made. It is, of course, entirely appropriate for business management to formulate general plans for resources and operations in the indefinite future. The expanding function of research in business firms is based primarily upon the premise that new products and new techniques will be developed and will benefit the company in some presently undeterminable future period. But such planning, however important it may be, is not budgeting. (Of course, a firm can and should budget the costs of its research activities in the immediate future even though the ultimate benefits therefrom, if any, will be derived in the indefinite future.)

Purposes of Budgets

As the title of this chapter implies, budgets are intended to facilitate the managerial functions of planning and control.[2] Good managers do

---

[2] The terms "planning" and "control" are used here in fairly well-understood contexts. However, the subject of management planning and control has been consid-

not enter into new periods blindly. They plan, as carefully as possible, the normal operations of the period, as well as the unusual occurrences to the extent that these can be foreseen. Good budgets compel management to plan in a comprehensive and coherent manner and to plan specifics, not vague generalities. Planning improved profits is of no value unless the planning involves the specific production, distribution, and financial programs necessary to yield higher profits.

The control implications of budgeting are inextricably linked with the planning aspects. For example, to plan delivery costs of $60,000 during the first quarter of the next year when such costs are viewed as reasonable and consistent with planned sales is to afford, simultaneously, a basis for evaluating the propriety of actual delivery costs. Of course, changes in sales as compared with the budget may reasonably necessitate changes in delivery costs. Perhaps a more useful approach to the budgeting of delivery costs would be to plan them in relation to units of sales volume so that changes in delivery costs may be anticipated and handled efficiently as actual sales volume is seen to deviate from the budgeted volume. This latter approach to the budgeting of costs and expenses is commonly referred to as *flexible budgeting* and will be discussed in detail in Chapter 9.

As a tool of control, the budget gives the responsible manager a guide to the conduct of operations and a basis for evaluating actual results. Actual revenues and expenses can be adjudged satisfactory or unsatisfactory in light of the relevant budgeted data and also in light of changes in conditions since the budget was prepared. The last portion of the preceding sentence is very important. The budget should not be regarded as a rigid requirement of performance. As already observed, many of the factors upon which a budget must be based are beyond the control of the firm's management; and all of them are subject to some degree of uncertainty. The budget is a plan, not an immutable commitment to performance; it is a means of control, but not a straitjacket on operations. Blind compliance with a budget may be worse than having no budget at all.

Another important aspect of budgetary planning and control is the efficient (i.e., profitable) allocation of the capital available to the enterprise. All expenditures require capital, in one form or another; and capital is invariably limited. Not unusually, the sum of all desirable expenditures exceeds the total amount of available capital. Where such

---

ered in much greater depth by many writers. Unfortunately, they are not all in agreement. While an exploration of the subject is beyond the scope of this text, interested readers will find it a very worthwhile area to investigate. A good reference is Robert N. Anthony, *Planning and Control Systems: A Framework for Analysis* (Boston: Division of Research, Graduate School of Business Administration, Harvard University, 1965). In addition to presenting his own framework, Anthony makes numerous references to other writers' conceptions of planning and control.

is the case, there must be some procedure and some person in the budget system to weigh the alternative uses of capital and to select those uses which offer the greatest profit potential for the firm. Thus, one of the functions of the budget is to plan the most efficient possible allocation of the capital resources of the firm.

As a final note here, it is important to remember that a budget is a tool of management to be employed appropriately in the pursuit of management's basic objective, the optimum long-run profit of the firm. Like all tools, budgets are costly; and the more detailed and carefully prepared a budget is, the more it will cost. In any firm, the cost of the budget should be justified in terms of the additional revenues and/or cost savings it produces. Not the same degree of budget sophistication is appropriate for all firms. The discussions of budgeting in this text assume a relatively large company which finds it economically expedient to employ a complete and carefully detailed budget. The concepts illustrated here, however, may be adapted with more or less modification to suit the needs and means of a firm of any size.

FRAMEWORK FOR BUDGETING

The Budget Period

In order to be operationally meaningful, a budget must be related to a specific time period, called the budget period. A detailed budget for all segments and activities of an enterprise is normally prepared for relatively short periods of time only, typically no longer than one year. A fully detailed budget would include all expected revenues, expenses, receipts, disbursements, and other financial activities for each segment (e.g., division) of the firm for each significant time interval (e.g., a month) in the budget period. For example, an operating budget for one year may include a complete breakdown of revenues and expenses for each of the 12 months of the year. Alternatively, it might provide monthly detail for the first half of the year only, with the budgeted data for the second six months given by quarters or in total only. Long-range plans looking further than one year into the future may be developed for those segments of the business in which they are considered useful. Detailed long-range planning for the enterprise as a whole is seldom practicable. However, in certain segments of the firm it is highly desirable, if not absolutely necessary. As examples, long-range planning is essential in the areas of product development, equipment replacement, plant expansion, and the procurement of long-term capital.

In a fully developed budget system, there may be two or more budget periods planned simultaneously, the differences among such periods being the relative amounts of detail in which they are planned. Following is a description of such a budget system for a hypothetical corporation: By December 15, 1971, the operating budget for 1972 is finalized. This budget is fully detailed, by months, for all phases of operations for the first half of 1972. It includes details of budgeted revenues, expenses, receipts, and disbursements by divisions of the corporation and by product lines. For the second half of 1972, estimated data for the entire company are summarized by quarters only. No detail is given for the several divisions or for the individual product lines. By June 15, 1972, a new budget will be prepared. This will provide full details for the second half of 1972 and summarized quarterly estimates for the first half of 1973. This procedure is repeated every six months. Thus, the budget system is constantly moving forward into the future but is able to build its short-range detailed budget partly upon the basis of an earlier semidetailed plan. In addition to this formalized annual budget, the corporation prepares annually an intermediate-range sales forecast for the next three years. Finally, long-term capital procurement and investment needs are planned in general terms five years ahead.[3]

Thus, there are three different time periods in the future for which financial plans are formulated. Each of these might be regarded as a unique budget period. Within the framework of the definition of a budget posited earlier, however, only the operating plan for the next year would qualify as a true budget. Even within that year, there are two subperiods of differing budget detail. While the terminology of budgeting is not so standardized that definitive conclusions can be stated here, there is a useful distinction to be made between budgeting, as such, and long-range planning. For purposes of discussion in this text, we shall regard any plans that are not comprehensive and coordinated for the entire enterprise and that extend further into the future than the normal detailed budget period as falling into the category of long-range planning. This distinction is adopted here only for purposes of simplifying discussion. Many businessmen and writers today are making very specific distinctions between intermediate and long-range planning. Such distinctions are beyond the scope of this text, however.

Environmental Factors

Once the budget period has been established, the persons responsible for preparation of the budget must attempt to determine the nature of the environmental conditions that will obtain during that period. By environment here we mean all factors and circumstances outside the firm that will influence the operations of the firm but will not be subject to

---

[3] Long-range planning is not limited to five years in the future, of course. It may be carried forward as far as is considered practical in the individual firm. Generally speaking, however, the longer the planning period the less certain the plans will be.

any direct control by the firm's management. These environmental factors may be classified as social, economic, and political. Actually, these separate classifications are useful only for explanatory purposes. Obviously, all political and economic factors have social implications. Similarly, any social or political condition influencing a business enterprise is, thereby, of economic significance. Hence, the factors discussed below will be categorized as social, economic, or political according to popular notions of these terms.

Social Factors. Any aspect of the way people act and think is a social factor of potential importance to business operations. Some examples will be considered along with their possible implications for business planning. Mass population movements out of urban and into suburban areas might reasonably be expected to have major impacts upon patterns of demand for consumer products. More recreational equipment and garden tools may be demanded. Automobiles may be operated over more miles, and thus the demand for them and for gasoline may rise. An increase in the proportion of the total population in one particular age group (e.g., over 60 or under 18) will have implications for product demand. A reduction in the average family size will have obvious implications for housing demand. Fads and styles have important effects upon certain industries, notably women's clothing. It is important to attempt to plan for these styles and fads but, at the same time, difficult to do so, for they typically influence demand for relatively short periods of time and are notoriously unpredictable. The reader can readily add further examples to this list of social factors which have business implications.

Business managers must be aware of these varied social developments and must attempt to determine their impacts upon individual firms' operations. Changing patterns of population composition and movement are reflected in statistics compiled and published by the U.S. government. Changes in styles and tastes are reflected in specific markets. Competent managers should be able to trace the implications of shifts in demand in other markets to the markets for their own products. For example, an increased demand for small automobiles relative to that for standard-size cars will have implications for the demand for basic steel. In some instances, advertising and other promotional programs may be able to cause or to restrict certain types of social change; but for the most part, these changes are beyond the direct control of the firm. They are part of the environment in which the firm must operate, and the firm must adapt to them rather than they being adapted to suit the firm.

Economic Factors. As already mentioned, anything that affects a business enterprise may be thought of as an economic factor bearing upon the firm's operations. However, there are certain types of circumstances which, in common parlance, are generally refererd to as economic conditions. Seasonal patterns of demand and/or supply affect many business enterprises. Budgets must take these seasonal factors into consideration. If the entire demand for a particular product (e.g., snow removal equipment) occurs during one season of the year, the manufacturer of that product must realize that substantially all of his sales will be made during or just prior to that season and that his production and financing must be planned accordingly. He may plan production in a number of ways. One possibility is to produce only during the season of peak demand and to leave facilities idle during the remainder of the year. Another approach would be to manufacture the product at approximately the same quantity throughout the year and to plan an inventory buildup prior to the peak sales season and an inventory reduction during that season. A third alternative would be to diversify and produce other products with different seasonal patterns (e.g., lawn and garden equipment).

Cyclical fluctuations in economic activity, or business cycles, have tended to recur in more or less regular patterns. Some fluctuations, such as the boom of the 1920s followed by the depression of the 1930s, are of great magnitude. Others, such as the recession and recovery in the period 1961–62, are comparatively slight. Cyclical fluctuations affect individual firms differently. Historically, producers of heavy equipment have usually experienced substantial and direct impacts from cyclical changes in demand. Food producers, on the other hand, typically experience relatively mild effects as the cycle ebbs and floods. While one might expect a direct effect of business cycles on sales and production—that is, sales and production to decline during the period of recession and to rise during the period of recovery—this is not always so. A manufacturer engaged almost exclusively with government contracts for defense materials might find that his sales demand varies inversely with the business cycle. As a part of its overall countercyclical effort, the federal government may increase purchases of defense items during the period of recession in order to bolster industrial production and employment and then reduce such purchasing to normal levels when the upturn occurs. While business cycles may be attributed to the aggregate behavior of all enterprises in the economy, the individual enterprise may regard them as entirely beyond its own control. Budget preparation should always incorporate consideration of the stage of the business cycle expected to obtain during the budget period and of the influence that this stage will have upon the firm's operations.

Long-term and apparently permanent shifts in demand or supply are referred to as secular trends in economic activity. These secular trends frequently relate to basic social changes and are likely to be irreversible. If a firm finds that there is a permanently decreasing demand for its product, it must either shrink with that demand or add new products to its line. If, on the other hand, the secular trend is upward and demand for a product can be expected to expand at an increasing rate, the manufacturer should plan to expand his productive facilities in order to maintain his relative share of this market.

Political Factors. The line between political and economic factors is impossible to draw. For example, countercyclical monetary and fiscal policies employed by the federal government are politically designed economic stimulants. There are certain types of conditions, however, whose origins are quite distinctly political. Perhaps the extreme political circumstance is war. The impact of World War II on the American economy and on individual business firms was enormous. Even without actual war, a period of international tension (cold war) necessitating a continually improving defense posture has major economic implications. The sudden termination of such a period would entail very serious consequences for individual firms. Examples of other political factors that might influence the planning for an enterprise include new directions in antitrust legislation, more aggressive enforcement of existing antitrust laws, direct or indirect price and wage controls, and changes in the income tax law.

The combination of social, economic, and political conditions make up the environment within which business budgets must be developed. To some extent, these conditions are predictable and fairly easily incorporated in the budget. There remain a great many unpredictable environmental factors, however, which make even the most carefully worked out budget tenuous and subject to substantial deviations from actual operating results.

Company Policies

In addition to the environmental factors, there are many internal conditions and policies that must be taken into account in the preparation of a budget. For example, a firm may have the policy of limiting itself to the production of a high quality, high-priced commodity. If such a policy is to be continued, then a number of additional avenues for distribution of the product must be regarded as closed. A family corporation may adhere to a policy of operating only within one region of the country because expansion into the national market would not permit the family to maintain effective control over the corporation. While management may believe that entry into the national market would be highly profitable, it must exclude any such profits from its planning because of the policy imposed by the family owners of the firm. At this point we need not be concerned with whether such policies are wise. We merely note that they sometimes exist and form a part of the framework within which the budget must be developed.

HUMAN IMPLICATIONS OF BUDGETING

Thus far, we have discussed budgeting in an impersonal manner and have used the term management as an impersonal singular noun. But management is an aggregation of people, and these people must prepare and implement the budget. Insofar as the actual workings of a budget are concerned, the most important aspects are the effects of people upon the budget and, conversely, the effects of the budget upon people.

Personnel Involved in Budget Preparation

There is no standardized organization of people for budget preparation. Different firms use different procedures, but there are certain basic concepts which are applicable in all cases and should be given proper recognition. These basic concepts may be stated as follows:

1. The budget must be prepared and used in such a way that it helps the enterprise as a whole attain its objectives. In an organization with many separate responsibility centers, of course, the budget must also aid the managers of those centers in the attainment of their objectives. Consequently, the budget should be so devised as to facilitate the simultaneous achievement of both responsibility centers' goals and the entire firm's goals. That is, the budget should foster *goal congruence;* the goals of each segment of the organization should be congruent with those of the entity as a whole.

2. The budget must logically and effectively coordinate all segments and functions of the enterprise. Since the operations of one segment or function (e.g., manufacturing) inevitably interact with those of other segments or functions (e.g., marketing), personnel involved in budget preparation in one segment must work harmoniously with those in other areas. The development of a sound budget must be a cooperative venture.

3. The budget must be understood and accepted by those who will actually work with it and under it. Thus, these people should be involved in the budgetary process from the outset. They should want to make the budget work well. If they chafe under the budget and work against it, the results will inevitably be unsatisfactory.

The Budget Director. Every firm should have one executive who is responsible for the coordination, timing, and final presentation of the budget. He does not prepare the budget himself so much as he supervises its preparation. The ideal budget director would be a man with no other functional responsibilities, who reports directly to the top management (executive vice president or higher). Such a person would be as independent of special interest as any corporate executive could be. Being responsible for no functional operations and having a minimal staff working under him, he would have no personal motive for favoring one segment of the firm to the prejudice of others. Rather, he would be able to seek the best allocation of corporate resources for the enterprise as a whole.

If the vice president for manufacturing were also the budget director, no matter how hard he might try to avoid doing so, he would inevitably tend to favor his own division of the company in the allocation of scarce capital resources. This tendency would not indicate any dishonesty on his part but would be a perfectly natural consequence of his specialized knowledge of manufacturing problems and needs. In many firms, the chief budget officer is the controller. While he typically has no functional responsibilities, the controller may have a very large staff under him and may be responsible for a large number of staff services. In a situation involving a choice between the purchase of new production equipment and the purchase of a computer, the controller, in his capacity as budget director, may almost unconsciously build support for the computer purchase because of his greater appreciation of the benefits to be derived from the use of the computer. His bias may be unintentional, but it is nonetheless real. Probably few firms can actually afford to have the ideal budget director. In most companies, budget direction is not a full-time, year-round job. It typically is assigned to an executive with other responsibilities. Where a firm cannot afford a budget director with no other duties, the job might best be assigned to the executive vice president. While he is not free of functional responsibility, he has the next best qualification for unbiased judgment. He has responsibility for *all* functions of the business.

The Budget Committee. In order to ensure that all segments of the firm are properly coordinated in the final budget, all major segments should be represented on a committee of executives that compiles the budget in its final form. This committee would be chaired by the budget director and would include representatives of all major functional divisions of the firm—including manufacturing, distribution, finance, research, and any other distinct functions recognized in the firm's organization. The controller would also be a member of this committee. The composition of the budget committee would differ among firms, but the purpose would be the same in all cases—effective coordination of planning for the firm. The budget committee should not prepare the budget from the start but should compile it in its final form, after satisfactorily reconciling all initial conflicts in the various components.

Primary Budget Preparation. The initial development of budget data should come from those persons who will be responsible for performance under the budget. The preparation of the budget should be a "bottom-up" operation. Budget data should originate at the lowest level of operating management and should be refined and coordinated at higher levels. Thus, the initial budget of operating costs in a production department should be made by that department's supervisor. The initial sales plan for a particular territory should come from the sales manager in that territory, and he, in turn, should build his forecast on sales estimates provided him by his salesmen. These initial budget schedules may be revised considerably before the final budget is approved by top management, but it is essential that they start at the bottom.

The persons primarily responsible for operations within the budget or for explaining why such operations are impossible or undesirable are the lowest operating executives—the department foremen, for example. If these persons are not sympathetic with the budget, it will be of little practical value to the firm. Their sympathy or acceptance may be obtained, in part, by adequate education in the objectives of the budget. But it will be won principally by their own participation in the development of the budget. If they plan their own performances, they will be much more interested in striving to meet or better those performance levels. This approach might well be described as "before-the-fact responsibility accounting."

The manager of a single department cannot initiate his own budget schedule entirely by himself, of course. If he is a production department supervisor, there is no point in his attempting to plan his department's output for the coming year until he is given an indication of the expected sales demand for the product of his department. Thus, he must be provided with certain basic constraints before he can intelligently plan his own operations. It is unlikely that the initial budget schedule for a department will be identical to the final one. When all production departments' schedules are compiled and compared by the factory manager, he may find that they are not compatible. Similarly, when all divisions' budgets have been submitted to the budget committee, inconsistencies among them may well appear. The sum of the capital expenditure plans, for example, may exceed the available capital resources for the period. Some paring down of individual plans must be made, or else additional sources of capital must be located. Any changes made in initial budget estimates should be made first by the lowest responsible executive, however. The preliminary budget should be sent back to the bottom for revision and a second ascent through the several echelons of management to the budget committee. Perhaps this process will have to be repeated several more times. The goal of this repeated "bottom-up" budget development is complete acceptance of the budget at all levels of management. And this complete acceptance will be attained only if each manager really feels that the budget against which his performance will be evaluated is truly *his* budget.

The Final Budget. Once all internal inconsistences and conflicts have been resolved and the various operating managers have submitted budget schedules which are in harmony with each other, with the goals of the enterprise, and with the realities of the environment of the budget period, a final master budget is compiled by the budget director with the assistance of the budget committee. This budget is submitted to top management, the president and/or the board of directors, for final approval. Once approved at this level, the budget is disseminated among all managers responsible for performance under it. As a final caution, we should remember that, even in this final form, the budget is still only a plan, not a hard-and-fast requirement. The budget is only an aid to intelligent thinking and discretion, not a substitute therefor.

Budgets and Human Behavior

The interrelationships between management and the behavioral sciences are extensive and very important. They go far beyond the scope of this discussion, however. Hence, the comments in this section will be both brief and nontechnical. However, it is important for the student to have at least a general appreciation of the potential impacts of budgets on human behavior. If a budget is prepared realistically by a department supervisor and revised with his aid and approval, it may evoke a favorable response from him and serve as a stimulus to his efficient and profitable performance. If it is prepared by someone else without his aid or approval, it may generate hostility and act as a deterrent to his own intelligent thinking and, ultimately, may reduce efficiency and profits. However the budget is prepared, people will react to it. Their reactions will be either positive or negative, depending upon whether they feel the budget is reasonable and whether they were involved in its preparation. (Totally neutral reaction to a budget is conceivable but highly unlikely.) Thus, the budget is as much a tool of good human relations as of financial planning and control. The latter objectives will not be well served if the former is not carefully incorporated in the preparation and implementation of the budget.

Budget systems may include rewards and punishments for good and bad performances under the budget. Rewards might take the form of additional monetary compensation, faster advancement within the firm, public recognition, and/or other means. Punishment might involve simply the loss of additional compensation, promotion, or recognition; or it might take the form of positive unfavorable action such as demotion or dismissal. Where rewards and/or punishments are involved in a budget, it is extremely important that they be meted out in light of actual conditions during the budget period and not be based wholly upon the predetermined budget data. The rewards should be so conceived as to be given for performance which is in the overall best interests of the firm. A department supervisor may be able to minimize his operating costs and, hence, maximize his own reward by employing operating procedures that do not serve the best interests of the entire firm. Punishment for failure to meet reasonable budgeted achievement should be designed in such a way as to avoid fear and the blunting of initiative on the parts of responsible supervisors. Slavish adherence to budgets should not be the aim of budget reward and punishment schemes. Budgets must walk a narrow line between encouragement and discouragement, between motivation and fear. Specifically how this is to be accomplished is beyond the scope of this volume, but it is a critical importance to the success of a budget system.[4]

BUDGETARY REVIEW

Once the budget period has begun, the budget process must not cease to function until it is time to prepare the next period's budget. If the budget is to be an effective tool of control and an aid to dynamic planning, it must be reviewed periodically with views to both the past and the future. As regards the past, budgetary review is concerned with a comparison of actual operating performance with budgeted performance for a given period of time. As regards the future, budgetary review provides a basis for revising and/or extending future plans.

Budgetary review is commonly accomplished by preparation of periodic reports and holding periodic meetings of the budget committee to evaluate actual performance and to reappraise future plans. While there is no standard frequency for these formal reports and meetings, monthly review is found in many business firms. Probably budgetary review should be undertaken in a formal manner at least quarterly. Waiting until the end of a budget period before a careful comparison of actual and budgeted performances is made leaves no room for corrective action during that period. Only the next budget period can benefit from such review.

The comparison of actual and budget data is designed to afford a basis for controlling current and future operations. It is always possible that the conclusion from the comparison of actual and budgeted operating data will be that the budget was unrealistic to begin with or that actual conditions during the budget period are so different from those anticipated that the budget data are no longer valid. In any event, the causes of deviations of actual performance from the budget should be sought and, where appropriate, corrected. The mere fact that actual operating data

---

[4] There is a considerable body of literature on the behavioral implications of budgeting. Reports of empirical studies in this area may be found in Chris Argyris, *The Impact of Budgets on People* (New York: The Controllership Foundation, Inc., 1952); G. H. Hofstede, *The Game of Budget Control* (London: Tavistock Publications Limited, 1968); and Andrew Stedry, *Budget Control and Cost Behavior* (Englewood Cliffs, N.J.: Prentice-Hall, Inc., 1960).

differ from the budget and are so reported is only the prelude to managerial control. Identification of causes and corrective action are the essence of control.

In addition to evaluating past performance in light of the budget, the budget committee should review and reappraise the budget data for the remainder of the current budget period. Changes in actual conditions from those originally expected normally require parallel changes in operating plans. When such changes in the budget are deemed appropriate, they should be made and approved by all responsible managers. This revised budget, brought up to date by a discriminate budgetary review policy, then becomes the formal statement of operating plans for the remaining portion of the budget period. Further, in this process of reviewing conditions and prospects for the current budget period are the seeds of the budget for the subsequent period. Thus, budgeting can and should be a continuous, dynamic process.

CONSTRUCTION OF THE BUDGET

The mechanics of budget preparation are the topics of the following two chapters. At this point, however, it is appropriate to consider two general aspects of budget preparation.

Limiting Factor on Operations

In every enterprise, there is some factor which effectively restricts the total magnitude of operating activity during a given period. In the majority of industrial firms in the United States, this limiting factor is sales demand. Most of these firms find that the reasonably expected sales of their products determine the overall scope and size of their operations. In other firms, notably those engaged in gold mining and agriculture, production is usually the limiting factor on operations. A firm mining gold in the United States faces an unlimited demand at a fixed price set by Congress. In such instance, the amount of gold which the company can produce determines its sales for any period. Substantially the same situation obtains in agriculture,[5] although here the prices of commodities are not necessarily fixed. In some firms, the limiting factor is working capital. No matter how great the demand for its product and irrespective of available production facilities, a firm must have working capital in order to operate. Firms with a history of financial difficulties not infrequently find they are unable to obtain the necessary funds to produce and sell at a volume that would cure their financial ills.

[5] It is probably true that few farmers undertake any formal, comprehensive budgeting; but they must make some plans stated in financial terms. Large corporate farms do budget systematically, of course.

Whatever the limiting factor for a firm may be, it is the element which determines the size of total operations and, hence, the point at which the planning process should begin. There is no sense in planning production greatly in excess of forecasted sales unless some profitable use of the resultant inventory accumulation can be foreseen in the more distant future. It may happen that, as a budget is developed from one limiting factor, a different one is discovered. For example, the preparation of a budget may begin with a sales forecast on the assumption that sales demand is the limiting factor on operations; but the planning may reveal production limitations which cannot be exceeded and which require a reduction in the planned sales volume. Alternatively, it may be found that additional working capital would be needed to operate at the level called for in the sales forecast and that none is available.

Setting Budget Allowances

There is no one way in which the appropriate quantity for a particular budget item is determined. All budget data are, of course, estimates; but they are influenced strongly by past experience. After all, the only basis management has for judging the future is the past. This does not mean that budgeting simply presumes that what happened in the past will happen again. Changes in future conditions must be taken into account in applying the lessons of the past to the future. But even expectations of changes are necessarily conditioned by experience. Nevertheless, planning is essentially a future-looking activity. Actual data of the past are useful in budgeting only to the extent that they help to develop estimates of future data. Budget data must be drawn primarily from studies of the future.

One possible way to estimate future data is to extend the actual data of the past by means of an average rate of growth or decline in a particular quantity that has persisted over some significant period of time. Seasonal variations in historical data should also be considered. Thus, March of 1971 may be a useful basis for planning for March of 1972. Further, the relationship between March of 1971 and the fourth quarter of 1970 may be of some help in estimating data for March of 1972 when the data for the fourth quarter of 1971 are known.

For many items, standards may be used to set budget allowances. However, we must remember that standards indicate what should be achieved; budgets indicate what is expected to be achieved. The two are not necessarily identical. Management may be aware of certain circumstances during the budget period which will make it impossible to meet particular standards. For example, if management knows that an unusually large number of trainees will be on the job during a particular period, it may reasonably anticipate that the labor time standards will not be met but may decide that no change in those standards is necessary. In such a case, a variance from standard should be budgeted. Such variance must then be taken into account in using the labor time standard for control purposes during the budget period. All budget allowances must be evaluated against a criterion of reasonableness. An unreasonable budget is not only not useful to management but may actually be dangerous.

QUESTIONS FOR DISCUSSION

1. "Budgets may actually prove detrimental to effective managerial control. They provide preconceived plans as the criteria for evaluating actual operations. Thus, any errors in the planning process may be compounded in the control process." Comment on this criticism of budgets.

2. What are the essential elements of good budgeting?

3. Is it possible that the establishment of a formal budget period may impose arbitrary and potentially harmful limitations on management's planning function? Discuss.

4. In a company that uses both standards and budgets, should control be based upon standards or upon budget data when the two differ (i.e., when variances from standards are budgeted)? What, then, is the proper role or the significance of the other?

5. What social, economic, and political conditions existing currently and/or anticipated within the year would you expect to have the most significant identifiable impacts upon the budgeted operations of (a) an aircraft manufacturer, (b) a basic steel producer, and (c) a university?

6. You have recently been hired as budget director and systems analyst for a medium-sized manufacturer of industrial machinery. The firm has been in business for many years and has a history of steady growth, satisfactory profit margins, and work force stability. It has never made any formal use of budgets. The president has asked you to design and install a budgetary system as soon as practicable. After several months on the job, you have developed a basic outline of the budget system you believe is right for this company. The president has called a meeting of middle managers and factory supervisors to hear your initial presentation of this proposed budget system. He has asked you to describe the objectives of the system and, basically, how it will work. How will you begin your presentation at this meeting?

7. Inasmuch as the accounting department works closely with cost and expense data for an entire company, isn't it the logical unit to develop expense budgets for the several operating departments? Explain your position.

8. The Galena Company employs a merit system in compensating its supervisory personnel. In addition to a basic salary, each department supervisor receives a bonus based upon the relationship between his department's actual performance and its budget for the period. For most departments, this involves comparisons of actual and budgeted costs. An excess of actual costs over budgeted results in negative points. An excess of budget over actual costs produces positive points. The points are then added algebrai-

cally. Net negative points are ignored. Net positive points are multiplied by a predetermined bonus rate to determine the supervisor's merit compensation. Evaluate this bonus plan.

9. What benefits should a firm derive from the periodic meetings of its budget committee?

10. "Realistically, sales demand is the only limiting factor on the volume of a business firm's operations. Sales demand will inevitably generate the necessary capital and productive capacity to fill that demand." Discuss this assertion.

11. Define "goal congruence." Why is it important in budgeting?

12. How can a firm reconcile the notion of "bottom-up" budget development with top management's inescapable responsibility for planning the total operations of the firm?

13. "Do you know," said the president of the Streator Corporation, with a satisfied puff on his cigar, "Our budget system has saved us a half a million dollars since we began it three years ago." How would you expect such a financial saving to be measured? Is it important that such a saving be measured? Discuss.

14. How might statistical analysis be used to advantage in a budget system?

15. Read at least the first chapter of Robert N. Anthony's *Planning and Control Systems: A Framework for Analysis* (Boston: Harvard University, 1965). If this book is not available, substantially the same framework is summarized in the first chapter of Anthony, Dearden, and Vancil's textbook, *Management Control Systems* (Homewood, Ill.: Richard D. Irwin, Inc., 1965). How does budgeting relate to Anthony's framework of planning and control?

16. There has been considerable debate as to the merits of employee participation in budgeting. Some argue that employees work best when they have been involved directly in the budgetary process. Others suggest that at least some employees function best under an authoritarian budget system. An interesting discussion of these points of view appeared in an article by Selwyn Becker and David Green, Jr., "Budgeting and Employee Behavior" in the *Journal of Business* for October, 1962. A reply to this article by Andrew C. Stedry was published in the April, 1964, *Journal of Business* along with a rejoinder by Becker and Green. (All three of these items are reproduced in William J. Bruns, Jr., and Don T. DeCoster, *Accounting and Its Behavioral Implications* (New York: McGraw-Hill Book Co., 1969) and also in L. S. Rosen, *Topics in Managerial Accounting* (Toronto: McGraw-Hill Book Co., of Canada Ltd., 1970). Read this article and the subsequent discussions of it. If you were responsible for the decision, would you have your employees participate in the budget process? Explain your decision.

chapter 7

PROFIT PLANNING: THE OPERATING BUDGET

I N AN overall sense, it is impossible to plan the operations of a business firm on a piecemeal basis, for all segments and activities of the firm interact with each other. Nor is it possible to divorce the planning of profits from the planning of financial resources, for the two are interdependent. Profits cannot be obtained without capital resources, and, conversely, resources cannot be maintained indefinitely without profits (excepting in nonprofit institutions dependent upon contributions and in government units dependent upon tax revenue for their capital). Thus, the separate discussions of profit and resource planning in this and the following chapter are employed only to simplify the introduction of the problems involved. The interdependence will be evident.

A single, extended illustration of budgeting will be developed in this and the succeeding chapter. This illustration will depict the preparation of the master budget of Shadbolt Products, Inc., for the year 1972. Shadbolt Products manufactures light industrial equipment and has two distinct product lines, industrial pumps and chain saws. Industrial pumps are sold principally to industrial users, although a substantial number are also sold to dealers. Most chain saws are sold to dealers, but some are sold directly to users, particularly in foreign countries. For purposes of efficient distribution, the corporation has three sales divisions, the Western Division, the Eastern Division, and the International Division. All production is accomplished in the company's two plants located in Oakland and in Indianapolis. As the various component budgets are discussed in the pages that follow, they will be illustrated for Shadbolt Products, Inc.

THE SALES FORECAST

As mentioned in the preceding chapter, every firm faces some factor which effectively limits the magnitude of its total operations. In most industrial companies, this limiting factor is the demand for its product. While sales demand is not always the limiting factor with which the budget process must begin, it frequently is and will be regarded as such in the discussion and illustration in this chapter.

Factors Determining Sales

The Environment. The importance of the various social, economic, and political factors that go to make up the environment within which a business firm operates was discussed in the preceding chapter. In no respect are these environmental factors more important than in the preparation of the sales forecast. Sales represent one of the principal points of contact between a firm and its environment. Insofar as sales are concerned, the environment may be identified with the market (or markets) for a firm's products. In order for a firm to plan its sales for a coming period, it must be able to understand and evaluate the market for its products. Markets are enormously complex; they defy precise definition. Yet, management must not only arrive at an operational definition of its market but must also anticipate the behavior in that market during a particular future period. One of the best available indications of a market's behavior in the future is its behavior in the past. This is always a tenuous indicator, at best, however; for the future is always somewhat different from the past. It has been said that the only thing that is certain, in addition to death and taxes, is change. Thus, future market behavior must be predicted on the basis of past experience as adjusted for anticipated changes in behavioral patterns. The task of making such a prediction is difficult, and the cost of making a bad prediction may be very high, as witnessed by the large number of business failures in the United States each year.

For purposes of the Shadbolt Products, Inc., illustration, we shall assume that the year 1972 is expected to be one of general prosperity in the American economy, with probable record highs in such leading economic indicators as gross national product, personal income, business investment, and corporate profits. This prosperity will be reflected in most foreign markets as well. No unusual political or social changes are expected to have any major impact, favorable or unfavorable, upon sales during 1972. However, increasing concern for the preservation of American forest resources and a growing recovery and reuse of newsprint will probably cause the rate of growth in the market for chain saws to slow. This tendency is offset somewhat by the expanding housing market and by more effective programs of reforestation. On the basis of past years' experience and economic forecasts for 1972, the company's economist has estimated that the total sales of industrial pumps in the United States during 1972 will amount to approximately $500,000,000 and total sales of chain saws to about $300,000,000. (Neither of these figures includes sales abroad. Hence, they specifically exclude the market of the company's International Division.) An appraisal of environmental conditions can ordinarily lead no further than to a forecast of total demand for a product in a given market. What portion of that total demand may be expected to be filled by an individual firm can be predicted only after consideration of additional information. Past statistics on market shares are useful for this purpose, but they are hardly conclusive. One of the goals of many firms' managements is to increase their shares of the markets for their products.

Competition. Each firm's share of a market is determined, primarily, by competition among firms. Any time that two or more firms offer to sell the same product in the same market, there will be some degree of competition among them. Such firms may, of course, agree among themselves to restrict competitive activities in a manner that is designed to benefit all of them. Where such an agreement completely eliminated competition, the combination of the noncompeting firms (a cartel) would, in effect, be a monopoly. In the United States, such agreements to lessen competition are ordinarily illegal under the provisions of the antitrust laws. Even a monopolist is not wholly immune to competition, however. He must recognize the possibility of future competition from new firms entering his market and also of competition from substitute products in other markets (e.g., aluminum for steel, tea for coffee, etc.).

In economic theory, competition simply describes a situation in which there are many sellers of a product in a market. In common parlance, competition is used to denote rivalry. In this latter sense, competition among firms may take many forms; but all of these may be reduced to three basic forms—competition as to price, product (including customer services), and promotion. Whatever form it may take, competition entails the possibility of shifts in market shares among competing companies. Like the environmental factors discussed above, competitive forces are subject to much uncertainty and are difficult to predict. Nevertheless, these forces must be taken into account in preparing a sales forecast for an individual firm. The responsible executive must evaluate the effect of his own firm's and competing firms' various efforts to increase their respective market shares on the sales of his firm's products during the budget period. Pricing and promotional policies, as well as product changes, may be contemplated by the firm during the budget period. Such policies are, obviously relevant to the sales forecast and must be incorporated therein. At this point it might be appropriate to note that not all competitive efforts are aggressive and intended to increase a firm's market share at the expense of other firms. Much competitive effort is almost entirely defensive, designed simply to maintain an existing market share.

Shadbolt Products, Inc., enjoys a well-established position in the market for industrial pumps. This is a fairly stable market, insofar as relative shares are concerned. For several years Shadbolt's share of the market has amounted to approximately 10% of total domestic sales, and it is expected that approximately this same proportion of the market will be obtained in 1972. In the market for chain saws, Shadbolt is fairly new; and the sales manager believes the company's share of that market will continue to increase. In 1971, Shadbolt accounted for approximately 2% of the domestic sales of chain saws. The sales manager feels it is reasonable to expect this share to be increased to 4% in 1972. For both product lines, the company is unable to ascertain its percentage share of the foreign market. Statistics as to total foreign sales are difficult to obtain and unreliable. There are many very unpredictable factors, political and economic, which render foreign sales highly uncertain. However, the company's top management believes that its continued success in foreign markets is a reasonable expectation and that its export sales of chain saws, particularly to the developing nations, will continue to increase.

Company Policies. The sales of a company's products are obviously dependent largely upon a wide variety of company policies including pricing, product development, and promotion. These policies must be stated so that the responsible executives may plan sales realistically. Further, these policies interact with those of other firms in a competitive market, as described above. The ultimate consequences in terms of sales revenue of environmental conditions, competitive forces, and managerial actions cannot be predetermined with certainty. But a careful evaluation of these various factors can result in the avoidance of certain pitfalls in the budgeting process.

Developing the Sales Forecast in Detail

Personnel Involved. In the preceding chapter, it was suggested that the budget should be developed initially by the persons who will be responsible for performance under it. Thus, the sales forecast should originate with the division sales managers and their salesmen. However, any market information available to top management from its market research staff should be shared with the divisional sales managers so that it may be used by them in preparing their forecasts. Also, the company might have the research staff independently prepare its own sales forecast as a basis for evaluating the forecasts submitted by the divisions. Any discrepancies between these separate forecasts should be examined carefully, however. There should be no presumption that the market research staff's forecast is better simply because that staff reports directly to corporate management.

Initial sales estimates prepared by salesmen may have to be revised by the division sales managers on the basis of better information and also on the basis of salesmen's known propensities to over- or underestimate their territories' sales potentials. Such revisions should be discussed with those salesmen. Similarly, top management may find it necessary to revise the divisions' forecasts. Once again, these revisions should be made on the basis of consultations with the division sales managers. It should be the corporate objective to obtain the lower level managers' concurrence in all revisions of the sales forecast. If a salesman is handed a sales quota based on a forecast that he honestly believes to be unrealistic, his reaction and his subsequent sales efforts are almost certain to be less than ideal. He may contrive to meet a quota that he regards as excessive by offering unwarranted concessions to buyers (e.g., excessive discounts or unreasonable delivery schedules) or by other practices which are not in the best interests of the company as a whole.

Breakdown of the Forecast by Segments.   Given an estimate of total sales of a product in the market and the expected percentage share of a firm in that market, the anticipated sales of that firm might be computed by simple multiplication. For example, total domestic sales of industrial pumps for 1972 was estimated at $500,000,000; and Shadbolt Products' share of this market was estimated at 10%. These two data would yield planned domestic sales of industrial pumps by Shadbolt of $50,000,000. But this is an end figure, not an appropriate beginning for the sales forecast. A single total is not enough. The company must estimate which specific pumps will be sold, when, where, and how. In other words, the sales forecast must be built up by the various segments of the business in as much detail as is believed relevant in the individual firm.

Generally speaking, the sales forecast should always include detail as to the timing of expected sales. The forecast should indicate planned sales on a monthly basis, not merely totals for the entire budget period (typically one year). Sales data might be broken down further by product lines, by operating divisions, by sales territories, by channels of distribution, by sizes of customers, and by any other scheme of classification which suits the needs of management. In the Shadbolt illustration, the sales forecast for the year 1972 is subdivided by months, sales divisions, product lines, and channels of distribution. These subdivisions are merely illustrative and do not purport to be applicable to all industrial firms; they would, however, be suitable in a large number of firms.

In addition to a detailed breakdown of the sales forecast, it is common practice for the actual and budgeted data for the previous year to be included in the formal sales budget schedule. This comparative information affords management some frame of reference for appraising the new forecast. This is not to say that the past is always a valid basis for evaluating the future, but it often is the most readily available basis. Showing both actual and budgeted data for the previous year also affords some basis for appraising the efficiency of the budgeting process. In some instances it might be felt desirable to include actual and/or budgeted data

TABLE 7–1

Summary Sales Forecast for Shadbolt Products, Inc. (Fiscal Year 1972)
(thousands of dollars)

| | 1972 | | | | 1971 | |
	Western Division	Eastern Division	Inter-national Division	Total Company	Actual Total	Budget Total
January........	$ 3,410	$ 1,532	$ 865	$ 5,807	$ 5,187	$ 5,218
February.......	2,780	1,402	889	5,071	5,230	5,136
March.........	2,510	1,329	916	4,755	5,016	4,825
April..........	2,659	1,168	1,074	4,901	4,720	4,640
May..........	2,367	1,117	1,008	4,492	4,181	4,076
June..........	2,585	1,223	920	4,728	4,363	4,537
July..........	2,415	1,425	1,143	4,983	4,869	5,162
August........	2,995	1,540	994	5,529	5,381	5,375
September......	3,629	1,829	881	6,339	5,759	5,828
October.......	4,338	2,085	1,068	7,491	6,389	6,018
November......	4,745	2,148	1,101	7,994	6,780	6,598
December......	3,337	1,522	1,051	5,910	5,600*	5,087
	$37,770	$18,320	$11,910	$68,000	$63,475	$62,500

* Estimate.

for two or more previous years. Within certain limitations, the more comparative data available, the better can the new budget be evaluated. However, the reader of the budget must not be misled into thinking that the sales forecast for the coming period is nothing more than a statistical extension of actual data for several prior periods.

Tables 7–1 through 7–4 illustrate the several stages of the sales forecast for Shadbolt Products, Inc., for the fiscal year 1972. Each successive exhibit illustrates a different scheme of subclassification of the sales budget; and, with the exception of Table 7–4, each represents a different level of responsibility.

Table 7–1 is the summary sales forecast for the entire corporation for the budget period. The forecast is stated in terms of thousands of dollars of sales revenue only, and the only breakdown of the firm is by sales divisions. Budgeted sales are indicated for each month of the budget period.

Comparative data are provided in the form of the actual sales and the budgeted sales for 1971. Notice that the actual sales figure for December, 1971, is an estimate. As the 1972 budget must be completed prior to the end of 1971 (by December 15, 1971, in the case of Shadbolt Products), the final actual sales figure for December will not be available when the 1972 budget is completed. The monthly breakdown of sales must be based principally upon previous experience with seasonal variations in demand. Notice that approximately the same seasonal pattern obtains for the two domestic sales divisions. In the case of the International Division, however, no seasonal pattern is readily apparent. This situation follows from

TABLE 7–2

Sales Forecast for Shadbolt Products, Inc., Western Division
(Fiscal Year 1972)
(thousands of dollars)

	Industrial Pumps			*Chain Saws*			*Division Total*
	P-115	*P-85*	*Total*	*C-7*	*C-3*	*Total*	
January.....	$ 1,920	$ 1,050	$ 2,970	$ 240	$ 200	$ 440	$ 3,410
February....	1,440	875	2,315	240	225	465	2,780
March.......	1,200	700	1,900	360	250	610	2,510
April........	1,200	700	1,900	384	375	759	2,659
May........	960	525	1,485	432	450	882	2,367
June........	960	525	1,485	600	500	1,100	2,585
July........	960	525	1,485	480	450	930	2,415
August......	1,440	700	2,140	480	375	855	2,995
September...	1,920	1,050	2,970	384	275	659	3,629
October......	2,400	1,400	3,800	288	250	538	4,338
November...	2,880	1,400	4,280	240	225	465	4,745
December....	1,920	1,050	2,970	192	175	367	3,337
	$19,200	$10,500	$29,700	$4,320	$3,750	$8,070	$37,770

the fact that different parts of the world experience different seasonal changes. As a final caution, the rate of deviation of actual 1971 sales from that year's budget must not be taken as any indication of 1972 performance. Insofar as it is possible to predict, the sales forecast as prepared should be taken as the best estimate of the coming year's sales.

Table 7–2 takes a closer and more detailed look at the first sales forecast column of Table 7–1. It depicts the detailed sales forecast for the Western Division only. A similar forecast would be prepared for the Eastern Division. The same type might also be prepared for the International Division; however, in this instance, a somewhat different form is used for that division.[1] In Table 7–2, sales are still expressed in terms of dollar revenue only. Monthly breakdowns are again given. Divisional

---

[1] Cf. Table 7–4.

sales are now detailed by product lines, and these product lines are further subclassified. As may be seen in Table 7–2, two different types of industrial pumps are produced and sold by the company. Model P-115 is larger and has a higher selling price than model P-85. Similarly, chain saws are available in two models, the C-7 and the C-3, the former being larger and higher priced. Notice in this illustration that the seasonal sales pattern of the division is dominated by that of the industrial pump line but that the seasonal pattern of demand for chain saws tends to offset

TABLE 7–3

Sales Forecast—Industrial Pumps—for Shadbolt Products, Inc.,
Western Division (Fiscal Year 1972)
(units)

	P-115			P-85		
	Industrial Users	Dealers	Total	Industrial Users	Dealers	Total
January..........	3,000	1,000	4,000	2,250	750	3,000
February.........	2,200	800	3,000	1,900	600	2,500
March...........	1,900	600	2,500	1,500	500	2,000
April............	1,900	600	2,500	1,500	500	2,000
May.............	1,600	400	2,000	1,180	320	1,500
June............	1,500	500	2,000	1,180	320	1,500
July.............	1,400	600	2,000	1,100	400	1,500
August..........	2,200	800	3,000	1,500	500	2,000
September........	3,000	1,000	4,000	2,250	750	3,000
October..........	3,700	1,300	5,000	3,000	1,000	4,000
November........	4,800	1,200	6,000	3,200	800	4,000
December........	3,000	1,000	4,000	2,300	700	3,000
Total units....	30,200	9,800	40,000	22,860	7,140	30,000
Unit price........	$480	$480	$480	$350	$350	$350
Total sales (000s)...	$14,496	$4,704	$19,200	$ 8,001	$2,499	$10,500

that for pumps. Where seasonal sales patterns exist, there are numerous advantages of having two or more product lines whose seasonal patterns tend to counterbalance so that the total sales are fairly uniform throughout the year.

Table 7–3 goes one step further in the detailed development of the sales forecast. It shows the budgeted sales of the Western Division for one product line by channels of distribution. In this illustration, there are only two such channels, sales to industrial users and to dealers. Monthly detail is again given. In this forecast, sales data are given in terms of units of product and are converted to dollars of revenue only in total for the year. This schedule is a further breakdown of the first three columns of Table 7–2, and the relationship between the two exhibits should be clear. Note that no column is included in Table 7–3 for total units sold.

Such a total would be irrelevant, for the two models of pumps are not the same. Total dollar sales, of course, are relevant. Similar forecasts would be prepared for industrial pumps in the other divisions and for chain saws in all three divisions.

The three budget schedules illustrated and discussed above would be particularly relevant to different levels of responsibility within the firm. Table 7–1, the overall summary of expected sales, would likely be the only sales forecast used by top management (i.e., the board of directors, president, and executive vice president). Table 7–2 would be more pertinent to the interests of the vice president for marketing and the sales manager of the Western Division. Finally, Table 7–3 would probably be used only within the Western Division by the division sales manager and his subordinates. These relationships between levels of managerial responsibility and the budget schedules illustrated are intended to suggest the types of detail in a sales forecast which the various levels of management are likely to want and not to indicate standardized budget forms for the several management echelons cited.

For some purposes, specialized budget forms may be found appropriate. Thus, in Shadbolt Products, experience has led the vice president for marketing to employ a different form of divisional sales forecast for the International Division than that employed for the other two sales divisions. Specifically, he has found that a summary breakdown of foreign sales by country or region is more useful than that by product lines. The International Division sales forecast is presented as Table 7–4. This forecast is prepared in terms of sales revenue, by countries or regions, and on

TABLE 7–4

Sales Forecast for Shadbolt Products, Inc., International Division
(Fiscal Year 1972)
(thousands of dollars)

	Canada	Latin America	Western Europe	Other*	Total
January	$ 315	$ 119	$ 346	$ 85	$ 865
February	325	120	355	89	889
March	328	130	366	92	916
April	386	154	429	105	1,074
May	362	144	403	99	1,008
June	330	128	368	94	920
July	408	166	457	112	1,143
August	360	139	397	98	994
September	318	121	352	90	881
October	394	143	427	104	1,068
November	401	150	440	110	1,101
December	388	141	420	102	1,051
	$4,315	$1,655	$4,760	$1,180	$11,910

* Principally sales to Australia, Japan, and certain African nations.

a monthly basis. The last column in Table 7–4 is identical to the third column in Table 7–1. Details of expected foreign sales by product lines would be developed in budget schedules similar to those in Tables 7–2 and 7–3.

Budgeting Sales in Total Only

In the foregoing section, the sales forecast was developed by estimating unit sales volume for each product in each sales division and then multiplying those units by the selling prices to obtain budgeted sales revenue. This approach is feasible for Shadbolt Products, Inc., because it has only four different products and four selling prices. For many firms, this approach would be extremely difficult and time consuming, if not wholly impossible. It is difficult to imagine this approach being efficient for a firm selling several thousand different items at different prices, particularly where new products frequently are being added and old ones dropped from the line. A large department store, a mail-order house, or a drug wholesaler would find that sales forecasting based upon expected unit sales and selling prices was a practical impossibility. In such cases, the sales forecast may be developed from the start in terms of dollars of sales revenue. Breakdowns by sales divisions, by departments, by channels of distribution, and by sizes of customers may be feasible; but any complete breakdown by products is unlikely. Such an approach to the sales forecast is based almost entirely upon the firm's past experience, with adjustment for anticipated changes in the aggregate demand for the company's products and for expected average price changes. While this approach may appear to be less precise than the other, it is not necessarily less useful. A sales forecast prepared by this method may be every bit as reliable and useful for purposes of planning and control as one prepared initially from expected unit sales.

Long-Range Sales Planning

The sales forecast described in the preceding pages is normally adequate for purposes of budget preparation. Any attempt at long-range sales forecasting would be beyond the requirements of the immediate budget period. However, the studies and analyses upon which the short-run sales forecast is predicated should also provide some indication of sales demand in the more distant future. A long-range sales forecast is typically expressed in round totals for the company, with a minimum of detail. It is subject to considerably more error than the short-run forecast. Nevertheless, it is helpful to management in planning future plant capacity and future capital requirements.

Shadbolt Products, Inc., follows the practice of preparing a long-range sales forecast at the same time as its formal forecast for the coming budget period. This long-range plan is stated in terms of expected total revenues in each of the next five years, including the immediate budget period and the following four years. The only breakdown made is between domestic and foreign sales. Such a plan is illustrated in Table 7–5. Notice that this illustration shows a continually rising pattern of sales. This is, in part, because no period of recession in general business activity has been anticipated in preparing the long-range forecast. The firm's management does not, thereby, express its belief that no recession will occur during the next five years. It merely demonstrates its belief that the timing of business fluctuations is too unpredictable to incorporate in a plan of this nature. Because this long-range sales forecast is quite tenuous and

TABLE 7–5
Long-Range Sales Forecast for Shadbolt Products, Inc.
for Period 1972–76
(thousands of dollars)

	Domestic Sales	Foreign Sales	Total Sales
1972	$56,990	$11,910	$68,000
1973	57,500	12,500	70,000
1974	61,000	13,000	74,000
1975	65,000	14,000	79,000
1976	68,000	15,000	83,000

not relevant to normal operations in the coming period, it is circulated only among the top echelon of the company's management.

PRODUCTION BUDGETS

Factors Determining Production

Sales. In most cases, the volume of production is determined primarily by the anticipated volume of sales. With comparatively few exceptions, most companies' current output is designed principally to fill current sales demand. The timing of sales, as well as the total sales for the period, is important in planning output during the budget period. Production must flow from the factory according to a schedule that enables the firm to fill sales orders as they are received or within a reasonable time thereafter. Where there is a significant degree of seasonal variation in sales demand during a period, production may be scheduled either to vary with the fluctuations in sales or to ignore them. In the first instance, where output is scheduled to vary with sales, the firm must plan to expand its overall operating activities, including its work force probably, during or immediately prior to periods of peak demand and to reduce its operations and lay off workers during the slack seasons. In the second instance, where output is stabilized despite seasonal fluctuations in demand, the company must plan to build up its inventory of finished product during the slack period and to reduce these stocks during the peak sales season. Of course, there is also the opposite situation, in which production is subject to seasonal fluctuations but sales are not. Certain canning companies experience such conditions. In these cases, there is little alternative to periods of peak and low (if, indeed, any) production and inventory buildups and reductions.

Inventory Plans. While production normally is determined chiefly by budgeted sales, it should be planned with inventory requirements in mind also. For example, if a firm anticipates that future sales demand will continue to rise, it may decide that its inventory of finished product as of the end of the budget period should be greater than that at the start of the period. Obviously, if the inventory at the end of the period is planned to be greater than at the beginning of the period, production volume during that period must exceed planned sales volume. On the other hand, an enterprise may believe that it has been carrying too much inventory of finished product and may wish to reduce this balance as of the end of the budget period as compared with the beginning. In such case, planned output will be lower than the forecasted sales volume. Of course, it is not always easy to determine long in advance the level of inventory that will be needed at the end of a period; and the impact of inventory plans on production is unlikely to be nearly so significant as that of sales demand. Nevertheless, some plan for ending inventory should be incorporated in the production budget.

Capacity. Finally, production is necessarily limited by the productive capacity of the enterprise. Capacity, however, does not admit of any simple practical definition. It is not merely a matter of plant size. Capacity may be expanded by adding work shifts, by working the regular shift overtime, by working six or seven days a week, and by other schemes to increase the output of existing plant facilities. Such schemes increase operating costs, of course. Night shifts, overtime work, and weekend work command higher wages than those paid for regular straight-time work. Thus, insofar as practical operations are concerned, capacity is established by managerial decisions as well as by physical facilities. However defined, capacity places an upper limit on output. That limit may be somewhat flexible, but it cannot be stretched indefinitely.

Summary of Production Budget

While total budgeted production costs will be reported to top management in summary form, the first line of cost control is at the level of the operating department supervisors. Hence, the costs of production must be budgeted on departmental bases so that the individual responsible managers can plan and evaluate their own performances and so that their performances may be reviewed by their superiors within the proper framework of responsibility. These departmental budget schedules accumulate to make up the overall production budget for the firm.

Table 7–6 is a summary production budget for one of the two plants of Shadbolt Products, Inc. A similar budget schedule would be prepared for the other plant, and a further summarization might be made for the

TABLE 7–6

Production Cost Budget for Shadbolt Products, Inc., Oakland Plant
(Fiscal Year 1972)
(thousands of dollars)

	Materials	Labor	Variable Overhead	Total Variable Costs	Fixed Overhead	Total Costs
January............	$ 1,116	$ 904	$ 283	$ 2,303	$ 460	$ 2,763
February...........	1,116	904	283	2,303	460	2,763
March.............	1,118	904	283	2,305	460	2,765
April..............	1,123	906	285	2,314	460	2,774
May...............	1,127	905	286	2,318	460	2,778
June..............	1,118	905	283	2,306	460	2,766
July..............	1,116	904	283	2,303	460	2,763
August............	1,112	904	282	2,298	460	2,758
September..........	1,109	905	281	2,295	460	2,755
October...........	1,109	904	281	2,294	460	2,754
November..........	1,116	904	283	2,303	460	2,763
December..........	1,116	904	283	2,303	460	2,763
	$13,396	$10,853	$3,396	$27,645	$5,520	$33,165

entire company. The budget schedule in Table 7–6 would be directed principally to the manager of the Oakland plant and higher levels of authority within the manufacturing division of the corporation. Budgeted production costs are reported here as variable and fixed in order to facilitate management's appraisal of the effects of any changes in budgeted volume. The variable cost data were obtained by multiplying the budgeted unit output of the several products by their respective standard costs for materials, for labor, and for variable overhead. For the sake of simplicity, it is assumed here that no variances from these standard costs need be budgeted. The total planned fixed costs for the year were simply divided by 12 to obtain the monthly budget allowances. A comparison of this production cost schedule with the summary sales forecast in Table 7–1 reveals that the seasonal variation in sales is not reflected in the budget of output for the Oakland plant. (The output of the Oakland plant fills all sales orders for the Western Division and most of the orders for the International Division.) Thus, the inventory of the finished product at the Oakland plant is increased during the spring and summer and reduced during the peak sales period in the autumn and winter.

Production must also be budgeted in terms of units of output, of course. Table 7–7 is an example of a schedule of production for one product line, industrial pumps, in the Oakland plant of Shadbolt Products. Similar

TABLE 7–7

Unit Production Budget—Industrial Pumps—for Shadbolt Products, Inc., Oakland Plant (Fiscal Year 1972)

	P-115			P-85		
	Units Produced	*Units Shipped*	*Ending Inventory*	*Units Produced*	*Units Shipped*	*Ending Inventory*
Inventory, January 1.....			9,500			6,000
January................	4,850	5,300	9,050	3,850	4,400	5,450
February..............	4,850	4,100	9,800	3,850	3,600	5,700
March................	4,850	3,500	11,150	3,800	2,900	6,600
April.................	4,800	3,400	12,550	3,800	2,900	7,500
May..................	4,700	3,000	14,250	3,750	2,200	9,050
June.................	4,850	2,600	16,500	3,800	2,200	10,650
July.................	4,850	2,800	18,550	3,850	2,200	12,300
August...............	4,900	4,100	19,350	3,900	2,900	13,300
September............	4,900	5,400	18,850	4,000	4,400	12,900
October..............	4,950	6,800	17,000	3,900	5,800	11,000
November............	4,850	7,900	13,950	3,850	5,800	9,050
December............	4,850	5,800	13,000	3,850	4,400	8,500
	58,200	54,700		46,200	43,700	

schedules would be developed for the chain saw line and for the Indianapolis plant. The particular usefulness of this schedule lies in its comparison of the planned output of the plant with the budgeted shipments (sales) from it on a monthly basis. This comparison shows the month-by-month development of the inventory of finished pumps.

Labor Budget

Where the maximum practical output of a plant is not required to meet current sales demand, there is a degree of flexibility as to the scheduling of production. Within this range of flexibility, production may be planned so as to minimize the total costs of manufacturing. This end may be accomplished in different ways in different firms. However, in many firms it can best be achieved by making maximum use of a stabilized work force. In the Shadbolt Products' Oakland plant, for example, it apparently was determined to be better to level production throughout the year rather than to vary production with sales demand. More and more, the practical problems related to labor costs dictate as much stabilization of operations as is possible.

Traditionally, labor cost has been regarded as variable. Often, however, direct labor is a variable cost only by definition. When workers are not actually producing units of product, their wages are not accounted for as direct labor cost; but they are not necessarily stopped. Wages paid to workers during idle periods are accounted for as overhead, but they are still paid. The accounting treatment of labor costs cannot make them truly variable in an ultimate sense. For a variety of reasons labor costs have tended to become more nearly fixed than variable in large segments of American industry. This tendency is due largely to the efforts of labor unions, but it has not developed wholly as a result of external pressures. A stable work force with a minimum of turnover is likely to enhance employees' morale and efficiency and also to minimize training costs and operating inefficiencies during training periods. Where labor is substantially a fixed cost, total labor cost can usually be minimized by utilizing the work force in production on a level basis. If there are significant seasonal variations in sales, stable production will entail inventory buildups during periods of slack demand. The costs of financing, handling, and storing these inventories tend to offset some of the costs saved by stabilizing the labor force. In any particular company, the production schedule selected should be based upon the lowest total budgeted costs.[2] As labor moves more toward becoming a fixed cost, level output during the period is more likely to result in the lowest total cost.

Mechanically, a direct labor budget schedule is not difficult to prepare. Any planned level of output can be converted quite readily into the necessary number of labor hours in each production process. These hours may then be multiplied by either budgeted or standard wage rates to determine the total direct labor cost by processes. These total labor costs may then be accumulated for whatever cost centers management wishes to use. If standard costs are used, total labor cost would normally be the standard labor cost of budgeted production. If temporary variances from standards are anticipated, however, these variances should be added to the standard costs to determine the most realistic budgeted labor cost for the period.

---

[2] Determination of the production schedule that will minimize total cost may be accomplished by use of linear programming. This mathematical technique has many useful applications in budgeting. Problem 11 at the end of this chapter, for example, may be solved directly by use of linear programming. It may also be solved in a more tedious process of trial and error. Even then, it will be difficult to be confident that the minimum-cost solution has been reached.

Materials Budget

As in the case of direct labor, raw materials cost has traditionally been regarded as a variable cost of production. Unlike labor, materials cost has, in most instances, remained very nearly perfectly variable. The principal reason for this is that materials can be stored by themselves and used only as needed in production. Most materials cannot be stored indefinitely, of course. Some raw materials, notably in the food-processing industry, must be used quite promptly after their acquisition. Others can be stored for considerable periods of time, but very few are wholly immune to the value-erosive influences of physical deterioration and obsolescence. Because of the capacity of most raw materials to be stored for some period of time, materials cost typically is quite readily adaptable to variations in the level of output, whereas labor cost is comparatively inflexible in many industrial companies.

Purchase Planning. The fact that the usage of raw materials is quite flexible does not necessarily mean that they may be purchased in a manner dictated simply by fluctuations in production. There are many factors which bear upon materials purchasing policies. In an ideal situation, materials would be purchased just prior to their being required for use in production. In this way, the amount of capital tied up in materials inventory would always be at a minimum. There may be many cogent reasons for purchasing more than will be needed in production in the immediate future, however. Some examples of such reasons are to take advantage of quantity discounts, to increase inventory in advance of an announced or anticipated price rise, and to build stocks as a hedge against expected strikes in suppliers' plants.

In any case, there are certain general rules pertaining to the scheduling of materials purchases. The schedule for purchases of a particular material should be keyed to the schedules of production of the products in which that material is used. Purchasing policies should give proper recognition to normal time lags (lead time) between the placement of orders and the receipt of materials from suppliers. Generally speaking, it is safer to overestimate the lengths of these time lags than to attempt to plan purchases so that materials will arrive just when they are needed for production; stock-outs are far too disruptive and costly. Purchasing should be planned in such a way as to minimize the total cost of materials to the firm. One technique for the accomplishment of this objective is the determination of the most economical (i.e., the least costly) lot size in which to purchase materials.

Economical Lot Size Buying. There are certain factors that favor purchases in large lots. Discounts are frequently available for purchases of large quantities. Purchasing large quantities means fewer purchases and, consequently, costs saved by processing fewer purchase orders and related documents. Other factors tend to favor purchases in small quantities. Small purchases involve lower investments in inventory and, hence, lower interest costs. Small purchase quantities avoid the need for large and costly materials storage facilities. Purchasing in small lots leaves the firm in a more flexible position with regard to future operations. For example, a firm might more quickly discontinue an unprofitable product line if it did not have on hand a large stock of a material that could be used only in that line.

Several formulas have been developed to facilitate identification of the optimum lot size, or *economic order quantity* (EOQ), in which materials should be purchased. One such formula is as follows:

$$Q = \sqrt{\frac{2CS}{UI + A}}$$

where

Q = number of units in optimum purchase lot (EOQ);
C = cost of placing an order for materials,
S = number of units required for use each year,
U = cost of one unit of the material,
I = interest rate which firm must pay for capital,
A = cost of carrying one unit in inventory for a year.[3]

However precise this and similar formulas may appear, they involve a number of approximations. The cost of placing an order for materials is very difficult to measure. It should include only the avoidable costs of processing one order; the fixed costs of order placing are not relevant to any single order. The annual requirements for a particular material can usually be estimated fairly closely, given the budget of production. The unit cost of the material is also usually determinable with reasonable confidence. The interest rate which the firm must pay for its capital, however, is commonly subject to a great deal of uncertainty.[4] Finally, the annual carrying cost of materials inventory is difficult to allocate among the individual materials carried. Thus, economic order quantity formulas should be interpreted as reasonable indicators of optimum purchase quantities; but they cannot be taken as infallible guides to efficient purchasing.

The widespread use of computers in business firms is of considerable assistance in the planning of purchases. Economic order quantity formulas and other more sophisticated inventory models can be employed in conjunction with current data on materials usage, costs, and market con-

---

[3] Adapted from Robert I. Dickey (ed.), *Accountants' Cost Handbook* (2d ed.; New York: The Ronald Press Co., 1960), p. 5 · 16. In some EOQ formulas, A is expressed as a percentage of U. In this case, A and I may be summed and treated as a single factor to be multiplied by U.

[4] The problems of measuring the interest cost of capital will be considered at some length in Chapter 8.

ditions. This bank of inventory information can be updated daily as materials are ordered, received, and used. Changes in production schedules and/or in market factors can be injected promptly into inventory planning models; and revised order quantities and schedules can be developed immediately. Of course, the computer simply manipulates the data provided to it in accordance with the rules of the model. The determination of the relevant data and the structuring of the model remain

TABLE 7–8

SHADBOLT PRODUCTS, INC.
Materials Purchase Schedule for Fiscal Year 1972
(units)

Item	#310 gauge	Suppliers	Norton Gauges, Inc.
Uses	all industrial pumps		Lewellyn, Brown & Co.

	Orders	Receipts	Usage	Ending Inventory
December 31, 1971............				25,640
January...................	24,000		11,220	14,420
February..................		24,000	11,220	27,200
March....................	22,000		11,170	16,030
April.....................		22,000	11,120	26,910
May......................	24,000		10,965	15,945
June.....................		24,000	11,170	28,775
July......................	22,000		11,220	17,555
August...................		22,000	11,320	28,235
September................	22,000		11,425	16,810
October..................		22,000	11,375	27,435
November................	24,000		11,225	16,210
December................		24,000	11,220	28,990
	138,000	138,000	134,650	

the responsibilities of management. The computer endows sound management planning with timely and accurate analyses of information, but it does not substitute for good management judgment.

Materials Purchase Schedule. As a part of the overall production budget, there should be a schedule for the purchases of each raw material used in a company. This schedule should identify the material, its principal uses in the firm's production, the principal suppliers, and planned purchases, usage, and inventory balances by months. Table 7–8 is an illustration of such a schedule. It covers purchases of a particular gauge for both plants, as Shadbolt Products' purchasing is centralized in the home office. The schedule is based upon the following facts and policies: There is a normal delay of approximately 30 days between the date of sending an order and the date of receiving shipment on that order. The company has found that the most economical lot size for the purchase of this gauge is between 20,000 and 25,000 units. Thus, it has established the policy of ordering this item bimonthly, each order being sufficient to cover approximately two months' usage. Orders are planned not only with regard to current production but also with a view toward specific inventory plans. The company's policy is never to permit the inventory of a material to fall below 125% of the budgeted production requirements for that item for the following month. Further, in this instance, the company, anticipating increased production in 1973, plans that the inventory of gauges at the end of the budget period will be greater than at the start of the period. Usage of the gauge is based upon budgeted production of all industrial pumps in both plants plus a standard breakage allowance of 2%. Notice in Table 7–8 that only the receipts and usage affect the balance on hand at the end of each month; orders are not received in stock until the month following that in which they were placed.

Departmental Overhead Budgets

Where manufacturing operations are departmentalized, overhead costs should be budgeted by departments. These departmental overhead budgets are the bases for planning and controlling those costs during the budget period and also the bases for establishing normal or standard overhead rates. Because of differences among departments as to the types of overhead costs incurred and the behavior of those costs with respect to fluctuations in production volume, departmental budgets are practically mandatory. The departmental overhead budget schedule should detail the various cost items and should distinguish between the variable and the fixed items. The distinction between variable and fixed overhead costs permits the budget to be adjusted to conform to changing levels of production volume. The budgeting of overhead is discussed at length in Chapter 9.

BUDGETS OF NONMANUFACTURING COSTS

Budgets for distribution, administrative, and research costs are typically prepared in essentially the same way as are budgets for factory overhead. They are prepared on departmental bases as appropriate in the particular firm. To the extent feasible, they should be subclassified to identify variable and fixed costs. The basis for cost variability in a nonmanufacturing department will be quite different from that in a manufacturing department, of course. For example, in a shipping department the most suitable measure of volume might be the number of items or the number of separate shipments handled. In a billing department, the number of bills prepared or, possibly, the number of items on bills prepared would be a likely indicator of activity and cost behavior. For certain types of activities there may be no readily identifiable measure of activity nor any observed causal factor for cost fluctuations. This might be true of certain research operations. In such a case, the departmental budget would not include any volume measure nor would it be subclassified into variable and fixed costs. In effect, all costs would be budgeted as though they were fixed costs for the period, probably in the maximum amount approved by management for spending in that department during the budget period.

BUDGETED INCOME STATEMENTS

The operating budget is typically summarized in the form of a budgeted income statement for the budget period. This is usually prepared in the same format as the actual income statements used by management. Of course, the budgeted income statement contains the firm's profit plan for the period, not actual income. The details and the time periods covered in this budget statement normally coincide with those in actual reports. Thus, if quarterly income statements are used by management, the budgeted income statement will probably show all revenues and expenses by quarters.

Budgeted revenues for the year and for each quarter are obtained from the summary sales forecast (Table 7-1) and from other budget schedules for miscellaneous revenues (e.g., rents, royalties, dividends, and interest). Cost of goods sold in a manufacturing company may be determined simply by multiplying standard costs by budgeted sales volumes in units. Other variable expenses are usually functions of sales volume or of some other measure of volume. Fixed expenses are typically stated as quarterly amounts simply by dividing the budgeted annual total expense by four. Interest expense is derived from budgets for long-term and short-term capital financing; these are discussed in the next chapter. Income taxes are included by applying anticipated rates to budgeted income before tax.

QUESTIONS FOR DISCUSSION

1. Given the budgeted sales volume for a period, a planned inventory balance at the end of the period, and adequate working capital to finance operations, with which element of production (materials, labor, or overhead) would you begin the preparation of a production cost budget? Why?

2. If you were the budget director of a large manufacturing company with sales outlets in 12 different sales territories and several hundred salesmen, how would you go about preparing the initial draft of a sales forecast?

3. List all of the factors that you would take into consideration in preparing a materials purchase schedule, and list them in what you believe to be the order of their relative importance?

4. What would be the implications for production planning if direct labor were, substantially, a fixed cost?

5. "Where standard production costs are established, the preparation of the production cost budget is virtually automatic once the physical volume of production has been established." Comment on this statement.

6. It has been suggested that the planned level of inventory of finished product at the end of a budget period should be a partial determinant of the physical production volume budgeted for that period. How would management decide what the level of the ending inventory should be?

7. Some companies determine the compensation of their salesmen partly on the basis of sales in excess of predetermined sales quotas. Should such sales quotas be equal to budgeted sales for the period? If so, why? If not, what should be the relationship between the sales budget and sales quotas?

8. What alternatives with respect to the timing of production are available to a firm that experiences significant seasonal variations in the volume of its sales? Discuss the advantages and disadvantages of each of these alternatives.

9. How might a computer be used effectively in the preparation of an operating budget?

10. How would budgeting each of the following operating costs be different from the budgeting of the others:
    a) Direct materials?
    b) Repair and maintenance of production equipment?
    c) Research and development?
    d) Depreciation?

PROBLEMS

1. The Kalakaua Boat Corporation manufactures fiber glass boat hulls. Actual sales data for 1972 are summarized below:

First quarter	$ 2,000,000
Second quarter	5,000,000
Third quarter	4,000,000
Fourth quarter	3,000,000
	$14,000,000

The seasonal sales pattern experienced in 1972 is typical of the company's operations. For the past several years, the company has realized a steady growth in sales volume of 8% per year. This growth rate is expected to continue through 1973. In response to generally rising prices, the company plans to increase all selling prices by 6% effective January 1, 1973. This price increase is not expected to affect the pattern of growth in sales volume.

Required:

a) Prepare a sales forecast by quarters for 1973.

b) What would be the effect on total sales forecasted for 1973 if the price increase were expected not merely to halt the growth in sales volume but actually to cause a 5% reduction in volume in 1973?

2. The Kapiolani Company produces and sells a single product. The 1973 sales forecast in units of product is as follows:

First quarter...................................... 12,000
Second quarter.................................... 15,000
Third quarter..................................... 16,500
Fourth quarter.................................... 18,000

The inventory of finished product on January 1, 1973, is expected to contain 4,000 units. The planned inventory for the end of 1973 is 6,500 units.

Production is customarily scheduled to provide for two thirds of the current quarter's sales demand plus one third of the following quarter's demand. Thus, production anticipates sales volume by about one month.

The standard cost sheet for one unit of the product is as follows:

Materials (10 lbs. @ $.50)........................ $ 5.00
Direct labor (1½ hrs. @ $3.60).................... 5.40
Variable overhead (1½ hrs. @ $.80)............... 1.20
Fixed overhead (1½ hrs. @ $2).................... 3.00
                                                   $14.60

The standard fixed overhead rate was based upon a budgeted production volume of 90,000 direct labor hours for the year.

Required:

Prepare a production budget by quarters, showing the number of units produced and the total costs of materials, direct labor, variable overhead, and fixed overhead.

3. The Ala Moana Drug Corporation budgets sales in dollar volume only, as it sells a wide variety of individual items. The only breakdown of sales volume is according to four principal categories of products. Each category has demonstrated its own long-term rate of growth or decline in sales volume. Actual sales volumes in 1972 and long-term growth rates, by categories, are as follows:

Category	1972 Sales	Growth Rate
1.....................	$10,000,000	5%
2.....................	6,000,000	2
3.....................	15,000,000	−4
4.....................	9,000,000	10
	$40,000,000	

Required:

Prepare a long-range sales forecast, by categories, for the years 1973 through 1975.

4. The assembly department of the Kapahulu Toy Truck Company assembles each of the company's five models. The standard man-hours per toy in the assembly department and the budgeted output of each for the month of March, 1973, are given below:

Model	Standard Man-Hours	Budgeted Unit Output
Moving van..........................	½	3,600
Bulldozer...........................	¼	5,000
Cement mixer.......................	⅓	4,200
Trench digger......................	⅗	3,000
Dump truck........................	⅖	5,500

The budgeted variable overhead in the assembly department is $1.20 per man-hour. The budgeted fixed overhead for the year 1973 is $300,000. Budgeted volume for 1973 in the assembly department is 120,000 man-hours. The company uses absorption costing.

Required:

a) Compute the budgeted variable and fixed overhead costs, in total, for the assembly department for the month of March, 1973.

b) Does this budget include any budgeted under- or overapplied overhead? Explain.

5. The Hao Company uses 20,000 gallons of a chemical acid each year. This acid costs $50 per gallon, and the annual cost of carrying one gallon in inventory is $1. The company estimates that each purchase order, including all processing and handling, costs $125. The average interest rate paid by the company is 8%.

Required:

Compute the economic order quantity for purchases of this chemical acid.

6. The Piikoi Corporation wishes to purchase its raw materials in the most economical lot sizes. In order to achieve this objective, it applies the following economic order quantity formula to each of the various raw materials that it uses:

$$Q = \sqrt{\frac{2CS}{UI + A}}$$

For one of the company's raw materials, the cost of placing an order (*C*) is estimated to be $640. The annual usage (*S*) of this material is approximately 1,000,000 units. The unit cost (U) of the material is $1.50. The company's interest cost of capital (I) is 10%. The annual cost of carrying one unit in inventory (A) averages $.05.

Required:

a) Compute the economic order quantity (Q) in which this material should be purchased.

b) How would you expect each of the five variables under the radical to be measured? Which would you expect to be the most difficult to measure?

c) What additional factors, if any, not included in the formula might be considered in determining the lot size in which material should be ordered?

d) If each of the five variables, in turn, were increased by 50% with no change in any of the others, which increase would have the greatest effect on the economic order quantity? In other words, to which variable(s) is the economic order quantity most sensitive?

7. The Kaiulani Machine Tool Company manufactures precision instruments in its Ewa plant. There is no notable seasonal pattern to the sales of these instruments. The total production time for the instruments averages one and one-half months from start to completion. On December 31, 1972, there is an inventory of 2,400 finished units on hand. Unit sales for 1973 have been forecast as follows:

January	1,000	July	1,560
February	1,200	August	1,600
March	1,200	September	1,750
April	1,300	October	1,800
May	1,400	November	1,800
June	1,500	December	1,900

The productive capacity of the plant during 1973 is 2,000 units of product per month.

Required:

Prepare a monthly production schedule, in units, for precision instruments for 1973. This schedule should show units produced, units shipped to customers, and finished units in stock at the end of the month. Explain the inventory balance planned for December 31, 1973. On the basis of your production schedule, have you any further comments regarding the company's operations?

8. The Nuuanu Steel Corporation converts scrap steel into usable ingots. This conversion process requires just one working day. Finished ingots are shipped to customers as soon as they are completed. For every ton of scrap put into process, there is a yield of .75 ton of usable steel. In carload lots of 2,000 tons, scrap steel is purchased for $100 per ton. Freight charges for one carload are $6,000. In lots smaller than a carload, the price of scrap

steel is $120 per ton; and freight charges on these odd lots average $5 per ton.

Ordinarily, orders for scrap steel must be placed one month in advance of the date on which the materials are needed. The company's storage facilities can accommodate a maximum of 22,000 tons of scrap at one time. At December 31, 1972, the inventory of scrap consists of 14,000 tons. No scrap is on order at this date.

The sales forecast for the year 1973 is as follows:

Month	Ingot Tons	Month	Ingot Tons
January	9,000	July	13,800
February	10,200	August	12,600
March	11,400	September	12,000
April	15,000	October	12,000
May	15,000	November	10,800
June	14,400	December	9,900

Preliminary estimates indicate that about 10,200 ingot tons will be sold in January, 1974.

As a matter of company policy, all orders for scrap steel are placed on the first day of a month. Hence, all shipments may be expected to arrive on the first day of the following month. It is also the company's policy that the inventory of scrap steel not be allowed to fall below 2,000 tons at any time.

Required:

Prepare a schedule, by months, of scrap steel orders, purchases (i.e., receipts of orders), usage, and inventory balances and also of total purchase costs. The schedule should conform to production and inventory requirements as stipulated and should minimize total purchase costs for the year.

9. The Ala Wai Machine Company sells light machinery to manufacturers. Sales orders are obtained in two ways. Most are obtained by the company's salesmen when they call on customers. Others, called catalog orders, are placed directly by the customers. The salesmen leave catalogs with all of their customers for this purpose. Salesmen receive commissions of 5% of sales they obtain personally and 2% of catalog orders received from their territories.

Budgeted sales for 1973 are as follows:

Quarter	Total Sales	Salesmen's Orders	Catalog Orders
First	$ 5,000,000	80%	20%
Second	8,000,000	70	30
Third	10,000,000	60	40
Fourth	7,500,000	80	20

Shipping and billing expenses average 4% of sales revenue, regardless of the source of the order. Fixed selling expenses for 1973 have been budgeted as follows:

Sales salaries........................	$ 360,000
Advertising...........................	1,000,000
Travel................................	400,000

Sales salaries and travel expenses are paid out in a steady flow throughout the year. Advertising expenditures, however, will be made at irregular intervals in differing amounts. Actual advertising efforts are fairly steady throughout the year, however.

Required:

a) Prepare a budget of selling expenses, by quarters, for 1973.

b) Explain your allocation of fixed selling expenses to the several quarters.

c) It has been suggested that a 50% increase in budgeted advertising expenditures would double the proportion of catalog sales and would permit a 50% reduction in budgeted travel expenses. Would operations under this suggested plan be more profitable than presently budgeted operations? Support your answer with appropriate computations.

10. The Kamehameha Corporation manufactures two products, Kai and Lau. As of January 1, 1973, the inventory of finished products will include an estimated 20,000 units of Kai and 30,000 units of Lau. The sales forecast in units for 1973 is as follows:

Quarter	Kai	Lau
First......................	60,000	40,000
Second....................	40,000	40,000
Third.....................	50,000	50,000
Fourth....................	70,000	60,000

The unit selling prices of Kai and Lau are $8 and $12, respectively.

Both products are manufactured from a single raw material, the standard price of which is $.80 per pound. Standard usage per unit of Kai is 3 pounds and per unit of Lau is 4 pounds. At January 1, 1973, it has been estimated that the inventory of raw material will contain 140,000 pounds and that an additional 250,000 pounds will be on order. Delivery of materials is routinely made about one month after the order has been placed. Present storage facilities will hold no more than 400,000 pounds of raw material. The minimum stock of raw material considered safe at any given time is 100,000 pounds. All purchases must be in lots of 10,000 pounds.

The standard wage rate per hour in the factory is $2.50. The standard productions times are one man-hour for Kai and two man-hours for Lau. The standard variable overhead rate is $.75 per man-hour. The maximum productive capacity of the factory is 150,000 man-hours per quarter. This cannot be increased during 1973.

Variable selling expenses average 10% of selling prices. Budgeted fixed expenses for 1973 are as follows:

Manufacturing........................	$400,000
Selling...............................	150,000
Administration........................	200,000

The applicable income tax rate is 40%.

Planned inventory balances at December 31, 1973, have been set as follows:

Raw material......................	150,000 lbs.
Kai..............................	30,000 units
Lau..............................	25,000 units

The finished product warehouse will accommodate a maximum of 75,000 units of product—Kai and/or Lau. Any inventory in excess of that quantity must be stored in public warehouses at a cost of $1 per unit per quarter in storage. The company's production process is such that there is never any work in process at the end of a day.

Required:

Prepare the following budget schedules for the Kamehameha Corporation for the year 1973:

a)   Unit production schedule by products
b)   Production cost budget
c)   Materials purchase schedule
d)   Budgeted income statement in accordance with variable costing

Each of these schedules should show details by quarters. Where alternatives appear feasible, select that one which will tend to minimize the corporation's costs for the year.

11.   The Kalanianaole Company has three plants and manufactures two products. Because of technological differences in the production facilities, the cost to produce a unit of either product is not the same in all three plants. The difference between the unit costs of the two products in any one plant is wholly a consequence of differing materials contents. The time required to produce either product is the same in each plant. Hence, each plant's productive capacity in units is the same regardless of which product or mix of products is produced in it.

Following are the capacity and unit cost data for the three plants:

	Plant 1	*Plant 2*	*Plant 3*
Capacity in units........... 5,000		8,000	6,000
Unit cost to produce—			
Product A...............	$ 5	$ 8	$ 6
Product B...............	12	18	15

The sales forecast for the current period requires production of 10,000 units of Product A and 8,000 units of Product B. Naturally, management wishes to minimize the total cost of production.

Required:

Compute the budgeted output of products from the three plants that will minimize total production costs for the period. In other words, how many units of each product should be produced in each plant?

chapter 8

RESOURCE PLANNING: FINANCIAL BUDGETS

As STATED in Chapter 6, all budgets are expressed in financial terms, that is, in terms of money. There are, however, certain budgets which are concerned specifically with the financial function of the business enterprise. As is evident in the preceding chapter, the operating budget is concerned primarily with the functions of manufacturing, distribution, administration, and (where significant) research and development. The budgets discussed in this chapter involve the planning of the capital, both long-term and short-term, required in order for the budgeted operations to be carried on effectively. Hence, they are financial budgets in the narrow sense of relating to the planning of capital resources normally associated with the special area of responsibility of financial executives, such as the treasurer. If a firm is thought of as a complex operating machine, long-term capital may be thought of as the machinery and short-term capital, as the lubricant without which the machine cannot operate. The distinction between long- and short-term capital is not always readily identifiable, of course; but it is a useful one for purposes of discussion.

PLANNING SHORT-TERM CAPITAL

Short-term capital consists of those financial resources which flow into and out of a business in connection with the day-to-day operations of the firm and usually are provided by sources other than permanent or long-term investments by stockholders and creditors. This is not really a satisfactory definition, for it leaves many questions unanswered. If the proceeds of the sale of common stock are used to meet a current payroll, are those proceeds short-term or long-term capital? What is the status of

190

the proceeds of a two-year bank loan? While such questions are interesting, they need not be answered in order that we may have a workable concept of short-term capital. For practical purposes, we shall consider short-term capital to be synonymous with working capital, that is, the excess of current assets over current liabilities.[1] Whatever theoretical shortcomings this definition may have, it has the considerable practical advantage of ready measurability. In budgeting working capital, one current asset is of such great importance to the firm that considerable attention is given to it alone; and it is budgeted in great detail and with great care. This asset is, of course, cash.

Cash Budget

Cash is a critical asset in any firm, and its planning requires great care. Almost paradoxically, both too little and too much cash are undesirable from the viewpoint of good management. A certain amount of cash is necessary in order for a firm to carry on its day-to-day operations. Payrolls and other current obligations must be met on time. But cash is not an earning asset. No revenue derives from holding cash itself, whereas revenue does derive from such other assets as inventory, plant, and investments in securities. Thus, too little cash endangers the liquidity of a company and too much cash tends to restrict profitability. The basic objective of the cash budget is to plan cash profitably, that is, to plan for sufficient cash at all times to meet the needs of current operations and of such long-term projects as will require cash during the budget period but for no more cash than is reasonably necessary for these purposes. Unfortunately, cash planning, like all budgeting, is subject to a great deal of uncertainty. Hence, the cash budget normally calls for more than the minimum amount of cash required in order to allow some margin for error in planning. Further, management should always be prepared to obtain additional cash in the event that the normal sources fail to provide the amount needed for current operations. The sources and uses of cash in a business enterprise are commonly distinguished according to whether they relate to the ordinary operations of the firm or to other activities.

Operating Sources and Uses of Cash. In most firms, the principal source of cash is the sales of the company's products and/or services. In the case of cash sales, receipt of cash occurs at the time of sale. In the case of credit sales, receipt of cash occurs sometime after the sale. The average time required for cash to be received on credit sales is referred to as the average collection period for receivables. Obviously, this period must be taken into account in preparing a cash budget. For most firms, the

---

[1] Working capital can, of course, be a negative amount when current liabilities exceed current assets.

amount of credit sales will exceed the amount of cash that may be expected to be received as a result of those sales. Sales discounts, returns and allowances, and uncollectible accounts all reduce the amount of cash potentially collectible from credit customers.

Operating outlays of cash typically include payments to employees at regular payroll dates, remittances to the government and to others of amounts withheld from employees' wages and salaries, payments to suppliers for materials and supplies, payments for purchased services such as electricity and water, insurance premiums, property tax payments, and an almost endless variety of other items. Within quite restricted limits, the timing of cash outlays for current operations is subject to the control of management. Nevertheless, these outlays often must be made regardless of the timing of cash receipts from operations. Thus, the operating sources of cash during any given period may or may not be adequate to cover the operating outlays of that period. Where operating outlays are expected to exceed operating receipts during a period, the excess must be met either from a previously accumulated cash balance or from nonoperating sources.

Nonoperating Sources and Uses of Cash.   The principal nonoperating sources of cash are sales of long-lived assets and sales of securities. Assets sold may be either operating assets, such as plant and machinery, or nonoperating assets, such as stocks and bonds held as investments. It is important to remember that the sale of assets at a loss (i.e., at less than their book values), while reflected unfavorably on the income statement, still provides cash to the enterprise. Sales of securities should be interpreted broadly to include sales of stock (equity financing) and sales of all types of debt instruments, including bonds, commercial paper, and short-term notes (debt financing). Here again we see that the distinction between short-term and long-term capital is not a sharp one. Cash, the most liquid current asset, may be provided by either a 30-day note or a 30-year bond issue.

Nonoperating uses of cash include such transactions as purchases of long-lived assets, repayments of debt, retirements of stock, payments of dividends, payments of interest, and payments of income taxes. Even though an asset purchased is an operating asset (e.g., a production machine), the outlay for it is considered a nonoperating cash disbursement in the period of payment, for the asset will benefit the operations of several periods. Although interest and divdened payments may be normal and recurrent, they are generally not regarded as part of the operations of a business but, rather, as costs of obtaining the capital with which to conduct operations. Assuming continuous profitable operation, income taxes also are recurrent; but they are not costs of operations in the ordinary sense.

The Cash Budget Illustrated.   Table 8–1 is the cash budget schedule of Shadbolt Products, Inc., for the year 1972. It is prepared on a monthly

TABLE 8-1

Cash Budget for Shadbolt Products, Inc. (Fiscal Year 1972)
(thousands of dollars)

	Jan.	Feb.	March	April	May	June	July	August	Sept.	Oct.	Nov.	Dec.	Year's Summary
Operating receipts:													
Cash sales	$ 625	$ 600	$ 560	$ 500	$ 450	$ 450	$ 500	$ 600	$ 675	$ 750	$ 750	$ 650	$ 7,110
Collections on account	4,756	4,709	4,321	4,092	4,051	3,971	4,068	4,330	4,778	5,503	6,314	6,285	57,178
	$5,381	$5,309	$4,881	$4,592	$4,501	$4,421	$4,568	$4,930	$5,453	$6,253	$7,064	$6,935	$64,288
Operating outlays:													
Payrolls	$2,264	$2,263	$2,265	$2,264	$2,262	$2,265	$2,265	$2,264	$2,263	$2,266	$2,264	$2,264	$27,169
Payments to suppliers	1,475	1,481	1,486	1,488	1,487	1,485	1,491	1,487	1,488	1,485	1,489	1,485	17,827
Factory overhead	711	710	711	712	710	711	710	712	712	712	710	710	8,531
Distribution expenses	342	341	340	340	341	340	341	342	343	343	345	342	4,100
Administrative expenses	125	125	125	125	125	125	125	125	125	125	125	125	1,500
Research expenses	66	67	67	66	67	67	66	67	67	66	67	67	800
	$4,983	$4,987	$4,994	$4,995	$4,992	$4,993	$4,998	$4,997	$4,998	$4,997	$5,000	$4,993	$59,927
Net cash from operations	$ 398	$ 322	$ (113)	$ (403)	$ (491)	$ (572)	$ (430)	$ (67)	$ 455	$1,256	$2,064	$1,942	$ 4,361
Nonoperating receipts:													
Sale of land		$ 145											$ 145
Short-term borrowing					$ 394	$1,182	$ 394	$ 493	$1,379				3,842
		$ 145			$ 394	$1,182	$ 394	$ 493	$1,379				$ 3,987
Gross cash provided	$ 398	$ 467	$ (113)	$ (403)	$ (97)	$ 610	$ (36)	$ 426	$1,834	$1,256	$2,064	$1,942	$ 8,348
Nonoperating outlays:													
Interest				$ 150						$ 150			$ 300
Dividends	$ 100			100			$ 100			100			400
Income taxes			$ 350			$ 400			$ 400			$ 400	1,550
Repayment of short-term loans								$ 400	1,200	400	$ 500	1,400	3,900
	$ 100		$ 350	$ 250		$ 400	$ 100	$ 400	$1,600	$ 650	$ 500	$1,800	$ 6,150
Net cash provided	$ 298	$ 467	$ (463)	$ (653)	$ (97)	$ 210	$ (136)	$ 26	$ 234	$ 606	$1,564	$ 142	$ 2,198
Beginning cash balance	821	1,119	1,586	1,123	470	373	583	447	473	707	1,313	2,877	821
Ending cash balance	$1,119	$1,586	$1,123	$ 470	$ 373	$ 583	$ 447	$ 473	$ 707	$1,313	$2,877	$3,019	$ 3,019

basis. It is not sufficient to say that total cash receipts for the year will exceed cash disbursements. The sequence of the receipts and disbursements in relation to each other is extremely important so that temporary cash excesses or shortages may be foreseen and appropriate plans made. As a matter of fact, operational cash budgeting must be on a day-to-day basis. The fact that the net cash flow for a month is expected to be satisfactory is no assurance that a cash shortage will not develop sometime during that month. It would be impractical to construct a formal cash budget schedule for each working day of the year, but financial management's continuous planning of cash must assure that the firm's cash position will be adequate each day. In many firms, a weekly cash budget is prepared for a total period of less than one year—often for one quarter at a time. Additionally, a formal daily forecast may be prepared each day for the next working day.

In Table 8-1, budgeted cash receipts from and outlays for operations are reported first and the net cash provided by operations is shown. Then nonoperating sources and uses are added and deducted, respectively. The resultant figure at this point is the net cash generated by the firm during the period. Adding to this the cash balance at the beginning of the period yields the ending balance for the period. Cash provided by short-term borrowing is included in the body of Table 8-1. The need for this borrowing was first determined by preparing the cash budget without it and observing the timing and amounts of cash deficiencies which would have to be covered by borrowing.

Profitable Cash Management. As indicated in the preceding paragraph, the cash budget is used to determine the timing and amounts of short-term borrowings required to maintain liquidity in the enterprise. It should also be used to determine when excess cash is expected to be on hand so that financial management may plan to employ that cash productively. Where excess cash balances will be available temporarily, it is common business practice to invest such balances in short-term marketable securities. Among the most popular securities for this purpose are 90-day U.S. Treasury bills, certificates of deposit, and short-term commercial paper issued by large finance companies. Any security, however, including common stock, may be purchased and held as a short-term investment of temporarily idle cash. The advantage of converting idle cash into securities is obvious. The securities yield a return in the form of interest and/or dividends; cash, in itself, generates no earnings. Securities are, of course, subject to market fluctuations. Thus, their yields may be enhanced by gains when they are sold if the market has risen or offset by losses if the market has declined. Maximizing the total yield on these investments is the responsibility of financial management. Assuming that the management of Shadbolt Products believes that $750,000 is the maximum cash balance which it ever needs to carry, the cash budget in Table 8–1 indicates that excess cash balances could be turned to short-term investments during the first and fourth quarters of 1972. Conversely, assuming that the minimum acceptable cash balance is believed to be $400,000, short-term borrowing would be necessary during the second and third quarters. Even then, the cash balance would dip slightly below the minimum desired balance at the end of May; presumably, this minor deviation from the usual policy is here regarded as tolerable. Seasonal variations in cash flows and cash requirements are quite common.

Working Capital Budget

In addition to the cash budget, a firm may want a formal budget of total working capital, by months or quarters, for the budget period. This budget would include cash as indicated in the cash budget and short-term marketable securities, the purchase and resale of which would be suggested by the cash budget. In addition, the working capital budget would present expected balances of receivables, inventories, prepaid expenses, and miscellaneous current assets. The receivables, in most instances, would derive chiefly from planned sales to credit customers. There might also be receivables from employees, from affiliated companies, and from anyone else to whom the firm might extend credit for one reason or another. Budgeted inventories of materials, work in process, and finished product would be derived from budgeted production and, in the case of finished product, from the sales forecast also. Budgeted prepaid expenses would be determined on the basis of company policies, such as the use of a postage meter, and also on the basis of contractual commitments, such as insurance premium prepayments.

Current liabilities typically include such items as trade accounts payable, notes payable, and accrued expenses. Trade accounts arise principally from purchases of materials and/or supplies, and these are planned as part of the production budget. Notes payable would include the firm's own notes discounted at the bank; these obligations would be planned as part of the cash budget as explained in the preceding section. Among the commonest accrued expenses are accrued wages and salaries, which arise simply because the regular payroll dates do not always coincide with the dates on which financial statements are prepared.

Lest the discussion in the foregoing paragraphs be interpreted as suggesting that the working capital budget is prepared quite mechanically and is of little significance, we must observe that a firm's working capital position is of great importance to it as an indicator of its credit standing. Rightly or wrongly, institutions (notably banks) which grant short-term credit to business enterprises typically place considerable emphasis upon the existence and maintenance of a satisfactory working capital position, commonly measured by the current ratio (the ratio of current assets to current liabilities). Hence, planning working capital may be viewed as one facet of planning short-term borrowing.

LONG-TERM CAPITAL PLANNING

Budgeting cash and working capital is almost invariably restricted to the immediate budget period, usually no more than one year in the future. Continuous operation at a profit demands more extensive planning for future resources, however. There is no limit on the number of future periods for which capital resources should be planned. A good general rule is that capital planning should be extended as far into the future as is practicable and meaningful. For some industrial firms, this may be no more than five years. For other enterprises, such as public utilities, capital planning may reasonably be projected for 20 or more years into the future. For purposes of discussion here, we shall consider first the sources from which long-term capital may be expected to be obtained, then the cost of this capital, and finally the uses of the capital by the firm. Obviously, the sources and uses of capital are related. Firms often seek capital with a specific use in mind. A firm that has demonstrated its ability to make profitable use of the capital it obtains will typically find more sources of additional capital open to it. Conversely, persistent unprofitable uses of capital will have the effect of closing off sources. Nevertheless, obtaining capital and using capital are distinct activities and they entail separate decisions. Capital, once obtained, may be used for any legitimate purpose; and it may be used sequentially for various purposes. The decision to obtain capital and the selection of sources of capital is commonly referred to as the *financing decision*. Uses of capital are the objects of the *investment decision*.

Sources of Long-Term Capital

Debt Financing. Long-term capital sources are commonly classified as either debt or equity financing. Debt financing for long periods is usually accomplished by the sale of bonds, by mortgages, or by bank term loans. While considered as long-term borrowing, term loans are seldom of as long maturities as bonds or mortgages. There are, of course, differences among these various sources of debt capital; there are several different types of bonds alone. These differences are not of particular significance to the present discussion, however. All debt financing has certain common features which are relevant to long-term capital planning. To begin with, all debts have maturity dates at which they must be repaid. Even though a firm may plan to repay one long-term obligation with the proceeds of a new one, it must still make such a plan and arrange for the new borrowing. Perhaps the most important single aspect of debt financing is the interest charge which accompanies it. Interest payments must be made in stipulated amounts and at specified times, regardless of the profitability of operations or of the cash position of the firm. Failure to meet interest payments normally means that the principal amount of the debt becomes due immediately, and it may well precipitate the liquidation of the enterprise. Thus, a decision to obtain long-term capital by borrowing involves a concomitant commitment to fixed cash disbursements at regular intervals with the attendant threat of serious consequences should those disbursements not be made on schedule.

Long-term borrowing may impose additional restrictions upon a firm. Bond indentures frequently contain provisions designed to protect the bondholders by limiting further financial activities of the bond issuer. Examples of such restrictions are limitations upon dividend payments, prohibitions against additional borrowing, and requirements of minimum working capital balances. Each of these restrictions narrows the scope of management's discretion as to operations for as long as the debt is outstanding. For example, a requirement of a particular working capital position, typically measured by the current ratio, may prevent management from taking advantage of a potentially profitable opportunity because such action would temporarily reduce the current ratio below the required minimum.

Equity Financing.   Long-term capital provided by the owners of an enterprise is generally referred to as equity capital. It may be provided directly by them through investments of their personal wealth in the enterprise, or it may be provided indirectly by the reinvestment of enterprise earnings in the business. In a corporation, direct investments by owners are effected by sales of the corporation's stock. Indirect investments are usually measured by the amount of retained earnings in the corporation. Equity capital is normally regarded as permanently invested in the firm. With certain exceptions, such as the issuance of redeemable preferred stock, it is not contemplated that amounts paid for stock will ever be repaid to the stockholders by the corporation. This does not mean that equity capital is not subject to reduction. Just as retained earnings increase the stockholders' investment, accumulated losses may reduce their investment. In fact, continuous losses may completely eliminate the stockholders' capital investment and may erode capital provided by debt financing as well. (Such would be the case where total liabilities exceeded total assets.)

To the extent that future profits may be predicted, long-range capital planning may be predicated in part upon the expectation of the reinvestment of enterprise earnings. In an expanding company, however, it is likely that reinvested earnings will not be sufficient to meet all future capital needs. Further, stockholders' desires for dividends place a practical limitation on the amount of income that may be retained in the business. Thus, most successful firms find that they must periodically obtain additional long-term capital by selling additional shares of stock or by borrowing. Some of the considerations which should precede a decision to borrow were discussed in the preceding section. While stock does not command a regular fixed dividend comparable to the interest on bonds, the practical exigencies of good stockholder relations demand that reasonable dividends be paid more or less regularly. In a closely held corporation, such as a family business, sale of stock to outsiders may endanger the close control enjoyed by the present stockholders. Loss of control may be prevented by the sale of nonvoting stock. Most nonvoting stock is preferred stock, which normally carries a cumulative preference as to dividends. For a number of reasons, there is little market for nonvoting common stock.[2]

The Cost of Capital

One of the principal factors to be considered in any decision is the cost to be incurred. This is no less true of a decision regarding sources of capital than it is of any other decision. All capital has a cost. Any assumption that a particular type or source of capital is cost-free is erroneous. The cost of capital is not uniform, however. It may be different in different firms, at different times in a single firm, and for different sources of capital. Thus, one must be precise in discussing the cost of capital so that there is no confusion as to the particular cost in question. For purposes of discussion here, we shall deal with two concepts of the cost of capital. The first is the *specific cost of capital*. This is the cost associated with one specific source of financing. The second is the *average cost of capital*, a weighted average of the costs of all of the various sources of financing in a firm at a given time. These will be considered in greater detail below. One additional general observation is necessary at this point, however. The cost of capital that is relevant to management for decision making is the current cost, that is, the cost of capital that reflects current conditions in the capital markets. The cost that happened to obtain the last time the firm actually went into the markets for capital is no longer relevant. Only the current cost is.

Cost of Debt Capital. The specific cost of debt capital is the effective after-tax interest rate on the market value of the outstanding debt securities of a firm. Since there may be several different classes of debt securities outstanding at a given time, there may be several different effective interest costs to the firm. Interest on debt capital is unique among the various specific costs of capital in that it is deductible for income tax

---

[2] The New York Stock Exchange will not even list nonvoting common stock.

purposes. Thus, the actual cost to the firm is less than the effective interest on the debt. It is the effective interest rate multiplied by the complement of the income tax rate. For example, if the effective interest rate is 8% before tax and the income tax rate is 40%, the net cost of that particular debt capital is 4.8% (8% × 60%).

The effective interest rate on debt is determined by current market conditions. It is not necessarily the same as the nominal, or coupon, interest rate nor the same as the effective interest at the date on which the debt securities were initially issued. The effective interest rate on a particular debt security can be determined from the nominal interest rate, the remaining period of time prior to the maturity of the debt, and the current market price of the security. For example, a $1,000 bond with a nominal interest rate of 6% payable semiannually (i.e., $30 of interest is paid to the holder every six months), due after 10 years, and currently selling in the market for $864 has an effective interest rate of 8%. This, of course, is before tax. If the bond issuer's income tax rate is 40%, his net interest cost on this bond is 4.8%, as explained above. The effective interest on debt can be computed rather tediously by the use of formulas, or it can be determined quickly from published tables of bond interest. The 8% current effective interest rate on the $1,000 bond above differs from the 6% nominal rate. It may very well differ also from the effective rate at which the bond was initially issued. If the bond had originally been issued 10 years ago at a price of $955, it then had an effective interest rate of 6.4%. Neither that original market rate nor the nominal rate is now the appropriate measure of the cost of capital from that bond, however.

Although the formulas for the precise computation of the effective interest rate on debt are complex and involve present value concepts that we shall not discuss until Chapter 15, a fairly simple formula will provide a reasonable approximation of the effective interest rate. It is as follows:

$$k = (1 - t) \frac{R + \left(\dfrac{P - M}{n}\right)}{\frac{1}{2}(P + M)}$$

where

k = the specific cost of debt capital
t = the applicable income tax rate
R = the nominal interest rate on the debt multiplied by the par or face value (P) of the outstanding debt
P = the par or face value of the outstanding debt
M = the market value of the outstanding debt
n = the number of years to maturity of the debt

If this formula is applied to the $1,000 bond in the preceding paragraph, the result is very close to the effective interest cost of 8% before tax and 4.8% after tax.

$$k = (1 - .40) \frac{60 + \left(\dfrac{1,000 - 864}{10}\right)}{\frac{1}{2}(1,000 + 864)} = .60(.079) = .0474$$

This formula indicates an effective interest cost of 7.9% before tax and 4.74% after tax. While not exact, these figures are certainly useful approximations of the true interest costs.

Cost of Preferred Stock. Legally, preferred stock is part of a corporation's equity capital. It represents an ownership interest, not a creditor's claim. Economically, however, it has characteristics more like long-term debt than like common stock. There is a fixed annual dividend payable on preferred stock. Generally, this dividend must be paid before any dividends can be paid to common stockholders; and it cannot be increased, regardless of the amount of profits earned.[3] The cost of preferred stock capital is computed simply by dividing the amount of the fixed annual dividend by the current market price of the stock. Thus, if the dividend is $7 per share and the market price is $78 per share, the specific cost of capital is 9%. This is essentially the same calculation used for a bond, except that it is simplified by the absence of any maturity date and it is not tax deductible.

Cost of Common Equity. The specific costs of debt and preferred stock derive basically from fixed periodic interest and dividend payments. There is no fixed periodic dividend on common stock. If earnings or cash balances do not warrant dividend payments for a particular year, none need be paid. Conversely, where earnings and cash are sufficient, there is no other upper limit on the dividends that may be distributed to common stockholders. Thus, the current dividend payout is not a valid indicator of the specific cost of common equity capital. When an investor purchases a share of common stock in a corporation, he is looking toward earnings and dividends over an indefinite future period. This is true whether he expects to realize his return on the investment by holding the stock indefinitely and receiving dividends or by reselling the stock to someone else at a later date. Thus, the relationship between expected future dividends and the current market price of the stock is the basis for determining the specific cost of capital. Inasmuch as future dividends may reasonably be expected to increase over time, no single dollar amount readily

---

[3] This statement is true of most preferred stock. Some preferred stock, however, is classified as participating. That is, the preferred stockholders have the right to participate with the common stockholders in distributions of relatively large dividends. In this case, the specific cost of preferred stock would tend to be equal to the specific cost of the common equity.

represents those dividend expectations. Hence, the cost of common capital may be approximated by dividing the current dividend by the market price of the common stock and adding to the quotient a factor that represents the anticipated rate of growth in dividends in the future. This may be shown as follows:[4]

$$k = \frac{D}{M} + g$$

where

k = the specific cost of common equity capital,
D = the current dividend per share of common stock,
M = the current market price per share of common stock,
g = the expected average annual rate of growth in dividends.

The specific cost determined in accordance with the foregoing formula is applicable to all of the capital provided by common stockholders. This includes both amounts directly invested by stockholders when they purchased shares of stock from the corporation (i.e., contributed capital) and amounts reinvested from earnings (i.e., retained earnings). When an investor purchases a share of common stock, he obtains an equity in the corporation. The total of all common shareholders' equities appears in the corporate balance sheet as the sum of the contributed common capital plus the retained earnings (or total stockholders' equity minus preferred shareholders' equity). Retained earnings are as much a part of the common equity as the common stock itself. Hence, the market price of the common stock reflects the sum of the contributed capital and the reinvested earnings—as well, of course, as future earnings and dividend prospects.

Some might be tempted to consider depreciation as another source of capital, but this would be an error. It is true that net income plus depreciation usually provides a reasonable approximation of the amount of working capital generated by operations during a period. However, only the net income portion of that represents an increment to total capital. And even that increment is typically reduced by current dividend payments. Depreciation, however, reflects simply a conversion of capital held in the form of long-lived assets to working capital. Thus, it represents a change in the composition of the assets derived from the total invested capital of the firm; but it is not in any sense an increase in that total capital.

Average Cost of Capital. It is common practice to regard current liabilities as an offset to current assets rather than as a distinct portion of total invested capital. Thus, total capital (or capitalization, or capital

---

[4] Harold Bierman, Jr., and Seymour Smidt, *The Capital Budgeting Decision* (2d ed.; New York: The Macmillan Co., 1966), p. 157.

structure) is usually considered to comprise long-term debt and stock-holders' equity. The average cost of capital is then computed from the specific costs of these sources. It is an average of the specific costs, weighted by the respective market values of the total capital provided from each source. This is illustrated in Table 8–2. In lines 1 through 8 of the table, the specific cost of each source of capital is computed. Each specific cost listed in line 8 is then multiplied by the percentage that the

TABLE 8–2

Computation of Average Cost of Capital

	\multicolumn{5}{c}{*Source of Capital*}
	\multicolumn{2}{c}{*Bonds*}	\multicolumn{2}{c}{*Stocks*}	
	1st Mortgage	*Debenture*	*Preferred*	*Common*	*Total*
Basic Data:					
1. Maturity Value......	$20,000	$100,000			
2. Nominal Interest Rate..........	6%	7½%			
3. Years to Maturity...	8	22			
4. Annual Interest or Dividend.......	$ 1,200	$ 7,500	$ 3,000	$ 12,000	
5. Market Value of Capital.........	$17,700	$ 85,800	$40,000	$200,000	$343,500
Specific Cost of Capital:					
6. Preliminary.........	8.0%	9.0%	7.5%	6.0	
7. Growth Factor......	—	—	—	5.0%	
8. After Tax at 40%...	4.8%	5.4%	7.5%	11.0%	
Percentage of Total Market Value.......	5.2%	25.0%	11.6%	58.2%	100.0%
Average Cost of Capital...	.25%	1.35%	.87%	6.40%	8.87%

market value of that particular source of capital bears to the total market value of all capital. The sum of the resultant products (in the total column) is the average cost of capital for the firm. In this illustration, the average cost of capital is computed as 8.87%. For all practical purposes, this would probably be taken as 9%. This illustration is not advanced as representative of what the actual cost of capital is likely to be in any particular company. It simply demonstrates the mechanics of computing the average cost of capital.

Long-Term Capital Investments

Resource Allocation. The problems and procedures associated with the planning of long-term capital investments are popularly referred to as *capital budgeting*. The basic problem of capital budgeting is to ascertain the most profitable uses of the scarce capital available to the firm. In most firms, the various opportunities for investment exceed the available capital. Thus, the capital budgeting process must strive to identify the most profitable of the alternative investment opportunities in order that the scarce capital of the enterprise will be employed most effectively. Profitability, it must be remembered, is a long-run objective; and the maximum long-run profit is never determinable in advance with certainty. Thus, management must weigh a variety of factors relative to each alternative investment opportunity; and not all of these factors are readily translatable into rates of profit. Despite the difficulties involved in estimating the profit potentials of alternative investments, it is very important that management be able to forecast investment profitability and to do so with a high degree of success. Long-term capital investments, by definition, commit the enterprise's capital to particular projects and/or assets for long periods of time. Just as the profits from such investments are expected to continue for a long time, losses resulting from them are likely to persist also. And the abandonment of unprofitable long-term projects or long-lived assets is likely to entail the loss of a substantial portion, if not all, of the capital invested therein.

Chapter 15 will discuss quantitative techniques for evaluating the relative profit potentials of alternative investment opportunities. Before considering these techniques, however, we must examine the relevance of particular types of costs in specific decision-making situations. At this point it is appropriate only to make one observation concerning these techniques. While the mathematical methodologies of the techniques are precise, so long as the data to which the techniques are applied are estimates, the conclusions drawn from the techniques are estimates also.

Project Planning. Long-term capital investments may take many forms. They may involve the acquisition of long-lived tangible assets, such as buildings and machinery. They may involve purchases of intangible assets such as franchises, leaseholds, and patents. Major advertising and other promotional programs frequently entail long-term commitments of substantial amounts of capital. An investment in a going concern—the acquisition of a subsidiary corporation, for example—is likely to include all of the foregoing types of investments. Whatever the nature of the particular investment, it should be defined and measured carefully. Most investments involve some initial outlay of capital, but this outlay may not be the full measure of the investment. The construction of a factory, for example, commits the firm not only to the purchase price of the building and equipment but also to many years' operating costs and to the additional working capital necessary to support the operation of the plant. Both the amounts and the timing of these several outlays are very important to effective capital budgeting. Outlays must be compared with receipts expected to be derived from the investment over its useful life in order to evaluate its profit potential. Commonly, the profit potential of long-term investment projects is stated as a rate of return on the amount invested.

Typically, the need for or desirability of a particular long-term investment is first determined by the responsible executive who would be most concerned with it. The sales manager is likely to originate the idea for a major promotional program; a department supervisor will probably first suggest the replacement of a piece of machinery or the purchase of additional machines; and the controller may propose the acquisition of a computer. Executives request that corporate funds be allocated to particular projects. It is not at all unusual for the sum of such requests to exceed the amount of available capital. Thus, priorities must be assigned by top management. These priorities are based upon an analysis of the relative profit potentials of the several projects. The responsible executives prepare estimates of total outlays required for their respective projects, along with the timing thereof, and estimates of the revenues to be derived from them. Each executive requesting an allocation of capital must justify it in terms of the long-run objectives of the entire firm. Top management then coordinates the various requests for capital expenditures with the expected amount of available long-term capital and determines which projects will be undertaken and in what sequence.

Effective control over capital expenditures requires that actual spending be consistent with planned outlays for approved projects. Often, of course, it proves necessary to spend more or less for a particular project than was originally anticipated. Any excess spending should be specifically justified and approved. It must be observed here, however, that it may be difficult to avoid additional expenditures once a project has been started and capital committed to it. For example, a building may be planned at a total cost of $8,000,000. After construction has begun and several millions of dollars have been spent, it may be determined that the total cost will actually be $12,000,000. Despite the fact that this represents a 50% increase over the amount originally budgeted, management may feel that it has no alternative to spending the additional $4,000,000. At this point, the choice may be between spending the additional money for a completed building which can be used to produce revenue or abandoning the construction project and any hope of revenue from it. In a situation such as this, the expected revenues from use of the building must be adequate to justify the *future* outlays necessary to complete the structure. The amount already expended is not relevant; it is a sunk cost. It cannot be recovered if the building is left unfinished. Even if only a portion of it can be recovered by completion of the building, such completion would be financially advantageous. The future costs are the relevant ones for decision making.

THE BUDGETED BALANCE SHEET

In current accounting practice, the financial resources of a firm are summarized periodically in the form of a balance sheet or statement of financial position. As a part of the master budget, a budgeted balance sheet is sometimes included to indicate the anticipated financial position of the firm at the close of the budget period and, perhaps, at selected dates during the period. Just as the actual balance sheet has come to be regarded by many as less important than the income statement, the budgeted balance sheet is likely to be viewed as less useful to management than the budgeted income statement and related component operating budget schedules. One study of budget practices showed that only 56% of the firms observed prepared budgeted balance sheets, whereas 98% of them prepared budgeted income statements.[5] Nevertheless, a budgeted balance sheet should be of some use in identifying the anticipated consequences of budgeted operations for a period.

BUDGET REVIEW REPORTS

The importance of budgetary review in the managerial control process was mentioned in Chapter 6. At the periodic meetings of the budget committee, budget review reports comparing actual and budgeted performances are studied and discussed. In order that these discussions may be pointed and fruitful, the reports should be prepared and disseminated in sufficient time before the meeting that the responsible executives may study them, pursue any material variations of actual data from the budget, and attempt to identify the causes thereof.

Shadbolt Products, Inc., holds its monthly budget review meeting on the 10th of each month to consider performance of the previous month and of the year to date. Table 8–3 is an example of a budget review report. It is a sales report for the Western Division and is broken down by products. Actual data for the last month and for the year to date are compared with the pertinent budgeted sales data. The budgeted sales figures are taken from the sales forecast for the Western Division (Table 7–2). This report indicates that sales of industrial pumps have been exceeding budgeted volume. While both models of pumps sold more than the budgeted amounts for the month of October, the sales of the P-85 pump for the first 10 months of the year (in total) have been below budgeted volume. A substantial excess of actual over budgeted sales of the P-115 model has more than compensated for the reduced sales of the

---

[5] Burnard H. Sord and Glenn A. Welsch, *Business Budgeting: A Survey of Management Planning and Control Practices* (New York: Controllership Foundation, Inc., 1958), pp. 277 and 280.

P-85, however. For both the month and the year to date, sales of both models of chain saws have lagged behind budgeted volume. It will be recalled that the company planned sales of chain saws for 1972 on the assumption that its share of the total market for these products would increase from 2% to 4%. Evidently this assumption has not been validated by actual sales.

Knowing the amounts of deviations of actual data from the budget is only the beginning of the control process, of course. The really important step is the next one, attempting to determine why these deviations occurred. Causes of favorable deviations are just as imporant as causes

TABLE 8–3

Sales Report for Shadbolt Products, Inc., Western Division, for the Month Ended
October 31, 1972
(thousands of dollars)

	October			Year to Date		
	Actual	*Budget*	*Variance*	*Actual*	*Budget*	*Variance*
Industrial pumps:						
P-115...........	$2,520	$2,400	$120	$15,504	$14,400	$1,104
P-85...........	1,435	1,400	35	7,770	8,050	(280)
Total.......	$3,955	$3,800	$155	$23,274	$22,450	$ 824
Chain saws:						
C-7...........	$ 258	$ 288	$(30)	$ 3,672	$ 3,888	$ (216)
C-3...........	248	250	(2)	3,250	3,350	(100)
Total.......	$ 506	$ 538	$(32)	$ 6,922	$ 7,238	$ (316)
Total sales........	$4,461	$4,338	$123	$30,196	$29,688	$ 508

of unfavorable ones. If the company is able to identify the reasons for the increased demand for the P-115 model pump, it may be able to direct its efforts toward those reasons to reinforce and extend them. On the other hand, the causes of the lower demand for the company's chain saws should be sought out and, if possible, corrected. If the company has failed to obtain the percentage of the chain saw market that it forecast, it should attempt to learn the reason. Perhaps the price is too high and/or the product quality is too low relative to competing saws. Perhaps promotion of the chain saw line is inadequate. And perhaps the sales goal, which represented a doubling of the company's share of the market, was unrealistic to begin with. Whatever the reason, the essence of control is finding that reason and taking such action as is appropriate to correct the situation.

Similar budget review reports would be prepared for all segments of the firm and for all aspects of operations. Expense reports with comparative budget data will be illustrated in the following chapter.

QUESTIONS FOR DISCUSSION

1. Distinguish between short-term and long-term capital. Of what significance to management is this distinction?

2. What basic rules should be observed in effective cash planning?

3. Cash budgeting has sometimes been described as the process of reconciling conflicting objectives regarding cash in the most satisfactory possible compromise. To what conflicting objectives does this description refer? Is the conflict real?

4. If a firm already has prepared a good cash budget, of what further value is a budget of working capital?

5. How might alternative accounting principles affect a budget of working capital? How might they affect a budgeted balance sheet?

6. What is the cost of capital? Why is it an important factor in the managerial function of planning?

7. What is the difference between a specific cost of capital and a firm's average cost of capital? Why might the specific costs of various sources of capital differ from one another?

8. Does a charitable organization, whose only source of capital is donations, have a cost of capital?

9. What are the essential problems involved in capital budgeting?

10. "In the implementation of any long-term investment project, there is always some 'point of no return' beyond which it is impractical and unreasonable to abandon the project." Assuming for the moment that this assertion is valid, how would one identify this "point of no return"? Now, is the assertion really valid? Explain.

11. Why do you suppose more business firms prepare budgeted income statements than prepare budgeted balance sheets? Do you believe their reasons are valid?

12. What improvements might be made in the budget review report in Table 8–3 in this chapter to make it more useful to management?

13. "The operating budget must be prepared before the financial budgets, for the latter are dependent upon the former, particularly as regards cash and working capital generated by operations. The operating budget is independent of financial budgets, however, and may be completed without regard to them." Discuss the validity of these statements.

PROBLEMS

1. The Kern Corporation manufactures and sells a single product. All sales are for cash at a standard price of $25 per unit. All out-of-pocket costs are paid

in cash at the time they are incurred. This includes the cost of raw materials, which are purchased locally every other day as they are required in production. Goods are produced only to order; there are no inventories.

The sales forecast, in units of product, for 1973 is as follows:

First quarter...................................... 8,000
Second quarter.................................... 12,000
Third quarter..................................... 16,000
Fourth quarter.................................... 14,000

The standard cost sheet for one unit of product appears below:

Raw materials (10 lbs. @ $.50)................ $ 5
Direct labor (2 hrs. @ $4).................... 8
Variable overhead (2 hrs. @ $1.50)............ 3
Fixed overhead (2 hrs. @ $2).................. _4_
                                             $20

Fixed overhead was budgeted at $200,000 for the year, and production volume was budgeted at 100,000 labor hours for the year.

Variable selling expenses amount to $.50 per unit sold. Fixed selling expenses average $30,000 per quarter.

Depreciation of $25,000 per quarter is included in budgeted fixed overhead, and depreciation of $10,000 per quarter is included in the budgeted fixed selling expenses.

Required:

Prepare a schedule of cash generated by operations, by quarters, for 1973.

2. The Cohan Corporation has the following capital structure as of December 31, 1972:

	Market Value of Outstanding Securities	Specific Cost of Capital
Debenture bonds...............	$20,000,000	6%
Mortgage bonds...............	10,000,000	5
Preferred stock................	15,000,000	8
Common stock.................	55,000,000	12

Required:

Compute the average cost of capital of the Cohan Corporation.

3. The Romberg Steel Products Company's operating budget for 1973 includes the following revenues and expenses involving cash receipts and disbursements:

	First Quarter	Second Quarter	Third Quarter	Fourth Quarter
Sales on account........	$2,000,000	$1,500,000	$1,800,000	$2,400,000
Purchases of materials on				
account.............	400,000	400,000	450,000	500,000
Payroll...............	700,000	700,000	800,000	900,000
Miscellaneous expenses..	300,000	300,000	300,000	300,000

The company's experience indicates that 70% of accounts receivable are collected in the quarter in which the sales are made; 20% are collected in the following quarter; 6% are collected in the second following quarter; and 4% prove to be uncollectible. Sales in the third and fourth quarters of 1972 were $1,600,000 and $1,800,000, respectively.

Half of the materials purchased during a quarter are paid for in that quarter, and the other half are paid for in the following quarter. Purchases during the fourth quarter of 1972 totaled $420,000. Payrolls and miscellaneous expenses are paid for in the quarter in which incurred.

Nonoperating cash outlays call for dividend payments of $75,000 on the last day of each quarter. In addition, bond interest in the amount of $50,000 is payable on June 30; and $30,000 is payable on December 31. Further, serial bonds in the principal amount of $800,000 will mature on June 30, 1973, and must be paid from the regular cash account.

The cash balance at January 1, 1973, will be $120,000. The minimum cash balance considered necessary is $100,000.

Required:

Prepare a cash budget, by quarters, for 1973. If borrowing is necessary at any time during the year, include it in this budget. Assume that all borrowing will be for a period of one quarter (but may be renewed by new loans for additional periods of one quarter) and will bear interest at 8% per annum.

4. The Berlin Chemical Corporation has the following long-term capital outstanding as of December 31, 1972:

Bonds with a face value of $20,000,000 were issued in 1955 and are due on December 31, 1984. The nominal interest rate on these bonds is 6% per annum. They are currently selling in the market at 96. (That is, a bond with a face value of $1,000 is selling for $960.)

One hundred thousand shares of preferred stock with a par value of $100 are outstanding. The annual dividend is $7.50 per share. This stock is presently selling on the market at $108 per share.

One million shares of $5 par value common stock is issued and outstanding. The current market price per share is $45. Annual dividends per share on this common stock for the past 10 years have been as follows:

1963	$1.00	1968	$1.47
1964	1.08	1969	1.59
1965	1.17	1970	1.72
1966	1.26	1971	1.86
1967	1.36	1972	2.00

The income tax rate is 40%.

Required:

Compute the corporation's average cost of capital. Include all necessary preliminary computations.

5. The Porter Company has completed its operating budget for 1973 and has prepared the following monthly analysis of budgeted cash provided by (or consumed in) operations:

January	$100,000	July	$(80,000)
February	60,000	August	10,000
March	30,000	September	30,000
April	(20,000)	October	70,000
May	(50,000)	November	100,000
June	(100,000)	December	120,000

The company adheres to a strict policy of cash management that is designed to provide adequate cash balances at all times and to avoid excessive balances. If the cash balance is between $50,000 and $100,000, the cash position is regarded as satisfactory and no specific action is taken. If the balance exceeds $100,000, the excess is invested in short-term marketable securities. These securities will be purchased and, when necessary, resold in even multiples of $1,000. They will earn interest at an annual rate of 6%, collectible when the securities are resold. For budget purposes, it is assumed that securities are resold at neither a gain nor a loss.

If the cash balance falls below $50,000, any short-term securities held will be sold. If the proceeds from such sales are not sufficient to restore the balance to $50,000, cash will be borrowed in even multiples of $1,000 at an annual interest rate of 8%, payable when the loans are repaid. As soon as the cash position permits, these short-term loans will be repaid.

As of January 1, 1973, the cash balance is expected to be $70,000. There will be no marketable securities on hand and no outstanding loans payable.

Required:

Prepare a schedule, by months, showing (*a*) anticipated cash balances, (*b*) cash provided by or consumed in operations, (*c*) amounts to be invested in short-term securities, (*d*) resales of short-term securities, (*e*) short-term borrowing, and (*f*) repayments of short-term loans. For simplicity, it may be assumed that all cash transactions occur on the last day of the month. Apply a first-in, first-out assumption when short-term marketable securities are sold.

6. The Friml Beverage Company plans to introduce a new soft drink, called Sparkle-Up, in 1973. Forecasted sales volume, in cases, for the company's five sales territories during 1973 is as follows:

Month	East	South	Midwest	West	Foreign
January..........	10,000	5,000	8,000	10,000	2,000
February.........	10,000	6,000	8,000	10,000	2,000
March...........	12,000	7,000	10,000	15,000	3,000
April............	15,000	8,000	12,000	18,000	3,000
May.............	18,000	9,000	14,000	24,000	4,000
June............	20,000	10,000	17,000	28,000	4,000
July............	25,000	12,000	20,000	30,000	4,000
August..........	25,000	15,000	20,000	35,000	5,000
September.......	22,000	15,000	18,000	35,000	5,000
October.........	20,000	14,000	16,000	30,000	5,000
November.......	18,000	13,000	15,000	27,000	5,000
December.......	18,000	12,000	15,000	25,000	5,000

Actual sales data for the first six months of 1973 show the following numbers of cases sold in the five territories:

Month	East	South	Midwest	West	Foreign
January..........	11,450	4,670	6,400	12,240	1,200
February.........	12,220	5,600	6,550	12,660	1,200
March...........	14,300	6,240	7,000	14,800	860
April............	14,850	6,180	8,420	16,750	620
May.............	15,160	5,800	9,860	18,000	1,080
June............	15,700	6,250	12,850	21,260	1,440

All domestic sales were made at the standard list price of $1.85 per case. Foreign sales were at a standard price of $2.10 per case.

Required:

a) Prepare a budget review report of sales for the month of June, 1973.
b) Can you draw any generalizations about the sales forecast from this report? Can you draw any generalization about the validity of the seasonal sales pattern anticipated in the forecast?

7. The Herbert Doll Company makes five different dolls. All sales are to toy wholesalers and large retailers at the same prices. The budgeted sales volume in units and the list prices planned for the month of December, 1973, are as follows:

Doll	Budgeted Units	List Price
Dancing Dolores.................	7,500	$ 8.50
Raggedy Randy..................	12,000	3.00
Sleepy Sally....................	6,000	7.50
Sophisticated Suzette............	4,500	12.00
Talking Tammy.................	8,000	9.00

Actual sales in units and in total dollars for December were reported as follows:

Doll	Units	Dollars
Dancing Dolores...................	8,200	$ 67,650
Raggedy Randy....................	9,600	24,000
Sleepy Sally......................	6,400	48,000
Sophisticated Suzette..............	4,800	59,520
Talking Tammy...................	6,500	55,250
		$254,420

Required:

a)   Prepare a sales report for the month of December to compare actual and planned sales in whatever manner you believe would be most useful to management.

b)   What differences between actual and budgeted sales volumes would you consider worthy of special attention by management?

c)   What additional information might be helpful to management in evaluating the sales report for December?

8.   The Rodgers Corporation is in the midst of a major expansion program. Its new plant building is scheduled for completion by September 30, 1973. Construction contract payments must be made as the work progresses, according to the following fixed schedule:

February 1, 1973.............................	$ 200,000
April 1, 1973................................	200,000
June 1, 1973................................	250,000
August 1, 1973..............................	400,000
September 30, 1973..........................	550,000
	$1,600,000

As of January 1, 1973, the corporation has a sinking fund for plant expansion consisting of marketable securities with a total market value of $800,000. This market value is not expected to change during the first nine months of 1973. The sinking fund securities yield a return of 5% per annum. All sinking fund earnings as of December 31, 1972, have already been collected. Earnings in 1973 will be collected as the securities are sold to meet contract payments.

The cash balance as of January 1, 1973, is $50,000. Cash provided by (or consumed in) normal operations during 1973 is budgeted as follows:

January..............	$40,000	July..................	$30,000
February.............	50,000	August...............	60,000
March................	20,000	September............	80,000
April.................	(30,000)	October..............	50,000
May..................	(70,000)	November............	40,000
June.................	(10,000)	December............	20,000

A minimum cash balance of $50,000 is considered necessary. Balances in excess of that amount will be held as cash rather than being invested, however.

Any construction payments that cannot be met from operating sources or from the liquidation of sinking fund securities will be financed by borrowing at 8%. These loans will be repaid as soon as possible.

Required:

Prepare a schedule, by months, showing (a) cash from operations, (b) cash realized on sales of sinking fund securities, (c) cash borrowed, (d) construction contract payments, (e) loan repayments, and (f) cash balances. Assume that securities will be sold and that loans will be made and repaid in even multiples of $1,000 (exclusive of interest).

9. Gershwin's Appliance Store plans to begin operations on January 1, 1973. Estimated sales, in units, for the first six months of that year are as follows:

January	100
February	160
March	180
April	220
May	380
June	360

Each appliance will be sold at a list price of $200. It is anticipated that 25% of sales will be for cash and the remainder on installment contracts. The installment contract will require a down payment of 10% of the price and 10 monthly payments of $20 each, including all finance charges.

The store will purchase appliances for $125 each. Purchases will be financed by paying 20% down and giving a noninterest bearing note for the balance. This balance must be paid at the end of the month in which the appliance is sold. An average inventory of 200 units is to be kept in stock.

The store plans to use the installment contracts as collateral for bank loans equal to 60% of the unpaid balance on all new installment contracts obtained each month. These loans must be repaid monthly in an amount equal to 60% of the installment collections for the month. The interest charge on these bank loans will be 6% per annum on the balance of loans outstanding at the end of the preceding month. Interest will be paid monthly.

Salesmen will receive a commission of $20 on each appliance sold. The commission is payable in the month of sale. Other variable out-of-pocket expenses will be $30 per unit sold. Fixed out-of-pocket expenses are expected to average $1,200 per month.

Receipt of the bank loans and repayments thereof will be effected on the last day of the month.

Required:

Prepare a cash budget, by months, for the first half of 1973. Include any appropriate supporting schedules. It will be the company's policy to maintain a minimum cash balance of $5,000. Any deficiency of cash provided from the business will be made up by additional investments by the owner of the store.

(Adapted from CPA Examination)

chapter 9

FLEXIBLE EXPENSE BUDGETS

W<small>E HAVE</small> already seen that the operating budget for an enterprise includes budget schedules of operating costs and expenses in all of the various departments within the firm. Among manufacturing costs, those that are directly traceable to the product and that vary in direct proportion to the volume of production—direct materials and labor costs—are relatively easy to budget. They are direct functions of the volume of production. If the actual volume of production deviates from the planned volume, planned materials and labor costs can be adjusted quite readily to conform to the new volume. For indirect manufacturing costs, however, this direct functional relationship does not obtain. Overhead costs are, of course, incurred because of production; but the direct input-output relationship existing between materials and labor costs and production volume is lacking. Even those overhead costs which vary with the volume of production typically do so in a vaguely defined manner. For example, experience may indicate that indirect materials cost varies quite nearly in direct proportion to output; but it may be impossible to identify any specific indirect materials input per unit of output. Fixed manufacturing costs, of course, are incurred in amounts unrelated to variations in output.

What is true of overhead in this context is largely true of nonmanufacturing costs also. These latter costs usually vary, in part, with the volume of activity to which they are logically related. Thus, selling costs may vary with the volume of sales; clerical costs, with the volume of clerical work done; etc. However, as in the case of overhead, there is usually no direct relationship between the amount of a particular nonmanufacturing cost and the volume of activity. (Sales commissions are the classic exception here.) Certain nonmanufacturing costs are fixed in amount, regardless of the volume of activity. In summary, then, there is some degree of variation of overhead and of most nonmanufacturing costs with approprite measures of volume; but the variation is partial and the total costs cannot readily be expressed as a certain amount per unit of volume.

If indirect costs are budgeted simply at a given amount for the budget period, with no indication as to how those costs would behave if volume were to deviate from the planned level, such a budget would be of limited usefulness to management. If, however, the budget schedule is developed in some way that indicates what the overhead or nonmanufacturing costs may be expected to be at various levels of volume, its utility for purposes of cost planning and control is greatly enhanced. Budgets of indirect costs at a single volume only, with no basis for determining the impact of a change in volume on the budgeted costs, are called *fixed budgets* or *static budgets*. Budgets which do provide a basis for determining the costs anticipated at various levels of operating activity are referred to as *flexible budgets, variable budgets,* or *sliding budgets.* The first term seems most descriptive of the essential character of these budgets and will be used consistently throughout this book.

CONSTRUCTION OF FLEXIBLE BUDGET

Departmentalization of Costs

In any firm large enough to have significant departmental distinctions for operating purposes, flexible budgets should be prepared individually for the indirect costs of each department, whether it be a manufacturing, administrative, selling, or other type of department. The development and construction of flexible budgets are the same, whether they pertain to manufacturing or nonmanufacturing oprations. Flexible budgets for indirect manufacturing costs may have more uses than nonmanufacturing cost budgets, however. For example, a flexible budget for overhead is ordinarily used to establish a normal or a standard overhead cost of the product. Since nonmanufacturing costs are treated as period costs rather than as product costs in current accounting practice, this particular application would not be pertinent to a flexible budget for a nonmanufacturing department. The remainder of the discussion in this chapter will have reference to flexible budgets for overhead costs only. This limitation is solely for the sake of uniformity and clarity in the presentation. The same concepts are applicable to nonmanufacturing cost budgets. Nonmanufacturing costs will be given specific attention in Chapter 12.

An illustration of a flexible overhead budget is presented in Table 9–1. This budget is for the light machinery department of the M-G

Stanley Corporation. Similar schedules would be prepared for the other manufacturing departments and for the various nonmanufacturing departments. Because the M-G Stanley Corporation prepares monthly operating reports for its management and wishes to analyze and evaluate its operating costs monthly, the budgeted overhead data in this illustra-

TABLE 9–1

M-G STANLEY CORPORATION

Monthly Expense Budget

Department Light machinery						*Approved* 12/10/71	
Supervisor W. S. Gilbert							
	Variable Rate per Hour	*Fixed Cost per Month*	*Volume in Labor Hours*				
			15,000	*18,000*	*21,000*	*24,000*	
Controllable costs:							
Indirect labor..........	$ .90		$13,500	$16,200	$18,900	$21,600	
Labor-related costs.....	.20	$ 800	3,800	4,400	5,000	5,600	
Indirect materials......	.50		7,500	9,000	10,500	12,000	
Fuel and power........	.08	2,000	3,200	3,440	3,680	3,920	
Repairs and							
maintenance.......	.10	4,000	5,500	5,800	6,100	6,400	
			$33,500	$38,840	$44,180	$49,520	
Noncontrollable costs:							
Supervision...........		3,200	$ 3,200	$ 3,200	$ 3,200	$ 3,200	
Taxes and insurance....		800	800	800	800	800	
Depreciation..........		25,000	25,000	25,000	25,000	25,000	
			$29,000	$29,000	$29,000	$29,000	
Total costs........	$1.78	$35,800	$62,500	$67,840	$73,180	$78,520	
Normal rates per labor hour:							
Variable rate..........			$1.7800	$1.7800	$1.7800	$1.7800	
Fixed rate............			2.3867	1.9889	1.7048	1.4917	

tion are for one month. Obviously, the data in the flexible budget can be expressed in terms of any period of time—a month, a quarter, a year. As a practical matter, the flexible budget would rarely, if ever, apply to more than one year.

The Measure of Volume

The essence of a flexible budget is the presentation of estimated cost data in such a manner that permits their determination at various levels of volume. As a practical matter, this means that all costs must be identified as to how they behave with changes in volume—whether they vary or remain fixed. In order to identify the behavior of the various cost items in a department, it is necessary first to define volume in the most meaningful way. For a department which is engaged in the production of several substantially different products (e.g., refrigerators, clothes dryers, and ranges), units of output would not be an appropriate measure of volume, for the various units are not alike. In such a case, volume is typically expressed in terms of some unit of input, such as direct labor hours, direct labor cost, or machine-hours. The volume measure selected for any given department should be that quantity which displays the greatest degree of correlation with those costs of the department that do vary with the level of operating activity. The various cost items may be tested by appropriate statistical methods against two or more alternative measures of volume. That measure which shows the highest degree of correlation with the variable costs would then be chosen as the volume indicator for the department.[1]

Different departments are likely to use different measures of volume. The light machinery department in Table 9–1 uses direct labor hours as its volume measure, presumably because observations and studies have shown that the variable cost items tend to vary more nearly in proportion to the labor hours worked in the department than to any other possible indicator of departmental activity. In the same firm's heavy machinery department, it might be found that machine-hours afford the best indication of cost behavior. There is no reason why the same volume measure should be used in all departments within a single firm. One might even raise the question as to whether it is necessary that only one measure be employed in each department. Correlation analyses might show that some costs in a department vary in proportion to labor hours, while others vary in proportion to machine-hours. Should both measures of volume be used for the department, or should only one be selected? In theory, there would be no objection to two or more volume indicators being used in a single department. In practice, this would require two or more flexible budgets for the department. Whether the additional precision would be worth the additional clerical cost involved in such a plan is dubious. In the discussion in this chapter, a single measure of volume for each department will be assumed.

Budget Cost Allowances

Cost Variability. Once the measure of volume has been selected, the next step in the development of the flexible budget is the determination of the behavior of each cost item with respect to that volume indicator. In the illustration in Table 9–1, this means that each cost item had to be studied in conjunction with direct labor hours to determine how it

---

[1] The student is referred to any basic statistics text for the specific technique to be employed for this correlation analysis.

behaved as the hours increased and decreased. The first two money columns in this budget schedule depict the behavior of each cost item with respect to labor hours worked in the department. Fixed costs are budgeted as total amounts. Variable costs are budgeted as amounts per labor hour. Some of the cost items—labor-related costs, fuel and power, and repairs and maintenance—comprise both variable and fixed components. In total, therefore, these are semivariable costs. For reasons to be explained shortly, semivariable costs restrict the usefulness of the flexible budget. Hence, in practice, they are most frequently treated as wholly variable, as absolutely fixed, or as consisting of separable variable and fixed components.

These first two columns, showing the variability and/or fixedness of the departmental cost items, are the essence of the flexible budget. In fact, if we were not interested in the individual cost items but only in the total departmental costs, the final figures in these two columns would be all we would need. The entire flexible budget could be reduced to a simple statement that variable costs in the department are incurred at the rate of $1.78 per direct labor hour and fixed costs are $35,800 per month.[2] With this information we could estimate total departmental cost at any volume. Even where the details of the several cost items are of interest, the first two columns provide an adequate statement of the flexible budget. With the information in these columns, we can provide budget estimates for any volume. To demonstrate this, the student should use the data in those first two columns to calculate the budget cost allowances for 16,000 and for 19,245 hours.

Cost Controllability. As a part of the overall plan of cost control, the flexible budget is commonly developed in such a way as to distinguish between those costs which are regarded as controllable by the department supervisor and those which are not. The noncontrollable costs in Tabel 9–1 include the supervisor's own salary and those of the assistant foremen in the department, for these are set by the plant manager. Taxes, insurance, and depreciation on departmental equipment are also regarded as beyond the control of the supervisor, as they derive from decisions made at higher levels of management. It must be understood that the noncontrollable costs in Table 9–1 are such only at the level of responsibility of the departmental supervisor. At some higher level of responsibility, they also would be controllable. All costs in a firm should be controllable at some level of responsibility.

Cost controllability must always be evaluated critically and cautiously. Not all of the items listed as controllable costs are necessarily completely

---

[2] Of course, this flexible budget might just as well be expressed as a fixed cost of $35,800 per month plus a variable rate of $1.78 multiplied by the production volume of the period. In this arrangement, it is easily recognizable as a specific application of the general form of a linear equation (i.e., $y = a + bx$).

subject to the discretion of the department supervisor. A certain amount of maintenance cost, for example, is inevitably incurred as a consequence of the decision to acquire and use equipment. If this decision is not made by the department supervisor, it is doubtful that this basic maintenance cost can be said to be truly controllable by him. Nevertheless, the identification of controllable and noncontrollable costs at the several levels of responsibility is so important to effective cost control that a practical distinction between the two is needed. That distinction must then be interpreted reasonably.

Normal Overhead Rates

Given budgeted overhead costs and budgeted volume, normal overhead rates can be computed from either a fixed or a flexible budget. The important difference is that only one set of rates can be computed from a fixed budget, whereas rates for any level of volume can be calculated from a flexible budget. The normal variable overhead rate is the same at any volume, as illustrated at the bottom of Table 9–1. The normal fixed overhead rate, however, is a function of a constant total cost and budgeted volume. Thus, the normal fixed rate is lower at higher volumes, as can be seen in Table 9–1. It is extremely important that the student understand the nature of a normal fixed overhead rate. Fixed overhead can be expressed as a rate per unit of volume only at a given volume. At any other volume, that rate is not really valid. What has been said here for normal overhead rates is basically applicable to standard overhead rates as well, except that the volume at which the standard fixed overhead rate is determined is not necessarily the budgeted volume for the period. Standard overhead rates are discussed in the next chapter.

ESTABLISHING BUDGET ALLOWANCES

As with so many things in life, the most important step in the development of a flexible budget is the most difficult. A flexible budget is only as good as the cost allowances included in it and the separation of these costs into variable and fixed components. At the outset, we must recognize that no flexible budget can be perfect, because the composite budgeted cost allowances cannot be perfect. In a practical situation, it is unlikely that there will be any perfectly variable costs that vary in direct proportion to volume over the full range of possible operating volumes. Likewise, there will probably be few absolutely fixed costs that do not change at all over the entire range of possible operations. Nevertheless, the concepts of variable and fixed costs are so useful to effective planning and control that it is better to make a reasonable assumption regarding the variability or fixedness of a cost than to throw up one's hands in frustration at a fruitless search for perfection.

Variable Costs

Despite the fact that there may be no costs which are perfectly variable over all ranges of volume, there may be a substantial number of cost items which come fairly close to being so. In addition, there may be cost items which approach perfect variability over the relevant range of volume, that is, the range within which the department is almost certain to operate. For example, if a particular department regularly operates between 60% and 90% of capacity, there is little merit in the accountant's being concerned with the behavior of departmental costs at 20% or 30% of capacity. In such a case, the flexible budget may be entirely valid over the range of activity which may reasonably be expected. The fact that it is not valid at some operating level which would be reached only under highly unusual circumstances—such as a strike—is then of little practical consequence. Thus, many cost items which do not meet the strict definition of a variable cost are commonly treated as variable costs for purposes of establishing flexible budget allowances and for subsequent analyses. The attendant degree of imprecision is greatly outweighed by the utility of the flexible budget to management.

Fixed Costs

For purposes of planning and control, it is useful to distinguish between two types of fixed costs. First, there are some costs that are fixed in amount and that must be incurred each period as a consequence of a decision made at some time in the past. These are referred to as *committed costs*. The most familiar examples of committed fixed costs are those that derive from an earlier decision to acquire and use plant property. Depreciation, property taxes, and property insurance are examples of committed costs. It is true that management has some discretion as to the amount of periodic depreciation by virtue of its choice of a depreciation method. However, this choice affects only the timing of depreciation charges; and it is available only once, when the asset is acquired. The second type of fixed cost is fixed in amount as a result of a current management decision. Such costs are called *managed costs* or *programmed costs*. Implicit in the concept of a managed cost is periodic managerial discretion as to the amount of the cost in the ensuing period. Perhaps the best examples of managed costs are in the area of nonmanufacturing costs. Certain elements of factory overhead also tend to fit the category, however. The amount budgeted for supervision is usually determined by a management judgment as to the optimal ratio of supervisory to operating employees. As technology and other conditions change, that judgment may change. Fixed maintenance costs are largely committed in that the earlier decision to acquire plant facilities necessitates current expenditures to maintain them. However, management usually has some discretion as to the amount of fixed maintenance costs. To some extent, there is a tradeoff between the amount spent on maintenance and the frequency of replacement of machinery. Thus, the distinction between committed and managed costs is not always a clear one; but it is a useful one for planning and control purposes.

Some fixed costs may meet the strict definition of the concept. Such items as depreciation, property taxes, and insurance are likely to be the same at full capacity as they would be if the plant were temporarily shut down. Others, such as supervision, are more likely to remain fixed only over certain ranges of volume. Perhaps one supervisor can handle operations in a department up to 30% of capacity; a second becomes necessary when operations exceed 30%; a third must be added when volume reaches 60%; and a fourth is required at 90% of capacity. Obviously, supervision cost in this case does not qualify as a true fixed cost. However, if the department's operations are almost certain to fall somewhere between 60% and 90% of capacity, supervision may validly be treated as a fixed cost. Changes in the cost outside the relevant range of operations are irrelevant. As in the case of variable costs, utility is a much more significant criterion than perfection.

Semivariable Costs

Step Budgeting. Unfortunately, not all costs are so nearly variable or fixed that they may be treated as one or the other without further study. Many cost items do vary with volume even within fairly small ranges, but they do not do so in a manner even close to direct proportionality. One possible method of dealing with such costs is to budget them at each of the several levels of volume which are to be tabulated in the formal flexible budget schedule, without reference to how they might behave at nontabulated levels. This method is usually described as *step budgeting.* While this solution to the problem would permit the preparation of a formal budget schedule, it would limit the flexibility of the budget. Step budgets do not provide for any direct determination of the budgeted cost at some volume not tabulated. This amount might be estimated by interpolation between tabulated amounts. However, interpolation implies a linear relationship between the cost and volume; whereas the use of step budgeting denies the existence of such a relationship. In any event, it is important that management be able to determine the budgeted cost at any given volume; and step budgets are of limited value for this purpose. The alternative to step budgeting is to eliminate semivariable costs from the budget by treating them as variable, as fixed, or as a combination of the two.

Classification by Dominant Characteristics. The simplest and, unfortunately, the least precise method of disposing of semivariable cost items is to treat them as either variable or fixed according to their dominant characteristics. Thus, if observation shows that a particular semivariable cost is closer to being variable than fixed, it is treated as variable and an average rate of variability is established on the basis of past experience, as adjusted for expected changes in conditions. If inspection indicates that the item is closer to being fixed, it is treated as such in an amount which would be expected to be incurred at the most likely level of

TABLE 9–2

	Machine-Hours	Maintenance Cost
January	120,000	$90,000
February	130,000	91,000
March	115,000	84,000
April	105,000	85,000
May	90,000	82,000
June	80,000	73,000
July	70,000	72,000
August	80,000	78,000
September	95,000	75,000
October	110,000	89,000
November	125,000	95,000
December	140,000	93,000

operations. Obviously, this solution to the problem of semivariable costs introduces a considerable degree of imprecision into subsequent analyses based upon the flexible budget allowances. In a study of practices in 58 firms, the National Association of Accountants found that identification of variable and fixed costs on the basis of their dominant characteristics was a common, if not the commonest, practice.[3]

Least Squares Regression Method. This method is based upon the assumption that a semivariable cost can be separated into fixed and variable components. This separation is usually based upon an analysis of past experience, adjusted appropriately for expected changes in costs or in other conditions. Several actual costs and the volumes at which they occurred are analyzed to determine a general trend of cost in relation to volume. For example, assume that a production department measures its operating volume in machine-hours and management believes that its maintenance costs are partially related to the number of

---

[3] NAA, "Separating and Using Costs as Fixed and Variable," *N.A.A. Bulletin,* Accounting Practice Report No. 10, Vol. XLI (June, 1960), sec. 3, p. 15.

machine-hours worked. Actual experience with volume in machine-hours and maintenance cost during the most recent year is shown in Table 9–2. If we may assume that there will be no change in maintenance operations or in prices during the coming budget period, these data may be used directly to determine the separate variable and fixed portions of maintenance cost. On the other hand, if there is reason to anticipate some change, this should be reflected in the data first. For example, if the prices of maintenance services were expected to rise by 5%, all of the amounts in the second column above would be multiplied by 105% before proceeding further with the analysis.

In our illustration, we shall assume that no change to the previous year's data is necessary. The variable and fixed components of the semivariable maintenance cost are computed by solving the following equations:

$$b = \frac{n\Sigma XY - \Sigma X\Sigma Y}{n\Sigma X^2 - (\Sigma X)^2}$$

$$a = \frac{\Sigma Y}{n} - b\left(\frac{\Sigma X}{n}\right)$$

where

n = the number of observations used (12 months' data in this case),
X = value of the independent variable (machine-hours here),
Y = value of the dependent variable (maintenance cost),
b = variable cost rate per unit of volume (per machine-hour),
a = fixed cost per period (per month).

From the data in our illustration, we find that $a = \$49,110$ and $b = \$.3315$. In other words, maintenance cost is budgeted at $49,110 per month plus $.3315 per machine-hour worked.[4] In practice, these figures might

---

[4] This solution to the least squares regression analysis is presented below. The student who is not familiar with this technique is referred to any standard textbook on statistics.

Months (n = 12)	Machine-Hours (X)	Maintenance Cost (Y)	XY	X²
January	120,000	$ 90,000	10,800,000,000	14,400,000,000
February	130,000	91,000	11,830,000,000	16,900,000,000
March	115,000	84,000	9,660,000,000	13,225,000,000
April	105,000	85,000	8,925,000,000	11,025,000,000
May	90,000	82,000	7,380,000,000	8,100,000,000
June	80,000	73,000	5,840,000,000	6,400,000,000
July	70,000	72,000	5,040,000,000	4,900,000,000
August	80,000	78,000	6,240,000,000	6,400,000,000
September	95,000	75,000	7,125,000,000	9,025,000,000
October	110,000	89,000	9,790,000,000	12,100,000,000
November	125,000	95,000	11,875,000,000	15,625,000,000
December	140,000	93,000	13,020,000,000	19,600,000,000
Σ	1,260,000	$1,007,000	107,525,000,000	137,700,000,000

be rounded for convenience. Total budgeted maintenance cost at any given volume may now be found by solving the following equation:

$$Y = a + bX$$

where all of the symbols have the same meanings as in the previous equations.

The least squares method of analysis of semivariable costs is commonly accompanied by a graphic depiction of the relationship between cost and volume. Figure 9–1 is a graph of the maintenance cost illustration. It shows a scattergraph of actual maintenance costs incurred in the recent year (i.e., a plot of the maintenance cost incurred at the volume worked in each month). A least squares regression line is then drawn on the basis of computed values of a and b.[5] This line shows the budgeted total maintenance cost at any volume. The slope of the line is the variable rate per unit of volume. The total monthly fixed cost is found at the point where the regression line intersects the vertical axis. The graph, of course, is not essential to effective use of the least squares method. The least squares computations, however, are necessary if the line on the graph is to depict cost behavior accurately.

The study by the National Association of Accountants referred to earlier found that most of the firms whose practices were observed and who did separate semivariable costs into fixed and variable components used the least squares method to do so.[6] One final note of caution is appropriate here. The reader should not be mesmerized by the mathematical precision of the least squares method. The mathematics are precise, but they are applied in the development of an approximation of actual cost

---

Then

$$b = \frac{n\Sigma XY - \Sigma X\Sigma Y}{n\Sigma X^2 - (\Sigma X)^2} = \frac{12(107,525,000,000) - 1,260,000(1,007,000)}{12(137,700,000,000) - 1,260,000^2} = .3315$$

and

$$a = \frac{\Sigma Y}{n} - b\left(\frac{\Sigma X}{n}\right) = \frac{1,007,000}{12} - .3315\left(\frac{1,260,000}{12}\right) = 49,110$$

[5] This line is drawn by computing and plotting cost at two different volumes and then connecting those two points by a straight line. Thus, we might compute budgeted maintenance cost (Y) at 120,000 machine-hours and at 60,000 machine-hours by twice solving the equation $Y = a + bX$, where X has successive values of 120,000 and 60,000. This produces the following results:

$$Y_{120,000} = \$49,110 + \$.3315(120,000) = \$88,890$$
$$Y_{60,000} = \$49,110 + \$.3315(60,000) = \$69,000$$

Of course, the same line will be obtained by connecting any two points computed from this equation; and any solution to the equation will represent a point that lies on the line.

[6] NAA, *op. cit.*, p. 11.

FIGURE 9-1

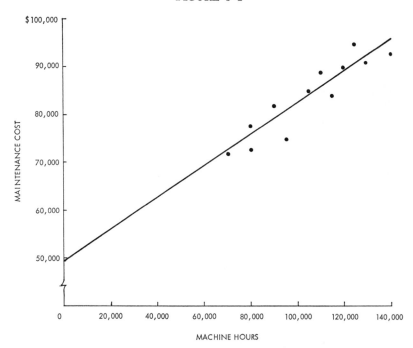

behavior. The separation of a semivariable cost into variable and fixed components is made because it is useful and it is a reasonable approximation of reality.

High-Low Method. Another method of separating semivariable costs into variable and fixed components is the *high-low method*. This method is based upon only two observations of actual cost behavior, one at a high volume of activity and a second at a low volume. Logically, the high and low volumes used should be the upper and lower limits of the relevant range within which actual volume is most likely to fall. Because it uses only two sets of data, the high-low method is much simpler to use than the least squares method. For the same reason, however, it is also less precise. Suppose, for example, that a production department determined that at a high production volume of 24,000 direct labor hours per month its fuel and power cost was $3,920. At a low volume of 15,000 direct labor hours, fuel and power cost was $3,200. With these data only, variable and fixed elements of fuel and power cost may be computed. The change in cost between the high and low volumes is assumed to reflect the pattern of cost variability. Thus, the variable rate per labor hour is computed as follows:

	Labor Hours	*Fuel and* Power Cost
High volume........	24,000	$3,920
Low volume.........	15,000	3,200
Differences.........	9,000	$ 720

As volume changed by 9,000 hours, cost changed by $720. Thus, fuel and power cost is assumed to include a variable component equal to $.08 per direct labor hour ($720 ÷ 9,000 hours). With this variable rate, we can compute the fixed cost component at either the high or the low volume or at both. The fixed cost is simply the difference between the total cost at either volume and the newly found variable cost component.

	High Volume	*Low Volume*
Total cost...........	$3,920	$3,200
Variable cost:		
24,000 hrs. @ $.08..	1,920	
15,000 hrs. @ $.08..		1,200
Fixed cost..........	$2,000	$2,000

Thus, we have determined that fuel and power cost should be budgeted at $2,000 per month plus $.08 per direct labor hour.

The high-low method is an acceptable way of approximating cost behavior when no better data are available. It is likely to be less accurate than the least squares method, however. The latter method is based upon numerous data, perhaps representative of various points in the relevant range of volume. The high-low method uses only data drawn from the extreme ends of that range.[7]

DEPARTMENTAL EXPENSE REPORTS

Report Form

Table 9–3 is a departmental expense report for one month. It reports the actual expenses incurred in the light machinery department of the M-G Stanley Corporation for the month of April, 1972. Actual expenses are compared with the budgeted expenses as presented in the departmental flexible budget, Table 9–1 in this chapter. Differences between the actual and budgeted cost data are identified as variances and provide the

---

[7] To illustrate the difference in results under these two methods, assume that the high-low method were to be applied to the maintenance cost and machine-hour data used in connection with the least squares illustration. The high volume was 140,000 machine-hours, with a cost of $93,000. The low volume was 70,000 hours, with a cost of $72,000. Using the high-low method with these data, we would compute a variable cost rate of $.30 per hour (instead of $.3315) and a fixed cost of $51,000 per month (instead of $49,110).

TABLE 9–3

M-G STANLEY CORPORATION
Monthly Expense Report

Department Light machinery   *Month of* April, 1972
Supervisor W. S. Gilbert

	Current Month			Year to Date		
	Actual Cost	Budgeted Cost	Spending Variance	Actual Cost	Budgeted Cost	Spending Variance
Direct labor hours......	19,150	19,150		72,600	72,600	
Controllable costs:						
Indirect labor........	$17,880	$17,235	$ 645	$ 68,465	$ 65,340	$3,125
Labor related costs....	4,675	4,630	45	17,982	17,720	262
Indirect materials.....	9,318	9,575	(257)	36,394	36,300	94
Fuel and power.......	4,120	3,532	588	15,820	13,808	2,012
Repairs and maintenance.......	5,200	5,915	(715)	21,640	23,260	(1,620)
Total..........	$41,193	$40,887	$ 306	$160,301	$156,428	$3,873
Noncontrollable costs:						
Supervision..........	$ 3,360	$ 3,200	$ 160	$ 13,120	$ 12,800	$ 320
Taxes and insurance...	800	800		3,200	3,200	
Depreciation.........	26,500	25,000	1,500	101,500	100,000	1,500
Total..........	$30,660	$29,000	$1,660	$117,820	$116,000	$1,820
Total costs.............	$71,853	$69,887	$1,966	$278,121	$272,428	$5,693
Budgeted cost for actual labor hours (19,150).		$69,887			$272,428	
Budgeted cost for budgeted labor hours (18,000)..........		67,840			271,360	
Planning variance.......		$ 2,047			$ 1,068	

focal point from which the process of cost control proceeds. Table 9–3 is
not offered as a standard report form, but it is representative of the type
of information usually contained in such expense reports. Inclusion of
data for the year to date as well as for the month just ended is not
essential to the basic nature of the report, but it does afford management
a basis for appraising the department's cost performance over a series of
months and for evaluating the effectiveness of cost control efforts suggested by prior months' reports. The various components of this report
will be discussed in the paragraphs that follow.

Adjusting the Budget to Actual Volume

If the M-G Stanley Corporation used fixed departmental budgets instead of flexible budgets, there would be only one level of budgeted
costs against which actual costs could be compared. Assume that the

corporation had originally estimated that operating volume in the light machinery department would be approximately 18,000 direct labor hours per month during the budget period under consideration. A fixed budget would present only the costs budgeted for that volume, with no indication of cost variability or fixedness. While this would afford some basis for evaluating actual costs, it would not permit management to distinguish between those variances which arise because actual operating volume has differed from that originally anticipated and those variances attributable to spending more or less than the budget calls for. A flexible budget enables management to distinguish between these two types of variances, for it allows the determination of budgeted costs at any volume.

In order to appraise departmental spending during a given period, management wishes to compare actual costs with the costs which the budget indicates should have been incurred at the operating volume actually achieved during the period. Thus, the budgeted costs tabulated in Table 9–3 are budgeted costs for 19,150 direct labor hours, the actual volume for April. To the extent that costs are variable (cf., Table 9–1), budget allowances for the actual volume are simply the products of 19,150 hours multiplied by the several variable cost rates per hour. To the extent that costs are fixed, they are the same dollar amount at any volume. Repairs and maintenance costs, for example, are budgeted at 19,150 hours by multiplying 19,150 by $.10, the variable rate per hour, and then by adding $4,000, the fixed amount per month. Similar computations are made to determine budgeted costs for the actual volume of the year to date. In this instance, the actual labor hours used (72,600) are the total actual hours worked in the department during the first four months of 1972.

Variances from the Budget

Spending Variance. The difference between actual costs and budgeted costs for the actual volume is described as the *spending variance.* This is not the ideal term, for not all of the cost items in a department necessarily involve current spending. Depreciation, for example, shows a spending variance in Table 9–3, although we know that depreciation does not involve current cash outlays. The term is fairly widely used, however, and will suit the purpose so long as we understand what it means. Insofar as cost control is concerned, this is the more important variance to management. It is the variance more likely to be subject to control by the department supervisor.

Planning Variance. The *planning variance* is the difference between the budgeted costs for the actual volume and the budgeted costs for the volume originally expected when the complete operating budget was prepared. In the illustration at hand, the planning variance for April is the difference between the costs budgeted at 19,150 direct labor hours and those budgeted at 18,000 hours. The planning variance for the year to date is the difference between the costs budgeted at the actual total direct labor hours of 72,600 and the costs budgeted at the originally planned labor hours, 72,000. This variance is only as controllable as the reason for the difference between actual volume and that originally planned. It does, however, complete an explanation of the difference between actual departmental costs and costs planned in the original operating budget.

As a final note, it is well to observe carefully that the variances discussed here are variances from budgeted overhead costs. In the next chapter we will consider variances from standard overhead cost. While a standard overhead cost is developed from budget data, it is quite different from a budgeted cost itself. Consequently, variances from standard are different from those variances illustrated here. The variances here have been computed and identified without regard to any standard or normal overhead rates. They are derived from a comparison of actual costs and budgeted costs only.

QUESTIONS FOR DISCUSSION

1. Why is a flexible budget a better technique for planning and controlling costs than a static budget?

2. "As long as the separation of overhead or of any other cost into variable and fixed components is inexact, the resultant flexible budget is inexact. When this budget is then applied to actual cost data for purpose of cost control, the comparisons produced will also be inexact. Consequently, they may produce confusion, ill feelings, and possibly even inappropriate managerial action." Discuss this allegation.

3. The flexible budget illustrated in Table 9–1 and the expense report in Table 9–3 in this chapter both could have been completed without identification of cost items as controllable and noncontrollable. Why then should this distinction be included in these exhibits?

4. Discuss the advantages and disadvantages of step budgeting of semivariable costs. What are the principal alternatives to step budgeting?

5. Discuss the relative advantages and disadvantages of the least squares regression method and the high-low method of separating semivariable costs into variable and fixed components.

6. For purposes of planning and control, what is (are) the essential difference(s) between committed and managed fixed costs?

7. What is the significance of the spending variance from budgeted costs? What is the significance of the planning variance? Which is more important to management in evaluating the operating performance of a department supervisor? Explain.

8. The controller of the Alpine Corporation is impressed with the success of flexible budgets for overhead in the corporation's manufacturing departments. He would like to use them also in the departments under his direct supervision—payroll, billing, and general accounting. What are the requirements for the establishment of useful flexible budgets in nonproduction departments such as these?

9. Flexible budgets involve, fundamentally, the distinction between variable and fixed costs. Are they, then, as useful in variable costing systems, where only variable costs are charged to production, as they are in absorption costing systems? Discuss.

10. Discuss the potential applicability of flexible budgets to the planning and control of (*a*) direct materials cost, (*b*) executives' salaries and bonuses, and (*c*) research and development costs.

PROBLEMS

1. The Almador Frozen Food Company packages all of its products in its packing department. The budgeted costs for the operation of the department in 1973 have been established as follows:

Variable costs:	
Raw materials............................	$1,600,000
Direct labor.............................	900,000
Packing supplies.........................	66,000
Indirect labor...........................	150,000
Labor-related costs......................	105,000
	$2,821,000
Fixed costs:	
Maintenance.............................	$ 65,000
Heat, light, and power..................	72,000
Taxes and insurance.....................	17,000
Depreciation............................	125,000
	$ 279,000
Total budgeted costs....................	$3,100,000

Management wishes to have flexible budgets prepared for all operating departments. Operating volume in the packing department may best be measured in direct labor hours. Direct labor cost in the department has been budgeted at the standard rate of $3 per hour.

Required:

a) Prepare, in its most elementary form, a flexible budget of overhead costs for one year in the packing department.

b) Compute the normal variable and fixed overhead rates for the department for 1973.

2. The following overhead costs may reasonably be expected to be incurred in the assembly department of the Plumas Office Furniture Company:

Indirect materials.................... $.20 per labor hr.
Indirect labor....................... $10,000 per mo. plus
                                          $.10 per labor hr.
Supervision.......................... $24,000 per mo.
Repairs and maintenance.............. $3,600 per mo.
Depreciation......................... $12,000 per mo.
Cleaning supplies.................... $.12 per labor hr.
Heat, light, and power............... $4,000 per mo. plus
                                          $.24 per labor hr.
Insurance and taxes.................. $1,500 per mo.

All of these cost items, excepting supervision, depreciation, and insurance and taxes, are regarded as controllable by the department foreman.

Required:

a) Prepare a tabular flexible budget for overhead in the assembly department at each of the following monthly levels of production volume: 70,000; 80,000; and 90,000 labor hours.

b) Assuming that the company uses absorption costing and that it budgets production volume at 80,000 labor hours per month, compute the normal overhead rates for the assembly department.

3. You have recently been appointed budget director of the Inyo Machine Corporation. One of your objectives is to establish flexible overhead budgets for all production departments. For this purpose, you asked each department supervisor to submit a report of his monthly costs. The following report was received from David Wong, the supervisor of the stamping department:

"My biggest cost item, of course, is labor. There are nine machines in the department. Each one needs an operator, a materials handler, and an assistant. Operators get $4.50 an hour; handlers, $3 an hour; and assistants, $2.50 an hour. Now, I have 10 operators. Nine are regularly assigned to machines. The 10th relieves the regular operators when they take their breaks and any other time they need relief. Then there is the janitor; he gets $500 a month. My own salary is $1,100 a month, incidentally.

"When the machines are operating the full eight-hour day, our monthly maintenance charges run about $20,000. Even when we were shut down for three months during the strike last year, though, routine maintenance cost $12,080 each month. Power is metered at each machine, and each one uses about 120 kilowatt-hours for each hour it is in operation. Supplies seem to depend on how much the machines are being used. For a full eight-hour day, we use about $126 worth of supplies. If the machines are working less, the supplies go down accordingly. I know there are other costs charged to the department on the monthly reports, but I don't know how they are arrived at."

Further investigation reveals that the monthly depreciation on the machinery in the stamping department is $25,000. Insurance and taxes on the machinery total $30,000 for a year. The rate paid by the corporation for electric power is $.04 per kilowatt-hour. From the payroll section, you learn that fringe benefits average 10% of gross wages and salaries.

Each month may be assumed to consist of 22 eight-hour working days.

Required:

a) What measure of operating volume would you use for the stamping department's flexible overhead budget? Why?

b) Construct a flexible budget schedule for overhead in the stamping department for one month. Include budget allowances for 75% and for 100% of full operating capacity.

4. The Modoc Corporation is developing flexible budgets for the first time. It appears that the indirect labor in the light machining department is a semivariable cost. Volume in this department is measured in direct labor hours. Management believes it is entirely reasonable to expect that this department will operate at no more than 48,000 labor hours per month and no less than 36,000 hours per month. Indirect labor cost has been budgeted at $44,000 for a volume of 48,000 labor hours and at $38,600 for a volume of 36,000 labor hours.

Required:

By use of the high-low method, resolve the budgeted indirect labor cost in this department into a variable rate per labor hour and a fixed cost per month.

5. The Sonoma Electric Company wishes to set flexible budgets for each of its various departments. A separate maintenance department performs all major and routine repair work on the company's equipment and facilities. It has been determined that maintenance cost is primarily a function of machine-hours worked in the various production departments. Total actual machine-hours worked and maintenance costs incurred during 1972 are as follows:

Month	Machine-Hours	Maintenance Cost
January	140,000	$238,000
February	125,000	228,000
March	120,000	220,000
April	105,000	200,000
May	90,000	188,000
June	80,000	171,000
July	100,000	190,000
August	110,000	205,000
September	125,000	233,000
October	30,000	160,000
November	140,000	240,000
December	150,000	255,000

The company's plant was shut down by a strike for three and a half weeks during October, 1972.

Required:

a) Assuming that maintenance costs are expected to be 10% higher in 1973 than they were in 1972, compute the variable cost per machine-hour and the fixed cost per month by use of the high-low method.

b) If the company wished to charge maintenance costs to production departments at a normal rate, how would such a rate be established? How, then, should the company account for any differences between actual maintenance costs incurred and maintenance costs charged to production departments by means of this normal rate?

6. The cost of heat, light, and power in the Tulare Valve Company tends to vary with the volume of direct labor hours worked in the factory but not in direct proportion thereto. Budgeted heat, light, and power costs in 1973, by quarters, are as follows:

Quarter	Cost	Labor Hours
First..........................	$75,000	60,000
Second.........................	84,000	70,000
Third..........................	95,000	90,000
Fourth.........................	88,000	80,000

Required:

a) By means of the least squares regression method, compute budgeted heat, light, and power cost as a variable rate per labor hour and a fixed cost per quarter.
b) Using the cost data computed in (a), calculate total budgeted cost at 60,000 labor hours and at 90,000 labor hours.
c) With the foregoing information, plot a least squares regression line on a graph of heat, light, and power cost.

7. The Placer Plastics Company is preparing a flexible overhead budget for its drill press department. Volume in this department is measured in machine-hours. Budgeted volume and budgeted power costs for the year 1973 have been projected as follows:

Month	Machine-Hours	Power Costs
January.........................	2,000	$ 18,000
February........................	2,500	20,000
March...........................	3,000	21,000
April...........................	3,300	22,000
May.............................	4,000	25,000
June............................	5,000	30,000
July............................	6,000	33,000
August..........................	5,000	28,000
September.......................	4,500	26,000
October.........................	4,000	22,000
November........................	3,500	20,000
December........................	3,000	20,000
	45,800	$285,000

Required:

a) Construct a graph of the relationship between machine-hours and power costs for 1973.

b) By the least squares regression method, compute the budgeted power cost allowances at 3,000 and 6,000 machine-hours. Draw the least squares regression line on the graph in (a).

8. The San Benito Explosives Corporation has prepared the following quarterly budget of conversion costs in its Hollister plant:

	Quarter 1	Quarter 2	Quarter 3	Quarter 4
Direct labor..............	$ 600,000	$ 750,000	$ 800,000	$ 700,000
Indirect materials.........	48,000	60,000	64,000	56,000
Indirect labor............	100,000	100,000	100,000	100,000
Repairs and maintenance....	170,000	200,000	210,000	190,000
Depreciation.............	200,000	200,000	200,000	200,000
Supervision..............	20,000	20,000	20,000	20,000
Power and light..........	85,000	100,000	105,000	95,000
Labor-related costs........	72,000	87,000	92,000	82,000
	$1,295,000	$1,517,000	$1,591,000	$1,443,000

Required:

Using direct labor cost as the measure of volume, prepare a flexible budget of overhead in good form for the Hollister plant.

9. The monthly flexible overhead budget for Department 44 of the Humboldt Manufacturing Company is as follows:

Cost Item	Variable Rate per Hour	Fixed Costs	40,000 Labor Hours	50,000 Labor Hours	60,000 Labor Hours
Indirect labor..............	$ .45	$ 24,500	$ 42,500	$ 47,000	$ 51,500
Supervision...............		33,000	33,000	33,000	33,000
Labor-related costs........	.20	5,750	13,750	15,750	17,750
Indirect materials.........	.18		7,200	9,000	10,800
Power and light...........	.09	6,600	10,200	11,100	12,000
Maintenance..............	.28	9,000	20,200	23,000	25,800
Depreciation..............		41,250	41,250	41,250	41,250
Miscellaneous.............		12,900	12,900	12,900	12,900
	$1.20	$133,000	$181,000	$193,000	$205,000

The volume of operations in Department 44 was expected to average 50,000 labor hours per month during 1973. For the month of August, actual operations in the department totaled 55,000 labor hours. The actual overhead costs incurred during August were as follows:

Indirect labor...........................	$ 52,200
Supervision.............................	34,400
Labor-related costs......................	17,450
Indirect materials.......................	9,650
Power and light.........................	11,700
Maintenance............................	21,800
Depreciation............................	44,000
Miscellaneous..........................	13,000
	$204,200

Required:

a) Prepare an expense report for Department 44 for the month of August, 1973. Show the variances of actual costs from budgeted costs in as much detail as you believe is relevant to management.

b) Under absorption costing, what would the normal variable and fixed overhead rates be in Department 44 for the year 1973?

10. The flexible overhead budget for the packing department of the Imperial Drug Company allows $50,000 per month plus $1.60 per man-hour worked in the department. Actual cost data for the first quarter of 1972 are summarized below:

Month	Variable Costs	Fixed Costs	Man-Hours
January.............	$ 99,000	$49,500	60,000
February............	108,000	51,000	68,000
March..............	115,000	51,600	75,000

Operating volume in this department for 1972 has been budgeted at 70,000 man-hours per month.

Required:

a) Prepare a report showing the spending and planning variances from the budget for each month and for the quarter in total.

b) What inferences may be drawn from an examination of the variances in this report?

11. Following is the overhead budget for the shearing department of the Contra Costa Swimwear Company for one month:

Direct labor hours.........	15,000	20,000	25,000	30,000
Indirect labor.............	$15,000	$17,000	$19,000	$21,000
Supplies.................	3,750	5,000	6,250	7,500
Space occupancy..........	12,000	12,000	12,000	12,000
Total overhead...........	$30,750	$34,000	$37,250	$40,500

Volume for 1972 had been budgeted at 25,000 direct labor hours per month. During September, 1972, the department worked a total of 18,600 direct labor hours, and the following overhead costs were incurred:

Indirect labor...........................	$16,600
Supplies.................................	4,500
Space occupancy.........................	12,800
	$33,900

Required:

a) Identify each cost item in this budget as variable, fixed, or semivariable.
b) Convert the budget above into the basic format of a flexible budget.
c) Prepare a brief expense report for September, 1972. Show variances between actual and budgeted costs.

12. The flexible budget for the smelting department of the Kern Copper Company appears as follows:

Cost Item	Variable Rate per Machine-Hour	Fixed Cost per Quarter
Indirect materials..............	$ 2.50	
Indirect labor.................	6.00	$ 45,000
Power and water..............	1.20	20,000
Maintenance..................	12.00	150,000
Taxes and insurance...........		5,500
Depreciation.................		225,000
Labor-related costs............	3.30	4,500
	$25.00	$450,000

Production volume in this department had been budgeted at 24,000 machine-hours per quarter for the year 1972. During the third quarter of 1972, actual production volume was only 18,000 machine-hours. The following actual overhead costs were incurred in the smelting department during the third quarter:

Indirect materials........................	$ 48,000
Indirect labor...........................	142,000
Power and water.........................	44,000
Maintenance.............................	350,000
Taxes and insurance.....................	6,200
Depreciation............................	216,000
Labor-related costs......................	66,000
	$872,200

Required:

a) Prepare an expense report for the smelting department for the third quarter of 1972. Show variances of actual costs from the budget in a way most useful to management.

b) How could there be a spending variance for a committed fixed cost like depreciation?

13. You have been engaged as a management consultant to the Calaveras Manufacturing Corporation. The firm is not large, and its entire factory is treated as a single cost center for purposes of charging overhead to production. The corporation manufactures three products: Dese, Dem, and Dose. Standard production times for these products are two labor hours, eight labor hours, and three labor hours, respectively.

You have learned that budgeted output for 1972 called for production of 100,000 units of Dese, 20,000 units of Dem, and 70,000 units of Dose. Factory overhead for the year was budgeted at $684,000 for variable costs and $1,026,000 for fixed costs. Variable overhead varies in relation to labor hours. You are satisfied that the budgeted cost allowances were reasonable and that the classifications of costs as fixed and variable are proper.

The company's chief accountant established normal overhead rates per unit of product by means of the average labor time per unit of budgeted output. This average labor time was computed as follows:

Product	Budgeted Units	Labor Hours per Unit	Total Labor Hours
Dese..............	100,000	2	200,000
Dem..............	20,000	8	160,000
Dose..............	70,000	3	210,000
	190,000		570,000

Average labor time per unit of output = 570,000 hours ÷ 190,000 units = 3 hours per unit.

The normal overhead rates used for product cost accounting were then determined as follows:

	Total Cost	÷	Total Hours	=	Normal Rate per Hour	×	Average Hours per Unit	=	Normal Rate per Unit
Variable costs.....	$ 684,000		570,000		$1.20		3		$3.60
Fixed costs.......	1,026,000		570,000		1.80		3		5.40
Totals...........	$1,710,000				$3.00				$9.00

Actual output for 1972 consisted of 80,000 units of Dese, 40,000 units of Dem, and 40,000 units of Dose. Standard production times for the three products were met exactly throughout the year. Actual variable overhead costs for the year totaled $700,000 and actual fixed overhead, $1,050,000. The chief accountant submitted the following analysis of underapplied overhead to the factory manager at the end of the year:

Actual overhead costs incurred............................	$1,750,000
Overhead applied to production (160,000 units produced @ $9)......................................	1,440,000
Net underapplied overhead.............................	$ 310,000

The factory manager expressed surprise and disappointment upon receiving this analysis. He said that he was under the impression that operations in the factory were exceeding plans, and he could not understand how almost 18% of total overhead could have been unabsorbed by production. He has asked you to review the cost and production records and submit a report to him.

Required:

a) Evaluate the overhead costing procedure developed by the chief accountant.

b) Prepare for the factory manager a report showing what you believe to be the most useful comparison of actual and planned overhead costs for 1972.

c) The company's inventory of finished product at December 31, 1972, consists of 3,000 units of Dese, 2,000 units of Dem, and 1,500 units of Dose. There is no inventory of work in process at the end of the year. Finished product is costed by the first-in, first-out cost flow assumption. As a consequence of the cost procedures used by the chief accountant, are the Finished Product and Cost of Goods Sold accounts correctly stated as of December 31, 1972? If not, what adjusting entry or entries should be made to correct them? Support any adjustments with appropriate computations. (Assume that the inventory of finished product was costed correctly at January 1, 1972.)

chapter 10

ACCOUNTING FOR STANDARD MANUFACTURING COSTS

STANDARD COSTS were introduced in Chapter 5. At that point, however, we were concerned only with the basic nature of standard costs and the manner of their determination. We then saw in Chapter 7 that standard costs are useful in the development of the operating budget, particularly in the budgeting of materials and labor costs. In Chapter 9 we saw that flexible budgets are employed in the development of standard overhead costs. In this chapter we shall consider some of the technical aspects of accounting for standard costs and the related variances of actual costs from standard. The control applications of standard costs will be discussed further in the following chapter. While management is concerned primarily with the control aspects of standard costs, the technical aspects are important to managers as well as to cost accountants. A manager cannot make effective use of a control device which he does not understand.

USES OF STANDARD MANUFACTURING COSTS

The principal purpose of standard manufacturing costs in a business enterprise is to facilitate control of actual manufacturing costs. Standard costs provide criteria against which actual costs may be compared and evaluated. Where actual costs deviate materially from standard, appropriate managerial action should be taken. If standard costs were used only for cost control, they might be employed in budgets and in operating reports without ever affecting the cost accounting system directly. Business experience has shown, however, that standard costs are useful in the accounting system itself. Quite commonly, they are used in lieu of actual costs as the basis for costing manufacturing inventories. When inventories are valued at standard costs, the cost of goods sold will be measured in terms of standard costs also. Thus, standard costs quite regularly find their way into the balance sheets and the income statements of manufacturing enterprises.

The incorporation of standard costs in the accounting system is likely to save clerical time and effort and, consequently, to reduce the cost of operating the accounting system. For example, if an inventory of finished product is valued at standard cost, the perpetual inventory records may be maintained in terms of physical quantities only, for the cost of the inventory may be determined at any time simply by multiplying the quantity on hand by the standard cost per unit. This use of standard costs in inventory accounts avoids the necessity of employing some inventory cost flow assumption such as Fifo, Lifo, or average cost, except when the standard cost for the particular inventory is changed. So long as the standard costs in use are current and reasonably attainable, they are acceptable bases for reporting inventories and cost of goods sold in financial statements prepared for stockholders, creditors, and other interested parties. In other words, standard costs are included in the framework of generally accepted accounting principles.

From one point of view, the valuation of inventories at standard costs may be regarded as not only acceptable but actually preferable to valuation at actual costs. If standard costs represent the costs which should be incurred in the manufacture of a product, one might argue that only they should be charged to that product. Any excess of actual costs over standard costs, then, would be regarded as costs of inefficiency of one sort or another rather than as costs of production. This argument may appear less reasonable in the opposite case, where actual costs are less than standard costs. However, in such case, one might view the cost difference as cost savings attributable to unusual efficiency in operations rather than to production itself.

VARIANCE COMPUTATION

Differences between actual costs and standard costs are called variances. Where actual cost is greater than standard cost, the variance is unfavorable. Where actual cost is less than standard, the variance is favorable. These terms are used in a specialized sense here to denote the direction of the variance from standard cost. A qualitative evaluation of variances as good or bad can be made only after the variances have been studied and their underlying causes identified. In this text, variances are computed by subtracting actual costs from standard costs, so that favorable variances will appear as positive amounts and unfavorable variances as negative amounts. Obviously, the opposite arithmetic approach could be taken to arrive at exactly the same variances. The approach used here has been selected simply because there seems to be an intuitive logic in variances identified as favorable appearing as positive figures and those identified as unfavorable appearing as negative figures.

Variance computation, discussed in the following sections, is the mathematical technique for determining the amount of a variance. Variance analysis, discussed in the next chapter, is the investigative process of ascertaining the causes of variances. Obviously, the latter is the more important procedure insofar as management is concerned; but computation of variances ordinarily must precede their analysis. Variance computation may be learned by committing to memory a series of variance formulas. Such an approach to learning, however, cannot relate the mathematical technique to the ultimate managerial objective. Hence, the discussion of each variance in the paragraphs that follow will begin with a description of the fundamental meaning of the variance. If one understands what a variance is intended to depict and understands the natures of the standard and actual quantities from which the variance is derived, the variance formula should follow logically.

Materials Variances

The cost of materials in a manufactured product is determined by two basic factors, the price paid for materials and the quantity of materials used in production. The time of purchase and the time of usage are not ordinarily the same. Materials may be purchased in one period and used in a subsequent period. To the extent that a materials cost variance arises from purchasing, it should be associated with the period in which the purchase was made. To the extent that it arises from usage, it should be associated with the period in which the materials were used in production. Thus, a single net materials variance, comprising both price and usage elements, cannot be computed directly. Of course, a single variance may be computed as the algebraic sum of the separate price and usage variances. It is doubtful that such a net variance would be useful to management, however.

Materials Price Variance. When materials are purchased, they may be bought either at the established standard price or at some price other than standard. In the latter instance, a variance will arise because of the price differential from standard. This is the *materials price variance.*

While this variance is not necessarily attributable to good or bad purchasing practices, it does arise at the time of purchase and, logically, should be identified at that point. Obviously, the total amount of the variance will be greater the more units of materials are bought. Thus, the materials price variance is a function of the difference between the standard and actual prices per unit of material and the quantity of material purchased. The formula then follows logically:

> The materials price variance is equal to the difference between the standard price and the actual price per unit of material multiplied by the quantity of materials purchased,

or

$$(1) \qquad\qquad MPV = (SP - AP) \times Q$$

This variance, as well as the others discussed in this chapter, will be illustrated for a hypothetical manufacturing company with a highly simplified manufacturing cost structure. The Rapa Nui Company makes imitation Polynesian statues. It uses a single raw material in the production process. This material, a chemically treated clay substance, has a standard price of $10 per pound.[1] During the month of October, 1972, the company purchased 14,000 pounds of this material at a price of $9.96 per pound. The materials price variance for the month is computed as follows:

$$MPV = (\$10.00 - \$9.96) \times 14,000 = \$.04 \times 14,000 = \$560$$

As the actual price in this instance is lower than the standard price, the variance is favorable and, hence, a positive number.

Materials Usage Variance. The *materials usage variance* (or *materials quantity variance*) seeks to identify the difference between actual and standard materials costs attributable to the use of more or less materials in production than the standard quantity. The actual usage of materials is determined from a summary of materials issue reports during the period under study. For the Rapa Nui Company, this summary shows total actual usage of 12,500 pounds in October, 1972. The standard quantity of materials in production depends upon two factors, the standard quantity of materials required for each unit of product and the number of units produced during the period. The standard cost card of the Rapa Nui Company calls for an input of 8 pounds of material for each statue produced. During the month of October, 1972, 1,560 statues were completed; and there was neither a beginning nor an ending inventory of work in process. Where there is a beginning or an ending inventory of work in process or both, the degree of completion of such inventories must be determined; and the units produced during that

---

[1] Refer to Chapter 5 for the manner of establishing price and quantity standards for both materials and direct labor.

period must be expressed in terms of equivalent units of production.[2] For the Rapa Nui Company, the standard quantity of material in production for October, 1972 is 12,480 pounds (1,560 units produced, each requiring 8 pounds of material).

If the materials usage variance is to do what it is intended to do, namely, to measure the cost variance attributable to usage of materials, it must abstract from the problem of price differences. As the difference between actual and standard price (if any) is determined at the time of purchase of materials, the usage variance ignores such difference and translates physical quantities to costs by means of the standard price only. Thus, the materials usage variance is a function of the difference between the standard and actual materials input quantities and the standard materials price. The formula is as follows:

> The materials usage variance is equal to the difference between the standard quantity of materials in production and the actual quantity used multiplied by the standard materials price,

or

(2) $$MUV = (SQ - AQ) \times SP$$

For October, 1972, the materials usage variance of the Rapa Nui Company is computed thus:

$$MUV = (12,480 - 12,500) \times \$10 = (20) \times \$10 = (\$200)$$

In this and in subsequent illustrations, negative amounts are shown in parentheses. As here, where the actual usage exceeds the standard quantity in production, a negative variance is unfavorable.

Labor Variances

Unlike materials, labor cannot be stored. Hence, the purchase and usage of labor may be viewed as simultaneous. Actually, payment for labor services is usually made at regular paydays after the work has been performed. Wages and salaries accrue as work is done, however, so that the purchase and usage of labor services are effectively simultaneous. Hence, a single net labor variance for a given period can be computed. It is the difference between the actual and standard labor costs of the period. It is, however, both feasible and useful to break this net variance down into components attributable to price and quantity differences. Unlike the two materials variances described above, these two labor variances do sum to a single significant variance.

Labor Rate Variance. The difference between standard and actual labor costs attributable to a difference between the standard and actual

---

[2] Refer to Chapter 4 for the method of computing equivalent units of production.

hourly wage rates is identified as the *labor rate variance* (or *wage rate variance*). (As mentioned in Chapter 5, weekly or monthly salaries are controlled by budgets and are not expressed as standard rates.) In order to isolate the effect of wage rate differentials, the labor rate variance ignores the question of whether the number of labor hours worked during the period was above or below the standard number that should have been worked. It is concerned only with the number of hours that actually were worked and, hence, that were paid at the actual wage rate and should have been paid at the standard rate. The labor rate variance, thus, is a function of the difference between the standard and actual wage rates and the actual labor hours worked. The formula is as follows:[3]

> The labor rate variance is equal to the difference between the standard wage rate per hour and the actual wage rate multiplied by the actual number of hours worked,

or

(3) $$LRV = (SR - AR) \times AH$$

The Rapa Nui Company has only one class of direct laborers; their standard wage rate is $2 per hour. During October, 1972, the actual payroll shows 31,100 hours worked at an actual wage rate of $2.03 per hour. Computation of the company's labor rate variance for the month is as follows:

$$LRV = (\$2.00 - \$2.03) \times 31,100 = (\$.03) \times 31,100 = (\$933)$$

As the actual hourly rate is higher than the standard rate, the variance is unfavorable.

Labor Efficiency Variance.   The quantity of labor used in a period is measured in units of time (usually man-hours). The time required for production is commonly thought of as an indication of the efficiency of the labor force. Hence, the variance which seeks to identify the impact of working more or less hours than the standard hours in production is called the *labor efficiency variance* (or *labor time variance*). It abstracts from problems of rate differences, which are identified in the labor rate variance, and is concerned only with the standard wage rate. The actual hours worked are determined from payroll summary sheets. The standard hours in production are determined by the established standard hours required for the production of one unit of product and the number of units produced during the period under study. Again, where there are partially completed inventories of work in process at the beginning and/or end of the period, production must be stated in terms of equivalent

---

[3] Less frequently today, the standard labor rate is a rate per piece of production rather than per hour worked. In this case, the labor rate variance would be equal to the difference between the standard piece rate and the actual piece rate multiplied by the actual units produced during a period.

units. Thus, the labor efficiency variance is a function of the difference between standard and actual labor hours worked and the standard wage rate. The formula is as follows:

The labor efficiency variance is equal to the difference between the standard and the actual labor hours worked during a period multiplied by the standard wage rate per hour,

or

(4) $$LEV = (SH - AH) \times SR$$

The standard cost card of the Rapa Nui Company calls for 20 man-hours of work for each statue manufactured. Actual production for the month of October, 1972, totaled 1,560 statues. Standard hours in production, then, total 31,200 (1,560 units $\times$ 20 hours). The labor efficiency variance for the month is computed as follows:

$$LEV = (31,200 - 31,100) \times \$2 = 100 \times \$2 = \$200$$

Since the actual hours worked are less than the standard hours in production, the variance is favorable.[4]

Overhead—Measures of Volume

As explained in Chapter 5, standard overhead costs are based upon budgets and, typically, upon flexible budgets such as the one illustrated in Table 9–1 in Chapter 9. Standard variable overhead costs are determined independently of the level of volume planned, but standard fixed overhead costs can be determined only at some specified level of volume. An understanding of standard overhead costs and overhead variances requires a prior understanding of several concepts of production volume.

Normal Volume. A standard fixed overhead cost per unit of volume must be set at one given level of volume which is considered representative of the company's operations. The volume level most commonly selected for this purpose is *normal volume*. Normal volume is usually defined in either of two ways, which may or may not prove to be equivalent in any given situation. The first definition of normal volume is

---

[4] If direct laborers were compensated by a piece rate instead of an hourly rate, there would be no labor efficiency variance as described here. Under a pure piece-rate system, direct labor cost (after allowance for any labor rate variance) would be a direct function of output. However, as a practical matter, workers in a piece-rato system must still be paid at least a minimum hourly wage. Thus, an inefficient worker whose output was insufficient to make his piece-rate compensation at least equal to the minimum hourly wage would receive an additional amount so that his total earnings equaled the minimum wage for the number of hours he worked. Such additional payment is referred to as a "makeup to minimum" and amounts to a labor efficiency variance. This type of variance, of course, could only be unfavorable. As noted in footnote 3, piece-rate compensation plans are no longer common in American industry.

the preferred rate of operating capacity in a firm's manufacturing facilities. Each firm identifies a particular rate of capacity at which it would most like to operate its plant. Logically, this is that level of capacity at which the mix of productive inputs is optimized and, hence, manufacturing cost per unit of product is minimized. It is easy to see that such a concept of normal volume would be consistent with the notion of standard cost. In a large segment of American industry, the preferred rate of operating capacity in recent years has been between 90% and 95% of full capacity.

The second definition of normal volume is the average level of production activity over a complete business cycle. This is a difficult concept to quantify because business cycles are not always easily defined and because, in most firms, there is a secular growth trend superimposed upon cyclical fluctuations. In other words, this average would normally be an upward moving average. While management might wish that the average production volume would be equal to the preferred rate of capacity, it is more likely that it would be lower. The preferred rate is more likely to be achieved only during periods of prosperity. Of course, these periods may be more prolonged than periods of recession.

However it is defined, normal volume will not necessarily be equal to budgeted production volume for any given period. While the standard fixed overhead cost may be based upon normal volume, the operating budget should be predicated upon the best estimate of what volume actually will be during the budget period. As is true of any concept of volume, normal volume may be measured either in units of output or in units of input.

Actual Output Volume. *Actual output volume* is simply the number of units of product actually produced during a given period. Output measures the results of production. These may be regarded as good or bad, satisfactory or unsatisfactory, according to established plans for output. There is no such concept as "standard output volume," however, as the term "standard" is used here. In this context, "standard" refers only to inputs, such as materials, labor hours, and machine-hours. In October, 1972, the actual output of the Rapa Nui Company totaled 1,560 units of product. Although the company uses input rather than output in measuring production for purposes of charging overhead costs to products, actual output is necessary to determine the standard materials usage and the standard labor hours in production.

Standard Input Volume. Production volume may also be measured in units of input. The input quantity used as a measure of production volume in the illustration in this chapter is direct labor hours. *Standard input volume* is the total quantity of labor hours (or of some other input quantity) that the labor time standard indicates is necessary to produce the actual output of a period. Thus, standard input volume and actual output volume, although stated in different quantities, are equivalent measures of the results of operations. The standard input volume for the Rapa Nui Company in the month of October, 1972, is simply the 31,200 standard direct labor hours in production. This total is determined by multiplying the 1,560 units of output (i.e., completed statues) by the labor time standard of 20 man-hours per statue. Standard input volume is always a direct function of the actual output and the relevant standard (labor time, in this case) per unit of output.

Actual Input Volume. Where volume is measured in labor hours, *actual input volume* is simply the actual labor hours worked during a period. This may be greater than standard input volume by the amount of excess, or wasted, hours worked or less than standard by the amount of hours saved. Actual input volume measures the firm's total productive effort during a period, whether that effort was fruitful in terms of output or not. For October, 1972, the actual input volume of the Rapa Nui Company was 31,100 labor hours. This amount includes the 31,200 standard labor hours minus the 100 hours saved.

Overhead Variances in General

As in the case of direct labor, a single variance for overhead is significant. This is the net difference between the standard overhead cost of production for a period and the actual overhead costs incurred in the period. Where volume is measured in units of output, standard overhead cost is computed by multiplying the actual units produced by the standard variable and fixed overhead costs per unit of product. Where volume is measured in units of input, standard overhead cost is computed by multiplying the standard input volume by the standard variable and fixed overhead rates per unit of input. If input is stated in labor hours, these are standard rates per hour. A variable overhead rate is simply the budgeted amount per unit by which variable overhead costs are expected to change in response to changes in volume. It is used in both variable and absorption costing. A fixed overhead rate is determined by dividing total budgeted fixed overhead costs for a period by the normal volume for that period. The fixed rate, of course, is used only in absorption costing. As absorption costing is the more inclusive alternative, we shall discuss standard overhead costs here within that framework.

The flexible overhead budget of the Rapa Nui Company allows total variable overhead costs of $1.20 per direct labor hour plus total fixed costs of $51,200 per month. (The entire company is treated here as a single cost center having a single flexible budget. This is done merely to keep the size of the illustration easily manageable.) Normal volume has been established as 32,000 labor hours per month. Thus, the standard fixed overhead rate is $1.60 per labor hour ($51,200 ÷ 32,000 hours).

The total standard overhead cost in production for the month of October is computed by multiplying the 31,200 standard direct labor hours in production by the variable and the fixed rates per hour, thus:

Standard variable overhead (31,200 × $1.20).............	$37,440
Standard fixed overhead (31,200 × $1.60)................	49,920
Total standard overhead cost for month..................	$87,360

The actual overhead costs incurred during October totaled $89,000, including $37,650 of variable costs and $51,350 of fixed costs. The net overhead variance, then, is the difference between the total standard and actual overhead costs:

Total standard overhead cost...........................	$87,360
Total actual overhead cost.............................	89,000
Net overhead variance.................................	$(1,640)

As the actual costs are greater than the standard cost, the net overhead variable is unfavorable.

Overhead Variances—Three-Variance Plan

Where volume is measured in units of input, the net overhead variance can be further broken down into three component variances.

Overhead Spending Variance. The *overhead spending variance* seeks to identify and isolate that portion of the net overhead variance that is attributable to differences between actual and budgeted spending on overhead cost items. It ignores any differences that may exist between actual and standard input volumes or between standard input volume and normal volume. It accepts actual input volume at face value and measures the difference between the budgeted overhead spending for the actual input volume and the actual overhead costs incurred. Flexible overhead budgets are essential for the computation of this variance, for the budget must be adjusted from whatever volume was originally planned to the actual input volume of the period. The formula for this variance is as follows:

The overhead spending variance is equal to the difference between the budgeted overhead costs for the actual input volume and the actual overhead costs incurred,

or

$$(5) \qquad\qquad OSV = BCAIV - AC$$

Note that this is exactly the same as the spending variance computed in Table 9–3 of Chapter 9.

For the month of October, 1972, the actual input volume of the Rapa Nui Company was 31,100 direct labor hours. The flexible budget allows

$1.20 per labor hour plus $51,200 per month. The actual overhead costs were given in the preceding section. The company's spending variance for October is computed as follows:

Budgeted costs for actual input volume:		
Variable costs (31,100 hrs. × $1.20)........		$37,320
Fixed costs.............................		51,200
		$88,520
Actual costs:		
Variable costs.........................	$37,650	
Fixed costs...........................	51,350	89,000
		$ (480)

As the actual costs exceed the budgeted costs, the variance is unfavorable. Separate spending variances for variable and fixed overhead could be computed easily from the data above. In this illustration, both would be unfavorable variances—$330 for variable overhead and $150 for fixed overhead.

The spending variance computed in the preceding paragraph includes both variable and fixed overhead cost items, for the Rapa Nui Company uses absorption costing. The question arises as to whether both variable and fixed overhead would be included in the determination of the spending variance in a company using variable costing. If the variance is to conform to the definition of product cost under variable costing, fixed overhead would be excluded from it. Thus, it might be referred to as the variable overhead spending variance. This approach would be consistent with the exclusion of any fixed overhead from standard production cost under variable costing. On the other hand, just because fixed overhead is not charged to production, its control cannot be ignored. Costs must be controlled regardless of how they are accounted for. Thus, for cost control purposes, a total overhead spending variance, including both variable and fixed costs, would still seem more appropriate. Perhaps the simplest solution to this question would be to compute separate spending variances for variable and fixed overhead, recognize only the variable cost variance in the accounts, but use both for control purposes.

For effective cost control, the spending variance should be determined separately for each item of overhead cost, as was done in Table 9–3 in Chapter 9. The causes of the total overhead spending variance may be quite varied. The variance may be caused, in part, by differences between the actual prices paid for goods and services included in overhead and the prices assumed in the development of the budget. It may also be caused, partly, by differences in the actual usage of such goods and services as compared with the usage planned in the budget. For example, assume that the flexible budget includes a variable allowance of $.10 for indirect materials. This allowance may be based upon a price of $.05 per pound and an expected rate of consumption of 2 pounds per direct labor hour. If the actual price is more than $.05 per pound and the actual consumption rate is greater than 2 pounds per hour, the actual cost of indirect materials will be higher than the budgeted indirect materials cost for the actual input volume. That higher cost will be caused by both price and usage factors. Other overhead items may involve either more or less spending than the budget calls for. If a depreciation rate on factory equipment is changed after the flexible budget is established, actual and budgeted depreciation will differ; and this difference will appear in the overhead spending variance.

Overhead Efficiency Variance. This variance exists only where volume is measured in units of input. The *overhead efficiency variance* measures the excess cost incurred or the cost saving due to the fact that actual input volume is more or less, respectively, than standard input volume. Logically, this variance relates only to variable overhead costs, for only variable costs are affected by variations in volume. The formula for the efficiency variance is as follows:

The overhead efficiency variance is equal to the difference between the standard input volume and the actual input volume multiplied by the standard variable overhead rate per unit of volume,

or

(6) $$OEV = (SIV - AIV) \times SVOR$$

Where labor hours are the input quantity used to measure volume, the overhead efficiency variance is caused directly by labor efficiency. Thus, some have argued that the overhead efficiency variance should be regarded as part of the labor efficiency variance. Certainly, they have a common cause; but there is no objection to these two efficiency variances being stated separately.

For the Rapa Nui Company in October, 1972, the standard input volume is 31,200 direct labor hours. The actual input volume is 31,100 hours, and the standard variable overhead rate is $1.20 per hour. The variance is then computed thus:

$$OEV = (31,200 - 31,100) \times \$1.20 = 100 \times \$1.20 = \$120$$

Since the actual input volume is less than the standard input volume, variable overhead costs should have been saved, and the variance is favorable. Whenever volume is measured in labor hours, the labor efficiency variance and the overhead efficiency variance will always both be favorable or both be unfavorable.

Overhead Volume Variance. The *overhead volume variance* is attributable to differences between the standard input volume and normal volume. Specifically, it arises because a standard fixed overhead rate is computed at normal volume and applied to production at standard input volume. Strictly, a fixed overhead rate per unit of volume is valid only at the volume at which the rate is computed. This is so because fixed overhead costs are constant in total and, hence, are different per unit at each different level of volume. Nevertheless, in a standard cost system, a fixed overhead rate computed at normal volume is charged to production at standard input volume, which is most likely to be different from normal volume. Thus, this practice almost invariably causes a variance. The standard fixed overhead rate is strictly conceived to absorb total budgeted fixed overhead only at normal volume. If used at any other volume, the fixed overhead rate will result in either more or less than the total budgeted fixed overhead being absorbed by production. As fixed overhead is charged to production only in absorption costing, the volume variance can exist only in that method. The formula for the overhead volume variance is as follows:

> The overhead volume variance is equal to the difference between the standard fixed overhead cost charged to production and the budgeted fixed overhead cost,[5]

or

(7) $$OVV = SFOC - BFOC$$

For the Rapa Nui Company, the standard fixed overhead charged to production during October, 1972, was $49,920 (31,200 standard hours × $1.60 per hour). The budgeted fixed overhead is given as $51,200 per month. The volume variance, then, is computed thus:

$$OVV = \$49,920 - \$51,200 = (\$1,280)$$

The variance is unfavorable because the standard input volume is not sufficient to absorb all of the budgeted fixed overhead costs at the standard fixed overhead rate of $1.60 per hour. Any time that a fixed overhead rate is applied at a volume lower than the normal volume at which it was computed (as is the case here), the standard fixed overhead cost will be less than the budgeted fixed cost, and the volume variance will be unfavorable. Conversely, if a fixed overhead rate is applied at a volume higher than normal volume, the volume variance will invariably be favorable.

Summary of Three-Variance Plan. We have observed the determination of three separate overhead variances. Their algebraic sum should be equal to the net overhead variance of $1,640 computed earlier. That this is, in fact, so may be demonstrated simply.

---

[5] An alternative method of calculating the overhead volume variance is to multiply the difference between the standard input volume and the normal volume by the standard fixed overhead rate. Actually, this is not a different formula but a different arrangement of the same formula.

Overhead spending variance.................... $ (480)
Overhead efficiency variance...................   120
Overhead volume variance.....................   (1,280)
Net overhead variance........................ $(1,640)

The spending variance relates to both variable and fixed overhead cost items; the efficiency variance relates exclusively to variable cost items; and the volume variance relates exclusively to fixed overhead.

Overhead Variances—Two-Variance Plan

Where production volume is measured in units of output rather than input, only two separate overhead variances can be computed. As the Rapa Nui Company uses an input measure of volume, we must construct a different illustration for the two-variance plan. Assume that the following budgeted and actual data are taken from the records of the Easterland Company for the month of June, 1972:

Normal volume........................... 15,000 units of output
Budgeted variable overhead.............. $.60 per unit of output
Budgeted fixed overhead................. $13,500 per month
Actual output........................... 15,800 units of product

Actual overhead costs:
    Variable............................ $ 9,500
    Fixed............................... $13,900

The standard fixed overhead rate is $.90 per unit ($13,500 ÷ 15,000 units at normal volume). The net overhead variance is then computed as follows:

Standard overhead cost for month:
    Variable cost (15,800 units × $.60)......... $ 9,480
    Fixed cost (15,800 units × $.90)............   14,220
                                                         23,700

Actual overhead cost for month:
    Variable cost........................... $ 9,500
    Fixed cost.............................   13,900   23,400
    Net overhead variance...................... $ 300

The net variance here is favorable.

Overhead Budget Variance. Where overhead is charged to production on the basis of output rather than input, there is no basis for measuring overhead efficiency and, hence, no overhead efficiency variance. Thus, the two-variance plan identifies overhead variances attributable to spending and volume differences only. The *overhead budget variance* in the two-variance plan is fundamentally similar to the spending variance in the three-variance plan. The use of a different name for the variance in the two-variance plan is common practice and is helpful in distinguishing the two plans. Further, the budget variance is not identical to the spending variance. Even though overhead efficiency is not measurable separately in the two-variance plan, it may still exist. If it does, the budget variance includes both spending and efficiency factors; whereas the spending variance in the three-variance plan specifically excludes the efficiency factor. The budget variance is the difference between the actual costs incurred and the costs which the flexible budget indicates should be incurred at the actual output volume achieved. The formula is as follows:

> The overhead budget variance is equal to the difference between the budgeted overhead cost for the actual output volume and the actual overhead cost incurred,

or

(8) $$OBV = BCAOV - AC$$

For cost control purposes, the budget variance should be determined separately for each distinct overhead cost item.

For the Easterland Company for the month of June, 1972, the overhead budget variance is the difference between the budgeted costs for the actual output volume of 15,800 units of product and the actual costs incurred in June. It is computed as follows:

Budgeted cost for actual output volume:		
Variable (15,800 units × $.60)...............		$ 9,480
Fixed..................................		13,500
		$22,980
Actual cost:		
Variable...............................	$ 9,500	
Fixed.................................	13,900	23,400
		$ (420)

As the actual costs exceed the budget allowances for the actual volume, the variance is unfavorable.

The budget variance can be employed in firms which use an input measure of volume also. In such firms, it is simply the algebraic sum of the spending and efficiency variances in the three-variance plan. It is computed as the difference between the budgeted cost for the standard input volume and the actual cost. Because of the basically different sources of the spending and efficiency variances, however, the three-variance plan is normally more useful to management.

Overhead Volume Variance. The volume variance is identical under both the two-variance plan and the three-variance plan. It is the difference between the standard fixed overhead cost charged to production and the budgeted fixed overhead cost. Where volume was measured in units of input, standard fixed overhead cost was computed by multiplying the standard fixed rate by the standard input volume. Where volume is stated in units of output, standard fixed overhead cost is determined by multiplying the standard fixed rate by the actual output volume. But standard input volume and actual output volume, it should be recalled, are equivalent concepts. Both measure the results of production. For the Easterland Company, the volume variance for June, 1972, is computed thus:

Standard fixed overhead cost (15,800 × $.90
    standard fixed rate per unit)................. $14,220
Budgeted fixed overhead cost per month.........   13,500
                                                  $ 720

The variance is favorable because actual output volume is greater than normal volume.

Summary of Two-Variance Plan. The algebraic sum of the overhead budget and volume variances computed for the Easterland Company should be equal to the net overhead variance of $300, computed earlier. That this is so is shown below:

Overhead budget variance...................... $(420)
Overhead volume variance......................   720
Net overhead variance......................... $ 300

The budget variance deals with both variable and fixed costs, while the volume variance relates exclusively to fixed costs.

Summary of Variance Formulas

For the sake of ease in studying and reviewing variances, the formulas for the eight variances discussed in the foregoing pages are summarized below. In each case, the formula is so stated that a positive variance is favorable and a negative variance, unfavorable.

Materials and Labor:

(1) Materials price variance = (standard price per unit of material − actual price) × quantity of materials actually purchased.

(2) Materials usage variance = (standard quantity of materials in production − actual quantity used) × standard price per unit.

(3) Labor rate variance = (standard wage rate per hour − actual wage rate) × actual labor hours worked.

(4) Labor efficiency variance = (standard labor hours in production − actual hours worked) × standard wage rate per hour.

Overhead—Three-Variance Plan:

(5) Overhead spending variance = budgeted overhead costs for actual input volume − actual overhead costs.

(6) Overhead efficiency variance = (standard input volume − actual input volume) × standard variable overhead rate.

(7) Overhead volume variance = standard fixed overhead cost in production − budgeted fixed overhead cost.

Overhead—Two-Variance Plan:

(8) Overhead budget variance = budgeted overhead cost for actual output volume − actual overhead cost.

(7) Overhead volume variance—same as under three-variance plan.

RECORDING STANDARD MANUFACTURING COSTS

There is no uniform system of accounting by which standard costs are incorporated in the recording process of the cost accounting cycle. There are at least three basic types of standard cost systems, and there are variations in the techniques used under each system. All of these differences are methodological, however, and not conceptual. The same variances would be computed under any of these systems,[6] although they might be recorded differently in the accounts. In this chapter we shall illustrate the so-called *single plan* of standard cost accounting, wherein all manufacturing inventory accounts are charged and credited only for standard costs. Differences between standard and actual costs are charged or credited to variance accounts. Favorable variances appear as credit balances, for they represent cost savings (or offsets against cost) as compared with standard costs. Unfavorable variances appear as debit balances, for they are additional costs in excess of standard amounts.

The cost accounting cycle for the Rapa Nui Company for October, 1972, will be illustrated here. Fundamentally, the entries here are the same as those illustrated in Chapter 3 for an actual cost system. The variances recorded in the entries below are those computed in the foregoing sections and will not be explained further.

1. *Purchase of Materials.* Fourteen thousand pounds of raw materials were purchased at a price of $9.96 per pound. The standard price is $10 per pound.

Materials Inventory	140,000	
Materials Price Variance		560
Vouchers Payable		139,440

The inventory account is charged for the standard price of the units purchased. The liability to the supplier, of course, is recorded at the actual price; for this is the amount that will have to be paid to him.

---

[6] There is one exception to this statement. Under one variation of any of the basic standard cost systems, the materials price variance is computed for the units used only, rather than for the total number of units purchased. From the standpoint of managerial control, this approach to the materials price variance seems to be less useful than the one employed in this chapter; hence, it will not be discussed or illustrated.

2. *Usage of Materials.* Twelve thousand five hundred pounds of materials were actually used. The standard input is 8 pounds per statue produced. As 1,560 statues were manufactured during the month, standard materials usage amounts to 12,480 pounds.

```
Work in Process.................................... 124,800
Materials Usage Variance...........................    200
    Materials Inventory............................           125,000
```

Work in Process is charged for the standard quantity of materials at the standard price. Materials Inventory must be credited for the actual quantity used at the standard price.

3. *Manufacturing Payroll.* The actual hours worked by direct laborers totaled 31,100 for the month. The standard hours in production amounted to 31,200. The actual wage rate paid was $2.03 per hour, as compared with the standard rate of $2 per hour.

```
Work in Process.................................... 62,400
Labor Rate Variance................................    933
    Labor Efficiency Variance......................            200
    Payroll Summary................................         63,133
```

Work in Process is charged for the standard hours in production at the standard wage rate. The Payroll Summary is credited for the actual direct labor cost of the month (the actual hours at the actual rate). This entry is deliberately simplified to focus attention on the basic labor cost accounting procedures. Actually, it is likely that some amount of indirect labor would be included in the payroll; this would be charged to an overhead control account, of course. The entry for payment of the payroll is no different from the same entry under an actual cost system. The payroll department is concerned with actual labor cost data only. Standards do not affect the amounts paid to workers and withheld for subsequent remittance to the government or some other third party.

4. *Actual Overhead Cost Incurrence.* The actual overhead costs incurred are recorded in the same way under a standard cost system as in an actual cost system. The $89,000 of actual overhead costs incurred comprised $37,650 of variable costs and $51,350 of fixed costs.

```
Variable Overhead Control.......................... 37,650
Fixed Overhead Control............................. 51,350
    Various accounts...............................          89,000
```

5. *Application of Overhead Cost to Production.* Work in Process is charged for the standard overhead cost of the units produced during the month. Under absorption costing, this will be the sum of the standard variable cost rate ($1.20 per labor hour) and the standard fixed cost rate ($1.60 per labor hour), each multiplied by the standard labor hours in production for the month (31,200 hours).

Work in Process......................................	87,360	
Variable Overhead Applied.........................		37,440
Fixed Overhead Applied...........................		49,920

Under variable costing, only variable overhead would be charged to the product. The fixed Overhead Control account would be closed directly to Revenue and Expense Summary.

6. *Recording Overhead Variances.* The entries illustrated in paragraphs 4 and 5 above do not show the overhead variances directly. Rather, they leave the net overhead variance as the difference between the debit balances in the Overhead Control accounts and the credit balances in the Overhead Applied accounts. This may be an entirely satisfactory method of accounting for these variances. If, however, management wishes to have them recorded in individual accounts as are the materials and labor variances, the Overhead Control and Applied accounts may be closed and the desired variance accounts set up. This procedure will be illustrated below for the absorption costing method only and for the three-variance plan only. Similar entries for variable costing and/or for the two-variance plan should be obvious.

Variable Overhead Applied............................	37,440	
Fixed Overhead Applied..............................	49,920	
Overhead Spending Variance..........................	480	
Overhead Volume Variance............................	1,280	
Overhead Efficiency Variance......................		120
Variable Overhead Control.........................		37,650
Fixed Overhead Control............................		51,350

7. *Completion of Production.* The standard cost sheet (or standard cost card) for the product of the Rapa Nui Company under the absorption costing method is as follows:

Materials (8 lbs. @ $10).....................		$ 80.00
Labor (20 hrs. @ $2).........................		40.00
Overhead:		
Variable (20 hrs. @ $1.20).................	$24.00	
Fixed (20 hrs. @ $1.60)....................	32.00	56.00
		$176.00

Thus, the total standard cost of one statue is $176. Under variable costing, it would be $144 per statue, the $32 of fixed overhead being omitted. Since Work in Process has been charged only for the standard cost of goods put into production, logically it will be the standard cost of completed units that will be transferred from that account to Finished Product. The entry for this transfer, under absorption costing, is as follows:

Finished Product.....................................	274,560	
Work in Process...............................		274,560

The standard cost of 1,560 finished statues is $274,560 (1,560 @ $176). Under variable costing, the standard cost of the finished production would be less, totaling only $224,640 (1,560 statues @ $144).

8. *Sales.* During October, 1972, the Rapa Nui Company sold 1,500 statues at a unit price of $240. The entry to record the sales revenue is, of course, unaffected by the costing method employed by the firm.

Accounts Receivable.............................. 360,000
    Sales.. 360,000

The cost of sales depends upon the costing method used, however. Under absorption costing, the cost of goods sold would be the product of the 1,500 statues sold multiplied by the standard unit cost of $176.

Cost of Goods Sold................................ 264,000
    Finished Product............................... 264,000

Under variable costing, the cost of sales would be equal to 1,500 statues sold at a standard variable cost of $144 per statue.

DISPOSITION OF VARIANCES

Charge or Credit to Current Period's Income

Once the variances have been computed and have been charged or credited to individual variance accounts,[7] the question arises as to what should be their final disposition. In most cases, as a practical matter, variance accounts are charged (unfavorable variances) or credited (favorable variances) to the income of the current period. This may be accomplished by closing the variance accounts either to the Revenue and Expense Summary account or to the Cost of Goods Sold account. Net income, of course, would be the same under either alternative. In the income statement, the net total of all the variances is treated as an adjustment to the cost of goods sold figure. If the net variance is favorable, it is deducted from cost of goods sold; if the net variance is unfavorable, it is added to cost of goods sold.[8] Showing each variance in detail would seem unnecessary in a summarized report such as the income statement. Individual variances should, of course, be reported to appropriate levels of management for action.

So long as standards are current and attainable and so long as flexible budgets for overhead are based upon reasonable current cost estimates, charging or crediting manufacturing variances to current income appears to be a theoretically sound and practically satisfactory method of disposing of them—with one possible exception to be noted shortly. If, on the other hand, standards and budgets are not current and attainable, standard cost is not a satisfactory measure of current production costs;

---

[7] The same effect can be achieved by charging or crediting all variances to a single Variance Summary account.

[8] This is essentially the same method of reporting as suggested in Chapter 3 for net under- or overapplied overhead.

and, hence, the variances are not valid indicators of departures from cost levels that should have been attained. In such instance, it would be better to dispose of the variances by adjusting the several manufacturing cost accounts from the invalid standard cost to the actual cost of the period.

Allocation of Variances to Manufacturing Cost Accounts

If standards and budgets do not reflect current attainable cost levels, charging or crediting variances to income may result in an overstatement or understatement of inventories and cost of goods sold. In such a case, it is better to adjust the inventory and cost of goods sold accounts to actual costs by allocating the manufacturing variances among them. Variances would be allocated among the several accounts to which the standard manufacturing costs had been charged—Work in Process, Finished Product, and Cost of Goods Sold. The amount allocated to each of these accounts would be determined by the amount of the relevant standard cost in each account as of the end of the period relative to the total amount of that standard cost charged to production during the period. For example, labor variances would be allocated on the basis of standard labor cost of the period. Assume that a total of $600,000 of standard labor cost had been charged to Work in Process during a given period. Of that total, $540,000 had been transferred to Finished Product and $420,000 had been further transferred from Finished Product to Cost of Goods Sold. At the end of the period, the standard labor cost of the period in each of these accounts would be as follows:

Work in Process.....................	$ 60,000
Finished Product....................	120,000
Cost of Goods Sold.................	420,000
	$600,000

The net labor variance would then be allocated as follows: one tenth to Work in Process, two tenths to Finished Product, and seven tenths to Cost of Goods Sold. Allocation of materials and overhead variances would be accomplished in a similar manner; standard materials cost and standard overhead cost, respectively, being used as the bases for allocations. It should be noted that the materials price variance would likely be allocated partly to Materials Inventory as well as to the three accounts listed above.

Special Problem of the Volume Variance

The discussions in the preceding two sections is sufficient for all of the variances from standard cost except one, the overhead volume variance. Even if the flexible budget contains current attainable fixed cost estimates, the standard fixed overhead rate may not provide for a reasonable assignment of current fixed overhead to production. This fixed rate is computed on the basis of normal volume, which, as explained earlier, may deviate substantially from the budgeted and/or from the actual volume in any single period. Thus, a substantial volume variance could actually be anticipated in most periods. If normal volume is the average level of operations expected over the course of the business cycle, one would expect that favorable and unfavorable volume variances would tend to offset one another over a complete cycle. If normal volume is defined as the company's preferred rate of operating capacity, however, and if that rate is not always reached and almost never exceeded, the volume variance over long periods of time would be unfavorable.

Where the amount of the volume variance is not very material in relation to total inventory cost or to net income for the period, it may safely be treated as an adjustment to cost of goods sold along with the other variances. If the amount is very material, it would have to be allocated among the accounts affected. However, it should be noted that in most cases, most of the volume variance would be charged or credited to cost of goods sold even if it is allocated among the several accounts. This is a result of the fact that most of the goods produced currently are also sold currently. Thus, the volume variance would be unlikely to have a substantial effect on income except in cases of substantial changes in the level of inventories of manufactured products at the end of a period as compared with the beginning of that period.

If it is expected that favorable and unfavorable volume variances will offset each other over time, a firm might wish to defer the volume variance at the end of each period. It would be a deferred credit (a liability) if favorable and a deferred charge (an asset) if unfavorable. This practice is usually restricted to monthly financial reporting. Annual financial statements almost invariably provide for a final disposition of the volume variance. Where there are significant monthly variations in production volume, deferral of the volume variance at the end of each month seems appropriate. Deferral at the end of a fiscal year, however, seems questionable. The volume variance derives from the practical exigencies of an absorption costing system. It is not so much a consequence of operations as it is a consequence of how operations are accounted for. Further, a defered volume variance would be a dubious asset or liability in any event.[9]

---

[9] The proponent of variable costing in published financial statements may smile at this point and observe that, if people would only listen to him, there would be no volume variance to worry about at all.

QUESTIONS FOR DISCUSSION

1. "Inasmuch as standard costs reflect costs that should have been incurred rather than costs that actually were incurred, they are useful only for purposes of cost analysis and control. They may not be used in the valuation of inventories or in the measurement of income. If standard costs are used for the latter purposes, the balance sheet and the income statement will reflect, in part, the operating goals of the firm rather than its operating results." Comment on this statement.

2. Explain the essential source of each of the variances listed below. That is, from what conditions or factors do they derive?
   a) Materials price variance
   b) Labor rate variance
   c) Materials usage variance
   d) Labor efficiency variance
   e) Overhead spending variance
   f) Overhead efficiency variance
   g) Overhead volume variance

3. Which of the variances listed in Question 2 above would be different under variable costing as compared with absorption costing? What causes these differences?

4. Can any of the variances listed in Question 2 be computed without knowledge of the volume of output during the period? If so, which one(s) and why?

5. Define each of the following terms: (a) normal volume, (b) actual output volume, (c) standard input volume, and (d) actual input volume. What is the role of each of these four concepts of volume in the determination of three overhead variances for a company that charges overhead to production on the basis of direct labor hours?

6. Why is it generally invalid to sum the materials price and usage variances algebraically and to describe the total as the "net materials variance" for the period?

7. The labor rate variance computed in this chapter is the difference between the standard and actual wage rates per hour multiplied by the total actual hours worked. Some writers have suggested that this might be further broken down into two subvariances: (a) the excess wage rate multiplied by the standard labor hours in production and (b) the excess wage rate multiplied by the excess (or saved) hours above (or below) the standard hours. Do you believe this further refinement of the labor rate variance would be useful to management for purposes of cost control? Explain your answer.

8. What is the basic difference between the two-variance plan and the three-variance plan for analyzing overhead costs? Under what circumstances may only one of these plans be used? Under what circumstances may either be used? When either may be used, which would be preferable? Why?

9. How may variances be disposed of in the accounts and reported in the financial statements? If there are alternatives, which is the most appropriate way? Why?

10. A corporation has approximately 800 different materials that are used in its various products. It would like to have daily reports of materials usage and the usage variance, but it does not feel that a detailed analysis of the usage of each material every day is practicable. Can you suggest a procedure that would yield reasonably reliable *and complete* daily materials usage reports without the necessity of analyzing each individual material every day?

11. What criteria might be established by management for determining whether a variance is significant and requires special corrective action?

PROBLEMS

1. The Roberts Corporation manufactures ceramic ash trays. A standard cost system is used to account for production. The standard cost sheet for one ash tray is as follows:

Raw materials:
Clay (1½ lbs. @ $.32)............................ $ .48
Pigment (5 oz. @ $1.24)......................... 6.20
Direct labor (¼ hr. @ $4.60)..................... 1.15
Overhead:
Variable... .52
Fixed... .65
$9.00

During the month of October, 1972, actual production totaled 40,000 ash trays. Actual production data for that month are summarized below:

Materials purchases: 66,000 lbs. of clay @ $.35 and
180,000 oz. of pigment @ $1.20
Materials usage: 62,400 lbs. of clay and 208,000 oz.
of pigment
Direct labor: 9,800 hrs. @ $4.75
Variable overhead: $21,600
Fixed overhead: $27,000

There were no beginning or ending inventories of work in process for the month. Sales for October totaled 36,500 ash trays.

Required:

Compute the following quantities and show all computations:
a)   Standard materials, labor, and overhead costs in production for October, 1972
b)   Standard cost of finished production
c)   Standard cost of goods sold
d)   Materials price and usage variances
e)   Labor rate and efficiency variances

2. The Buck Manufacturing Company makes widgets and employs a standard cost accounting system. The standard cost of one widget is as follows:

Materials (3 units @ $1.75)............		$ 5.25
Labor (2 hrs. @ $3.80)...............		7.60
Overhead:		
Variable (2 hrs. @ $1.50)...........	$3.00	
Fixed (2 hrs. @ $2.40).............	4.80	7.80
		$20.65

During the year 1972, actual output included 80,000 finished widgets. The inventory of work in process at January 1 consisted of 10,000 widgets, complete with respect to materials and half complete with respect to labor and overhead. At December 31, 20,000 widgets were in process, complete with respect to materials and half complete with respect to conversion costs.

Materials purchases for the year totaled 300,000 units at a price of $1.82 each. The total materials usage for the year was 278,000 units. The factory payroll for the year included a total of 166,000 direct labor hours at an average rate of $3.95 per hour.

Required:

Compute the materials price and usage variances and the labor rate and efficiency variances. Show all computations.

3. The Fitzgerald Corporation manufactures a variety of children's clothing. All products require some work in the stitching department. Normal production volume in that department is 60,000 direct labor hours per month. The budgeted monthly overhead cost for the stitching department is $135,000 plus $.75 per direct labor hour. The company uses absorption costing.

During June, 1972, the stitching department recorded a total of 64,500 labor hours, 1,500 of which were in excess of the standard hours allowed for the department's output that month. Actual overhead costs for the month included $140,000 of fixed costs and $45,000 of variable costs.

Required:

Compute three variances from standard overhead cost for the month of June, 1972. Show all computations.

4. Following is the flexible overhead budget for the Crane Company for one month:

Percent of full capacity...	70%	80%	90%	100%
Standard machine-hours..	28,000	32,000	36,000	40,000
Variable costs..........	$70,000	$80,000	$90,000	$100,000
Semivariable costs.......	34,400	37,600	40,800	44,000
Fixed costs.............	60,000	60,000	60,000	60,000

Management believes that the range of volume tabulated in this budget encompasses any volume that might reasonably be expected to occur. Normal volume has been set at 90% of capacity. Both variable and fixed overhead costs, including variable and fixed components of the semivariable costs, are charged to production at standard rates per machine-hour.

Actual operating data for the month of April, 1972, are as follows:

Actual machine-hours.....................	33,500
Standard machine-hours..................	32,000
Variable overhead costs....................	$81,000
Semivariable overhead costs...............	40,000
Fixed overhead costs......................	60,000

Required:

a) Separate the semivariable costs in the budget into variable and fixed components. Then compute standard variable and fixed overhead rates per machine-hour.

b) Calculate three variances from standard overhead cost for the month of April, 1972.

c) Explain briefly the essential meaning of each of these three variances.

5. The Ferber Products Company uses a standard cost system and variable costing. Overhead is applied to production on the basis of direct labor cost (i.e., dollars of standard direct labor). The flexible budget for the company's overhead allows $50,000 per month plus $1.10 per direct labor dollar. Budgeted direct labor costs for the month of October, 1972, are $100,000. Actual operations for October are summarized below:

Actual direct labor cost....................	$88,000
Standard direct labor cost.................	85,000
Actual variable overhead..................	99,000
Actual fixed overhead.....................	52,500

Required:

a) Compute the standard overhead cost of production for the month of October, 1972.

b) Compute as many variances from standard overhead for October as you can.

6. The Melville Company produces a single product. Both variable and fixed overhead costs are charged to production at standard rates per unit of product. The flexible budget for overhead allows $3.60 per unit of product plus $48,000 per month. Normal volume is 8,000 units per month. During the month of July, 1972, a total of 7,500 units were produced. Actual variable overhead totaled $24,600 and actual fixed overhead, $48,800.

Required:

a) Compute the standard overhead cost of production for July, 1972.

b) Compute as many variances from standard overhead cost for July as you can.

7. The Jackson Manufacturing Company processes its three products in three separate production departments. Product A is processed in Department 9. Overhead is charged to production in this department at standard rates per unit of Product A. The standard variable overhead rate is $.60; the stan-

dard fixed overhead rate is $1.20. Normal production volume is 750,000 units of Product A annually.

At January 1, 1972, 60,000 units of Product A were in process in Department 9. They were complete as to materials and half complete as to conversion costs. A total of 680,000 units of Product A were finished during the year, and 55,000 units remained in process at December 31, 1972. These unfinished units were 80% complete with respect to materials and 40% complete with respect to conversion costs. Actual overhead for 1972 included variable costs of $392,000 and fixed costs of $920,000.

Required:

Compute as many variances from standard overhead cost in Department 9 during 1972 as you can.

8. The Hemingway Corporation manufactures a single product. Production is costed at standard variable cost. The standard cost sheet for one unit of product is as follows:

Materials (10 pcs. @ $.60).................	$ 6.00
Labor (3 hrs. @ $3.50)....................	10.50
Overhead (3 hrs. @ $1.50).................	4.50
	$21.00

The flexible budget for overhead allows $1.50 per direct labor hour plus $240,000 per year.

Actual production data for 1972 are summarized below:

> Unit output: 110,000 units of product
> Materials purchases: 1,200,000 @ $.57
> Materials usage: 1,185,000 pcs.
> Direct labor hours: 312,000
> Direct labor cost: $1,138,800
> Variable overhead: $485,000
> Fixed overhead: $265,000

Required:

Compute as many variances from standard cost for 1972 as you can.

9. The Mitchell Frock Company manufactures women's clothing. Work in Process is charged with standard manufacturing costs, including both variable and fixed factory overhead. The Kismet nightgown is the sole product of the sheer department and is produced in standard lots of 125 units. The relevant standards and budget data are as follows:

> Raw materials:
> Silk: 500 yds. per lot @ $3.60 per yd.
> Lace: 360 yds. per lot @ $5.50 per yd.
> Direct labor: 60 man-hrs. per lot @ $3.50 per hr.
> Overhead: $1.50 per man-hr. plus $12,000 per mo.

Normal volume is 50 lots of production per month.

The actual operations in the sheer department for the month of December, 1972, are summarized below:

Purchases of materials:
  Silk: 30,000 yds. @ $3.50 per yd.
  Lace: 20,000 yds. @ $5.75 per yd.

Usage of materials:
  Silk: 26,850 yds.
  Lace: 22,280 yds.

Direct labor: 3,500 man-hrs. @ $3.66 per hr.

Overhead:
  Variable: $5,450
  Fixed: $12,750

Output: 56 lots of Kismet nightgowns

Required:

Compute as many variances from standard cost for the month of December as you can.

10. The Faulkner Company uses the single plan of standard cost accounting and absorption costing in its production records. The standard cost sheet for one of its principal products is as follows:

Product W

Materials (4½ lbs. of Material K @ $.80)...		$3.60
Labor (¼ hr. @ $4.40)..................		1.10
Overhead:		
Variable (¼ hr. @ $2).................	$ .50	
Fixed (¼ hr. @ $6)...................	1.50	2.00
		$6.70

Normal production volume of Product W has been set at 5,000 labor hours per month.

Actual operation for the month of April, 1972, are summarized below:

(1) Purchased 75,000 pounds of Material K at $.76 each.
(2) Used 82,500 pounds of Material K in production.
(3) The total actual payroll included 4,375 hours of work on Product W at an average rate of $4.50 per hour.
(4) Actual variable overhead applicable to Product W amounted to $8,500. Applicable fixed overhead totaled $32,500.
(5) During April, 17,600 units of Product W were completed and transferred to finished stock. On April 1, there were 800 units in process; these were complete with respect to materials and half complete with respect to labor and overhead. At the end of April, 1,200 units remained in process, complete as to materials and half complete as to labor and overhead.

Required:

a) Prepare a schedule showing all postings to Work in Process—Product W for the month of April, 1972, including the opening and closing balances.

b) Compute as many variances from standard production cost for April as you can.

11. The Updike Products Company produces a single product. Absorption costing and the single plan of standard cost accounting are used in the valuation of inventories and in the measurement of periodic income. The standard cost sheet for the company's product appears as follows:

Materials (5 lbs. @ $.90).................. $ 4.50
Direct labor (2 hrs. @ $3.75)............... 7.50
Overhead................................ 3.00
$15.00

The flexible budget for overhead allows $.75 per unit of product plus $22,500 per month. Normal production volume is measured in units of output, and overhead is applied to production on the same basis.

Transactions for the month of January, 1972, the first month of the company's operations, are as follows:

Materials purchased: 50,000 lbs. @ $.96
Materials used: 45,000 lbs.
Direct labor: 17,200 hrs. @ $3.65
Variable overhead: $6,000
Fixed overhead: $22,500
Completed production: 7,800 units
Ending inventory of work in process: 600 units, complete with respect to materials and half complete with respect to conversion costs

Required:

Compute as many variances from standard costs for January, 1972, as you can.

12. The Cooper Boat Corporation produces a single product, concrete boat hulls. Absorption costing and standard cost accounting are employed. The standard direct production costs of one unit of product are as follows:

Materials:
  60 lbs. of cement @ $.12.................. $ 7.20
  15 yds. of wire mesh @ $1.20............. 18.00
$25.20
  Labor (16 hrs. @ $4)...................... 64.00

The flexible budget for overhead allows variable costs of $1.25 per direct labor hour and fixed costs of $3.50 per labor hour, based upon a normal volume of 64,000 direct labor hours per year.

Actual operations during 1972 were as follows:

(1) 3,800 units of product were completed. Twenty units were in process at the end of the year; they were complete as to materials and half complete as to labor time. There was no work in process at the start of the year.

(2) Two hundred fifty thousand pounds of cement were purchased at an average price of $.14 per pound. Sixty-five thousand yards of wire mesh were purchased for $1.15 per yard.

(3) The factory used 245,000 pounds of cement and 60,000 yards of wire mesh during the year.

(4) The factory payroll included 64,000 direct labor hours at an average wage rate of $4.15 per hour.

(5) Variable overhead costs totaled $76,250; fixed overhead amounted to $235,000.

(6) Thirty-seven hundred fifty finished hulls were sold at a price of $220 each.

Required:

a) Compute as many variances from standard cost as you can.

b) Prepare journal entries to record the operations of 1972.

13. The Salinger Rubber Company manufactures rubber washers and employs a standard cost system with absorption costing. Standards have been set for production lots of 1,000 washers. Materials standards call for 16 pounds of rubber per lot at a standard price of $.25 per pound. Labor standards call for 2.4 man-hours per lot at a standard wage rate of $3.20 per hour. The flexible budget for overhead for one month is as follows:

Output (in lots)........	12,000	15,000	18,000
Machine-hours.........	36,000	45,000	54,000
Variable costs..........	$57,600	$72,000	$86,400
Fixed costs............	99,000	99,000	99,000

Overhead is applied to production on the basis of machine-hours. Normal production volume has been set at 15,000 lots of washers per month.

Operations for October, 1972, are summarized below:

Purchases: 300,000 lbs. of rubber @ $.275 per lb.
Materials usage: 292,000 lbs. of rubber
Direct labor: 45,000 hrs. @ $3.40 per hr.
Variable overhead: $75,000
Fixed overhead: $105,000
Machine-hours worked: 50,000
Output: 17,500 lots
Sales: 19,000 lots

Required:

Prepare journal entries to record operations for the month of October, 1972. Show variance computations to support these entries.

14. Grey Electric Products, Inc., manufactures condensers in Department 101. Standard costing and absorption costing are used in accounting for production. The standard cost sheet for one condenser is as follows:

Materials:
Part No. 98736 (1 unit @ $3.29).......... $ 3.29
Part No. 6485 (2 units @ $1.44)........... 2.88
Labor (.8 hr. @ $4.25).................... 3.40
Overhead:
Variable (.8 hr. @ $.75)................. .60
Fixed (.8 hr. @ $1.30)................... 1.04
                                          $11.21

The flexible budget for Department 101 allows variable overhead of $.75 per labor hour and fixed overhead of $422,500 per year. Normal volume is 325,000 labor hours per year.

During 1972, a total of 375,000 condensers were produced. The average actual prices paid for parts No. 98736 and No. 6485 were $3.41 and $1.41, respectively. Four hundred thousand units of part No. 98736 and 700,000 units of part No. 6485 were purchased. The total direct labor cost in Department 101 during 1972 was $1,284,800; total labor time was 292,000 hours. A summary of materials requisitions shows that 380,000 units of part No. 98736 and 762,000 units of part No. 6485 were used during the year. Variable overhead for the year totaled $238,000; fixed overhead totaled $439,000.

During 1972, 360,000 condensers were sold at an average price of $18.

Required:

Prepare journal entries to record the operations of 1972. Present variance computations to support these entries.

15. The Tarkington Corporation manufactures turnbuckles in lots of 250. A single plan standard cost accounting system is used. The standard cost of one lot of production is as follows:

Materials (400 lbs. @ $.75)..................		$300
Labor (14 hrs. @ $3.50).....................		49
Overhead:		
Variable (14 hrs. @ $1.50)...............	$21	
Fixed (14 hrs. @ $3).....................	42	63
		$412

Normal production volume has been established at 40,000 direct labor hours per month.

Actual operating data for the month of February, 1972, are summarized below:

> Output: 2,500 lots
> Materials purchases: 1,200,000 lbs. @ $.77
> Materials usage: 988,000 lbs.
> Labor: 37,000 hrs. @ $3.35
> Variable overhead: $60,000
> Fixed overhead: $112,000
> Sales: 600,000 turnbuckles @ $2.25
> Selling and administrative expenses:
>   Variable: $117,400
>   Fixed: $130,250

The applicable income tax rate is 40%.

Required:

a) Compute as many variances from standard cost as you can.
b) Prepare journal entries to record the operating transactions for the month of February.
c) Prepare an income statement for February, 1972.

16. The Wharton Engine Company produces engine blocks in its forging department. Blocks are charged with the standard variable costs incurred in production. The standard cost sheet for one engine block is as follows:

Materials (60 lbs. @ $.30).................	$18.00
Direct labor:	
Machine operators (2¼ hrs. @ $4.20)......	9.45
Handlers (½ hr. @ $2.80)...............	1.40
Variable overhead (2 machine-hrs. @ $2.50)....	5.00
	$33.85

The output of the forging department is budgeted at 15,000 units annually. Fixed overhead in the department is budgeted at $120,000 per year.

During 1972, the actual output of the forging department was 12,000 engine blocks. Seven hundred thousand pounds of material were purchased at an average price of $.33 per pound. Materials usage reports show that a total of 775,000 pounds were used during 1972. The cost accounting department's records show that machine operators worked 30,000 hours at an actual wage rate of $4.08 and that handlers worked a total of 5,800 hours at a wage rate of $2.95. Forging department cost records show that total variable overhead was $68,000 and total fixed overhead was $125,000. The total actual machine-hours worked during the year amounted to 26,000.

Required:

Prepare journal entries to record the operations of the forging department during 1972. Show variance computations in support of these entries.

17. The Hawthorne Company assembles power drills in two successive production departments. Actual assembly work is done in Department 10. The drills are then tested and boxed in Department 20. The company uses variable costing and a single plan standard cost system. The standard cost sheet for one drill is as follows:

Materials:		
Drill housing (1 @ $3.18)..............	$3.18	
Electric motor (1 @ $5.44).............	5.44	
Cord with plug (1 @ $.87).............	.87	
Box (1 @ $.12)......................	.12	$ 9.61
Direct labor:		
Department 10 (¼ hr. @ $3.60)........	$ .90	
Department 20 (⅓ hr. @ $3.30)........	1.10	2.00
Variable overhead:		
Department 10 (¼ hr. @ $1.80)........	$ .45	
Department 20 (⅓ hr. @ $2.52)........	.84	1.29
		$12.90

During 1972, a total of 450,000 power drills were assembled in Department 10. In Department 20, 435,000 drills were tested, boxed, and transferred to the finished stock room.

Actual materials purchases during 1972 were as follows:

Drill housings: 440,000 @ $3.25
Electric motors: 425,000 @ $5.32
Cords: 480,000 @ $.85
Boxes: 500,000 @ $.11½

Materials usage is summarized below:

In Department 10:
    Drill housings: 450,660
    Electric motors: 450,200
    Cords: 451,200
In Department 20:
    Boxes: 450,000

The payroll for 1972 included the following summary charges to the two production departments:

Department 10:   118,000 hrs. @ $3.75
Department 20:   142,000 hrs. @ $3.40

Actual overhead costs incurred during the year were as follows:

	Department 10	Department 20
Variable...................	$225,000	$360,000
Fixed.....................	135,000	195,000
	$360,000	$555,000

Required:

a) Compute as many variances from standard cost as are appropriate.
b) Prepare an analysis showing all debits and credits to the accounts for Work in Process—Department 10 and Work in Process—Department 20.

18. The Steinbeck Paper Company began operations in 1972. During that year, it completed production of 180,000 reams of paper. Materials standards called for 4 pounds of pulp per ream at a price of $.24 per pound. Actual materials usage in 1972 totaled 1,200,000 pounds of pulp. A total of 1,440,-000 pounds were purchased at an average price of $.32 per pound. At the end of the year, the inventory of work in process consisted of 20,000 reams of paper, half complete with respect to all cost elements. The ending inventory of finished product contained 40,000 reams of paper.

The company's auditors have stated that they regard the materials price and usage variances as excessive because the pertinent standards were not realistic. Accordingly, management has agreed to adjust the affected accounts to reflect the average actual cost of raw materials. The single plan of standard cost accounting has been used.

Required:

a) Determine the proper allocations of the materials price variance and the materials usage variance to the appropriate accounts.

    b)   Prepare a journal entry to adjust the accounts to conform to the auditors' requirements.

19.   The O'Hara Manufacturing Company produces a single product. The standard costs for materials and labor total $28 per unit of product. The flexible budget allows $2 per machine-hour for variable overhead and $2,500,000 per year for fixed overhead. Normal volume is 500,000 machine-hours per year. During 1972, the company was shut down by a strike for five months. Actual production and cost data for 1972 are as follows:

> Actual output volume: 75,000 units of product
> Standard input volume: 300,000 machine-hrs.
> Actual input volume: 320,000 machine-hrs.
> Actual variable overhead: $660,000
> Actual fixed overhead: $2,500,000
> Sales: 80,000 units of product @ $80
> Variable nonmanufacturing expenses: $400,000
> Fixed nonmanufacturing expenses: $1,200,000

There were no materials or labor variances in 1972. Income taxes may be ignored.

Required:

a)   Assuming that the company uses absorption costing, compute as many overhead variances as you can.

b)   Prepare an income statement for 1972 in the absorption costing format.

c)   Now assuming that the company has consistently used variable costing, prepare an income statement for 1972 in that format.

20.   The Allen Drug Company produces a patented cough syrup in its San Jose plant. The standard cost sheet for one case of 24 5-ounce bottles is as follows:

> Raw materials:
> Glycerine (84 oz. @ $.11).............. $9.24
> Alcohol (12 oz. @ $.18)................ 2.16
> Cherry flavoring (30 oz. @ $.15)........ 4.50
> Bottles (25 @ $.04).................. 1.00 $16.90
> Direct labor:
> Blending department (½ hr. @ $3.60)... $1.80
> Bottling department (¼ hr. @ $4.40)... 1.10   2.90
> Overhead:
> Blending department:
>   Variable (½ hr. @ $.80)............. $ .40
>   Fixed (½ hr. @ $1.60).............. .80
> Bottling department:
>   Variable (¼ hr. @ $1).............. .25
>   Fixed (¼ hr. @ $3)................ .75   2.20
> $22.00

    Normal volume is 10,000 labor hours per month in the blending department and 5,000 labor hours per month in the bottling department.

    The glycerine, alcohol, and cherry flavoring are mixed together in 25-

gallon batches in the blending department and then piped to the bottling department, where it is placed by machine into 5-ounce bottles and then moved to the warehouse pending shipment to customers.

During August, 1972, a total of 24,000 cases of cough syrup were prepared and bottled. There were no inventories in process in either department at the beginning or at the end of the month.

Purchases of raw materials during August are summarized as follows:

> Glycerine: 18,000 gals. @ $14
> Alcohol: 2,400 gals. @ $23.50
> Cherry flavoring: 6,000 gals. @ $20
> Bottles: 4,000 gross @ $5.70

Actual materials usage during August was as follows:

> Glycerine: 17,000 gals.
> Alcohol: 2,180 gals.
> Cherry flavoring: 5,800 gals.
> Bottles: 4,125 gross

The actual payroll included 11,600 hours in the blending department at an average wage rate of $3.80 per hour and 6,400 hours in the bottling department at an average wage rate of $4.50 per hour. Actual overhead costs incurred were as follows:

> Blending department:
> Variable............................. $ 9,900
> Fixed............................... 16,800
> Bottling department:
> Variable............................. 6,750
> Fixed............................... 15,750

During August, 22,000 case of cough syrup were sold at an average price of $33 per case. Variable selling expenses amounted to 10% of sales revenue. Fixed administrative expenses totaled $65,000. The applicable income tax rate is 40%.

Required:

a) Compute as many variances from standard cost for August, 1972, as are appropriate.

b) Prepare journal entries to record the operating transactions for August.

c) Prepare an income statement for the month of August.

chapter 11

COST CONTROL
THROUGH VARIANCE
ANALYSIS

VARIANCE computation answers the comparatively simple question of by how much actual costs differed from standard costs. This answer is of significance to management, but only as a starting point from which to pursue the objective of cost control. The more crucial questions remain to be answered. Why did actual costs differ from standards? Was the difference favorable or adverse to the enterprise in view of its basic objectives? Who was responsible for the difference? What, if anything, can or should be done about it? These questions cannot be answered by simple mathematical formulas, although mathematical analyses may be useful in answering some of them. Nor are the answers to be found directly in accounting data, although the accounting system may be so structured as to facilitate finding the answers. In this chapter we shall consider some of the problems associated with management's attempts to answer these questions. In doing so, we shall encounter more problems than solutions; but solutions can never be attained until problems have been identified.

CAUSAL ANALYSIS OF VARIANCES

In Chapter 10 we saw that variances may be resolved into components or elements. The net difference between actual and standard labor costs, for example, may be subdivided into a price component and a quantity component. Merely knowing that the actual price paid for labor

274

services during a particular period exceeded the standard price, however, does not explain why it did. Computing specific variances identifies areas for further investigation, but it does not pinpoint reasons for cost differences. In the paragraphs that follow, we shall consider briefly each of the variances computed in Chapter 10 and attempt to suggest some of the types of reasons why they may arise. Specific reasons, however, can be determined only in specific cases.

Materials Price Variance

The materials price variance is simply the difference between the actual price and the standard price paid for raw materials purchased. As it arises at the point of purchase, one might be inclined to take it as an indicator of the efficiency or inefficiency of the purchasing function in a firm. Such a conclusion would be tenuous at best, however, and might prove to be completely erroneous. For example, if the actual price exceeded the standard price because of a marked shift in market conditions, whether temporary or permanent, the resulting price variance might be wholly beyond the control of the purchasing department or, for that matter, of anyone in the firm. If the average market price for a particular material has increased by 5% from the level implicit in the firm's price standard and the firm's price variance for the period is 4% in excess of standard, the situation seems to reflect unusually efficient purchasing practices. Here a nominally unfavorable variance would be traceable ultimately to a combination of uncontrollable circumstances and exceptionally good performance. On the other hand, an unfavorable price variance may reflect the purchasing department's negligence in failing to seek the most advantageous sources of supply. A favorable price variance might be achieved by purchasing from an unreliable supplier, but consequent delivery delays may precipitate a partial shutdown of production facilities and delays in filling customers' orders, if not the actual loss of orders. Such a favorable variance, obviously, is favorable in name only; it is clearly adverse in effect.

A particular price variance or some portion thereof may be attributable to a department other than purchasing. For example, if the foreman of a production department fails to notify purchasing of a shortage of materials on hand, an emergency order may become necessary at a price above standard—perhaps because special handling and airfreight charges must be incurred in order to obtain delivery in time to avert a production stoppage. In this example, a price variance is caused by inefficiency in a materials using department.

In an actual situation, it is likely that several different causes will combine to produce a net price variance. To begin with, variances of different directions and various causes may occur in connection with purchases of different raw materials. Different types of variances may be encountered in connection with successive purchases of a single material. In such a case, the net materials price variance may not be very useful to management. A net variance of $800, for example, may appear negligible when compared with total purchases of $4,000,000. But that net variance may be the algebraic sum of very substantial offsetting favorable and unfavorable variances. Obviously, the apparently negligible net variance here masks significant component variances; and the latter are important to effective cost control.

Materials Usage Variance

A materials usage variance may be traced to a great variety of causes. Excessive usage may be caused by careless handling of materials by production personnel, by inefficient or poorly adjusted machinery, by pilferage, by a tightening of quality control requirements, or by an almost endless list of other possible circumstances and events. Changes in product specifications may cause either favorable or unfavorable usage variances for which the only solution is to alter materials usage standards. Purchasing of substandard materials may result in excessive materials consumption. This may or may not be desirable, depending upon the net impact on total cost. For example, a firm's price and usage standards for copper tubing may be based upon purchases of pre-cut pieces of uniform length. The purchasing department may learn that it can effect substantial savings by buying random mill lengths instead, but use of these random length pieces will result in greater amounts of scrap in the factory. The consequent unfavorable materials usage variance may be more than offset by a favorable price variance. If so, the unfavorable usage variance is actually a reflection of a profitable change in policy and will ultimately be eliminated by a change in the materials usage standard to conform to the new policy.

Separate materials usage variances should be determined for each type of material used and for each production center. Tracing variances to cost centers is at least the beginning of an answer to the question, "Who is responsible for the variances?" Responsibility must be determined before control can be effected.

Materials Mix Variance. In some production processes, two or more different raw materials are combined in a standard formula to produce a product. In such a situation, it may be possible to vary the mix of materials used (i.e., to change the quantities of certain materials relative to the quantities of others) and still produce a satisfactory product. Such variations in the standard materials mix could be reflected simply in the materials usage variance. Thus, an unfavorable usage variance for one material might be offset by a favorable variance for another. However, the net effect of these two variances is not likely to be zero. If the material whose usage was increased is more expensive than that whose usage was reduced, the net financial effect of the two variances will be unfavorable. Thus, substituting one raw material for another, even though the total input quantity of all materials does not exceed the standard amount, can cause a special type of materials usage variance. This is usually referred to as a *materials mix variance*. It is a consequence of materials usage, but a consequence of relative rather than absolute differentials in usage. Hence, where it can be identified separately, it is useful to do so. Substantial deviations from the standard product mix may not only cause variances from standard cost; they may also impair product quality, possibly to the point that the output is useless.

Labor Rate Variance

A difference between the actual and standard wage rates may be attributed simply to a negotiated wage increase not yet reflected in the standard wage rate. While management may not be pleased about the wage increase, the resultant wage rate variance, as such, is a normal and proper consequence of the change in the rate. Of course, the net labor rate variance should be analyzed according to different classes of laborers. A wage increase may not be uniform among all classes of workers, and variances in different classes may have significantly different causes.

Part of a labor rate variance may be caused by the assignment of higher paid workers to jobs regularly performed by lower paid employees. Such practice is not desirable but sometimes is unavoidable. For example, a temporary reassignment of highly paid workers may be necessary to reduce a production bottleneck. During a period of reduced demand and output, the company may prefer to lay off the lower paid employees and reassign the higher paid ones in order to retain the more highly skilled and, hence, more highly paid members of its work force. This particular type of labor rate variance is sometimes reported separately as a *labor substitution variance*.

Of the variances considered here, the labor rate variance is probably the least susceptible to direct control by management. This does not mean that its causes are of no interest, however. Knowing the causes of variances assists management in planning future costs as well as in controlling current costs.

Labor Efficiency Variance

The root causes of a labor efficiency variance may be personal to the workers and/or inherent in the work situation. The first type of cause is more difficult for management to deal with. A worker's personal efficiency may be affected by his health, family or financial problems, a real or imagined grievance against management, fear of a layoff, imminent retirement, and the World Series. There is usually little, if anything, management can do directly about such matters. However, there is also little likelihood that all workers will be affected by the same personal problems at the same time. Management, of course, is primarily interested in the average efficiency of the labor force. Concern for an individual worker's inefficiency is usually restricted to his immediate supervisor and then only if his inefficiency is persistent. To combat personal causes of labor inefficiency and to foster efficiency in general, the most management can do ordinarily is to provide a work environment conducive to satisfying the workers' personal needs and goals.

The second type of cause of a labor efficiency variance—that inherent in the work situation—is of more general concern to management. Examples of such causes are the introduction of new equipment or tools in a factory, a failure to maintain machinery in proper working condition, use of substandard raw materials, production bottlenecks, and changes in production processes. These situations can cause general efficiency or inefficiency in an entire department or, perhaps, throughout a plant. Thus, their potential impact upon production costs and profits is greater than that of purely personal problems. At the same time, these situations are likely to be more readily identifiable and more amenable to managerial action.

The mere existence of a labor efficiency variance does not necessarily indicate good or bad performance by workers. The variance might be caused by poor planning on the part of management. It might reflect changes in the factory layout, in production equipment, or in quality control standards. Finally, the labor efficiency variance may be affected by the firm's manner of accounting for idle time. If all idle time is recorded and charged to overhead rather than to direct labor, a significant unfavorable labor efficiency variance may be avoided—but only by an increase in the overhead spending variance. On the other hand, during a period of temporarily reduced output, workers may be assigned makework tasks to avoid temporary layoffs. This could cause a substantial unfavorable efficiency variance that reflected a conscious managerial decision and not the quality of labor performance at all.

Overhead Spending Variance

The flexible budget, upon which the standard overhead rates are based, presumes a particular amount of cost for each item in the budget. For the variable cost items, this amount is expressed as a cost per unit of the relevant measure of volume. For the fixed cost items, it is a total dollar amount per time period. In either case, if the actual cost incurred differs from the amount presumed in the budget, the difference will be reflected in the spending variance. If, for example, indirect materials cost is greater than budgeted, the excess will appear in the spending variance. That excess may be caused by an increase in the price paid for indirect materials or by an increase in the rate of use thereof or by some combination of the two. Price and usage differences may be traced to the same types of causes mentioned earlier in connection with direct materials. Similarly, indirect labor cost may differ from the budgeted amount because of rate and/or time differences, which, in turn, may be attributed to any of the causes discussed in connection with direct labor. Power costs may be affected by rate changes and by a difference in the rate of power consumption per unit of volume from the consumption rate assumed in the establishment of the budget. Property tax rates may change from those initially estimated and/or the assessed valuation of the firm's taxable property may be changed.

A change in the depreciation charged to production will be included in the spending variance. Depreciation changes may be caused by changes in the estimated useful lives of depreciable assets or by acquisitions and/or disposition of those assets. Whatever the cause, it seems questionable to describe a change in depreciation as a *spending* variance, for depreciation is usually considered the classic example of a noncash expense. In pursuing its objective of cost control, management is certain to be aided by a separation of that portion of the overhead spending variance due to a change in the depreciation rate from the portion due to such causes as excessive usage of indirect materials.

Overhead Efficiency Variance

This variance is concerned exclusively with variable costs, and it abstracts from the question of their deviation from budgeted amounts. It seeks to identify solely the impact upon total variable overhead costs of a difference between the actual and standard input volumes. As mentioned in Chapter 10, this variance can exist only where volume is measured in terms of some input quantity and, consequently, there can be some measurable concept of efficiency. If volume is measured in labor hours, the causes of the overhead efficiency variance will be the same as those of the labor efficiency variance. If, on the other hand, machine-hours are used as the volume measure, the causes of the overhead efficiency variance must be sought independently. In a real sense, given its operating capacity, machinery cannot be efficient or inefficient of itself. If a machine is running slower than its normal operating speed, the reason must be human at its ultimate source. The machine operator may be unskilled or unfamiliar with the particular piece of equipment.

The plant foreman may be negligent in his observance of the prescribed maintenance schedule. In any event, the overhead efficiency variance is caused not by changes in overhead costs as such but, rather, by changes in the volume of activity requiring the incurrence of overhead costs.

Overhead Budget Variance

The budget variance of the two-variance plan is basically comparable to the spending variance in the three-variance plan. Hence, the discussion of the spending variance above is applicable to the budget variance also. Even where volume is measured in units of output, overhead costs may be influenced somewhat by labor efficiency or inefficiency. Hence, some of the causes of the overhead efficiency variance described in the preceding section may be present in the budget variance.

Overhead Volume Variance

The volume variance is unique among variances from standard cost in that its dollar amount is determined by the mechanics of the cost accounting system itself. Since the volume variance relates exclusively to fixed costs, it is encountered only where the absorption costing method is employed. Under variable costing, no fixed overhead would be charged to production at all; hence, there could be no such quantity as standard fixed overhead cost and no variance therefrom. In absorption costing, however, fixed overhead is charged to production. Differences between the actual and budgeted amounts of fixed overhead will appear in the spending (or budget) variance. The volume variance is attributable solely to the fact that a standard fixed overhead rate is computed at a normal volume and is then applied to production at some actual volume which is unlikely ever to be exactly equal to the normal level. For example, if fixed overhead is budgeted at $480,000 and normal volume is set at 150,000 direct labor hours, the standard fixed overhead rate will be $3.20. If the standard input volume for a given period totals 160,000 hours, the standard fixed overhead cost will total $512,000. Thus, there will be a $32,000 volume variance. This variance is simply the consequence of applying a standard rate of $3.20 to 10,000 more hours than were presumed when that rate was established. In this case, had the standard fixed overhead rate been set at 160,000 labor hours, it would be $3 per hour and there would be no volume variance. In effect, the $3.20 rate is too high in light of the greater than normal volume. The total budgeted fixed costs could be spread over the higher volume of production at a lower rate per unit of volume.

Lest the foregoing discussion suggest that management need not be concerned at all with the volume variance, we should hasten to point out that the cause of the difference between actual and normal volumes may require investigation. If normal volume is an average level of operations over a complete business cycle, management may reasonably expect that it will not be achieved in any one period. Here the real question is why actual volume differed from that planned for the particular period. Volume changes may be attributed to shifts in demand, to labor disputes, to materials shortages, to shortages of working capital, to ineffective marketing practices, to poor product quality, or to any one or combination of a number of other factors. As may be seen quite readily, some of these causes may be within the control of management and some may not be. Some businessmen make the mistake of regarding volume as inherently uncontrollable. Actually, the difference between a successful and an unsuccessful businessman may be their relative abilities to influence their operating volumes.

Problems of Finding Causes of Variances

In the foregoing paragraphs we have mentioned some of the possible causes of variances of actual cost from standard. Identifying actual causes in actual instances may be extremely difficult, if not impossible. Some causes are fairly easily identified—such as machinery breakdowns, wage increases, and usage of substandard materials. Others may be too elusive to be determined specifically. This should not be taken as grounds for despair, of course. It simply means that cost control can never be complete. But some control is infinitely better than none.

SIGNIFICANCE OF VARIANCES

As one may easily conclude from the discussions in the preceding sections, determining the cause(s) of a variance from standard cost can be a difficult, time consuming, and, hence, expensive task. Management's goal of cost control will hardly be furthered if the firm spends more in uncovering the causes of variances than the variances are likely to amount to in the future. Thus, variance analysis is customarily restricted to those variances that are considered significant. The significance of a variance is a function of both its amount and its recurrence. That is, the larger a variance is in relation to standard cost, the more significant it will be considered by management. Even more importantly, the more likely a variance is to recur, the greater significance management will accord it. Obviously, the significance of a variance is heightened if it is both large in amount and persistent in occurrence.

How large a variance must be in order to be considered significant is a difficult problem that must be resolved largely on the basis of managerial judgment. Probably no one would disagree that a variance equal to 25% of standard cost was material in amount or that a 1% variance was immaterial. Where the line separating materiality from immateriality lies, however, would be less easily agreed upon. Is a 5% variance material? Some firms do use this particular figure as a threshold for materiality of variances. The significance of a variance of a particular size depends partly upon the tightness of the underlying standard. The tighter a standard is, the larger an unfavorable variance from it may be expected to be. Consequently, management ought to set a higher significance threshold for an unfavorable variance from a tight standard than for one from an easily attained standard. An unfavorable variance is specified here because a variance is more likely to be unfavorable as the standard is set tighter. Also, most managers are predisposed to be more concerned about unfavorable variances. As we have observed before, however, favorable variances should not be ignored. An investigation of their causes may lead the way to long-run cost reductions.

The size of a variance, of course, is known when it is computed. Thus, a decision as to its significance on that basis may be made as soon as the variance has been calculated. Unfortunately, the same is not true of a variance's likelihood of recurrence. Until one has made a determination of the cause(s) of a variance, he can hardly decide how likely it is to occur again. Thus, some preliminary investigation of substantial variances is necessary in order to determine whether they are the results of nonrecurring circumstances or of continuing conditions. Obviously, the latter situation is of greater concern to management. Once a variance has been determined to have been caused by circumstances that may be expected to persist, a more extensive study of the problem and of possible solutions should be made.

REPORTING VARIANCES BY RESPONSIBILITY

Determining the cause of a variance will usually entail the fixing of responsibility for it at the same time. Additionally, in many cases, it is possible to fix responsibility without ascertaining the precise cause of a variance. For example, a labor efficiency variance may be traced to a particular production department fairly readily if cost data are departmentalized. Fixing responsibility for the variance upon an individual department supervisor does not, of course, assure effective control; but it does set the problem at the level at which it may be controllable. Hence, one of the most important facets of a standard cost system is the variance reporting mechanism. This mechanism must be so structured as to get the right information to the right people at the right time and in the most useful manner.

Timing of Reports

Reports are expensive. There are costs involved in their preparation, their transmittal, their reading, and their storage. These costs, like all costs in a business enterprise, should be justifiable in terms of basic objectives. Too many reports can be just as bad as too few. It might be possible to report daily all manufacturing variances to all supervisory personnel in a plant. If this were done, however, it is quite likely that the surfeit of information would only confuse the readers of the reports and obscure the truly relevant facts. A much more practicable and useful practice might be to report daily *some* variances to *some* supervisors. Other variances might be reported less frequently and only to selected persons.

Daily reports are most useful in connection with those variances which may arise and, hence, may be controlled from day to day. This is likely to be particularly true of the materials usage and the labor efficiency variances. It may be true of the overhead spending variance, at least as regards some components of it. The latter is such a conglomerate variance, however, that day-to-day control might be prohibitively expensive. Where overhead is applied to production on the basis of labor hours, control of the overhead efficiency variance should be regarded as part of the control of labor efficiency. Even if some materials are purchased each day, it is unlikely that the same materials would be purchased daily. Hence, daily reports of the materials price variance would not appear to be desirable. In some industries, however, daily purchases of the same materials may be common; if so, daily price variance reports may be very useful. The labor rate variance is not likely to lend itself to day-to-day control efforts and, consequently, seems an unlikely candidate for daily reporting. Finally, daily reports of the overhead volume variance would almost certainly be both useless and meaningless. For those variances where daily reporting and control are inapplicable, monthly reports may be adequate. It is not possible to state general rules for the frequency of reporting specific variances. It is pertinent to observe, however, that once a frequency has been established, reports should be disseminated as promptly as possible. Late reports are of as little value as last week's newspaper.

Addresses of Reports

As a general rule, variance reports should be directed only to those persons in the organization who may reasonably be held responsible for the variances. Thus, a departmental foreman should probably receive reports of materials usage and labor efficiency. If materials prices and labor rates are beyond his scope of authority, there would seem to be little value in reporting price and rate variances to him. While his conduct may on occasion be the cause of price variances (as when he delays requesting a reorder of materials until the stock is so low that an emergency purchase must be made at an unfavorable price), his responsibility in such instance can be fixed without furnishing him copies of all price variance reports. The plant manager should receive reports of all manufacturing variances, with the possible exception of the volume variance, for which he is not likely to be responsible. Reports to him would usually be less detailed than those submitted to the department foremen; the only breakdown may be by departments. If an individual is not responsible for a variance, the only valid reason for reporting it to him would be to broaden his perspective of the enterprise's operating problems. In such case, the report would seem to be a training rather than an operating device. Variance reports to top corporate management are typically submitted in summary form on a monthly basis. Even if certain variances are reported to immediate supervisors daily, it is unlikely that they would be made available to top management so frequently.

Format of Reports

It is not possible to formulate a standard variance report which might be used by any firm. However, certain fundamental ideas should be considered. Where variances are analyzed by causes in the report, some effort should be made to distinguish between amounts which are and which are not controllable at the level of responsibility to which the report is directed. Controllability is quite often a very difficult concept to identify operationally, but some effort in that direction is likely to be beneficial to management. Comparison of current variances with those of some prior period and/or with those of the year to date is often helpful in establishing a frame of reference within which the current data can be appraised. Variances may be stated as percentages of standard costs, particularly where comparative data are presented. Percentages often afford a more meaningful basis for comparison than do absolute figures. Materials usage and labor efficiency variances may be reported to departmental foremen in terms of physical quantities only. If a foreman knows that his time is excessive on certain operations, it is questionable whether his capacity to control the excess would be improved by his knowing the dollar impact of the excess time.

Finally, variance reports should be prepared in accordance with the principle of exceptions. That is, significant variances should be highlighted and separated from immaterial ones. This is often accomplished by presenting the variance report in a tabular format with four columns for standard cost, actual cost, variances, and those variances that exceed the established significance threshold (e.g., 5% of standard cost). The fourth column, then, would be the one to which the managerial reader's attention would be most directed, for it would indicate the exceptions from established levels of acceptable performance.[1]

VARIANCES FROM BUDGETED COSTS

Thus far in this chapter and in the preceding one, we have been concerned with computing, accounting for, and analyzing variances from standard costs. While such variances are generally useful in the managerial process of cost control, they are not necessarily the most significant bases for control. Often, particular variances will be expected during a future period and will be incorporated into the operating budget for that period. For example, a materials price variance may be budgeted in the anticipation of a temporary market shortage of raw materials. If an unusually large number of trainees will be on the job during a budget period, it would be reasonable to budget an unfavorable labor efficiency variance. And as long as fixed overhead is charged to production (under absorption costing) at a rate established at normal volume, it is quite likely that a volume variance may be budgeted each year, for no one year is likely to be the average year implicit in the concept of normal volume.

Where variances are included in the budgeted manufacturing costs for a period, the more significant variances are those not budgeted, that is, those which reflect deviations of actual costs from budgeted levels. For example, a substantial favorable volume variance may be budgeted in a period of peak business activity. If the actual volume variance is favorable, as compared with standard cost, but is not as great as the budgeted variance, the indication is that actual volume, while still above the normal level, was not as high as originally planned for the period. Thus, there may be an unfavorable variance from the budget included in a favorable variance from standard. (Remember that the terms favorable and unfavorable are used in this context to indicate the direction of a variance, not a qualitative evaluation of it.) Once variances have been included in the formal operating plan for the year, management will be better served by concentrating upon any additional, unplanned variances. A budgeted variance is a part of the operating plan rather than a deviation therefrom. Of course, changing conditions during the budget period may require adjustments to any of the budgeted data, including budgeted variances. As long as the budget is considered a valid basis for planning and control, however, budgeted variances should be considered as parts

---

[1] An illustration of a graphic variance report that highlights significant variances in a similar fashion appears in Figure 19–1 in Chapter 19.

of the base from which operating deviations are measured rather than as parts of the deviations.

DETERMINATION OF VARIANCES BY STATISTICAL SAMPLING

In all of our discussions of variances thus far, we have implicitly assumed that separate variances are computed for each different raw material, each class of labor, and each production department. This is not always practicable, however, particularly in cases of materials and labor variances that are to be reported frequently. A factory or even a single department may use so many different materials or classes of labor that regular determination of price and usage variances for each would be prohibitively expensive. As an alternative, variances might be computed for only a sample of the materials or labor classes. If this were a statistically valid random sample, the average variances determined for the sample could be extended to the entire population by statistical inference. For example, suppose that the average materials usage variance found in a sample were 4% of standard materials cost in the sample. It might then be inferred that the average usage variance for all materials was within a specified range on either side of 4% of standard cost. Further, the probability that this sample result fairly represented the entire population could be quantified. To illustrate this procedure, it might be said that, on the basis of the sample results, there is a 95% probability that the total materials usage variance was between 3.2% and 4.8% of total standard materials cost. (In statistical terminology, it would be said that there was a 1.6 percentage point confidence interval about the sample mean of 4% at the 95% confidence level.) Then, if the materials usage variance were taken to be 4% of standard cost, management would have to recognize that this figure is only an estimate and that the actual variance might be as low as 3.2% or as high as 4.8% without violating the statistical requirements specified in computing it. Further, there still remains a 5% probability that the variance is yet lower or higher than the limits specified. When variances are computed by sample procedures, management should determine that the resultant variances are statistically significant and not merely a consequence of the limitations of the sampling process.

Computer-based standard cost accounting systems make computation of all variances for all items more feasible than manual accounting systems. Sampling procedures are usually employed to avoid the excessive time and cost requirement of a complete survey. If all of the necessary data are already stored in computer-accessible memory devices, it may be quite simple and economical to obtain variances based upon data for the entire population rather than only a sample.

QUESTIONS FOR DISCUSSION

1. The production manager of a manufacturing company notices that the usage of a particular raw material has consistently exceeded the standard for several weeks. A review of production techniques and quality control practices indicates that the materials quantity standard for this item is still reasonable and attainable. How might the production manager go about determining the specific cause(s) of this materials usage variance and identifying the person(s) responsible for it?

2. If a labor rate variance can be traced directly to a negotiated increase in wage rates and, thus, is regarded as uncontrollable, is there any useful purpose served in reporting the variance to management? Explain.

3. The prices of some commodities are established in well-organized markets and may fluctuate from day to day. Agricultural products are typical examples of such commodities. Are materials price standards and price variances practicable control techniques in firms that use such commodities as raw materials? Explain.

4. Where a standard cost system is employed, is "variance control" the same thing as "cost control" in production departments? In other words, can management effectively control costs by focusing its attention only upon variances and their control? Discuss.

5. What is the difference between variances from standard costs and variances from budgeted costs? In a firm which uses both budgets and standard costs, might these variances prove to be different in amounts? If so, which variances would be more useful to management for purposes of cost control—variances from standard costs or variances from the budget? Explain.

6. Is the overhead volume variance controllable? If so, by whom? If not, why not?

7. The management of a manufacturing firm has noticed that the variable cost portion of its overhead spending variance is almost invariably favorable when production volume exceeds normal and unfavorable when operations fall below normal volume. Conversely, the fixed cost portion of the spending variance is favorable when operations are below normal and unfavorable at volumes above normal. Without further information, what condition(s) might this situation suggest?

8. Is there any relationship between the analysis of variances from standard production cost and the evaluation of the results of quality control tests and inspections? Is it possible that the results of these two procedures might indicate that a single cause had produced favorable variances and poor product quality or unfavorable variances and superior product quality? If so, illustrate such causes.

9. In a company that charges overhead to production at standard rates per direct labor hour, what would be appropriate time schedules for the reporting of the three overhead variances? In other words, how frequently should each variance be reported to management?

10. Is fixing responsibility for a variance equivalent to ascertaining its cause? Explain.

11. "In general, materials usage control can be tighter under a job order cost system than under a process cost system." Do you agree with this statement? Explain your position.

12. Where variable costing is used, should fixed overhead be included in the computation of the overhead spending variance? Explain your answer.

13. What does a materials mix variance disclose that a conventional materials usage variance does not?

14. How can management decide whether a variance is significant or not?

PROBLEMS

1. The net labor efficiency variance for the stamping department of the Long-fellow Lamp Corporation for the month of November, 1972, was computed as follows:

Standard labor hours................................	28,500
Actual labor hours.................................	30,200
Excess hours......................................	(1,700)
Standard wage rate per hour........................	$ 3.60
Unfavorable variance...............................	$(6,120)

The factory superintendent is responsible for all production operations. He asked the stamping department foreman to explain the reasons for the excess labor hours in his department. The foreman submitted the following analysis of excess labor time for November:

Standard hours in production.........................		28,500
Excess hours:		
Trainee operating machine..........................	48	
Experienced operator instructing trainee.............	12	
Rework time on units rejected by inspector...........	420	
Rework time on Job No. 337; original specifications had been in error...............................	80	
Raw materials received from storeroom were too thick..	75	
Work done on obsolete standby equipment; regular equipment was overloaded........................	600	
Partial lot run on Job No. 345......................	20	
Extra setup time required after machine breakdown....	15	
Idle time; no production scheduled...................	420	
Unexplained......................................	450	2,140
		30,640
Hours saved:		
New tools used....................................	360	
Consecutive jobs run for same product; no setup time required for second job........................	40	
Assistant foreman assigned to machine operation for one week.......................................	40	440
Actual hours worked...............................		30,200

Required:

Prepare a report that classifies the various causes of the labor efficiency variance as controllable by the department foreman, controllable by the factory superintendent, or uncontrollable at the level of the factory. Indicate which causes you believe require further attention by managment. Comment on any further action that might be taken with respect to the various causes of the variance.

2. Die casting in the Dickinson Tool & Die Company is done in three separate but basically identical departments. The company's management has decided that total volume is too great to be handled efficiently in a single department. Monthly materials usage reports are used to compare performances in the three departments. These reports detail standard usage, actual usage, and the variance for the current month and for the year to date. A tabular summary of the data reported in the first half of 1972 is presented below:

	Pounds of Metal		
	Standard Usage	*Actual Usage*	*Variance*
Department 1:			
January...................	29,000	31,200	(2,200)
February.................	28,700	30,500	(1,800)
March...................	29,800	31,400	(1,600)
April....................	30,500	31,400	(900)
May.....................	31,200	31,800	(600)
June....................	31,000	31,200	(200)
Year to date..........	180,200	187,500	(7,300)
Department 2:			
January...................	30,600	31,000	(400)
February.................	29,800	30,000	(200)
March...................	28,800	28,700	100
April....................	29,900	30,200	(300)
May.....................	30,800	30,400	400
June....................	31,300	31,100	200
Year to date..........	181,200	181,400	(200)
Department 3:			
January...................	29,900	29,300	600
February.................	29,500	29,200	300
March...................	30,600	30,500	100
April....................	31,000	31,000	
May.....................	31,300	31,500	(200)
June....................	31,400	31,900	(500)
Year to date..........	183,700	183,400	300

Required:

Draft a report in what you believe to be the best form for purposes of a comparative analysis of the operating performances of the three departments with respect to materials usage during the first half of 1972.

3. Riley Creative Toys, Inc., manufactures toy metal trucks and similar items in three successive production departments. Labor time records in these departments during 1972 show the following data:

	Standard Hours	Actual Hours	Variance
Stamping department:			
First quarter.............	52,000	54,750	(2,750)
Second quarter...........	48,000	50,250	(2,250)
Third quarter.............	54,000	57,000	(3,000)
Fourth quarter............	58,000	60,800	(2,800)
	212,000	222,800	(10,800)
Assembly department:			
First quarter.............	130,000	127,200	2,800
Second quarter...........	120,000	124,000	(4,000)
Third quarter.............	135,000	133,500	1,500
Fourth quarter...........	145,000	145,900	(900)
	530,000	530,600	(600)
Painting department:			
First quarter.............	26,000	24,600	1,400
Second quarter...........	24,000	23,400	600
Third quarter.............	27,000	27,500	(500)
Fourth quarter...........	29,000	30,100	(1,100)
	106,000	105,600	400

Required:

Draft a report in what you believe to be the best form for purposes of a comparative analysis of the labor efficiencies of the three departments during 1972.

4. Refer to Problem 16 in Chapter 10. The output of the forging department of the Wharton Engine Company in that problem is substantially (20%) below the budgeted annual output. Can the effects of this reduced volume on costs be measured within the framework of the standard cost system employed by the company? Explain.

5. Refer to Problem 19 in Chapter 10. Discuss alternative presentations of the overhead volume variance computed in that problem under the absorption costing method. Which alternative do you feel would be most useful to management and to stockholders in this case? Are the same alternatives available under variable costing? Discuss.

6. The Whitman Chemical Corporation manufactures an automobile oil additive from three basic raw materials. Standard materials cost for a batch of 25 gallons of this additive is as follows:

Material X (50 qts. @ $2)................... $100
Material Y (30 qts. @ $4)................... 120
Material Z (20 qts. @ $9)................... 180
                                          $400

During 1972, 5,000 batches of the additive were produced. Actual materials usage for this output is summarized below:

	Quarts
Material X	225,000
Material Y	140,000
Material Z	135,000

Required:

a) Compute the materials usage variance for 1972 in quarts only.

b) Compute the materials usage variance for 1972 in dollars.

c) Explain any notable difference between the two variances computed above.

7. The Frost Frozen Foods Company prepared the following graphic analysis of its labor cost for August, 1972:

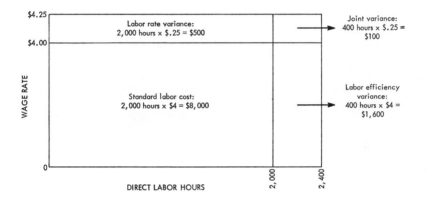

The area of the largest rectangle represents total actual labor cost for the month. The areas of the four smaller, internal rectangles are labeled on the graph. (These are not drawn accurately to scale.)

Required:

Comment on the usefulness of this graphic variance analysis to management.

8. The Holmes Manufacturing Corporation produces small refrigerators that are used primarily in home bars and in small apartments. There are five successive production departments. Steel frames and sides are manufactured in Department No. 1. The basic frame is assembled and painted in Department No. 2. Various pieces of hardware are installed on the frame, insulating fiber is inserted in the sides, some packing materials are put into place, and the frame is repainted in Department No. 3. Shelves and interior compartments are installed in Department No. 4, along with additional interior packing materials. Finally, in Department No. 5, the motor is installed,

insulation fiber is placed in the motor compartment, and the last packing materials are put into place. The refrigerators are then transferred to a warehouse pending shipment to dealers.

During 1972, a total of 120,000 refrigerators were manufactured completely and transferred to the warehouse. There were no beginning or ending inventories of work in process.

The following materials usage report was submitted to management for the year 1972:

Material	Standard Quantity @ Standard Price	Actual Quantity @ Standard Price	Materials Usage Variance
Steel parts:			
Department 1...........	$1,440,000	$1,620,000	$(180,000)
Department 3...........	240,000	246,000	(6,000)
Plastic parts:			
Department 2...........	150,000	165,000	(15,000)
Department 4...........	720,000	691,200	28,800
Insulating fiber:			
Department 3...........	180,000	185,400	(5,400)
Department 5...........	90,000	87,600	2,400
Paint:			
Department 2...........	60,000	68,000	(8,000)
Department 3...........	96,000	98,400	(2,400)
Packing materials:			
Department 3...........	24,000	25,200	(1,200)
Department 4...........	60,000	69,000	(9,000)
Department 5...........	12,000	11,700	300
Motors:			
Department 5...........	1,800,000	1,878,000	(78,000)
	$4,872,000	$5,145,500	$(273,500)

Required:

Evaluate this report critically.

9. The Sandburg Seating Company manufactures armchairs for classroom use. The standard cost of manufacturing one chair is as follows:

Raw materials:
Tubular steel (8 lbs. @ $.90)........... $7.20
Wood (2 bd. ft. @ $.25)............... .50
Chrome casters (4 @ $.09)............. .36 $ 8.06
Direct labor (¾ hr. @ $4.60)............   3.45
Overhead:
Variable (¾ hr. @ $1.20).............. $ .90
Fixed (¾ hr. @ $2.80)................ 2.10   3.00
$14.51

The standard overhead rates were derived from the following flexible budget for indirect manufacturing expenses:

Cost Item	Variable Rate per Labor Hour	Fixed Cost per Month
Indirect labor...................		$ 60,000
Labor-related costs..............	$ .69	9,000
Indirect materials...............	.15	
Power and light.................	.08	25,000
Depreciation....................		130,000
Taxes and insurance.............		16,000
Repair and maintenance.........	.28	40,000
	$1.20	$280,000

For the past five years, the company's sales and production have grown steadily. Actual output, in units, during this period is summarized below:

Year	Units
1967................................	1,060,000
1968................................	1,200,000
1969................................	1,320,000
1970................................	1,500,000
1971................................	1,700,000

After the first six months of 1972, it appears that this pattern of growth in output is continuing. Production during the month of June, 1972, totaled 160,000 units.

A total of 675 tons of tubular steel was purchased during June, 1972, at an average price of $1,880 per ton. Materials usage reports indicate that 650 tons were used in production during the same month. Four hundred thousand board feet of wood were purchased for $.17 per board foot. All of this wood was used up in production during June. It was very green wood and proved to be quite difficult to work with. In addition, cracking and warping in the production process was far in excess of normal. Five thousand hours of rework time were required for chairs on which the wood originally installed proved to be defective and had to be replaced prior to shipment. Two thousand two hundred cases of brass casters were purchased at an average cost of $17.50 per case. Each case contains 250 casters. These brass casters were purchased because of a temporary market shortage of the chrome casters. They are substantially similar to the standard item, although they tend to have a somewhat shorter life in service. Five hundred cases of chrome casters (250 casters per case) and 2,100 cases of brass casters were used in production during June.

Production workers recorded a total of 128,000 direct labor hours in June, 1972. Of these, 124,000 were straight-time hours at a wage rate of $4.90 per hour; and the other 4,000 were overtime hours at one and one-half times this hourly wage rate. Employees were granted a $.30 per hour wage increase in the new labor agreement signed on March 20, 1972.

Actual overhead costs incurred during June were as follows:

Indirect labor...........................	$ 69,000
Labor-related costs.......................	105,900
Indirect materials........................	18,500
Power and light..........................	37,500
Depreciation.............................	137,500
Taxes and insurance.....................	16,000
Repair and maintenance..................	82,600
	$467,000

The company's president has recently expressed concern that cost control in the factory is not tight enough. He has called a meeting of the policy committee for July 21, 1972, to discuss the situation, to determine whether a problem really exists, and to consider remedies if it does. To narrow the focus of discussion at this meeting, he has announced that June will be examined as a representative month. The controller, a member of the policy committee, has been directed to provide appropriate cost data for the month of June for discussion at this meeting.

Required:

a) Prepare an analysis of production costs for the month of June.

b) Discuss the usefulness of your analysis for the announced purpose of the July 21 meeting.

PLANNING AND CONTROL OF NONMANUFACTURING COSTS

DISCUSSIONS in the preceding three chapters have focused almost exclusively upon procedures for the effective planning and control of manufacturing costs. This relative emphasis upon production costs reflects typical business practice. Cost accounting has always been concerned primarily with manufacturing costs, and the most significant efforts toward efficiency and cost control have been directed at production operations. There is an increasing interest in extending these efforts into the area of nonmanufacturing operations, however. The costs of distributing goods and services, of administering large and complex organizations, of financing those organizations, and of conducting substantial research represent a large and an increasing share of the total costs of business enterprises and of our gross national product. In total, these costs exceed all manufacturing costs. Thus, they are too big to be ignored. They should be planned and controlled as carefully as are manufacturing costs. To the extent that they are similar in nature to production costs, similar control techniques may be used. To the extent that they are dissimilar, special techniques must be devised to control them.

The relatively high degree of controllability of manufacturing costs may be ascribed to two basic factors. First, most manufacturing costs are functionally related to manufactured products, and a fairly clear cause-

and-effect relationship exists. If the cost item is variable, it is controlled in relation to units of product. If it is fixed, it is usually related to productive capacity and is incurred as a consequence thereof. The relationship of semivariable costs to production is more complex and uncertain, but it is customarily assumed to exist.[1] The second factor contributing to the controllability of manufacturing costs is the routine and repetitive nature of most manufacturing operations. Mass production has resulted in the standardization of manufacturing operations and, hence, of manufacturing costs. When a task is done the same way over and over, it becomes increasingly easy to predict and to control the cost of performing that task. While most manfacturing costs are functionally related to output and are incurred in routine, repetitive activities, not all are. Such activities as quality control, factory accounting, and value analysis involve nonstandardized operations only remotely related to specific units of product. Hence, their costs are not controllable as are most other manufacturing costs. Rather, they must be controlled in the same way as most nonmanufacturing costs.

Nonmanufacturing costs characteristically are not functionally related to units of product. Some of them, however, are related to some other measure of operating volume. Those that are may be controlled in relation to that volume, much as manufacturing costs are controlled in relation to the volume of production. Many nonmanufacturing costs are unrelated to any useful volume measure, and these must be controlled by other methods. Similarly, many nonmanufacturing activities are neither routine nor repetitive. Each successive task may be different from any previous one. Obviously, the inability to apply the lessons of experience complicates the problems of planning and control. Nevertheless, these problems may not be ignored. Positive procedures for planning and controlling these costs must be devised and implemented.

VARIABLE COSTS

Any cost item that varies in direct proportion to some volume of activity may be planned and controlled in terms of that volume. The measure used for these purposes is the cost per unit of volume. For planning and control, this unit cost is allowed for each expected and each actual unit of volume. Material deviations from this unit cost are investigated and, hopefully, corrected if they are unfavorable. This use of a unit variable cost for managerial purposes requires that it be the *right* unit cost, that is, the amount that each unit of volume *should* cost. Determining the right unit cost is fairly easy in some cases and quite difficult in others. Thus, the mere fact that a cost has been identified as variable does not mean that it is readily controllable.

---

[1] See Chapter 9, pages 221–26.

Flexible Budgets for Nonmanufacturing Costs

For certain nonmanufacturing operations, costs may effectively be controlled by means of departmental flexible budgets, much in the manner of factory overhead costs. In order for a flexible budget to be operative, it is essential that the operations of the department be expressible in terms of some measure of volume that bears a significant relationship to the costs incurred in that department. Further, a significant amount of the total departmental costs must vary in reasonably direct proportion to the volume measure selected. A flexible budget comprising almost nothing but fixed costs would be little more useful than a static budget. The appropriate measure of volume will vary from department to department. For example, some selling expenses are likely to vary in proportion to sales volume, whether in dollars or in units. Salesmen's commissions are the classic example here, but other costs, such as credit losses and packing and shipping expense, may also be very close to perfectly variable with sales volume. Administrative costs may vary with respect to some specialized volume of administrative work done. Such specialized measures of volume are often referred to as *work units*. For example, the number of bills prepared might provide a useful basis for planning and controlling many of the costs in a billing department. The number of documents typed might be taken as a measure of the volume of work in a typing pool. A more precise measure here might be the number of lines typed. However, the time consumed in actually measuring volume (i.e., counting lines) might be considered excessive in relation to the potential benefits from the added precision.

Once a relevant volume measure has been selected for a particular nonmanufacturing department, the flexible budget is constructed in the manner described in Chapter 9. Variable costs are stated as rates per unit of volume and fixed costs, as total dollar amounts per time period. Semivariable costs are resolved into variable and/or fixed components by one of the methods discussed in Chapter 9. Actual departmental costs may then be compared with the flexible budget, adjusted to actual volume, to provide a basis for an evaluation of performance and a start for positive cost control efforts. All of this is exactly the same as the use of flexible budgets for overhead. The only significant difference is in the measure of volume that is used.

Standard Nonmanufacturing Costs

Only infrequently have standards been applied to nonmanufacturing operations and costs. There seem to be two reasons for this. First, standard manufacturing costs are customarily used for inventory valuation as well as for control; and nonmanufacturing costs are not charged to inventory accounts. Second, and probably more importantly, standard costs are applicable only to routine, repetitive operations. Rightly or wrongly, businessmen have generally concluded that most nonproduction operations are not sufficiently standardized to admit of useful standard costs. Actually, there are many nonmanufacturing activities that are standardized and for which standard costs are feasible. Thus, the infrequent use of standard costs in these areas is probably largely attributable to the fact that managers have found budgets to be satisfactory means of cost control.

Standard nonmanufacturing costs based upon price and quantity standards are feasible if there is a direct functional relationship between some readily measurable unit of volume and the cost items in question. Thus, usage of certain types of supplies (e.g., preprinted forms and packing materials) might be controlled by use of price and quantity standards, just as are direct materials used in production. Similarly, certain nonmanufacturing operations (e.g., check preparation and invoice processing) may lend themselves to the establishment of labor time and rate standards, as in the case of direct factory labor. In all likelihood, however, the aggregate amount of nonmanufacturing costs for which price and quantity standards could be set is small. The cost of a multicopy preprinted purchase order, for example, is only a small portion of the total cost of making a purchase. The work involved in purchasing is not likely to be standardized.

A greater amount of nonmanufacturing cost items could be included in flexible budgets. With such budgets and with defined normal volumes of activity, standard nonmanufacturing costs could be established in the same way as are standard overhead costs for production. However, these standard costs would not be needed for inventory valuation; and they would be no better for purposes of cost control than the flexible budgets from which they were derived. For control purposes, the most significant overhead variance is the spending variance. As seen in Chapters 9 and 10, this is exactly the same whether flexible budgets alone or standard costs based upon them are used. Inefficiency in the use of an input factor, such as labor time, can be identified and investigated without first determining an efficiency variance in dollars. Also, deviations of actual volume from expected volume do not demand the computation of a dollar variance. And deviations of actual volume from normal volume in the short-run are not usually considered significant to management. Thus, development of standard nonmanufacturing costs from flexible budgets would appear to be superfluous.

The Importance of the Volume Measure

Both flexible budgets and standard costs depend upon the existence of a readily measurable and useful concept of volume. Measurability is obviously important, but usefulness is even more so. In manufacturing, flexible budgets and standards are usually based upon the volume of output of goods or upon the volume of some productive input that bears a direct relationship to output. As long as the goods produced can be sold, output volume can fairly easily be identified as good (sufficient to meet sales demand) or bad (insufficient). Such a qualitative appraisal of volume is very important to management. Volume must be compatible with the basic objectives of the firm. Cost control would hardly be effective simply because cost per unit of output was equal to or less than budgeted or standard cost, if the output so exceeded demand that much of it would have to be scrapped.

Making a qualitative appraisal of the volume of some activity other than sales (usually considered good because they increase revenue and income) or production (normally considered good as long as the goods can be sold) may be difficult. For example, assume that the volume of activity in a purchasing department is measured by the number of purchase orders prepared, and that variable costs are stated as a rate per purchase order. Now, variable costs may be controlled in relation to the number of actual orders processed; but such control does not necessarily mean that spending in the purchasing department is in harmony with the firm's basic goals. Perhaps too many or too few purchase orders are being prepared. Management's objective of cost control is not fully achieved if the purchasing department is very efficiently preparing an excessive quantity of purchase orders. There remains to be answered a very important question. Given more fundamental objectives, what volume of purchase orders may be considered appropriate for the period? A purchase order is a means to an end, not an end in itself. The same is true of many other items whose volumes might be used to measure activity in nonmanufacturing departments—e.g., the number of paychecks prepared, credit applications processed, advertising circulars distributed, bills prepared, reports written, and miles traveled. Too few of any of these items may inhibit sales, profits, growth, and other managerial objectives. Too many of them, on the other hand, will be wasteful. Hence, management must first define the appropriate volume of nonmanufacturing activity in light of its basic goals and then seek to control costs in terms of that volume. In many instances, unfortunately, the former requirement may prove to be very difficult. Few objective standards for the "right" volume of these activities exist.

COMMITTED FIXED COSTS

Committed fixed costs were defined in Chapter 9 as fixed costs that must be incurred in each period as a consequence of a major decision made at some time in the past. Most committed fixed costs are associated with contracts (e.g., a long-term employment contract with the corporation's president) or with the acquisition of long-lived assets (e.g., a plant or a warehouse). The identifying characteristic of a committed cost is that its amount, as well as its incurrence, is predetermined and can be altered only by another major decision to reverse or to amend the earlier commitment. There are many costs, of course, to whose incurrence management is effectively committed. One cannot visualize an organization functioning unless wages and salaries are paid, but the amounts of wages and salaries paid to specific individuals need not be predetermined. Thus, a committed cost is one whose amount is not subject to periodic control by management. Consequently, committed costs must be planned and controlled at the time that the basic commitment is made. Chapters 15 and 16 discuss the planning of major capital expenditures, such as for plant and equipment. This capital budgeting process should explicitly include consideration of the consequent committed fixed costs.

The concept of a committed fixed cost is easy to define, and its control implications are easily explained. Once a major commitment has been made, the resultant committed costs must be included at a given amount in the annual budget. Further control is not feasible. Unfortunately, determining just exactly what is a committed cost in a particular situation may not be quite so easy. For example, the decision to construct a factory commits the firm to certain costs over the factory's life. Some of these costs, such as depreciation and property taxes, are truly uncontrollable in amount each year. Other costs are equally necessary as a consequence of the construction decision, but their annual amounts are not so rigidly fixed. For example, every factory requires periodic maintenance. Therefore, the incurrence of annual maintenance costs cannot be avoided. A managerial decision to omit maintenance altogether would entail such dire consequences that it could not be seriously considered at all. However, the exact amount that must be spent on maintenance in any single year need not be fixed. To some degree, there is a tradeoff between maintenance costs and productive efficiency or between maintenance costs and factory life. Management might conceivably make this tradeoff decision differently in one year as compared with the previous year. (Obviously, the tradeoff between maintenance and factory life is not perpetually flexible. Reduced maintenance expenditures in any one year may irrevocably shorten the plant's life.) Thus, is factory maintenance a committed cost? Probably the most accurate answer is that there is some absolute minimum level of maintenance cost that is properly regarded as committed. Over and above this minimum, the amount spent is subject to periodic managerial discretion. Hence, the additional, discretionary amount may be thought of as a managed cost.

MANAGED COSTS

A large number of fixed costs are fixed in amount for a given period as a result of a current management decision. Management has some significant range of discretion as to the amount of cost it will budget for the particular purpose or program in question. There are referred to variously as *managed costs, programmed costs,* or *discretionary costs.* The first term will be used consistently here. It is most descriptive of the essential character of these costs; they are subject to current control by management. Some common examples of managed fixed costs are the costs of advertising, public relations, research and development, employee training, executive development, and various other types of staff assistance. A managed cost is fixed in amount because management has determined that that amount is all that need be, should be, or can be spent for the purpose in the current period. The amount allowed for that purpose may change significantly from period to period, however. In this respect, a managed cost is quite different from a committed cost. At the same time, variations in the amount spent over time may bear no meaningful relationship to any measure of volume. There is, thus, no similarity to variable costs. Herein lies the great difficulty in planning managed costs. If the cost is not a function of any observable volume measure and if it is not predetermined as a consequence of some earlier commitment, how does management decide on the appropriate amount to spend in any given period?

There are many ways of answering this question, and they are not necessarily mutually exclusive. One approach is to determine how much competitors are spending for the same purpose. This is a particularly useful method in dealing with items that are directly related to the firm's competitive position—such as advertising, other promotional programs, and product development and testing. Much advertising (in the cigarette market, for example) is regarded as defensive. Its goal is not so much to gain new customers as to avoid losing old customers to competitors. If management believes that its advertising budget is primarily a defensive weapon, amounts spent by competitors logically become a dominant factor in determining the current amount of this particular managed cost. Of course, some firms may consciously decide to behave differently from their competitors. A company that prides itself on product leadership, for example, may deliberately choose to spend substantially more than the industry average on research and development. An industry leader may feel it can safely cut its promotional outlays, whereas a new or an ambitious firm may decide it must spend more than the average on promotion.

There are many programs in any organization which are largely internal in their implications and effects. They have little direct impact upon competitors. Examples of such programs are general accounting, order processing, purchasing, and legal services. The complete absence of any of these functions might have dire competitive consequences, but the level of spending for them is not likely to have any observable short-run effect on competition. What criteria can management apply to determine appropriate spending levels for such items? Once again, average levels of spending for the same item in other firms, particularly those in the same industry, may be a useful, if rough, guide. If trade association data indicate that firms in a particular industry annually spend an average of 2% of net sales on general accounting or an average of $300 per employee on general personnel functions, these averages may be taken as presumptive guidelines for any single firm's spending. Essentially, management asks, "If others are spending this much, how can we justify spending significantly more or less?" Of course, there may be a very sound answer to that question. While management may begin by presuming it should spend about what the rest of the industry does for an item, it should be willing to accept reasons for deviating from industrial averages. For example, a firm may attribute its employees' loyalty and work force stability to relatively high expenditures for employee recruitment and training. Thus, it may justify higher than average costs in terms of better than average results.

Another possible criterion for controlling managed costs that have primarily internal implications is a subjective notion of effectiveness. For example, management may decide that personnel administration will be more effective if some specified level of spending is allowed for that purpose. This spending level is necessarily related to some level of work performed in the personnel function. These subjective notions are difficult to justify, however; and they are likely to differ considerably among individual managers. It is ordinarily impracticable to test the effectiveness of various levels of funding for a program such as personnel administration, but it may be possible to simulate the effects of various levels of spending if a suitable model of that program's impact upon the entire firm can be constructed. Computer-based simulation may offer some significant opportunities for improved planning and control of managed costs. Such opportunities are largely unexplored at this time, however.

A substantial portion of managed costs, particularly in the area of administration, represents salaries. Thus, one way of controlling these costs is to impose personnel ceilings on departments. This is a useful device, for the efficiency of a department may often be appraised better in terms of the number of persons working in it than in terms of the dollars that it spends. Personnel and dollars are closely related, of course. A reduction in personnel entails a cost saving. Personnel ceilings are not very popular, of course. Department supervisors tend to regard them as unwelcome restrictions. Other personnel may view them as potential threats to their own jobs. These adverse implications should be considered before such ceilings are imposed. Nevertheless, control of managed costs in many areas inevitably means control of salaried personnel.

A very pragmatic approach to controlling managed costs is to allow spending in an amount that management believes it can afford. Some firms, for example, budget research and development costs as a percentage of expected sales. Logically, this appears to be a somewhat backward approach to the problem. One would expect sales to be determined, at least partially, by research and development programs. Budgeting for the latter on the basis of the former seems to suggest just the opposite relationship. Actually, sales are selected as the basis for the research and development budget not because of any presumed causal relationship but because they are one useful indicator of how much the firm can afford to spend for that purpose. Nevertheless, management must recognize that declining sales may be the result of insufficient product research and development. Hence, it may be appropriate to increase spending for this purpose as sales decline. Other managed costs are likely to be budgeted on the basis of ability to spend also. Public relations and charitable contributions are typical examples.

One writer has suggested that managed costs may usefully be separated further into policy costs and operating costs.[2] Policy costs are dependent almost entirely on managerial judgment and would include such items as advertising, research, and executive development. Changes in amounts budgeted for these items would be unlikely to have any direct and immediate effect on current production and sales operations. Operating costs, on the other hand, are closely tied to these current operations; and changes in spending levels might have immediately recognizable impacts on production or sales. Examples are supervision, purchasing, and quality control. While this distinction may have conceptual validity, it would be a difficult one to define in practice. A reduction in advertising, for example, may have as prompt an effect on sales volume as would a cutback on quality control inspections. Rather than using a dual classification of managed costs, it may be useful to think of them as a broad spectrum, ranging from close to slight relationships to current operations.

The spectrum of managed costs may also be visualized as comprising degrees of variability of spending levels. It might be feasible for a firm to vary its charitable contributions at will, with no effect other than on the financial positions of its beneficiaries. It might be very damaging for the firm to vary its research and development expenditures widely from year to year, however. A budget cut in this area may mean that an ongoing project, in which much has already been invested, would have to be terminated. It might mean that valuable scientific personnel would have to be laid off one year and recruited anew in some later year. While such great variations may be unavoidable in some instances, they are not conducive to stable growth in sales and profits. This illustration again highlights the essential characteristic of managed costs. The program for

---

[2] Marshall K. Evans, "Profit Planning," *Harvard Business Review,* Vol. XXXVII (July–August, 1959), p. 46.

which these costs are incurred may well be indispensable, but the dollar amount spent on it in any single year is subject to considerable managerial discretion. That discretion must include adequate consideration of a wide range of factors, some of which are likely to suggest conflicting decisions. These conflicts cannot be avoided, and they must be resolved.

PROGRAM PLANNING IN THE DEPARTMENT OF DEFENSE

The United States Department of Defense annually spends billions of dollars on what may properly be considered nonmanufacturing programs. (It also spends billions on activities essentially equivalent to manufacturing operations—notably materials procurement, shipyard work, and aircraft repairs.) It has, of course, a great need to plan and control these costs effectively and some very serious obstacles to overcome in doing so. To meet this challenge, it has developed a fairly complex system for financial planning and control. This system has also been implemented throughout most of the federal government, in many state and local governments, and in numerous private organizations. The details in the application of the system may have to be varied to meet the special situation of any individual organization, but the basic ideas are generally applicable. Hence, it is worthwhile to examine this system briefly.

Prior to 1961, planning in the Department of Defense was not as systematic and comprehensive as it is now. While longer range plans were made, the formal planning process was tied very closely to the annual budget submitted to Congress. As a consequence, planning tended to follow the budgetary structure employed by the Congress and focused excessively on each year alone. Congress' consideration of the Defense budget was centered on the individual services (Army, Navy, and Air Force) and on specific spending items (e.g., wages and salaries, materials, equipment, etc.). The emphasis on the distinction among the services was more practicable when each service had fairly clear and distinct responsibilities. During World War II, for example, the Navy was concerned almost exclusively with the war at sea. Navy planes ordinarily did not fly the same types of combat missions as did the Army Air Corps (now the Air Force). Even the types of combat missions assigned to the Marine Corps and the Army infantry were quite different, and the Marines' activities were limited almost exclusively to the Pacific theater. These mission distinctions among the services no longer exist. Carrier-based Navy planes and land-based Air Force planes flew essentially the same tactical missions in Korea and in Viet Nam. Hence, they may legitimately be thought of as interchangeable, at least partially. The nation's nuclear defense forces are manned by all three of the services. Indeed, the operational military commands are coordinated. Thus, financial planning and control along service lines has limited value today.

The budgetary emphasis on individual cost items has never been a satisfactory means of effective planning. It was intended originally to give Congress effective control over government spending, as the Constitution provides. However, if spending items are too narrowly defined, the result could be to make governmental management all but impossible. This danger was recognized very early. Thomas Jefferson had argued that Congress ought to appropriate funds for "every specific purpose susceptible of definition." In challenging this view, Alexander Hamilton raised an admittedly extreme example of the consequent danger. He observed that funds might be appropriated separately to purchase oats and hay as feed for Army horses. Should the appropriation for oats be fully expended but not that for hay and should only oats be available at a particular moment, the horses might starve and their riders with them—and all because the supply officer lacked the authority to spend hay money on oats.[3] As a matter of fact, cost items were never that narrowly defined; and in 1951, spending categories in the Defense appropriations were consolidated into fewer, broader classes (e.g., military personnel, civilian personnel, operation and maintenance, construction, and research and development). While this consolidation is an obvious improvement, it still entails budgetary emphasis upon the items for which government funds will be expended rather than upon the goals to be achieved as a result of the expenditures.

In 1961, the Department of Defense formally inaugurated a new planning system referred to as the Planning-Programming-Budgeting System (PPBS). As a matter of fact, these terms had been used since 1949, when Congress required a "performance budget" from the Department as a whole. However, prior to 1961, this approach was limited largely to the annual budgetary process. To be sure, long-range planning did occur; but it was not systematically related to the annual budgets and it did not coordinate the three services' plans. The essence of PPBS is both simple and logical. At the planning stage, basic objectives are formulated for American defense policy as far into the future as is considered practical and useful. These objectives are formalized in the Joint Strategic Objectives Plan, prepared by the Joint Chiefs of Staff and approved by the President. After approval of these objectives, specific programs are developed to meet the objectives; this is the programming phase. Approved programs are planned in detail for five years and are incorporated in the Five-Year Defense Program. This is both a military plan and a financial

---

[3] Arthur Smithies, *The Budgetary Process in the United States* (New York: McGraw-Hill Book Co., Inc., 1955), pp. 51–52.

forecast. Ideally, the annual budgeting process would simply draw the financial requirements for the next year from the five-year plan and present them both in terms of programs and in terms of spending items for consideration by Congress. In recognition of the fact that conditions and estimates can change, the system formally provides for program change requests that may be submitted in advance of the annual budget to obtain changes in the approved programs contained in the five-year plan. The annual budget process does not actually function quite so easily, of course. There is much give-and-take between the Department and the Congress and also among the members of Congress.

In summary, then, PPBS approaches the planning process by defining first what the government wishes to achieve in the way of defense (planning), then determining what means of reaching these goals are to be used (programming), and finally providing resources to implement the chosen means (budgeting).

The Joint Strategic Objectives Plan deals with political and military assessments of potential threats to national security and with projections of force levels required to cope with them. For example, the threat of nuclear attack is evaluated and the forces necessary to deter it are determined. Deterrent forces must then be establishd in specific programs, such as retaliatory strike missiles (ICBMs), antimissile missiles (the Safeguard system), and civil defense. All three of these are specific program elements within a single major program titled Strategic Forces, which is only one of nine major programs. The complete list at the time of this writing is as follows:[4]

Strategic Forces	Transportation	Logistics
General Purpose Forces	Guard and Reserve Forces	Personnel Support
Specialized Forces	Research and Development	Administration

Within each major program there are several program elements or subprograms. Strategic Forces, for example, include the land-based Minuteman missile system, the submarine-based Polaris/Poseidon missile system, and the air-borne Strategic Air Command. These are all means of nuclear retaliation. Since an increase in any one of the three would diminish the need for the other two, given certain objectives, it is clear that financial planning for defense must focus on missions rather than on objects or on the services, as was formerly the case. With plans and programs defined, the budgeting process can be more meaningful to governmental managers. A cut in the Defense budget can be translated into a reduction in specific programs. Conversely, a call for additional Posei-

---

[4] The major programs have changed before and undoubtedly will change again. This list gives the reader a general idea of the types of distinctions that are involved, however. The programs are obviously interrelated. General Purpose Forces for use in so-called "limited wars" depend upon Transportation and Logistics if they are to fulfill their mission.

don missiles, for example, can be converted to annual cost increases for the missiles, the submarines to carry them, the men to operate these craft, their training, and all of the other necessary support facilities. Further, knowledge of lead times permits each of these increased costs to be placed in a particular year's budget.

An obvious question that arises in connection with the defense planning process is, "How much is enough?" How are force levels justified? There is no convenient measure of effectiveness. Sales promotion, for example, may be justified in terms of sales volume. A new plant may be justified in relation to output. There is no similar measure of volume to support defense spending, however. The ultimate objective of our Strategic Forces, for example, is to *deter* attack. Thus, our nuclear retaliatory weapons are truly effective only if they are never used. But how can one decide how many of them are required in order to ensure that they won't be used? The answer to this question is inevitably subjective, but some measurable concepts of defense capability have been developed to support requests for specific weapons. Such measures as target coverage (i.e., number of targets that could be struck by a weapon system), flight distance, payload (commonly measured in tons of destructive force), and invulnerability to enemy attack are used as indexes of defense capability. Yet, these are only intermediate aims; the basic objective is still deterrence. Similar measurement problems arise in nondefense areas. PPBS is now used throughout the federal government. It is easy to see that it could be a valuable tool in planning water resources, urban improvements, transportation, and other national needs. Yet, how does one measure an improvement in something as complex as the urban environment? An increase in housing units is one measure, but it may be achieved in different ways, some of which might aggravate other urban problems. Transportation needs may be met by building freeways, but these often impinge on housing and recreational areas and they add to air pollution problems. Thus, not only are the objectives of any single program difficult to measure but they may also conflict with the goals of other programs.

In the final analysis, PPBS is a useful approach to the planning and control of expenditures for a wide variety of programs. In industrial firms, it would seem particularly applicable to research and development, sales promotion, training, and other programs whose payoffs are expected to be realized only sometime after the expenditures have been made. It is by no means a panacea, of course. It does not resolve the problem of defining goals; and, yet, it depends upon a resolution of that problem. It does not obviate the need for judgment nor avoid disagreements as to the effectiveness of specific programs (witness the heated disputes in Congress over the necessity for and even the feasibility of certain weapon systems). Finally, one cannot demonstrate that PPBS has always worked better than the earlier, less systematic methods. The Polaris missile program is often cited as a model of good military planning and development, and it was operational before PPBS was initiated. The widely publicized operational and financial problems of the F-111 aircraft (known as the TFX in its developmental stage) is painfully dramatic evidence that PPBS cannot compensate for unwise decisions. It can significantly enhance the efforts of good management, however.[5]

FUNCTIONAL COST CLASSIFICATIONS

One of the most familiar and widely used schemes of cost classification is by functions.[6] This classification scheme is reflected in the traditional income statement. Typical functional classifications of nonmanufacturing costs include distribution or marketing costs, administrative costs, research and development costs, and financial costs. These functional categories are quite useful for certain purposes, and there is no reason why they should not be retained. However, they are less useful for purposes of planning and control than the classification of costs as variable, managed, and committed. Flexible budgets, for example, may be used in exactly the same way to control manufacturing, marketing, or administrative costs that are partly variable with some measurable concept of volume. Functional classification may be of some value as a very gross tool of cost control. Thus, a corporate president may compare what his firm spends on administration with amounts spent in similar companies to determine very roughly whether his firm's administrative costs seem excessive, too low, or about right. There is a very real danger in this approach. To begin with, "similar" companies are not identical. Organizational structures and administrative practices vary among companies, and there is no reason to presume that one way is necessarily better than others. Administrative efforts and costs are validated by success in the attainment of the organization's goals. If success may be achieved in a variety of ways, one may legitimately conclude that administrative standardization is neither necessary nor desirable. In addition, different firms may define administrative costs differently. One firm may treat sales executives' salaries as administrative costs, while another reports them as marketing costs. Similarly, the cost accounting department's costs might be charged either to administrative cost or to factory overhead.

Whatever limitations functional cost categories may have for control purposes, they very often must be used. If a firm is organized along

---

[5] The reader interested in pursuing PPBS further is referred to Stephen Enke (ed.), *Defense Management* (Englewood Cliffs, N.J.: Prentice-Hall, Inc., 1967); and to David Novick (ed.), *Program Budgeting* (2d ed.; New York: Holt, Rinehart & Winston, Inc., 1968).

[6] Functional classifications of costs were discussed previously in Chapter 2, pp. 19–22.

functional lines (i.e., manufacturing departments, sales departments, research department, etc.), cost data will be collected and reported along the same lines. This is required for effective responsibility accounting. Hence, a brief consideration of some of these function classifications is appropriate.

Distribution Costs

Distribution, or marketing, encompasses a wide range of activities; and there is no clearly defined distinction between distribution and other functions. For example, are credit losses (bad debts) distribution costs or financial costs? Is the sales manager's salary a distribution cost or an administrative cost? These questions need not be answered in order to plan and control the individual cost items, but they do highlight the difficulty of broad functional cost classifications. For purposes of discussion here, we shall subclassify distribution costs into three categories: direct selling, promotion, and customer servicing.

Direct selling costs are those incurred in the course of making sales and attempting to make sales. They include such items as salesmen's salaries and commissions, salesmen's travel expenses, and cost of operating sales and display facilities. In the long run, of course, such costs must be related to and justified in terms of results—that is, sales. For purposes of short-run control, however, they may more effectively be related to effort than to accomplishment. Travel expenses, for example, may vary greatly among salesmen and over time insofar as they relate to sales volume. On the other hand, they may bear readily definable and logical relationships to calls made and miles traveled. In the long run, of course, sales calls and travel must be justified in terms of sales revenue. In the short run, however, the frequency and duration of calls are usually established as a matter of policy. Given such a policy, travel expenses may be largely controllable by reference to the volumes of calls and mileage. Thus, these costs may be viewed as managed costs for purposes of policy planning. Once the managerial decisions have been made, however, the costs vary partially with volume and may be controlled accordingly.

Promotional costs are intended to stimulate demand for a company's products and services. Hopefully, this demand will then be translated into actual sales. Promotion includes such things as advertising, catalogs, premium offers, and contests. It is difficult to relate these costs to actual sales, because they are intended to stimulate future sales. Even after the fact, it is seldom possible to attribute specific amounts of sales to particular promotional projects. Hence, promotional costs are unlikely to be controllable in terms of any measure of sales volume. Advertising costs may be related to some measure of volume of effort, however. Minutes of network television time, pages of national magazine space, numbers of readers reached, and numbers of direct mailings might be useful bases for appraising the efficiency of advertising expenditures; but they could not easily be translated into effectiveness, as measured by increased sales. Thus, promotional costs must be regarded essentially as managed costs. Possibly, over fairly long periods of time, useful measures of effectiveness might be derived from statistical analyses of actual promotional cost and sales data.

Customer servicing costs include activities attendant upon sales, such as billing, shipping, credit analysis, accounts receivable maintenance, and handling claims and complaints. Many of these operations, notably billing, shipping, and accounting, may be so routine and repetitive as to permit cost control by techniques similar to those used for production costs—especially flexible budgets. The important distinctive feature of customer servicing is that it involves activities primarily internal to the firm. So long as these activities are performed properly, there is no interface between the firm and its customers, as there must be in the cases of direct selling and promotion. (Such customer service activities as handling complaints and collecting overdue accounts may become exceptions to this general statement if established routine procedures fail to produce the desired results.)

Administrative Costs

The 20th century has witnessed a significant increase in the number of white-collar, or administrative, workers relative to blue-collar, or production, workers. Since most administrative personnel are paid weekly or monthly salaries and are laid off only in unusual circumstances, administrative labor costs are largely fixed. And salaries normally constitute the majority of all administrative costs. Such nonlabor costs as office rent, depreciation, and maintenance are also largely fixed. Hence, the bulk of administrative costs are typically managed or committed fixed charges. Some, however, are likely to vary with the volume of work done. For example, the payroll department might be considered part of the administrative structure of a firm. Some part of the cost of preparing and distributing paychecks and maintaining pay records is likely to vary in direct proportion to the number of checks prepared. Similarly, stenographic costs may be controllable, at least partially, on the basis of the number of documents typed.

Research and Development Costs

The problems of planning and controlling these costs have been discussed before in the section on managed costs.[7] Research and development

---

[7] See page 303.

is an excellent example of an activity in an industrial firm that may be viewed as a major program, designed to meet the objective of long-term growth and expansion, and comprising many subprograms (individual research projects). Thus, the planning-programming-budgeting procedures used in the Department of Defense might prove very useful for cost planning and control in this area. Research may be considered essential to future sales, but there is no practical way of relating current research outlays to future revenues—except long after it is too late to control those outlays. Moreover, it is an unhappy reality that research will often entail fairly expensive projects that must ultimately be abandoned as fruitless. Regrettably, investigation of several blind alleys is frequently unavoidable if any significant accomplishments are to be made. This is similar to drilling for oil, where many dry wells may have to be drilled in order to get one producing well. Perhaps the best control that can be exercised over research costs is to ensure that all costs directly traceable to a particular project are charged to it. In this way, management will have an idea of how much is being spent on fruitful projects and how much on projects that yield no return at all. The performance of research administrators may be evaluated to some extent by reference to project cost analysis. Finally, management must recognize that much spending on research and development actually constitutes capital investments made in anticipation of benefits in the future. Analysis of such investments is the subject of Chapters 15 and 16.

Financial Costs

Financial costs include interest, costs of issuing securities, bank service charges, and other costs incurred in the process of obtaining and holding capital. Control of these costs is in the province of financial managers, such as the corporate treasurer. This aspect of capital management is beyond the scope of this text. The primary contribution that management accounting can make in this area is to provide information that will facilitate profitable operations, given some actual or target sales volume, with the lowest practicable investment in assets. Reductions in assets mean reduced interest cost on invested capital. While reduction of assets is always a secondary goal after more important objectives, such as growth, profits, and stability, it should not be ignored.

QUESTIONS FOR DISCUSSION

1. Discuss the problems associated with the establishment of useful standard costs for nonmanufacturing operations.
2. "As a general rule, variable costs are more easily controllable than fixed costs, simply because the former have some defined relationship to a meas-

urable volume of operating activity." Do you agree with this statement. Explain your position.

3. How would you go about establishing a flexible budget for the cost accounting department in a manufacturing company? Compare this process with that of establishing a flexible budget for one of the company's production departments.

4. Suggest work units that would be practicable measures of operating volumes in the nonmanufacturing departments listed below. Explain briefly why you chose each work unit suggested. If you believe no practicable measure of volume is available for a particular department, give your reasons.
   a) Customer billing department
   b) Purchasing department
   c) Legal department
   d) Shipping department
   e) Factory first-aid station

5. The sales promotion department of the Wilkes Publishing Company promotes sales of encyclopedias by magazine advertising and by direct mail solicitations. Advertising costs are budgeted and controlled in relation to the number of magazine readers reached, as determined by the magazine publishers' circulation statistics. Mailing costs are budgeted and controlled in relation to the number of promotional brochures mailed. Evaluate these bases for planning and controlling promotional costs.

6. "It would be hard to imagine a cost to which management is more committed than income tax. Of course, income tax is not fixed; it varies with the firm's taxable income. So, I have discovered a new cost concept—the committed variable cost." Comment on this assertion.

7. How does management manage managed costs?

8. Suggest some useful criteria for the planning and control of research and development costs in a manufacturing corporation. Rank these criteria in what you believe to be the order of their importance. Justify your choice of the most important criterion.

9. While sipping coffee in the Student Union after a particularly trying managerial accounting class, three students were discussing the controllability of faculty salaries. "Basically, they're variable costs," said the first; "because the number of faculty members depends on the student enrollment." "No," argued the second student, "faculty salaries are managed costs; they are set by the Board of Regents and voted by the legislature." The third student smiled and replied, "You're both wrong! Most of those professors have tenure; so, their salaries are committed costs." What kind of cost are faculty salaries?

10. "If the Planning-Programming-Budgeting System is such a wonderful thing, how can the Department of Defense keep coming up with such tremendous cost overruns and production delays on programs like the C5A transport and the Mark 48 torpedo?" Can you answer this question?

11. How can we measure the effectiveness of such social programs as public education and recreation? Is it necessary that their effectiveness be measured? If not, how can we decide how much money to spend on them?

12. "Technical advances in business information systems and data processing will ultimately provide the same degree of control over nonmanufacturing costs as over manufacturing costs." Do you agree or disagree with this prediction? Why?

PROBLEMS

1. The O'Hara Company has established standard costs for the operation of its payroll department. The standard time allowed for the preparation of one paycheck and related documents and records is one quarter of an hour. The department's costs have been budgeted at $4.50 per man-hour plus $9,000 per month. Normal volume in the department has been set at 6,000 paychecks per month, as the company's normal work force consists of 3,000 people, each paid twice a month. During May, 1972, a total of 5,600 paychecks were prepared and distributed. Timekeeping records show that the payroll department worked 1,460 hours during June. Actual variable costs for the month were $6,600, and actual fixed costs, $9,400.

Required:

Compute as many variances from standard cost in the payroll department for the month of June as you can.

2. Hamilton Shoe Co., Inc., has established standard costs for its invoicing department. These standard costs are as follows:

Variable cost per invoice prepared....................	$.75
Variable cost per invoice line typed...................	.02
Fixed cost per invoice prepared......................	.50

In a normal year, 40,000 invoices are prepared. During 1972, 42,500 invoices were prepared. A random sample of 642 invoices showed that the average number of lines typed on an invoice was 12. The total fixed cost incurred in the department during 1972 was $21,000. The total variable cost was $43,000.

Required:

Compute as many variances from standard invoicing cost for 1972 as you can.

3. The management of the Benteen Corporation believes that its planning and control of nonmanufacturing costs are less efficient that the procedures used for production costs. Accordingly, it is seeking to establish departmental budgets for most of its nonmanufacturing operations. The facts outlined below were developed from a study of the costs incurred in the purchasing department.

The purchasing department supervisor receives a monthly salary of $1,600. His secretary receives $540 per month. There are five purchasing clerks who are paid an hourly wage of $4.80. Typists are paid $2.40 per hour. The standard six-part purchase order form used costs $.20 per set; one set is required for each purchase order. Experience indicates that approximately

10% more sets are spoiled and must be discarded. Typing supplies are estimated to cost $.32 per hour of typing time. Rent on the office space occupied by the purchasing department is charged on the basis of floor space; this charge amounts to $420 per month. Property taxes and insurance on this portion of the building are $600 per year. Labor-related costs average 10% of hourly wages and 15% of monthly salaries. During a normal month, 2,000 purchase orders are issued. It takes a purchasing clerk about one quarter of an hour to process an order and give it to a typist with the necessary instructions. Typists can type approximately 120 lines per hour. The average purchase order contains 15 lines. When not working on purchase orders, purchasing clerks update vendors' files and review vendors' catalogs. Typists are reassigned to the typing pool when not needed in the purchasing department.

Required:

Prepare a flexible expense budget for the purchasing department for one month. Include budgeted cost allowances for the normal monthly volume of 2,000 purchase orders.

4. During the month of November, 1972, the purchasing department of the Benteen Corporation (cf. Problem 3 above) processed a total of 1,650 purchase orders. The actual costs recorded in the department for the month were as follows:

Wages and salaries:	
Supervisor....................................	$1,600
Secretary.....................................	560
Purchasing clerks.............................	2,160
Typists.......................................	540
Labor-related costs...........................	594
Supplies:	
Purchase order forms used.....................	345
Typing supplies used..........................	72
Space occupancy charges:	
Rent..	450
Taxes and insurance...........................	50
	$6,371

Required:

Prepare an expense report for the purchasing department for November. Compare actual costs with budgeted costs.

5. The marketing division of the Butler Corporation is responsible for promotion, sales, and delivery of the company's products. It comprises five sales territories, all of which are served by two regional warehouses. These warehouses were substantially expanded early in 1971 and are expected to meet the corporation's requirements for the storage of finished products for at least five more years.

A summary of the operating statistics for the marketing division for the preceding five years is presented below:

	1972	1971	1970	1969	1968
Number of shipments..........	10,300	10,000	9,900	9,800	9,600
Sales revenue in thousands of					
dollars...................	$67,000	$60,000	$58,000	$55,000	$50,000
Costs in thousands of dollars:					
Advertising..................	$ 6,200	$ 5,500	$ 5,500	$ 5,600	$ 5,000
Salesmen's travel.............	2,600	2,200	2,350	2,100	1,800
Salesmen's commissions.......	4,020	3,600	3,480	3,300	3,000
Order processing..............	309	300	297	294	288
Executives' salaries...........	900	860	840	880	800
Warehousemen's wages........	598	570	545	515	480
Depreciation.................	1,200	1,200	900	900	900
Labor-related costs..........	738	669	648	627	570
Total costs..............	$16,565	$14,899	$14,560	$14,216	$12,838

The business prosperity of the 1960s continued throughout 1968 and most of 1969. A fairly mild, though persistent recession occurred during 1970 and the first three quarters of 1971. Rapid economic recovery ensued, and 1972 was again a year of general prosperity.

Required:

Classify each of the marketing division's costs as variable, managed, or committed. Propose guidelines for budgeting these costs in 1973. The preliminary sales forecast for 1973 is for about 10,700 shipments and for sales of $75 million.

6. The research division of Pittypat Petrochemicals, Inc., has recently been reorganized and expanded. It is directed by a vice president for research and development who has overall administrative responsibility for the division. The chief of research is Dr. Gunther Hansson, who is responsible for the technical direction of the division. He is assisted by a research staff of 8 graduate scientists and 24 laboratory technicians. The personnel complement of the division is completed by secretaries, maintenance men, janitors, and watchmen. The division occupies its own building in Albuquerque.

The work of the division is carried on in a series of distinct research projects of widely varying lives. Each project is assigned to the immediate supervision of one of the eight staff scientists. Each of these men is ordinarily responsible for two or more projects at any one time. Dr. Hansson, of course, has general responsibility for all research projects.

Most projects involve the testing of materials for desired properties and efforts to develop new materials with desired characteristics. Some projects require the use of special equipment which cannot be reused within the division and must be sold at nominal prices to universities or for scrap. All equipment and materials used in the research division are procured by the company's central purchasing office in Dallas.

When a project culminates in the development of a new and valuable material, a patent is obtained and the new product is produced and marketed.

Many projects, however, result in no useful achievement and must be abandoned.

For the past several years, all costs incurred in the research division have been charged to current expense as they were incurred. As the total costs of research and development have grown rapidly, management has become concerned that this practice may be obscuring the true financial implications of the division's activities. You have been engaged as a consultant to management, with instructions to study the situation and make recommendations.

Required:

In your report to management, outline a proposal for the recording and analysis of research and development costs in Pittypat Petrochemicals, Inc. Consider individual cost items as well as total research and development costs. Indicate how these costs should be reported to management and to readers of the corporations annual financial statements.

PART III
Decision Making

——————————————— chapter 13

COST-VOLUME-PROFIT
RELATIONSHIPS

As THE title of Part III suggests, the chapters in this part of the book will be concerned chiefly with the analysis and application of financial data in specific business decision-making situations. This must not be interpreted to mean that the costs and procedures discussed in the previous parts of the book have no impact upon business decisions. A budget, for example, is a decision in itself; and budgeted costs are integral parts of that decision. Cost control, however effected, requires that specific decisions be made; these decisions must be based primarily upon accumulated cost data, including actual, planned, and standard costs. The same fundamental types of costs are involved in decision-making analysis, but here they are classified and analyzed in accordance with their relationships to the specific facts of the decision at hand. A great many business decisions affect directly the revenues, the costs, and/or the operating volume of the enterprise. Thus, at the outset, it will be useful to examine the relationships among these quantities and the implications thereof for the firm's profit. At this point, before proceeding, the reader may wish to review the discussion of cost behavior in relation to volume in Chapter 2.[1] Much of the material in this and in the following chapters assumes a full understanding of the natures of variable and fixed costs, as well as of the practical difficulties involved in attempting to identify specific costs as variable or fixed.

Costs identified as variable are assumed to vary in direct proportion to volume, however volume may be measured. Fixed costs are assumed to be absolutely fixed over the relevant range of volume. So long as these

---

[1] Pages 22–27.

basic assumptions are reasonably valid, the behavior of an enterprise's costs with respect to changes in the volume of its operations can be predicted and analyzed quite accurately. The existence of truly semivariable costs, however, clouds the cost-volume picture. The effective elimination of such costs by one of the methods described in connection with the development of flexible budgets[2] simplifies the analysis but also renders it that much less precise. Nevertheless, the usefulness of cost-volume analysis to management justifies this simplification and overrides the degree of imprecision created thereby.

Revenues, like variable costs, are assumed to vary in direct proportion to the volume of units sold. Where sales volume is expressed in terms of sales dollars, it is definitionally equal to revenues (excluding from consideration here such nonoperating revenues as interest, dividends, and rent). As both revenues and variable costs vary directly with volume, the net difference between them—variable profit—must also vary in proportion to volume. Thus, the effects of changes in operating volume may be analyzed simply in terms of a variable profit which varies, in total, in direct proportion to changes in volume (and, hence, is constant per unit of volume) and fixed costs which are constant in total regardless of volume fluctuations. Such analysis is quite simple, but there may be some fairly complicated problems underlying it. The most appropriate measure of volume is not always obvious. In a single product firm, volume may be measured quite readily in terms of units of product. In a multiproduct firm, however, it is more likely that sales volume will be measured in terms of dollar sales and production volume in terms of some measure of input (e.g., labor hours). Further, the volumes of sales and production are not necessarily equal. Thus, no one volume measure may be a suitable common denominator for total operations. This problem will be discussed further in a subsequent section. Finally, as observed in Chapter 2, the concepts of variable and fixed costs are simple and definite; the task of classifying actual costs as one or the other may be quite difficult, however. The discussions in this and the following chapter will assume that these practical problems have been resolved satisfactorily and will be concerned only with the basic analysis.

BREAK-EVEN ANALYSIS

The most familiar form of cost-volume profit analysis is break-even analysis. In fact, many businessmen and accountants regard these two ideas as synonymous. More precisely, though, the latter is a specific type of the former. Break-even analysis involves the study of revenues and costs in relation to volume and, specifically, the determination of that

---

[2] Cf., Chapter 9, pp. 221–26.

volume at which the firm's revenues and expenses will be exactly equal. The *break-even point* may be defined as that level of operations at which total revenue is equal to total expense and, hence, net income is equal to zero.

Determining the Break-Even Point

In Units of Product. For a single product firm, the break-even point may be computed very conveniently in terms of units of product. The break-even volume for a given period is the number of units of product that must be sold in order to create enough revenue just to cover all expenses, both variable and fixed. Each unit sold will cover its own variable costs and leave a remainder, the variable profit per unit, to contribute to covering fixed costs. When enough units have been sold so that the total variable profit is equal to the total fixed expenses, the break-even point has been reached. Thus, the break-even volume in units may be expressed algebraically as follows:

$$\text{Break-even volume} = \frac{\text{Total fixed costs}}{\text{Variable profit per unit}}$$

Assume that a small manufacturing company produces a single product. The selling price is $8 per unit and the variable costs are $5 per unit. These variable costs include all items that vary in proportion to volume—both manufacturing and nonmanufacturing costs. The company's annual fixed costs total $150,000. In order to break even, the company must sell 50,000 units of product annually. This volume is computed as follows:[3]

$$\text{BE} = \frac{\$150,000}{\$3} = 50,000 \text{ units}$$

That the company's net income is equal to zero at a volume of 50,000 units may be demonstrated quite easily.

Revenues (50,000 units @ $8).................	$400,000
Variable costs (50,000 units @ $5).............	250,000
Variable profit............................	$150,000
Fixed costs...............................	150,000
Net income...............................	$ 0

In Dollar Sales Volume. There are few single product companies in our modern industrial society, and most multiproduct firms are not able to measure volume in terms of any common unit of product. Such firms typically express sales volume in terms of total dollar sales. The basic requirement of the break-even point in unchanged, however; total

---

[3] Here and in subsequent illustrations, the abbreviation "BE" is used to represent the break-even volume.

revenue must just cover total expense. In this situation, variable costs and variable profits are expressed as amounts per dollar of sales or, more simply, as percentages of sales. The break-even volume is then computed by equating total variable profit to total fixed costs, as before. Since the variable profit is a known ratio, or percentage, of total sales revenue, the sales volume necessary to generate sufficient variable profit just to cover fixed costs may be computed thus:

$$\text{Break-even volume} = \frac{\text{Total fixed costs}}{\text{Variable profit ratio}}$$

Assume that a medium-sized multiproduct manufacturing corporation compiles the following budgeted operating data:

Budgeted sales for one year...................	$20,000,000
Budgeted variable costs for one year............	14,400,000
Budgeted fixed costs for one year...............	3,920,000

The variable costs can be seen to be equal to 72% of sales; hence, the variable profit is 28% of sales. The break-even volume is then computed as follows:

$$\text{BE} = \frac{\$3,920,000}{.28} = \$14,000,000$$

Proof of this break-even computation is as follows:

Revenues......................................	$14,000,000
Variable costs (72% of $14,000,000)..............	10,080,000
Variable profit.................................	$ 3,920,000
Fixed costs....................................	3,920,000
Net income....................................	$ 0

As a Percentage of Full Capacity. Many business managers are accustomed to thinking of their firm's operations in terms of percentages of full productive capacity. Full capacity is usually defined as the greatest volume presently attainable, given the firm's production facilities and its operating policies. This concept is sometimes termed *practical capacity*. It is not necessarily the maximum possible volume. Unusual amounts of overtime by both men and machines may stretch a firm's capacity considerably, but ordinarily only for fairly short periods of time. Whatever volume is selected as full capacity, it is established as 100% of capacity. While the break-even point as a percentage of full capacity cannot be determined by direct computation, it may easily be determined indirectly. If the operating volume at full capacity is known in terms of units or dollar sales and the break-even point has been determined in comparable terms, the latter may be stated as a percentage of the former very simply. In the illustration of the single product company above, assume that full capacity is 100,000 units of product. The break-even point, 50,000 units, is reached at 50% of capacity. If full capacity for the multiproduct corporation illustrated in the preceding paragraph is set at an annual sales volume of $21,000,000 and the break-even sales volume is $14,000,000, the break-even point is achieved at 67% (two thirds) of full capacity.

Break-Even Graphs

Break-even analysis is very commonly presented in graphic form. Break-even graphs can depict the profit-volume position of the firm clearly and simply. The traditional break-even graph is illustrated in Figure 13–1. This is a graphic depiction of the break-even point com-

FIGURE 13–1

Break-Even Graph

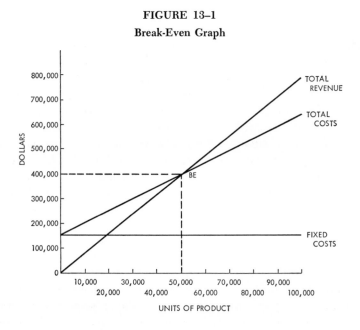

puted in units of product for the single product firm in the preceding section. Units of product are measured on the horizontal axis, and dollars (both revenues and costs) on the vertical axis. Fixed costs are shown as a constant amount, $150,000, at all levels of operation. Variable costs are then plotted over and above total fixed costs. The resultant line is the total cost line, including both variable and fixed costs. There is no variable cost line in the graph; variable costs are depicted as the vertical distance between the fixed cost and the total cost lines. The total cost at any point is the sum of the $150,000 fixed costs plus the $5 variable cost per unit of product multipled by the number of units sold at that point.

Total revenue at any point is the product of the unit price of $8 and the number of units sold. The upper limits of the graph are determined on the basis of the firm's full capacity, 100,000 units of product in this illustration. The break-even point (BE) occurs at the intersection of the total revenue and total cost lines. Dropping a perpendicular from the point BE to the horizontal axis shows the break-even point in units of product. Dropping a perpendicular from BE to the vertical axis shows the break-even point in dollar sales volume. Below (to the left of) point BE, total costs are higher than total revenue and operations are unprofitable. Above (to the right of) BE, total revenue exceeds total costs and operations are profitable. The amount of the profit or loss at any volume is simply the vertical distance between the total revenue and total cost lines. Thus, given budgeted sales volume, the budgeted profit may be read directly from the graph. The excess of budgeted volume over the break-even volume is commonly referred to as the *margin of safety.* If budgeted volume here were 80,000 units of product, the margin of safety would be 30,000 units.

Where the break-even point is measured in terms of dollar sales volume rather than in units, the break-even graph remains basically the same as in Figure 13–1. The only difference is that volume on the horizontal axis is measured in sales dollars. In that case, a perpendicular from the point B to either axis would show the break-even dollar sales volume. The same type of graph could depict the break-even situation in relation to full capacity; in this case, the horizontal axis would measure percentages of capacity. Thus, except for the quantity on the horizontal axis, the break-even graph is the same regardless of the concept of volume used.

Profit-Volume Graph. An increasingly popular variation on the traditional break-even graph is the profit-volume graph. This is a plot of an enterprise's profit in relation to volume. It is illustrated in Figure 13–2, using the data for the multiproduct manufacturing corporation whose break-even point was computed in dollar sales volume earlier. Total profit or loss is measured on the vertical axis—profit above the horizontal axis and loss below it. Volume is measured on the horizontal axis, which is drawn at the point of zero profit (i.e., the break-even point). Volume may be expressed in whatever terms desired by management. Here, it is stated in terms of percentages of full capacity. The maximum loss, which occurs at a volume of zero, is simply the total fixed costs of the enterprise. As volume increases, a proportionate variable profit appears and increases with it. Total profit, however, is negative until the break-even point is reached. The operating loss declines and ultimately disappears at that volume at which the total variable profit is equal to total fixed costs—the break-even volume. Beyond this point, there is a positive net income. On this graph, the break-even point is measured on the horizontal axis at the point where that axis is intersected by the profit line.

In Figure 13–2, the total fixed costs and, hence, the maximum loss are $3,920,000. The variable profit rate is 28% of sales. As already demonstrated, this company breaks even at a sales volume of $14,000,000, or two thirds of the firm's capacity. The graph shows the amount of profit or loss which may be expected at any level of operations. At full capacity, for example, the budgeted profit would be just below $2,000,000 ($1,960,000 to be precise). This profit may be read from the

FIGURE 13–2

Profit-Volume Graph

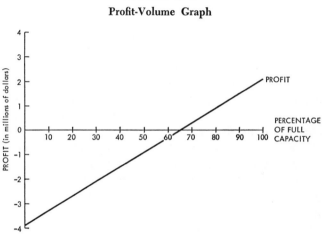

profit-volume graph or computed by applying the variable profit rate (28%) to all sales in excess of the break-even volume. (Sales at full capacity here exceed break-even sales volume by $7,000,000.)

Assumptions Underlying Break-Even Analysis

The validity of the break-even analysis explained and illustrated above is based upon several assumptions. Effective use of break-even analysis demands an appreciation of the significance of each of these assumptions.

Uniform Prices. The assumption that all financial data are comparable underlies all of accounting, not merely break-even analysis. If dollar amounts are to be compared in any meaningful way, the dollars involved should have the same real value (i.e., the same purchasing power). In break-even analysis, the dollars of revenue and the dollars of cost should be uniform in terms of their purchasing powers. Dollars of depreciation on assets acquired in past periods should be adjusted to conform to the current price level before a break-even point is determined. Unfortunately, price-level adjustments are only infrequently made in present business practice. Hence, a great many break-even computations violate the uniform price assumption without even specifically recognizing it.

Completely Predictable Cost Behavior. As is evident in both the formulas and the graphs in the preceding sections, conventional break-even analysis presumes that all of an enterprise's costs are either perfectly variable or absolutely fixed over all ranges of operating volume. Total variable cost is assumed to be a positive linear function of volume, and total fixed cost is assumed to be wholly unaffected by volume. As a practical matter, it is not necessary that these assumptions be valid over all ranges of volume. If they are basically true over the relevant range of volume, that range within which the firm is most likely to operate, break-even analysis is valid. Even within the relevant range of volume, it is probable that there will be some degree of imprecision in the assumptions regarding cost-volume relationships. Nevertheless, managers have found the analysis useful despite its imprecision.

Perfectly Variable Revenue. A third assumption, related to the second, is that an enterprise's total revenue is perfectly variable with its physical volume. Like variable cost, revenue is assumed to be a positive linear function of volume. For some firms, this assumption may be completely valid; selling prices per unit may be the same at all volumes. For others, however, it is not valid. The same products may be sold to large customers at lower prices than to small customers. Price reductions may be necessary in order to attain high levels of sales volume. Once again, however, the assumption is generally useful and not so unrealistic as to impair the analysis seriously.

Effect of Imperfect Cost or Revenue Behavior. If revenue and/or variable costs are not perfectly variable with physical volume—that is, if they are nonlinear functions of volume—and/or if fixed costs are not absolutely fixed, the revenue and/or cost lines in the break-even graph (Figure 13–1) will not be straight. If one or more of these lines is curved or kinked, it is possible that the total revenue and total cost lines will intersect at two or more points. Such a situation would imply multiple break-even points. These might be caused by a nonlinear revenue function, a nonlinear variable cost function, a fixed cost line that is other than perfectly horizontal, or by any combination of these circumstances. Figure 13–3 illustrates a graph of multiple break-even points in which each of the three possible circumstances is present. (Notice the similarity between the cost lines in this exhibit and those in Figure 2–2 in Chapter 2.)

The existence of multiple break-even points in Figure 13–3 is caused

FIGURE 13–3

Illustration of Multiple Break-Even Points

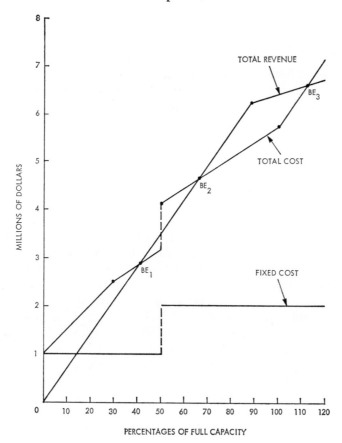

by three factors. First, total revenue is not a perfectly linear function of volume. At 90% of capacity, the revenue line is kinked. This reflects the fact that the average net selling price is expected to decrease beyond this point, presumably because of quantity discounts to large purchasers and price reductions offered to induce new customers to purchase from the company. In reality, these price discounts and reductions would more likely occur gradually as volume increases. Thus, the total revenue curve might be curved gradually rather than kinked abruptly. The second factor at work in the illustration is the change in the rate of variable costs. At 30% of capacity, the variable cost rate decreases. This decrease might be caused by materials price reductions attributable to purchasing in larger quantities. Also, labor costs may be reduced by more efficient utilization of the larger work force required to handle an increasing volume. As with the price reductions, these cost decreases might well occur in stages. If so, the total cost curve would be curved, not kinked. At 100% of capacity, the variable cost rate increases because of diseconomies of operating above the preferred rate of capacity. In other words, plant capacity is used more intensively and less efficiently above 100%. The third factor causing multiple break-even points is an increase in fixed costs in a single step at 50% of capacity. This may reflect the use and maintenance of additional machinery and an increase in the supervisory staff. As a consequence, both the fixed cost line and the total cost line are discontinuous at that point. Both are pushed upward by the amount of the increase in fixed costs.

As a result of these three circumstances and their relationships to each other, there are three break-even points. The first is reached, much as in Figure 13–1, when total revenue is sufficient to cover total costs; this is at point BE_1. Above BE_1, operations are profitable until the firm reaches the volume at which the fixed costs are increased. Between that point and BE_2, operations are again unprofitable. Between BE_2 and BE_3, profits are once more realized. Finally, beyond BE_3, operations are unprofitable because of a decline in revenue per unit of volume and an increase in unit variable cost. Such a graph would be enormously useful to management if cost behavior could be budgeted so precisely. Even apart from the existence of multiple break-even points, knowledge of alterations in cost behavior at critical levels of volume would be extremely useful. As a practical matter, business managers have found that break-even analysis is more feasible and still useful where the conventional assumptions about cost and revenue relationships to volume are employed.

The profit-volume graph (Figure 13–2) would be affected in much the same way as the break-even graph by nonlinear revenue and cost functions. The profit line would not be straight; it might be discontinuous; and it might intersect the horizontal axis at two or more points.

Stable Product Mix. A fourth assumption underlying break-even analysis relates only to multiproduct firms. As such firms are characteristic of our economy, however, this assumption is generally applicable. We have seen that for a multiproduct firm, the break-even point is determined by dividing total fixed costs by an average ratio of variable profit to sales. If each product has the same variable profit ratio, the break-even point is unaffected by changes in the product mix. However, if, as is more likely, different products have different variable profit ratios, a shift in the product mix can cause a shift in the break-even point. This is illustrated in the following example: A manufacturing corporation produces and sells three products; its annual fixed costs total $420,000. Budgeted sales and variable profits, by products, are shown in Table 13–1. The average variable profit ratio in this budget is 28%

($560,000 ÷ $2,000,000). The break-even sales volume, then, is $1,500,000 ($420,000 ÷ .28). This break-even point is based upon a weighted average variable profit ratio computed from the budgeted product mix. If the product mix is altered, the average variable profit ratio and the break-even point may be changed also. Assume, for example, that the actual sales and variable profit data for the budget period turn out to be as shown in Table 13–2. The average variable profit is now 23.5% ($470,000 ÷ $2,000,000), and the break-even volume is $1,787,235 ($420,000 ÷ .235). The raising of the break-even point is caused by a shift in the product mix, with no change whatever in total sales volume. In comparison with the budget, there has been an increase in the sales of products with low variable profit ratios and a

<table>
<tr><th colspan="4" align="center">TABLE 13–1</th><th colspan="4" align="center">TABLE 13–2</th></tr>
<tr>
<th>Product</th>
<th>Budgeted Sales (in $000)</th>
<th>Variable Profit (in $000)</th>
<th>Variable Profit Ratio</th>
<th>Product</th>
<th>Budgeted Sales (in $000)</th>
<th>Variable Profit (in $000)</th>
<th>Variable Profit Ratio</th>
</tr>
<tr>
<td>X . . . . .</td><td>$ 600</td><td>$120</td><td>20%</td>
<td>X . . . . .</td><td>$1,000</td><td>$200</td><td>20%</td>
</tr>
<tr>
<td>Y . . . . .</td><td>900</td><td>315</td><td>35</td>
<td>Y . . . . .</td><td>200</td><td>70</td><td>35</td>
</tr>
<tr>
<td>Z . . . . .</td><td>500</td><td>125</td><td>25</td>
<td>Z . . . . . .</td><td>800</td><td>200</td><td>25</td>
</tr>
<tr>
<td></td><td>$2,000</td><td>$560</td><td></td>
<td></td><td>$2,000</td><td>$470</td><td></td>
</tr>
</table>

decrease in the sales of the product with the high ratio. The impact of this change in product mix on income before taxes is substantial. Budgeted income was $140,000; actual income is $50,000.

Equality of Sales Volume and Production Volume. A final assumption underlying conventional break-even analysis is that the volume of sales and the volume of production are equal. Everything produced is sold; there is no significant change in the level of inventory of goods on hand. This assumption is necessary because the analysis matches total costs and total revenues for the period and relates them jointly to a single measure of volume. It is, of course, very possible that some of the costs of one period will be incurred in the production of goods to be sold in a subsequent period. This is quite a normal business occurrence, but it tends to complicate the calculation of a break-even point for one period. Where this assumption is clearly invalid (i.e., where sales and production volumes are significantly different), the break-even point may still be computed as shown above if the sales value of production is substituted for current revenue in the computation. In effect, this alternative assumes that goods produced for inventory will eventually be sold at the current selling price.

Utility of Break-Even Analysis

Probably the best summary evaluation of break-even analysis is to say that it is a useful tool of managerial planning and decision making but not a sharp tool. Because of the several restrictive assumptions underlying the analysis, the computation of a break-even volume should be regarded as an approximation rather than as a precise measurement. Nevertheless, even if the analysis yields only an approximate break-even operating volume, this estimate is much superior to no such information at all. The break-even point is of special interest to management, for it identifies that level of operations below which the objective of profit would be missed altogether. A corollary of the profit motive is the desire to avoid losses. Some managers may feel a stronger desire to avoid a loss of a given amount than to obtain a profit of the same amount. If management places a proportionately higher value upon a situation that involves some profit (and avoids any loss) than upon one that involves an increase in an existing level of profit, then the break-even point represents the operating volume at which management's scale of values (or utility function) changes. As such, it is of unique significance.

Even if the break-even point is not considered uniquely useful, the analysis underlying it may be. Often management is more interested in the general pattern of the relationships among volume, costs, and profit than in the break-even point itself. The popularity of the profit-volume graph (Figure 13-2) attests to this interest, for that graph focuses attention upon expected profits at all levels of operations.

ANALYSIS OF CHANGES IN PRICES, COSTS, AND VOLUME

One of the most useful and simplest applications of cost-volume-profit relationships is the analysis of changes in one or more of the basic elements—revenue, cost, and volume. This type of analysis can be employed to answer questions such as the following: What would be the impact upon profits of a price increase if that increase caused volume to decline? Can profits be improved by increasing the advertising budget and thereby boosting volume? Can prices be raised to offset the impact on profits of a wage increase? What sales volume must be achieved in order to attain some target profit? The analysis of problems of these types will be illustrated in the following paragraphs.

Effect of Price Increase

If a price increase has no effect upon volume, the effect upon profit will be very simple. Profit before taxes will rise by the amount of the price increase multiplied by the present volume. Net income after taxes will be increased by the before-tax profit rise multipled by the complement of the applicable income tax rate (i.e., 100% minus the tax rate). As a matter of fact, however, it is likely that volume will decline in response to a price increase. The extent of the volume decline depends upon the degree of competition in the market and upon the price elasticity of demand for the product (i.e., the extent to which buyers' demand for it is influenced by its price). Assume that a manufacturer is contemplating a 5% price increase on all of its products in 1972. Its sales in 1971 totaled $6,000,000 and its variable costs, $4,800,000. The 5% price increase would raise total revenue by $300,000. However, the company expects that the sales volume of all products will be 8% lower in 1972 because of the higher prices. Since volume affects both revenue and variable costs proportionately, the impact of the volume reduction may be computed directly in terms of the variable profit. Without a change in volume, variable profit in 1972 would be $1,500,000 ($6,300,000 − $4,800,000). The volume decline, however, means that the variable profit will be 8% lower than this amount, or 92% of it. Thus, the budgeted variable profit would be $1,380,000. This is still better than the 1971 variable profit of $1,200,000. If the applicable income tax rate is 40%, the after-tax increase in profit is $108,000 (60% of $180,000, the increase in variable profit). The company's fixed costs may be ignored in this analysis, for they will be unaffected by the proposed change.[4]

Effect of Increase in Fixed Costs

An increase in the total annual fixed costs of an enterprise may be caused either by external circumstances (e.g., an increase in property taxes) or by a managerial decision (e.g., an increase in executives' salaries). In either event, the effect is to raise the break-even point of the firm, assuming no change in the variable profit. Any increase in price or decrease in variable costs would tend to offset this effect, for either would

---

[4] It may be tempting to try a shortcut in working with problems of this type. If there is to be a 5% price increase and an 8% volume decrease, one might reason, won't the net effect be a 3% decrease in total revenue? Unhappily, the answer is, "No!" The base of the 5% price increase is not the same as the base of the 8% volume decrease. Hence, there is no net 3% change. First, the 5% price increase is applied to the prior year's sales of $6,000,000. This produces a tentative sales revenue of $6,300,000. The 8% volume decrease is then applied to this new figure, not to the original $6,000,000. Thus, the volume decrease will reduce sales by $504,000 (8% of $6,300,000). Total sales revenue, then, will be $5,796,000 ($6,300,000 − $504,000). Exactly the same result would be obtained if the 8% volume decrease were first applied to the original $6,000,000 sales and the 5% price increase were then applied to the amount so computed. Applying a net 3% reduction to the original $6,000,000 would indicate that sales, after both price and volume changes, should be $5,820,000. And this is not correct.

increase the variable profit ratio. Of course, an increase in fixed costs might cause an increase in volume; while not affecting the variable profit ratio, this could increase the total variable profit. For example, assume that a small company producing and selling a single product sold 25,000 units during 1971 at a price of $80. Variable costs per unit are $60 and fixed costs total $400,000, including $50,000 of advertising costs. The company's management is dissatisfied with the present rate of income on sales volume. The market research firm engaged to study the problem suggests that a 20% increase in the advertising budget would boost sales volume by 6%. Would such a move be profitable? The question can be restated as follows: Will the additional variable profit generated by the higher volume cover the increase in fixed costs? The variable profit of $20 per unit would be obtained on an additional 1,500 units (6% of 25,000); in total, then, variable profit would be increased by $30,000. This would be three times the amount of the increase in fixed advertising cost—$10,000 (20% of $50,000). After income tax at a rate of 40%, net profit would be greater than in 1971 by $12,000 (60% of $20,000).

This profit-volume analysis must be employed carefully; it is not always appropriate. A very different type of situation is presented by the firm that finds it is unable to meet the demand for its products because of limited production facilities. It is considering doubling its productive capacity by building a new plant. Such a move would increase annual fixed costs by $7,500,000. Present sales volume is $72,000,000 annually; annual variable costs total $48,000,000. It is expected that the additional capacity would result in a 25% increase in sales volume during the first year of operations in the new plant. This would mean a 25% increase in the current variable profit, or an increase of $6,000,000. Obviously, this additional profit does not justify a $7,500,000 increase in fixed costs. But, just as obviously, it is not valid to seek to justify an increase in productive capacity in terms of one year's sales increase alone. The new plant will last for many years, and it must be justified or defeated in light of the expected impact upon variable profit over all of those years. For reasons to be explained in Chapter 15, simple profit-volume analysis is inadequate for an evaluation of effects that will occur over a period of several years. Unlike the increase in the advertising budget, the construction of a new plant commits the enterprise's resources to a specific use for a long period of time. Its profitability must be evaluated by means of long-term investment analysis, not by any short-run profit measurement.

Effect of Wage and Price Increases

A great deal has been written in recent years about the so-called wage-price spiral, in which wage increases trigger price increases which, in turn, cause further wage and price rises ad infinitum. If given credence at all, this spiral is usually thought of as a phenomenon of the economy as a whole. For the individual firm, the wage-price problem is unlikely to be so clear or so nearly automatic. A firm may wish to raise prices to offset the decline in profits attendant upon a wage increase. As we have already observed, however, a price increase may result in a volume decline, which tends to reduce profits also. As an example, assume that a firm prepares a budgeted income statement in the variable costing form shown in Table 13–3.

Shortly after the preparation of this forecast, it is learned that a wage increase will cause variable costs to be 4% higher than originally budgeted. With no change in price or volume, this would reduce variable profit and profit before tax by $1,200,000. The firm wishes to

TABLE 13–3		TABLE 13–4	
Sales..................	$50,000,000	Sales..................	$50,727,500
Variable costs..........	30,000,000	Variable costs..........	30,732,000
Variable profit..........	20,000,000	Variable profit..........	19,995,500
Fixed costs.............	15,000,000	Fixed costs.............	15,000,000
Net profit before tax.....	5,000,000	Net profit before tax.....	4,995,500
Income tax (40%).......	2,000,000	Income tax (40%).......	1,998,200
Net income.............	$ 3,000,000	Net income.............	$ 2,997,300

raise its prices to compensate for this wage boost. Market research indicates that a 3% price increase would result in a volume decline of $1\frac{1}{2}\%$. If a 3% price rise were adopted, the budgeted income statement would appear as in Table 13–4. This revised budget reflects the impact of only one combination of price increase and volume decrease. Similar computations might be made for other percentage price rises and volume declines. Such computation, of course, does not mean that the requisite price increase is feasible; factors of competition must also be considered before any price decision can be made.

Volume Needed to Attain Target Profit

The basic mechanics of break-even analysis may be adapted very easily to determine the operating volume necessary for a firm to attain a specific target profit. Assume, for example, that a corporation seeks a minimum rate of return on invested capital of 8% after taxes. For a given budget period, this objective requires a net income of $2,400,000. The company's variable costs average 60% of selling prices; fixed costs total $18,000,000 per year; and the applicable income tax rate is 40%. The volume here must be sufficient to produce a total variable profit that will cover fixed costs plus the target profit. Since fixed costs are a before-tax quantity, the profit employed in the analysis must also be measured before taxes. The target profit before taxes here is $4,000,000 ($2,400,000 ÷ .60). Thus, sales volume must be sufficient so that 40% of it—the variable profit—will be equal to $22,000,000, the sum of the fixed costs and the target profit before tax. This volume is computed thus:

$$\text{Target volume} = \frac{\$22,000,000}{.40} = \$55,000,000$$

This and the other analyses illustrated in the foregoing paragraphs are but examples of the types of situations and problems that may be analyzed in terms of the relationships among revenue, cost, and volume.

ADVANTAGE OF VARIABLE COSTING

Throughout the discussion in this chapter, the importance of an effective separation of variable and fixed costs and of the variable profit as a unique figure has been obvious. The distinction between variable and fixed costs and the identification of the variable profit are essential to the variable costing method and to variable costing reports. While the same data may be derived from absorption costing records, they are incidental to rather than inherent in that method. In practice, it has been observed that firms using absorption costing usually do not separate variable and fixed costs in the accounting records. Consequently, when such cost data are required for special analyses, they must be developed in a manner not characteristic of the cost accounting system in use and, hence, at extra cost. Under variable costing, on the other hand, separate reporting of variable and fixed costs is basic to the system. Hence, the distinction is always available for analysis. Further, the variable costing income statement shows directly the variable profit. Thus, without additional information, management can make analyses of the anticipated impacts of volume, price, and/or cost changes. Such analyses are ordinarily not possible from absorption costing income statements without supplementary information. Thus, variable costing appears to be clearly superior insofar as the utility of the income statement for profit-volume analysis is concerned. This does not mean, of course, that variable costing is preferable to absorption costing as a general rule; but it certainly is a notable point in its favor.

QUESTIONS FOR DISCUSSION

1. Describe the effects on a company's profit of a change in sales volume only, when all other pertinent variables remain unchanged. What are the effects on profit of a change in production volume only?

2. "Since business firms seldom operate at their break-even points for any prolonged period of time, break-even analysis is of very limited use to management." Evaluate this statement.

3. What would be the impact on a firm's break-even point if there were a uniform general increase in the price level, i.e., an increase of the same proportion in all prices? Consider the case of a firm which holds a sufficient inventory of merchandise to meet all anticipated sales demand during the coming fiscal year. Effective on the first day of that period, all prices are doubled as a consequence of a devaluation of the currency. In that period, when would this firm break even—when revenues equaled the original dollar cost of the merchandise sold or when revenues equaled the current market value of the goods sold? Ignore any costs other than the cost of the goods sold.

4. Does the choice between absorption costing and variable costing have any implication for the break-even point of a firm? Explain.

5. Is it a fair generalization to say that the product with the highest variable profit ratio is the most profitable product in a company's product line? Explain.

6. If a firm's management believed that its anticipated break-even sales volume for a particular budget period were too high, what action(s) might it take to lower that break-even volume?

7. Will a firm that plans to liquidate previously accumulated inventory during a period break even at a different volume from that at which it would break even if it were planning to build up its inventory during the period? Explain.

8. If, as is typically assumed in economic analysis, there is an inverse relationship between sales volume and selling price, what is the effect on profit when selling price is increased and costs remain unchanged? Does the assumption of a linear relationship between sales volume and total revenue in break-even analysis conflict with the customary economic assumption that volume and selling price vary inversely with each other? Explain.

9. How might a profit-volume graph be used by management in the process of developing a comprehensive operating budget?

10. How should income taxes be considered in break-even computations? In cost-volume-profit analyses generally?

11. If a multiproduct firm's break-even point depends upon the product mix sold, what is the firm's true break-even point?

12. The break-even graphs in this chapter show fixed costs on the bottom, with variable costs on top of them. Why can't these graphs show variable costs on the bottom and fixed costs on top?

PROBLEMS

1. The Bellini Bell Company, which produces a single model, reports the following summarized budget data:

Unit selling price...................	$15
Unit variable costs.................	$ 9
Annual fixed costs.................	$5,400,000
Full productive capacity............	1,500,000 units

Required:

Compute the company's break-even point in terms of—
a) Units sold
b) Dollar sales volume
c) Percentage of full capacity

2. The income statement of the Bizet Cigarette Company for 1972 appeared as follows:

BIZET CIGARETTE COMPANY
Income Statement
For Year Ended December 31, 1972

Sales..............................		$600,000
Variable expenses:		
Cost of goods sold.................	$390,000	
Distribution......................	78,000	468,000
Variable profit......................		$132,000
Fixed expenses:		
Production........................	$ 76,000	
Administration....................	45,000	121,000
Income before tax....................		$ 11,000
Income taxes.......................		4,400
Net Income........................		$ 6,600

Required:

a) Assuming that the operating data for 1972 are representative of future periods, what is the company's break-even point?
b) Draft a break-even graph for this company and label all important parts of it.

3. The Verdi Company sells anvils for $25 apiece. Variable costs of producing and selling anvils average $18.50 per unit. Annual fixed costs of operation total $200,000. The income tax rate is 40%.

Required:

How many anvils must the company sell in order to earn a net income after tax of $75,000?

4. The Rossini Products Company is considering purchasing an old lumber mill in Coos Bay, Oregon, as a plant site for the manufacture of widgets. The mill would cost $2,400,000 initially, and an additional $3,600,000 would have to be spent to convert it to an efficient widget factory. The converted plant would have an estimated useful life of 30 years and an expected salvage value of $600,000 at the end of that time. It would have a productive capacity of 75,000 widgets per year.

Widgets sell for $23 apiece. Variable costs for one widget are as follows:

Materials..........................	$4.80
Labor.............................	5.50
Overhead..........................	3.30
Distribution.......................	1.50
Franchise fee......................	.50

The annual fixed out-of-pocket costs of operating the factory would amount to $249,200.
a) Compute the annual break-even point for the widget factory in terms of both units and dollar sales volume.
b) Draft a properly labeled break-even graph for the company.

5. The graph below depicts the conventional break-even analysis. Physical units of product are measured on the x axis. Budgeted sales volume in units of product is depicted by the line segment $c \rightarrow k$.

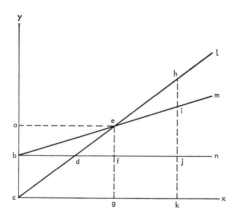

Required:
By use of the letters on the graph above, identify the point, line segment, or area on the graph that represents each of the following:
a) Total revenue at any volume
b) Total variable cost at any volume
c) Fixed costs
d) Break-even point in dollar sales
e) Break-even point in units
f) Margin of safety
g) Total budgeted revenue
h) Total budgeted variable cost
i) Total budgeted costs
j) Budgeted operating profit
k) Maximum possible total loss

6. The Massenet Corporation manufactures a variety of hand tools. The following summary data are taken from the operating budget for 1973:

Sales......................	$35,000,000
Variable expenses.............	25,200,000
Fixed expenses...............	7,700,000

Required:

a) Compute the break-even point.

b) Draft a profit-volume graph for the Massenet Corporation. Show on it the budget profits before tax for sales volumes of $20,000,000 and $40,000,000.

c) What sales volume would have to be achieved to yield a net income after tax of $2,000,000? The income tax rate is 40%.

d) List some of the assumptions underlying the break-even computation in (a).

7. On the profit-volume graph below, dollar sales volume is measured on the x axis. The line segment $b \rightarrow f$ represents budgeted sales volume.

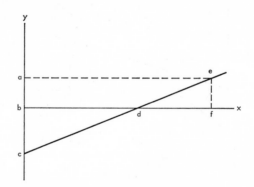

Required:

Identify the quantity represented by each of the following:

a) Line segment $b \rightarrow a$.

b) Line segment $b \rightarrow c$.

c) Line segment $b \rightarrow d$.

d) Line segment $d \rightarrow f$.

e) $? = \dfrac{b \rightarrow c}{d \rightarrow b}$

8. The budgeted income statement, by product lines, of the Meyerbeer Corporation for 1973 is as follows:

	Product A	Product B	Product C	Total
Sales....................	$200,000	$500,000	$300,000	$1,000,000
Variable expenses:				
Cost of goods sold......	$ 90,000	$270,000	$150,000	$ 510,000
Selling...............	30,000	90,000	45,000	165,000
	$120,000	$360,000	$195,000	$ 675,000
Variable profit..........	$ 80,000	$140,000	$105,000	$ 325,000
Fixed expenses:				
Overhead..............	$ 36,000	$ 90,000	$ 54,000	$ 180,000
Administrative.........	16,000	40,000	24,000	80,000
	$ 52,000	$130,000	$ 78,000	$ 260,000
Income before tax........	$ 28,000	$ 10,000	$ 27,000	$ 65,000
Income tax (40%)........	11,200	4,000	10,800	26,000
Net Income.............	$ 16,800	$ 6,000	$ 16,200	$ 39,000

All products are manufactured in the same facilities under common administrative control. Fixed expenses are allocated among the products in proportion to their budgeted sales volumes.

Required:

a) Compute the budgeted break-even point of the corporation from the budget data provided.

b) What would be the effect on budgeted income if half of the budgeted sales volume of Product B were shifted to Product A and C in equal dollar amounts, so that total budgeted sales volume would remain the same?

c) What would be the effect of the shift in the product mix suggested in (*b*) on the budgeted break-even point?

9. The budgeted sales of the Donizetti Company for 1973 amount to $500,000,000. Variable costs are expected to average 70% of sales. Fixed costs are budgeted at $60,000,000 for the year.

Required:

a) What is the company's break-even point in 1973?

b) What sales volume would be necessary in order to increase budgeted profit before tax by 50%?

c) Would it be profitable for the company to increase budgeted sales volume by 20%, without changing prices, by improving product quality and thereby increasing variable costs by 20%?

10. The Halevy Company manufactures a single product in one continuous process. The standard cost sheet for one unit of this product is as follows:

Raw material............................	$18.00
Direct labor (8 hrs. @ $3.50)...............	28.00
Variable overhead (8 hrs. @ $.90)...........	7.20
Fixed overhead (8 hrs. @ $2.50).............	20.00
	$73.20

Normal production volume is 400,000 units of product per year. Sales and production for 1973 have been budgeted at 350,000 units. The product is sold at a price of $140 per unit. Variable selling expenses average 12% of selling price. Fixed selling, administrative, and research and development costs are budgeted at $6,000,000 per year.

Required:

a)   What is the company's break-even point for 1973?

b)   Would the break-even point be different if volume were budgeted at 450,000 units instead of 350,000? Explain.

c)   Would it be profitable for the company to raise its selling price to $160 if such a move would result in a loss of sales of 80,000 units? What effect, if any, would such a move have on the break-even point?

11. In government, an industrial fund (or working capital fund) activity is a business-type operation that renders essentially commercial services to other governmental units. Typical examples are printing plants, supply depots, and shipyards. Because it is a governmental unit providing services to other governmental units, an industrial fund activity attempts to set its prices so that it will just break even. Both profits and losses are avoided.

The Cilea Naval Shipyard is an industrial fund activity. Its budgeted variable costs are $8.50 per man-hour; budgeted fixed costs are $3,000,000 per quarter. On the basis of ship repair schedules and other information, shipyard management has estimated that its volume of work in 1973 will be about 750,000 man-hours per quarter.

Required:

What pricing policy should the Cilea Naval Shipyard announce to its customers for 1973?

12. The income statement of the Strauss Steel Strapping Company for the year 1972 appeared as follows:

STRAUSS STEEL STRAPPING COMPANY

Income Statement
For Year Ended December 31, 1972

Sales..............................		$58,000,000
Cost of goods sold (at standard cost)......	$42,050,000	
Add overhead volume variance..........	2,450,000	44,500,000
Gross margin...........................		$13,500,000
Selling and administrative expenses........		11,800,000
Income before tax......................		$ 1,700,000
Income tax............................		680,000
Net Income............................		$ 1,020,000

The company's president is very dissatisfied with the year's operating results. He considers the 1972 income of less than 2% of sales revenue disgraceful, in view of the fact that the industry average is 9% of sales. Further, he is concerned by the fact that the company has not been able fully to utilize its productive capacity.

Further study of the cost records shows that fixed overhead of $7,350,000 was included in the standard cost of good sold in 1972. Three million dollars of fixed selling and administrative expenses were incurred during that year. Production and sales volumes were equal in 1972. The applicable income tax rate is 40%.

Required:

The president has announced that it will be the company's goal in 1973 to earn a net income comparable to the industry average as a percent of sales. Assuming no changes in prices or in costs, what sales volume would be necessary to achieve this goal? Do you believe this goal is currently feasible for the company?

13. The Leoncavallo Corporation manufactures and sells industrial machinery in two sales territories. Budgeted income statements for these territories and for the company as a whole for the year 1973 are presented below:

	Northern Territory	Southern Territory	Corporate Totals
Sales....................	$6,000,000	$3,600,000	$9,600,000
Variable expenses:			
Materials................	$1,500,000	$ 900,000	$2,400,000
Direct labor.............	1,800,000	1,080,000	2,880,000
Overhead................	600,000	360,000	960,000
Selling..................	300,000	180,000	480,000
Fixed expenses:			
Overhead................	600,000	600,000	1,200,000
Selling..................	175,000	105,000	280,000
Administrative...........	350,000	210,000	560,000
Total expenses..............	$5,325,000	$3,435,000	$8,760,000
Income before tax...........	$ 675,000	$ 165,000	$ 840,000
Income tax (40%)..........	270,000	66,000	336,000
Net Income................	$ 405,000	$ 99,000	$ 504,000

All of the fixed expenses, excepting overhead, are incurred in the home office and are allocated between the two territories on the basis of their expected sales volumes. Fixed overhead is actually traceable to the individual territories.

The manager of the Southern Territory has argued that his sales volume could be increased by 10% with no changes in prices if he were allowed to spend $75,000 annually on sales promotion in his territory. The vice president for sales feels that a price reduction of 5% in both territories would increase sales volume in both by 15%. The manager of the Northern Territory contends that sales efforts should be concentrated in his territory, which he believes to be the more profitable one. He points out that the Southern Territory expects sales equal to 60% of his but a profit equal to less than 25% of his. Thus, he argues, every dollar of increased sales in the Northern Territory will add more to corporate profit than another dollar of sales in the Southern Territory.

Required:

a) Accepting the validity of the underlying assumptions, determine the profitability of the suggestions made by the manager of the Southern Territory and by the vice president of sales.

b) Evaluate the argument of the manager of the Northern Territory.

14. The Wagner Corporation plans to introduce a new product in 1973. The variable costs to produce and sell one unit will total $60. The annual fixed costs incurred directly because of this new product will be $200,000. Market research studies of the demand for this new product indicate that 5,000 units could be sold at a price of $150 per unit during 1973 and that sales volume will decline by 10 units as price is increased by $1 or rise by 10 units as price is reduced by $1. It is the corporation's policy that new products should return a profit margin before tax of 20% of sales revenue.

Required:

What price, if any, will yield the target profit margin of 20% on sales of this new product in 1973?

15. Sales of the Puccini Company's product have been declining over the past several years. In 1972, 300,000 units were sold. For 1973, sales volume has been budgeted initially at 250,000 units, which represent only half the company's productive capacity. Several plans have been proposed to reverse this downward sales trend.

The sales manager recommends reducing the price of the product by 10%. This, he contends, will result in a 25% increase in sales volume over the amount initially budgeted for 1973.

The production engineer argues that the difficulty lies with product quality. He asserts that an additional 50,000 units over the initial 1973 sales forecast could be sold if a higher quality raw material were used in the product. Use of this new material would increase materials cost by 16%.

A management consultant has recommended that the production engineer's proposal be adopted and coupled with a 5% price increase. This, he estimates, would increase budgeted sales volume for 1973 by 10%.

In any event, the company's direct labor cost will be increased by 5% as of January 1, 1973.

Income for 1972 was reported as follows:

Sales..............................		$27,000,000
Raw materials cost..................	$7,500,000	
Direct labor.......................	5,400,000	
Variable overhead..................	2,400,000	
Fixed overhead.....................	5,000,000	
Variable selling expenses............	1,800,000	
Fixed selling expenses...............	2,500,000	
Fixed administrative expenses........	3,000,000	27,600,000
Net Loss...........................		$ (600,000)

Required:

Analyze the effects of each of the three plans proposed for 1973 and identify the plan that would result in the greatest budgeted profit before tax. Unless something to the contrary is stated, assume that all financial data in 1972 will be applicable in 1973.

16. Gounod & Company, Inc., has a maximum productive capacity of 750,000 units per year. Normal volume is regarded as 700,000 units per year. Standard variable manufacturing costs are $3 per unit. Fixed factory overhead is $840,000 per year. Variable selling expenses are $.60 per unit, and fixed selling expenses total $600,000 per year. The unit selling price is $6.
   The results of operations for 1972 are summarized below:

	Units
Sales.............................	600,000
Production........................	625,000

   There was a net unfavorable variance from standard variable manufacturing costs of $20,000. All variances are disposed of as adjustments to the cost of goods sold.

   Required:

   For (a), (b), and (c) below, assume no variances from standard manufacturing costs and no differences between sales and production volumes.
   a) What is the break-even point in dollar sales?
   b) How many units must be sold to earn a net income of $300,000 per year before tax?
   c) How many units must be sold to earn a net income before tax equal to 10% of sales?
   d) Compute the company's income before tax for 1972 under (1) absorption costing and (2) variable costing.
   e) Explain any difference between the two incomes computed in (d).

   (Adapted from CPA Examination)

17. The Macagni Specialties Company is engaged in the manufacturing and wholesaling of two principal products. As special assistant to the president, you have been asked for your advice on sales policy for the coming year. Two different plans are under consideration by management. Management believes that either will (a) increase sales volume, (b) reduce the ratio of selling expenses to sales, and (c) decrease unit production costs as compared with the preceding year. These two plans are outlined below:

   Plan 1: Premium Stamp Books

   Each package of Product A would contain three premium stamps, and each package of Product B would contain two premium stamps. Premium stamp books would be given to consumers. When a book is filled with 50 stamps, it would be redeemed by the award of a cash prize, the amount of which is indicated under an unbroken seal attached to the book. Every 5,000 books distributed would provide for prizes in accordance with the following schedule:

Number of Books	Prize per Book	Total Prizes
1	$500	$ 500
4	250	1,000
10	100	1,000
20	50	1,000
50	10	500
100	5	500
4,815	1	4,815
5,000		$9,315

The costs of this plan would be as follows:

Books, including distribution . . . . . $25 per 1,000 books
Stamps . . . . $2.24 per 1,000 stamps
Prizes . . . . See schedule above

This plan would take the place of all previous advertising; previous selling prices would be maintained.

Plan 2: Reduced Selling Prices

The selling price of Product A would be reduced by 8⅓% and that of Product B by 7½%. Advertising expenditures would be increased by 33⅓% of the rate of advertising cost incurred in the preceding year.

These two plans are mutually exclusive alternatives. In addition to the information above, you have obtained the following data regarding operations during the preceding year and expected changes therein under the alternative plans:

	Product A	Product B
Preceding year's operations:		
Units sold	80,000	240,000
Production cost per unit	$2	$1.50
Selling price per unit	$3	$2
Selling expenses (one third of which was advertising)	18% of sales	18% of sales
Administrative expenses	8% of sales	8% of sales
Expected changes:		
Increase in unit sales volume:		
Plan 1	50%	33⅓%
Plan 2	45%	40 %
Decrease in unit production cost:		
Plan 1	8%	10 %
Plan 2	7%	10 %
Administrative expenses:		
Plan 1	5% of sales	5% of sales
Plan 2	Same total dollar amount as last year for both products.	

Selling expenses other than advertising would be incurred at the same rate as last year under either plan.

Required:

a) Prepare a report for management comparing the operations of the preceding year with those proposed for the coming year under both of the alternative plans.

b) Is management correct in its expectations as to the three specific improvements in operations that were mentioned in the first paragraph of this problem?

(Adapted from CPA Examination)

chapter 14

INCREMENTAL PROFIT ANALYSIS FOR DECISION MAKING

AT ONE time, accounting data were accumulated in business firms almost solely for the purpose of reporting the results of operations after they had occurred. Accounting, consequently, was regarded primarily as a backward-looking function. Accounting reports were required for investors but were of limited use to management. Recent years have witnessed a marked departure from this point of view. The importance of reports to investors has not diminished, but the uses of accounting data by management have grown to the point that they are often regarded as more important than reports to investors. Actually, accounting reports are equally important to both groups, but often in quite different ways. The types of data required by management and the manner of their presentation frequently differ greatly from the data in and form of conventional reports to investors. Investors' reports continue to emphasize historical data; this emphasis may be debated, but it remains a fact of "generally accepted accounting principles." Management, on the other hand, is not bound by the constraint of general acceptance. Managers are concerned chiefly with data pertinent to the future, and they are not satisfied with historical reports as indicators of future operations. Managers want to know very specifically what costs and profits can be and should be, not just what they were. Further, management must be concerned with the details of operating problems and prospects for individual segments or components of the enterprise. Investors, on the other hand, are ordinarily interested in the operations of the enterprise as a whole only. The accounting system should be designed so as to meet the needs of both management and investors as completely as possible.

Accounting data are generally recognized to be indispensable tools of management in the making of business decisions. These financial data alone do not make decisions, but they are essential elements to be considered in the process of deciding. For purposes of discussion in this book, business decisions will be classified as two general types, short-term operating decisions and long-term investment decisions. The distinction between these two types is one of time. Short-term decisions may be implemented and, if desired, reversed within a short period of time. (As a practical expedient, a "short period of time" is often considered as one year or less.) Long-term investment decisions affect the operating position of a firm for a sufficiently long period of time that their financial consequences must be evaluated in light of the impact of time upon them. Investment decisions involve the commitment of capital resources to some asset (e.g., a building) or to some project (e.g., a new product line) for an anticipated long period of time. Abandonment of the asset or project before the end of its expected economic life may entail a substantial loss of capital. Short-term decisions, on the other hand, do not involve long-term capital commitments. If a short-term decision proves to be unwise, it may be reversed promptly without significant loss of capital. Hence, the element of time may be ignored in the decision-making analysis. Short-term decisions will be discussed in this chapter. Long-term investment decisions will be considered in Chapters 15 and 16.

FINANCIAL DATA FOR DECISION MAKING

Relevant Costs

For purposes of inventory valuation and profit reporting, the distinction between manufacturing and nonmanufacturing costs is an important one. In profit-volume analysis, the distinction between variable and fixed costs is most important. For purposes of making a specific decision among alternative possible courses of action, however, these distinctions are merely incidental. The essential distinction for decision making is between relevant and irrelevant costs. Any costs that will be affected by a particular decision—whether they will be increased or decreased—are relevant costs insofar as that decision is concerned. Costs that will be the same regardless of how a particular decision is made are irrelevant costs.[1] There are no general rules for distinguishing between relevant

---

[1] Refer to Chapter 2, pages 29–32, for a more extensive discussion of cost classifications for purposes of decision making.

and irrelevant costs. They can be determined only in the context of the circumstances surrounding a specific decision. The very same cost item may be relevant to one decision and irrelevant to another. The discussions in the following paragraphs are concerned with how to look for relevant costs.

Variable Costs. It would be wrong to say that variable costs are always relevant costs.[2] Of course, any cost that varies with volume will be affected by a decision that will cause a change in volume. A decision may, however, have some relationship to variable costs without affecting their amounts. For example, a decision among alternative methods of handling and storing raw materials will not affect the cost of the materials themselves; yet, raw materials cost is almost always regarded as variable. Relevant costs can be identified only in light of the particular decision at hand. By their very nature, however, variable costs are highly susceptible to change. Hence, it is probably a good rule always to scrutinize variable costs very carefully to determine whether or not they will be affected by a decision.

Fixed Costs. In a short-term decision-making situation, fixed costs may be either relevant or irrelevant. If a fixed cost is wholly traceable to a specific decision and will be incurred if and only if that decision is made, it is a relevant cost. For example, opening a new sales territory would likely entail the salary of a new sales manager for the territory. His salary would be a fixed cost if it were incurred, but it would be incurred only if the decision to open the new territory were made. If a fixed cost would be incurred in the same amount regardless of how a particular decision is resolved, it is an irrelevant cost. Thus, the salary of the vice president for marketing would probably be a fixed cost; and it would most likely be unaffected by the opening of a new sales territory, even though the vice president may be deeply involved in the operations of the new territory. The vice president's salary here would be an irrelevant cost, not because it is unrelated to the object of the decision at issue but because it would not be affected in amount by that decision. It is not necesary that there be relevant fixed costs in every decision situation, of course; but the possibility of their existence should always be investigated. They might be easy to overlook and, yet, quite significant in amount.

Interest. In strict theory, interest cost is independent of individual decisions. It is the cost of obtaining capital and, as such, is not affected by decisions as to the utilization of that capital. In practice, however, sources and uses of business capital are often viewed as interdependent,

---

[2] The computer acquisition decision discussed on pages 29 and 30 in Chapter 2 involves irrelevant variable costs.

particularly in connection with short-term decisions. One of the alternatives under consideration in a given case may necessitate short-term borrowing, while the other(s) do not. In such case, the interest on that borrowing may be considered a relevant cost in the decision-making process. If all of the alternative courses of action would require equal short-term borrowing, of course, the interest would be common to all of the possible choices and would be an irrelevant cost. Inclusion of short-term interest among the relevant costs of a particular alternative is appropriate only if the short-term borrowing would be undertaken if and only if that course of action were adopted.

In theory, the firm is thought of as faced with a wide range of possible sources of capital, whether short-term or long-term, not all of which alternatives would be related to one specific decision. Thus, short-term borrowing would be entered into in any event so long as there were some profitable use for the capital. As a practical matter, however, business managers usually are unable to evaluate all possible sources and uses of short-term capital in so broad a perspective. Business decisions are often made within the framework of a single problem or program. In such cases, it would be acceptable to regard short-term borrowing and the interest thereon as peculiar to one possible decision. This could be true only for short-term interest, however. In the long-run, a broad overview of all possible investment opportunities must be adopted.

Depreciation. Depreciation is the periodic amortization of the cost of a long-lived asset acquired at some time in the past. As such, it necessarily derives from a long-term investment decision. Once the investment decision has been implemented and the asset purchased, the subsquent depreciation expense is determined in light of the asset's expected useful life and in accordance with one of a number of alternative depreciation methods available at the option of management. Thus, depreciation is inherently related to what we have described as a long-term decision. To include depreciation as a relevant cost in any short-term decision-making situation is erroneous and may be seriously misleading. If a particular decision would have the effect of increasing periodic depreciation, the increase could be attributed to an investment in a new asset, to a shortening of the life of an old asset, or to a change in the depreciation method used. Either of the first two causes would entail an investment decision which would have to be analyzed in relation to the relatively long period of time involved. The third possible cause would involve no substantive financial implications, except in the event that the change in depreciation charges were acceptable for income tax purposes. Any reduction in depreciation attendant upon the disposition of a long-lived asset would also be a consequence of a long-term investment decision. Actually, in this case, it would be a disinvestment decision. Thus, depreciation should be ignored in short-term decision-making situations. If depreciation cannot be ignored, then the decision cannot be analyzed by the procedure to be described in this chapter.

Incremental Profit

A full analysis of the expected accounting implications of a specific decision, including both costs and revenues relevant to it, will yield the amount of profit which that decision would contribute to the enterprise as a whole. This amount is referred to as the *incremental profit* from the decision. The incremental profit is that portion of the total income of the firm which can be traced directly to a particular decision. It may be either positive or negative. It may be the net difference between incremental revenues and incremental costs generated by the decision; as such, it would be either positive or negative depending upon whether the revenues or the costs, respectively, were greater. Revenues need not be involved, of course. The incremental profit may be simply the amount of a cost reduction (positive incremental profit) or of a cost increase (negative incremental profit). A change in the method of handling materials, for example, would not be likely to affect revenues; but it could reduce or increase the materials handling costs.

It should be noted here that all business decisions need not produce positive incremental profits. In order for a decision to be profitable in the short run, the incremental profit must be positive. But short-run profits may be sacrificed in the anticipation of improved long-run profits, however vague the expectation may be. A negative incremental profit is certainly an adverse feature of a possible course of action, but it does not necessarily mean that the decision must go against that course. Financial data are indispensable parts of the decision-making process, but they do not make the decision by themselves.

Determination of the incremental profit in a given situation begins with an identification of the relevant costs and the incremental revenues that would obtain if a particular decision were made. The incremental profit may be computed as follows:

Additional revenues.............		xxx
Plus: Cost savings.............		xxx
		xxx
Less: Lost revenues............	xxx	
Cost increases............	xxx	xxx
Incremental profit..............		xxx

Any one or all but one of the items in this computation might be equal to zero, of course. If all of them were zero, the decision would appear to have no direct financial implications. Such a decision might be illustrated by the choice of a new production manager. The choice made may well have very substantial long-run and/or short-run profit implications, but it is highly unlikely that they could be quantified in advance.

SHORT-TERM DECISION-MAKING PROBLEMS

In the paragraphs that follow, we shall examine and analyze several short-term decision-making situations in terms of their incremental profits. Some of the nonfinancial considerations which would be pertinent to the decisions will also be noted briefly. The nature and purposes of this text demand that the financial data be emphasized in these illustrations, but they are still only parts of the total decision-making process, albeit essential parts.

Extent of Processing a Product

The Facts. The Blaine Corporation manufactures a single product which it sells to other firms who process it further for ultimate sales to clothing manufacturers. The normal monthly operating volume for the corporation is 100,000 units of product produced and sold. The unit selling price and standard unit costs under the present operations are shown below:

Selling price..........................		$6.50
Standard costs:		
Direct materials.....................	$1.20	
Direct labor........................	1.75	
Variable overhead...................	1.10	
Fixed overhead.....................	.85	
Variable selling expense...............	.90	
Fixed selling expense.................	.30	6.10
Unit profit before tax.................		$ .40

The corporation's management is considering the possibility of performing the further processing necessary for the corporation itself to sell directly to clothing manufacturers. A study has shown that this further processing would require no added investment in productive facilities. After further processing, the product could be sold to clothing makers for $8 per unit. The additional costs of the further processing are estimated as follows:

Direct labor....................	$.65 per unit
Variable overhead..............	$.25 per unit
Variable selling expense.........	$.10 per unit
Fixed overhead.................	$15,000 per month
Fixed selling expense...........	$10,000 per month

The decision at hand is whether to process the product further or to continue selling it as is now done.

Incremental Profit Analysis.   Before commencing an analysis of the alternative choices here, it is well to observe the way in which fixed costs have been presented above. The current fixed costs are stated as standard amounts per unit of product. By definition, fixed costs can be expressed per unit only at one given volume. Here, that volume is 100,000 units per month. Thus, the present fixed overhead amounts to $85,000 per month and fixed selling expense, to $30,000 per month; and *this* is how fixed costs *should* be stated. In this particular case, no change in volume is contemplated in connection with the decision; but the practice of stating fixed costs per unit of volume is potentially misleading and should be avoided.

The analysis of the financial data in this situation may be made by preparing comparative budgeted income statements for the two alternatives which may be selected. Such statements, in the variable costing form, are presented below:

	Present Processing	Further Processing
Sales revenue	$650,000	$800,000
Variable costs:		
Direct materials	$120,000	$120,000
Direct labor	175,000	240,000
Overhead	110,000	135,000
Selling expense	90,000	100,000
	$495,000	$595,000
Variable profit	$155,000	$205,000
Fixed costs:		
Overhead	$ 85,000	$100,000
Selling expense	30,000	40,000
	$115,000	$140,000
Income before tax	$ 40,000	$ 65,000
Federal income tax (40%)	16,000	26,000
Net income	$ 24,000	$ 39,000

So long as the income tax rate is less than 100%, inclusion of the tax in the analysis only reduces the absolute amount by which further processing would increase profits; but the relative advantage of further processing remains. Nevertheless, it is good practice always to include income taxes in decision-making analyses. In some cases, tax implications may be controlling factors in the decisions.

The same result as developed above can be obtained from a much shorter analysis, dealing only with the incremental revenues and costs associated with the decision to engage in further processing.

Incremental revenue per unit.............	$	1.50
Incremental variable cost per unit.......		1.00
Incremental variable profit per unit.....	$	.50
Monthly volume in units..................		100,000
Incremental variable profit per month....	$	50,000
Incremental fixed cost per month.........		25,000
Monthly incremental profit before tax....	$	25,000
Federal income tax (40%).................		10,000
Incremental profit.......................	$	15,000

Inasmuch as the incremental profit is positive, the decision to undertake further processing would be more profitable in the short-run than continuing the present operating policy.

Other Considerations. The facts in this illustration indicate that a decision to engage in further processing would not require additional capital investment. This is a very important condition. If further capital investment were necessary, the decision would have to be evaluated as an investment proposal; incremental profit analysis as illustrated above would not be adequate. The analysis above also presumes that additional laborers could be obtained and laid off on short notice. Even if hiring new workers presents no problem, laying them off might; periodic hirings and layoffs are discouraged by the provisions of many union labor agreements. The Blaine Corporation must also question whether its production personnel have the technical knowledge and skill to perform the further processing efficiently. The decision to process further entails the marketing of the company's product in an unfamiliar channel of distribution. Establishing effective working agreements with clothing manufacturers may make new demands on the abilities of the sales force and it may take some little time. Not all of these considerations lend themselves to precise financial measurement, but they must not be ignored. Thus, the monthly incremental profit of $15,000 is an important factor in the decision-making process; but it is not the final answer in itself.

Make or Buy

The Facts. The Bonham Radio Company manufactures a variety of electronics equipment. Several of the items produced contain one or more units of a small capacitor, part No. 63812 in the company's list of standard materials. This capacitor is manufactured by the company in its own parts plant. The standard cost for one capacitor is as follows:

Materials.........	$3.20
Direct labor......	2.40
Variable overhead.	1.10
Fixed overhead....	1.40
	$8.10

All of these are current attainable standards. Monthly usage of this part averages 60,000 units. At a budget meeting, the purchasing agent suggested that the company might save money by purchasing this part from an independent supplier. He stated that he knew it could be purchased in the quantity used by the Bonham Company for $7 per unit. Buying the part would increase clerical purchasing costs by approximately $1,000 per month. The supervisor of the stores department estimated that the additional costs of storing and handling the part, if purchased, would be about $.25 per unit. No additional facilities would be needed to store the part, nor would any production facilities be abandoned if its production were discontinued. The parts plant manager reported that the manufacture of this capacitor is not so significant a portion of his total operation that its discontinuance would have any impact upon the plant's fixed overhead.

Incremental Profit Analysis. A cursory glance at the facts in this situation might suggest that a decision to buy the capacitor would indeed be a cost saving. Eighty-five cents per unit ($8.10 − $7.25) would appear to be saved, and this amounts to $51,000 per month for 60,000 units. Even after the additional clerical cost of $1,000 per month, there appears to be a $50,000 monthly cost saving (before taxes, of course). The saving is purely illusory in this case, however. Part of the standard cost of $8.10 for this part is fixed overhead. For inventory costing purposes, it is perfectly correct to assign $1.40 of the parts plant's fixed overhead to this capacitor, assuming that the absorption costing method is employed and that a valid cost allocation scheme is applied. However, discontinuing the manufacture of this part will not affect the parts plant's fixed overhead at all. The fixed cost now charged to part No. 63812 would either be reallocated to other parts or be charged to the volume variance. In either event, the plant's fixed overhead would not be reduced. Thus, fixed overhead is an irrelevant cost in respect to the decision to make or buy part No. 63812. Only the variable production costs—materials, direct labor, and variable overhead—are relevant to the decision. The variable costs to manufacture total $6.70. Thus, there is an incremental cost of $.55 per unit ($7.25 − $6.70) inherent in the decision to purchase this part. At a monthly usage of 60,000 units, the decision to purchase the capacitor would be analyzed as follows:

Monthly purchase cost (60,000 units @ $7.25)...........	$435,000
Plus: Incremental monthly clerical cost.................	1,000
	$436,000
Variable manufacturing costs per month (60,000 units @ $6.70).....................................	402,000
Incremental cost to purchase (before taxes)..............	$ 34,000
Federal income tax (40%).............................	13,600
Incremental cost per month to purchase part No. 63812..	$ 20,400

Thus, an apparent incremental cost saving is actually an incremental cost. The incremental profit of the suggested change in policy is a negative $20,400 per month.

Other Considerations. If a decision to make a part would require an investment in new production facilities or if a decision to buy a part would permit the disposal of existing facilities, the alternatives would have to be evaluated as long-term investment decisions. The situation described here suggests that any decision made could be reappraised and reversed within one month. Other factors must also be considered. If the part were purchased, could the capacity of the parts plant thus idled be employed in some other profitable manner? The analysis above implies that the answer to this question is "No," but the question was not really raised. It should be. Would there be any difference in the quality or technical characteristics of the purchased capacitor as compared with the present part No. 63812? Would an independent supplier be as reliable as the company's own parts plant? Even if the relevant costs of purchasing the part were lower, the danger of a costly stock-out due to an unreliable source of supply might outweigh the computed cost saving. Finally, the incremental profit analysis in the preceding paragraph presumed that direct laborers could be laid off if the production of the capacitor were discontinued. Even if such a layoff were feasible, it might create long-run labor relations problems which would offset the short-run cost saving. The impact of a decision on labor relations can seldom be quantified, but it should never be ignored.

Dropping a Product Line

The Facts. The Turandot Products Company produces and markets three products. It has prepared the income statement shown in Table 14–1, in the absorption costing form.[3] The company's management is considering dropping Pong from the line of products because it has consistently shown a loss.

Incremental Profit Analysis. A useful starting point in this analysis is to recast the income statement presented in the variable costing form and to eliminate the allocation of fixed costs among the products. However valid such an allocation may be for purposes of inventory costing and income measurement, it is not relevant to the question of the profitability of the individual products. Here we shall assume that all of the company's fixed costs are common to the three products. We also assume that the sales and production volumes for the year were equal, so that the same total amount of fixed manufacturing costs will be charged to revenue

---

[3] The distinction between variable and fixed costs is not ordinarily made in absorption costing statements, but it is included here to facilitate subsequent analysis. If not included in the income statement, it could be derived from the cost records.

under variable costing as under absorption costing.[4] The report of profits by product lines in the variable costing form and under the assumptions postulated is as illustrated in Table 14–2. Now it is clear that each product has a positive variable profit. So long as there are no relevant fixed costs, each product also has a positive incremental profit. Here Pong's contribution to the total profit of the firm (before taxes) is $30,000. The apparent loss from its continued sale can be seen to be attributable to the allocation of a portion of the common fixed costs of the company to it. Even if relevant fixed costs were present in the analysis, Pong would have a positive incremental profit as long as its relevant fixed costs were less

TABLE 14–1
TURANDOT PRODUCTS COMPANY

	Ping	Pang	Pong	Total
Sales....................	$600,000	$450,000	$150,000	$1,200,000
Cost of goods sold:				
Variable................	$360,000	$270,000	$105,000	$ 735,000
Fixed..................	120,000	90,000	30,000	240,000
	$480,000	$360,000	$135,000	$ 975,000
Gross margin.............	$120,000	$ 90,000	$ 15,000	$ 225,000
Selling expenses:				
Variable................	$ 40,000	$ 30,000	$ 15,000	$ 85,000
Fixed..................	30,000	22,500	7,500	60,000
	$ 70,000	$ 52,500	$ 22,500	$ 145,000
Net income before tax.......	$ 50,000	$ 37,500	$ (7,500)	$ 80,000
Income tax (40%)...........	20,000	15,000	(3,000)	32,000
Net income................	$ 30,000	$ 22,500	$ (4,500)	$ 48,000

than $30,000. Whenever a decision is to be made on the basis of the relative profitabilities of several product lines, their respective profits should be measured by their incremental profits. Allocations of fixed costs common to all products are irrelevant and misleading.

On the basis of the information given, the incremental profit of a decision to discontinue production and distribution of Pong would be a negative $18,000 after tax ($30,000 × .60). This may be proved by subtracting all data relevant to Pong from the totals for the company in the income statement above and then recomputing the income tax accordingly.

Other Considerations. Any decision concerning the continuation of one product in a company's line must take into account a wide range of possible implications. Product income statements can be very mislead-

---

[4] See Chapter 4, pages 98–101, for a discussion of the impact of differences between sales and production volumes on reported incomes under these alternative costing methods.

ing; they may show only the apparent profitability of each product. For example, if one product is dropped from the line, there may be adverse effects on the sales of other products. If two or more products are complementary, discontinuing one is almost certain to result in reduced sales of the other(s). As an illustration, a manufacturer of machinery could reasonably expect to sell fewer machines if he stopped making and selling spare parts for the machinery. Buyers may place orders with a particular seller because they can obtain a complete line of merchandise from him. If he reduces that line, the buyers may look elsewhere for suppliers from whom they can purchase the complete line. Thus, in the

TABLE 14–2
TURANDOT PRODUCTS COMPANY

	Ping	*Pang*	*Pong*	*Total*
Sales....................	$600,000	$450,000	$150,000	$1,200,000
Variable costs:				
Production..............	$360,000	$270,000	$105,000	$ 735,000
Selling.................	40,000	30,000	15,000	85,000
	$400,000	$300,000	$120,000	$ 820,000
Variable profit.............	$200,000	$150,000	$ 30,000	$ 380,000
Fixed costs:				
Production..............				$ 240,000
Selling.................				60,000
				$ 300,000
Net income before tax.......				$ 80,000
Income tax (40%)..........				32,000
Net income...............				$ 48,000

case analyzed above, discontinuance of Pong might involve a negative incremental profit of more than the amount computed because of reduced sales of Ping and/or Pang. Unfortunately, such interproduct demand relationships usually cannot be measured accurately; but they can be extremely important.

The discontinuance of a product line was illustrated here as a very simple situation. Ignored was the very pertinent question of what might be done to fill the void left by the abandoned product. If a company discontinues making and selling one product, there will be some amount of idle capacity in both production facilities and the sales force. This idle capacity may be diverted to production and sales of a new product or of one or more of the other products already in the line. For example, the decision to discontinue Pong would take on new and significant dimensions if we knew that the capacity thus idled could be diverted to additional output and sales of Ping and/or Pang. Suppose that the loss of all Pong sales could be replaced with an equal dollar volume of some combination of Ping and Pang sales. The latter two products both have a variable profit ratio of one third of sales, as compared with Pong's variable profit ratio of 20%. Thus, additional sales of either or both of these products in the amount of $150,000 would add $50,000 to total variable profit. The incremental profit of the decision to discontinue Pong would then be positive, as shown below:

Increase in variable profit from Ping/Pang...........	$50,000
Less: Loss of variable profit from Pong...............	30,000
Incremental profit before taxes.....................	$20,000
Incremental profit after tax ($20,000 × .60).........	$12,000

Finally, there are other factors which may not lend themselves to short-run financial analysis. What will be the impact of the discontinuance of a product line on the overall company image? What will be the impact of the decision on the company's employees—specifically, their job security? What psychological effect, if any, might this decision have upon the salesmen in their subsequent promotion of the other products? The fact that these questions may be unanswerable does not mean that they must not be asked.

COMMON PRODUCTION COSTS

In some manufacturing enterprises, two or more different products emerge from a single, common production process and a single raw material. A familiar example is the variety of petroleum products derived from the refining of crude oil. Such products present some peculiar and important problems to cost accountants and to managers. They are identifiable as separate products only at the conclusion of the common processing. This point of separation is commonly referred to as the *split-off point*. The costs incurred up to the split-off point are true common costs; they cannot be traced to the separate products in any direct or logical manner. For inventory costing purposes, however, it is necessary that all production costs be charged to products and, more particularly here, to separate products. For purposes of managerial analysis, of course, costs need not be identified with individual products unless it is both meaningful and useful that such identification be made. Thus, common production costs must be allocated among the products manufactured jointly in order that inventory values and income may be determined in accordance with generally accepted accounting principles. In certain decision-making situations, however, such allocations may not only be unnecessary but may be invalid. Both the inventory costing and the decision-making implications of common costs will be considered in the sections that follow.

Allocation of Common Production Costs

Joint Products. Where two or more products are derived from a common production process and a single raw material and each is regarded as a major product of the company, they are usually referred to as *joint products* or as *coproducts*. For purposes of inventory valuation and income determination, the common costs of producing joint products are allocated among them according to some reasonable scheme. The most widely accepted basis for this allocation is the relative sales values of the several joint products at the split-off point. This may be illustrated by a simple example. Products A, B, and C are obtained from a single raw material. Each product is salable as it comes from the common processing; that is, each has a readily determinable market value at the split-off point. The common production costs—including raw materials, direct labor, and all overhead—total $600,000 for a given period. The unit output and market value of each product is indicated below, along with the allocation of the common production costs in proportion to the relative market values of the products at the split-off point:

Product	Unit Output	Market Value at Split-off	Allocation of Common Cost
A........	20,000	$ 600,000	$300,000
B........	25,000	200,000	100,000
C........	15,000	400,000	200,000
	60,000	$1,200,000	$600,000

This illustration assumes the absorption costing approach. Under variable costing, fixed overhead would be excluded from the cost of the coproducts; but the same allocation problem would remain for the common variable costs.

It has sometimes been suggested that the common costs be allocated among joint products in proportion to the number of units produced. If such an allocation scheme were applied to the three products above, their respective costs would be as follows:

> Product A.............. $200,000
> Product B.............. 250,000
> Product C.............. 150,000

Since the cost allocated to product B under this scheme is greater than its sales value, product B would appear to be unprofitable. Of course, its lack of profitability in that case could be traced directly to the cost allocation method employed. Hence, the common cost allocation is usually made on the basis of relative sales values. This is a neutral method insofar as individual product profitability is concerned. Allocation by relative sales values assures that each product will have the same gross margin ratio at the split-off point. In the illustration above, each product has a gross margin ratio of 50% of sales value.

If a product is not readily salable at the split-off point, its market value at that point may be approximated by subtracting from its ultimate sales value the further costs of processing it separately. Thus, if product C above could be sold at a final price of $500,000 but only after further processing costs of $80,000, its market value at the split-off point would be estimated to be $420,000. Obviously, such an approach assumes that no profit attaches to the product beyond the split-off point; sales value added beyond that point is presumed to be exactly equal to the separate processing costs. Despite the logical invalidity of this assumption, the approach is quite widely used. Where separate processing costs are not substantial in relation to the common costs, this method would not appear to be seriously objectionable. If the separate costs are substantial and, particularly, if they differ significantly among the several joint products, sales value at the split-off point may be estimated in a slightly different manner to allow for a portion of the profit to be associated with the separate processing. The ratio of the total gross margin on all products to total production costs, both common and separate, would be computed. Given this ratio, it would then be assumed that the same percentage gross margin attaches to each dollar of production cost. Sales at the split-off point would then be approximated by subtracting both the separate processing costs and the gross margin assumed to attach thereto from the final sales value of each product.

By-Products. If one of the products emerging from a common material and production process is regarded as relatively unimportant in the overall product line of the company, it is described as a *by-product*. A by-product is usually regarded as produced incidentally to the manufacture of a principal product, or main product. Generally speaking, a by-product is identified as such if its revenue is not considered a significant portion of total revenue and if little special effort is required in its manufacture and distribution. No portion of the common production costs is allocated to a by-product. Rather, all of the common costs are charged to the principal product(s). The net realizable value (final sales value minus any separate costs of processing and selling) of the by-product is then credited to the total cost of manufacturing the principal product(s). This may be illustrated by a very simple example. A corporation produces two products, Mapo and Bypo; the former is the principal product and the latter, a by-product. Output, cost, and sales data for a year are as follows:

	Mapo	*Bypo*
Units produced.................	100,000	8,000
Unit selling price................	$5.00	$.40
Common production costs.........	$300,000	
Separate costs..................	$ 60,000	$1,200

The cost of the principal product would then be determined thus:

Common costs.........................		$300,000
Separate costs........................		60,000
		360,000
Less net realizable value of Bypo:		
Sales value.......................	$3,200	
Less separate costs................	1,200	2,000
Total cost of Mapo....................		$358,000
Units produced.......................		100,000
Unit cost............................		$3.58

If all of the by-product is sold in the period in which it is produced, its full net realizable value is realized; there is no inventory of by-product. If there remains an inventory of by-product, it must be valued at its net realizable value in order that the full amount of the net realizable value of by-product produced during a period may be credited to the cost of the principal product manufactured in the same period. This deviation from the customary practice of valuing inventories at cost is generally accepted and, in view of the relative insignificance of by-products, is not likely to have a material effect upon total asset valuation or upon reported income.

There are no set rules for distinguishing between joint products and by-products. The distinction is a matter of judgment to be made in each individual situation. Similarly, the distinction between by-products and scrap is a question of judgment. Salable scrap is ordinarily accounted for in substantially the same way as by-products. Unsalable scrap, of course, requires no accounting, except to the extent that costs are incurred in order to dispose of it.

Common Production Costs in Decision Making

When a decision concerning the production of an entire group of joint products or of principal product(s) and by-product(s) is under consideration, the common production costs are relevant to the decision to the extent that they would be avoided if the entire product group were abandoned. The relevant common costs in such a case would include materials, labor, and variable overhead and might include some fixed costs. If the decision at hand involves only one product in the group, however, the common production costs are not relevant to it. Abandonment of only one of a group of joint products (or of a by-product) would not reduce the common costs at all.[5] The incremental profit of the entire group is measured by the difference between the revenue obtained from all of the products and the total costs, both common and separate, directly traceable to the group. The incremental profit of an individual product in the group, however, is measured by the excess of its own revenue over its own separate costs. Any allocation of common cost to one product is irrelevant to its incremental profit. Common cost allocations can be dangerously misleading for decision-making purposes, particularly if the allocations are made on some basis other than relative market values.

It may seem somewhat bothersome that the incremental profits of two joint products can be determined without regard to the very significant common costs of making those products. But incremental profit is not the same thing as net profit. Incremental profit is the amount which an individual product (or a decision) contributes to total enterprise profit, recognizing that the sum of all incremental profits from the several products (or other segments) of the enterprise must be greater than the common costs if a net profit for the firm as a whole is to be realized. The relationship of the profit contributed by one segment of an enterprise to the total enterprise profit will be amplified in Chapter 18.

Incremental Profits of Joint Products. The preceding paragraphs suggested that the incremental profit of an individual joint product is simply the difference between its sales value and its separate costs. This is true if "separate costs" are properly defined and measured. The relevant separate costs of a product are those which are directly traceable to it and would be avoided if the product were discontinued. Thus, if the cost accounting system allocates a portion of general factory administrative cost and other general factory overhead to all operations in the plant, that portion of the separate processing costs which represents such allocations is irrelevant to the incremental profit of an individual product. The same is true of fixed selling and administrative expenses which may be allocated among the various products for some reporting purpose (not inventory valuation, of course). Only those selling and

---

[5] This statement implicitly assumes that the proportions of joint products (or of main products and by-products) emerging from the common process are fixed. In some instances, it is possible to alter the product proportions by varying the inputs of labor or materials. For example, the proportion of one joint product might be reduced if certain labor tasks were omitted from the common processing. Thus, a decision to abandon that product alone could possibly entail a reduction in common costs with no change in the output of the other joint product(s). However, the reduced total of common costs would have to be allocated over fewer joint products after such a change had been made.

administrative expenses directly traceable to the individual product may be included in the determination of the product's incremental profit.

Everything said above concerning joint products is equally true of by-products. In the case of a principal product (as distinguished from a by-product), on the other hand, it would seem that the revenue from the sales of that main product should normally be adequate to cover not only its own separate costs but also the production costs common to it and the by-product. There are instances where this is not so and where the overall profitability of the combination of principal product and by-product is assured only by sales of the by-product. In such instance, it would appear that the by-product is such only by arbitrary definition; in a very real sense, it is a joint product.

Extent of Processing a Joint Product or By-Product. Sometimes a firm has an alternative with respect to the disposition of a particular joint product or by-product. It may sell the item in its stage of completion at the split-off point or may subject it to further processing and sell it in a more advanced stage of completion at a higher price. Such an alternative should be evaluated as any other decision concerning the extent of processing a product. The analysis for such a decision was illustrated earlier in this chapter.[6] The incremental profit from a decision to process the item further would be equal to the *additional* revenue realized from selling the product at the advanced stage of completion minus the further processing and other costs directly traceable to the product. If that incremental profit is positive, the decision to process further would be advantageous from the point of view of short-run profit maximization. As in all decisions, there may be other considerations which cannot be quantified or reduced to financial consequences but which are, nevertheless, critical to the decision. And, of course, if the decision to engage in further processing would require the purchase or construction of additional productive facilities, the proposal would have to be analyzed as a long-term investment decision. Simple incremental profit analysis would not be appropriate.

QUESTIONS FOR DISCUSSION

1. For purposes of decision making, what are relevant costs?
2. Is the incremental profit from a decision the same as the variable profit from the decision? Explain.
3. Distinguish clearly among the following three concepts: relevant cost, direct cost, and variable cost. Distinguish among these three concepts: fixed cost, indirect cost, and irrelevant cost.

---

[6] Pages 351–53.

4. Suggest an operational distinction between short-term and long-term decisions. Into which category would you expect each of the following decisions to fall:

   a) A decision to purchase a new building?

   b) A decision to rent a new building?

   c) A decision to sell products in new market areas?

   d) A decision to create a long-term planning committee of the board of directors?

5. "Since fixed costs are unaffected by a change in the volume of operations, they are always irrelevant to any business decision short of a decision to discontinue operations altogether." Evaluate this statement.

6. Is incremental profit analysis pertinent to decision making in nonprofit institutions such as schools and hospitals? Discuss.

7. The uses of cost data in income measurement and inventory valuation are not always compatible with the uses of cost data for decision making. How can a single cost accounting system provide data for both of these purposes? Would such a system include all of the cost data necessary for financial accounting purposes? Would it include all of the cost data necessary for decision making?

8. Describe the procedures that the management of a manufacturing firm might employ to identify and measure all of the costs relevant to a decision whether to make or to buy a part used in the manufacture of a product.

9. This chapter suggests that the common costs of producing two or more joint products are relevant to the valuation of inventories of the individual products but irrelevant to a decision regarding any one of the joint products. This appears to be inconsistent. If a cost is irrelevant to whether a product is produced or not, how can such a cost reasonably be included in the cost of an inventory of that product? In this connection, would it make any difference whether absorption or variable costing were used?

10. "Unlike the common costs of joint products, the costs associated with by-products are handled essentially the same way for financial accounting purposes as they are for decision making." Is this statement true? Explain.

11. A lumber company is planning to build a new mill. It has two basic alternatives with regard to the disposition of sawdust. The sawdust can be swept up, placed in sacks, and sold; or it can be burned in an incinerator. Assuming that the incinerator will be needed for other refuse, regardless of the decision regarding the sawdust, what factors would be relevant to the decision as to how sawdust should be disposed of? Would this decision situation be changed materially if the incinerator would not be needed if the sawdust were not to be burned?

12. How should the lumber company in the preceding question determine whether sawdust is to be accounted for as a joint product, a by-product, or as scrap in the event that the decision is made to sell the sawdust?

13. If depreciation on manufacturing equipment is recorded by the productive hours method and the company is considering adding a second production shift, is depreciation a relevant cost in connection with the decision regarding the second shift? Why or why not?

14. Are income taxes relevant costs with respect to decisions that are expected to have the effect of increasing or decreasing taxable income? Could income tax considerations ever be the deciding factors in such decisions? Explain.

15. Should the incremental profits of all decisions actually made by management sum algebraically to the net income subsequently reported for the firm? Why or why not?

PROBLEMS

1. The Spenser Electronics Company produces most of its own parts and components. The standard wage rate in the parts department is $3.90 per hour. Variable overhead is applied at a standard rate of $.80 per hour and fixed overhead, at a standard rate of $2.40 per labor hour.

For its 1973 output, the company will require a new part that it has never used before. This part could be made in the parts department without any expansion of the existing facilities. However, it would be necessary to increase the monthly cost of product testing and inspection by $750. Estimated labor time for the new part will be one half of an hour per unit. Raw materials cost has been estimated at $6.25 per unit. Alternatively, the part could be purchased from an independent supplier for $9.50 per unit, delivered. The company has estimated that it will use 50,000 units of the new part during 1973.

Required:

Would it be more profitable for the company to make or to purchase this new part in 1973? Support your answer with appropriate financial analysis.

2. The Dryden Company produces a single product in its Leeds plant. This product is manufactured in three successive production departments. Following are the budgeted annual production costs for an output of 75,000 units, which is regarded as normal volume:

	Department A	Department B	Department C
Direct materials...............	$150,000	$ 52,500	
Direct labor..................	90,000	120,000	$ 60,000
Variable overhead.............	45,000	60,000	30,000
Fixed overhead...............	135,000	180,000	90,000
	$420,000	$412,500	$180,000

Fixed overhead is applied to production at a plantwide rate of 150% of direct labor cost. None of the fixed overhead is considered to be directly traceable to individual departments.

Recently, the company has learned that it can purchase a semifinished product, ready for work in Department B, from a Birmingham manufacturer at a unit price of $3.75, delivered. If this semifinished product were purchased instead of the basic raw material, Department A could be closed down. However, direct labor costs in Department B would be increased by 15% because of changes in operations necessitated by the introduction of this semifinished product into that department.

Required:

a) On the basis of short-run profitability, would it be better for the company to purchase the semifinished product or to continue producing in Department A?

b) What additional factors should the company's management consider before making the decision in this situation?

3. The Donne Engine Company produces most of its engine parts in its own plant. Recently, it has been weighing the merits of purchasing some finished parts instead of manufacturing them. At present, it is studying the advantages of buying Part No. 88 from an outside supplier for $12 per unit. If this were done, monthly purchasing costs would be increased by $900.

Part No. 88 is now manufactured in the stamping department along with several other parts. The department would continue operations on a somewhat reduced basis if Part No. 88 were no longer produced there. The average monthly usage of Part No. 88 is 7,500 units. The direct costs of producing the part include $5 per unit for materials and two labor hours per unit at a wage rate of $3.20 per hour. Overhead is applied to production in the stamping department on the basis of direct labor hours. The monthly overhead budget for this department is as follows:

Direct labor hours	150,000	180,000	210,000
Variable costs	$120,000	$144,000	$168,000
Fixed costs	198,000	198,000	198,000
	$318,000	$342,000	$366,000

Normal production volume in the stamping department is 180,000 labor hours per month, and current actual production volume is at about the same level. Discontinuation of the production of Part No. 88 would cause an unfavorable volume variance in the department of about $16,500 per month.

Required:

Would it be more profitable for the company to continue making Part No. 88 or to purchase it?

4. The Marvell Bakery sells two very popular specialty cakes, a butter cream delight and a German chocolate layer cake. Both are baked in the same oven, which will accommodate 15 cakes at one time and can be operated for a maximum of 60 hours per week. The demand for both cakes is so great that the bakery could sell the maximum output of the oven in any combination of the two cakes, including all of one or all of the other. The

only direct costs of these cakes are their respective ingredients costs. A comparison of the prices, ingredients costs, and oven times of the two cakes is as follows:

	Butter Cream Delight	German Chocolate
Price.....................	$2.00	$1.65
Ingredients cost.............	.80	.75
Oven time.................	30 min.	20 min.

Required:

What would be the most profitable sales mix of these two cakes?

5. The Milton Products Company produces Product X. This product sells for $7.50 per unit. Variable costs to make and sell the product are $2 per unit, and fixed costs are $4 per unit at a normal output of 500,000 units per year. Sales volume in recent years has been equal to normal output.

Rearbuck Stores, Inc., has offered the Milton Products Company a contract for 150,000 units of Product X each year at a price of $6 per unit. As these units would be distributed under Rearbuck's private brand name, they would not adversely affect regular sales of Product X. The company could avoid $.20 of variable selling expenses for each unit sold under this proposed contract. Fixed production costs would have to be increased by $500,000 in order to increase production volume to 650,000 units.

The production engineer has recommended a plan to improve product quality and, thereby, increase sales volume. His proposal would increase variable production costs by $.25 per unit and fixed costs by $350,000 per year. Sales volume would be increased by 100,000 units annually with no change in the selling price.

The sales manager has suggested still another plan to boost sales volume. He would reduce the selling price by 10%. This price reduction would increase sales volume by 40%. This additional output could be achieved by an increase in fixed costs of $600,000 per year.

None of the three proposed changes in operations would necessitate any new capital expenditure.

Required:

Accepting the assumptions underlying each of the three proposals for increased sales volume and assuming that the three proposals are mutually exclusive, evaluate the profitability of the alternative courses of action open to management.

6. The Pope Plumbing Company manufacturers a wide variety of component parts. Two of these, the Type C Valve and the Type K Elbow Joint, are currently suffering greatly reduced sales volumes because of competition

from lower priced substitutes. Data relevant to these two products are as follows:

	Type C Valve	Type K Elbow Joint
Selling price.................	$12.50	$3.00
Units currently sold annually...	6,000	20,000
Unit production costs:		
Materials..................	$ 5.25	$ .75
Labor.....................	3.20	.80
Variable overhead...........	1.60	.40
Fixed overhead.............	2.40	.60
	$12.45	$2.55

Unabsorbed fixed overhead currently is about $25,000 per year.

The sales manager has suggested that selling prices of $10.95 for the Type C Valve and $2.50 for the Type K Elbow Joint would make these products competitive and would restore the company's normal market shares for these items—15,000 units per year of the valve and 40,000 units annually of the elbow joint.

The purchasing agent has pointed out that identical items could be purchased from Japanese manufacturers below the company's own cost and then resold to the company's customers. Such an arrangement, he claims, would partially mitigate the impact of the suggested price reductions. Type C Valves could be purchased from Japanese suppliers for $11 each and Type K Elbow Joints, for $2.25 each. Both of these prices include all freight and import duties.

The volume of production of the two items in question here is not so great than any decision affecting them would have any impact on investments in production or distribution facilities. All selling and administrative expenses are considered fixed costs and are currently allocated among the company's products at a rate of 20% of full manufacturing costs.

Required:

Submit a report showing the relative profitabilities of the alternative selling prices suggested for the two products in question and of the profitability of buying either or both of the items from Japanese suppliers.

7. The Gray Corporation produces a single product in its plant. This product sells for $25 per unit. The standard cost per unit produced is as follows:

Raw materials (4 lbs. @ $2)...............	$ 8
Direct labor (2 hrs. @ $2.50)..............	5
Variable overhead.......................	2
Fixed overhead........................	5
	$20

The plant is currently operating at full capacity of 800,000 units per year on a single shift. This is inadequate to meet sales demand, and the sales manager has estimated that the firm will lose sales of 400,000 units next year if the capacity constraint is not eased.

Plant capacity could be doubled by adding a second shift. This would require additional out-of-pocket fixed overhead costs of $3,500,000 annually. Also, a night-work wage premium of 10% would have to be paid on direct labor in the second shift. However, if annual production volume were 1,200,000 units or more (but not less), the corporation could take advantage of a 5% quantity discount on its raw materials purchases.

Required:

a) Would it be profitable to add the second shift in order to obtain the additional sales volume of 400,000 units per year?

b) What would be the minimum annual increase in production volume over the present 800,000 units necessary to justify adding the second shift?

8. You are the independent auditor for the Burns Company. When you had completed your audit for the preceding year, management asked your assistance in arriving at a decision whether to continue manufacturing a part or to buy it from an outside supplier. The part, called a Faktron, is a component used in several of the company's finished products.

From your audit working papers and from further investigation, you have developed the following data relative to the company's operations:

(1) The annual requirement for Faktrons is 12,000 units. The lowest price quotation from a supplier was $21.50 per unit.

(2) Faktrons have been manufactured in the precision machinery department. Following are the total costs in this department during the preceding year, when 12,000 Faktrons were produced:

Materials..............................	$ 350,000
Direct labor............................	400,000
Indirect labor..........................	160,000
Light and heat..........................	20,000
Power.................................	30,000
Depreciation...........................	200,000
Property taxes and insurance............	15,000
Payroll taxes and other fringe benefits........	84,000
Miscellaneous..........................	27,000
	$1,286,000

Discontinuing production of Faktrons would reduce the operating volume of the precision machinery department but would not permit the disposal of any of the department's assets.

(3) The following proportions of the variable costs in the precision machinery department are avoidable if Faktron production is halted:

Materials.........................	30%
Direct labor......................	35
Indirect labor....................	25
Power............................	20

(4)   If Faktrons are purchased from an outside supplier, shipping charges would average $.75 per unit; and indirect labor cost in the precision machinery department would be increased by $20,000 annually for receiving, inspecting, and handling the purchased parts.

Required:

Prepare a schedule showing the relative costs of making and buying Faktrons to assist management in reaching a decision. What considerations other than this cost comparison would you bring to management's attention in helping them to arrive at a decision?

(Adapted from CPA Examination)

9. The Coleridge Theater has shown the motion picture, "Uneasy Flyer," for the past two weeks. It has been the most successful film that has played at the theater for several years. Because of the earthy language, negligible costuming, and compromising positions in which the heroine repeatedly finds herself, the manager of the theater has scrupulously restricted admission to adults only. The manager is convinced that attendance will continue to be above normal for another two weeks if the run of "Uneasy Flyer" is extended. Another movie, "Red Ryder and the Chocolate Mine," is booked for the next two weeks, however. Even if "Uneasy Flyer" is extended, the theater will have to pay the regular rental on "Red Ryder" as well.

Normal attendance at the Coleridge Theater is 2,000 patrons per week, approximately one fourth of whom are children under the age of 12. Attendance for "Uneasy Flyer" has been 50% greater than the normal total, despite (or possibly because of) the "adults only" policy. The manager believes that this would taper off during a second two weeks. He estimates that attendance would be 25% below that of the first two weeks during a third week and 33⅓% lower during a fourth week. Attendance for "Red Ryder and the Chocolate Mine" would be expected to be normal throughout its run, regardless of how long that was.

All features at the theater are shown at the regular prices of $2 for adults and $1.20 for children under 12. The rental charge for "Uneasy Flyer" is $900 for one week or $1,500 for two weeks. For "Red Ryder and the Chocolate Mine," it is $750 for one week or $1,200 for two. All other operating costs are fixed in the amount of $4,200 per week, except for the cost of popcorn and candy, which averages 60% of its selling price. Sales of popcorn and candy regularly average $.20 per patron, regardless of age.

Required:

The manager of the Coleridge Theater has three courses of action open to him for the next two weeks. He can extend the run of "Uneasy Flyer" for two weeks; he can extend its run for one week and show "Red Ryder and the Chocolate Mine" for one week; or he can show "Red Ryder" for the full two weeks for which it was originally booked. Which alternative would be the most profitable?

10. The Wordsworth Company has asked your assistance in determining the most economical sales and production mix of its products for 1973. The com-

pany manufactures a line of dolls and a doll dress sewing kit. The sales department has provided you the following information:

Product	Estimated Demand in Units in 1973	Net Price per Unit
Laurie doll...............	50,000	$ 6.00
Debbie doll...............	80,000	3.50
Sarah doll...............	30,000	10.00
Kathy doll...............	40,000	7.50
Sewing kit...............	250,000	2.50

To promote sales of the sewing kit, as well as the dolls, there is a 20% reduction in the established net selling price for a kit sold to a customer who purchases a doll at the same time. Based on past experience, the company estimates that sewing kits will be sold in conjunction with 80% of the sales of each of the four dolls.

From the accounting records, you have developed the following data:
(1) Standard direct production costs per unit:

Product	Materials	Labor
Laurie......................	$1.50	$2.00
Debbie......................	.90	1.00
Sarah.......................	3.10	3.00
Kathy.......................	2.22	2.40
Sewing kit..................	.82	.60

(2) The standard wage rate is $4 per hour and is expected to continue unchanged throughout 1973. The plant has an effective production capacity of 120,000 labor hours per year on a single shift basis. Present equipment can produce any and all of the products.
(3) Variable overhead will amount to $1.20 per direct labor hour. Total fixed overhead for 1973 will be $240,000.
(4) There will be no inventories of work in process or of finished products on January 1, 1973.

Required:
a) Prepare a schedule showing the incremental profit of each product in whatever manner will be most useful to management.
b) Is the present effective capacity on a single shift adequate to meet estimated sales demand in 1973? If not, how would you recommend that the company alter its budgeted product mix in order to keep production within the limits of a single shift capacity?
c) Irrespective of your answer in (b), assume now that capacity is not sufficient to meet 1973 sales demand. How might the company expand

capacity to meet that demand? Under what conditions would each of these methods of expanding capacity be profitable in 1973?

(Adapted from CPA Examination)

11. Following is the budgeted income statement of the Byron Products Company for the year 1973:

	Product X	Product Y	Product Z	Total
Sales......................	$200,000	$75,000	$100,000	$375,000
Cost of goods sold:				
Materials..................	$ 29,000	$18,500	$ 17,000	$ 64,500
Direct labor...............	75,000	20,000	25,000	120,000
Variable overhead...........	30,000	8,000	10,000	48,000
Fixed overhead.............	37,500	10,000	12,500	60,000
	$171,500	$56,500	$ 64,500	$292,500
Gross margin................	$ 28,500	$18,500	$ 35,500	$ 82,500
Selling and administrative expenses:				
Variable..................	$ 16,000	$ 6,000	$ 8,000	$ 30,000
Fixed....................	5,000	3,000	2,000	10,000
	$ 21,000	$ 9,000	$ 10,000	$ 40,000
Income before tax.............	$ 7,500	$ 9,500	$ 25,500	$ 42,500
Income tax (40%)............	3,000	3,800	10,200	17,000
Net Income.................	$ 4,500	$ 5,700	$ 15,300	$ 25,500
Units produced and sold........	5,000	3,000	2,000	

The factory is expected to operate at full capacity during 1973. It takes twice as long to produce one unit of Product X as it does to produce one unit of Product Y. And it takes half again as long to produce one unit of Product X as it does to Product one unit of Product Z.

All fixed costs are common to all three products.

Required:

a) Rank the three products in the order of their contributions to total company profit per unit of factory time.

b) Assume that the company has decided to discontinue production of the least profitable product, as shown by the ranking in (a), and to produce equal quantities of the remaining two products. Operations would continue at full capacity. Which two products would be produced and in what quantities?

c) What would be the incremental profit of the proposed shift in product mix determined in (b)?

12. The management of the Keats Cottonseed Company has engaged you to assist in the development of information to be used for managerial decision making. The company has the capacity to process 50,000 tons of cottonseed per year. The output yield of one ton of cottonseed is as follows:

Product	Average Yield per Ton of Cottonseed	Average Selling Price per Trade Unit
Oil......................	300 lbs.	20¢ per lb.
Meal....................	600	$60 per ton
Hulls...................	800	$30 per ton
Lint....................	100	$ 4 per cwt.
Waste..................	200	No value

A marketing study has indicated that the company can expect to sell its maximum output during the coming year at the average selling prices listed above. You have determined that the company's costs are as follows:

> Processing costs:
> Variable: $18 per ton of cottonseed put into process
> Fixed: $500,000 per year
> Marketing costs (variable): $40 per ton of output sold
> Administrative costs: $300,000 per year

From the foregoing information, you have prepared and submitted to management an analysis of the company's break-even point. In view of almost continually fluctuating prices in the cottonseed market, management has asked you to determine the maximum amount that the company can afford to pay for a ton of cottonseed and suffer an operating loss no greater than the loss that would be incurred if operations were shut down. You have been advised that all fixed costs would still be incurred if operations were shut down.

Required:

a) Compute the maximum amount that the company can afford to pay for a ton of cottonseed during the coming year.
b) The board of directors considers that a net profit before taxes of 20% of stockholders' equity is the minimum satisfactory return in a fairly risky industry such as this. Stockholders' equity currently totals $1,500,000. Compute the maximum average price that the company can afford to pay for a ton of cottonseed during the coming year and still realize the minimum rate of return desired.
c) Assuming the company does produce at full capacity during the coming year, what would the average price per ton of cottonseed have to be in order for the company to break even?

(Adapted from CPA Examination)

13. Shelley Hosiery Mills, Inc., manufactures and sells women's stockings. Productive capacity is 5 million pairs per year. All pairs produced are carefully inspected. Twenty percent of the output is unavoidably flawed and must be sold as "seconds." The remaining 80% of the output is sold under the brand name "Shelley Sheers" for $2 per pair. The seconds are presently being sold under the brand name "Shelley Seconds" for $1.20 per pair.

Budgeted sales volume for 1973 is as follows:

	Pairs
"Shelley Sheers"	3,500,000
"Shelley Seconds"	800,000

Budgeted costs for 1973 are as follows:

Variable production costs	$.60 per pair produced
Fixed production costs	$2,200,000
Variable selling expenses	$.10 per pair sold
Fixed selling expenses	$1,500,000

A marketing consultant has advised management that the sales of seconds under the Shelley brand name are injuring sales of the "Shelley Sheers." He has estimated that sales volume of "Shelley Sheers" could be increased by 20% in 1973 if sales of seconds under the company's brand name were discontinued.

The sales manager has learned that the entire output of seconds could be sold to a chain of discount stores with no brand identification for $.70 per pair. The usual variable selling expenses on these sales would be avoided, but additional shipping and billing costs of $20,000 per year would be incurred.

There was no significant inventory of either "Shelley Sheers" or seconds in stock as of December 31, 1972.

Required:

Assuming the validity of the marketing consultant's estimates, determine the most profitable way of disposing of seconds during 1973. Present a report to management in support of your conclusion.

14. The Browning Corporation produces five joint products from a common raw material and common processing. The budgeted annual outputs of these products and their unit market values at the completion of the common processing are as follows:

Product	*Units Produced*	*Market Value*
A	10,000	$ 5.00
B	25,000	4.00
C	5,000	15.00
D	40,000	1.50
E	20,000	2.25

The basic raw materials used in a year cost $179,000. Labor and overhead incurred in the common processing cost $85,000 per year.

Required:

Allocate the common production costs among the five joint products.

15. The Arnold Company produces a main product, M, and a by-product, B. During 1972, the company's first year of operations, common production costs totaled $750,000. Output consisted of 90,000 units of M and 10,000 units of B. Separate processing costs amounted to $270,000 for M and $25,000 for B. Sales during the year included 80,000 units of M at $15 apiece and 8,000 units of B at $5.50 apiece.

Required:

a) Compute the values of the inventories of M and B at December 31, 1972.

b) Determine the income before tax that should be reported for 1972.

16. The Dodgson Corporation manufacturers two products, Dum and Dee. Under present operations, raw materials are processed in Department A and the two products are separated at the end of this process. For every unit of Dum, two units of Dee are obtained. Dum is then finished in Department B and Dee, in Department C. Actual operating data for 1972 are as follows:

	Dept. A	*Dept. B*	*Dept. C*	*Total*
Units produced:				
Dum.......................	40,000	40,000		40,000
Dee.......................	80,000		80,000	80,000
Costs incurred:				
Raw materials...............	$120,000			$120,000
Direct labor.................	70,000	$50,000	$60,000	180,000
Variable overhead............	40,000	20,000	20,000	80,000
Avoidable fixed overhead.......	20,000	10,000	10,000	40,000
Common fixed overhead (allocated on basis of floor space)...............	50,000	25,000	25,000	100,000

At present, Dum is sold for $6.25 and Dee, for $4 per unit. Both products are also readily marketable at the completion of processing in Department A—Dum for $4.50 per unit and Dee for $2.75 per unit. Department B and/or Department C could be closed down completely if Dum and/or Dee, respectively, were sold at the split-off point.

Required:

a) Under an absorption costing system, what was the average unit cost of Dum and of Dee during 1972? Show supporting computations. Accept the allocation of common fixed overhead among departments as given.

b) From the point of view of short-run profit maximization, when should each product have been sold during 1972—after final completion or at the split-off point?

17. The Swinburne Corporation manufactures three different products from a single raw material. A summary of operating data for 1972 is presented below:

	Product A	Product B	Product C	Total
Output in pounds..............	90,000	60,000	30,000	180,000
Selling price per pound.........	$.50	$.90	$2.00	
Production costs:				
Materials...................				$50,000
Direct labor................	$4,000	$6,000	$5,000	40,000
Variable overhead............	2,000	3,000	2,000	15,000
Fixed overhead..............	3,000	5,000	4,000	29,000

No allocation of the common production costs incurred up to the split-off point has been made in the foregoing data. All of the output of 1972 was sold. The company uses absorption costing.

Required:

a) Allocate the common production costs among the three products in some reasonable manner.

b) Would it be profitable for the corporation to alter the output mix by reducing output of Product B by half and thereby increasing outputs of Products A and C by 15,000 pounds each at the cost of increasing the common production costs by 10%?

18. The Hopkins Packing Company prepares and packs a variety of meat products. Bones are cleaned of all usable meat and then are ground into meal, which is packed in 50-pound sacks and sold to fertilizer manufacturers. The company's output and sales in 1972 were as follows:

	Meat	Bone Meal
Production (in pounds)...........	750,000	60,000
Sales (in pounds).................	720,000	50,000
Sales revenue received...........	$540,000	$25,000

Total operating costs for 1972 were as follows:

Raw materials used.............................	$201,000
Direct labor......................................	88,000
Variable overhead applied.......................	70,400
Fixed overhead applied..........................	105,600
Selling and administrative expenses...............	65,000
Underapplied overhead..........................	9,200

Variable overhead is applied to production at a normal rate of $.80 per dollar of direct labor cost. Fixed overhead is applied at a rate of $1.20 per direct labor dollar. The direct labor cost of grinding and bagging the bones was $4,000 in 1972. This work was done in facilities and with equipment used in the production of meat products. No fixed overhead or nonmanufacturing expenses could be avoided simply by scrapping the bones. Bone meal is accounted for as a by-product.

Inventories are accounted for by the average cost method. The inventory of finished product at December 31, 1971, consisted of 20,000 pounds of meat products at a total cost of $9,675. There was no inventory of unsold bone meal at December 31, 1971. There were no inventories of work in process at the beginning or at the end of 1972.

The applicable income tax rate is 40%.

Required:

Prepare an income statement and a supporting statement of cost of goods manufactured and sold for the year 1972.

19. The basic processing of raw materials in the Yeats Chemical Corporation's plant yields three semifinished products, Worlon, Nantron, and Extron. The budgeted cost of the basic processing for 1973 is $3,470,000. Budgeted production, price, and separate cost data for the three products are as follows:

	Worlon	*Nantron*	*Extron*
Output in units...........	400,000	200,000	50,000
Selling price per unit.......	$9	$15	$2
Separate processing costs:			
Variable cost per unit....	$2	$1.50	$.80
Fixed cost.............	$400,000	$200,000	$20,000

Worlon and Nantron are accounted for as joint products. Extron is treated as a by-product.

Required:

a) Compute the budgeted unit cost of each of the joint products for 1973. Absorption costing is used.

b) By increasing the basic processing cost for the year by $250,000, the product mix could be altered to yield one-fifth more of Nantron and one-fourth more of Extron with no change in the total number of units of all products produced. Would such a change in production plans for 1973 be profitable?

c) By increasing the basic processing cost for the year by $400,000, all production of Extron could be converted to equal quantities of Worlon and Nantron. Would this change in the planned production for 1973 be profitable?

20. In 1946, A. F. Slicko developed and patented a heat-resistant paint which has the additional properties of being long wearing and easy to clean. He found a ready market for this new paint among manufacturers of ovens and other equipment used under conditions of extreme heat. At the outset, Slicko and 12 employees produced this paint in a small rented plant and delivered it to customers in the Chicago area only. By 1949, however, it was apparent that a much broader market for this product existed and could be served only by a major expansion of production and distribution

facilities. Accordingly, Slicko incorporated under the name Asbestone Paint Company and constructed a large plant in East Chicago. An expanded sales force began distribution of the paint under the trade name "Asbestone" throughout the East and Midwest.

In 1952, Slicko obtained a patent on a graphite-base industrial lubricant, subsequently marketed under the trade name "Glideze." The combined demand for this new product and for Asbestone soon exceeded the capacity of the East Chicago plant. In 1958, a new and larger plant was completed in Gary; and all paint production was shifted to that location. This left the East Chicago plant temporarily far below capacity. Growth in demand for Glideze and the introduction of another new product soon corrected this situation, however.

In 1967, the company introduced a lightweight heatproof liner for use in ovens, kilns, and similar equipment. This liner, marketed under the trade name "Heatrap," quickly proved to be a good seller, especially to customers who could also use Asbestone. Indeed, while the growth in sales of Asbestone had been very steady for the previous several years, it accelerated rapidly as demand for Heatrap grew. And salesmen who found a customer willing to buy Heatrap soon learned that they also had a good prospect for sales of Asbestone in place of competing products.

By the end of 1972, it had become apparent that the combined capacities of the two plants could no longer meet demand. In fact, the sales forecast for 1973 seemed to exceed existing capacity. After considerable discussion, the board of directors voted to construct a major new plant near Highland on property Slicko had purchased some years earlier as a speculative investment. When this plant is completed, the East Chicago plant will be sold. The Highland plant will not be ready until the spring of 1974, however. Hence, it will not help to solve the immediate problem of inadequate capacity for 1973.

Sales in units of products for the 10 years prior to 1973 were as follows:

Year	Asbestone (Gallons)	Glideze (Pounds)	Heatrap (Square Yards)
1963	2,500,000	500,000	
1964	2,600,000	600,000	
1965	2,704,000	640,000	
1966	2,812,000	695,000	
1967	2,974,000	735,000	200,000
1968	3,191,000	800,000	600,000
1969	3,663,000	850,000	2,000,000
1970	4,040,000	880,000	3,000,000
1971	4,522,000	960,000	4,400,000
1972	5,059,000	1,000,000	6,000,000

Sales for 1973 have been budgeted as shown below:

Asbestone.................... 5,500,000 gals.
Glideze...................... 1,100,000 lbs.
Heatrap...................... 7,200,000 sq. yds.

Standard production cost data for the three products are as follows:

	Asbestone	Glideze	Heatrap
Standard production lot.......	100 gals.	50 lbs.	1,000 sq. yds.
Standard labor hours per lot....	20	25	75
Standard wage rate............	$3.60	$3.60	$3.60
Standard materials cost per lot........................	$504	$80	$140

The flexible budgets for overhead in the two plants are summarized below:

	East Chicago Plant	Gary Plant
Variable rate per direct labor hour.............	$1.20	$1.20
Fixed cost per year......................	$2,000,000	$6,000,000

The annual productive capacity of the East Chicago plant is 500,000 direct labor hours. Capacity in the Gary plant is 1,500,000 direct labor hours. Both of these quantities are also used as normal volumes. Both plants can produce any or all of the three products, although no paint has actually been manufactured in East Chicago since 1958.

Inventories of finished products and work in process at December 31, 1972, are the minimum stocks required for continuous sales and production operations.

The company's income statement for 1972, by products, appeared as follows:

ASBESTONE PAINT COMPANY
Income Statement
For Year Ended December 31, 1972

	Asbestone	Glideze	Heatrap	Total
Sales................	$50,590,000	$10,000,000	$ 3,600,000	$64,190,000
Standard cost of goods sold...............	34,401,200	6,000,000	4,800,000	45,201,200
Gross margin.........	$16,188,800	$ 4,000,000	$(1,200,000)	$18,988,800
Unfavorable overhead volume variance....				$ 152,800
Fixed selling and administrative expenses...				12,336,000
				$12,488,800
Income before tax.....				$ 6,500,000
Income tax (40%).....				2,600,000
Net income.........				$ 3,900,000

Required:

Given the present capacity constraint, what would be the most profitable product mix for the company in 1973? Assume that prices and costs will not change from 1972.

chapter 15

CAPITAL BUDGETING: ANALYSIS OF INVESTMENT DECISIONS

L ONG-TERM investment decisions, often called capital budgeting decisions, involve commitments of capital to specific assets or projects for long periods of time. Once made and implemented, such decisions ordinarily cannot be reversed easily without significant loss of the invested capital.[1] This does not mean that capital budgeting decisions are irreversible, of course; but it does mean that their implications are more extensive than those of the short-term decisions discussed in Chapter 14. Investment decisions typically require fairly long periods of time for their full financial justifications. A simple make-or-buy decision regarding components may be justified by cost savings almost at once. A decision to purchase a building, on the other hand, ordinarily can be justified financially only over a period of many years. The purchase is made in contemplation of continued economic benefits from occupancy of the building throughout a long useful life.

The critical element in an investment decision is time. It is the factor that necessitates analysis by techniques different from those

---

[1] The types of investment decisions discussed here do not include decisions to invest in marketable securities. Since these securities may readily be resold, the investment decision is easily reversed. The possibility of a capital gain or loss still exists, of course.

explained in Chapter 14. The time factor requires financial planning into the fairly distant future, and it entails a long delay before the benefits of the investment are fully realized. The time factor injects the element of interest on the invested capital into the decision. In Chapter 14, we saw that interest is theoretically irrelevant to the short-term decisions considered there.[2] It is not possible to ignore interest in capital budgeting decisions, however. The commitment of capital to specific purposes for long periods entails an interest cost too large to be ignored. Indeed, interest is the crucial difference between the analyses of a long-term investment decision and a short-term decision. The time factor in capital budgeting may also inject a greater degree of uncertainty into the planning process than is usually encountered in annual budgetary planning.

BASIC OBJECTIVE AND APPROACH

Optimum Allocation of Scarce Capital

The basic goal of long-term investment decision making is to maximize the wealth of the investor over the long run. In a business firm, this goal is usually stated as the maximization of long-run profit. In a governmental agency, it would logically be stated as the maximization of public benefits from the available capital resources. Whatever the nature of the organization, it has a limited supply of capital available to it. Therefore, it must attempt to make the best possible use of that capital. Management must invest capital in projects most likely to achieve the basic goal of maximizing wealth. As capital is a scarce economic resource, it has a cost. This cost of capital is expressed as an interest rate.[3] The return from an investment must be at least equal to the cost of the capital invested. Otherwise, the firm would be financially better off if it didn't have the capital at all. The problem of capital investment may be more complicated than simply determining whether individual investment opportunities offer a sufficient return relative to the cost of capital. Frequently, the potentially profitable investment opportunities exceed the capital available for investment. Thus, management must select those investments that are *most* profitable.[4] In general, then, capital budgeting is the analytical process of allocating a firm's scarce capital to the most advantageous possible uses.

---

[2] Page 348.

[3] The determination of the cost of capital was discussed and illustrated in Chapter 8, pages 198–202.

[4] An excess of investment opportunities over available capital defines the condition known as "capital rationing." It is discussed more fully in Chapter 16.

Investment and Financing Decisions

In a broader context, capital budgeting might be thought of as comprising two principal types of decisions. One is the investment decision: How should the available capital be employed? The other is the financing decision: How should the necessary capital be obtained? The former decision is concerned with uses of capital; the latter, with sources of capital. Obviously, there is an important interrelationship between the two decisions. Capital cannot be invested unless it can first be obtained. Conversely, it would be pointless to obtain capital that could not advantageously be invested. Nevertheless, these are two separate and distinct decisions; they are not merely two facets of a single decision. Moreover, these two decisions must be analyzed separately by management. If the investment and financing decisions are combined, serious error may be the result. In this book, we shall be concerned only with the investment decision. Financing decisions are usually considered at great length in business finance courses.

Types of Investments

Before analyzing them, management must understand the natures of the various investment opportunities available and any relationships among them. Some investments are complementary: making one investment either necessitates or, at least, suggests making another. The full benefits will not be obtained unless both are made. In this case, it is desirable (perhaps mandatory) that the two investments be combined into a single package for purposes of managerial analysis. For example, a decision to invest in mineral rights would be pointless (assuming that the rights were not to be held for speculative purposes) unless an investment in mining equipment were also made. Neither investment would produce any benefits unless the other were also made. Thus, there is really only a single investment decision to be made. As another example, a decision to invest in company-owned trucks may suggest a decision to invest also in a company-owned garage for repair and maintenance of the trucks. In this instance, the first investment could be made alone, although it might prove more advantageous if the second were made also. Similarly, the garage alone might offer some benefits; but its full justification depends upon the investment in the trucks.

Some investments are mutually exclusive: acceptance of one necessarily involves rejection of the other(s). For example, if either of two machines would perform a particular manufacturing operation satisfactorily but only one can be used, the decision to buy one automatically entails a decision not to buy the other. Where mutually exclusive investment opportunities exist, they should be identified and dealt with directly.

A choice among the alternatives should be made first, and only then should the best alternative be considered along with other possible investments.

Finally, many investments are essentially independent. No significant interrelationship can be detected. For example, a decision to invest in a computer would appear to be independent of a decision to invest in a company airplane. Either or both investments might be made or rejected without regard to the other. The only relationship that might exist in such a case would arise if the otherwise independent investments were competitors for the firm's limited available capital. In this case, however, rejection of one investment would not be caused by acceptance of the other. Rather, it would be caused by the shortage of capital.

Importance of Cash Flows

Investment decisions should be analyzed in terms of the cash flows directly traceable to them. These cash flows include both receipts and outlays. They should be the *incremental cash flows* that will occur in the future if and only if the particular investment is made. Both the amounts and the timing of these cash flows must be estimated carefully if a sound investment decision is to be made. The natures of these future cash flows will vary. Almost every investment will require some substantial initial cash outlay; this is usually referred to as the amount invested. Subsequent receipts and outlays may differ considerably among investments. For example, a decision to purchase new production machinery may generate cash receipts in the form of reduced out-of-pocket operating costs. Such cash cost savings are, for practical purposes, equivalent to cash receipts. A decision to undertake a long-term promotional program is usually expected to generate cash flows in the form of increased variable profit—the net excess of increased sales receipts over the increased variable expenses of such sales. It is important to identify clearly those cash flows which are directly traceable to a specific investment decision. Some increase in sales and, hence, in variable profit may be anticipated as a normal consequence of a secular growth in demand. This additional variable profit should be separated from that directly attributable to a specific investment, such as a promotional program.

An investment in a new plant or in a plant expansion would entail an initial cash outlay for purchase or construction of the plant. (Actually, if the plant had to be constructed, the "initial" outlay would probably be spread over some period of time, possibly several years. Illustrations and problems in this book will assume that the initial outlay must be made in total immediately.) In addition to the initial outlay, periodic repairs and maintenance would necessitate fairly regular cash outlays throughout the plant's useful life. The principal expected cash receipts from the

investment would be the cash profit realized from sale of products manufactured in the new plant. At the end of the plant's life, there might be
some final cash receipt representing the terminal salvage or scrap value
of the building. While the foregoing cash flows associated with an investment in a plant are those that most readily come to mind, there is
another that may be very significant in a given situation. This is the
investment in incremental working capital required for the operation of
the plant. Plant operations will require, in most cases, an increased investment in inventories of raw material, work in process, and finished
products. They will also necessitate a larger work force and other
supporting activities. In order to finance these increased operations, the
firm may have to increase its total investment in working capital. The
incremental working capital should be included as part of the initial
outlay for the new plant. Of course, at the end of the plant's life, that
incremental investment in working capital would no longer be needed for
the specific plant and it should be included as part of the cash receipt
from terminal salvage value.

Cash Flows and Income Taxes.   For a business enterprise, most cash
receipts and outlays must be analyzed after consideration of their income
tax implications. The relevant cash flows are after-tax cash flows. We
shall continue to assume an income tax rate of 40% on all income. Thus,
taxable cash receipts may be converted to their after-tax amounts by
multiplying them by 60%. (This is equal to the amounts of the cash receipts before tax less the 40% income tax payable.) Similarly, tax deductible cash outlays must be multipled by 60% to determine their after-
tax amounts. Some cash flows have no direct tax effects because of the
provisions of the Internal Revenue Code. These, obviously, have the
same before-tax and after-tax values. It would be possible to treat all
of the tax effects pertinent to an investment decision as a single cash flow.
There are some analytical advantages in relating tax effects to individual
cash flows, however; and this method will be employed consistently here.

Depreciation is a noncash expense and, as such, would not be relevant
to capital budgeting analyses. However, depreciation is also a deductible expense in the computation of taxable income. Thus, although it has
no before-tax cash implications, it does generate after-tax cash receipts
in the form of reduced income tax payments. That is, the cash outlay for
taxes is lower because of the tax deductibility of depreciation. Different
depreciation methods involve different time patterns of these after-tax
cash flows. Accelerated depreciation methods cause higher depreciation
deductions and lower tax payments in the early years of an asset's life
than does the straight-line method. As we shall see, the timing of cash
flows is an important determinant of their significance in the decision-
making process. Consequently, the depreciation method to be used should

be regarded by management as a part of the decision to invest in a depreciable asset. It is not merely a technical accounting matter.

The federal income tax law in the United States is extremely complex. It contains many special provisions that may be applicable to particular investment decisions. Certain gains, for example, are identified as long-term capital gains and currently are taxed at a rate lower than that applicable to ordinary income. The after-tax cash benefits from capital gains, thus, are greater than those from ordinary income of the same amount before tax. Operating losses of one period may be carried over to subsequent periods and offset against operating profits. Thus, tax effects are not always bounded by the limits of a single year. If, for example, a proposed investment in a subsidiary corporation is not expected to be profitable for the first year or two of its existence, the tax savings from the early years' operating losses need not be lost. They may be realized in a later profitable year. For purposes of the discussions, illustrations, and problems in this text, no technical knowledge of the income tax law is assumed. In the absence of any statement to the contrary, the reader may assume simply that all revenues and gains are taxable at 40% and that all expenses and losses are deductible at the same rate. Any special tax considerations pertinent to an illustration or a problem will be explained explicitly. To ignore tax implications altogether in these illustrations would be unrealistic. Tax planning is an integral part of good capital budgeting.

TECHNIQUES OF INVESTMENT ANALYSIS

The mechanical process of analyzing the budgeted cash flows relevant to a particular investment proposal is only part of the total investment decision-making process, but it is an important part. It will be the subject matter of the remainder of this chapter. The assumptions underlying these analytical techniques, as well as their mechanics, should be clearly understood by managers responsible for decision making. Generally, all analytical techniques for capital budgeting may be classified in two broad categories: those that do recognize the time value of money and those that do not. Any technique that does not fall into the first category is thereby deficient. Money does have time value, and any analysis of money flows over extended periods of time that ignores this fundamental fact is consequently invalid. Our discussion will be devoted primarily to valid analytical techniques. We will, however, also consider two methods that ignore the time value of money, simply because these methods are fairly often used in practice. The techniques of analysis to be examined in the sections that follow include the following:

1. Those that recognize the time value of money:
   a) Net present value.
   b) Present value index.
   c) Discounted rate of return.
2. Those that ignore the time value of money:
   a) Payback period.
   b) Simple rate of return.

Before turning to these analytical techniques, however, it is important that we clearly understand the concept of the time value of money. All of the valid methods of investment analysis depend upon this concept.

TIME VALUE OF MONEY

Cash flows have both face values, or dollar values, and time values. Thus, $100 today is not equal to $200 today. This is obvious. Nor is $100 today equal to $100 one year from today. If this does not appear equally obvious, ask whether a rational person would be just as satisfied to wait a year for $100 as to receive the same amount immediately. Clearly, he would prefer to have the money now. If he receives it now, he can invest it to earn interest over the ensuing year. Thus, one year from now he can have the original $100 plus one year's interest on it. If he could earn interest at 10% compounded annually, $100 now could be invested to become $110 one year from now. Thus, $100 today is equal in time value to $110 one year from today at 10% interest. Likewise, $100 one year from today is equal to $90.91 today, because $90.91 plus 10% interest for one year amounts to $100. This is the essence of the time value of money. It is a consequence of the fact that money can be invested to yield a return. Therefore, one would prefer to have a given dollar amount of money sooner rather than later. Conversely, he would be unwilling to exchange a given dollar amount today for the same amount in the future. He would insist upon receiving a larger amount in the future. How much larger that amount would have to be would depend upon the interest rate applicable and the number of years he would have to wait for his money. The value to which $100, invested now at 10% interest compounded annually, will grow at the end of each of the next five years is computed thus:

$$
\begin{array}{lr}
\text{Year 0 (i.e., now)}\dots\dots\dots\dots\dots\dots\dots\dots & \$100.00 \\
\text{Year 1 } [\$100 + .10(\$100)]\dots\dots\dots\dots\dots & 110.00 \\
\text{Year 2 } [\$110 + .10(\$110)]\dots\dots\dots\dots\dots & 121.00 \\
\text{Year 3 } [\$121 + .10(\$121)]\dots\dots\dots\dots\dots & 133.10 \\
\text{Year 4 } [\$133.10 + .10(\$133.10)]\dots\dots\dots\dots & 146.41 \\
\text{Year 5 } [\$146.41 + .10(\$146.41)]\dots\dots\dots\dots & 161.05 \\
\end{array}
$$

These same values could be computed from the following more compact formula:

$$F = \$100(1 + .10)^n$$

where F is the value to which $100 will grow at the end of n years at 10% interest. Obviously, any values for the initial dollar amount and the interest rate could be substituted for $100 and 10%.

In the tabulation above, all of the end-of-year values shown are equal insofar as time value is concerned. However, no two of them are directly comparable at any single moment in time, for each is expressed at a different time. One of the problems of capital budgeting is to express cash flows that will occur at various times in a common time dimension. This is done by converting all of these cash flows to their values at the same point in time. Mathematically, any point in time might be chosen. Thus, all six of the figures above are equal to $100 at year 0, to $110 at year 1, to $121 at year 2, etc. While any point in time might be used, logically one should use the point in time at which he must make a decision—that is, the present time. Thus, all of the cash flows would be stated in terms of their value at year 0, which is a common way of identifying the present time in capital budgeting analyses. Of course, all of the dollar amounts in the tabulation above have a present value equal to $100, so long as the appropriate interest rate is 10%. The process of converting a future cash flow to its present value by use of an interest rate is called *discounting*, and the resultant present value is frequently referred to as a *discounted present value*. The interest rate used may also be referred to as the *discount rate*.

Discounting future cash flows to their present values is essential in any analytical technique that properly recognizes the time value of money. It may be done by solving the appropriate present value formula, or it may be done by reference to published tables of present values, such as those in Appendix A to this book. The use of tables is a much easier alternative, for the present value formulas have already been solved for a large number of cases. The reader not already familiar with tables of present values is advised to read the introductory comments preceding the tables in Appendix A. These tables contain present values of $1. These may be converted to the present value of any given cash flow by multiplying the amount of that cash flow by the appropriate present value of $1. Hence, the tabulated present values are frequently referred to as *present value factors*. Note that there are three different tables for three distinct types of cash flows. A cash flow may occur only once in a lump sum at the end of some future period. Present values of such cash flows are found in Table A–3. A cash flow may also occur in a uniform stream throughout a single future period. For example, a total of $100,000 might be received or paid in small regular installments during one future year. The present value of such a cash flow would be found in Table A–2. Finally, a cash flow might occur in a uniform stream throughout each of several successive future years. Such a cash flow is commonly called an annuity. The same amount is received or paid each period. Present value factors for annuities are found in Table A–1.

TECHNIQUES THAT RECOGNIZE THE TIME VALUE OF MONEY

As was stated earlier, any valid method of analysis for purposes of investment decision making must recognize the time value of money. We shall discuss and illustrate three generally valid methods for investment analysis. Each of these methods deals with the present values of all of the cash flows relevant to an investment proposal. The only basic differences among them is in the interest rate used to discount cash flows to their present values. Both of the first two methods presented use the same predefined discount rate; hence, they are really two variations of a single basic method. The third method uses an unknown discount rate that must be determined in the analytical process.

Net Present Value

The net present value of an investment is the difference between the present value of the budgeted cash receipts and the present value of the budgeted cash outlays directly traceable to the investment. If the net present value is positive (i.e., the present value of the receipts exceeds that of the outlays), the investment is profitable. If the net present value is negative (i.e., the present value of the receipts is less than that of the outlays), the investment is unprofitable. All future cash flows relevant to the investment are discounted to their present values by use of an interest rate equal to the enterprise's weighted average cost of capital.[5] This cost of capital is the logical discount rate to use, for it is the break-even rate for long-term investments. That is, the interest rate earned on invested capital must equal the average interest cost of that capital if the firm is to break even on its investments. If the net present value of an investment is exactly equal to zero when the cost of capital is used as the discount rate, that is a break-even investment. The interest rate earned on it is exactly equal to the cost of capital. If the net present value is positive, the investment is profitable; and the interest rate earned on it is greater than the cost of capital.

The mechanics of computing the net present value of an investment proposal are quite simple when tables of present values are used. We shall illustrate this computation first for a very simple investment. An investor has the opportunity to purchase a truck now at a cost of $16,000.

---

[5] See Chapter 8, pages 201–2, for an explanation of the weighted average cost of capital.

This truck would have a useful life of five years. It could be used to haul cargo and earn annual cash revenues of $10,000. The annual out-of-pocket costs of operating the truck would be $3,700. Thus, the principal cash receipt from operation of the truck would be a net $6,300 each year for five years. For income tax purposes, the investor would depreciate this truck by the straight-line method (i.e., $3,200 of depreciation would be deductible each year). His income tax rate is 40%. Therefore, the net receipts from operation would be reduced by 40% from $6,300 to $3,780 after tax. However, the investor would save income taxes each year in an amount equal to the annual depreciation deduction ($3,200) multiplied by the income tax rate (40%). This $1,280 annual tax saving is also an

TABLE 15–1

Analysis of Proposed Investment in Truck

	Cash Flow before Tax	Tax Effect	Cash Flow after Tax	Present Value Factor at 10%		Present Value
				Table	Factor	
Cash receipts:						
Annual net cash receipts from operations..............	$ 6,300	$(2,520)	$ 3,780	A–1	3.9347	$ 14,873
Tax saving from depreciation...	—	1,280	1,280	A–1	3.9347	5,036
						$ 19,909
Cash outlay:						
Purchase of truck.............	(16,000)		(16,000)			(16,000)
Net present value..............						$ 3,909

after-tax cash receipt. The tax saving derived from depreciation is commonly referred to as the *depreciation tax shield*. Finally, this investor's weighted average cost of capital is 10%.

The proposed investment in this truck is analyzed in Table 15–1. Each cash flow is discounted to its present value by using the appropriate factor from the 10% column of the tables in Appendix A. In this illustration, the only present value factor used is 3.9347, the present value of a five-year annuity of $1 at 10%. Since the initial outlay to purchase the truck would be made at the present time, its present value is equal to its face value. No discounting is required. Alternatively, we might say that the present value factor applicable to a present cash flow is always 1.0000, regardless of the discount rate used. In Table 15–1 and in subsequent illustrations, cash receipts are shown as positive cash flows and cash outlays or reductions in cash receipts are shown as negative cash flows. Negative flows are enclosed in parentheses. Note that the tax saving from depreciation is a cash flow only after tax; before tax, it is a noncash expense. Note also that the cash outlay for purchase of the truck has no direct tax effect. In fact, the tax effect of this purchase is the tax saving from depreciation of the truck. This tax effect cannot be combined directly with the purchase, however, because the timing of the two cash flows is not the same. Cash flows may legitimately be combined only if they have the same timing. In this illustration, thus, the two cash receipts might have been added together *after tax* and discounted by one multiplication instead of two. Note carefully, however, that these two items are totally dissimilar before consideration of their tax effects. Finally, it would be equally correct to include the operating revenues of $10,000 as receipts and the operating expenses of $3,700 separately as outlays instead of using only the net receipts of $6,300. This alternative would increase the present values of the receipts and of the outlays by the same amount. Hence, the net present value would remain exactly the same— $3,909. It is unlikely that such additional detail would improve the analysis in any way, and it would involve slightly more work.

Confusion sometimes arises as to the correct use of the income tax rate in determining after-tax cash flows. As may be seen in Table 15–1, an item that is a before-tax cash flow and is directly taxable (a receipt) or tax deductible (an outlay) is reduced by the product of itself multiplied by the tax rate. The remainder is the amount of the after-tax cash flow, and it is equal to the before-tax cash flow multiplied by the complement of the tax rate. An item such as depreciation, that is not a cash flow at all before tax, is also multiplied by the tax rate to compute its tax effect. In this case, however, that tax effect *is* the after-tax cash flow. Thus, two general rules may be followed in determining after-tax cash flows. *If an item is a cash flow before tax, multiply it by one minus the tax rate to determine its after-tax amount. If an item is not a cash flow before tax, multiply it by the tax rate to determine its after-tax amount.*

A somewhat more complex illustration of the net present value method is presented in Table 15–2. The pertinent facts in this example are as follows: A corporation has an opportunity to purchase a laborsaving machine now at a cost of $110,000. The machine would have a useful life of eight years, at the end of which time it could be sold for a salvage value of $10,000. For tax purposes, the machine would be depreciated by the straight-line method. In order to keep the machine running properly, its motor and gears would have to be replaced at the end of the fourth year of its life. This replacement would cost $20,000 and would be deductible at that time for tax purposes. Use of the machine would save labor costs each year, but the amount of these cost savings would not be the same each year. The annual cost savings are estimated thus:

First four years (years 1–4).............	$20,000
Next three years (years 5–7)............	25,000
Last year (year 8)....................	18,000

TABLE 15-2

Analysis of Proposed Investment in Labor-Saving Machine

	Cash Flow before Tax	Tax Effect	Cash Flow after Tax	Present Value Factor at 10%		Present Value
				Table	Factor	
Cash receipts:						
Annual labor cost savings:						
Years 1–4.........	$ 20,000	$ (8,000)	$ 12,000	A–1	3.2968	$ 39,562
Years 5–7.........	25,000	(10,000)	15,000	A–1	1.7374	26,061
Year 8............	18,000	(7,200)	10,800	A–2	.4726	5,104
Tax saving from depreciation.......	—	5,000	5,000	A–1	5.5068	27,534
Terminal salvage value............	10,000		10,000	A–3	.4493	4,493
						$ 102,754
Cash outlays:						
Purchase of machine..	(110,000)		(110,000)			$(110,000)
Replacement of motor and gears........	(20,000)	8,000	(12,000)	A–3	.6703	(8,044)
						$(118,044)
Net present value (negative)...........						$ (15,290)

While such a pattern may not be typical of most investment proposals, it will serve to illustrate the mechanical flexibility of the net present value method. The corporation's weighted average cost of capital is 10%. The applicable income tax rate is again assumed to be 40%.

A line-by-line examination of Table 15–2 will show how each of the various cash flows pertinent to this investment proposal is discounted to its present value. The principal cash receipt from the investment in this machine is the saving of annual labor cost. This cost saving is not received in a uniform annuity over the entire eight-year life of the machine, however. Hence, the cost savings must be discounted in three separate steps. The $20,000 that will be saved in each of the first four years constitutes a four-year annuity. After adjusting for the tax effect, the after-tax saving is discounted by the present value factor from the 10% column and the four-year row of Table A–1. The $25,000 cost saving in each of the next three years is also an annuity. However, it is a three-year annuity that will not commence for four years. It cannot be discounted by the three-year factor in Table A–1, because that factor is for a three-year annuity beginning at once. The proper discount factor must be computed by subtracting the four-year factor (3.2968) from the seven-year factor (5.0342). The remainder (1.7374) is the factor for

the intervening three years, that is, the years 5, 6, and 7. Since these
are the years in which the $25,000 annual saving will be realized, this
remainder is the appropriate discount factor.[6] Finally, the cost saving
in the last year occurs in a uniform stream throughout only one year.
The present value factor for such a cash flow is found in Table A–2 in the
10% column on the eight-year row. This factor is then multiplied by the
after-tax amount of the cash flow as in the previous instances.

Straight-line depreciation is handled in exactly the same way as in
the preceding illustration. Annual depreciation expense is $12,500 (the
difference between the $110,000 cost and the $10,000 salvage value divided
by the eight-year life of the machine). As this amount is tax deductible
at a rate of 40%, it produces an after-tax cash flow of $5,000 per year for
eight years. This eight-year annuity is discounted to its present value by
the eight-year factor in the 10% column of Table A–1. The terminal
salvage value is a lump-sum cash receipt at the end of the eighth year.
Hence, it is discounted by the eight-year, 10% factor from Table A–3.
This salvage value constitutes recovery of that portion of the cost of the
machine not earlier charged to depreciation. Hence, so long as no more
nor less than $10,000 is expected to be received, there will be no gain or
loss on final disposition of the asset. Consequently, the terminal salvage
value has no tax effect.

The initial outlay for the purchase of the machine has a present value
equal to its face value, for there is no time delay in its incurrence. Its
tax effect has already been handled separately in the tax saving from
depreciation. The outlay for replacement of the motor and gears at the
end of the fourth year will be tax deductible in that year. Hence, the
after-tax cash flow will be only $12,000. This is discounted by multiply-
ing it by the present value factor for the fourth year in the 10% column
of Table A–3. Since the present value of all outlays exceeds that of all
receipts, the net present value is negative. At a cost of capital of 10%,
the proposed investment in the machine would not be profitable.

Present Value Index

The present value index is simply a variation of the net present value
method. It is the ratio of the present value of cash receipts to the present

---

[6] This same factor may be computed by taking the three-year factor from Table
A–1 and multiplying it by the four-year factor from Table A–3. In essence, this approach says that there is a three-year annuity that has a present value factor of
2.5918 (from Table A–1). This present value will not exist until the end of the
fourth year in the future, however. Hence, it is discounted by the present value
factor for a lump sum at the end of four years—.6703 (from Table A–3). This produces the same result as that obtained by subtraction in Table A–1: 2.5918 × .6703 =
1.7373. The trivial difference is due to rounding. This approach is a bit more cumber-
some, for it involves two tables instead of one and multiplication instead of subtraction.

value of cash outlays. The appropriate discount rate is still the weighted average cost of capital. If the present value index is less than 1.00, the investment is unprofitable; if it is greater than 1.00, the investment is profitable. This is consistent with the results of the net present value method, for the index could be less than 1.00 only if the net present value were negative. Similarly, an index of more than 1.00 follows from a positive net present value. An index of exactly 1.00 and a net present value of zero would be compatible and would indicate a break-even investment.

The present value index for the proposed investment in a truck (Table 15–1) is computed as follows:

$$\text{Present value index} = \frac{\text{Present value of cash receipts}}{\text{Present value of cash outlays}} = \frac{\$19,909}{\$16,000} = 1.24$$

The index for the investment in a laborsaving machine (Table 15–2) is calculated in the same way:

$$\text{Present value index} = \frac{\text{Present value of cash receipts}}{\text{Present value of cash outlays}} = \frac{\$102,754}{\$118,044} = .87$$

This index is sometimes referred to as a *discounted benefit/cost ratio*, since it is a ratio of the discounted cash receipts (benefits) to the discounted cash outlays (costs).

In connection with the example of the investment in a truck, we noted previously that cash flows having the same time dimension could be combined or handled separately with no change in the net present value. The operating revenue of $10,000 could have been treated as a cash receipt each year, and the out-of-pocket operating expenses of $3,700, as an annual cash outlay instead of combining them into a single net cash receipt of $6,300. This alternative would have increased the present values of both the cash receipts and the cash outlays by the same amount. Hence, the net present value would be unchanged. The present value index, however, would be different under this approach. This effect may be seen by recomputing the net present value in Table 15–1 as shown in Table 15–3, with cash flows shown initially at their after-tax amounts. This net present value is identical to the one determined in Table 15–1. However, the present value index computed from these data is lower than the one originally computed.

$$\text{Present value index} = \frac{\text{Present value of cash receipts}}{\text{Present value of cash outlays}} = \frac{\$28,644}{\$24,735} = 1.16$$

Obviously, an alternative method of processing exactly the same basic data cannot really reduce the profitability of an investment. It is simply a characteristic of a ratio that its value is affected by the absolute magnitude of the two variables (the present values of the cash receipts

TABLE 15-3

	Cash Flow after Tax	Present Value Factor at 10% Table	Factor	Present Value
Cash receipts:				
Annual revenue............	$ 6,000	A-1	3.9347	$ 23,608
Tax saving from depreciation............	1,280	A-1	3.9347	5,036
				$ 28,644
Cash outlays:				
Annual expenses..........	(2,220)	A-1	3.9347	$ (8,735)
Purchase of truck.........	(16,000)			(16,000)
				$(24,735)
Net present value...........				$ 3,909

and outlays here), even though the absolute difference between them (the net present value here) remains the same. As a practical matter, the present value index is most accurate and useful when all of the cash flows that may legitimately be combined (that is, all that have the same timing) are combined. Thus, the proper index for the truck investment is 1.24, as originally calculated from the data in Table 15–1.[7]

Discounted Rate of Return

The discounted rate of return on an investment is the true interest rate earned on that investment over the course of its economic life. It is a *discounted* rate of return because it specifically provides for the time

---

[7] The superiority of the alternative that combines, or nets, all cash flows having the same timing may be seen from a comparison of two very simple investment proposals. Both have three-year lives and both require initial outlays of $40. Investment A will produce annual cash revenues of $250 and will require annual cash expenses of $225. Investment B will generate annual cash revenues of $100 and entail annual cash expenses of $80. (All of these dollar amounts are already stated after taxes.) It is already evident that investment A is more attractive, for it returns $5 more each year with no difference in the initial outlay. If both investments are discounted at 10%, the preference for investment A still appears. It has a net present value of $25, while investment B's net present value is only $12. This same ranking appears when the present value indexes are calculated from the net cash flows (i.e., $25 per year for A and $20 per year for B). The index for investment A is then 1.63, while that for investment B is 1.30. However, if the gross cash receipts and outlays are used in calculating the indexes, the ranking of the two investments is reversed. Investment A has an index of 1.04; and investment B, 1.05. Clearly, this second approach cannot be correct, for investment A is unquestionably superior. Of course, this particular pair of alternatives cannot be considered typical. One would not ordinarily expect two investments of the same initial outlay to produce such widely differing annual receipts and outlays. Nevertheless, the fact that a fallacious ranking *can* occur when the present value index is computed without first combining time-comparable cash flows is sufficient basis for using the other approach.

value of money. This same measure is sometimes referred to as the *effective yield* of an investment. Economists usually refer to it as the *internal rate of return* on an investment. By whatever name, it is an interest rate determined from an analysis of all of the cash flows relevant to an investment proposal and their timings. Operationally, the discounted rate of return is that interest rate which, when used to discount all cash flows pertinent to an investment, will equate the present value of the cash receipts to the present value of the cash outlays. In other words, it is that discount rate that will cause the net present value of an investment to be equal to zero. While the calculation of the discounted rate of return does not involve the average cost of capital, any evaluation of its significance must. If the discounted rate of return is greater than the cost of capital, the investment is profitable. If the discounted rate of return is lower than the cost of capital, the investment is unprofitable. Thus, the cost of capital is just as important in this method as in the net present value and the present index methods. The difference is that it enters the analysis after the mechanics of computation are completed rather than as a part of those mechanics.

The procedure for computing the discounted rate of return is essentially the same as that for the net present value. All of the cash flows pertinent to an investment proposal are discounted to their present value. The interest rate used as the discount rate is not specified in advance, however. Rather, it is an unknown rate that will cause the net present value to be zero. Thus, the procedure usually involves several trial-and-error discountings of the cash flows with successive guesses at the appropriate discount rate. When the net present value is equal to zero, the correct rate has been found. As a practical matter, it is sufficient to find a rate that will make the net present value of the investment almost equal to zero. This rate is then taken as a satisfactory approximation of the discounted rate of return.

We shall illustrate this trial-and-error procedure for the proposed investment in a laborsaving machine (Table 15–2). We have already seen that the investment has a negative net present value when its cash flows are discounted at the 10% cost of capital. Consequently, we know that the discounted rate of return must be less than 10%. It may be found by repeating the discounting procedure at interest rates lower than 10% until we find one that produces a net present value equal or close to zero. Suppose we guess that the appropriate discount rate is 7%. After discounting all of the after-tax cash flows in Table 15–2 at 7%, we find that there is a negative net present value of −$3,797. This tells us that the correct rate of return is still lower than 7%. If we next discount all of the relevant cash flows at 6%, we find a positive net present value of $474. Thus, the correct rate must be higher than 6%. As a practical matter, knowing that the discounted rate of return is between 6% and 7%

should be sufficiently precise for purposes of decision making. We have straddled the true rate and defined a range of only one percentage point within which it falls. Further, since the positive net present value at 6% is much smaller than the negative value at 7%, we may say that the discounted rate of return in approximately 6%.[8]

Of course, there is no guarantee that the trial-and-error process will take us so quickly to the rate we seek. Particularly for a very complex investment proposal, many iterations of the process might be required before we found the discounted rate of return. While the tedium of repeated discounting may once legitimately have been considered a disadvantage of this method, it no longer is. The trial-and-error approach can be programmed for a fast and accurate computer solution.

For certain investments, the discounted rate of return can be determined very easily by reference to tables of present values. If the cash flows associated with an investment can be reduced to cash receipts in the form of an annuity of uniform value over the life of the project and cash outlays in a lump sum at the beginning of the project's life, the discounted rate of return can be found directly in Table A–1 after one simple computation. Fortunately, quite a number of investment proposals typically are of this type. The proposed investment in a truck (Table 15–1) is an example. Both of the two items of cash receipts are uniform-value annuities after taxes. Thus, they may be combined into a single after-tax annuity of $5,060 per year for five years. The only cash outlay, $16,000, occurs at the beginning of the life of the investment, that is, at the present. Remember that, when the discounted rate of return is used to discount all cash flows to their present values, it will make the present value of the receipts equal to the present value of the outlays. Since the outlays all occur at the present time in our example, their present value is equal to their face value regardless of the discount rate used. Thus, our problem is to find some interest rate that will equate a five-year annuity of $5,060 to a present value of $16,000. If we had a table of present values of an annuity of $5,060, we would only have to find $16,000 in the five-year row to determine the rate of return. Of course, we have a table of present values of an annuity of $1 only. Thus, we must divide both the annuity and the initial outlay, which is the present value of the annuity, by $5,060. The same discount rate that will equate $5,060 per year for five years to $16,000 will equate $1 per year for five years to $3.16. In the five-year row of Table A–1, we find the factor 3.1605 in the 20% column. This factor is so close to 3.16 that we may accept 20% as the discounted rate of return on the proposed investment in the truck.

---

[8] By interpolation between 6% and 7% (cf., Appendix A), we can determine that the discounted rate of return is 6.11%. So precise a result from the discounting of estimated future cash flows is not really very meaningful, however.

Critical Evaluation of Methods

All three of the analytical techniques discussed in the preceding sections are conceptually valid and complete methods of analyzing capital investment proposals. All explicitly recognize the time value of money; hence, they are sometimes described collectively as discounted cash flow methods. All three indicate whether the investment would be profitable, with the average cost of capital used as the criterion for profitability. That is, the investment must yield a return greater than the cost of capital in order to be considered profitable. The net present value and the present value index methods incorporate the cost of capital directly in their calculations, while the discounted rate of return is compared to the cost of capital. There are some differences among these techniques, however, and also some potential difficulties in the use of any one of them.

The discount rate used in the net present value method and in the present value index method is the firm's cost of capital. The discount rate used in computing the discounted rate of return is that rate of return itself. This distinction is the source of a substantive difference. All three methods entail the implicit assumption that cash receipts from an investment are immediately reinvested in some project to yield a rate of return equal to the discount rate used in the basic analysis. Thus, the first two methods assume that cash receipts will be reinvested to yield a rate of return equal to the cost of capital. The discounted rate of return method, on the other hand, assumes that those cash receipts will be reinvested to earn the same rate of return as that calculated for the original investment. For example, the proposed investment in a truck (Table 15–1) has a net present value of $3,909 and a present value index of 1.24, when the cash flows are discounted at 10%, only so long as the cash receipts can be reinvested to earn 10%. Similarly, the discounted rate of return on this investment is 20% only if the cash receipts can be reinvested to earn 20%. If it appears that one or the other of these alternative reinvestment assumptions is more realistic, there is a logical argument for using an analytical technique that involves the better reinvestment assumption. Unfortunately, it is seldom practicable to make a reliable forecast of reinvestment opportunities several years in the future. Hence, reinvestment plans are not typically included in investment analyses in any explicit fashion. Thus, management might decide that the best implicit assumption is that the rate of return available on current investments will also be available in the future. Alternatively, management might prefer the more conservative assumption that cash receipts can be reinvested to earn no more than the cost of capital. Whichever method of analysis is chosen, its implicit reinvestment assumption should be recognized.

The discounted rate of return method suffers a technical shortcoming that does not afflict the other two methods. The net cash flow associated with an investment in any single period is either positive (a net cash receipt) or negative (a net cash outlay). In a simple situation, the net cash flow is negatively only at the present, the time of the initial outlay. Subsequently, the net cash flow is consistently positive, even though it may fluctuate somewhat in amount. In this simple case, the algebraic sign of the successive net cash flows over time changes only once; it is negative at the outset and then positive in all future periods. If the sign of the net cash flows in successive periods changes more than once, the discounted rate of return may be indeterminate. There *may be* (but not necessarily *will be*) as many rates of return as there are sign changes.[9] Each of these rates would equate the present value of total cash receipts with that of total cash outlays. Obviously, such a solution to the analysis of the investment proposal is not satisfactory. While multiple rates of return may be mathematically meaningful, only one rate is economically significant in determining whether an investment is profitable. As a matter of fact, if an adequate analysis of the multiple rates of return is made, one of them may be identified as the relevant one for purposes of investment decision making.[10] Fortunately, the majority of business investment proposals fit into the simpler case that produces a single, determinate discounted rate of return. Thus, the multiple-rate-of-return situation is not typical. It ought not be ignored, however; for when it occurs, its effect may be very important to the investment analysis. This problem has led many writers to reject the discounted rate of return as a generally useful technique of investment analysis.

On a very pragmatic plane, the net present value and present value index offer an advantage of simplicity. These methods require only one discounting of the cash flows relevant to an investment. As was demonstrated above, the determination of the discounted rate of return, except in very simple cases, is a trial-and-error procedure that might entail several discountings until the appropriate rate is found. While this is not a real problem for a manager with access to computing equipment, it may be a genuine consideration for the harried student who must rely on nothing more powerful than a slide rule. The problems at the end of this chapter and the next can be solved by any of the methods discussed here. The student who does not have access to a computer (a regrettable circumstance that, hopefully, will be rectified in the near future) will find them solved more quickly in most cases by use of the net present value or the present value index.

The discounted rate of return does have one practical advantage of

---

[9] This phenomenon is an illustration of Descartes' rule of signs.

[10] An analysis to resolve the problem of multiple rates of return is described in G. David Quirin, *The Capital Expenditure Decision* (Homewood, Ill.: Richard D. Irwin, Inc., 1967), pp. 49–55.

its own. It is stated as an interest rate, a very familiar concept to business-men and to investors generally. The other two methods, while equally valid, present their results in less familiar forms. Of course, as these methods become more widely understood and used, this problem of un-familiarity should disappear.

TECHNIQUES THAT IGNORE THE TIME VALUE OF MONEY

As was stated earlier, any technique for analyzing investments is defective if it fails to consider the time value of money. The two methods discussed below are included here only because they are used with some degree of frequency in practice. Neither, however, may be relied upon to provide an indication of an investment's true profit potential.

Payback Period

The payback period of a proposed investment is the length of time required for the net cash receipts from the investment to equal, in total, the amount of the initial outlay. It is often described as the time re-quired for an investment to pay for itself. The basic premise of this technique is that, other things being equal, an investment that will pay for itself soon is better than one that will require a long time before the initial outlay is recovered. The payback is expressed in units of time, usually years. The customary formula for its computation is as follows:

$$\text{Payback period} = \frac{\text{Initial outlay}}{\text{Average annual net cash receipts}}$$

By this formula, the payback period for the proposed investment in a truck (Table 15–1) would be computed thus:

$$\text{Payback period} = \frac{\$16,000 \text{ initial outlay}}{\$5,060 \text{ annually}} = 3.16 \text{ years}$$

Since this period is less than the five-year life of the truck, one might be tempted to conclude that the investment would be profitable. As it hap-pens, we know that this investment is profitable; but we cannot safely conclude that simply from the payback period.

The formula above is not appropriate in determining the payback period of the investment in a laborsaving machine (Table 15–2). In this case, the annual cash receipts vary considerably over time. Also, there is an additional cash outlay four years after the initial outlay. Hence, the payback period must be determined by accumulating positive and negative cash flows sequentially until the algebraic sum of all of them is exactly zero. This is done in the chronological analysis of the cash flows relevant to the laborsaving machine shown in Table 15–4. The positive

TABLE 15–4

	Cash Flow	Cumulative Sum
Present...........................	$−110,000	$−110,000
First year........................	17,000	−93,000
Second year......................	17,000	−76,000
Third year.......................	17,000	−59,000
Fourth year......................	17,000	−42,000
End of fourth year................	−12,000	−54,000
Fifth year........................	20,000	−34,000
Sixth year.......................	20,000	−14,000
First 7/10 of seventh year..........	14,000	0

cash flows for all years include the sum of the after-tax labor cost savings plus the tax saving from depreciation. Assuming that the $20,000 to be received during the seventh year is received in a uniform stream, $14,000 will have been received after seven tenths of the year is over. Thus, the payback period would be 6.7 years. This is shorter than the machine's life of eight years, but it does not indicate that the investment is profitable. We have already seen that, at a cost of capital of 10%, this is an unprofitable investment. The problem, of course, is that the payback computations ignore the very important fact that future cash receipts cannot validly be compared with an initial outlay until they have been discounted to their present values.

The payback period could be made a valid indicator of the time required for an investment to pay for itself, if all cash flows were discounted to their present values. This is seldom done, however. Even if it were done, the payback period would not be a complete measure of an investment's profitability. It could only indicate *whether* the investment was profitable, not *how profitable* it was. For example, an investment calling for an initial outlay of $1,000 and having annual cash receipts of $300 for five years would have exactly the same payback period as an investment of $1,000 initially with annual cash receipts of $300 for 10 years. Yet, the latter investment, with its longer life, is obviously preferable. The payback period, however, even if computed from present values, would not show the advantage of the second investment. The net present value, present value index, and discounted rate of return methods all would show the greater profitability of the longer lived investment.

Simple Rate of Return

The simple, or undiscounted, rate of return is often called the financial statement method of computing a rate of return because it uses the type of data found in the conventional balance sheet and income statement. Unlike any of the methods discussed previously, it does not deal only with cash flows. Rather, it divides the estimated average annual net income (or contribution to net income) from an investment by the initial outlay for that investment. If the investment involves the purchase of a depreciable asset, depreciation is deducted from operating revenues along with cash operating expenses to determine net income. While this treatment of depreciation is entirely appropriate in the determination of periodic net income after it has been earned, it is incorrect in a forecast of future benefits from an investment. The simple rate of return on the proposed investment in a truck (Table 15–1) is computed below:

Annual revenue from operations.............		$10,000
Annual cash operating expenses.............	$3,700	
Annual depreciation......................	3,200	6,900
Income before tax.......................		$ 3,100
Income tax at 40%.......................		1,240
Annual net income.......................		$ 1,860
Divided by initial outlay.................		16,000
Simple rate of return ($1,860 ÷ $16,000)....		11.6%

This result is significantly below the true (discounted) rate of return of 20%.

In an alternative method of computing the simple rate of return, the annual net income is divided by the average investment rather than the initial outlay. The average investment is defined as the unrecovered portion of the initial investment that remains at the midpoint of the life of the investment. It is computed by taking one half of the sum of the initial outlay plus the terminal salvage value. In cases such as the investment in a truck, where there is no terminal salvage value, the average investment is simply one half of the initial outlay. Thus, the simple rate of return on the average investment in the truck is 23.2% ($1,860 ÷ $8,000). This is still not the same as the discounted rate of return.

Possibly one attraction of the financial statement method of computing a rate of return is that it conforms to the methodology used in computing the rate of return on the investment in assets in a company for a fiscal period.[11] There is no reason, however, why the computation of the rate of return in prospect on a proposed investment over its entire life should be the same as the computation of the rate of return in retrospect for a firm or a part of a firm during a single period. These two distinct rates of return are conceptually different. They are designed to serve different purposes, and it is entirely proper that they are computed in different ways. The discounted rate of return on an investment proposal is the interest rate earned on that investment *over its entire life*. There is nothing in the method that implies that the same rate is earned *in each year* of that life.

---

[11] This after-the-fact rate of return will be discussed in Chapter 18.

QUESTIONS FOR DISCUSSION

1. What are the distinctive characteristics of an investment decision as contrasted with a short-term decision of the type discussed in Chapter 14?

2. This chapter is concerned almost entirely with the financial analysis of long-term investment decisions confronting business managers. While financial analysis is indispensable to an intelligent decision, it is not the sum and substance of the decision-making process. What other factors are relevant to the decision? Have these factors any financial implications? If so, why are they not incorporated in the formal financial analysis? If not, how should they be analyzed in the decision-making process?

3. Are the principles of capital budgeting discussed in this chapter relevant to governmental and other nonprofit organizations as well as to business firms? Discuss.

4. Discuss the relevance of each of the following expenses commonly appearing in corporate income statements to the financial analysis of an investment decision:
   a)   Depreciation
   b)   Interest
   c)   Income taxes

5. Why does money have time value? Is present value the same as time value? Explain.

6. Define the net present value of an investment in a way that should be clear to a reasonably informed layman (i.e., one who is not an accountant nor an expert in financial matters).

7. Why is the discounted rate of return preferable to the simple rate of return on an investment proposal?

8. What are some of the practical disadvantages in using the discounted rate of return as a method of evaluating capital investments?

9. Is it a safe generalization to say that any investment having a payback period shorter than its economic life is profitable? Why or why not? Is it a safe generalization to say that any investment with a payback period longer than its economic life is unprofitable? Why or why not?

10. Of what general utility is the payback period in capital investment analysis?

11. What are some of the advantages and disadvantages of the present value index as compared with the net present value?

12. What do the net present value, the present value index, and the discounted rate of return all have in common?

13. Your rich uncle has an opportunity to purchase for $100,000 a small retail store that will produce an annual net income after taxes of $10,000. He plans to make this investment, as it will yield a rate of return of 10% on his capital and, in his own words, "that beats government bonds." Criticize your uncle's analysis of this investment opportunity.

14. A friend of yours is planning to start his own business. He will have to purchase a store building, display counters, other furnishings, and an inventory. In talking with you about his plans, he mentions that he is fortunate

in not having to worry about interest because all of the money he invests will be his own savings, which are now on deposit in his checking account. How would you react to this observation?

PROBLEMS

1. Following are the basic financial data pertinent to three independent investment opportunities:

> Wholesale distributorship:
> | | |
> |---|---|
> | Initial cash outlay................................ | $180,000 |
> | Annual cash receipts............................. | 25,000 |
> | Economic life...................................... | 15 years |
> | Cost of capital.................................... | 8% |
>
> Diamond mine:
> | | |
> |---|---|
> | Initial cash outlay................................ | $500,000 |
> | Annual cash receipts............................. | 150,000 |
> | Economic life...................................... | 6 years |
> | Cost of capital.................................... | 15% |
>
> Farm:
> | | |
> |---|---|
> | Initial cash outlay................................ | $300,000 |
> | Annual cash receipts............................. | 30,000 |
> | Terminal cash salvage value.................... | 100,000 |
> | Economic life...................................... | 20 years |
> | Cost of capital.................................... | 10% |

Required:

Compute the net present value of each of these investments.

2. The basic financial facts pertinent to five independent investment proposals are outlined below:

> Investment A:
> | | |
> |---|---|
> | Initial outlay..................................... | $ 600,000 |
> | Annual cash receipts............................. | 110,000 |
> | Life... | 10 years |
> | Cost of capital.................................... | 10% |
>
> Investment B:
> | | |
> |---|---|
> | Initial outlay..................................... | $ 50,000 |
> | Annual cash receipts............................. | 8,000 |
> | Terminal salvage value.......................... | 10,000 |
> | Life... | 15 years |
> | Cost of capital.................................... | 12% |
>
> Investment C:
> | | |
> |---|---|
> | Cost of capital.................................... | 15% |
> | Life... | 15 years |
> | Annual cash receipts: | |
> | First five years................................ | $ 100,000 |
> | Next five years................................. | 200,000 |
> | Last five years................................. | 150,000 |
> | Terminal salvage value.......................... | 200,000 |
> | Initial outlay.................................... | 1,000,000 |

Investment D:
Annual cash receipts:
  First year............................   30,000
  Second year...........................   60,000
  Last 23 years.........................   100,000
Life.....................................   25 years
Initial outlay........................... $ 500,000
Outlay at end of 8 years.................   200,000
Outlay at end of 16 years................   300,000
Cost of capital..........................   9%

Investment E:
Initial cash receipt..................... $ 400,000
Annual cash outlay.......................   75,000
Cost of capital..........................   11%
Life.....................................   7 years

Required:

Compute the net present value of each of these five investments.

3. An investment proposal promises to yield $25,000 in cash annually for a period of 12 years and requires an initial investment of $95,000.

Required:

Determine the discounted rate of return on this investment.

4. An investment of $500,000 today promises to return net cash proceeds after taxes of $70,000 per year for the next 20 years.

Required:

What is the discounted rate of return on this investment?

5. An investor whose cost of capital is 8% has an opportunity to purchase a 20-year mortgage note that provides for monthly payments of $650 over the entire term of the note.

Required:

What is the maximum amount that the investor could pay for this mortgage note without suffering a loss on his investment?

6. The U.S. Coast and Geodetic Survey has been leasing the land for its Furnace Creek Testing Grounds. The lease has five more years to run at the current annual rental of $100,000. A development company has recently purchased this land and has advised the government that it plans to construct a retirement community on it after 10 years. Hence, the new owner would be willing to renew the government's lease when it expires for only five additional years; and it has notified Coast and Geodetic Survey officials that the rent would then be raised to $150,000 per year. The government is contractually committed to restoring the land to its natural condition at the termination of the lease for an estimated $200,000. After further discussions, the development company has offered to sell the land to the government now for $1,000,000.

The Coast and Geodetic Survey does not plan to continue the testing activities being conducted at Furnace Creek for longer than 10 more years in any case. If it did purchase the land, it would simply add it to the Death Valley National Monument at the end of 10 years.

Federal regulations specify that major capital expenditures of this type should be evaluated by using a discount rate of 10%.

Required:

Present a financial analysis that will show whether it would be cheaper for the government to purchase the land or to continue renting it for 10 more years.

7. Robin Oakapple has an opportunity to purchase a large cruiser that is used commercially for fishing parties off the Kona Coast. The boat has a remaining useful life of 12 years. It would cost $750,000 now and could be resold at a scrap value of $30,000 after 12 years. Annual receipts from passengers are expected to average $600,000, and annual out-of-pocket operating expenses are estimated at $450,000. Oakapple would pay income taxes at a rate of 40% and would deduct depreciation on the boat by the straight-line method. His cost of capital is 10%.

Required:

a) Compute the payback period for the investment in the boat.
b) Compute the simple rate of return on (1) the initial investment and (2) the average investment.
c) Compute the net present value of the proposed investment.
d) Compute the present value index of the investment.
e) Determine the discounted rate of return on the investment.

8. Following is a summary of the important financial data applicable to five independent investment proposals?

Investment	Initial Outlay	Annual Cash Receipts	Life in Years
A............	$ 90,000	$ 17,380	10
B............	100,000	12,960	12
C............	50,000	19,300	5
D............	250,000	28,910	20
E............	600,000	217,920	4

The applicable cost of capital is 10%.

Required:

Rank these five investments in the order of their—

a) Payback periods
b) Discounted rates of return
c) Present value indexes
d) Net present values

9. The Cholmondeley Paper Products Corporation is considering the construction of a new plant to produce facial tissue. The initial cost of the plant would be $7,500,000. It would have a useful life of 25 years and no terminal salvage value. Depreciation on this plant would be deducted for tax purposes by means of the straight-line method. Annual cash revenues from sales of the plant's output are budgeted at $5,000,000 and annual out-of-pocket operating costs, at $3,500,000. The corporate income tax rate is 40%. The company's cost of capital is 10%.

   Required:

   Would the investment in the new plant be profitable? Support your answer with appropriate financial analysis.

10. The Jos. Porter Realty Company is contemplating the purchase of an old apartment building on Nob Hill for $1,700,000, $300,000 of which would be the cost of the land. Extensive renovations to the building would be required and would cost an estimated $2,800,000. This work would be done and paid for in stages over the coming year. The renovated building would then have an economic life of 20 years. For tax purposes, it would be depreciated by the straight-line method.

   Apartments would be rented to wealthy tenants at exorbitant rentals. At full occupancy, which may reasonably be anticipated over the full 20-year period, annual rent collections would total $1,200,000. Regular operating and maintenance expenditures would average $400,000 per year. At the end of the building's economic life, the land could be sold for an estimated $500,000. The salvage value of the building at that time would just cover the cost of demolishing it.

   The company's cost of capital is 8%. The income tax rate is 40%.

   Required:

   Would the contemplated real estate investment be profitable? Support your answer with appropriate financial analysis.

11. Adam Goodheart, 50 years of age, has received an inheritance of $250,000 from his uncle. He is currently employed as store manager of a large metropolitan haberdashery. His salary is $20,000 per year, and he does not anticipate that this will change if he remains in his present position until retirement at age 65. He is considering two alternative uses of his inheritance. The first plan would be to continue in his present job and to invest the $250,000 in safe 15-year term bonds yielding 8% interest, tax free. The second plan would be to purchase and operate his own store.

   Goodheart knows of a haberdashery that he could buy for $200,000, which includes $80,000 for inventory and the balance for the building and fixtures. The land is leased. He would have to invest an additional $50,000 for working capital purposes. Expected annual sales in this store would be $400,000. Annual out-of-pocket operating expenses, including land rent, would total $350,000. As Goodheart would manage his own store, he would have to leave his present job. At the end of 15 years, the land lease would terminate and the building and fixtures would become the property of the lessor. Goodheart would recover his original working capital investment, however.

The applicable personal income tax rate is 30%. Straight-line depreciation would be deducted for income tax purposes.

Required:

Prepare an analysis showing which of Goodheart's two alternatives would be more profitable for him. Assume that he has no third alternative.

12. The Buttercup Home Products Company has developed a new kitchen appliance that it plans to introduce in the coming year. It is estimated that this product will have a market life of 10 years. An initial expenditure of $800,000 for equipment to manufacture the product will be necessary. After two years, additional equipment costing $1,400,000 will have to be purchased. The original equipment will have no significant salvage value at the end of the product's market life. The equipment purchased two years later, however, will be sold for approximately $200,000 at the end of the market life. For tax purposes, straight-line depreciation will be used.

Projected annual sales volumes of this new appliance over the course of its market life are as follows:

1st year.	$ 500,000
2d year.	1,000,000
3d–8th years.	2,500,000
9th–10th years.	1,000,000

Variable out-of-pocket costs to manufacture and distribute the product will average 60% of selling prices. Fixed out-of-pocket operating costs will average $250,000 annually. In addition, a special sales promotion campaign is planned. Its annual costs will be as follows:

1st year.	$400,000
2d year.	200,000
3d–10th years.	50,000

The applicable income tax rate is 40%. It may be assumed that the company, as a whole, will have net taxable income in every year, regardless of profit or loss on any single product line. The company's cost of capital is 10% after taxes.

Required:

Will it be profitable for the company to market this new appliance?

13. Mountarrat Productions, Inc., is planning a super-spectacular motion picture to be titled "The Last Days of Los Angeles." Production is scheduled to begin at once and is expected to take two years to complete. Operating cash outlays, including actors' salaries (except as noted in the next paragraph), are budgeted at $5,000,000 each year while the film is in production. In addition, the producers will have to make an immediate payment of $1,500,000 for a large-scale model of the city of Los Angeles. The model will

be depreciated for tax purposes by the straight-line method over the first two years that the film is in release. There will be no salvage value recovered on this model, as it will be completely destroyed during the filming of the movie's final scene.

To enhance the dubious artistic flavor of the picture, the producers have engaged the distinguished character actor, Earl Tolloller, to play the small but pivotal role of a prophet of doom. Tolloller has agreed to accept either an annual salary of $250,000, to be paid in weekly installments over the two-year period of production, of simply 5% of the gross receipts from the film during the first two years it is in release. The latter alternative would require two payments to Tolloller at the end of each of the first two years that the film is exhibited. Each of these payments would be equal to 5% of the gross receipts for the year just ended. No salary or percentage for Tolloller is included in the $5,000,000 annual production costs mentioned earlier.

The producers have estimated that the gross cash receipts from the film would be $8,000,000 during the first year it is in release, $5,000,000 in the second year, and $2,000,000 per year during each of the following five years. Then, at the end of the seventh year, television rights would be sold for $5,000,000. Theater receipts thereafter would be negligible.

The applicable income tax rate is 40%. The production company's cost of capital is 12%.

Required:

a) Assuming that the picture will be made, should the producers pay Earl Tolloller the salary or the percentage of the first two years' gross receipts?

b) A major stockholder named Strephon has challenged the soundness of this project. He argues that "big budget" movies are passe and that the budgeted gross is not adequate to cover the costs of making the picture anyway. Would the picture be a profitable venture?

14. The Hildebrand Electronics Corporation has developed a revolutionary new remote control device for television sets. It can be installed easily and inexpensively on any set. The corporation plans to build a new factory for the production of this device. The initial cost of the factory will be $10,000,000. Its useful life is estimated at 20 years and its terminal salvage value at $1,000,000.

The remote control device will be sold for $18 per unit. Variable costs of production and marketing will be $8 per unit. In addition, there will be annual fixed factory costs of $1,250,000, including salaries, maintenance, taxes, insurance, and straight-line depreciation on the factory.

An initial sales promotion campaign is planned. It calls for an immediate outlay of $200,000 and subsequent outlays throughout each of the first three years of the product's market life in the following amounts:

1st year	$200,000
2d year	100,000
3d year	50,000

After the third year, promotion of this device will simply be a part of the company's regular annual advertising program at no additional cost. This advertising program currently costs an average of $400,000 per year.

Forecasted annual sales volumes for the device are as follows:

	Units
1st year	50,000
2d year	100,000
3d year	200,000
4th–20th years	250,000

The income tax rate is 40%. The company's cost of capital is 10%.

Required:

Prepare a report showing the budgeted profitability of the proposed investment in the new factory.

15. Fairfax bought an apartment building 25 years ago for $675,000. It has a remaining economic life of 20 years and no terminal salvage value. His annual income statement for the operations of this building appears as follows:

Rent revenue		$375,000
Expenses:		
Out-of-pocket	$135,000	
Depreciation	15,000	150,000
Income before tax		$225,000
Income tax at 40%		90,000
Net income		$135,000

Meryl has expressed an interest in buying this building "if the price is right." It may be assumed that rents and out-of-pocket expenses will continue as shown above for the remaining life of the building. Meryl is in the 30% income tax bracket.

Fairfax has a cost of capital of 12%. Meryl's cost of capital is 10%.

Required:

a) What is the least for which Fairfax can afford to sell the building?

b) What is the most Meryl can afford to pay for the building?

16. The Willis Land Development Company has an opportunity to purchase the mineral rights on a small plot of land known to be rich in limestone. It would have to pay $20,000 now for those rights, which it would then hold for 20 years. The company estimates that its net cash flow from extraction and sale of the limestone would amount to $5,000 per year for the entire 20-year period. At the end of 20 years, the company would have to restore the land to its natural condition. This would cost an estimated $100,000 at that time. The company's cost of capital is 10%. All of the cash flows mentioned above already include their income tax effects.

The controller of the company asked one of his new assistants to determine the discounted rate of return that the company would earn on the proposed investment. The assistant submitted a report showing a rate of return of approximately 22½%. The controller decided to double-check the new man's work. To his dismay, he came up with a discounted rate of return of only 3½%. Annoyed, he returned the assistant's report with a sharply critical note attached to it. The next morning, the assistant walked into his office with a smile on his face. "Chief," he announced, "We are both right." And he placed the following report on the controller's desk:

Analysis of Limestone Mineral Rights, December 5, 1972

Discount Rate	Net Present Value	Discount Rate	Net Present Value
0%.......	$ −20,000	16%.......	$ +4,550
2%.......	− 5,550	18%.......	+3,070
4%.......	+ 2,350	20%.......	+1,750
6%.......	+ 6,150	22%.......	+ 400
8%.......	+ 7,590	24%.......	− 850
10%.......	+ 7,670	26%.......	−1,960
12%.......	+ 6,950	28%.......	−2,970
14%.......	+ 5,820	30%.......	−3,920

While the controller was pleased to have his faith restored in the new assistant, he now had a new concern. "How do I explain this?" he asked. "And what do I tell the boss when he asks me whether that blasted piece of land would be a good investment?"

Required:

Answer the two questions posed by the controller in the last paragraph above.

—————————— chapter 16

CAPITAL BUDGETING: APPLICATIONS AND COMPLICATIONS

IN THE PRECEDING chapter, techniques for analyzing the cash flows pertinent to an investment decision were explained and illustrated. The importance of recognizing the time value of those cash flows was emphasized. The subject of capital budgeting covers much more than techniques of financial analysis, however. It embraces the various types of investment decisions that may face managers and the problems of measurement and analysis that may be encountered. Some of these situations and problems will be discussed in this chapter. The potential implications and complications of capital budgeting decisions extend far beyond the scope of this discussion, however.

Most probably, the greatest practical problem of capital budgeting is the development of reliable estimates of the future cash flows relevant to an investment proposal. This is similar to the problems of forecasting for annual budgets, but it is more acute because of the long time horizon over which plans must be formulated. Unless reasonable cash flow estimates can be made, the most sophisticated analytical techniques will yield unreliable results. While the techniques provide correct analysis, they cannot compensate for inaccurate basic data. Also, the precision (to four decimal places) of the present value factors in Appendix A does not mean that the present values of future cash flows computed by use of those factors are very accurate. An approximation of a future cash flow may be discounted to a *precise* present value, but this does not increase the *accuracy* of the original estimate. Thus, care should be taken in the development of cash flow estimates. The validity of the subsequent capital budgeting analysis depends largely upon this critical first step.

ASSET REPLACEMENT DECISIONS

A fairly common illustration of a capital budgeting decision is the asset replacement decision. Managers frequently must consider the possibility of replacing an asset presently in service with a new and presumably better one, even though the old asset's useful life has not expired. Obviously, if the old asset can no longer be used, the replacement decision takes on a different character. It is then a decision either to replace the asset or to discontinue the operation for which the asset has been used. Assuming that operations can be carried on with either the present asset or a new one, the replacement decision will depend upon which alternative is more profitable or otherwise more advantageous. Capital budgeting analysis, of course, can deal directly only with the matter of profitability. Such other legitimate considerations as safety and public responsibility can be incorporated in the financial analysis only if they have measurable effects on future cash flows.

The profitability of replacement may be indicated by a positive net present value, a present value index greater than 1.00, or a discounted rate of return greater than the cost of capital for the investment in the new asset *in place of* the old one. That is, the analysis will focus on the cash flows that will occur if the new asset is substituted for the old one. These will not be the same cash flows that would occur if the same new asset were purchased to perform a function that had not previously been performed at all. The relevant cash flows, then, are the incremental flows associated with use of the new asset instead of the old one.

For purposes of the replacement decision, whether the old asset is fully depreciated or has only recently been purchased is not normally a critical consideration. The original cost incurred for the old asset is now a sunk cost; it has no direct bearing on the decision. As a matter of fact, a loss on the disposition of an old asset has a favorable implication for the replacement decision if that loss is tax deductible. The basic factors entering into the analysis are the incremental cash flows from operating the new asset in place of the old one, the price that must be paid for the new asset, the incremental depreciation tax shield on the new asset, the current salvage value of the old asset, and the terminal salvage values of both. A typical replacement decision is illustrated in Table 16–1.

The data for this illustration are as follows: A corporation purchased a large production machine two years ago for $775,000. This machine was then estimated to have a useful life of 10 years and a terminal salvage value of $50,000. Now, a new automated machine is available to

TABLE 16-1

Analysis of Proposed Asset Replacement Decision

	Cash Flow before Tax	Tax Effect	Cash Flow after Tax	Present Value Factor at 10% Table	Present Value Factor at 10% Factor	Present Value
Cash receipts:						
Incremental operating cost savings	$ 250,000	$(100,000)	$ 150,000	A–1	5.5068	$ 826,020
Incremental tax saving from depreciation*	. . . . . .	28,000	28,000	A–1	5.5068	154,190
Incremental terminal salvage value	10,000		10,000	A–3	.4493	4,493
Proceeds from sale of old machine	250,000		250,000			250,000
Tax saving from loss on sale of old machine†	. . . . . .	152,000	152,000			152,000
						$ 1,386,703
Cash outlay:						
Purchase of new machine	(1,200,000)		(1,200,000)			(1,200,000)
Net present value						$ 186,703

* Incremental tax saving from depreciation:

Depreciation on new machine [($1,200,000 − $60,000) ÷ 8 yrs.]		$142,500
Depreciation on old machine [($775,000 − $50,000) ÷ 10 yrs.]		72,500
Incremental depreciation		$ 70,000
Income tax rate		40%
Incremental tax saving		$ 28,000

† Tax saving from loss on sale of old machine:

Original cost of machine		$775,000
Accumulated depreciation (2 yrs. @ $72,500)		145,000
Book value at date of proposed sale		$630,000
Proceeds from sale		250,000
Loss on sale		$380,000
Income tax rate		40%
Tax saving		$152,000

perform the same function as the two-year-old-machine. It would cost $1,200,000, would have a useful life of eight years, and would have a terminal salvage value of $60,000. It would reduce annual out-of-pocket operating costs by $250,000 as compared with continued operation of the old machine. The old machine could be sold now for $250,000. It is being depreciated by the straight-line method for tax purposes, and the same method would be used if the new machine is purchased. The corporation's cost of capital is 10%, and the income tax rate is 40%.

The largest cash receipt from the replacement investment is the present value of the operating cost savings. There is also a positive cash flow resulting from the greater tax deduction for depreciation. Note that only the excess of the tax saving from depreciation on the new machine over that on the old machine is included, for that is the amount by which the cash flow will change if the replacement decision is made. The proceeds from the sale of the old asset are also a positive cash flow. Although the old asset must be sold at a loss of $380,000, this loss involves no cash outlay. On the contrary, the tax saving from deduction of this loss is a positive cash flow, tending to make the replacement investment more attractive.[1] It would be a mistake to think of the loss on disposition of an old asset as a negative factor tending to inhibit replacement. A very minor cash receipt in this case is the present value of the incremental terminal salvage value of the new machine over that of the old one. It should be included in the analysis, of course. The only cash outlay in this illustration is the initial expenditure to purchase the new machine.

The analysis in Table 16–1 concludes with the determination of the net present value of the proposed replacement decision. The present value index might also be computed. If it is, the proceeds from the sale of the old machine and the tax saving from deduction of the loss on this sale should first be offset against the outlay for purchase of the new machine. The combination of cash flows with the same timing, it should be recalled, is appropriate in order to compute the present value index correctly. In this case, the effect of the combination is to reduce the present values of both the cash receipts and the cash outlay in Table 16–1 by $402,000. The present value index would then be calculated as follows:

$$\text{Present value index} = \frac{\text{Present value of cash receipts}}{\text{Present value of cash outlay}} = \frac{\$984,703}{\$798,000} = 1.23$$

---

[1] Losses on sale of assets used in business operations are generally deductible for tax purposes in the year of the sale. An exception is made, however, if the old asset is traded in for a new asset. In that case, a loss on the trade-in is not immediately deductible. Rather, it must be added to the cost of the new asset and then deducted in the form of depreciation over the life of the new asset. In total, the same dollar amount of tax deduction is allowed for the loss, but the timing is different. Since the present value of a cash flow diminishes the longer in the future that cash flow is deferred, there is a clear advantage in being able to deduct the loss all at once instead of having to include it as part of the depreciation allowed on the new asset.

If this same combination were used in computing the net present value, of course, there would be no change in that value. It would still be $186,-703. The discounted rate of return on the replacement decision might also be computed. In this case, the rate of return is approximately 16%.[2]

SELECTION OF DEPRECIATION METHOD

In financial accounting, the primary criterion for selection of a depreciation method is the best possible matching of costs with revenue. In capital budgeting, this criterion is totally irrelevant. The only way in which depreciation is relevant to an investment decision is through its tax effect. Hence, the criterion for selection of a depreciation method to be used for income tax purposes in connection with a proposed new asset is maximization of the present value of the asset's depreciation tax shield. Whether the depreciation method chosen for tax purposes is the same as that used for financial reporting is irrelevant. In general, one of the accelerated depreciation methods will produce a higher present value for the tax saving from depreciation than the straight-line method, so long as the income tax rate is not expected to rise substantially during the course of the asset's life. This tendency to prefer the accelerated methods reflects the fact that they allow greater depreciation deductions in early years, and, of course, the present value of a cash flow is greater the earlier that cash flow will occur. The two popular accelerated depreciation methods are the double-declining balance method and the sum-of-years'-digits method. As a general rule, the double-declining balance method will result in a higher present value of the depreciation tax shield if the life of the asset is fairly short and/or the asset has a substantial terminal salvage value. The sum-of-years'-digits method tends to be more favorable in connection with an asset having a very long life and/or little if any salvage value. Both of these methods are illustrated below in comparison with the straight-line method that has been used in all of the investment analyses illustrated thus far.

Consider a depreciable asset with an original cost of $100,000, no terminal salvage value, and a life of five years. Assume that the company's cost of capital is 10% and its income tax rate is 40%. Regardless of the depreciation method chosen, the total depreciation deductible over the asset's life will be $100,000 and the total tax saving from this deduction will be $40,000—at face value! The present value of this tax saving will depend upon the timing of its realization, however. Under the straight-line method, $20,000 of depreciation will be deducted each year

---

[2] Because of the limited number of columns in the tables in Appendix A, the closest one could come to this rate of return by reference to those tables would be to say that it is between 15% and 20%, but much closer to the former.

for five years. The tax saving, thus, will be in the form of a five-year annuity of $8,000. At 10%, the present value of this annuity is $31,478 ($8,000 × 3.9347). If the double-declining balance depreciation method is used, depreciation each year is equal to 40% (i.e., double the straight-line rate) of the annually declining book value of the asset. Thus, the tax saving is not a level annuity. Each year's tax saving is unique in amount and, hence, each must be discounted separately by the appropriate factor from Table A–2. The calculation of the present value of the tax saving from double-declining balance depreciation is as shown in Table 16–2.

TABLE 16–2

Year	Beginning Book Value	Depreciation Rate	Depreciation	Tax Rate	Tax Saving	Present Value Factor	Present Value
1........	$100,000	.40	$40,000	.40	$16,000	.9516	$15,226
2........	60,000	.40	24,000	.40	9,600	.8611	8,267
3........	36,000	.40	14,400	.40	5,760	.7791	4,488
4........	21,600	.50	10,800	.40	4,320	.7050	3,046
5........	10,800	1.00	10,800	.40	4,320	.6379	2,756
							$33,783

Thus, the present value of the tax saving from depreciation by the double-declining balance method is $2,305 more than by the straight-line method. Notice that the company switches to the straight-line method in the fourth year of the asset's life. This switch is a standard part of the double-declining balance method. It should be made whenever the depreciation deduction would be greater by applying a new straight-line rate to the *remaining* life and book value than by continuing to apply the doubled rate used in prior years.

In the sum-of-years'-digits method, an annually declining depreciation rate is applied to the original cost of the asset. The calculation of the present value of the tax saving from depreciation of the asset described above by the sum-of-years'-digits method is as shown in Table 16–3.

TABLE 16–3

Year	Original Cost	Depreciation Rate	Depreciation	Tax Rate	Tax Saving	Present Value Factor	Present Value
1........	$100,000	5/15	$33,333	.40	$13,333	.9516	$12,688
2........	100,000	4/15	26,667	.40	10,667	.8611	9,185
3........	100,000	3/15	20,000	.40	8,000	.7791	6,233
4........	100,000	2/15	13,333	.40	5,333	.7050	3,760
5........	100,000	1/15	6,667	.40	2,667	.6379	1,701
							$33,567

This result is $2,089 higher than the present value under the straight-line method, but it is $216 lower than that under the double-declining balance method. Hence, management should select the double-declining balance method for tax purposes if this $100,000 asset is purchased. It is conceivable that the choice of a depreciation method might make the difference between an investment being profitable and it being unprofitable. For example, if the net present value of the proposed investment in the asset discussed above were positive but less than $2,300 when the double-declining balance method was used, that net present value would become negative if the straight-line method were used instead.

To illustrate the effect of a longer life, suppose that the $100,000 asset in the foregoing illustration had a life of 20 years instead of five and that all other facts remained the same. The present values of the tax saving from depreciation under each of the three methods illustrated would be as follows:[3]

Method	Present Value
Straight-line............................	$17,293
Double-declining balance..............	20,117
Sum-of-years'-digits..................	22,435

All three present values are lower than those in the previous illustration, because the same total tax saving is spread over 20 years rather than only five. As before, the straight-line method is the least advantageous of the three. This time, however, the sum-of-years'-digits method is the most favorable one to use. In every capital budgeting analysis involving a depreciable asset, the most favorable method of depreciation should be determined before the rest of the analysis is completed. Most of the problems at the end of this chapter and the preceding one specify the straight-line method in order to simplify the computations. This should not be interpreted to mean that this is the best method to use. Unless tax rates are expected to rise substantially in the future, the straight-line method is usually the least advantageous one to use.

SEPARATION OF INVESTMENT AND FINANCING DECISIONS

The preceding chapter noted that there are two basically different types of decisions involved in the capital budgeting process. One is the

---

[3] The computations underlying these present values are exactly the same procedurally as those illustrated above when the asset's life was five years. The computations for the double-declining balance and the sum-of-years'-digits methods are much longer, of course. This is unavoidable if one has access only to the tables in Appendix A. There are tables available elsewhere, however, that show the present value of the total (not the annual) tax saving from depreciation under the two accelerated depreciation methods directly by a single discounting calculation. See, for example, Tables C and D in Harold Bierman, Jr., and Seymour Smidt, *The Capital Budgeting Decision* (2d ed.; New York: The Macmillan Co., 1966), pp. 404–11.

investment decision, relating to uses of capital. The other is the financing decision, concerned with sources of capital. It is important that these two decisions be analyzed separately in order to avoid possible errors. If the cash flows associated with financing are mingled with those pertinent to an investment, the result may be an erroneous conclusion that a basically unprofitable investment proposal is acceptable. This error is illustrated below in connection with a proposed investment in an asset that would generate after-tax cash receipts of $12,000 per year for five years and would require an initial cash outlay of $50,000. If the average cost of capital for the investor is 10%, this proposal's net present value would be determined as follows:

Annual cash receipts (5-year annuity)......................	$ 12,000
Present value factor for 5 years and 10% (Table A-1).........	3.9347
Present value of cash receipts............................	$ 47,216
Present value of cash outlay..............................	(50,000)
Net present value..	$ (2,784)

The proposed investment would be unprofitable. This fact may also be seen by computing a present value index of .94 ($47,216 ÷ $50,000) or by determining that the discounted rate of return is about $7\frac{1}{2}\%$.[4]

Logically, if an investment proposal is unprofitable at the average cost of capital, it should not be made profitable simply by changing the means of financing it. Yet, that is exactly the impression that may be created if the financing decision is confused with the investment proposal. Suppose that the investor is offered the alternative of purchasing this asset on an instalment plan. A down-payment of $5,000 would be required. Thereafter, annual instalment payments of $10,420 after taxes would be required for five years. This instalment plan is merely one way of financing the proposed investment. As such, it should have no effect on the profitability of the investment itself. But see how the combining of the investment and the financing cash flows makes the investment *appear* to be profitable.

Annual cash receipts.................................	$12,000
Annual instalment payment...........................	10,420
Net annual cash receipts.............................	$ 1,580
Present value factor.................................	3.9347
Present value of cash receipts........................	$ 6,217
Present value of cash outlay (down-payment)............	(5,000)
Net present value....................................	$ 1,217

Similarly, the present value index would *appear* to be 1.24, and the discounted rate of return, almost 20%. All of these values are erroneous,

---

[4] The discount rate that will equate $12,000 per year for five years to $50,000 is the same rate that will equate $1 per year for five years to $4.17. In Table A-1, a present value factor of 4.17 in the five-year row falls about midway between the 7% column and the 8% column.

however, and are inappropriate for purposes of investment decision making.

The investment was correctly analyzed to begin with, and it would be unprofitable as long as the average cost of capital is 10%. A separate analysis should be made of the proposed financing alternative. The five instalment payments of $10,420 are an alternative to expending an additional $45,000 immediately. This is equivalent to borrowing $45,000 now and repaying it with interest at a rate of 6%.[5] The fact that a single source of financing entails an interest cost of 6% does not mean that the *average* cost of capital is that low. In this case, it is given as 10%. It is the average interest cost of capital, not any single cost associated with a particular source of financing that is the criterion for investment profitability. As a matter of fact, borrowing additional capital at an after-tax interest cost of 6% could actually increase the average cost of capital to more than 10%, if the consequence were a reduction in the attractiveness of the company's equity securities to investors.[6]

MUTUALLY EXCLUSIVE INVESTMENTS OF DIFFERENT LIVES

Present value analysis of future cash flows is inherently involved with the time frame of those cash flows. For comparison purposes, it would be very convenient if all investment proposals had the same life, for this would provide a common time horizon for the capital budgeting process. Obviously, not all projects can be expected to have the same life. When two or more projects must be compared directly, however, a difference between their lives causes a complication. Mutually exclusive alternative investments typify projects that must be considered in direct comparison with each other. When such alternatives have different lives, this comparison is made more difficult. A perfect comparison would require knowledge about future alternatives that will be available for the period of the difference in the lives of the projects currently under consideration. For example, assume that a company needs to replace its furnace. Two models are available. Model X would cost $25,000 now, would involve annual after-tax operating costs of $10,000, and would have a useful life of five years. Model Y would cost $40,000 now, would entail annual after-tax operating costs of $8,000, and would have a life of eight years. Comparison of these alternatives is complicated by the

---

[5] The discount rate that will equate $10,420 per year for five years to $45,000 is the same rate that will equate $1 per year for five years to $4.32. In Table A–1, a present value factor of 4.3197 is found in the five-year row and the 6% column.

[6] The relationship between the cost of any one source of financing and the average cost of capital is discussed more expansively in numerous books and articles. For example, see Bierman and Smidt, *op. cit.*, chap. ix; and G. David Quirin, *The Capital Expenditure Decision* (Homewood, Ill.: Richard D. Irwin, Inc., 1967), chap. vi.

fact that they have different lives. Yet, complicated or not, the comparison must be made. The two models are genuine alternatives.

Since neither furnace will generate any cash receipts, it is not feasible to compute any of the customary measures of an investment's profitability. The financial objective of the investment in the furnace is to minimize total costs. One approach that might appear useful is to determine the present value of the total cost of each alternative. This is done in Table 16–4. The cost of capital is assumed to be 10%.

TABLE 16–4

	Model X	Model Y
Annual operating costs....................	$10,000	$ 8,000
Present value factor for 10% and		
model's life (Table A-1)................	3.9347	5.5068
Present value of annual costs.............	$39,347	$44,054
Initial purchase cost.....................	25,000	40,000
Present value of total costs...............	$64,347	$84,054
Useful life..............................	5 years	8 years

Unfortunately, this comparison is not conclusive, for Model Y has a life three years longer than model X. Hence, its greater present value of total costs is not necessarily a disadvantage. Presumably, the company would need a furnace for the sixth, seventh, and eighth years in the future regardless of the model purchased now. Thus, if model X is chosen, a new furnace will be required afer five years. The characteristics and costs of furnaces that will be available then cannot be predicted accurately now. A perfect solution to the present choice problem, however, requires complete knowledge about future replacement furnaces. In the absence of such knowledge, management must seek to convert the financial analysis of the present alternatives to a common time horizon. While such conversion is useful for decision making, it does not eliminate the problem of different lives. Rather, it simply removes that difference from the comparison.

Replacement Chains

One method of achieving a common time horizon is to assume that each model, if purchased, would be replaced at the end of its useful life by an identical furnace. These sequential replacements, or replacement chains, would be continued as long as necessary to obtain a common time horizon. As a practical matter, this is usually done over a number of years equal to the lowest common multiple of the lives of the alternatives. In our illustration of the furnaces, this would be a period of 40 years. For model X, this analysis would involve a 40-year annuity of $10,000 plus an outlay of $25,000 at the beginning of the first year and every fifth year thereafter, through and including the 36th year. For model Y, there would be a 40-year annuity of $8,000 plus outlays of $40,000 now and every eighth year thereafter, through and including the 33d year. When all of these cash flows were discounted to their present value at 10%, the present values of the total costs of the two alternatives over a 40-year time period would be as follows:

Model X................ $171,497
Model Y................ 158,607

In the absence of any compelling nonfinancial considerations, model Y, with its lower lifetime cost, would be selected. While this replacement chain analysis does neutralize the time differential, it also presumes that technology and prices will stagnate for the next 40 years. This is hardly a reasonable presumption.

Salvage Values at End of Shortest Life

A second means of dealing with the time difference is to make a comparison of present values over the life of the shortest lived alternative. In the case of the two furnace models, that would be model X with a life of five years. The estimated salvage value of the longer lived alternative, model Y, would be included as a cash receipt in the present value analysis. The alternative with the lower net cost (i.e., operating cost over five years plus initial outlay minus salvage value after five years) would then be selected. This approach, of course, depends upon a reasonable estimate of the salvage value of the longer lived alternative(s). If that value is highly uncertain, the approach is not very satisfactory.

Equivalent Annual Costs

A third technique for eliminating the time difference is to compute the annual cost that is equivalent to the present value of the total cost of each alternative. This entails adding to the annual operating cost an annuity whose present value over the life of the alternative is equal to the initial outlay for that alternative. This annuity is the equivalent annual cost of purchasing the asset. The equivalent annual costs of the two alternatives in our furnace illustration are computed as shown in Table 16–5.

TABLE 16–5

	Model X	Model Y
Initial cost......................................	$25,000	$40,000
Divided by present value factor for 10% and life of the model (Table A–1)............	3.9347	5.5068
Equivalent annual purchase cost...............	$ 6,354	$ 7,264
Annual operating cost........................	10,000	8,000
Equivalent annual cost......................	$16,354	$15,264

In other words, spending $6,354 each year for five years is equivalent to spending $25,000 now, if the cost of capital is 10%. Similarly, an annuity of $7,264 for eight years is equivalent to an immediate expenditure of $40,000 at a 10% cost of capital. The operating costs, of course, are already stated on an annual basis. We may now compare the alternatives directly and choose the one with the lower equivalent annual cost— model Y.

The foregoing analysis does not say that there would actually be an annual expenditure of $15,264 if model Y is selected. Rather, it says that such an annual expenditure is equivalent to the actual proposed expenditures of $40,000 at once and then $8,000 annually for eight years. Further, this procedure does not cancel the difference in the lives of the two models. It simply removes the difference from the analysis. It says nothing, however, about what might be done during the sixth, seventh, and eighth years if model X were purchased. Of the three techniques discussed here, the equivalent annual cost method is recommended as the simplest and as valid as either of the other two. It avoids the necessity for an estimate of salvage value, which is required in the second method above. Insofar as a choice among alternatives is concerned, it will give the same result as the replacement chain method. However, it usually requires fewer calculations; and it would probably be easier to explain to management.

MUTUALLY EXCLUSIVE ALTERNATIVES WITH DIFFERENT INITIAL OUTLAYS

When two or more mutually exclusive alternative investments have different initial outlays, even though they have equal lives, a question arises as to the appropriate method of comparing them. The net present value method tends to favor the larger alternatives, although these are not necessarily the better ones. The net present value is affected directly by the absolute size of the cash flows associated with a proposal. This is not true of the present value index and the discounted rate of return. Both of these are relative measures of profitability. That is, they express the profitability of an investment in relation to the amount invested. Which technique is best for choosing among mutually exclusive alternatives depends upon the circumstances surrounding the investment and the investor. An example will help explain the problem of choice of a technique. A company with an average cost of capital of 10% is considering buying one or the other of two laborsaving machines; it could not use both. Both machines have lives of 10 years. Machine L costs $50,000 and saves costs of $10,000 per year after tax. Machine M costs $80,000 and saves costs of $15,000 per year after tax. Table 16–6 shows a comparison of the results of determining the profitabilities of these alternative machines by the three techniques. By the net present value method, machine M appears more profitable. By either of the other two methods, machine L seems preferable. Which actually is the better alternative?

The answer to that question depends upon the answer to another. Will the choice between these two alternatives affect the company's ability to

TABLE 16–6

	Machine L	Machine M
Net present value..................	$13,213	$14,820
Present value index................	1.26	1.19
Discounted rate of return...........	15–16%	14–15%

make any other investment? If it will not, machine M should be chosen. While it is not as profitable per dollar invested as machine L, it would increase the total wealth of the investor by a larger amount. In other words, in this case, the greater net present value indicates the investment to be selected. However, if investing in machine M would limit the firm's ability to make other investments because of a limitation on the total amount of capital available for investing, the net present value is not a suitable basis for the choice between these mutually exclusive alternatives. In this situation, the fact that machine L would consume $30,000 less of the firm's investible capital becomes significant. The choice now depends upon what return might be obtained by some other investment of that $30,000 if machine L were chosen in preference to machine M. Thus, the two machines cannot now be compared all by themselves. Machine M must be compared with machine L plus some other profitable investment of the differential $30,000.

The best way to make the choice between mutually exclusive investment proposals, when that choice has an effect on other investment possibilities, is to compute the profitability of the additional investment required to make the larger of the alternative investments under consideration. In the example of machines L and M, this would entail determining the return from investing an additional $30,000 in machine M. This is often referred to as the *incremental investment*. The incremental investment of $30,000 in this case will produce an incremental annual cash receipt of $5,000 ($15,000 − $10,000) for 10 years. The three measures of profitability for this incremental investment are as follows:

Net present value.................... $1,607
Present value index...................   1.05
Discounted rate of return.............. 11–12%

These measures should now be compared with those for other possible investments of the same $30,000. If this incremental investment proves to be more profitable than any alternative use of the capital, machine M should be purchased. On the other hand, if the incremental investment is found to be less attractive than other projects that would use the $30,000, machine L should be chosen.

CAPITAL RATIONING

In all of our discussions and illustrations of investment decisions thus far, with the exception of that in the immediately preceding section, we have been concerned simply with determining whether an investment would be profitable. By implication, then, if the investment was profitable, it would be undertaken. This rule is valid so long as the firm is able to obtain all the capital necessary to make all profitable investments available to it. In such a situation, the capital budgeting process is relatively simple—once estimates of future cash flows have been made. First, choices among mutually exclusive alternatives would be resolved by selecting the one with the largest net present value in every case. Then, all investments with positive net present values would be made. This statement assumes that unprofitable investments would not be made. This may not be realistic. It may sometimes be necessary to make certain investments (e.g., installation of warning signals at railroad crossings) because they are required by law. Actually, such an investment might be truly profitable if it would avoid recurring fines or other financial penalties. Also, a firm may make investments (e.g., a cafeteria or plant landscaping) to improve its relations with employees or with the community at large. Such investments may be thought to yield certain intangible benefits that are hoped to enhance profits in the long run, although not in any measurable amount.

It may happen, however, that a firm is not able to obtain all of the capital necessary to make all potentially profitable investments. In this case, the firm is faced with the necessity of rejecting some investments that meet established criteria of profitability. Such a situation is described as *capital rationing*. That is, the capital available to the firm is rationed to it in an amount less than the firm might profitably invest. Consequently, management must allocate the limited available capital in a way that produces the greatest possible benefit. It is no longer sufficient to determine *whether* an investment is profitable. Management must also *rank* the alternative investment opportunities according to their relative profitabilities. Only the most profitable investments will be made. (Again, exceptions may be made for "necessary" or desirable investments not offering identifiable financial returns.) Thus, under conditions of capital rationing, the analytical technique used for evaluating investment opportunities must be capable of ranking the alternatives or of determining the optimal combination of investments that fits the constraint of limited capital.

Causes of Capital Rationing

Capital rationing may be caused by factors external to the firm or by internal restrictions imposed by management. The primary external cause of capital rationing is an imperfect capital market. In a perfect capital market, every firm will be able to obtain all of the capital it needs as long as it has profitable uses for that capital. The total amount of capital available to all investors at a given time is fixed, of course. Consequently, the average cost of capital to any single firm is partially determined by the aggregate supply of capital in the market. Given its cost of capital, however, the firm will then be able to obtain capital so long as it has investment opportunities offering rates of return greater than the cost of capital. In an imperfect capital market, each firm may not be able to obtain all of the capital it could profitably invest. Imperfection may be caused by deficiencies in market information, by rigidities that hamper the free flow of capital between firms, and by a difference between the interest rate at which the firm can obtain capital in the market (i.e., the borrowing rate) and the interest rate it could earn by loaning its own capital to others in the market (i.e., the lending rate). One reason why the borrowing rate is typically greater than the lending rate is the costs that must be incurred when a firm seeks additional capital by selling securities in the market. Fees must be paid to register the securities with the appropriate federal and/or state authorities, and a fee must be paid to the investment banking syndicate that will handle the marketing of the securities. In a government agency, the funds authorized by the legislature constitute an external limitation on the amount that the agency may invest.

Internal causes of capital rationing are sometimes more difficult to justify, as they reflect self-imposed restrictions on potentially profitable investments. Nevertheless, where they exist, the capital budgeting analysis must recognize them. A firm's management may decide that it will not incur debt to obtain additional capital, perhaps as a matter of conservative financing policy. A closely held corporation may reject the opportunity of selling additional shares of common stock, for this would threaten the present stockholders' control of the firm. In a large, decentralized corporation, top management may arbitrarily limit the funds it is willing to make available for investment by the division managers. Finally, management may insist that any investment undertaken yield a rate of return greater than the average cost of capital. The reason for requiring a rate of return greater than the cost of capital may be to provide for overly optimistic estimates of cash receipts or simply to enforce a conservative investment policy. Whatever the reasons for or the logic of internal capital rationing, it constrains the capital budgeting process in the same way as external rationing.

Effects of Capital Rationing

Regardless of its cause, capital rationing affects the investment decision-making process in several important ways. First, as has already been observed, it requires that independent investment opportunities be ranked according to profitability. This is largely a technical problem and is discussed in the next section. Second, under conditions of capital rationing, a firm really should extend the decision process to include investment opportunities both at the present time and in the future. Unless capital rationing is considered to be a temporary constraint, the investments chosen now may constrain the choices of future periods. Thus, management might decide to make a minimally profitable investment today because it has a very short payback period. Thus, additional funds will be available in some future period to permit the firm to take advantage of a particularly profitable investment then. Unfortunately, few firms are likely to have enough information about future investment opportunities to make this multiperiod analysis practical.

Finally, capital rationing changes the effective cost of capital relevant to investment decisions. It raises that cost from the average cost of capital explained in Chapter 8[7] to the rate of return that must be foregone on the most profitable investment proposal that is rejected because of the limitation on available capital. This is an opportunity cost. For example, if a firm's weighted average cost of capital, determined in the usual manner, is 10% and if that firm must reject investment opportunities offering rates of return of 12%, 13%, and 14%, its effective cost of capital has increased to 14%, the highest yield that had to be foregone because of the capital rationing constraint. This is the effective cost of capital, for it measures the sacrifice the firm had to make in order to use its limited capital for the investments that it was able to undertake.

---

[7] Pages 201–2.

Methods of Ranking Independent Investment Proposals

The ranking of investment opportunities according to their relative profitabilities may vary with the technique of measuring profitability that is used. The net present value method, for example, tends to make investments of large amounts appear relatively attractive because it expresses profitability in absolute dollar amounts. Thus, unless all investments are of equivalent size—an unlikely situation—the net present value cannot be relied upon for ranking purposes. Both the present value index and the discounted rate of return are relative measures and are not affected by the size of the investment. Thus, they tend to produce accurate rankings. It is possible that these latter two methods will not produce the same ranking, however, because of their different implicit reinvestment rate assumptions.[8] Difficulties of ranking independent investments will be seen in the illustration below.

Suppose that a company operating under the constraint of capital rationing has six independent investments from which to choose. For simplicity, we shall assume that each alternative requires an initial cash outlay and will generate cash receipts in the form of a level annuity over the next 10 years. All cash flows are stated after consideration of tax effects. The company's average cost of capital is 10%. The six alternatives and their profitabilities according to the three analytical techniques are summarized in Table 16–7.

TABLE 16–7

Investment	Annual Cash Receipts	Present Value of Cash Receipts	Initial Cash Outlay	Net Present Value	Present Value Index	Discounted Rate of Return
A..............	$19,309	$122,058	$100,000	$22,058	1.22	15%
B..............	9,291	58,731	50,000	8,731	1.17	14
C..............	9,252	58,485	40,000	18,485	1.46	20
D..............	8,171	51,651	30,000	21,651	1.72	25
E..............	3,574	22,592	20,000	2,592	1.13	13
F..............	1,649	10,424	10,000	424	1.04	11

If these six alternatives are now ranked by the three measures of profitability, we find the same ranking by the present value index and the discounted rate of return methods. The ranking by the net present value method is different, however, as shown in Table 16–8.

Which investments will actually be made depends not only upon the ranking but also on the amount of capital available for investment. Sup-

---

[8] Chapter 15, page 397.

TABLE 16–8

Ranking by Net Present Value	Ranking by Present Value Index and Discounted Rate of Return
A	D
D	C
C	A
B	B
E	E
F	F

pose that exactly $100,000 is available. Neither of the rankings above directly indicates the investments that should be made. The net present value ranking suggests investment A, but that is actually the least profitable possible use of the $100,000. The other two methods suggest investments D and C, but their selection precludes the making of either of the next two investments in that ranking because of the limit on available funds. Thus, the best way to determine the optimal investment program is to determine the net present values of the various combinations of investments that would sum to $100,000 and to choose the largest. The four feasible investment packages that total $100,000 and their net present values are given in Table 16–9.

TABLE 16–9

Investments	Net Present Value
C, D, E, and F...................	$43,152
B, D, and E.....................	32,974
B, C, and F.....................	27,640
A..............................	22,058

Any other combination would either exceed $100,000 or would use less than all of the available capital. The first alternative is considered impossible here; the second would be inefficient. Given another set of alternatives, however, it is possible that the optimal investment package would include projects totaling less than $100,000, with the balance simply loaned to other firms to earn a rate of return equal to the cost of capital. In this particular illustration, however, no other combination of projects totaling $100,000 or less would be more profitable than the package of C, D, E, and F.[9] Exactly the same conclusion would be reached if the

---

[9] This particular illustration is quite simple. In even a modest sized organization, there may be so many investment proposals that the search for the optimal investment program by listing all possible packages would be too tedious to be practicable. In such cases, the optimal investment package may be found by the use of linear programming or, perhaps, integer programming. For a discussion of this approach to the capital rationing problem, see H. Martin Weingartner, *Mathematical Programming and the Analysis of Capital Budgeting Problems* (Englewood Cliffs, N.J.: Prentice-Hall, Inc., 1963).

four feasible investment *packages* were compared by their aggregate present value indexes or discounted rates of return.

Of course, capital rationing does not necessarily imply that a fixed amount of money is available for investment. It simply means that not enough is available to fund all potentially profitable projects. Presumably, the amount available is somewhat flexible. Thus, management might be able to obtain sufficient funds to make the top group of investments on a list ranked by the present value index or the discounted rate of return. With this kind of flexibility, a ranking by one (or both) of these methods could be a valid basis for direct selection of projects to be undertaken.

RISK AND UNCERTAINTY

In our discussions thus far, we have tacitly assumed that the future cash flows pertinent to an investment can be budgeted accurately. Any budget, of course, is subject to some degree or risk and uncertainty. It is possible that the actual outcome of an investment (or of any other plan, for that matter) will be any one of many alternative results, not necessarily the particular result predicted. This is the essence of risk. The approach to decision making under risk is to determine the probability of each possible outcome and to compute the average or expected value of these alternatives. It is possible, of course, that the decision maker will not have information permitting him to determine the probabilities of the alternative outcomes. In this case, he is faced with uncertainty. One approach to decision making under uncertainty is to seek to protect against the worst possible outcome. Alternatively, the decision maker might make a subjective estimate of the probabilities of alternative results and use these in the same way as objectively determined probabilities. Investment decisions under conditions of risk and uncertainty are illustrated in the paragraphs that follow.

A decision maker faces risk when the outcome of his decision will depend partly upon conditions over which he is unable to exercise any control. For example, suppose that a trucking company is considering the construction of a truck depot at the terminus of a small railroad's freight spur. This railroad is presently the principal source of transportation of goods into and out of the region beyond the terminus. Like most railroads, its financial condition is not very secure. However, it is currently negotiating a possible merger with a larger and more stable railroad. If this merger is consummated, shipment of goods on the freight spur would be increased considerably. On the other hand, if the merger fails, it is possible that the small railroad will discontinue operations on this marginally profitable freight spur. The trucking company can do nothing about the railroad's situation, but that situation will significantly affect the profitability of the investment in a trucking depot. Construction of the depot would cost $500,000 now, and the facilities would have an economic life of 20 years. The annual variable profit from the depot would depend upon the railroad's situation. If the railroad continues to operate as it presently is doing, the trucking depot's annual variable profit would be $100,000. Should the merger with a larger railroad be consummated, the trucking depot would produce an annual variable profit of $150,000. However, if the railroad were forced to discontinue operations on the freight spur, the variable profit from the truck depot would be only $50,000 per year. The trucking company's management has estimated that the probability of the

TABLE 16–10

Analysis of Proposed Investment in Trucking Depot

Computation of expected value of variable profit:

Situation	Variable Profit	Probability	Expected Value
Closing of freight spur.............	$ 50,000	.2	$ 10,000
Continuation of *status quo*..........	100,000	.5	50,000
Railroad merger...................	150,000	.3	45,000
Expected variable profit..............			$105,000

Analysis of profitability of investment:

	Cash Flow before Tax	Tax Effect	Cash Flow after Tax	Present Value Factor at 10% Table	Present Value Factor at 10% Factor	Present Value
Cash receipts:						
Expected variable profit.............	$ 105,000	$(42,000)	$ 63,000	A–1	8.6466	$ 544,73
Tax saving from depreciation........	......	10,000	10,000	A–1	8.6466	86,46
						$ 631,20
Cash outlay:						
Construction of depot..............	(500,000)		(500,000)			(500,00
Net present value...................						$ 131,20
Present value index..................						1.2
Discounted rate of return.............						13–14

railroad's continuing to operate as at present is .5 (i.e., 5 chances out of 10); the probability of the merger is .3; and the probability of closing down operations on the freight spur is .2. With these data, the trucking company can estimate the expected value of the proposed investment in a depot.

The analysis of this proposed investment is shown in Table 16–10. The cost of capital is assumed to be 10%, and the income tax rate, 40%. The straight-line depreciation method would be used for tax purposes. The first part of this table shows the computation of the expected value of the variable profit from the trucking depot. This is simply the sum of the three alternative variable profits, each weighted (or multiplied) by the probability of the situation that would produce it. The second part of the table shows the determination of the projected profitability of the investment in the same way as in previous illustrations. The expected value of the variable profit is reduced by its tax effect and then discounted to its present value in the usual way. The tax saving from depreciation is not affected by the various probabilities because it will be realized if the investment is made, regardless of the railroad's future. Strictly speaking, decision making under risk requires objective knowledge of probabilities—as in a game of cards or dice. For practical purposes, however, decision making under uncertainty is equivalent to that under risk when subjective estimates of probabilities are used. The results, of course, are dependent upon the validity of the probabilities used.

If the investment decision must be made under conditions of uncertainty without the use of probabilities, management can, at best, predict the financial implications of the alternative possible outcomes. No expected value can be computed, however. Hence, management must make an inherently subjective judgment as to the financial danger it is willing to accept. One approach in this case is to pursue a course of action that will maximize the minimum profit that might result from the decision made. This approach employs the so-called *maximin* criterion; it is basically pessimistic. Management presumes that the worst will happen (the minimum profit will be realized) no matter what choice is made. Consequently, management seeks to obtain the best of the alternative bad results. A similar approach employs the *minimax* criterion. Here management chooses the alternative that will minimize the maximum loss that might be incurred. This is a conservative approach to decision making. Under both of these approaches, of course, all financial data should be discounted to their present values. The *maximin* and *minimax* criteria are most appropriate when management is faced with a wider range of alternatives than simply to accept or reject a proposed investment. For example, if the decision regarding the trucking depot involved not only a choice between building it and not building it but also a choice as to its size, one of these criteria might offer a particularly useful way for management to evaluate the implications of the choices facing it.[10]

CHANGES IN PRICES AND INTEREST RATES

Even after discounting, dollars received or paid in the future may not be directly comparable to cash flows at the present. Inflation and deflation alter the real values of cash flows. If the rate of general price inflation or deflation can be predicted, future cash flows can be adjusted for it

---

[10] For a more expansive discussion of decision making under conditions of risk and uncertainty, see David W. Miller and Martin K. Starr, *Executive Decisions and Operations Research* (2d ed.; Englewood Cliffs, N.J.: Prentice-Hall, Inc., 1969), pp. 104–20.

before they are discounted to their present values. The impact of price changes on investment decisions can be significant, particularly if the annual rate of price change is expected to be substantial. Some investments generate future cash flows that may be expected to change approximately in direct proportion to the general price level. Investments in common stocks, production facilities, and retail stores typically fall into this category. If the cash flows from the investment would follow the pattern of the general price level exactly, then price changes could be ignored in the capital budgeting process. Future cash flows would be adjusted "automatically" for price inflation or deflation. Other investments, such as in bonds, generate cash flows that are fixed in dollar amount. Consequently, the real value of these cash flows declines in periods of price inflation and rises during periods of deflation. For example, investment in a bond that yields a rate of return of 6% is unprofitable, regardless of the cost of capital, if the annual rate of inflation is higher than 6%. Obviously, expected price changes are factors to be considered in the investment decision-making process.

Interest rates, the price of money, may change over time just as any other price. Such changes have important implications for capital budgeting. To begin with, they mean that the cost of capital for a firm cannot be expected to remain constant over time. Similarly, future investment opportunities may be expected to have different rates of return than current investments. This fact complicates the precision of investment analysis, for we know that all of the analytical techniques that recognize the time value of money entail an implicit assumption about the interest rate that will be earned on the reinvestment of the cash receipts from a current investment. Changes in interest rates tend to undercut the validity of such assumptions. Also, prospective interest rate changes should be considered when investment alternatives have different lives. An expectation that interest rates in the future will be lower than currently would tend to make the longer lived investment more attractive. Conversely, anticipated increases in interest rates tend to favor shorter lived investments now. Of course, these expectations must be weighed carefully with other pertinent factors, including any differences between expected rates of return on the current investment opportunities.

INTANGIBLE BENEFITS FROM CAPITAL INVESTMENTS

Not every investment may be expected to generate specific cash receipts. If an investment produces neither revenues nor cost savings, it cannot be justified on financial grounds. Yet, such investments cannot be rejected out of hand. Corporations frequently invest in such nonremunerative projects as plant beautification, art objects in executives' offices, and employees' recreational facilities. Apparently, these firms believe that such investments will yield intangible benefits that more than justify the outlays. They are unable to assign a specific financial value to those benefits, however.

Intangible benefits are particularly important in investments made by governmental and nonprofit organizations. For example, the primary benefits of government funded public housing developments are usually alleged to be the physical and psychic satisfactions that the residents derive from living in decent conditions. In effect, the majority, through their tax payments, invest in facilities intended to benefit personally a minority. Even such public investments may produce some recognizable financial benefits, however. Elimination of substandard slum dwellings may reduce the public cost of fire protection. Particularly if coupled with expanded job opportunities, public housing projects may lead to reduced crime rates and, hence, lower costs of police protection and lower property insurance rates. The incremental earnings of construction workers and contractors are also relevant financial benefits to the public as a consequence of the public housing project. Similar evaluations might be made of other public investment projects, notably dams, harbors, recreational facilities, and waste-treatment plants. Of course, the more explicitly financial techniques of capital budgeting are also applicable to investments intended chiefly to produce intangible benefits. Present value analysis can indicate which of various alternatives is the least costly means of achieving a specified goal. Such analysis is extremely important in the public sector, for it may lead to savings of capital on certain projects so that more is available for other beneficial investments.

QUESTIONS FOR DISCUSSION

1. A small manufacturing corporation has two machines of the same basic type. One was purchased 10 years ago and is now fully depreciated, although still in service. The other was purchased just one year ago and is being depreciated over a useful life of 10 years. A revolutionary new machine has recently appeared on the market. It really makes the old type of machine obsolete, even though still physically usable. Both of the old type machines the corporation is now using could be sold for the same low scrap value. Management is planning to scrap the machine purchased 10 years and replace it with one of the new type. The machine purchased one year ago will be retained, however; for management does not believe the company can afford to bear the loss that would be incurred by scrapping it now. Evaluate the two decisions management has made regarding the two machines now in service.

2. "Because of the time value of money, it is always advantageous for a taxpayer to elect one of the accelerated depreciation methods rather than the straight-line method." Do you agree with this assertion? Why or why not?

3. Why is it so important for management to distinguish clearly between investment and financing decisions?

4. What are the alternative methods for analyzing mutually exclusive invest-

ment proposals that have differing economic lives? What limitation is inherent in all of them?

5. "The discounted rate of return and the present value index are common denominators of investment profitability. They are not affected by the size of the initial investment. The net present value, on the other hand, tends to vary directly with the size of the investment. Hence, it is a biased measure of investment profitability." Discuss this statement.

6. How should mutually exclusive alternative investments of different initial amounts be compared?

7. What are the implications of capital rationing in the capital budgeting process?

8. What are some of the principal problems encountered in an attempt to rank several independent investment proposals in the order of their profitability?

9. Weighting alternative estimates of the cash flow associated with an investment proposal by their respective probabilities of occurrence is one way of coping with the problem of uncertainty in capital budgeting. The results, of course, are no better than the data used in the analysis. How might management go about determining the probabilities of two or more alternative patterns of cash flows from a single investment proposal?

10. Some firms have attempted to incorporate uncertainty in their capital budgeting analyses by using higher discount rates on investments considered to be relatively more risky than others. Evaluate this method of coping with the problem of uncertainty.

11. Assume that the general price level in the economy will rise at an annual rate of 5% for the forseeable future. How should this inflation factor be included in the analysis of an investment of $100,000 in—

   a) A public utility's bonds?
   b) A department store?
   c) Commercial real estate?

12. When a state legislature appropriates public funds for the construction of new academic facilities on the campus of a state college, it is making a capital investment decision. How might such an investment be justified financially?

PROBLEMS

1. Palmieri Bros. Winery is now using a bottling and corking machine purchased four years ago for $200,000. This machine has a remaining useful life of six years and no terminal salvage value. Accumulated depreciation on the machine totals $80,000. Annual out-of-pocket operating costs associated with the use of this machine are $600,000. The machine could be resold today for $25,000.

   A new bottling and corking machine has recently appeared on the market. It sells for $350,000, has an economic life of six years, and would have a terminal salvage value of $50,000. The company has estimated that annual out-of-pocket operating costs with this new machine would be $500,000.

The company's cost of capital is 8%. The income tax rate is 40%. The company always uses straight-line depreciation for tax purposes. Any loss on resale of assets is tax deductible at the time of sale.

Required:

Prepare a financial analysis to show whether it would be profitable for the winery to replace its bottling and corking machine now with one of the new type.

2. The Gama Tool & Die Company now uses a die stamping machine that was purchased two years ago at a cost of $400,000. It is being depreciated by the straight-line method over a life of eight years and is assumed to have no terminal salvage value. Recently, there has been developed a new machine that performs the same operation much more efficiently. This new machine could be purchased for $600,000. It would reduce annual out-of-pocket operating costs by $150,000 throughout its useful life of six years. The new machine would have a terminal salvage value of $6,000. The old machine could be sold now for $100,000.

The company's cost of capital is 10%. The applicable income tax rate is 40%. Straight-line depreciation would be used on the new machine if it is purchased.

Required:

Would replacement of the old die-stamping machine now be profitable for the company?

3. The Pointdextre Corporation manufactures small electronic components largely by hand labor. Recently, a machine has been developed to automate part of this work. The machine would cost $980,000 delivered and installed and would have a useful life of 12 years. Its salvage value at the end of that time is estimated at $20,000. Acquisition of this machine would render useless a number of work benches now in use. These benches originally cost $40,000 eight years ago and are being depreciated over a useful life of 20 years with no assumed salvage value. These benches could be sold now for about $4,000.

A comparison of annual operating costs under the present hand-labor method and with the machine in service is as follows:

	Hand Labor	Machine
Raw materials....................	$250,000	$270,000
Direct labor......................	400,000	120,000
Indirect labor....................	80,000	100,000
Heat, light, and power............	50,000	80,000
Depreciation.....................	2,000	80,000
Taxes and insurance..............	8,000	20,000
	$790,000	$670,000

The corporation will use straight-line depreciation for both financial reporting and income tax returns. The applicable income tax rate is 40%. The corporation's cost of capital is 10%.

Required:

Would it be profitable for the corporation to purchase the machine?

4. The Bunthorne Dredge and Dock Company is currently using a harbor dredge purchased two years ago at a cost of $5,000,000. This dredge was estimated to have a useful life of 10 years and a terminal salvage value of $500,000. A substantially improved dredge is now available at a cost of $8,000,000. It operates faster than the one presently in service and would increase the corporation's annual revenues by $1,250,000. It would also increase annual operating costs, exclusive of depreciation, by approximately $600,000.

The new dredge would have a useful life of eight years and an expected terminal salvage value of $800,000. If the new one is purchased, the company would have no further use for the old dredge, which can be sold currently for about $1,100,000.

The firm's cost of capital is 9%. The income tax rate is 40%. Straight-line depreciation is used on all assets for income tax purposes.

Required:

Prepare an analysis showing whether it would be profitable to replace the old dredge now.

5. The Sangazure Printing Company is considering replacing its present press with a new one that would double capacity and improve the overall quality of the printing work done. The new press would cost $75,000 and would have a useful life of 10 years, with an expected terminal salvage value of about $5,000. The old press has a book value (i.e., cost less accumulated depreciation) of $30,000. It could be sold now for $5,000. If held for the remaining 10 years of its useful life, the old press would have a terminal salvage value of $2,000.

Annual operating costs under each press at the present volume of work are compared below:

	Old Press	New Press
Variable costs:		
Materials and supplies.............	$40,000	$40,000
Labor.........................	25,000	35,000
Fixed costs:		
Miscellaneous out-of-pocket		
expenses......................	20,000	10,000

While the new press would double capacity, the company anticipates that actual volume would increase by only 80%. The company now bills all jobs at variable cost plus 40% thereof. It would not be possible to raise prices with the new press in service, even though quality would be improved thereby.

Straight-line depreciation has been used on the old press and would be used also for the new one. The income tax rate is 40%. The company's cost of capital is 11%.

Required:

Prepare an analysis to assist management in deciding whether or not to replace the printing press.

6. The Pitti-Sing Nursery needs a new sprinkler system installed. The system would cost $100,000 and would last for four years. The terminal salvage value of the old piping would then just cover the cost of removing it. The nursery has a cost of capital of 10% and is subject to an income tax rate of 40%.

Required:

What would be the most advantageous depreciation method for the nursery to use in its income tax returns?

7. Pish-Tush Products, Inc., has plans to purchase a new machine for $500,000. This machine would have a useful life of five years and a terminal salvage value of $100,000. The company's cost of capital is 12%, and the income tax rate is 40%.

Required:

What would be the most advantageous method of depreciation for the corporation to elect for income tax purposes.

8. The Katisha Company is contemplating the acquisition of several new machines at a total cost of $800,000. These machines would have useful lives of 10 years and no significant terminal salvage values. If they are purchased and put into service, the company would save out-of-pocket operating costs of $155,000 each year.

The company could use either the straight-line method of depreciation or the double-declining balance method for income tax purposes. If the latter method were chosen, the company could switch to straight-line whenever it would be to its advantage to do so.

The income tax rate is 40%. The company's cost of capital is 10%.

Required:

a) Which tax depreciation method would be more advantageous?
b) Would the proposed investment in the machines be profitable?

9. The Hilarion Company is considering purchasing a 20-year lease of mineral rights for $250,000. It would finance the purchase by signing a 20-year note payable in the amount of $200,000 and paying the balance in cash at once. Annual cash income from operations, including all tax effects, would be

$51,000. The annual payment on the note would total $26,400, after considering the tax deductibility of interest on the note.

Required:

Determine the discounted rate of return on the investment in mineral rights.

10. Calverley Products, Inc., was considering the purchase of a laborsaving machine that would increase its after-tax cash flow by $12,000 per year for five years and would cost $49,500 installed. Inasmuch as the proposed investment appeared to yield less than the company's cost of capital of 12%, management decided against buying the machine. When the machine salesman learned of this decision, he proposed that Calverley buy the machine on an installment contract. Under this contract, Calverley would pay only $1,000 down and then monthly installments of $966.67 for five years. The salesman pointed out that this arrangement offered the company an increase in its annual cash flow of $400 per year for the next five years for an investment of only $1,000—a rate of return of more than 30%. Management decided to reconsider its earlier decision.

Required:

Advise Calverley's management as to the profitability of the proposed investment and the desirability of the installment contract.

11. J. W. Wells has an opportunity to purchase a lease on a service station for $60,000. The purchase would be financed by a cash payment of $20,000 and a 12-year note for the balance. Monthly payments of $650 would be required for the term of the note. The lease has a remaining term of 12 years and is not renewable. All property rights revert to the lessor at termination of the lease. Annual cash receipts from operation of the station are estimated at $30,000, and annual out-of-pocket operating costs, at $15,400.

The income tax rate is 40%. Wells' cost of capital is 10%.

Required:

a) Compute the net present value of this investment proposal.
b) Determine the discounted rate of return on the proposed investment.
c) What is the specific interest cost of the 12-year note?

12. The Grosvenor Corporation sells computer services to its clients. The company recently completed a feasibility study and decided to obtain an additional computer on January 1, 1973. Information regarding this new computer is as follows:

(1) The purchase price of the computer is $500,000. Maintenance, property taxes, and insurance would cost the purchaser $40,000 annually. If the computer is rented, the annual rent charge is $175,000 plus 5% of gross annual billings to clients. The rental contract includes main-

tenance, taxes, and insurance as the responsibility of the computer manufacturer.

(2) Because of competitive conditions, the company feels it would have to replace the new computer at the end of three years with one that is larger and faster. It is estimated that the computer will have a resale value of $200,000 at the end of three years. If purchased, the computer would be depreciated on a straight-line basis for both financial reporting and income tax purposes.

(3) Estimated annual billings for the services performed on the new computer will be $400,000 during the first year and $500,000 during each of the second and third years. The estimated annual expenses of operating the computer is $150,000 in addition to those expenses mentioned above. Also, $25,000 of start-up costs would be incurred as soon as the computer is installed.

(4) The corporate income tax rate is 40%. The company estimates its cost of capital to be 15%.

Required:

a) Prepare a schedule comparing the estimated annual net incomes from the new computer under the purchase and rental alternatives.

b) Prepare a schedule showing the annual cash flows under the purchase and rental alternatives and comparing their net present values.

c) Should the new computer be purchased or rented?

(Adapted from CPA Examination)

13. The Murgatroyd Corporation must construct acid bath facilities for cleaning its tools and dies used in molding aluminum forms. It has a choice of either a dip process or a spray process. Dip process facilities would cost $330,000 and would have a useful life of 15 years. Annual operating costs for this process would average $25,000. Spray process facilities would cost $200,000 and would have a useful life of eight years. Their annual operating costs would average $40,000. Neither facilities would have any terminal salvage value. The straight-line depreciation method would be used in either case.

The corporation's cost of capital is 10%. The applicable income tax rate is 40%.

Required:

Which type of acid bath facilities would be more economical for the corporation to purchase and operate?

14. The Maybud Diaper Laundry can buy either a Saf-Steem boiler for $20,000 or a Hot-Mor boiler for $11,000. The Saf-Steem model has a service life of 12 years and would cost about $800 per year to maintain. The Hot-Mor model would last for seven years and would cost about $1,100 per year to maintain. Either would be depreciated by the straight-line method, and neither would have a significant terminal salvage value.

The laundry has a cost of capital of 9%. Its income tax rate is 40%.

Required:

Which boiler would be more economical for the laundry to install?

15. Jack Point, a truck driver and mover, is eager to be his own boss. He wants to buy his own moving truck and become a Venetian Van Lines contractor. There are two used trucks available to him. He could afford either one, but he would have no interest in buying both, as he doesn't want to be anyone's boss either.

   A Putterbuilt truck would cost $24,000, has a cargo capacity of 3,000 cubic feet, and would have a useful life of five years and a terminal salvage value of $4,000. An Internal Harder truck would cost $18,000, has a cargo capacity of 2,500 cubic feet, and would have a useful life of three years and a terminal salvage value of $3,000.

   From others' experience, Point estimates that his annual operating receipts would be about $20 per cubic feet of cargo handled. His annual out-of-pocket costs would be about $12,000 regardless of which truck he bought.

   Point has estimated that his cost of capital is 12%. He is in the 30% income tax bracket.

Required:

Assuming that Jack Point wishes to maximize his annual receipts, which truck should he buy?

16. The Partlet Corporation has $10,000,000 available for investment in its 1973 capital budget. The six independent investment proposals listed below are the only remaining candidates for consideration by management. Each of these six proposals would have an economic life of 10 years. The corporation's cost of capital is 10%. If the entire $10,000,000 is not invested, the remainder will be loaned for short terms to other firms to yield a net rate of return of 10%.

   The six investment proposals and their budgeted cash flows are as follows:

Investment	Initial Outlay	Net Annual Cash Receipts
A..............	$4,000,000	$ 800,000
B..............	2,000,000	357,400
C..............	3,000,000	579,200
D..............	5,000,000	1,156,500
E..............	1,500,000	408,500
F..............	2,500,000	429,300

Required:

a) Rank the six investment proposals in the order of their profitability. Which investments should the corporation undertake?
b) What is the corporation's effective cost of capital for 1973?

17. The Poo-Bah Products Company has a total of $5,000,000 available for investment. The cost of capital is estimated to be 8%. The company is considering the following five independent investment opportunities, each having the indicated budgeted financial characteristics:

Investment	Initial Outlay	Annual Cash Receipts	Annual Cash Outlays	Life in Years
A....................	$2,500,000	$3,000,000	$2,300,000	10
B....................	1,500,000	2,150,000	1,800,000	12
C....................	1,000,000	850,000	660,000	15
D....................	2,000,000	2,500,000	2,000,000	12
E....................	2,000,000	1,860,000	1,220,000	8

The income tax rate is 40%. Initial outlays may be amortized, for tax purposes, by the straight-line method.

Required:

a) Rank these five investments in the order of their profitability.
b) What would be the most profitable total investment program for the company to undertake?
c) What factors complicate investment decision making in this case?

18. The Deadeye Distillery Corporation is considering three alternative promotional plans for new products. They involve various combinations of prices, development expenditures, and promotional outlays. High, medium, and low forecasts of revenues under each plan have been formulated; and their respective probabilities of occurrence have been estimated. These budgeted revenues and probabilities, along with other pertinent data, are summarized below:

	Plan A	Plan B	Plan C
Budgeted revenue (with probability):			
High..................	$3,000,000 (.3)	$2,400,000 (.2)	$5,000,000 (.2)
Medium................	2,000,000 (.3)	2,000,000 (.7)	2,500,000 (.5)
Low..................	500,000 (.4)	1,500,000 (.1)	0 (.3)
Variable costs as percentages of revenues............	60%	75%	70%
Initial investment..........	$2,500,000	$2,000,000	$2,400,000
Life in years..............	8	8	8

The corporation's cost of capital is 12%. The income tax rate is 40%. Investments in promotional programs will be amortized by the straight-line method. The corporation will have net taxable income in each year, regardless of the success or failure of the new products.

Required:

a) Which promotion plan would be expected to be the most profitable? Show supporting analysis.

b) In the event the worst happened, which plan would result in the lowest total loss?

19. The Carruthers Cartage Company is considering expanding its fleet of barges by purchasing 12 new barges, each with a freight capacity of 600 tons. Maximum operating capacity for a barge is 500,000 ton-miles per month. Each barge would cost $250,000 and would have an estimated useful life of 20 years. Depreciation would be computed by the straight-line method for income tax purposes.

The company's standard freight rate is $.08 per ton-mile. Variable out-of-pocket operating costs average $.03 per ton-mile. Fixed monthly out-of-pocket costs are $10,000 per barge. The income tax rate is 40%, and the company's cost of capital is 10%.

Management has estimated that the chances are 6 out of 10 that the new barges will be utilized at a normal volume of 75% of maximum capacity. (Routes and schedules would make it impossible for the company to buy and operate nine barges at 100% of capacity instead of 12 barges at 75% of capacity.) The actual operating rate may be affected by the result of a pending situation over which the company can exert no control. One of its chief competitors is the G&S Railroad, which is presently actively discussing a merger with the larger and stronger Midcontinent Railroad. If this merger is approved—and the chances are 3 in 10 that it will be— the G&S Railroad's competitive position will be substantially improved. It could then attract freight now handled by barges on the rivers. In that case, Carruthers' management estimates that the new barges would be operated at only 50% of maximum capacity. On the other hand, there is 1 chance in 10 that the merger will not be approved and that, consequently, the G&S Railroad will be forced to discontinue operations. In that event, the new barges would be utilized at 100% of their maximum capacity.

Required:

Would the proposed investment in the new barges appear to be profitable? Present a supporting analysis to management.

20. Alhambra Aluminum Products, Inc., is a medium-sized manufacturer of aluminum and aluminum products. Corporate sales volume in 1972 totaled $96 million, on which the company earned $6.7 million after taxes. Most of Alhambra's customers were relatively small users of aluminum extrusions and/or custom-designed aluminum products. Thus, Alhambra had found a segment of the aluminum market in which it was able to compete quite effectively with the three giants of the industry.

Alhambra fared less well in competition for bauxite, the basic raw material of aluminum production, however. Getting the bauxite required to meet the company's annual production requirements was one of its biggest problems. The demand for aluminum products was fairly stable. Unfortunately, the supply of bauxite was neither stable nor predictable. The causes of this supply problem were both natural (weather conditions and discoveries of new bauxite deposits) and economic (widely varying outputs from marginal mines in various parts of the world). There seemed to be no way that anything could be done about this supply situation; it was just a fact of life that had to be faced.

It was a problem that hit Alhambra harder than it did the big three aluminum producers, however. These companies had their own bauxite mines and, in addition, long-term supply contracts with large independent mines. Alhambra, on the other hand, relied entirely upon bauxite produced by smaller independent mines. But it was precisely these mines that were the most unstable sources of supply. In some years, they could meet all of Alhambra's needs at very favorable prices. In other years, they were able to mine little if any bauxite. Then Alhambra had to "beat the bushes" to find the supplies that it needed, and it had to pay premium prices for them. What was worse, the bauxite that the company could get in the bad years was usually a low grade of ore that yielded less aluminum and caused higher conversion costs as a result. Following is a summary of Alhambra's bauxite purchases over the preceding 10 years and the net costs per ton:

Year	Tons Purchased	Net Cost per Ton
1972	518,000	$35.40
1971	402,000	32.00
1970	390,000	31.60
1969	493,000	33.25
1968	385,000	30.50
1967	484,000	32.90
1966	473,000	32.50
1965	457,000	32.70
1964	350,000	29.30
1963	342,000	29.25

Thus, the market for bauxite was an aggravated "feast or famine" situation. In a good year, such as 1971, Alhambra could fill its requirements by purchasing relatively smaller quantities of high-grade ore at favorable prices. In a bad year, such as 1972, the company had to buy larger quantities of low-grade ore and pay higher prices. Competitive conditions in the aluminum products market did not allow the company to pass those higher prices on to its customers. It simply had to accept lower profits in the bad years.

For several years, one of Alhambra's important bauxite suppliers had been del Bolero Mines, Ltd., a Brazilian corporation. Recently, del Bolero's American representative advised Alhambra that his firm was investing heavily in newly discovered deposits in Indonesia and felt that it had to cut back on some of its operations in the Western Hemisphere. Accordingly, del Bolero planned to sell its Plaza-Toro mine in Honduras. The American representative knew of Alhambra's supply problems and suggested that del Bolero would be willing to sell the Plaza-Toro mine directly to Alhambra for $30 million, without soliciting competing bids. This mine was a known producer of high-grade ore, and reliable geological surveys indicated that it had the capacity to continue producing an annual output of about 750,000 tons for the next 20 years.

The market research staff at Alhambra estimated the company's bauxite requirements for the next 20 years at an annual average of 520,000 tons of high-grade ore. If it had to buy low-grade ore, annual requirements would be about 650,000 tons. An average market price of $40 per ton was forecast for the same 20-year period. This price was an average of the lower and higher prices that could be expected in good and bad years. Inasmuch as the productive capacity of the Plaza-Toro mine exceeded Alhambra's own requirements, the excess output could readily be sold at prevailing market prices. With data provided by the market research staff, his own cost accounting department, and the management of the del Bolero mining division, the corporate controller prepared a financial analysis of the proposed investment. This appears in Exhibit 1. There was general agreement within the corporation that the basic estimates underlying this analysis were as good as could be obtained in the circumstances. There was some controversy about the question of risk, however.

Exhibit 1

Capital Budgeting Analysis of Investment in Plaza-Toro Mine

Cash receipts:

Cost savings from use of high-grade ore:			
Annual tonnage saved (650,000 − 520,000).....			130,000
Estimated market price per ton...............	$	40.00	
Estimated conversion costs per ton............		3.20	$ 43.20
Annual saving............................			5,616,000
Profit on sale of excess output:			
Excess tonnage mined (750,000 − 520,000).....			230,000
Market price per ton.......................	$	40.00	
Variable mining costs per ton................		28.00	$ 12.00
			2,760,000
Gross cash receipts...........................			8,376,000
Less income taxes, net of percentage depletion*...			2,838,000
Net cash receipts............................			5,538,000
Discount factor for 20 years at 10%............			8.6466
Present value of cash receipts..................			$47,885,000

Cash outlays:

Investment in mine.........................	$30,000,000	
Additional working capital needed to operate mine......................................	6,000,000	36,000,000
Net present value of investment...............		$11,885,000
Present value index of investment..................		1.33
Discounted rate of return on investment...........		14½%

*Income taxes are charged at a rate of 50%. The net tax due is substantially reduced by a percentage depletion allowance of $1,350,000 per year, however.

For some time, Alhambra had used 10% as its cost of capital. This was used as the discount rate for proposed capital investments only when they were relatively riskless, however. In other cases, a higher discount rate was used to compensate for the element of risk. In the case of the Plaza-Toro mine, the president of the company wondered whether a discount rate of at least 15% would not be more appropriate. If that were used, of course, the investment would appear to be unprofitable. The controller defended his use of 10% on the grounds that purchase of the mine would actually reduce risk by eliminating the year-to-year fluctuations in materials purchase quantities and prices. In fact, he contended that 10% was a conservative discount rate in view of the fact that the company would use capital borrowed at 6% to finance the purchase of the mine.

Required:
a) Evaluate the capital budgeting analysis prepared by the controller. Indicate any revisions you believe should be made in it.
b) What do you believe the appropriate discount rate for the investment in the mine should be? Explain.

chapter 17

THE ROLE OF COSTS
IN PRICING DECISIONS

Probably the most important single decision which the management of a business enterprise must make is setting the price for the firm's product or service. In a multiproduct firm, many pricing decisions must be made. The pricing decision is critical not only at the outset, but it must be reappraised and, possibly, revised regularly. The pricing decision affects the entire enterprise and must be made with this fact in mind. It is not simply a marketing or a financial decision. It is the genesis of the revenues which the firm realizes. If those revenues persistently fail to cover the costs of the firm, the enterprise as a whole will ultimately fail. The accountant, as a planner, compiler, and analyst of financial data, is importantly involved in the price-setting decision. Fnancial data and, more specifically, cost data are fundamental elements in the price-setting process; but they are only part of that process. Their relevance to the pricing decision must be neither exaggerated nor underestimated; either error could be financially fatal. This chapter is concerned with the proper role of cost data in price-setting decisions. It does not purport to offer a comprehensive analysis of pricing.

ECONOMIC THEORY OF PRICE DETERMINATION

It is not the purpose of this section to expound or to summarize price theory as commonly developed in the discipline of economics. A few basic notions will be reviewed, however, to establish a general framework for the ensuing discussion of the pertinence of costs to pricing decisions.

Supply and Demand

The basic factors determining price in economic theory are the supply of a product (or service) and the demand for it. If there is an actual market for a product, there must be some price at which the physical volume of product that suppliers are willing to sell is equal to that volume which customers (i.e., "demanders") are willing to buy. That is the price at which the product is traded. This relationship between supply and demand is commonly depicted graphically by a positively sloped supply curve and a negatively sloped demand curve, as illustrated in Figure 17–1. (These curves need not be straight lines, of course.) The price of the product (p in Figure 17–1) is determined at the point of inter-

FIGURE 17–1

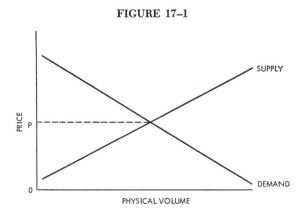

section of the supply and demand curves. The conceptual validity of this analysis is readily apparent. Its practical applicability, however, is not always so apparent. Managers do not have access to neat supply and demand curves such as those in Figure 17–1. They may be able to estimate the general patterns of supply and demand for their products, but these estimates are subject to varying and indeterminate degrees of error.

Elasticity of Demand. One of the most critical characteristics of the demand for a product is its price elasticity, that is, the relative degree to which changes in the price of the product cause changes in the volume of sales of that product. Obviously, knowledge of the elasticity of demand for a product is crucial to any price change decision. Yet, the elasticity of demand for most products is subject to a considerable degree of uncertainty. The demand for certain products, such as salt, is usually agreed to be highly inelastic. A substantial increase in the price of a pound of salt may have no appreciable impact upon consumers' purchases of it. Other products, however, have definitely elastic demand schedules. Substantially more units will be purchased at low prices than at high prices. (The demand curve in Figure 17–1 obviously is elastic.) Observing that the demand for a product is generally elastic or inelastic is one thing. Measuring its elasticity—determining the impact upon physical sales volume of a specific price change—is quite another. Yet, it is just this determination that is important to the business manager contemplating a change in the price of his product.

His problems are further complicated by the factor of cross-elasticity of demand. This is the relative degree to which the sales of one product are affected by changes in the price of a substitute product (e.g., the impact on the sales of steel of a reduction in the price of aluminum). The problem of measuring cross-elasticity is further clouded by the prior problem of identifying substitute products.

A review of the discussions in the preceding three paragraphs suggests that management cannot measure accurately the most basic factors underlying the price-setting decision. Nevertheless, these economic factors cannot be ignored. Subsequent discussions of the role of costs in pricing decisions will not deal extensively with the factors of supply and demand, but these factors will always be present as the basic constraints within which the pricing decision must be made.

Competition

Price-setting decisions must be weighed and evaluated with adequate consideration of the impact of competition upon the decision and the impact of the decision upon competition. In the perfect competition of economic theory, the individual seller is, in effect, the captive of competition. He has no price-setting discretion at all. One of the requisites of perfect competition is homogeneity of product; all sellers' products must be identical. If there exists an element of product differentiation among sellers, the market is described as imperfectly competitive. In an imperfect market, the individual seller has some range of discretion within which he may set his price. The extreme of price-setting discretion is the monopolist. He is the only one selling his particular product and, therefore, is limited in his pricing decisions only by the factors of supply and demand. However, as in the case of public utilities, the government may step in and impose additional constraints on the monopolist's pricing policies.

Subsequent discussions of pricing decisions in this chapter will assume some degree of imperfect competition in the market for the product whose price is in question. The seller will always be assumed to have some range of discretion in setting his price. This assumption is generally valid in respect to the operations of most American manufacturers and distributors.

PRICING STANDARD PRODUCTS

Not all pricing decisions have the same dimensions. There may be great differences between a decision as to the price of one of a company's standard products and a decision regarding the pricing of a special order. The former type of decision will be considered here. Pricing special orders will be discussed in a later section. Standard products here include all items regularly produced and sold by the company, whether they are produced continuously for inventory or on individual customers' orders only.

Cost-Plus Pricing

One of the simplest approaches to price-setting decisions is to set the price at an amount equal to the standard or budgeted cost of production (or purchasing, in the case of a merchandising enterprise) plus a normal markup. This normal markup is usually a target gross profit, intended to cover nonmanufacturing costs and leave a remainder for net profit before taxes. The normal markup is customarily stated as a percentage, either of selling price or of cost. Normal markups are fairly widely employed in retailing, where they are regularly expressed as percentages of selling prices. Thus, in a retail store, a markup of 30% for an item with a cost of $3.50 means a selling price of $5. Whenever one encounters a normal markup percentage, he should be careful that he understands whether selling price or cost is the base of that percentage.

Unfortunately, while pricing at cost plus a normal markup is attractively simple, it lacks economic logic and is not generally valid. This approach to pricing assumes that it is possible to make an equitable allocation of all manufacturing costs among the several products of a firm. But there are no criteria for what constitutes an "equitable" allocation. Common costs are inherently not traceable to individual products. Allocation is an arbitrary expedient used for purposes of inventory valuation and income determination because generally accepted accounting principles require that all manufacturing costs be assigned to specific products. The same allocations are not necessarily appropriate or even acceptable for purposes of decision making.[1] And pricing is very definitely a decision-making situation. Further, adding a normal markup to production cost and establishing the total as the selling price presumes either that there is no competition or that the resultant selling price is competitive. A manufacturer may find that his production cost plus a

---

[1] See the discussion of the different treatments of common production costs for inventory accounting and for decision making in Chapter 14, pages 358–63.

normal markup results in a price that is either too high or too low for the existing market. As long as buyers recognize some difference between his product and substitute products in the market, they will accept a commensurate difference in price. The range of the individual seller's price-setting discretion in such a case varies with the degree of substitution among the several sellers' products. The closer the degree of substitution, the narrower is the individual seller's range of pricing discretion.

In a dynamic market, characterized by change and uncertainty, pricing at cost plus a normal markup is not a generally valid or sustainable policy. It may be a useful starting point for the pricing decision, but the seller must be prepared to deviate from such a target price and, perhaps, to deviate greatly from it. What is basically unsound in this approach is not its recognition of the need to cover costs but its insistence upon a normal margin.

Relevant Costs for Pricing Decisions

Direct Costs. In a single product firm, all of the costs incurred may be regarded as traceable to the one product. Hence, all costs are direct costs with respect to the product. In setting a price for such a product, management would properly expect it to cover all of the company's costs and provide a profit margin. In a multiproduct firm, however, not all costs are directly traceable to individual products. Some are true common costs; any assignment of these to individual products is purely arbitrary. Which costs in the multiproduct firm, then, are relevant for pricing decisions? When a decision is to be made regarding the price of an individual product, only those costs directly traceable to that product, those costs which could be avoided by discontinuing production and sale of the product, should be considered directly. In other words, this type of pricing decision should be approached by means of the incremental profit analysis described in Chapter 14. In the incremental profit approach, the selling price must cover all direct costs—both manufacturing and nonmanufacturing, both variable and fixed—that are attributable to a product. The price should also contribute to the covering of common costs and the realization of a profit. The common costs are not ignored in this approach; they are provided for by the excess of the selling price over the direct costs. Common costs are not assigned to the individual products for the simple reason that they bear no direct relationship to those products. Thus, if cost plus a normal profit margin is to be the target price for a product, the cost involved should be the total of all costs directly traceable to that product. Once again, however, this target price may have to be regarded only as a starting point in the pricing decision.

For a short period of time it is tolerable for the price of a product to do no more than cover its direct costs or even, possibly, only the direct variable costs. This may be the case, for example, when a new product is introduced. The initial direct promotional costs may be unusually high relative to sales volume, and special price concessions may be granted in connection with introductory offers. In this case, the negligible contribution to common costs in the short run is accepted in anticipation of long-run profits. In other cases, a very low contribution from one or more products may be accepted for want of a more profitable alternative. A low contribution is better than none at all.

In the long run, of course, the aggregate revenues from all products must cover the common costs as well as the direct costs. Ideally, each product should make a significant contribution to common costs; but it is not possible to state any general rule for determining satisfactory and unsatisfactory contributions. If factors of demand and/or competition prevent a firm from setting a price for one of its products that will cover direct costs, there may be no alternative to discontinuation of that product. If a competitive price does cover direct costs and yields some contribution to common costs, however, how high must that contribution be to justify long-run continuance of the product in the company's line? This question can be answered only in light of the available alternatives. If the product is discontinued, are there others which may be substituted for it and which will yield a higher contribution to common costs? What effect will discontinuance of this product have upon the demand for other products in the line? The elimination of one product from the line may cause the loss of sales of other, complementary products.[2] Product-pricing decisions should be made with a view toward maximum company profit in the long run. This objective should be regarded as a total company accomplishment, not a piecemeal result of several independent pricing decisions.

Full Cost Pricing. Pricing decisions should be made in recognition of the need for the firm to cover all costs, at least in the long run. A fairly popular extension of this recognition is the practice of *full cost pricing*, wherein all costs or, at least, all manufacturing costs are assigned to individual products. This extension, however, is not valid. It seeks to establish specific cost-product relationships in cases of common costs where no such relationships actually exist. If only manufacturing costs are assigned to individual products, full cost pricing ignores the fact that some nonmanufacturing costs may be directly traceable to products. Under the incremental profit approach, each product's price must cover its own direct costs, whether manufacturing or nonmanufacturing. Once this requirement is met, then the sum of all products' incremental profits must cover common costs.

---

[2] See Chapter 14, page 357.

At this point, the reader may raise the question of how management can assure that all common costs will be covered if individual products' prices are set on the basis of directly traceable costs only. To begin with, basing prices on direct costs is, at best, only a starting point in the pricing decision. Market conditions must be considered, and these may dictate prices that provide a very substantial contribution to common costs. In any event, to the extent that costs are relevant in the pricing decision, they must include only those costs that bear some definable functional relationship to the product in question. Allocations of common costs among products and prices based upon the resultant full costs must be regarded as nothing more than tentative targets. For certain products, such targets have proved realistic and attainable. For others, however, these targets must quickly be abandoned. A low contribution from a single product does not necessarily mean that the price is too low or that the product ought to be discontinued. If the economic determinants of price are such that the combined prices for all of a company's products are insufficient to cover common costs in the long run, the conclusion is not that the individual prices are wrong but rather that the firm is economically inefficient. Such a firm must either improve its operating efficiency or cease operations and liquidate.

Pricing a New Product

The introduction of a new product in a company's line may entail some additional problems. If it is significantly different from any product already available, there is no established market for it. Until its introduction, there has been no supply of the product and, hence, no demonstrated demand for it. The company may believe firmly that the demand will be substantial, but this has yet to be proved in the market. In all likelihood, there are some near-substitute products currently on the market; but their actual degree of substitution is as yet unknown. Thus, the competitive influence on the price of the new product can only be estimated. Further, the firm may have no reliable estimate of the direct costs of manufacturing and marketing the new product. Its cost patterns are likely to change as the firm obtains experience with the product and as its sales volume increases. In summary, then, pricing decisions for new products involve essentially the same considerations as those discussed earlier for established products. These considerations are subject to considerably greater uncertainty, however.

Test Marketing.   One fairly popular technique employed to obtain valuable experience with a new product is test marketing. The product is introduced in selected areas only, often at different prices in different areas. Such tests afford the firm's management some idea as to the amount and elasticity of the demand for the product, the competition it will encounter, and the contribution to common costs and profit it may be expected to yield at various prices and volumes. Test marketing, of course, is not a perfect simulation of full-scale production and distribution. It may, however, provide very useful information for better planning of the full-scale marketing effort. It also permits initial pricing mistakes to be made in miniature rather than on a large scale.

Pricing for a Target Rate of Return. In most cases, the introduction of a new product involves some capital investment outlays and should be evaluated, in part at least, as a long-term investment decision. The price set for the product should be sufficient to yield at least the minimum acceptable rate of return on investment required by the firm. In other words, the price must be high enough that the net present value of the investment is positive. In capital investment analysis, management is concerned with the net cash inflow to be derived from a decision. For a new product, the net cash inflow is a function of both price and volume. If volume were a fixed quantity, the required price could be determined quite easily by means of discounted cash flow analysis. However, as long as there is some elasticity of demand for the product, the price and volume will vary inversely with each other. The pattern of this variation may be determined from test marketing or estimated from experience with near-substitute products.

To illustrate the relevance of capital investment analysis to pricing decisions, assume that a company is introducing a new product for which it feels it has considerable latitude in setting price. The product has been test marketed in three areas at three different prices. As a result of these tests, the firm estimates that the three alternative prices will yield the annual sales volumes indicated in Table 17–1. Variable costs are budgeted at $4 per unit for the two volumes in excess of 100,000 units per year. For the low volume of only 60,000 units, however, variable costs would be $5 per unit. This difference reflects cost savings obtainable at larger scales of operation. The required investment outlay is all for production equipment that would have an economic life of three years and no terminal salvage value. It would amount to $450,000 if volume is to exceed 100,000 units. Both this investment and the avoidable fixed costs of production and distribution would be reduced if the low volume alternative were planned. As in previous illustrations, the company's average cost of capital is assumed to be 10% and the applicable income tax rate, 40%. It is evident from the table that either the $6 price or the $7.50 price would be profitable but that the latter is much more so. In the absence of other conflicting evidence, thus, the price would be set at $7.50.

The foregoing illustration is greatly simplified. It assumes that only three alternative prices are possible. Actually, the price might be set anywhere within a fairly broad range. This assumption merely reduces the size of the illustration, however. It does not impair the basic point. Also, a constant annual sales volume is planned for the first three years.

TABLE 17–1

Analysis of Test Market Data

	Test Area		
	1	*2*	*3*
Test selling price per unit.....................	$ 6.00	$ 7.50	$ 9.00
Variable costs per unit........................	4.00	4.00	5.00
Variable profit per unit.......................	$ 2.00	$ 3.50	$ 4.00
Estimated annual unit sales volume............	150,000	120,000	60,000
Total variable profit..........................	$300,000	$420,000	$240,000
Avoidable fixed costs.........................	100,000	100,000	80,000
Incremental profit before tax.................	$200,000	$320,000	$160,000
Income tax at 40%...........................	80,000	128,000	64,000
Incremental profit after tax...................	$120,000	$192,000	$ 96,000
Tax saving from straight-line depreciation ($\frac{1}{3}$ × investment outlay × 40%)............	60,000	60,000	53,333
Annual cash receipts after tax.................	$180,000	$252,000	$149,333
Present value factor for 3 years at 10%........	2.5918	2.5918	2.5918
Present value of cash receipts.................	$466,524	$653,134	$387,041
Investment outlay............................	450,000	450,000	400,000
Net present value............................	$ 16,524	$203,134	$(12,959)
Present value index..........................	1.04	1.45	.97
Discounted rate of return.....................	12½%	38%	7½%

In reality, one would expect the sales volume of a new product to grow over the period of its introduction and initial market penetration. Further, sales potential and additional capital investments after the first three years are not considered at all. Unless the market life of the product is expected to be only three years, this omission is also unrealistic. Finally, pricing to obtain a target rate of return on invested capital is subject to all of the imprecisions and uncertainties that characterize capital budgeting decisions in general. In fact, the element of uncertainty may be greater than normal in this case. Some firms attempt to compensate for this additional uncertainty by requiring a higher than normal rate of return on an investment in a new product. For example, the firm in the illustration above might demand that a new product offer a discounted rate of return of 20% or more rather than one which merely exceeds the cost of capital of 10%. Although it is conceptually valid, this approach still demands some practical decision as to how much additional return is needed to compensate for the increased uncertainty.

PRICING SPECIAL ORDERS

For purposes of the present discussion, special order pricing decisions include only nonrecurring, or "one time only," decisions. These will be classified according to two general types: orders for special products and orders for standard products at special prices. The important distinguishing characteristic of both of these types of special pricing decisions is that they pertain to individual sales only. They are not intended to influence the regular prices of the seller's standard products.

Orders for Special Products

The first type of special order is for a custom-made product, designed and manufactured to a single customer's specifications by a firm that does not regularly handle such orders. If a firm routinely processes special items to customers' orders, it should set the price for each such order on the basis of an established general pricing policy, for it is then not a special situation. In firms regularly producing custom-made goods more than in any others, pricing at cost plus a normal profit margin has merit. There is no market and no competitive price for such goods. The producer quite reasonably seeks to recover his costs plus a profit. If that profit is too great, other producers will win orders away from him. If the profit is too low, on the other hand, the producer will lose money on such orders. Thus, the profit margin will tend to be normalized by the threat of competition on one side and by the manufacturer's profit objectives on the other.

Incremental Profit Analysis. The decision as to the price of an order for a custom-made item should be made in consideration of the alternatives. If such an order is received when a firm is producing at full capacity, acceptance of it would necessitate either a reduction in the output of standard products or overtime. If the order is taken at the cost of regular production, its price must be adequate to yield an incremental profit at least equal to that foregone on the standard products which cannot be produced because of the special order. In order to determine their respective incremental profits, management must know the direct costs of both the special order and the standard products. These will include variable costs and, possibly, direct fixed costs. Special setup and training costs incurred in connection with the special order must be assigned to it, even though they may derive from sources normally included in general plant overhead. For example, indirect labor for machinery setup and maintenance is commonly a part of overhead, charged to standard products at a normal or standard rate. If the special order requires setup and maintenance costs in excess of those that would routinely be incurred for production of standard items, that *excess* is a direct cost of the special order.

If an order for a custom-made product is received at a time when the firm is operating below capacity and its acceptance would involve simply the utilization of otherwise idle facilities, the price of such order need cover its own direct costs only. Here the alternative to the special order is no output at all. If the order yields any incremental profit at all, the firm's net income will be increased. The alternative of sales of regular products does not exist.

Capital Investment Analysis. Acceptance of an order for a custom-made product was discussed above as a short-run decision. Implicit in this analysis is the assumption that the order could be produced without additional capital investment in production facilities. If new investments were necessary in order for the firm to accept the order, either the price of the order would have to cover the full amount of such investments or the firm would have to have reasonable expectations of further profitable employment of the new facilities. In the latter instance, those other profitable opportunities should be quantified; and the proposal should be evaluated as any capital investment decision.

Other Considerations. Handling special orders occasionally may afford a company the opportunity of examining the possibilities of entering new markets without committing itself thereto. On the other hand, a firm's unfamiliarity with a special product may present peculiar difficulties. The costs of processing the order may be increased beyond the planned amount because of unexpected overruns on time and/or expenses. If the order is priced in advance on the basis of budgeted costs (as would often be the case), any significant cost overrun could convert a planned profit to a loss. With this possibility in mind, management may accept orders for new and unfamiliar items only if the buyer agrees to bear any reasonable and unforeseen additional costs.

Cost-Plus-Fixed-Fee Pricing. Perhaps the extreme expedient in pricing special orders for special products is to charge the customer for the total actual costs of producing the goods plus a predetermined profit. That profit, agreed to by the parties in advance, would be the "fixed fee" added to cost in order to determine price. Obviously, such a contract benefits the seller, for he is guaranteed a profit. There is no risk of loss on the order. It is not necessarily beneficial to the buyer, however; for the seller has no incentive to control production costs on the order. At one time, cost-plus-fixed-fee contracts were quite common in government purchases of specialized goods—including very costly defense equipment. Recently, however, the government has sought to purchase such goods under cost-plus-incentive-fee contracts or other incentive arrangements. Under this type of contract, the seller will be reimbursed for actual costs plus a predetermined profit only if his actual costs equal the estimated costs that were used by both parties in negotiating the contract. If his actual costs are lower than estimated, his profit is increased by a predetermined percentage of the cost saving. Conversely, if actual costs exceed the estimate, his profit is reduced or even completely eliminated. These incentive contracts are intended to offer the seller part of the cost recovery advantages of cost-plus-fixed-fee contracts and, at the same time, to encourage him to cut costs and, thereby, benefit both himself and the government. Similar agreements would be equally appropriate in contracts between two private firms. The size of the predetermined profit margin will be established by negotiations. Presumably, the seller would seek a larger profit margin if there was a high degree of uncertainty associated with his cost estimate.

Orders for Standard Products at Special Prices

Incremental Profit Analysis. Not uncommonly, manufacturers are asked to supply large quantities of standard products to individual customers at prices below regular list prices. If such an order is received when a manufacturer is operating at full capacity, it will almost certainly be rejected. Why should a firm cut prices when it can sell the same quantity at regular list prices? If, however, the manufacturer is producing below capacity, the special order affords an opportunity to employ idle facilities in the production of the company's standard products. In this situation, any price that yields some incremental profit will increase net income in the short run. From the viewpoint of incremental profit analysis, the only costs relevant to the decision are those direct costs that would be avoided if the order were not accepted. Ordinarily, these will be the variable production and delivery costs.

As an example, assume that a company operating at 70% of normal capacity is asked to produce 25,000 units of one of its regular products for a large drugstore chain at the special price of $1.65 per unit. The regular selling price is $2.25 per unit. The standard production cost of the item is as follows:

Raw materials...................	$ .48
Direct labor.....................	.65
Variable overhead...............	.29
Fixed overhead..................	.38
	$1.80

Acceptance of the order would place no strain whatever on production facilities and would not affect output of items for sale at regular prices. The incremental administrative cost of handling this order is estimated to be $900. At first glance, the order might appear unprofitable, for the proposed selling price is less than the standard cost of the product. However, it must be remembered that the fixed overhead will be incurred in any event. Whether it is charged to production or charged to the volume variance, it is incurred. The proposed price of $1.65 does exceed the variable production costs (raw materials, direct labor, and variable overhead) by $.23 per unit. Thus, the total variable profit on the order would be $5,750 (25,000 units × $.23). After deducting the direct fixed administrative cost of $900, the incremental profit before tax would be $4,850.

Capital Investment Analysis. The illustration in the preceding paragraph involved a special order for a large quantity of a standard product at a lower price only once. However, a manufacturer might be offered a similar proposition on a continuing basis. A distributor might offer to purchase annually a minimum quantity of a particular product at a reduced price. Such an offer would involve a long-term commitment of resources to one sales contract. Hence, it would have to be evaluated as an investment opportunity. If the only alternative to acceptance of this order were employment of the same resources to produce the same product for sale at the regular price, a decision to reject the offer could be made without resort to discounted cash flow analysis. However, if the alternative is idle capacity, the decision may be very different. The unusable idle facilities could probably be disposed of, at least in part, for their current salvage value. The special order would be profitable, then, if the present value of the after-tax cash inflow from it exceeded the current salvage value (after consideration of the tax effect) of the idle facilities. A third alternative might be to construct new plant facilities specifically to handle the special order. Such an investment should be analyzed as any capital investment proposal. Management should bear in mind, however, that the implications of the decision upon cash flows may extend beyond the special order itself.

Other Considerations. Before any decision is made to sell a regular product at a special low price, consideration should be given to the possible repercussion upon sales of that product at the regular price. If other customers learn that the item has been sold at a reduced price, they may demand a similar price or they may even threaten to cancel their orders. If it becomes common knowledge that a product is being sold at a "cut-rate" price, the image of the product's quality may be impaired. If the buyer at the low price is a private brand distributor, however, the manufacturer's name might never be associated with the item when resold below the usual selling price. Thus, if the special sale can be kept secret, the dangers suggested above might not arise. If the manufacturer enters into a long-term contract to supply a private brand seller with a product, knowledge of the arrangement is likely to spread. To some extent, this depends upon the nature of the product. If the product is a radio, minor changes in the exterior of the cabinet might effectively mask the manufacturer's identity. If it is an automobile tire, however, the tread design might reveal the manufacturer despite the presence of the distributor's private brand name on the casing. As a manufacturer's sales volume is obtained increasingly from one or a few large buyers, his bargaining position with them deteriorates. Ultimately, his continued solvency may depend upon their will. Obviously, this possibility should be considered before entering into sales contracts of the type described here. As a final consideration, the offering of standard products to individual buyers at reduced prices might be in violation of the federal antitrust law.

ROBINSON-PATMAN ACT

In 1936 the Congress passed and President Franklin D. Roosevelt approved the Robinson-Patman Act. This law amended the Clayton Act of 1914 and added to the federal government's arsenal of antitrust legislation. Specifically, the Robinson-Patman Act deals with price discrimination—situations in which a seller offers the same product to different buyers at different prices. Section 2(a) of this act provides that it is unlawful for a seller to discriminate in price between different purchasers of goods of like grade and quality if such discrimination would tend to lessen competition or to create a monopoly.[3] However, the seller who so discriminates may justify price differentials by showing that they are attributable to actual cost differences. This cost defense provision of the law reads as follows:

> *Provided*, That nothing herein contained shall prevent differentials which make only due allowance for differences in the cost of manufacture, sale, or delivery resulting from the differing methods or quantities in which such commodities are to such purchasers sold or delivered.[4]

The Robinson-Patman Act is enforced and the cost defense interpreted by the Federal Trade Commission. The following paragraphs do not purport to contain an exhaustive discussion of the act or of the cost defense alone. They simply attempt to indicate the role of cost accounting in one important area of antitrust legislation.[5]

The cost defense has not played a major role in formal proceedings of the Federal Trade Commission in cases of alleged price discrimination. It has, however, been of considerable importance in many of the commission's investigations which have terminated without formal complaints.[6] Thus, managers responsible for price-setting decisions should be cogni-

---

[3] 49 Stat. 1526 (1936).

[4] *Ibid.*

[5] For more expansive treatments of this act and the cost defense in particular, see Corwin D. Edwards, *The Price Discrimination Law*, (Washington, D.C.: The Brookings Institution, 1959), chap. xviii on the cost defense; and Wright Patman, *Complete Guide to the Robinson-Patman Act* (Englewood Cliffs, N.J.: Prentice-Hall, Inc., 1963), pp. 70–83 on the cost defense. A detailed analysis of experience with the cost defense in actual cases may be found in Herbert F. Taggart, *Cost Justification* (Ann Arbor: Bureau of Business Research, School of Business Administration, The University of Michigan, 1959).

[6] Edwards, *op. cit.*, pp. 587–89; and Patman, *op. cit.*, pp. 75–76.

zant of the relevance of the antitrust law to their work and of the particular pertinence of cost data to the legality of price differentials. As the Robinson-Patman Act deals with price discrimination between different buyers of the same product, it is relevant only to pricing decisions respecting standard products. The pricing of custom-made products does not come within the scope of the act.

Although the cost defense includes within its scope both manufacturing and nonmanufacturing costs, there is no question that distribution costs are the most important ones in establishing an effective cost defense. Some cost differentials are easy to show; lower freight charges on carlot shipments are examples. Other cost differentials may be more difficult to demonstrate. For example, it is generally agreed that the costs of order taking, invoicing, and billing are lower per sales dollar on large orders than on small orders. If the seller's cost accounting system is not set up so as to develop these costs as amounts per sales dollar, however, he may have difficulty in establishing an acceptable cost defense on such basis.

Earlier in this chapter, the prime importance of direct costs in pricing decisions was emphasized. For purposes of the cost defense in the Robinson-Patman Act, however, both direct and indirect costs are relevant. The Federal Trade Commission will not accept the assignment of only the direct costs of a product or of a particular method of distribution to that product or method in a cost defense. A reasonable allocation of common costs to all products or to all business activities of the firm is required.[7] In determining what is a reasonable cost allocation scheme, the commission has shown a general inclination to accept widely employed cost accounting practices. If a seller wishes prior approval of his cost allocation practices, he may submit them to the commission's accounting staff for review. The commission may then indicate approval or suggest modifications. In order to avoid future difficulties, the seller probably will conform to the commission's suggestions. In this way, a cost defense is established before the fact. As costs and other operating conditions change, of course, cost differences justifying price differentials are likely to change also. In other words, a cost defense, once established, is not immutable; it must be kept current.

The cost defense provision in the Robinson-Patman Act offers a challenge to the cost accountant. It requires him to develop and defend detailed cost analyses that may go beyond the ordinary requirements of product costing or of managerial analysis. It demands more detailed analysis of distribution costs than most firms have yet developed. Finally, it imposes upon the accountant the professional responsibility for developing cost accounting systems that entail the most appropriate

---

[7] Edwards, *op. cit.*, p. 586.

and reasonable cost classifications and allocations. To some extent, the reasonableness and equity with which the price discrimination law is administered depend upon accountants' acceptance of this responsibility.

QUESTIONS FOR DISCUSSION

1. The suggestion that an individual seller's costs have some relevance to his pricing decisions implies that he can set his prices at his own discretion and based upon his own situation. Isn't this implication inconsistent with the generally accepted notion that prices are set by forces of demand and supply in markets?

2. The president of a medium-sized manufacturing corporation makes the following statement at a meeting of the company's policy committee: "When we get around to setting prices, every cost we incur had better be charged to one or another of our products if we expect to make any money. I don't care how or why a cost is incurred, if it's there it has to be covered by some price. Anybody who thinks differently just doesn't understand the realities of business." How would you respond to this statement?

3. Under what circumstances, if any, is pricing at cost plus a target profit margin a valid approach to the pricing decision?

4. What are the relevant costs in a decision regarding the price of one of a company's regular products?

5. How does the level of operating capacity affect a special order pricing decision?

6. What are the relevant costs in a decision regarding the price of a custom-made product?

7. What are the relevant costs in a decision regarding a special, low price for an order of one of a company's regular products?

8. "Although it may be conceptually valid, the practice of pricing new products so that they will yield a specified rate of return on their investments is extremely difficult, if not impossible, to implement effectively." Do you agree or disagree with this statement? Explain.

9. Your company is planning to introduce a new product in the home appliance market. Initial market research indicates that demand for this product will eventually be large enough to justify the expansion of the company's production facilities. Forecasted sales in the first year or two of the product's market life can probably be met by production in existing facilities, however. What factors should management consider in setting a price for this new product? What factors should be considered in the decision as to the timing of expansion of production facilities?

10. A manufacturer has been approached by a large chain of discount stores with an offer to purchase a large quantity of a particular electrical appliance at a price 20% below the regular price. This quantity would represent almost 25% of the manufacturer's current annual output of the appliance. Existing capacity is adequate if the offer is accepted, however.

What costs and other factors should the manufacturer consider in its process of deciding whether to accept or reject this offer?

11. Assume that the manufacturer has accepted the offer described in Question 10. Another customer has learned of the 20% discount and has filed a complaint, alleging price discrimination, with the Federal Trade Commission. How should the manufacturer go about establishing a cost defense against the price discrimination charge? Would his cost analysis for this defense be the same as the cost analysis used earlier in deciding whether to accept the discount chain's offer? Explain.

PROBLEMS

1. Woglinde Wineries, Inc., produces and sells a variety of wines. Among the company's products is a cocktail wine called Krystyl Brite. This wine has been on the market for three years. When it first appeared, it was the only wine of its kind in it general price range; and initial sales were very satisfying to management. In the most recent year, however, other producers have introduced their own low-priced cocktail wines; and sales of Krystyl Brite have declined substantially.

Krystyl Brite was originally introduced at a retail price of $2.19 per bottle. Woglinde Wineries sold it to retailers for $15.75 per case of 12 bottles. The competing wines that have appeared in the past year sell at retail for $1.59 per bottle. Retailers pay $11.45 per case of 12 bottles for these other wines. Woglinde Wineries has received numerous complaints from retailers who reported that many customers still called for Krystyl Brite but finally bought one of the competing brands because of the substantial price difference. Some retailers have cut the price of Krystyl Brite to as low as $1.69 per bottle, but they contend that they cannot make a profit on it at that price. In recent monhs, Woglinde Wineries has begun cutting its price per case to retailers.

Summary sales data for Krystyl Brite during its three years on the market are as follows:

Year	Cases Sold	Average Price per Case
1970	20,000	$15.75
1971	30,000	15.75
1972	24,000	14.50

Variable production and distribution costs average $7.50 per case. Fixed overhead is assigned to all wines at a normal rate of $3.60 per case. Fixed selling and administrative expenses are allocated among products at a rate of 20% of total sales. Production facilities are common to all of the company's wines. The only fixed distribution costs directly traceable to Krystyl Brite are advertising costs budgeted at $50,000. The company's management believes this advertising is necessary if any substantial sales volume of the product is to be maintained.

A survey of retailers and consumers indicates that Krystyl Brite still has a superior product image in the cocktail wine market, but that it is not great enough to warrant the existing retail price differential. Retailers who sold Krystyl Brite for $1.69 per bottle reported that their sales of the product were not materially affected by the introduction of the competing wines. Woglinde Wineries has a generally acknowledged reputation for higher quality products than the producers of the competing cocktail wines. The president is concerned that reducing the price of Krystyl Brite in the face of low-price competition might adversely affect this reputation. He agrees, however, that even further decline in sales of Krystyl Brite may be expected in the coming year if some positive action is not taken to reverse the trend.

Required:

a) What would be the lowest price per case the company could accept if sales volume in the coming year were 25,000 cases?

b) If $1.69 per bottle were considered an effectively competitive retail price, what would be the highest competitive price per case the company could set?

c) What price would you recommend the company set for a case of Krystyl Brite during the coming year? Why?

2. The Wellgunde Corporation plans to introduce a new product in 1973. Sales volumes, consistent selling prices per unit, and consistent variable costs per unit have been estimated as follows:

Sales in Units	Selling Price	Variable Costs
10,000	$15	$10.00
20,000	14	9.50
30,000	13	9.00
40,000	12	8.50
50,000	11	8.00
60,000	10	7.50
70,000	8	7.00
80,000	5	6.50

The volumes listed are limits for their respective prices and variable costs. That is, any sales above each volume would have to be made at the next lower price and variable costs.

Fixed costs directly traceable to the new product are expected to be $25,000 for any volume up to and including 40,000 units. Above 40,000 units, these costs would be $40,000.

Required:

At what price should the corporation introduce this new product if it wishes to maximize its profit on the product?

3. Flosshilde Products, Inc., has recently developed a new electric bottling machine. While operating on the same principle as machines currently on the market, it is faster and results in less spillage and breakage. The com-

pany's management is seeking the most advantageous price at which to introduce this new machine and has requested your assistance in making this pricing decision. You have been provided the following information:

(1) There are four basically competitive bottling machines on the market at present. Their selling prices are shown below:

$$
\begin{array}{ll}
\text{Alberich Bottler} \ldots \ldots \ldots \ldots \ldots \ldots & \$78{,}000 \\
\text{Fafner Automatic Filler} \ldots \ldots \ldots \ldots & 82{,}500 \\
\text{Fasolt Bottling Machine} \ldots \ldots \ldots \ldots & 75{,}000 \\
\text{Mime Fast-Filler} \ldots \ldots \ldots \ldots \ldots & 80{,}000 \\
\end{array}
$$

Management is convinced that the new machine will save users operating costs in comparison with these competing machines and, hence, believes a higher price would be justifiable.

(2) Cost estimates for producing and selling the new machines have been prepared by the product engineering staff. Variable production costs per unit have been budgeted as follows:

$$
\begin{array}{ll}
\text{Materials} \ldots \ldots \ldots \ldots \ldots \ldots \ldots & \$16{,}000 \\
\text{Direct labor} \ldots \ldots \ldots \ldots \ldots \ldots & 12{,}000 \\
\text{Overhead} \ldots \ldots \ldots \ldots \ldots \ldots \ldots & 9{,}000 \\
\end{array}
$$

Fixed overhead is applied to all of the company's products at a normal rate of 125% of direct labor cost. Variable distribution costs are expected to average $800 per machine. Fixed nonmanufacturing expenses are allocated among products in proportion to total revenues. In recent years, this allocation has averaged 10% of sales revenue.

(3) Additional manufacturing equipment costing $500,000 and having a useful life of five years will be required to produce the new bottling machine. Otherwise, existing facilities and personnel are considered adequate to meet the expanding operations of the company.

(4) The company's products currently are yielding a net profit before tax of approximately 15% of revenues, after deductions for both direct costs and allocated indirect costs.

Required:

a) Prepare a preliminary report summarizing your analysis of the factors management should consider in this pricing decision.

b) What additional information, if any, would you want to have before making a specific price recommendation?

4. The Gerhilde Specialties Corporation has developed a golfer's "cart bag," replete with novel gadgets. If the clubs are properly stored in the bag, the desired club is extended automatically at the touch of a button. There is a built-in ball washer, an 18-hole scorekeeper, and a retractable umbrella for sudden showers. The cart bag has its own wheels and handle and, because of its size and weight, is self-propelled by a small battery-powered motor.

The corporation's management has decided to "skim the cream" off the market for several years before introducing the cart bag to the mass market at a price within the means of the average golfer. Consequently, initial production facilities will be limited to produce an output below the expected total demand. Early promotional efforts will be directed at the high-income golfer. Because of this very selective distribution plan, management believes it has quite wide latitude in setting its price. There is no effectively competitive product on the market.

The cost of the production facilities required to manufacture the cart bag in the initial low volume will be $2,500,000. The annual output of these facilities will be 8,000 units, and management is confident that all of them can be sold. The facilities will have an economic life of four years and no significant terminal salvage value. Promotional outlays are planned at $150,000 during each of the first four years. Variable costs of producing and distributing the cart bag will average $250 per unit. Additional fixed operating costs incurred because of this new product are budgeted at $75,000 per year.

The company's profit goals call for a discounted rate of return of 15% after taxes on investments in new products. The cost of capital is 10%. The income tax rate is 40%. Straight-line depreciation will be used for tax reporting.

Required:

a) What initial selling price is necessary to obtain the desired rate of return on investment?

b) If management had decided instead to seek the broadest possible market for this new product immediately, what financial variables in the pricing decision would you expect to be changed? Why?

5. The Ortlinde Company plans to introduce a new product in 1973. Initial tests and studies indicate that the product might be sold at any of four alternative prices. Pertinent data for each of these prices are as follows:

Price...................	$8.00	$12.00	$15.00	$20.00
Variable cost per unit.......	3.50	4.00	4.50	5.00
Units sold annually.........	600,000	400,000	300,000	150,000
Annual fixed costs..........	$ 750,000	$ 800,000	$ 800,000	$ 600,000
Initial capital investment required...............	7,000,000	6,000,000	5,000,000	3,500,000

Whatever the capital investment amount, it will be amortized by the straight-line method over a useful life of eight years. The applicable income tax rate is 40%. The company's cost of capital is 11%.

A total of $500,000 has already been expended over the past two years in research and development on this new product.

Required:

Prepare an analysis of the alternative prices for this new product. Which would be the most profitable price for the company to set?

6. The Waltraute Manufacturing Company produces a variety of precision instruments and components. Most are sold to manufacturers of electronics

equipment and to laboratories. The company's policy is to price all of its regular products at 150% of the variable costs to produce and sell them. Because of the specialized character of these products, this has proved to be a viable pricing policy.

Recently, the Coast Guard has requested bids on a compact, long-range radio direction finder for use on small craft. Specifications call for 750 units. The company's president is interested in the possibility of the firm entering the government contracting market as a prime contractor and has asked the controller to prepare a cost estimate for this radio direction finder. Based upon the Coast Guard specifications, the controller has prepared the following cost estimate:

Raw materials....................................	$260,000
Direct labor.....................................	180,000
Variable overhead...............................	120,000
Fixed overhead..................................	270,000
Production setup costs...........................	40,000
Special tools and dies...........................	90,000
Clerical costs of processing government forms and reports..	15,000
Total cost......................................	$975,000
Unit cost ($975,000 ÷ 750 units).................	$ 1,300

Coast Guard specifications required delivery of all 750 direction finders within the next 12 months. In order to meet this schedule, Waltraute would have to forego regular sales orders totaling $600,000.

Required:

What would be the lowest price the company could bid for the radio direction finder without sacrificing short-run profit?

7. In late 1972, the Fricka Corporation invited the Brunnhilde Company to submit a design for a fork-lift truck to meet the special requirements of Fricka's warehousing facilities and also to submit a bid for a contract to produce 40 of these trucks. Similar invitations were sent to four other equipment manufacturers.

The Brunnhilde Company has suffered from considerable excess capacity during the past two years and has seen little hope of improving the situation. Consequently, it readily accepted the Fricka Corporation's invitation and has already spent a total of $25,000 on design and cost studies in connection with it. As a result of this work, a bid of $8,000 per truck has been submitted. In support of this bid, the controller of the Brunnhilde Company has prepared the following budgeted profit statement on the contract:

Revenue (40 units @ $8,000).................		$320,000
Costs:		
Materials (40 @ $3,000)....................	$120,000	
Direct labor (40 @ $1,500).................	60,000	
Variable overhead (40 @ $750)..............	30,000	
Fixed overhead (40 @ $1,200)..............	48,000	
Shipping (40 @ $125)......................	5,000	
Design and cost study.....................	25,000	288,000
Net profit before tax.......................		$ 32,000

The Fricka Corporation has indicated that it prefers the Brunnhilde design to any of the others submitted but that the bid price of $8,000 is excessive. It has made a counteroffer to award the contract to Brunnhilde at a price of $6,750 per truck.

Required:

Should the Brunnhilde Company accept the Fricka contract at the proposed price of $6,750 per unit?

8. The Schwertleite Company produces a wide variety of plumbing and heating products. One of these products is the Loge thermal control unit, the standard cost of which is as follows:

Materials........................	$ 7.50
Direct labor......................	10.00
Variable overhead.................	2.50
Fixed overhead...................	8.00
	$28.00

The Loge thermal control unit is produced in a series of manufacturing departments, each of which also works on many of the company's other products. It is sold to wholesalers and industrial users at a unit price of $35. Variable selling expenses average $1.20 per unit. Fixed selling expenses are budgeted at 10% of sales revenue.

The Schwertleite Company has been approached by a large manufacturer of furnaces and boilers with an offer to buy 8,000 of the Loge units annually at a special price of $27.50 per unit. If accepted, this offer would increase Schwertleite's output considerably and would necessitate an increase in annual fixed manufacturing costs of $35,000. No new capital investment would be required, however.

Required:

a) On the basis of short-run profitability, would you recommend acceptance of the special-price offer?

b) What other factors should management consider before reaching a decision on this offer?

9. The Helmwige Corporation produces a single product. Its maximum annual productive capacity is 840,000 labor hours. Currently, it is producing at an annual rate of 600,000 labor hours. Normal volume is 800,000 hours.

Recently, a private-brand distributor has offered to buy 100,000 units of the corporation's product at a special price of $22.50 per unit. The regular selling price is $35 per unit. The standard cost sheet for one unit of the product is as follows:

Materials (8 lbs. @ $.70)...........................	$ 5.60
Labor (3 hrs. @ $3.60)..............................	10.80
Variable overhead (3 hrs. @ $1.20).................	3.60
Fixed overhead (3 hrs. @ $1.50)....................	4.50
	$24.50

Required:

a) In the short run, would it be profitable to accept the private-brand distributor's offer?

b) Would your answer to (a) be different if the offer called for 60,000 units instead of 100,000 units? Why?

10. The Siegrune Company manufactures a toaster-oven, the unit standard cost of which is as follows:

Materials	$ 6.40
Labor	4.80
Variable overhead	2.00
Fixed overhead	3.50
	$16.70

Variable selling costs of $.80 per unit are incurred when the toaster-oven is sold under the Siegrune brand name. The regular selling price is $25 per unit. Annual fixed selling and administrative expenses total $800,000.

The productive capacity of the company is 360,000 units per year. Budgeted sales and output for 1973 are both 250,000 units. Normal volume is 300,000 units per year.

The company has received three offers for special purchases of the toaster-oven at reduced prices. These three offers, none of which has been included in the budgeted sales and output for 1973, are outlined below:

Offer A: The prospective buyer would take 80,000 units during 1973 at a price of $15.75 per unit. He would sell the toaster-oven under the Siegrune brand name.

Offer B: The prospective buyer would take 100,000 units during 1973 at a price of $15 per unit. These units would be sold under the buyer's private brand name and would have slightly modified housings to disguise the manufacturer's identity. This modification would not change unit costs.

Offer C: The prospective buyer would take 200,000 units during 1973 at a price of $18 per unit. These units would also be sold under the buyer's private brand name and in modified housings. Unit cost would not be affected by the modifications.

Required:

Evaluate each of the three offers from the point of view of short-run profitability in 1973. What other factors might be relevant to the decision to accept or reject any or all of the offers?

11. The Rossweise Fruit Products Company produces and bottles four different fruit juices. Most of its output has been sold to grocery wholesalers. Sales of one of these juices, lime juice, have never come up to the company's expectations. Sales, in cases of 8-ounce bottles, during 1972 were as follows:

Product	Cases	Price per Case
Prune juice..................	90,000	$5.60
Apple juice.................	150,000	4.20
Lemon juice................	60,000	7.00
Lime juice.................	20,000	6.50

Actual operating costs for 1972 are summarized below. No changes have been anticipated in the budget prepared for 1973.

	Variable Cost per Case	Fixed Cost per Year
Raw materials:		
Prunes..........................	$1.80	
Apples..........................	1.10	
Lemons..........................	2.40	
Limes..........................	2.75	
Bottles..........................	.20	
Direct labor........................	1.20	
Overhead..........................	.50	$200,000
Selling expenses......................	.25	90,000
Administrative expenses..............		120,000

A chain of "cut-rate" liquor stores has offered to purchase 30,000 cases of lime juice in 1973 at a price of $4.75 per case. These sales would not involve any variable selling expenses. In addition, because of the substantial increase in volume, the cost of limes would be reduced by $.25 per case.

Required:

a) Would it be profitable for the company to accept the liquor stores' offer?

b) Irrespective of your answer in (a), assume that the company did accept the offer and that one of its wholesale grocery customers has now filed a complaint alleging price discrimination by the Rossweise Company. Can an effective cost defense, as provided for in the Robinson-Patman Act, be established in this case? Support your answer with some appropriate cost analysis.

12. Schooner Harbor has long been one of the most popular seafood restaurants in eastern Connecticut. It is most famous for its boiled-live lobster with a special butter sauce made from a secret recipe. The national reputation of this particular dish has led to numerous requests from restaurateurs all over the country for the right to serve it in their establishments under the Schooner Harbor name. Several years ago, the proprietor of Schooner Harbor sensed in these requests an opportunity for very lucrative additional business at the cost of a fairly modest investment.

Thus, the proprietor set up a separate corporation, Noank Live Lobsters, Inc., to pack and ship live lobsters and jars of sauce. Sauce is prepared in the restaurant's kitchen and put into 2-pound jars. It is then transferred to a packing plant purchased especially for the new corporation. In the packing plant, 20 live lobsters and three jars of sauce are packed in specially designed cases. All cases are packed for specific customers' orders. The cases are then taken by company-owned trucks to New York for delivery to local restaurants, or for air shipment to out-of-town buyers.

Shipments of live lobsters have increased steadily since this business was begun, until, today, the packing plant is operating at its practical capacity. Even so, orders frequently must be delayed because of a back-log of demand. Initially, orders were received only from "exclusive" restaurants in large cities. Recently, however, orders have started to come in from a wider variety of restaurants. Some chains of restaurants have asked the company to ship large orders at reduced prices. Thus far, the proprietor has not been able to fill any such orders because of the heavy demand from regular customers. However, he has begun to wonder whether he may not have conceived the live lobster shipping business on too small a scale. He currently is considering the feasibility and financial advisability of shipping large quantities at special prices, and of shipping to a wider variety of customers. Realistically, the latter course of action would have to involve lower basic prices.

Each case of live lobsters is now sold for $80 plus air freight charges from New York. This price was arrived at by assuming that restaurants serving Schooner Harbor lobster and sauce would price the item at $6 per serving and that they would be willing to pay an average of $4 per serving for the distinction of including the dish on their menus. Information from present customers suggests that most do charge about $6 for the dish. The costs of producing, packing, and transporting the lobsters have been estimated by the proprietor as follows:

Cost of packing case (empty)	$3.60
Cost of 2-pound jar (empty)	.03
Packing labor per case	.80
Cost of sauce:	
Ingredients per pound	1.10
Labor per pound	.20
Trucking costs per month	$800
Packing plant overhead per month (wholly fixed)	$500
Cost of lobsters (see below)	

The cost of lobsters varies widely, depending upon seasonal changes, weather, and market conditions. Within a single year, the cost may range from $.75 to $1.50 per lobster.

Several restaurants which price their meals considerably below those sold in the corporation's present customers' establishments have indicated that they would be eager to buy if the price could be reduced to $3 per lobster or less. One restaurant chain has offered to purchase regularly in quantities of at least 50 cases per order at a price of $50 per case. The proprietor of Schooner Harbor believes similar arrangement could be made with other chains.

Required:

a) Evaluate the corporation's present pricing system.
b) Define the decisions facing the proprietor in connection with the growing demand for live lobsters and sauce. Suggest approaches to the solution of each of these decisions.
c) If the proprietor does decide to reduce the price and to offer quantity discounts, would the prices of $3 per lobster and $50 per case to chains for large orders, as suggested by potential customers, be satisfactory? Discuss.

chapter **18**

DIVISIONAL
PERFORMANCE
MEASUREMENT

As BUSINESS enterprises and other organizations grow larger in size, more complex in structure, and more diverse in operations, they are typically subdivided into several segments or divisions. Each division is a separately identifiable center of operating activity and of managerial responsibility. The degree of autonomy enjoyed by divisions varies widely. Some operate within the constraints of narrowly defined policies dictated by top management. Others may be charged broadly with the task of operating efficiently or profitably. Whatever the situation may be, top management clearly retains a very positive concern for the operations of all divisions. Consequently, top management wishes to establish and maintain a dependable method of measuring performance in each division and a regular system of performance reporting. Of course, divisional managers also are interested in having reports on their own divisions' performances.

It should be noted that the term "division" is being used here in a very general sense to describe any logical segment or subcomponent of an organization. That segment may be a distinct organizational subcomponent and may be formally designated as a division (e.g., the Chevrolet Division of General Motors Corporation). It may also be designated as a department, a branch office, a district, a service center, or any of a variety of other titles. It need not be a separate organizational entity at all, however. A product line, a channel of distribution, or a class of customers might be regarded as a "division" of a firm for purposes of this discussion. The important characteristic of a division here is that its operating performance is separately identifiable and measurable in some way that is of practical significance to management.

The methods of divisional performance measurement discussed in this chapter all involve financial data. Thus, they are essentially measures of financial performance. While this emphasis is entirely appropriate in this book, the reader should be aware that there are many other very useful measures of performance that do not employ financial data. A division might be evaluated on such nonfinancial matters as employee attitudes, customer relations, innovative technology, maintenance of equipment, and delivery schedules. While all of these matters may be expected to have financial implications, at least over a long term, their direct measurement would likely be in nonfinancial quantities. Such measures are important to management, but they will not be considered directly here.

OBJECTIVES OF DIVISIONAL PERFORMANCE MEASUREMENT

Any system of divisional performance measurement and appraisal must begin with a clear statement of its objective(s). If it doesn't, the system may measure the wrong things; management may draw the wrong inferences from these measures; and the wrong action may be taken as a consequence. In a specific situation, the objective(s) must be very explicitly defined. In general, however, such objectives may be classified into three basic categories, as follows:

1. Measures designed to determine the contribution that a division, as an entity, makes to the total organization.
2. Measures designed to provide a basis for evaluating the quality of the divisional manager's performance.
3. Measures intended to motivate the divisional manager to operate his division in a manner consistent with the basic goals of the total organization.

These are by no means mutually exclusive objectives of a divisional performance measurement, and a single measure might serve all three. There are certain measures of divisional performance, however, which are not appropriate for one or more of these objectives. If such a measure is used improperly, it may do serious harm to the organization and may impede the attainment of basic goals.

If management wishes to evaluate the contribution of a division as a distinct entity, it must be careful that the measure chosen includes all factors directly traceable to that division and excludes all others. Only the incremental data directly pertinent to the division in question are properly included in the measure. If management wishes to evaluate the division manager's performance, it must select a measure that deals only with factors subject to that manager's control. Thus, the relevant data must fall with the scope of the division manager's responsibility. At first thought, it may seem artificial, if not impossible, to distinguish between the performance of a division and that of the division's manager. It is true that, in the long run, the two performances might be indistinguishable. The long run is made up of many short periods, however. In the short run, a very useful and, perhaps, necessary distinction may be made. It is conceivable, for example, that a manager could do a very good job of managing a highly unsuccessful division. Perhaps his job would be to liquidate the division at minimum loss to the firm. In such a case, the division could hardly be said to have made a satisfactory contribution to the company as a whole. Yet, the division manager may be adjudged to have discharged his responsibility very well. The distinction between the performance of a division as an entity and the personal performance of a division manager will be pointed out more specifically in subsequent sections.

Any performance measurement system may be expected to influence the behavior of the managers affected by it. In general, managers may be expected to attempt to make themselves look good. Further, if there is any potential personal benefit from the measurement (e.g., a bonus for good performance), managers will seek to attain that benefit. Such behavior is perfectly normal and should not be deplored. On the contrary, it should be turned to the firm's advantage. Top management should design the divisional performance measurement in such a way that, in seeking to achieve their own goals, the division managers will simultaneously be working toward the goals of the firm. Such a result is described as *goal congruence*. It should be foremost in the mind of anyone attempting to design a system of performance measurement and evaluation.

As a final note here, it is useful to distinguish between the measurement and the evaluation of performance. Measurement seeks to determine in an objective fashion what performance actually is. Evaluation is then a somewhat subjective judgment as to whether that performance is good or bad. The former is appropriately within the province of the management accountant; he should be an expert in financial measurements for all purposes. The latter, however, is the responsibility of operating management. An evaluation of performance must be made in light of the circumstances within which the division or the manager had to perform. These circumstances may change over time, and it may be difficult to determine the extent to which they control performance. It is not practicable to make the measurement system so sensitive and flexible that it can cope with the effects of changing circumstances directly. Rather, the necessary adjustments and allowances must be part of the evaluation process.

EXPENSE CENTERS

For purposes of measuring financial performance, the divisions of a firm may be classified according to the types of financial data used in the measurement. Three basic classes of divisions have been identified on these grounds—expense centers, profit centers, and investment centers. Each of these is considered in some detail below.

An *expense center* may be defined as a segment or division whose financial performance is measured by comparing its actual expenses with either budgeted or standard expenses for a given period. The essential requirement for an expense center is that the costs of operating the division be directly traceable to it. This requirement is both necessary and sufficient. The performance of an expense center is measured by financial measures of inputs only. No measure of output, or accomplishment, is needed. The analysis of performance compares actual and planned (or standard) consumption of resources in the division. There is no reference to what the division achieved as a consequence of consuming those resources. Thus, the performance measured in an expense center is the efficiency of operation in that center. "Efficiency" is used here in the engineering sense of the quantity of inputs used in producing some given output. Actual inputs are compared to some predetermined level that represents efficient utilization. In an expense center, these inputs are measured in dollars. Thus, efficiency is expressed by variances from budgeted or standard costs. Whether the output of an expense center is good or bad is a question that is not addressed by this measurement.

In many cases, the output of an expense center cannot reliably be measured in financial quantities. Hence, financial efficiency is the only feasible measure of divisional performance. Examples of such centers are legal departments, public relations staffs, the accounting department, and most personnel department activities. Each of these divisions may be regarded as necessary for the effective functioning of the firm as a whole. Further, each has a conceptually identifiable output—e.g., legal advice, good public relations, reliable accounting reports, and better qualified personnel. The difficulty is that these outputs cannot be expressed in terms of money. Indeed, there may be no quantitative measures of such things as good public relations. In cases such as these, the only practicable financial performance measure is one of efficiency. Such divisions can be evaluated only as expense centers. In other divisions, there may be financial measures of both inputs and outputs available. This does not mean that they must be treated as something more than expense centers, however. Management may elect to treat such a division as an expense center even though its inputs could be related to its outputs as well as to planned or standard inputs. For example, a production department in a factory may be regarded as an expense center for performance reporting purposes even though the goods that it produces have a readily determinable financial value. The choice of a performance measure should depend upon what management finds most useful.

If the objective of expense center analysis is to appraise the performance of the division as an entity, the relevant costs are the incremental costs of operating that division. These are the costs that would be avoided if the division were shut down permanently. In most instances, these incremental costs would include both variable and fixed costs. Irrelevant to this analysis are costs common to several divisions and allocated among them on some arbitrary basis. While such allocations may be appropriate for purposes such as inventory valuation, they are misleading in analyses of performance. If the objective is to evaluate the performance of the division manager, only those incremental costs controllable by that manager are relevant. These distinctions are illustrated in Table 18–1, a simplified and summarized expense report for a division formally organized as a factory department. (The reader will note that this report is simply an abridged version of the form used in Table 9–3 on page 227, with an additional distinction made between incremental and allocated common costs.) In order to be fully useful in a real situation, this report would have to show details by cost items under each of the three basic cost categories included. The variance from the budgeted controllable costs is a measure of the department manager's performance during the month. Any qualitative evaluation of his performance, however, must depend also upon an analysis of the causes for the variance. The variance from total incremental costs is a measure of the efficiency of the performance of the department as a segment of the firm. This is an impersonal measure, for it includes variances that the department manager is not responsible for.

The last line of the report includes the department's allocated share of common costs. Consequently, the variance on this line cannot be interpreted as any indication of the performance of the department as a separate entity. Managers differ in their views as to the validity of including this last line at all. Some argue that it is appropriately included, for these common costs must be incurred if all departments are to continue to operate. Hence, they should be allocated among the departments in some equitable fashion. Some claim that inclusion of these cost allocations makes the division manager more aware of the relationship of his particular division to the entire organization and, thus, helps prepare him for greater responsibilities in later years. Others contend that only those costs directly traceable to the division should be included in its report. They argue that inclusion of the allocated portion of common costs can only cause confusion and, possibly, mistrust. Actually, the most important requirement is that such cost allocations not be misunderstood. The best way to ensure that they are not mis-

TABLE 18–1

FRACTILE PRODUCTS CORPORATION
Monthly Expense Report

Department Factory Maintenance Supervisor H. A. Cassidy	Month of August, 1972		
	Actual Cost	Budgeted Cost	Spending Variance
Incremental costs of department:			
Controllable costs (measure of department manager's performance).........	$420,000	$400,000	$(20,000)
Noncontrollable costs...................	275,000	250,000	(25,000)
Total incremental costs (measure of department's performance as an entity)...........................	$695,000	$650,000	$(45,000)
Allocated portion of common costs.........	160,000	150,000	(10,000)
Total department costs.........	$855,000	$800,000	$(55,000)

understood is to avoid them altogether. If management feels that it is desirable to allocate all costs among the various divisions, then, at the least, they should clearly be segregated and labeled so that their natures and significance are not confused. Table 18–1 shows a spending variance from the department's allocated share of the budgeted common costs. This variance clearly has nothing to do with the division's performance. It would be much better if it were not shown in the report at all. This can be achieved by allocating only budgeted common costs to divisions. In this way, the actual and budgeted amounts in the divisional reports will always be equal and there will be no variances. Variances from budgeted common costs would then appear only in reports for the entire company, and that is exactly where they belong.

PROFIT CENTERS

A *profit center* may be defined as a division for which separately traceable revenues and expenses are matched to determine the division's profit. Thus, it is one step above an expense center in terms of its financial data requirements. Both revenues and expenses must be identified with the division. In a profit center, there are financial measures of the outputs as well as of the inputs. Consequently, it is feasible to measure the effectiveness of the division's performance in financial terms. Of course, it is also possible to measure efficiency in terms of actual and budgeted cost data. A profit center requires all of the data needed in an expense center as well as the additional data regarding revenues. Hence, management can determine whether the division is efficient in its utilization of resources and, further, whether the division was effective in attaining its objective. This objective is, presumably, to earn a satisfactory profit. The criterion for a "satisfactory" profit may be budgeted profit, past profit performance in the division, profits of other similar divisions, profits of other companies, or some combination of two or more of these. There is considerable potential danger in comparing the profit of a division to that of a separate company, however, even if both are approximately the same size and are in the same industry. A division can rely upon corporate management for many services that a separate company must provide for itself. Allocations of the costs of such services among divisions is not likely to neutralize this difference. Consequently, one might expect a division to be more profitable per dollar of sales volume than a separate company. If this expectation proves wrong consistently, one must then question the desirability of having a large firm with many operating divisions. The usual advantage alleged for such firms is that they foster economies of operation because of their size. If these economies are not reflected in relatively higher profits, the advantage would appear to be illusory.

Profit center analysis may be used as a basis for evaluating the performance of a division as an entity or for evaluating the performance of a division manager. While one would expect that these two performances would become indistinguishable over a long period, they might diverge significantly in any single short period. Further, division managers may be transferred often enough to warrant explicit efforts to distinguish their sequential personal performances from the ongoing operations of the division itself. In evaluating the performance of a division per se, external criteria are relevant. That is, it is reasonable to assess a segment's performance in light of its performance in prior periods or in comparison with performances of other similar divisions. In evaluating the division manager's performance, however, external criteria are less applicable. They entail factors over which the manager cannot reasonably exert any control. Hence, budgeted profit would be a more realistic performance criterion. Ideally, any profit measure of a division manager's performance should be made up exclusively of revenue and expense items subject to his control. Thus, a specially constructed "responsibility profit" would be desirable. In practice, this may prove simply to be the difference between revenues and controllable expenses. Noncontrollable revenues may exist, as in the case of a division that has a sister division as a captive customer as a result of a directive from top management. Such revenues are usually not reported separately, however. Profit measures for the division as an impersonal entity should be based only on revenues and expenses directly traceable to the division and avoidable if the division were closed down. Hence, the incremental profit concept discussed in Chapter 14 is the appropriate measure.[1]

---

[1] Page 350.

Natural and Constructive Profit Centers

In general, a profit center is visualized as buying resources in one market (the input market) and selling goods and services in another (the output market). Thus, its revenues are measured by output market prices and its expenses, by input market prices. To this extent, the profit center is much like an independent firm. A profit center that deals directly in both input and output markets is called a *natural profit center*. This is the most familiar type of profit center. A product division is the classic example. There is also a second type of profit center that may be identified and that may be very useful to management. For want of a better term, let us call it a *constructive profit center*. It is not naturally a profit center, but it may be made to appear as one. An example is the computer center or data processing department in a corporation. It purchases the resources that it requires in input markets, but it does not sell its product. Rather, it performs computing services for other divisions at no charge to them. On the face of it, the computer center would appear to be a logical expense center. So it might be. However, management might wish to know whether it is better to own and operate its own computer or to purchase computer time from a data processing service bureau. In order to answer this type of question, the computer center may be treated as a constructive profit center.

Assume, for example, that computing time may be purchased from an independent service bureau at a price of $250 per hour of processing time. Assume further that the corporation operates its own computer center at a monthly fixed cost of $20,000 plus variable costs of $150 per hour of processing time.[2] If the company-owned computer is used for 400 hours of processing during a given month, the following constructive profit statement may be prepared for the computer center for that month:

Revenue (400 hrs. @ $250)		$100,000
Expenses:		
Variable (400 hrs. @ $150)	$60,000	
Fixed	20,000	80,000
Divisional profit		$ 20,000

The "revenue" in this case is not actual revenue in the customary sense. Rather, it is an alternative cost avoided. Thus, this constructive profit

---

[2] An adjustment to a common denominator of processing time may be necessary here if a valid analysis is to be made. A large computer may be able to process jobs in considerably less time than a smaller one. In that case, an hour of processing time on the large machine is obviously not equivalent to an hour on the smaller one. Thus, the hourly cost rates of the two machines could be compared only after adjusting them for the difference in the speed of processing. For example, in the illustration above, if the service bureau's computer could complete any job in half the time the company's computer would take and the service bureau charged $500 per hour for processing, the appropriate comparison would be $250 per hour and $150 per hour (as indicated above) or, equivalently, $500 per hour and $300 per hour.

analysis shows that the corporation saved $20,000 during the month by operating its own computer rather than buying computer time from a service bureau. Implicit in this analysis is the assumption that all 400 hours of processing time would have been used regardless of where the data processing was done. This assumption is not always valid. It may be economical for a firm to perform certain jobs on its own machine but not on the service bureau's machine. This would be the case in our illustration if the value of a job to the firm were more than $150 but less than $250 per hour.

The illustration above is based on the premise that the firm already has its own computer. It would also be valid if the company were considering renting a computer on a contract that could be canceled at short notice. If the decision were to purchase a computer or to rent one on a long-term lease contract, however, it would have to be analyzed as a capital budgeting decision. The monthly cost savings would have to have a present value great enough to justify the initial outlay.

Divisional profit data may be used to evaluate the performance of the division per se or of the division manager in the case of a natural profit center. In the case of a constructive profit center, however, profit analysis can be used only to appraise the performance or contribution of the division as an entity. Thus, the computer center in our example made a contribution of $20,000 to the corporation's profit before taxes during the month studied. Corporate profit would have been $20,000 less if computing services had been purchased from an independent service bureau. This profit cannot be attributed to the computer center manager, however, for the "revenue" involved is wholly beyond his responsibility or control. Hence, the division manager's performance might best be appraised by comparing the actual and budgeted costs of operating the computer center. It is quite possible for the division to show a constructive profit (a favorable performance measure) but an unfavorable spending variance from budgeted cost (an adverse performance measure).

Divisional Profit and Corporate Profit

From the discussion to this point it is possible to infer an important point. The sum of the profits of all divisions is not necessarily equal to the profit of the corporation as a whole. Divisional profits are incremental profits. Costs not directly traceable to any single division are intentionally excluded from consideration in the computation of the profit of any division. Yet, they must be considered in determining corporate profit. This nonadditivity of divisional profit to corporate profit reflects the fact that these are two conceptually different measures. Divisional profit does not sum to corporate profit because it was never intended to do so. Divisional profit is a unique concept, designed to serve specific managerial needs. This is especially true in the case of a constructive profit center where the "revenue" is not recognized as revenue to the corporation at all.

Divisional Break-Even Analysis

The break-even point for a division, like a division's profit, is computed from revenue and cost data directly traceable to that division. Since costs common to two or more divisions would thus be excluded from all divisional break-even computations, the total of all divisions' break-even volumes would not be equal to the corporation's break-even volume. Further, in the case of constructive profit centers, the company's break-even volume would not even consider the "revenues" used in the divisions' break-even calculations. The computer center used in the illustration earlier in this chapter would break even when the costs avoided by not having data processing done by an independent service bureau (i.e., the "revenues") were exactly equal to the costs of operating the company's computer center. The break-even volume (BE) in hours in this case would be computed as follows:[3]

$$BE = \frac{\text{Total fixed costs}}{\text{Variable profit per hour}} = \frac{\$20,000}{\$250 - \$150} = 200 \text{ hours}$$

The variable profit, of course, is the difference between the service bureau's hourly charge and the company's own variable cost per hour. From this break-even analysis, management may conclude that it is more profitable to operate their own computer center as long as monthly processing volume exceeds 200 hours. Below that volume, it would be more profitable to have the work done outside.

Divisional Profit Reporting in Diversified Companies

The published income statements of business corporations have traditionally disclosed only summary data on revenues and expenses for a period. In recent years this practice has been reexamined, particularly in the cases of diversified companies, or conglomerates. In 1969, the Securities and Exchange Commission initiated a requirement that all corporations subject to its jurisdiction must report revenues and income by major "lines of business." Companies whose annual sales exceed $50 million must disclose revenues and income for each line of business that accounts for 10% or more of total revenue or of total income before tax. Smaller companies need disclose this information only for lines of business representing at least 15% of their total revenue or income.

---

[3] This is essentially the same analysis used in Chapter 13, page 321, to compute the break-even volume in units of product.

To date, the SEC has allowed companies considerable latitude in their interpretation of this divisional reporting requirement. A line of business may be defined, at management's discretion, as an organizational division, a product line, a market, or any other logical segment of the individual firm's operations. Divisional revenues and incomes may be reported either in dollar amounts or as percentages of company totals. The income for a line of business may be its incremental profit, or it may be calculated after an allocation of common costs among all lines of business.[4] At the time of this writing, these divisional reporting requirements have not been applied to firms not subject to the jurisdiction of the SEC. There is considerable likelihood that they will, however. Even before the SEC's action, the Accounting Principles Board of the American Institute of Certified Public Accountants urged diversified companies to consider voluntary disclosure of divisional operating data.[5]

INVESTMENT CENTERS

An *investment center* is essentially a profit center in which profit is related to the investment in the assets used in the division. The basic premise of this additional information is that profit is most meaningful when stated in terms of the capital investment required to produce it. Investment center analysis permits an assessment of the efficiency (in the economic sense of returns on resources used) with which division management has utilized the assets entrusted to its care. This analysis may be used as a basis for evaluating the contribution of the division as an entity and also the performance of the division manager. In both cases, however, it must be used very carefully. Misuse of this analysis may cause a serious lack of goal congruence between the division and the company as a whole.

Rate of Return on Investment

Unquestionably, the most common device for reporting performance in an investment center is the rate of return on investment in assets, or simply return on investment (ROI). The rate of return on investment is the ratio of net income to total assets. It may be computed directly as follows:

$$\text{ROI} = \frac{\text{Income}}{\text{Total assets}}$$

[4] For additional discussion of these requirements and examples of several companies' actual reports in compliance with them, see Paul A. Pacter, "Line-of-Business Earnings Disclosures in Recent SEC Filings," *The Journal of Accountancy*, Vol. CXXX (October 1970), pp. 52–63.

[5] "Statement of the Accounting Principles Board: Disclosure of Supplemental Financial Information by Diversified Companies," September, 1967, p. 4.

Frequently, however, the same result is attained by means of two intermediate calculations. The first is the ratio of income to sales revenue.

$$\text{Rate of income on sales} = \frac{\text{Income}}{\text{Sales}}$$

Then the ratio of sales to total assets is computed; this is called the asset turnover.

$$\text{Asset turnover} = \frac{\text{Sales}}{\text{Total assets}}$$

The rate of return on investment is then computed as the product of the rate of income on sales and the asset turnover, thus:

$$\text{ROI} = \text{Rate of income on sales} \times \text{Asset turnover}$$

Clearly, this three-step method of computing the rate of return can be collapsed to the direct computation shown initially. The three-step method is sometimes preferred because it shows more detailed information that may be particularly significant in individual industries. For example, financial performance in the retail grocery business is characterized by a low rate of income on sales (or a low markup) and a high (rapid) asset turnover. Conversely, the petroleum refining industry has a fairly high rate of income on sales but a much lower asset turnover. A knowledgeable person analyzing the performance of a company or a division in one or the other of these industries might well consider himself better informed in an important way if he knew all three of these statistics instead of the return on investment only.

As noted earlier, the rate of return on investment must be used very carefully to avoid serious misunderstandings and erroneous actions. To begin with, a rate of return is a useful index of performance only if there is some reasonable criterion available for comparison. That criterion may be the rate of return in the same division in prior periods, the rate in other divisions, the rate in independent companies, or some target rate of return. Independent companies are not likely to be good bases for comparison, however, for the same reasons mentioned in connection with profit center analysis.[6] Corporate headquarters would relieve its divisions of substantial asset investments and operating expenses that would have to be borne directly by an independent company.

Danger of Unprofitable Behavior by Division Manager. A danger in the rate of return on investment is that a division manager may feel compelled to maximize a ratio rather than the financial welfare of his division and the firm as a whole. For example, assume that a division holds assets valued at $500,000 and earns income of $100,000 per year. Its annual rate of return on investment is 20% ($100,000 ÷ $500,000). The company's average cost of capital is 10%. The division manager has an

---

[6] Cf. page 478.

opportunity to purchase for $100,000 an asset that would increase his division's income by $15,000; and the corporate treasury has the necessary $100,000 available in surplus cash that might otherwise be invested in marketable securities yielding 6%. From the point of view of the corporation, the new asset would yield a rate of return of 15%, which is higher than the cost of capital and vastly better than the return on marketable securities. Yet, the investment would reduce the division's rate of return to 19% ($115,000 ÷ $600,000). If the division manager understood that his performance would be measured only by the *rate* of return on his assets, with no attention to the absolute amount of his division's income, he would be tempted to forego the new asset. Conversely, if he held an asset valued at $100,000 that could be disposed of with a consequent reduction in divisional income of less than $20,000, he might be inclined to dispose of the asset and thus increase his rate of return. The fact that cash recovered from the sale of the asset might then be invested in marketable securities yielding only 6% would not appear to be his problem. One way of averting this danger is to evaluate the divisional manager's performance by several different measures and to impress upon him that the rate of return on investment is only one of the measures that should concern him.

Problems of Measuring Investment in Assets. Perhaps the most difficult problem of all is the appropriate measurement of a division's assets for purposes of the rate of return computation. The most readily available measure in most cases is the book value of the assets, the amount at which they are recorded in the company's accounts. This may also be the least useful measure, unfortunately. Assuming that some significant portion of the division's assets are depreciable, using book value as the basis for the investment in assets would tend to produce a rate of return that increased over time as the assets aged and were increasingly depreciated. Thus, so long as divisional income did not decline as rapidly as the book value of the division's assets, the divisional rate of return would rise as the assets became more worn and obsolete. A very popular way of correcting for this tendency is to use the gross book value of assets, that is, the original cost without any deduction for depreciation. While this does avoid the problem of a meaningless rise in the rate of return as time passes, it still is not a measure of the current economic value of the assets involved. For purposes of rate of return computations, valuation of assets at their current replacement cost would be the most generally appropriate solution to the problem. Although replacement cost data are not found in the accounts, they may usually be determined quite easily for a large number of assets. The replacement costs of inventories and of equipment for which an active market exists may be obtained directly from quoted market prices. Replacement costs of buildings may be approximated by periodic appraisals or by applying a construction price index to the original costs. Appraised values for land are usually reliable estimates of replacement costs. Special equipment and intangible assets may present more difficult problems, but some estimate of replacement cost is normally possible, even if it is no more than an adjustment of original cost for change in the general price level.

The assets included in the investment base for a division should be only those assets used exclusively in that division. Allocations of portions of the values of assets controlled by corporate headquarters and used for the general benefit of all divisions are not appropriate. Some firms have excluded from a division's investment base any assets that are currently idle (e.g., standby equipment). The resultant rate of return is said to be the return on invested capital *employed* rather than on the total available invested capital. This approach would tend to raise the rate of return, for idle assets presumably generate no income. Yet, this practice would seem to defeat one of the objectives of the measure—the determination of how efficiently assets have been used. The presence of idle assets suggests inefficient utilization of resources. If this is the case, it should be reflected in the rate of return on investment and not artificially excluded from that measure.

Problems of Measuring Divisional Income. All of the problems of profit center analysis are encountered also in investment centers. There are also some special problems of income measurement when a rate of return is to be computed. If assets are valued at replacement cost for this purpose—and they should be—depreciation expense should also be based upon replacement cost. The rate of return on investment for a company is customarily computed by reference to income after tax. A division pays no tax, however. Its incremental income is normally determined without regard to taxes. Consequently, any attempt to compare a division's rate of return with that of a company will probably encounter a very fundamental inconsistency. It is possible to compute divisional income after tax by applying the income tax rate to the division's incremental income. This is seldom done, however.

Residual Profit

There is an alternative measure of financial performance in an investment center that avoids some (but not all) of the problems associated with the rate of return on investment because it is not expressed as a ratio. *Residual profit* is the incremental profit of a division minus an interest charge based on the division's investment in assets. The interest rate used for this computation would normally be the company's average cost of capital. Residual profit is computed below for the division whose rate of return was 20% in the illustration in the preceding section.[7]

---

[7] Page 483.

This division had income of $100,000 and assets of $500,000. The company's cost of capital was 10%. It's residual profit is determined as follows:

Incremental profit.............................	$100,000
Interest on invested capital (10% × $500,000)...	50,000
Residual profit................................	$ 50,000

While the form of this measure is like that used in a profit center, the effect of a costly investment in assets is reflected in the final figure. Now, when the division in the example has the opportunity of purchasing a new asset for $100,000 in order to increase income by $15,000, the division manager would be induced to do so. Incremental profit would rise to $115,000. The interest charge also would increase to $60,000 (10% × $600,000). But the residual profit would increase, too—from $50,000 to $55,000.

Residual profit is not as widely used in investment center analyses as is the rate of return on investment. Actually, either measure is equally useful to management if it is properly interpreted and if the division manager's performance is intelligently evaluated. The problems and dangers associated with the rate of return are not inherent in that method. Rather, they reflect potential misuses of the method. Residual profit could also be misused, of course. Whichever method is used, it should be used correctly; and all parties concerned should understand clearly what it means and how it relates to top management's assessment of their performances.

INTERDIVISIONAL TRANSFER PRICING

Systems of measuring profit or return on investment in separate divisions are inevitably complicated when two or more divisions in the same company trade with each other. A division that purchases goods or services from independent suppliers and sells its products to independent customers has been described as a natural profit center. (If its investment in assets is clearly defined, it might also be referred to as a natural investment center.) This status is not appreciably changed if the division also purchases from a sister division and/or sells to a sister division *and if it deals with such sister divisions essentially as it does with independent companies.* If the latter condition is not met, the buyer-seller relationship between sister divisions is not the natural, or arm's-length, bargaining situation. As a consequence, profit responsibility may become blurred and divisional profit measurements may be tenuous, at best. Hence, we may distinguish between two basic situations. In the first, each division manager is free to trade with sister divisions or not as he chooses. This is the simpler—and the rarer—situation. Where it exists, divisional performance measures should not be complicated by the interdivisional trading that does occur. In the second situation, divisions are required to trade with each other by a top-management policy decision. While this decision may be entirely appropriate from the point of view of top management, it causes potential problems in measuring the performance of any one division. These problems are critical in the selection of the interdivisional transfer price.

A *transfer price* is the price at which goods or services are exchanged between sister divisions of the same company. This price may be set either by the division managers involved or by top management. If the divisions are free to decide whether or not to trade with each other, it is logical that the division managers should also set the transfer price for goods they actually agree to exchange. In that case, the transfer price would be equivalent to a price for goods exchanged between two independent firms. Consequently, the factors determining the transfer price would be the same as those that determine prices in general.[8] On the other hand, if the divisions are required to trade with each other, it is reasonable to expect top management to establish the price at which the exchanges will take place. Hence, part of the determination of the revenue of the selling division and the costs of the buying division is beyond the control of the respective division managers. Evaluation of division managers' performance in terms of any of the financial measures discussed earlier in this chapter would then be more difficult and would be potentially disruptive of harmonious relations among divisions and between individual divisions and top management.

A considerable variety of transfer prices has been proposed and used. Many of these are merely minor variations of a single method, however. In the sections that follow, we shall consider five basic types of transfer prices:

1. Cost.
2. Cost plus a normal markup.
3. Market price.
4. Incremental cost.
5. Negotiated price.

It is possible that more than one of these types would be used in the same company and even for the same transfer. Any or all of the first four may be used when top management requires that the divisions trade with each other. A negotiated transfer price, on the other hand, is appropriate only when the divisions are free to deal with each other or not, according to their own determinations of their own best interests.

---

[8] Some of these factors were discussed in Chapter 17.

Cost

Perhaps the simplest method of transfer pricing is cost, usually defined as the selling division's unit cost to produce and ship the product. This information is routinely collected in the cost accounting system in any event. Further, unit cost is the basis of inventory valuation in corporate accounting records. Thus, no unique information is required for purposes of transfer pricing. If it is management's intent to evaluate both the selling and the buying divisions as expense centers, pricing transfers at cost is appropriate. If standard cost data are available, the transfer price should be standard rather than actual cost. In this way, efficiencies and inefficiencies (as reflected in variances from standard cost) will be reported in the selling division, where they presumably originate. Cost would be an inappropriate transfer price for purposes of profit center or investment center analysis, however. It would tend to reduce profit in the selling division, for there would be no profit margin on goods sold to a sister division. Conversely, it would inflate the profit of the buying division, for that division's purchase costs would be artificially low.

Cost Plus a Normal Markup

Some firms have attempted to take advantage of the simplicity of cost-based transfer prices and, yet, derive divisional profit data from them. The means of doing this is to set transfer prices at cost (actual or standard) plus some predetermined profit margin or normal markup. In this way, the selling division apparently realizes a profit on the interdivisional sale. That profit, however, is an artificial margin dictated by policy rather than one generated by market forces. Its validity as a basis for evaluating the performance of the division as an entity or of the division manager is questionable, at least, and may be very misleading. If the profit margin is a target profit set by management or is computed so as to ensure that the selling and buying divisions will share equally in the total profit realized by the company upon sale of the final product to an outside customer, it provides management no useful information for purposes of performance appraisal. If, on the other hand, the normal markup is equivalent to the profit margin that a competing firm might reasonably be expected to realize, then the total transfer price begins to approximate a market value. As such, it might be useful for managerial analyses. Its usefulness tends to be a function of the closeness to which it approaches a true market price. A transfer price based on cost plus a normal markup has no unique value of its own, however.

Market Price

If there is an active market for the goods or services transferred between divisions and there are readily determinable market prices, these prices are logical values for the interdivisional transfers. Market prices reflect the collective values of many buyers and sellers; they are neither arbitrary nor artificial. Most importantly, market prices represent the divisions' alternatives. The selling division could sell its goods to independent customers at market prices. Similarly, the buying division would have to pay an independent supplier market prices for its materials. Market prices may require adjustments in some instances, and these are appropriate as long as they are consistent with market conditions. For example, the buying division may purchase materials in such a large quantity that it could obtain a discount from any independent supplier. If so, the same discount is properly allowed on internal transfers.

To a large degree, internal transfers at market prices leave the divisions in the same situations they would be in if they dealt with each other at arm's length. Of course, there are still some advantages of their corporate relationship. For example, the selling division bears no risk of bad debts on sales to sister divisions. In most corporations, payment is made regularly by a transfer from the Cash account of the buyer to the Cash account of the seller in the books of the corporation. Also, if the internal transfer is required by management policy, the selling division incurs no direct promotional expenses on a sale to a sister division. The buying division also derives some special benefits from the internal transfer. Ordinarily, a sister division is regarded by the seller as a preferred customer. Hence, the buying division can usually rely on delivery schedules and full customer services.

Obviously, market prices exist only for standard products or specialized products that are made up of standard components. For example, there may be a readily determined market price for a specially equipped forklift if it is built entirely of standard parts, each of which has its own market price. In the case of custom-designed products, however, there are usually no easily identified market prices. In such situations, cost plus a normal profit margin is often suggested as a reasonable approximation of what the market price ought to be. As noted in the preceding section, this method may be acceptable if the profit margin is comparable to what a competitor might realize. A market price for a custom-made product may also be established by requesting bids from several different manufacturers. The low bid may then be taken as the market price and used for internal transfer pricing. While this approach may generate a useful market price, it is not without disadvantages. If outside bidders come to realize that their only function is to provide the bid requester with an internal transfer price and that they have no real chance of obtaining the order, they will quickly discontinue submitting bids or might even submit wholly spurious bids. This would clearly be an undesirable situation. No firm wishes to make enemies.

Incremental Cost

If internal transfers are required as a matter of policy and if the principal objective of the transfer price is to provide useful information for top-management decision making, the best transfer price is the incremental cost in the selling division. In most cases, incremental cost would include all variable costs of producing and shipping the goods in question plus any fixed costs directly and exclusively traceable to the internal transfer. Incremental cost transfer prices can then be compared by top management to market prices for the same goods for purposes of make-or-buy decisions.[9] Such a decision, of course, emphasizes the point of view of the company as a whole. The positions of the divisions are of secondary importance here. Transfer pricing at incremental cost is incompatible with the objective of measuring divisional profit. If top management wishes to have incremental cost data for its own purposes but still wants to evaluate the divisions as profit or investment centers, at least two different transfer prices will have to be used for these two distinct objectives. There is no reason why more than one transfer price should not be used for the same internal transfer, except for the added clerical cost of preparing and reporting the duplicative information.

In the preceding paragraph, we noted that incremental cost is equal to the directly traceable costs of production and shipping in the selling division "in most cases." This is the case when the selling division has adequate capacity to produce all goods demanded by both sister divisions and independent customers or when there are no outside customers for the goods in question. However, if there are outside customers and if the selling division lacks sufficient capacity to meet the full demand for its products, the situation is very materially changed. In this case, the incremental cost to the selling division and to the company as a whole is the revenue lost on sales to outside customers that must be foregone in order to make the internal transfer to a sister division. Thus, incremental cost would be equal to the market price for those goods. Of course, if the selling division filled all orders from independent customers first and, hence, was unable to meet the buying division's demand, the buying division would have to fill its requirements by paying the market price to an outside supplier. In such a situation, it is entirely reasonable that top management might prefer to decide whether the two divisions should

---

[9] Cf. Chapter 14, pages 353–55.

deal with each other or not. Incremental cost data are still the appropriate bases for that decision, but they are now equal to the market price and not to the internal production costs.

Negotiated Price

Division managers should be allowed to negotiate with each other on transfer prices only if they also have the discretion to trade with one another or with independent parties. If internal transfers are required by top management, transfer price negotiations would be a useless and probably damaging exercise in gamesmanship. Neither party would have the normal bargaining leverage of taking his business elsewhere. The division managers would simply be arguing about the sharing of a pre-determined total amount. At best, the result of such negotiations would be meaningless. At worst, the result would be damaging internal conflicts.

Where the selling division does have a choice of customers and the buying division, a choice of suppliers, however, negotiated transfer prices should work well. If there is a well-established market price, the negotia-tions should promptly settle upon that as the transfer price. In the absence of a firm market price, the selling division should be willing to agree to some price greater than its incremental cost; and the buying division should be happy to agree to a price no higher than it could expect to pay to an independent supplier. (Remember that the selling division's incremental cost is equal to the revenue it would have to forego on some other sale if it is already producing at full capacity.) If the buying division could purchase the goods outside at a price below the selling division's incremental cost, it would be to the advantage of both divisions and the company for it to do so. Otherwise, the negotiations should result in a transfer price mutually advantageous to both divisions and to the company as a whole.

QUESTIONS FOR DISCUSSION

1. How can one really distinguish between the performance of a division and the performance of that division's manager?
2. What kind of performance is measured in an expense center? What are the criteria for evaluating that performance?
3. What kind of performance is measured in a profit center? What are the criteria for evaluating that performance?
4. Distinguish between a natural profit center and a constructive profit center. Can the same performance analyses be made in both?
5. How do performance measures in investment centers differ from those in profit centers?

6. May divisional profits and divisional rates of return on investment be compared to the profits and rates of return of independent companies in the same industry? Explain.

7. What are the principal alternative bases for measuring a division's investment in assets? What are some of the problems involved in using each?

8. Should common costs be allocated among divisions for purposes of divisional performance measurements? Discuss.

9. What is a division's residual profit? What are its advantages as a measure of divisional performance?

10. What is a transfer price? Is it a true price in the same sense as the prices of goods exchanged between firms in normal markets?

11. How, if at all, is the selection of a transfer price dependent upon the identification of the divisions involved as expense centers or as profit centers?

12. Under what circumstances are incremental costs appropriate and useful transfer prices?

13. Under what circumstances are negotiated transfer prices appropriate and useful?

14. "It is meaningless to say that all of a company's divisions are profitable but that the company itself is not. A company is the sum of its divisions, and its profits inevitably depend upon theirs." Comment on this statement.

PROBLEMS

1. The maintenance department of the Wildman Corporation performs all routine maintenance work in the corporation's factory, as well as much of the major repair work. This department is evaluated as an expense center. Its flexible budget for one year's operations appears as follows:

	Variable Rate per Machine-Hour	Fixed Cost per Year
Indirect materials..........................	$ .75	
Indirect labor............................	1.50	$ 12,000
Supervision..............................		30,000
Labor-related costs.......................	.30	8,400
Power and light..........................	.45	10,000
Depreciation.............................		22,000
General factory overhead..................		20,000
	$3.00	$102,400

Indirect materials, indirect labor, and power and light are cost items regarded as controllable by the maintenance department supervisor. General factory overhead is allocated among all of the departments occupying space in the factory on the basis of square feet of floor space. It includes such things as depreciation, taxes, and insurance on the building.

During 1972, a total of 40,000 machine-hours were worked in the factory. The actual costs charged to the maintenance department during this year were as follows:

Indirect materials........................	$ 33,000
Indirect labor..........................	78,000
Supervision............................	34,000
Labor-related costs.....................	22,400
Power and light........................	25,000
Depreciation...........................	24,500
General factory overhead................	21,600
	$238,500

Required:

Prepare an expense report for the maintenance department that will be useful to management in evaluating both the department supervisor's performance and the performance of the department as an entity.

2. The Elwell Company has three distinct sales divisions, each of which is evaluated as a profit center. The company's budgeted income statement for 1972 appeared as follows:

	Industrial Sales	Wholesale Sales	Government Sales	Total Company
Sales...................	$30,000,000	$40,000,000	$20,000,000	$90,000,000
Expenses:				
Standard production costs................	$15,000,000	$20,000,000	$10,000,000	$45,000,000
Sales commissions.......	2,400,000	3,200,000	1,600,000	7,200,000
Sales promotion.........	2,000,000	2,500,000	1,000,000	5,500,000
Other selling costs......	1,500,000	2,000,000	1,000,000	4,500,000
Divisional administration................	2,500,000	2,500,000	1,800,000	6,800,000
General corporate costs..	4,500,000	6,000,000	3,000,000	13,500,000
	$27,900,000	$36,200,000	$18,400,000	$82,500,000
Earnings before tax........	$ 2,100,000	$ 3,800,000	$ 1,600,000	$ 7,500,000

Actual operations for the year 1972 are summarized below:

	Industrial Sales	Wholesale Sales	Government Sales	Total Company
Sales...................	$44,000,000	$32,000,000	$14,000,000	$90,000,000
Expenses:				
Standard production costs................	$22,000,000	$16,000,000	$ 7,000,000	$45,000,000
Production variances....	880,000	640,000	280,000	1,800,000
Sales commissions.......	3,520,000	2,560,000	1,120,000	7,200,000
Sales promotion.........	2,200,000	2,500,000	1,200,000	5,900,000
Other selling costs......	2,200,000	1,600,000	700,000	4,500,000
Divisional administration................	2,600,000	2,600,000	1,800,000	7,000,000
General corporate costs..	7,480,000	5,440,000	2,380,000	15,300,000
	$40,880,000	$31,340,000	$14,480,000	$86,700,000
Earnings before tax........	$ 3,120,000	$ 660,000	$ (480,000)	$ 3,300,000

Accounting for Managerial Analysis

General corporate costs include all of the company's costs not incurred directly in one of the sales divisions nor included as part of standard production costs. These are allocated among the three sales divisions on the basis of their sales volumes.

Required:

Evaluate the Elwell Company's practices regarding the measurement of performance in the sales divisions. What specific changes, if any, would you recommend? Why?

3. The power plant of the Hatfield Company produced a total of 7,500,000 kilowatt-hours in 1972. The variable operating costs of the power plant were $300,000 for the year, and the fixed costs directly traceable to it were $500,000. Additional fixed costs of $120,000 were allocated to the power plant as its share of general corporate expenses. The rate for electricity from the local power and light company is $.12 per kilowatt-hour.

In the past, the company has always evaluated the performance of the power plant by comparing its actual costs with budgeted costs. The new president of the firm, however, wants all operating segments of the company to be treated as profit centers, if possible.

Required:

a) Can the power plant be evaluated as a profit center? If so, present an analysis of its profit performance in 1972.
b) If it is a profit center, at what volume would the power plant just break even?

4. The transportation department of the Scovill Distributing Corporation maintains a fleet of 60 automobiles for use by authorized company personnel. The department budget allows $.10 per mile of operation plus $75,000 per year for general maintenance. During 1972, the 60 cars were operated an average of 60,000 miles each. Total cost in the transportation department was $475,000. The rental cost of similar cars would be $.15 per mile.

Required:

a) Evaluate the operations of the transportation department in 1972 if it is regarded as an expense center.
b) Evaluate the operations of the transportation department in 1972 if it is regarded as a profit center.
c) Was it more profitable for the company to have its own cars in 1972 than to rent them? At what volume of operations, if any, would it be more profitable to rent cars? (Ignore capital investment considerations in answering this question.)

5. The following summarized data are adapted from a recent study of one year's operation of the U.S. Post Office (prior to its reorganization as a semi-independent corporation on July 1, 1971). All dollar amounts are in millions of dollars.

	First Class	Second Class	Third Class	Fourth Class	Totals
Revenues......................	$3,000	$ 150	$ 600	$ 900	$ 4,650
Variable expenses................	1,680	330	300	600	2,910
Variable profit margin............	$1,320	$(180)	$ 300	$ 300	$ 1,740
Traceable fixed costs.............	600	400	400	500	1,900
Net margin.....................	$ 720	$(580)	$(100)	$(200)	$ (160)
Common fixed costs..............					1,100
Net operating deficit (made up by congressional subsidy)............					$(1,260)

Required:

a) At what volume does each class of mail service break even?

b) At what volume would the entire Post Office break even if the mix of classes of service (product mix) remains as shown above?

c) Would it be profitable to double second-class postal rates if this would result in a reduction of second-class mailing volume by half?

6. The Denver plant of the Madden Manufacturing Company produces control panels used on most of the company's final products. This plant and all of the equipment in it are leased; the lease is cancellable on six-months' notice. Budgeted production and cost data for this plant for 1973 are as follows:

Materials cost................................	$1,200,000
Direct labor.................................	800,000
Variable overhead............................	400,000
Fixed overhead (including rent).................	800,000
Variable shipping expense......................	50,000
Fixed plant administrative expenses.............	250,000
Plant's share of general corporate expenses........	500,000
Total costs.............................	$4,000,000
Output of control panels......................	5,000

The output of the Denver plant is planned to meet the production requirements of the company's principal manufacturing plants. Recently, the company has learned that it could purchase a comparable control panel from an independent supplier at a price of $750 per panel, delivered.

Required:

a) Would it be profitable for the Madden Company to continue operating the Denver plant during 1973?

b) At what operating volume would it be more profitable to operate the Denver plant than to purchase control panels?

7. The small appliance division of the Rittenhouse Electric Company reports the following assets on its divisional balance sheet:

Original cost.........................	$30,000,000
Accumulated depreciation..............	12,000,000
Book value........................	$18,000,000

These assets have an estimated current replacement cost totaling $25,000,000.

The division's income statement for 1972 is summarized below:

Sales..............................	$40,000,000
Avoidable expenses of division..........	$31,000,000
Allocated share of corporate expenses....	5,000,000
	$36,000,000
Income before taxes..................	$ 4,000,000

Required:

a) Compute the rate of return on investment in the division's assets, valued at (1) book value, (2) gross cost, and (3) replacement cost.

b) Which of the three rates of return computed in (a) would be most useful for comparative purposes? Explain.

8. The McKinsey Corporation has eight major product divisions. The financial statements of the turbine division at the end of 1972 appeared as follows:

MC KINSEY TURBINE DIVISION

Balance Sheet
December 31, 1972

Current assets.........	$ 4,000,000		Current liabilities.......	$ 3,000,000
Plant property.........	15,000,000		Corporate equity.......	15,000,000
Accumulated deprecia-				
tion................	(4,000,000)			
Intangibles...........	3,000,000			
	$18,000,000			$18,000,000

MC KINSEY TURBINE DIVISION

Income Statement
For Year Ended December 31, 1972

Sales................................	$20,000,000
Cost of goods sold.....................	14,000,000
Gross margin..........................	$ 6,000,000
Selling and administrative expenses.......	2,500,000
Income before tax.....................	$ 3,500,000
Income tax (40%).....................	1,400,000
Net Income..........................	$ 2,100,000

All expenses are incurred directly in the division, except for $1,000,000 of selling and administrative expenses that are allocated from general corporate expense.

The McKinsey Corporation's cost of capital is 10%.

Required:

a) Compute the rate of return on investment in the turbine division by the three-step method.

b) Compute the turbine division's residual profit for 1972.

9. The food products division of the Kester Company has assets valued at a current cost of $40,000,000. The budgeted revenue of the division for 1973 is $150,000,000, and its budgeted expenses are $140,000,000. The company's cost of capital is 12%.

   Early in January, 1973, the division was offered the opportunity of purchasing a going concern for $20,000,000. The budgeted revenues of this firm for 1973 are $80,000,000, and its budgeted expenses are $76,800,000.

   Required:
   a) Compute the budgeted rate of return on investment and the budgeted residual profit of the food products division for 1973 before consideration of the offered investment opportunity.
   b) If purchased, how would acquisition and operation of the going concern affect the budgeted rate of return and residual profit computed in (a)?
   c) Assuming that the division is evaluated as an investment center, would you accept the proposed investment opportunity if you were the division manager? Explain.

10. The Filbey Company is planning to invest in a new subsidiary corporation. The initial investment required would be $45 million, and the subsidiary would have an economic life of 15 years and no terminal salvage value. The investment would be amortized by the straight-line method for income tax purposes. Estimated annual sales receipts from this subsidiary are $75 million, and out-of-pocket expenses are estimated at $61.2 million per year. The income tax rate is 40%. The company's cost of capital is 10%.

    Required:
    a) What is the discounted rate of return on the proposed investment?
    b) Assume that the company decided to make the proposed investment and that the actual receipts and out-of-pocket expenses during the first year of operation of the new subsidiary proved to be exactly as originally estimated. What is the subsidiary's rate of return on investment in assets for the first year?
    c) How would you explain any difference between the rates of return computed in (a) and (b)?

11. The electric motor division of the Krebs Corporation manufactures a heavy-duty motor that it sells at a competitive market price of $66 per unit. The standard cost sheet for one of these motors is as follows:

Materials............................	$12
Direct labor........................	17
Variable overhead...................	6
Fixed overhead......................	15
	$50

   The furnace division of Krebs Corporation currently purchases this type of heavy-duty motor from the Himmelblau Electric Company. Because it purchases 5,000 motors annually, it obtains a quantity discount of $2 per unit off the market price of $66. Since the electric motor division is currently producing 22,000 of these motors annually and has the capacity to produce 30,000 per year, management is considering whether it might not be more advantageous to have the furnace division purchase the motor from the electric motor division instead of an outside supplier.

Required:

a) From the point of view of corporate management, what transfer price would be most useful in helping it decide whether the motor should be purchased from the electric motor division or from the Himmelblau Electric Company as presently done?

b) If both divisions are to be evaluated as profit centers, what would be the most useful transfer price?

c) Would your answer to either (a) or (b) be changed if the electric motor division was already producing at its full capacity of 30,000 units per year? Explain.

12. The Jackson Athletic Equipment Company manufactures trampolines in two plants. The casting plant makes tubular aluminum frames, which are then shipped to the assembly plant. The assembly plant affixes nylon nets to the frames and stores the finished trampolines until they are shipped out on customers' orders.

The company uses absorption costing in charging costs to products. The materials cost per frame in the casting plant is $22.50. Two man-hours at a wage rate of $3.50 per hour are required for the completion of each frame. The flexible budget for overhead in the casting plant allows costs of $1.10 per hour plus $500,000 per year. Normal volume is 250,000 man-hours per year. Trampoline frame production represents about 20% of normal production volume.

Comparable frames could be purchased from independent manufacturers for $33 each. Finished trampolines are sold for $65 apiece. Selling and shipping costs average $5 per unit sold.

Required:

a) If both plants are treated as profit centers, at what transfer prices should frames be transferred from the casting plant to the assembly plant? Explain.

b) Would it be advantageous for the company to buy frames from independent manufacturers rather than to make them in the casting plant? Explain.

c) Would your answer to (b) be different if the casting plant's only output was trampoline frames? Why?

13. The boiler division of Rosenkampff Industries, Inc., has redesigned several of its principal products. Consequently, it will now need 60,000 highly sensitive thermal control units each year. The corporation's controls division produces such a unit and sells it at the current market price of $30.

This unit requires two hours of production time and has a unit materials cost of $8. The controls division has a productive capacity of 800,000 labor hours per year. It is currently operating at 80% of capacity. Total conversion costs in this division amount to $6 per labor hour plus $1,750,000 per year.

It is the corporation's policy to permit each division to operated essentially as an independent company. Division managers are free to determine their own sources of supply and to set their own prices.

Required:

a) What is the most the boiler division can afford to pay for the thermal control unit?

b) What is the lowest price at which the controls division can afford to sell the thermal control unit?

c) Irrespective of your answers in (a) and (b), assume that the two divisions have negotiated a transfer price of $27.50 for the thermal control unit and have entered into a one-year supply contract with each other. Is this arrangement advantageous to each division? Is it advantageous to the corporation?

d) Assume now that the boiler division had entered into a one-year supply contract for the thermal control unit with an independent vendor at the unit price of $27.50. Would this arrangement be advantageous to each division? Would it be advantageous to the corporation?

chapter 19

EFFECTIVE REPORTS
TO MANAGEMENT

T HE END product of much of the work of accountants is a report. The end results of the financial accounting cycle are the familiar financial statements—the balance sheet, the income statement, the statement of funds or cash flow, and the statement of retained earnings. The conclusion of the tax accountant's work is usually the preparation of a tax return. In management accounting, too, reports represent the culmination of much of the accountant's effort. The present chapter offers some basic guides for the preparation of reports to management. External financial reports, such as balance sheets and income statements, are not discussed specifically; but many of the rules applicable to management reports are equally pertinent to external reports.

COMMUNICATION THROUGH ACCOUNTING

Accounting is fundamentally a means of communicating financial information. Accountants accumulate and process financial data so that others may use them in making decisions. Seldom do the users of these data gather them for themselves. The users with whom we are concerned here are business managers. Financial information is recorded and classified by accountants for use by management. Accounting reports serve as the bridge between the accumulation and the utilization of financial information. The effectiveness of managerial decisions depends to a considerable extent, therefore, upon the effectiveness of accounting reports. Effective reporting involves, basically, getting the right information to the right persons at the right time.

Identification of the right information for business planning, control, and decision making is the essence of management accounting. It is the basic theme of most of this book. Managers know (or should know) what they wish to accomplish and what information they need in order to accomplish it. Accountants know (or should know) what information is available, how it may be analyzed, and the cost of processing it as desired. Cost-conscious management must never forget that data processing and reporting activities involve significant costs. The supply of and demand for financial information must be harmonized in a meaningful and a reasonable manner. Managers, who need information, must work jointly with accountants, who accumulate information, to develop and implement the best possible data processing and reporting system at the lowest possible cost. This objective requires that managers be familiar with the potentialities and the limitations of accounting and that accountants be conversant with the aims and the problems of management.

For example, management may be considering reclaiming and using production waste now sold as scrap. In order to evaluate the profitability of such a proposal, management should know its opportunity cost. The real opportunity cost of such a proposal, of course, is a future quantity which cannot be predicted with certainty. Nevertheless, that future cost information can be approximated from actual cost data accumulated and analyzed from the past. The accountant must be able to prepare a report containing the correct information for this purpose, and that report must communicate such information to management in the most meaningful and comprehensible manner. The remainder of this chapter is concerned with some general rules for the development of meaningful and comprehensible reports for management.

BASIC RULES OF GOOD MANAGEMENT REPORTING

Accountants would do well to keep something akin to Kipling's "six honest serving-men"[1] as rules for report writing. As Kipling was a storyteller rather than a report writer, his particular servingmen may not be directly applicable to accountants' reports; but the basic notion most certainly is. Six rules of report writing are suggested in the sections that follow. They are timeliness, clarity, conciseness, written reports, responsibility reporting, and reporting exceptions.

Timeliness

If a report is to be useful to a manager in making a decision, he must receive it before the decision must be made. If it is to be useful in

---

[1] Rudyard Kipling, chapter heading for "The Elephant's Child," in *Just-So Stories* (New York: Doubleday, Doran & Co., Inc., 1907), p. 85.

planning future operations, it must be received well in advance of the period being planned. If it is to be used in controlling current operations, it must be received at once. A weekly report of actual and standard materials usage received on the third day of the week following that covered by the report is too late. It should be available on the morning of the first day of the following week. A monthly summary of operations received at the middle of the following month is too late. It should be submitted within the first five days of the next month. It is entirely appropriate to accept a tolerable degree of inaccuracy as the price of promptness. If more precise data can be reported by delaying a report for a few days, the loss of time may well outweigh the gain in precision. The use of high-speed computers in business has greatly facilitated promptness in reporting. Computations and summaries that formerly required days for manual preparation can now be prepared by machines in minutes.

Timeliness is not merely a matter of promptness, however. Timely reports should be received when needed and only when needed. Too many reports can be just as bad as too few. Daily reports to department foremen of materials usage and labor efficiency may be both feasible and desirable. They permit foremen to take corrective action as soon as the need for it appears. On the other hand, daily profit reports for a company would be considered excessive in most cases. Regular reports should be prepared as often as management actually needs them and no more often. Irregular, or special, reports also should be submitted when needed. Ideally, the reporting system should be so structured as to provide managers with reports for special purposes whenever they are pertinent, not merely when managers request them. For example, suppose that a factory manager requests a report as to the profitability of replacing a particular machine. The report submitted indicates that replacement is not presently profitable. The internal information system should not drop the matter at this point. It should be so designed as to keep a constant watch on this replacement question. When replacement of the machine would be profitable, the system should recognize the fact and submit an appropriate report to the factory manager without his having to ask for it. In other words, the reporting system should provide for automatic feedback of relevant information to management.

Clarity

It should go without saying that reports to management should be clear and understandable. Yet, this most obvious of reporting requirements is so often missed. The author has heard so many business executives and partners in public accounting firms complain that junior executives and accountants cannot prepare readable reports that the problem assumes almost alarming proportions. As most reports are prepared in preliminary drafts by hand, a neat and legible handwriting can hardly be overemphasized. Grammatically correct and structurally attractive written English is essential to intelligent communication in business or elsewhere. Most importantly, of course, clarity involves making the point of the report clear at once to the reader. If a report presents the financial analysis of a proposal to process further a product now sold in a semifinished state, it should be organized around the two alternatives and not around the usual functional or departmental account classification of the firm. Variance reports should highlight variances, not the actual and standard costs from which they are determined.

Conciseness

Conciseness is very closely linked with clarity. Conciseness is not simply brevity. A concise report is both brief *and to the point.* Unnecessary information and explanations are eliminated from reports so that the necessary information stands out clearly. In a report comparing the incremental profits of alternative courses of action, for example, sunk costs ought not appear. Reports to management should be as short as possible, consistent with the need for completeness. A manager's time is valuable. Typically he is hurried. Long reports slow him down. Worse, long reports may force him to scan quickly and thus, perhaps, to miss important points. In his capacity as Prime Minister and Minister of Defence during World War II, Sir Winston Churchill often required subordinates to submit important reports to him on a single sheet of paper.[2] The effectiveness with which he discharged his wartime responsibilities argues well for wider adoption of this practice.

Written Reports

As a general rule, all formal reports to management should be in writing. Oral reports should be limited to informal or emergency communications. (A written report that the storeroom is on fire ought not be necessary.) Oral reports are inconvenient and unreliable. They demand that the person to whom a report is directed receive, digest, and evaluate the report at the moment it is presented to him. Further, they leave no evidence of their having been made. They cannot be proved later or referred to again. Sir Winston Churchill insisted upon transacting all official business in writing and disavowed responsibility for

---

[2] Winston S. Churchill, *Their Finest Hour* (Boston: Houghton Mifflin Co., 1949), pp. 166 and 168.

oral directives attributed to him unless they were confirmed in writing.[3] Such a requirement facilitates fixing responsibility for reports and prevents subsequent minunderstanding of or disagreement about what was reported.

The requirement of written reports should not preclude oral discussion of them, of course. Extensive discussion of operating reports by members of a budget committee, for example, may be extremely useful in more effective and profitable planning of future operations. Department foremen should be encouraged to discuss reports of their operating performances with plant managers and with members of the accounting department. Such discussions can foster improved understanding and acceptance of reports and their objectives, enhanced rapport between operating personnel and management, and, ultimately, improved operating efficiency.

Responsibility Reporting

Operating reports should be developed according to areas of responsibility. Reports on the operating performance of a particular supervisor should cover only those items for which he is responsible or should clearly distinguish between such items and those for which he is not accountable. Departmental expense reports, for example, should distinguish between costs that are controllable and those that are noncontrollable at the level of the department supervisor.[4] Otherwise, the manager reported on is likely to develop antagonism toward the reporting system, the accounting staff, and the higher management that reviews the reports. And higher management's review of operations would be impaired by a lack of distinction between controllable and noncontrollable costs.

The level of responsibility to which a report is directed should dictate to a considerable extent the form and content of it. To illustrate this idea, let us consider only the operating costs incurred in a single department during a month. The cost report submitted to the department supervisor should detail the individual cost items, classified as controllable and noncontrollable. It should indicate both actual and budgeted costs for the month and, possibly, the year to date and the resultant variances. If preferred, noncontrollable costs might be omitted from the report altogether. The report submitted to the plant manager will include cost data for all of the departments in his plant. These data may be summarized simply by broad functional classifications (materials, labor, and overhead), by their variability or fixedness with respect to volume,

---

[3] *Ibid.*, p. 17.

[4] See Table 9–3 in Chapter 9, page 227.

and by controllability. The report submitted to the vice president for manufacturing may include summaries of cost data from several plants. The data for individual departments within a plant may not be identified separately at all at this level of responsibility. If the vice president is not the one to take action to correct excessive materials usage in a department (or any other deviation from budgets or standards), there is no point in cluttering his report with such detailed information. The reporting of variances from standard by responsibilities was discussed at some length in Chapter 11.[5] The reader may wish to review that discussion at this point.

Although reports of operations directed to lower levels of management should clearly distinguish between controllable and noncontrollable data, they need not omit the latter. As a matter of fact, inclusion of information which is beyond a manager's present scope of responsibility may be a useful technique for expanding his perspective of the firm's operations and, thus, helping prepare him for broader managerial responsibilities in the future. Also, reports to a manager of the operating results of other divisions as well as his own may help to stimulate healthy competition among divisional managers. This may be particularly beneficial in connection with sales divisions. Care must be exercised, however, to ensure that such competition does not result in improved divisional performances at the expense of optimal company profit.

Reporting Exceptions

The concept of management by exception was mentioned earlier in this volume.[6] It is an approach to management which focuses attention on situations and operations which deviate from plans or from normal conditions. It is predicated upon a belief that management's limited and costly time is best spent in matters requiring corrective action or other improvement, not in reviewing satisfactory performance. Regular reports of operations, therefore, should be so constructed as to draw management's attention to exceptions. In a variance report, for example, special treatment should be given to variances which are beyond the established range of tolerance, for these are the variances which call for managerial action. This may be accomplished by placing such variances in a special column in the report or by putting some identifying mark next to them. The importance of reporting exceptions does not mean that satisfactory operating results are unimportant. Management, naturally, wants to know the results of operations, whether good or bad; but the bad results should be clearly identified. The reporting of exceptions

---

[5] Pages 282–85.

[6] See Chapter 5, page 135.

obviously is one of the most critical features of reports prepared specifically for purposes of control.

Report Retention

There seem to be a pack rat instinct in human nature that manifests itself in business offices as well as in private homes. Once a report has been prepared and submitted, it is almost invariably filed. Once filed, the chance of its being thrown away all but disappears. Eventually, the report may be microfilmed and the original copy discarded in order to save storage space; but it remains a part of the company's archives. There should be a general rule in business firms that nothing is retained unless there is some real possibility of its further usefulness. Alternatively, there might be some system of short-term filing for items of only temporary significance, the short-term file being cleared out on a regular schedule. Many reports must be retained for some specified period of time in order that their data may be included in subsequent summary reports. Other reports may have some legal significance and should be retained for a period governed by the applicable statute of limitations. Finally, some reports, such as annual financial statements, may be retained permanently as part of the history of the firm. Reports of clearly temporary usefulness, however, should be discarded as soon as their utility has been exhausted. Daily materials usage reports, for example, are unlikely to be of further significance (except, perhaps, as support for later summaries) after the end of the next day.

FORMAT OF REPORTS

Universally standardized report forms do not exist, nor would it be desirable if they did. The organizational structures, operations, and managerial philosophies of business firms differ considerably. Reports should be adapted to fit the peculiar characteristics of each individual firm. Within a single firm, however, standardization of report forms, within reasonable limits, is desirable. It fosters economy in report preparation and facilitates comprehension of reports. Standardization, of course, is possible only for regular reports. Limited standardization is possible for some special reports, but there must be adequate room for variations necessary to fit the individual situation. Requests for capital investments, for example, may be submitted to top management on standard forms; but their contents are likely to vary considerably.

Tabular Reports

Most accounting reports are prepared in tabular form. They typically contain one or more columns of data and frequently present combinations and/or comparisons of information. Financial statistics lend themselves to tabular presentation, and there is every reason to expect that most accounting reports will continue to appear in that format. A review of the various reports illustrated in the tables throughout this book will show almost all in the tabular form. This preponderance of practice should not preclude experimentation and change in report forms, of course. For some purposes, tabular reports may advantageously be supplanted or, at least, supplemented by other forms.

Graphic Reports

The use of graphs and charts is becoming increasingly popular in all types of reports. Relationships between two quantities (e.g., actual cost and budgeted cost) can be shown more clearly and vividly in many cases by two lines on a graph than by a comparison of dollar amounts. Graphs also lend themselves particularly well to presentations of comparative data intended to depict trends and other quantitative relationships over time.

Figure 19–1 is an illustration of a graphic report of the materials usage variance in a production department over a period of three months. It is a cumulative report, one that is added to daily and is completed

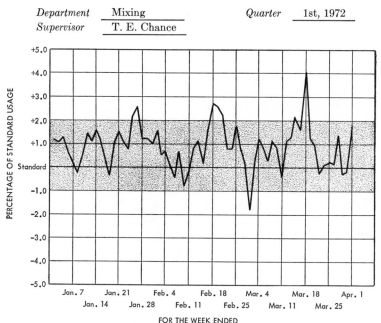

FIGURE 19–1

PARIAN MANUFACTURING CO.
Materials Usage Variance Report

only at the end of the quarter. This report is prepared for the plant superintendent, who uses it as a quick review of the operating performance of the department supervisor in one important area of his direct responsibility. Its cumulative content facilitates evaluation of the department's efficiency over time and of the results of efforts to correct prior variances. Separate daily reports of materials usage may be submitted to the department supervisor. Alternatively, as the variance data in Figure 19–1 are developed and entered daily, the same report could be presented to the department supervisor. The report in Figure 19–1 shows variances as percentages of standard usage rather than as physical amounts or dollars. The center line represents standard usage per unit of output. On either side of this line there is a line indicating the boundaries of the range of tolerable variances. Notice that the tolerable excess usage (2.0% of standard) is greater than the tolerable amount below standard (1.0%). This may be explained by the need to maintain product quality. If materials usage falls below the minimum, product quality may be so impaired that the units produced that day must be rejected. The area between the two lines bounding the range of tolerable variances is shaded on the graph so that variances outside that range—the exceptions requiring specific corrective action—are more readily identified.

Graphic reports, of course, are not always preferable to those in tabular form. Indeed, current reporting practices would seem to suggest just the opposite. Graphs tend to be less precise than tabulations. Further, they become increasingly difficult to read as additional data are reported in them. For simple reports, such as that in Table 19–1, and for long-term trend analyses, such as the growth or decline of the rate of return on investment in a firm over many years, graphs are especially appropriate. Probably their greatest advantage is that they enable the reader to grasp broad relationships or patterns quickly.

Narrative Reports

Although most accounting reports emphasize quantitative data, there is no reason why they should not also include textual material of a narrative or descriptive nature. Budget review reports, for example, might well include brief narratives of the operations for a period of time and the reasons for variances from the budget. Special reports covering such things as equipment replacement analyses, product line profit comparisons, and make-or-buy decisions ought to include some explanations of other pertinent factors which cannot presently be quantified. Quantitative information must be placed in its proper context, and this is properly the task of the written word. Almost anyone can fill in blanks with numbers, but this is not the essence of report writing. The good report writer can add succinct explanatory comments which give depth and meaning to the numbers. And management reports are nothing without meaning.

QUESTIONS FOR DISCUSSION

1. Discuss the relative advantages and disadvantages of tabular and graphic presentations of financial data in accounting reports.
2. What general rules may be stated for the frequency of issuance of regular reports?
3. Describe what you believe to be a good format for a monthly report of overhead costs incurred in a production department. If the data in the report would be classified, explain the reasons for the classifications. If any comparative data are included, explain what comparisons are made and why.
4. You are employed in a large, multiproduct firm that frequently must make decisions respecting product prices. You have been asked to draft a standard form on which the relevant financial data for pricing decisions can be reported to managers responsible for pricing. Describe the content of the form you would prepare and discuss its usefulness to management.
5. Are the data reported in the income statement which is usually included in the corporation's published annual report useful to the corporation's management for purposes of decision making? Explain your answer and discuss fully. If you feel they are not useful to management, of what value are these published data?
6. Variance reports were discussed in Chapter 11 as well as in the present chapter. What would you consider to be the basic guidelines for an effective variance report?
7. "*Resolved:* All reports submitted to the president and/or to the chairman of the board of a large industrial corporation should be no more than one page long." Do you concur with this resolution? Discuss fully.
8. Prepare a flow chart outlining the steps and procedures to be followed by a corporation's accounting department in preparing and distributing all types of financial reports.

APPENDIX

TABLES OF
PRESENT VALUES

THIS APPENDIX contains three tables of discounted present values of amounts to be paid or received in the future. These tables are based upon compound interest principles. They are included here primarily for use in the solution of problems in this text. They do not purport to be a complete set of compound interest tables useful to business managers and accountants. All three of the tables are based upon the principle of continuous discounting. That is, the factor of interest is assumed to operate continuously on the cash flows in question. This is equivalent to compounding interest each period, when the length of the period is infinitely small. Continuous discounting contrasts with discrete discounting, in which the interest factor operates on the cash flows only at the end of a period of substantial length. If this period is one year, this is equivalent to annual compounding of interest. Present value tables based upon discrete discounting are widely available in other books. Continuous discounting was chosen here because it seems more appropriate to the management of capital in a business firm or in any other organization with limited resources. Cash flows must be managed carefully on a daily basis, and opportunities to earn interest for even a few days should be taken advantage of.

Each of these tables contains three basic data, interest rates, time periods, and present values of $1. Given any two of these data, the third can be found in the tables, unless either the time period or the interest rate is beyond the limits of the tables. For most of the problems in this book, the interest rate and the time period will be given; the quantity sought will be the present value of some future cash receipt or payment. For some problems, the present value and the time period may be given, the interest rate being the unknown quantity. As a practical matter, the time period would seldom be unknown; but it could be found easily enough if the interest rate and the present value were given.

Although these are tables of the present value of $1, they can be used quite easily to determine the present value of any amount. The tabulated present values of $1 are often referred to as *present value factors*. These factors can be used to determine the present value of any dollar amount by simple multiplication. For example, the present value of $100 is simply 100 times that of $1; the present value of $.50 is half that of $1. The nature and the usage of each of the tables will be explained briefly in the sections that follow. Additional illustrations of their use will be found in Chapters 15 and 16 of the text.

Table A–1

Table A–1 is a table of present values of annuities of $1 to be paid or received in a steady stream throughout each of a given number of future periods. The word "annuity" suggests that the time periods involved be years, but this is not necessarily the case. The time period may be of any designated length, although often it will be a year. For most of the problems in this book, annual amounts received will be in the form of revenues or cost savings and amounts paid, in the form of expenditures or revenues foregone. The annuities discounted by means of this table are assumed to be received or paid in a steady stream during each year of their lives. Further, cash receipts are assumed to be reinvested as soon as they are received; and cash paid out is assumed to have been invested productively up to the time of its disbursement. Generally speaking, these assumptions are valid and fairly descriptive of the ordinary operating receipts and payments of a business. If a particular annuity involves annual lump-sum payments or receipts rather than a steady cash flow during the year, it cannot be discounted by use of Table A–1. Table A–3 can be adapted quite easily for this purpose, however.

An inspection of Table A–1 will show that the present value factors increase at a decreasing rate as the number of time periods increases. Each additional period involves an additional cash receipt or payment, but the successive present values of such additional amounts decline. Thus, the present value of the additional cash flow in the 10th year is less than that of the additional amount in the 9th year, etc. The total present value of the annuity continues to increase, however. Also, for any given period of years, the present value of the annuity decreases as the discount rate increases; there is an inverse relationship between the discount rate and the present value of a future cash flow.

To illustrate the use of Table A–1, assume that a firm has an opportunity to purchase a machine that will result in out-of-pocket operating cost savings of $15,000 per year for 12 years; the machine would have no terminal salvage value. Future cash flows are to be discounted at an interest rate of 9%. The projected annual cost saving of $15,000 is a 12-year annuity, the present value of which may be found from Table A–1. Enter the table at the column for 9% and the row for 12 years. The present value factor found at the intersection of the 9% column and the 12-year row is 7.3377. Multiply this factor by $15,000 to obtain a present value of $110,065.50 for this annuity. At a discount rate of 9%, a commitment to receive $15,000 annually in a steady stream for 12 years is presently worth $110,065.50. This is the maximum amount that the firm would be willing to pay to obtain the projected cost savings. Hence, the machine will be purchased only if its cost is $110,065.50 or less.

If an annuity will be received or paid over several future years not beginning with the first year, its present value can still be found from Table A–1. Suppose, for example, an investor can purchase an annuity which will pay him $10,000 per year for 15 years, starting in the 11th year hence. The tabulated present value factor for 15 years is for the first 15 years in the future and, thus, not appropriate here. This annuity will be received during the 11th through the 25th future years. Its present value factor is found by subtracting the factor for the first 10 years from that for the first 25 years. The remainder is the factor applicable to the 11th through 25th years. If the appropriate discount rate is 10%, the present value of this annuity is computed as follows:

Present value factor for 25 years..................	9.1790
Present value factor for 10 years..................	−6.3213
Present value factor for 11th–25th years............	2.8577
Face amount of annuity.........................	×$10,000
Present value of annuity.........................	$28,577

If the life and the present value of an annuity are known, the discounted rate of return (cf. Chapter 15) to be earned by purchase of the annuity may be found from Table A–1. For example, if we know that the present value of an annuity of $1 for 20 years is $7.58, we have but to enter the 20-year row of Table A–1 and look for a present value factor of 7.58 therein. We find it (7.5782 actually) in the 12% column; therefore, 12% is the discounted rate of return on the purchase of the annuity. Suppose, now, that the annuity is one of $12,000 per year for 10 years and that its present value is known to be $93,000. As the table is for an annuity of $1, not $12,000, both the annual amount of the annuity and the present value thereof must be divided by $12,000. An annuity of $12,000 for 10 years with a present value of $93,000 has the same discounted rate of return as an annuity of $1 for 10 years with a present value of $7.75 ($93,000 ÷ $12,000). In Table A–1, we find that a present value factor of 7.75 for a 10-year annuity falls between the tabulated amounts for 5% and 6%. For many purposes, this may be sufficiently precise. If a more exact rate of return is desired, it may be computed by interpolation.

Interpolation. The discount rate for a present value factor which falls between two tabulated factors may be determined by interpolation. The mathematical process of interpolation is illustrated below for the $12,000 10-year annuity described in the preceding paragraph. Its present value factor of 7.75 falls between tabulated factors of 7.8692 for 5% and 7.5198 for 6%. The total interval between these two tabulated factors is .3494 (7.8692 − 7.5198); this factor interval corresponds to a discount rate interval of 1% (6% − 5%). The interval between 7.8692 and 7.75 is .1192, and this corresponds to the interval between 5% and the exact discounted rate of return for the annuity in question. The difference between 5% and the exact discount rate is computed as follows, the difference being represented by x:

$$\frac{x}{.01} = \frac{.1192}{.3494}$$

$$\frac{x}{.01} = .344$$

$$x = .01(.344) = .00344$$

The exact discount rate (r) for this annuity then is equal to 5% plus x, or

$$r = .05 + .00344 = .05344$$

By interpolation, the discount rate for a present value factor of 7.75 for a 10-year annuity of $1 (or for a present value of $93,000 for a 10-year annuity of $12,000) is found to be 5.344%.

For most managerial purposes, interpolation to this degree of precision is not necessary or even useful. Further, interpolation does not always lead to such precise results. The rate of change of the present value factors as the discount rate increases is not linear, but the mechanics of interpolation are linear. This discrepancy does not cause any substantial error when interpolating between columns only 1% apart (e.g., between 5% and 6%, as above). However, interpolation between columns with a greater difference between them (e.g., between 30% and 40%) could result in a significant error.

Table A–2

Table A–2 contains the present values of amounts to be paid or received in a steady stream during only one future year. The basic mechanics of using this table are the same as those for Table A–1. Assume that a firm has an opportunity to purchase a machine with a life of five years and no terminal salvage value. The machine will cause an annual out-of-pocket operating cost saving for five years, but the successive annual cost savings will decrease in amount; they will not be in the form of a level annuity for five years. The cost savings expected are as follows:

Year	Cost Saving
1st....	$20,000
2nd....	16,000
3rd....	12,000
4th....	10,000
5th....	8,000

Because these savings are not in the form of a level annuity, no single present value factor can be used to discount them. Each annual cost saving (cash inflow) must be discounted separately. Assuming that the appropriate discount rate is 8%, these cost savings have a total present value computed as follows:

Year	Cost Saving	×	Present Value Factor at 8%	=	Present Value
1st....	$20,000		.9610		$19,220
2d....	16,000		.8872		14,195
3d....	12,000		.8189		9,827
4th....	10,000		.7560		7,560
5th....	8,000		.6979		5,583
					$56,385

If either Table A–1 or Table A–2 alone were given, the other could be developed from the one available. Notice that the first rows (the rows for the first year in the future) of the two tables contain identically the same present values. Each present value factor in the second row of Table A–1 is equal to the sum of the first two factors for the same interest rate in Table A–2. The factor for three years in Table A–1 is the sum of the factors for the first three years in Table A–2, etc. Conversely, the factor for the second year in Table A–2 is the difference between the factors for two years and for one year in Table A–1, etc.

Table A–3

Table A–3 is unlike either of the first two in that it contains present values for lump-sum cash receipts or payments at a single moment in the future. That moment is the end of the period indicated. The basic mechanics of its use, however, are the same as those for Tables A–1 and A–2. For example, the present value of a payment of one dollar 18 years in the future at a discount rate of 15% is $.0672 (the factor at the intersection of the 15% column and the 18-year row). If the payment were $10,000, the present value would be $672 ($10,000 × .0672).

Sometimes a business enterprise will anticipate a series of equal periodic payments in the future, as in the case of rental payments. The present value of such payments may be determined from Table A–3 also. Assume that a company enters into a 10-year lease agreement for a building. It agrees to pay annual rental of $40,000 on the first day of each of the next 10 years. This amounts to an initial payment of $40,-000 and an annuity of $40,000 payable annually in lump sums at the end of each of the succeeding nine years. (The first day of the second year is the end of the first year, etc.) Rather than to multiply 9 annual $40,000 payments by 9 separate present value factors, it is easier and quicker to add the first 9 tabulated factors in the appropriate interest rate column in Table A–3 and multiply their sum by $40,000. As the first year's rental must be paid at once, there is no time lapse and its present value is equal to its face value. Assuming a discount rate of 6%, the total present value of these rental payments is computed as follows:

Time of Payment	Face Amount	× Present Value Factor at 6%	= Present Value
Immediately..................	$40,000		$ 40,000
End of each of next 9 years.....	40,000	6.7476	269,904
			$309,904

The present value factor 6.7476 is the sum of the first 9 factors in the 6% column of Table A–3.

TABLE A–1

Present Value of Annuity of $1 Received or Paid in a Steady Stream throughout n Years in the Future

n	5%	6%	7%	8%	9%	10%	11%	12%	13%	14%	15%	20%	25%	30%	40%
1	0.9754	0.9706	0.9658	0.9610	0.9563	0.9516	0.9470	0.9423	0.9377	0.9332	0.9286	0.9063	0.8848	0.8640	0.8242
2	1.9032	1.8847	1.8663	1.8482	1.8303	1.8127	1,7953	1.7781	1.7611	1.7444	1.7279	1.6484	1.5739	1.5040	1.3767
3	2.7858	2.7455	2.7059	2.6671	2.6291	2.5918	2.5553	2.5194	2.4841	2.4497	2.4158	2.2559	2.1106	1.9781	1.7470
4	3.6253	3.5562	3.4888	3.4231	3.3591	3.2968	3.2361	3.1768	3.1190	3.0628	3.0079	2.7533	2.5285	2.3294	1.9952
5	4.4239	4.3197	4.2187	4.1210	4.0263	3.9347	3.8460	3.7599	3.6765	3.5958	3.5175	3.1605	2.8540	2.5896	2.1616
6	5.1835	5.0387	4.8993	4.7652	4.6361	4.5119	4.3923	4.2771	4.1660	4.0592	3.9561	3.4939	3.1075	2.7824	2.2731
7	5.9061	5.7159	5.5339	5.3599	5.1934	5.0342	4.8817	4.7359	4.5959	4.4621	4.3336	3.7669	3.3049	2.9252	2.3479
8	6.5935	6.3536	6.1256	5.9089	5.7027	5.5068	5.3202	5.1428	4.9734	4.8123	4.6586	3.9904	3.4587	3.0310	2.3980
9	7.2473	6.9542	6.6773	6.4157	6.1682	5.9344	5.7130	5.5037	5.3048	5.1168	4.9383	4.1734	3.5784	3.1094	2.4316
10	7.8692	7.5198	7.1917	6.8835	6.5936	6.3213	6.0649	5.8238	5.5958	5.3815	5.1790	4.3232	3.6717	3.1675	2.4541
11	8.4608	8.0525	7.6713	7.3153	6.9824	6.6714	6.3801	6.1077	5.8514	5.6116	5.3862	4.4459	3.7443	3.2105	2.4692
12	9.0236	8.5541	8.1185	7.7139	7.3377	6.9882	6.6625	6.3595	6.0758	5.8116	5.5645	4.5463	3.8009	3.2424	2.4793
13	9.5589	9.0265	8.5354	8.0819	7.6625	7.2748	6.9155	6.5828	6.2728	5.9855	5.7180	4.6285	3.8450	3.2660	2.4861
14	10.0681	9.4714	8.9242	8.4216	7.9593	7.5341	7.1421	6.7809	6.4458	6.1367	5.8501	4.6958	3.8793	3.2835	2.4906
15	10.5525	9.8904	9.2867	8.7352	8.2306	7.7688	7.3451	6.9566	6.5977	6.2682	5.9638	4.7509	3.9060	3.2965	2.4936
16	11.0133	10.2850	9.6246	9.0247	8.4785	7.9811	7.5270	7.1124	6.7311	6.3825	6.0617	4.7960	3.9268	3.3061	2.4957
17	11.4516	10.6567	9.9397	9.2919	8.7050	8.1732	7.6900	7.2506	6.8483	6.4819	6.1459	4.8330	3.9430	3.3132	2.4971
18	11.8685	11.0067	10.2335	9.5386	8.9120	8.3470	7.8360	7.3731	6.9512	6.5683	6.2184	4.8633	3.9556	3.3185	2.4980
19	12.2651	11.3363	10.5074	9.7663	9.1012	8.5043	7.9668	7.4818	7.0415	6.6434	6.2808	4.8881	3.9654	3.3224	2.4986
20	12.6424	11.6467	10.7628	9.9765	9.2741	8.6466	8.0840	7.5782	7.1208	6.7087	6.3345	4.9084	3.9730	3.3253	2.4990
21	13.0012	11.9390	11.0009	10.1705	9.4322	8.7754	8.1889	7.6637	7.1905	6.7655	6.3807	4.9250	3.9790	3.3274	2.4993
22	13.3426	12.2143	11.2229	10.3496	9.5767	8.8919	8.2829	7.7395	7.2517	6.8149	6.4205	4.9386	3.9836	3.3290	2.4995
23	13.6673	12.4736	11.4299	10.5150	9.7087	8.9973	8.3671	7.8068	7.3054	6.8578	6.4548	4.9497	3.9872	3.3302	2.4996
24	13.9762	12.7178	11.6229	10.6676	9.8294	9.0927	8.4426	7.8665	7.3526	6.8951	6.4843	4.9588	3.9900	3.3311	2.4997
25	14.2700	12.9478	11.8029	10.8085	9.9397	9.1790	8.5102	7.9194	7.3940	6.9275	6.5097	4.9663	3.9922	3.3317	2.4998

TABLE A-2

Present Value of $1 Received or Paid in a Steady Stream throughout the nth Year in the Future

nth year	5%	6%	7%	8%	9%	10%	11%	12%	13%	14%	15%	20%	25%	30%	40%
1st	0.9754	0.9706	0.9658	0.9610	0.9563	0.9516	0.9470	0.9423	0.9377	0.9332	0.9286	0.9063	0.8848	0.8640	0.8242
2nd	0.9278	0.9141	0.9005	0.8872	0.8740	0.8611	0.8483	0.8358	0.8234	0.8112	0.7993	0.7421	0.6891	0.6400	0.5525
3rd	0.8826	0.8608	0.8396	0.8189	0.7988	0.7791	0.7600	0.7413	0.7230	0.7053	0.6879	0.6075	0.5367	0.4741	0.3703
4th	0.8395	0.8107	0.7829	0.7560	0.7300	0.7050	0.6808	0.6574	0.6349	0.6131	0.5921	0.4974	0.4179	0.3513	0.2482
5th	0.7986	0.7635	0.7299	0.6979	0.6672	0.6379	0.6099	0.5831	0.5575	0.5330	0.5096	0.4072	0.3255	0.2602	0.1664
6th	0.7596	0.7190	0.6806	0.6442	0.6098	0.5772	0.5463	0.5172	0.4895	0.4634	0.4386	0.3334	0.2535	0.1928	0.1115
7th	0.7226	0.6772	0.6346	0.5947	0.5573	0.5223	0.4894	0.4588	0.4299	0.4029	0.3775	0.2730	0.1974	0.1428	0.0748
8th	0.6874	0.6377	0.5917	0.5490	0.5093	0.4726	0.4385	0.4069	0.3775	0.3502	0.3250	0.2235	0.1538	0.1058	0.0501
9th	0.6538	0.6006	0.5517	0.5068	0.4655	0.4276	0.3928	0.3609	0.3314	0.3045	0.2797	0.1830	0.1197	0.0784	0.0336
10th	0.6219	0.5656	0.5144	0.4678	0.4254	0.3869	0.3519	0.3201	0.2910	0.2647	0.2407	0.1498	0.0933	0.0581	0.0225
11th	0.5916	0.5327	0.4796	0.4318	0.3888	0.3501	0.3152	0.2839	0.2556	0.2301	0.2072	0.1227	0.0726	0.0430	0.0151
12th	0.5628	0.5016	0.4472	0.3986	0.3553	0.3168	0.2824	0.2518	0.2244	0.2000	0.1783	0.1004	0.0566	0.0319	0.0101
13th	0.5353	0.4724	0.4169	0.3680	0.3248	0.2866	0.2530	0.2233	0.1970	0.1739	0.1535	0.0822	0.0441	0.0236	0.0068
14th	0.5092	0.4449	0.3888	0.3397	0.2968	0.2593	0.2266	0.1981	0.1730	0.1512	0.1321	0.0673	0.0343	0.0175	0.0045
15th	0.4844	0.4190	0.3625	0.3136	0.2713	0.2347	0.2030	0.1757	0.1519	0.1314	0.1137	0.0551	0.0267	0.0130	0.0030
16th	0.4608	0.3946	0.3379	0.2895	0.2479	0.2123	0.1819	0.1558	0.1334	0.1143	0.0979	0.0451	0.0208	0.0096	0.0021
17th	0.4383	0.3717	0.3151	0.2672	0.2265	0.1921	0.1630	0.1382	0.1172	0.0994	0.0842	0.0370	0.0162	0.0071	0.0014
18th	0.4169	0.3500	0.2938	0.2467	0.2070	0.1738	0.1460	0.1225	0.1029	0.0864	0.0725	0.0303	0.0126	0.0053	0.0009
19th	0.3966	0.3296	0.2739	0.2277	0.1892	0.1573	0.1308	0.1087	0.0903	0.0751	0.0624	0.0248	0.0098	0.0039	0.0006
20th	0.3773	0.3104	0.2554	0.2102	0.1729	0.1423	0.1172	0.0964	0.0793	0.0653	0.0537	0.0203	0.0076	0.0029	0.0004
21st	0.3588	0.2923	0.2381	0.1940	0.1581	0.1288	0.1049	0.0855	0.0697	0.0568	0.0462	0.0166	0.0060	0.0021	0.0003
22nd	0.3414	0.2753	0.2220	0.1791	0.1445	0.1165	0.0940	0.0758	0.0612	0.0494	0.0398	0.0136	0.0046	0.0016	0.0002
23rd	0.3247	0.2593	0.2070	0.1654	0.1320	0.1054	0.0842	0.0673	0.0537	0.0429	0.0343	0.0111	0.0036	0.0012	0.0001
24th	0.3089	0.2442	0.1930	0.1526	0.1207	0.0954	0.0755	0.0597	0.0472	0.0373	0.0295	0.0091	0.0028	0.0009	0.0001
25th	0.2938	0.2300	0.1800	0.1409	0.1103	0.0863	0.0676	0.0529	0.0414	0.0324	0.0254	0.0075	0.0022	0.0006	0.0001

TABLE A–3

Present Value of $1 Received or Paid in a Lump Sum at End of n Years in the Future

n	5%	6%	7%	8%	9%	10%	11%	12%	13%	14%	15%	20%	25%	30%	40%
1	0.9512	0.9418	0.9324	0.9231	0.9139	0.9048	0.8958	0.8869	0.8781	0.8694	0.8607	0.8187	0.7788	0.7408	0.6703
2	0.9048	0.8869	0.8694	0.8521	0.8353	0.8187	0.8025	0.7866	0.7711	0.7558	0.7408	0.6703	0.6065	0.5488	0.4493
3	0.8607	0.8353	0.8106	0.7866	0.7634	0.7408	0.7189	0.6977	0.6771	0.6570	0.6376	0.5488	0.4724	0.4066	0.3012
4	0.8187	0.7866	0.7558	0.7261	0.6977	0.6703	0.6440	0.6188	0.5945	0.5712	0.5488	0.4493	0.3679	0.3012	0.2019
5	0.7788	0.7408	0.7047	0.6703	0.6376	0.6065	0.5770	0.5488	0.5220	0.4966	0.4724	0.3679	0.2865	0.2231	0.1353
6	0.7408	0.6977	0.6570	0.6188	0.5827	0.5488	0.5169	0.4868	0.4584	0.4317	0.4066	0.3012	0.2231	0.1653	0.0907
7	0.7047	0.6570	0.6126	0.5712	0.5326	0.4966	0.4630	0.4317	0.4025	0.3753	0.3499	0.2466	0.1738	0.1225	0.0608
8	0.6703	0.6188	0.5712	0.5273	0.4868	0.4493	0.4148	0.3829	0.3535	0.3263	0.3012	0.2019	0.1353	0.0907	0.0408
9	0.6376	0.5827	0.5326	0.4868	0.4449	0.4065	0.3716	0.3396	0.3104	0.2837	0.2592	0.1653	0.1054	0.0672	0.0273
10	0.6065	0.5488	0.4966	0.4493	0.4066	0.3679	0.3329	0.3012	0.2725	0.2466	0.2231	0.1353	0.0821	0.0498	0.0183
11	0.5770	0.5169	0.4630	0.4148	0.3716	0.3329	0.2982	0.2671	0.2393	0.2144	0.1921	0.1108	0.0639	0.0369	0.0123
12	0.5488	0.4868	0.4317	0.3829	0.3396	0.3012	0.2671	0.2369	0.2101	0.1864	0.1653	0.0907	0.0498	0.0273	0.0082
13	0.5220	0.4584	0.4025	0.3535	0.3104	0.2725	0.2393	0.2101	0.1845	0.1620	0.1423	0.0743	0.0388	0.0202	0.0055
14	0.4966	0.4317	0.3753	0.3263	0.2837	0.2466	0.2144	0.1864	0.1620	0.1409	0.1225	0.0608	0.0302	0.0150	0.0037
15	0.4724	0.4066	0.3499	0.3012	0.2592	0.2231	0.1921	0.1653	0.1423	0.1225	0.1054	0.0498	0.0235	0.0111	0.0025
16	0.4493	0.3829	0.3263	0.2780	0.2369	0.2019	0.1720	0.1466	0.1249	0.1065	0.0907	0.0408	0.0183	0.0082	0.0017
17	0.4274	0.3606	0.3042	0.2567	0.2165	0.1827	0.1541	0.1300	0.1097	0.0925	0.0781	0.0334	0.0143	0.0061	0.0011
18	0.4065	0.3396	0.2837	0.2369	0.1979	0.1653	0.1381	0.1153	0.0963	0.0805	0.0672	0.0273	0.0111	0.0045	0.0007
19	0.3867	0.3198	0.2645	0.2187	0.1809	0.1496	0.1237	0.1023	0.0846	0.0700	0.0578	0.0224	0.0087	0.0033	0.0005
20	0.3679	0.3012	0.2466	0.2019	0.1653	0.1353	0.1108	0.0907	0.0743	0.0608	0.0498	0.0183	0.0067	0.0025	0.0003
21	0.3499	0.2837	0.2299	0.1864	0.1511	0.1225	0.0993	0.0805	0.0652	0.0529	0.0429	0.0150	0.0052	0.0018	0.0002
22	0.3329	0.2671	0.2144	0.1720	0.1381	0.1108	0.0889	0.0714	0.0573	0.0460	0.0369	0.0123	0.0041	0.0014	0.0002
23	0.3166	0.2516	0.1999	0.1588	0.1262	0.1003	0.0797	0.0633	0.0503	0.0399	0.0317	0.0101	0.0032	0.0010	0.0001
24	0.3012	0.2369	0.1864	0.1466	0.1153	0.0907	0.0714	0.0561	0.0442	0.0347	0.0273	0.0082	0.0025	0.0007	0.0001
25	0.2865	0.2231	0.1738	0.1353	0.1054	0.0821	0.0639	0.0498	0.0388	0.0302	0.0235	0.0067	0.0019	0.0006	.....

INDEX

INDEX

This book has been set in 10 and 9 point Modern #21, leaded 2 points. Part numbers and titles are in 24 point (small) Helvetica. Chapter numbers are in 16 point Helvetica and chapter titles are in 24 point (small) Helvetica. The size of the type page is 27 x 45½ picas.